CASES IN

STRATEGIC MARKETING

Linda E. Swayne
Peter M. Ginter

PRENTICE HALL   Englewood Cliffs, New Jersey 07632

Library of Congress Cataloging-in-Publication Data

Cases in strategic marketing.

    1. Marketing—Decision making—Case studies.
2. Marketing—Management—Case studies. I. Swayne
Linda E. II. Ginter, Peter M.
HF5415.135.C37 1989   658.8'02   88-25300
ISBN 0-13-119108-X

Editorial/production supervision
   and interior design: York Production Services
Cover design: Wanda Lubelska Design
Manufacturing buyer: Margaret Rizzi

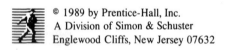
Printed in the United States of America
10 9 8 7 6 5 4 3 2 1

ISBN   0-13-119108-X

Prentice-Hall International (UK) Limited, *London*
Prentice-Hall of Australia Pty. Limited, *Sydney*
Prentice-Hall Canada Inc., *Toronto*
Prentice-Hall Hispanoamericana, S.A., *Mexico*
Prentice-Hall of India Private Limited, *New Delhi*
Prentice-Hall of Japan, Inc., *Tokyo*
Prentice-Hall of Southeast Asia Pte. Ltd., *Singapore*
Editora Prentice-Hall do Brasil, Ltda., *Rio de Janeiro*

Dedicated to our children—
Lisa and Heather
Robert and Karen
Unique and challenging case studies themselves.

CONTENTS

PREFACE

College education must be directed toward preparing students to enter complex decision-making environments. As Harvard President Derek Bok has indicated, an educated person must have a "curiosity in exploring the unfamiliar and unexpected, an open-mindedness in entertaining opposing points of view, tolerance for the ambiguity that surrounds so many important issues, and a willingness to make the best decisions he can in the face of uncertainty and doubt." For today's students, there will be few situations to which they can apply "classic" solutions developed in college classrooms. Rather, students will have to apply an independent critical intelligence and make judgments in a complex world of different and competing points of view.

The case approach has proven successful in allowing students to practice their decision-making skills without financial risk to an employer. Realizing the importance of the case method, marketing strategy and marketing management instructors have adopted the case approach to provide situations in which students may integrate and apply their marketing knowledge to gain experience.

THE CASE APPROACH

In order to effectively use cases it is essential that both students and instructors understand the nature of case studies and the teaching objectives of cases. A case typically is a record of a business situation that actually has been faced by business executives, together with surrounding facts, opinions, and prejudices upon which executive decisions have to depend.

A case study attempts to vicariously place students into a managerial position in which they will have to "size up" the situation and suggest some action for the organization. The action is typically a plan (set of decisions) that addresses the key issues of the case. Therefore, the case most often provides some degree of focus for the student, as well as the environment, in order to develop the decision-making situation.

The objective of the case approach is not to provide the "right" solution, or rote knowledge, that the student will be able to apply to a future situation. Rather, the case approach provides the student with perspective concerning the complexity of the issues that organizations face, practice in discerning the critical issues, application of theory, an understanding of the interrelatedness of business functions, and discussion concerning important issues faced by modern enterprise. Case studies provide the student an in-depth learning experience in a given business situation that is difficult to obtain elsewhere.

THE CASEBOOK

This casebook is designed to be used in upper-level marketing strategy and marketing management courses. Marketing Strategy or Marketing Management is usually the capstone course in marketing and is typically required for all marketing majors and marketing minors. The general objective of the capstone course is to pull together marketing theory and practice into a broad understanding of marketing and its application. Other courses in marketing provide an overview of marketing, as in the principles of marketing course, or an in-depth study of the various functional areas of marketing such as sales management, advertising, pricing, channels of distribution, and so on. The marketing strategy or marketing management course asks students to solve problems and develop comprehensive marketing strategies in situations that are not clearly predetermined as promotional, segmentation, or channels of distribution. Utilizing a top-management perspective, students must consider all of an organization's systems and their interrelationships in developing marketing recommendations.

THE CASES

The marketing case studies developed and chosen for the casebook offer students a broad exposure to a cross section of strategic marketing situations. We think you will find this collection of 42 cases to be pedagogically sound, appealing to students, stimulating to teach, and on target with respect to the leading problems and issues in strategic marketing.

All of the cases included in the casebook are current and are supported with extensive industry information to provide the background material necessary to understand and assess an organization's markets. However, the cases, as with tomorrow's marketing problems and opportunities, are not listed under predetermined categories that may indicate the nature of the problem or opportunity facing the organization. In addition, the book contains many new cases that have not previously appeared in marketing casebooks or texts.

Among the 42 cases, 15 deal with well-known national organizations, 12 with moderately sized regional companies, six are small businesses, and nine are concerned with international firms. These companies' products are in various stages of the product life cycle. Six of the companies have products in the introductory state of the product life cycle, nine in the growth stage, 21 in maturity, and six in the decline stage. The book also has excellent balance with regard to market position; 14 of the organizations are considered market leaders, nine are market challengers, ten are currently nichers, and nine are product/market followers. The cases are multidimensional and comprehensive in that all of the marketing functional areas, as well as the target market, must be considered in the analysis of the case.

ACKNOWLEDGMENTS

We are deeply indebted to many individuals for their assistance and encouragement in the preparation of this casebook. A special thanks to Dean M. Gene Newport of the School of Business at the University of Alabama at Birmingham and Dean Richard E. Neel of the College of Business Administration at the University of North Carolina at Charlotte who have always been supportive of our efforts. An additional thanks to all the fine people at Prentice Hall for their constant help and guidance, especially Whitney Blake who provided encouragement, enthusiasm, and ideas. Thanks to Susan Bogle and Marilyn James at York Production Services for their professionalism in all areas, particularly their willingness to put in extra hours to ensure timely publication. We would also like to thank the Prentice Hall reviewers of the cases. These colleagues were particularly helpful in balancing the types of cases and identifying "teachable" cases.

Finally, this book would not have been possible without the case writers. Case writing is a difficult art requiring many hours of library research, personal interviews, and detailed analysis. The case contributors listed in this text represent some of the finest case researchers anywhere. We think you will appreciate and enjoy their craft.

Linda E. Swayne
Peter M. Ginter

CASE CONTRIBUTORS

Robert L. Anderson
College of Charleston

Steven J. Anderson
Austin Peay State University

M. Edgar Barrett
Southern Methodist University

Alan Bauerschmidt
University of South Carolina

Daniel C. Bello
Georgia State University

Richard F. Beltramini
Arizona State University

Tana J. Bisch
M.B.A. Student, University of
Alabama at Birmingham

William R. Boulton
University of Georgia

Charles W. Boyd
Southwest Missouri State University

Lew G. Brown
University of North Carolina at
Greensboro

Mary K. Coulter
Southwest Missouri State University

Ronald L. Coulter
Southwest Missouri State University

Robert P. Crowner
Eastern Michigan University

James DeConinck
University of Arkansas

D. Keith Denton
Southwest Missouri State University

John Dunkelberg
Wake Forest University

Paul W. Farris
University of Virginia

Philip C. Fisher
University of South Dakota

Thomas F. Funk
University of Guelph

Janiece L. Gallagher
M.B.A. Student, University of South
  Florida

Kenneth Gardner
University of South Carolina

Robert R. Gardner
Southern Methodist University

Peter M. Ginter
University of Alabama at Birmingham

Delbert C. Hastings
University of Minnesota

Robert D. Hay
University of Arkansas

Diane Hoadley
University of South Dakota

William C. House
University of Arkansas

Jean-Pierre Jeannet
International Management
  Development Institute (IMEDE)

Lorraine Justice
Humana, Inc.

Daniel G. Kopp
Southwest Missouri State University

John D. Leonard
M.B.A. Student, University of
  Alabama at Birmingham

Robert O. Lewis
M.B.A. Student, University of
  North Carolina at Charlotte

Patricia A. Luna
Golden Enterprises, Incorporated

Eleanor G. May
University of Virginia

Patrick H. McCaskey
Millersville State University

John H. Murphy II
University of Texas at Austin

James E. Nelson
University of Colorado

Chistoph Nussbaumer
Austin Peay State University

Susan W. Nye

International Management
  Development Institute (IMEDE)

John E. Oliver
Valdosta State College

James Olver
University of Virginia

John A. Quelch
Harvard University

C. P. Rao
University of Arkansas

Betty R. Ricks
Old Dominion University

Andrew C. Rucks
Samford University

JoAnn K. L. Schwinghammer
Mankato State University

Lois Shufeldt
Southwest Missouri State University

Kenneth Simmonds
London Business School

Simon Slater
London Business School

Melvin J. Stanford
Mankato State University

Linda E. Swayne
University of North Carolina at
  Charlotte

Albert J. Taylor
Austin Peay State University

Jeff Totten
University of Wisconsin—Oshkosh

Dharmendra T. Verma
Bentley College

Robert P. Vichas
Florida Atlantic University

Charles Wagner
Mankato State University

Thomas L. Wheelen
University of South Florida

Terry Wheeler
Humana, Inc.

Jeanne Whitehead
Austin Peay State University

John S. Wright
Georgia State University

William R. Wynd
Eastern Washington University

CASE ABSTRACTS

CASE 4 **Golden Hybrids Inc.** 84

In the early 1960s, Golden Hybrids Inc., a medium-sized firm in the hybrid seed corn industry, embarked upon an expansion program. Although pretax profits had been declining since 1983, management became concerned about this situation only after it learned that profits in 1986 were $52,000 below those of 1985. Management felt that the real problem it faced was in marketing—too much money was being spent on a marketing program that was not effective. In order to remedy the situation, a new marketing manager was hired in October 1986. Peter Jenkin's responsibility was to develop a marketing strategy that would return Golden Hybrids to increasing profitability.

CASE 5 **Baldor Electric Company** 102

Baldor Electric Company manufactured electric motors for the industrial market. Company growth exceeded industry growth dramatically. Baldor was ranked sixth in the industry with sales of $150 million. Market share doubled in the period from 1973 to 1982 in spite of recessions in 1974–75 and 1981–82. The company's product line included electric motors sold through distributors and to original equipment manufacturers. The primary comparative advantage was energy efficient motors at competitive prices. In spite of Baldor's increase in market share, dollar and unit sales had declined for the first time in twenty-two years.

Industry Note **Electric Motors** 113

The electric motor industry is extremely concentrated with the top 11 (out of 340 nationally) companies accounting for over 80 percent of industry sales. The various kinds of motors, motor applications, major competitors, major markets, and market niches as well as industry forecasts are included as background material for the student.

CASE 6 **Peter Piper Pizza (B)** 124

In 1973, Anthony Cavolo opened the first Peter Piper Pizza restaurant in Glendale, Arizona. Currently there are 90 restaurants throughout eight southwestern states, of which 32 are company owned and 58 are franchised. Peter Piper Pizza is one of the fastest growing restaurant chains in the nation, selling approximately 7 million pizzas a year. In 1985, sales were $42 million, with 1986 sales expected to reach $60 million. Cavolo is very confident in his concept of quality pizza at a low price. Currently, he would like to limit expansion in the Phoenix market to company stores only. In other markets, there are no specific plans for the future. Peter Piper's has just penetrated the California market, which further challenged the small chain's marketing programs.

CASE 7 **British Airways** 137

By many criteria, British Airways was the largest international airline in the world, yet the government-controlled enterprise maintained a weak public image. While British Airways received the 1983 Airline of the Year award, many around the world considered the airline to be inefficient and incompetent. When Saatchi & Saatchi (ad agency) took over the advertising, dramatic changes were made in an attempt to position British Airways as the world leader in air travel. The "World's Favorite Airline" theme had mixed reactions and raised several important questions about British Airways' marketing strategy.

AmSouth Bancorporation was the state's largest banking institution with assets of over $5.9 billion. Its principal subsidiary, AmSouth Bank N.A., served the state through more than 140 full-service banking offices. Over the last fifteen years, the CEO directed AmSouth's aggressive growth within the state and had positioned AmSouth to be a buyer of out-of-state banks. In order to continue being a leader in the banking industry, CEO Woods believed that AmSouth must maintain an aggressive growth position.

Banking has operated in a relatively stable environment for many years. However, deregulation has allowed new forms of competition and new competitors and the passage of interstate banking legislation has widened considerably the "playing field." The strategies that worked in the past in the banking industry are no longer appropriate and bankers must consider a whole new set of contingencies in marketing their banks.

The Anheuser-Busch Company was founded in 1852. Since 1860, members of the Busch family led the corporation in developing and maintaining its position of leadership in the beer industry. Vertical integration to control the total production process (including raw materials, packaging, etc.) and diversification into food products (including Eagle-brand snacks) had been undertaken. Diversified operations included theme parks, the St. Louis Cardinals baseball team, railroads, and others. Diversification strategies were successful and continued growth seemed evident.

A backyard entrepreneur designed a novel stool and pail combination. "Sit 'n Pick" was the sole product of Essential Products, Incorporated, a recently formed small business. The entrepreneur and his sister, who agreed to market the product, were trying to determine the appropriate marketing strategy for Sit 'n Pick.

Home Baking Company, a family-owned bakery, marketed over forty products in three main categories—hamburger buns, hot dog buns, and brown 'n serve rolls. Most of the company's products were sold to McDonald's, Burger King, Hardee's, and Wendy's. Growth had always been an important objective at Home Baking and the president believed that if Home Baking was to continue to grow, some difficult decisions had to be made. These decisions concerned Home Baking's future position as a supplier to the fast-food industry, alternatives for new product and market development, alternatives for expanding production capacity, and methods for financing additional growth.

CASE 12 Three Bond Company, Ltd.: Serving the Customer 235

Three Bond's sealing products and technologies were used and respected by every automobile manufacturer in Japan and accounted for 50 percent of the company's sales. After experiencing growth rates of over 25 percent per year since 1955, Three Bond's growth had been increasing at about 15 percent per year for the past several years. The sales goal for 1986 was 28 billion yen (about $170 million), as compared to 22 billion yen in 1983, with an expected eight percent before tax profit. The company was taking steps to develop overseas bases of operations, in order to bring Three Bond's products and services to more nations around the world.

CASE 13 Dakotah, Inc. 246

In 1971, George Whyte started a cooperative of farmwives to alleviate some of the financial stress in the depressed agricultural region of northeastern South Dakota. The co-op manufactured bedcoverings and associated textile home furnishings enjoying record sales of over $13 million in 1986 and record profits of almost $400,000. Its products were marketed by department stores as top-of-the-line textile home furnishings. In May 1987, Dakotah appeared to be on the brink of a new era of growth and profitability. Taking advantage of marketing opportunities might require abandoning policies that were once the company's reason for existence.

CASE 14 Atlanta Cyclorama 259

A cyclorama is a 360-degree circular painting that when viewed from its interior gives the illusion that the viewer is in the scene. The Atlanta Cyclorama was created in 1885 and depicts the 1864 Battle of Atlanta. The masterpiece is a 50-foot-high, 400-foot circumference painting in the round, with a three-dimensional diorama complete with figures. The director of the Atlanta Cyclorama is struggling with devising long-range strategies for the attraction. Attendance will have to be increased from an estimated 300,000 in 1984 to 500,000 in 1987, and sales will have to exceed one million dollars per year by 1990 in order for the Cyclorama to survive.

CASE 15 Saunders Leasing System, Inc.: Coping with the 1980s 268

Saunders Leasing System, Inc. was one of the nation's major truck transportation service companies competing with the giants of the industry such as Ryder and Hertz. The early 1970s were a time of great pressure on Saunders because of rising fuel costs and high inflation. These influences were reduced by industry regulation which allowed for higher costs to be passed on to customers. The 1980s brought deregulation to the trucking industry creating an intensely competitive market with fewer entry controls. In 1986, Saunders was pursuing a strategy of geographic and product expansion offering a wide variety of services. However, it was the opinion of management that without additional capital resources or repositioning of the firm, they would no longer be able to effectively compete.

The trucking industry is comprised of a variety of types of companies supplying America's transportation needs. Private trucking, common carriers, and contract carriers are explored in order to understand the number of products that transportation companies can offer since industry deregulation. General industry problems as well as opportunities are included as background information to enable the student to focus on developing marketing strategy for Saunders.

In July 1981, five young artists from varied theatrical backgrounds started the Roxy Dinner Theatre with a $10,000 investment. They hoped to create "an atmosphere of high artistic values and lively community involvement." The group's energy, talent, and cohesiveness was pitted against their lack of business experience, a shortage of capital, and a difficult market. After one artistically successful month of operation, they were faced with a sizable loss, sparse audiences, and a lack of control. During their first month of operation, the Roxy staff traded free tickets for favors, lost money on dinners, bounced checks, kept inadequate records, advertised only in the local newspaper, and lost $10,000. Some sweeping changes had to be made if the theatre was to survive.

Ozark Glass, a division of Ozark-Mercantile, Inc., is a manufacturer of colored sheet glass used in making stained glass windows, etc. Founded in 1974 as an antique shop specializing in merry-go-round horses, the company expanded into a studio teaching interested consumers the hobby of stained glass. The company then started to actively pursue the profitable do-it-yourself market. Over the next several years, six franchise stores were opened. The rapid expansion of the company led to an inability to purchase enough glass to satisfy the demands of the franchise stores. Therefore, Ozark Glass started its own 16,700 square foot stained glass manufacturing facility. The company experienced impressive growth selling sheet glass in the United States and abroad.

Springfield Remanufacturing Corporation was formerly a diesel engine and engine component remanufacturing plant owned by International Harvester. Jack Stack, along with a group of employees, purchased the plant in 1983 and during the next four years, Stack positioned the diesel-engine rebuilding business mix into what he called the "four cylinders"—construction equipment, agricultural equipment, trucks, and automobiles. Annual sales grew from approximately $16 million in 1983 to $38 million in 1986. In 1985, Springfield received a contract from General Motors to remanufacture the 5.7 liter diesel engines used in the Oldsmobile and by early 1987, GM accounted for 50 percent of the company's business. But in April 1987, GM notified Springfield that the number of remanufactured engines needed during 1987 would be significantly less than previously planned. The firm had to reconsider its strategy.

While China was a major country with one billion people and significant resources, its economic development and personal income levels were still very low; most of the population was rural. 3M began planning to enter China in 1972 when Nixon began normalizing relations with the People's Republic. It was not until November 1984 that 3M was authorized to operate in China, primarily because the company was insistent on a fully owned subsidiary. While 3M was optimistic regarding the potential for operations in China, outside observers found that uncertainties surrounding the initial agreement represented potential problems that could endanger current plans and future prospects.

TenderCare diapers were different, offering a superior product that did indeed keep babies drier. Just under its liner was a wicking fabric that drew moisture from the surface around a soft, waterproof shield to an absorbent reservoir of filler. Pampers and all other disposable diapers on the market kept moisture nearer to the liner and, consequently, the baby's skin. It was important for the Rocky Mountain Medical Corporation (developer of TenderCare brand diapers) that the product reach the market as soon as possible. Every month of delay meant deferred revenue, other postponed benefits that would derive from a successful introduction, and the chance that an existing competitor might develop its own drier diaper and effectively block the company from reaping the fruits of its development efforts.

Software Publishing began operation in the early 1980s by developing an application program (software) for the Apple Computer called Personal Filing System, or PFS for short. Additional programs were gradually added to perform word processing, graphing, electronic spreadsheet, proofreading, and communication functions. In the mid 1980s, the PFS series was also adapted to run on IBM and IBM-compatible computers. Company sales revenues and profits steadily increased until 1986, when the company suffered a significant decline in both sales and net income. The company was faced with the task of evaluating marketing effort in relation to its principal competitors, and deciding which products and markets to emphasize in a dynamic, highly competitive environment.

The two owners of a small women's clothing store in a rural community desired to increase profits from the store. In the two years since they bought JJ's, the owners have improved the store's profitability somewhat. They believed that by increasing sales they would increase profits. The store's "young career" clothing lines are targeted to college or young career women, and ranged from casual to semi-dressy clothing, typically priced a few dollars below the competitors. The store is located one block off the main business area in a small town 40 miles from a larger city. The owners think the personal service they offer could attract young women from the nearby city.

CASE 23   The Dallas Morning News   394

The *Dallas Morning News* and the *Dallas Times Herald* had been battling for years, but in the first half of 1985, the *News* had gained a significant circulation advantage in Dallas County—long the *Times Herald*'s strongest market. Some industry analysts suggested the battle in Dallas for newspaper supremacy was over, won by the *Morning News*. But late in 1986, MediaNews Group purchased the *Times Herald* and immediately filed a circulation fraud suit against the *News*. MediaNews assembled an experienced and aggressive management team to lead the *Herald*. With a countersuit filed by the *News*, it appeared that rather than the battle being over, a new skirmish was underway.

CASE 24   MHA Safe Deposit, Ltd.   425

MHA Safe Deposit Company, Ltd. started with high hopes and expectations of success as a new private safe depository in the greater Boston, Massachusetts area. Approximately $800,000 in venture capital was raised, and an impressive office and vault complex was equipped. Unfortunately, the anticipated customer demand had not materialized. President Robert Hall recognized cashflow problems on the horizon, and knew decisive action must be taken.

CASE 25   AT&T and the Residential Long-Distance Market—(A) and (B)   443

Case A is set in early 1984 as AT&T prepared to implement the "equal access" provisions of Judge Harold Greene's order deregulating the telecommunications industry. Monica Barnes, a mid-level manager in AT&T's southern region marketing division, must prepare a marketing strategy for the residential customers to have them select AT&T as their long-distance provider. AT&T found itself in the position of having all its customers specifically asked to choose a long-distance provider. This unique situation provided a real marketing challenge in an industry not previously known for marketing prowess.

Case B is set one year later. AT&T had implemented a strategy based on the rules and regulations established in 1984. However, in mid-1985, the FCC published new rules that changed the "default" provisions of the earlier procedure. Whereas customers who failed to select a long-distance carrier had been "defaulted" to AT&T, the FCC decided that defaulters would be allocated based on the percentages of customers actually selecting each carrier in the first round. Further, customers already defaulted would be given another opportunity to decide. Monica must rethink the established strategy in light of these significant and unexpected decisions.

CASE 26   American Greetings   446

American Greetings is the world's largest publicly owned manufacturer of greeting cards and related social expression merchandise. In 1977, the company formulated a growth strategy to attack the industry leader, Hallmark. By the end of 1985, American Greetings had reached its objective of $1 billion in sales and had increased its market share from 24 percent to nearly 35 percent. However, 1986 performance was disappointing. Total revenue and earnings were flat and predicted to remain so for the next several years.

Immanuel-St. Joseph's Hospital, a private, nonprofit hospital, had a medical staff of more than 100 physicians, total assets of about $25 million, 700 employees, 180 beds, and was the leading hospital in south central Minnesota. However, it competed for both local and referral patients with the Mayo Clinic, the University of Minnesota hospital, and several other metropolitan hospitals. Immanuel-St. Joseph's marketing strategy was to maintain up-to-date health care technology, have competitive costs, market its own medical staff primarily to other physicians and secondarily to the public, and to market nonacute care programs directly to the public. Purchasing Magnetic Resonance Imaging equipment, while extremely expensive, was considered important to support the marketing strategy.

Volvo Bus of North America, a bus manufacturing subsidiary of the Swedish A.B. Volvo Company, entered the U.S. market after demand had peaked in the late 1970s and had yet to achieve profitability. From 1980 to 1985, demand for buses declined 50 percent, and prices dropped 25 percent. The first Volvo bus was produced in 1984, well after the Reagan administration had curtailed federal support for mass transit which had been initiated under the Carter administration. In March 1985, Volvo appointed Jan-Olof Rabe, former general manager of its Indonesian plant, as the new CEO of Volvo Bus-NA and gave him a 3-year charter to turn the United States operations around. Within 6 months of Rabe's appointment, Volvo's top management began a series of meetings to reassess the likelihood of a successful turnaround.

In 1986, the Army and Air Force Exchange Service (AAFES), a worldwide retail, food, and service organization, was one of the largest retailers in the United States, with sales of over $4.5 billion. The primary mission of AAFES was to provide authorized patrons (military personnel and their dependents) with merchandise and services of necessity and convenience at low prices. However, the 1980s had brought increased competition in retailing both in the U.S. and worldwide. General Long, Commander of AAFES, believed that some fundamental changes in the exchange system were required if it was to continue to be successful into the 1990s.

Humana Inc. is an international company that provides an integrated system of for-profit health care services that includes hospital care, prepaid health care and indemnity insurance plans, as well as medical care centers where independent physicians deliver primary medical care. At the end of fiscal 1985, company operations included 86 hospitals, 148 MedFirst clinics, and 359,200 members insured by Humana Care Plus. Over the years, Humana has enjoyed financial success. This performance was a direct result of acquiring or building new hospitals and selling unprofitable ones. However, the delivery of health care services has evolved and new strategies may be in order for Humana.

After more than a decade of declining sales, many people believed that the Swiss watch industry was again on the rise. Much of the credit for the resurrection had been given to Ernst Thomke, President of Ebauches SA, one of the Asuag-SSIH companies, and initiator of SWATCH. Thomke believed that the predictions of a revived Swiss watch industry were premature. He had recently accepted a new task of giving the Asuag brands, and particularly Tissot, a workable brand strategy to bring the Asuag group to profitability by the end of the 1980s. Specifically, his goal was to increase Asuag-SSIH total volume from 7 million to 50 million units.

SASSAFRAS! was a community cookbook developed and marketed by the Junior League of Springfield, Missouri, Inc. A second printing of 10,000 books was ordered less than one year after initial publication in April 1985. Selling to family, friends, neighbors, and the Springfield community had been relatively easy but SASSAFRAS! had been developed with the intent of the casebook becoming a long term, successful fund-raiser for the Junior League of Springfield. The organization needed unique, creative and effective marketing strategies to assure that SASSAFRAS! continued to sell as well or better than it did in its first year of publication.

The objective of Kraft, Inc. was to become recognized as the leading food company in the world. In order to accomplish this objective, the company's management team had to contend with a decline in the U.S. population growth rate, changing dietary habits, and a worldwide restructuring of major food processing companies. Kraft's top managers were coping with these changes through the product mix including retrenchment in fluid milk products, and growth in frozen desserts, such as the acquisition of Frusen Gladje, a premium ice cream. In 1986, Dart and Kraft, Inc. was separated into Kraft, Inc. and Premark International, Inc. which controlled Tupperware, West Bend, Hobart, and Wilsonart. As a result, Kraft, Inc. is now composed of the food lines and the Duracell Battery Division. In order to gain the top position in the world food processing industry, Kraft had to develop outstanding marketing strategies.

Circuit City, a very successful regional retailer of appliances, audio, video, and consumer electronics, had grown to 93 stores with $519 million in sales and $20 million in profit. The Circuit City strategy had shifted from small stores with various names and various merchandise selections to 30,000-to-40,000-square-foot stores with a vast selection of popular brand-name merchandise. The stores typically obtained a large share of the retail market. Growth had been accomplished by high levels of customer service, including repair services, along with guaranteed low prices on all merchandise. Circuit City must now develop a strategy to maintain growth and market position. One opportunity would be to reintroduce mail-order/catalog selling.

CASE 35   Rockwood Manor   635

Rockwood Manor is a residential-health facility that offers a full spectrum of services to meet the housing, nutrition, health, social, and spiritual needs of active, older persons. It is operated by a nonprofit corporation related to the United Methodist Church but receives no financial assistance from the church or any other organization. Recognizing the growing demand for housing, the board of directors has asked the administrator for a proposal to expand existing facilities. The administrator must assess the demand and recommend the appropriate marketing strategy for continued success.

CASE 36   Ryan's Family Steak Houses, Inc.   643

Ryan's is the second successful venture by Alvin A. McCall, Jr., in the family steak house business. Having previously developed the Quincey's concept with a group of partners, he wanted to follow his own philosophy. The first Ryan's restaurant was opened in Greenville, South Carolina in 1978, using the concept of quality products at reasonable prices. Mr. McCall took his firm public in 1982 and gained recognition by the stock market as a successful firm with an apparently assured future. However, the growth in sales for family steak houses was not predicted to increase as rapidly as other types of restaurants. In addition, the declining consumption of red meat could have a major impact on sales if the trend continued.

CASE 37   Knickers in a Twist   657

Peter Barnett decided he wanted to be self-employed. He investigated several business ideas before settling on Knickers in a Twist, a company he wanted to start to manufacture and sell ladies' knickers (underpants). Peter located an office, product designer, packager, suppliers, and other necessary people and agencies. He decided to have his knickers manufactured in Malta, returned to the United Kingdom to be packaged by a local firm, and then sold by some of Britain's best known retail stores. The product would be a high quality ladies' brief that would be sold in a clear plastic tube containing two different colored knickers twisted together. Initial research was encouraging and Peter was enthusiastic. He must either commit himself to the venture or abandon the idea.

CASE 38   Guest Quarters—Frequent Flyer   667

In January 1986, John Vernon, Vice President of Marketing for Guest Quarters, a small chain of all-suite hotels, decided that the firm should follow the rest of the industry and join at least one of the "frequent flyer" programs conducted by the major airlines. He knew that some action needed to be taken immediately to increase occupancy and profits at Guest Quarters. The newest hotels were experiencing problems in developing the kind of acceptance that Guest Quarters had gained in its older locations. Despite the fact that almost no data substantiating the benefits or costs of frequent flyer programs were available, Mr. Vernon believed that participation in such a program could help remedy the firm's situation. However, many options were open as to how and when to implement this strategy.

Housatonic Valley Workshop began as a father-and-son partnership in Oxford, Connecticut. The company manufactured and sold solid brass bookmarks that replicated early American weathervanes. They planned to market 19 distinct patterns including horse, rooster, eagle, Indian, fish, mermaid, and other designs. After eight months of operation, the owners were having second thoughts about their business venture. The product sold to a variety of retail outlets, but there were no repeat orders. Then a giftware distributor in California offered to "handle" the product.

Con-Way Central Express, as a regional less-than-truckload subsidiary of Consolidated Freightways, Inc., began operation in 1983 with 11 terminals. In 1986, just three-and-a-half years later, there were 38 locations and revenues had increased over twenty-five times. Con-way Central was in the top 25 in the country in terms of tonnage handled. This growth was quite significant considering the deregulation-induced shakeout in the trucking industry that caused many firms to enter bankruptcy. Management thought its commitment to on-time delivery was the primary reason for the company's success. The president's goal was to achieve 25 percent share of the midwest trucking market within the next few years.

Frank Rogers, Chairman of Ansafone Corporation, was concerned about how the company could exploit the recently liberalized United Kingdom market for telephone answering machines and reverse recent corporate losses. Ansafone's main business was the leasing of telephone answering machines including models ranging from simple dual tape machines to those with sophisticated remote control and extended recording capacity. Having made healthy profits until liberalization introduced new channels of distribution, a lower price level, and the option of buying machines, Ansafone had now come to a crisis. The rental base was rapidly eroding and Ansafone machines were over engineered and overpriced compared to competitive offerings. The company had experienced difficulty converting its recognition of changing competitive circumstances into a successful new strategy.

Matthew Robertson, previously a member of the highly successful development team for desktop publishing, had a new assignment. The engineering workstation market had been identified as having considerable potential for Apple's Macintosh II microcomputer. In terms of features and price, the Mac II was ideal for low-end workstation applications. Yet, engineers were going to be hard to convince that the Mac II was more than a toy and could handle sophisticated engineering software. Because the engineering workstation market was already established and included several formidable competitors, Matthew knew this new assignment was going to be more challenging than desktop publishing, a market that Apple established.

Golden Enterprises, Incorporated

COMPANY ORGANIZATION

Golden Enterprises, Incorporated, is a holding company that owns all of the outstanding shares of Golden Flake Snack Foods, Steel City Group, and the Sloan-Major Agency.

Golden Flake Snack Foods, Incorporated

The Golden Flake Snack Food Company accounts for 95 percent of Golden Enterprises's sales and over 96 percent of the operating profit. A full line of snack foods is manufactured including potato chips, corn and tortilla chips, cheese curls, popcorn, pork skins, roasted peanuts, onion rings, and cheese or peanut butter filled crackers. Golden Flake snack products are manufactured in Alabama, Tennessee, and Florida and are sold in thirteen states.

Steel City Group

The Steel City Group is comprised of Steel City Bolt & Screw, Incorporated, and Nall & Associates, a manufacturers' representative. Nall & Associates has only four employees and operates as part of Steel City Bolt & Screw. Steel City, founded in 1968 and acquired by Golden Enterprises in 1971, has become a leading manufacturer of custom-fabricated products, such as hot headed bolts, sag rods, anchor bolts, U-bolts, pole line fasteners, and other bent and threaded items. Its products are sold and shipped nationwide and some are exported.

Manufacturing is in a modern 80,000-square-foot plant in Birmingham, Alabama. A distribution warehouse in Greenville, South Carolina, was sold July 1986, to enable the company to concentrate its resources on manufacturing of specialty items. Customers include some of the leading American firms in such varied fields as electric utilities, lighting standard manufacturers, transmission towers, railroads, structured steel fabricators, farm equipment, metal buildings, and fastener distributors.

The Steel City Group contributed less than 5 percent to revenues and slightly over 3 percent in profit in 1986.

This case was written by Peter M. Ginter, Linda E. Swayne, and Patricia A. Luna as a basis for class discussion rather than to illustrate either effective or ineffective handling of an administrative situation. Used by permission from Patricia A. Luna.

Sloan-Major Agency

The Sloan-Major Agency is a full-service advertising agency with ten full-time employees. It was acquired by Golden Flake in 1980. Typical agency services are provided including media research and buying, creative development from concept to final copy (including package design), production, development and implementation of marketing programs, and public relations.

The account list for Sloan-Major has expanded from three to thirty clients, representing a variety of consumer, retail, industrial, and corporate accounts. Golden Flake Snack Foods has been its largest account. Billings for 1986 were $5 million, placing Sloan-Major among the top ten advertising agencies in the Birmingham area.

COMPANY HISTORY

Magic City Food Products was founded in 1923 in Birmingham, Alabama. Mr. Mose Lischkoff and Mr. Frank Mosher started the company in the basement of a Hills Grocery store in North Birmingham. Introduced as a new item, their fresh, kettle-cooked potato chips caught on quickly.

Helen Friedman was one of the first employees hired. Deemed the "Golden Flake Girl," she was the driving force in Magic City's rapid expansion. In fact, Helen and her mother financed the buy-out of Mr. Mosher's partner, Mose Lischkoff. Miss Friedman married Mr. Mosher in 1928, but later divorced him and received the company in settlement.

Under Helen Friedman's leadership, Magic City Food Products reached sales of almost one million dollars by 1946. That year the company was incorporated and sold to the Bashinsky family. One of the first moves of the new owners was to officially change the name of the company to be more descriptive: Golden Flake, Incorporated.

Sloan Bashinsky, the current chief executive officer, bought the company from his father ten years later in 1956. Although he had been one of the charter members of the board of directors and secretary-treasurer, Sloan Bashinsky had worked his way up through both route sales and production. He initiated the construction of Golden Flake's current Birmingham plant and later two additional plants in Nashville, Tennessee, and Ocala, Florida.

In 1968 the company became a public corporation and diversified into insurance, real estate, fasteners, and advertising. In 1977 Golden Flake Snack Foods became a wholly owned subsidary of the holding company, Golden Enterprises, Incorporated. (See Exhibit 1.1 for company history.)

The company has had steady sales growth. Since 1946 when one million dollars in sales was achieved, Golden Flake Snack Foods has doubled sales every five years. In the 1987 annual report, Golden Enterprises had total revenues of over $123 million. (See Exhibit 1.2.)

EXHIBIT 1.1	Company history summarized
1985	Ocala, Florida manufacturing plant began operation
1979	Sloan-Major Advertising Agency formed as a wholly owned subsidiary
1977	Golden Enterprises, Incorporated, a holding company was formed; Golden Flake Snack Foods became a wholly owned subsidiary
1968	Became public corporation
1966	Don's Foods (Nashville company) purchased
1948	Renamed Golden Flake, Incorporated
1946	Incorporated and purchased by the Bashinsky family
1923	Magic City Foods started by Lischkoff and Mosher

THE SALTED SNACK FOOD MARKET: INDUSTRY PROFILE

Snack foods have been around for over two centuries. Snack is actually a Dutch word that means "to bite." Thus, snacks are bite-sized foods perfect for quick meals or quick energy. Sales of salted snack foods have steadily increased, and in fact, tripled over the last decade. However, projections are that sales will slow to a 9 percent increase over the next ten years. Sales volume for 1985 was $7.05 billion and increased 8.19 percent in 1986 to $7.63 billion.

The salted snack food market has been a relatively small portion of the total snack food market. Confectionary items (candy bars, candy morsels, etc.) constitute the greatest percentages of snack food sales. (See Exhibit 1.3.)

Forty-seven percent of the salted snack food market was potato chip sales. Corn/tortilla chips represented 23.3 percent of industry sales. The remaining one-fourth of the market consisted of popcorn, cheese curls, pork rinds, pretzels, and salted nuts sales. (See Exhibit 1.4.)

Sales volume in 1986 was up 8.19 percent over 1985, which had been a disappointing year in the industry. One regional executive speculated that the reason 1985 sales were "off" was the relatively prosperous economy. "The snack food market does well in recessionary times and suffers when the economy is better and people spend part of their greater disposable income to dine out." Fast-food

EXHIBIT 1.2 **Golden Flake snack foods sales and income history**
(In thousands of dollars, fiscal year)

	1979	1980	1981	1982	1983	1984	1985	1986	1987
Total revenues	$42,831	$50,348	$58,681	$70,253	$81,218	$95,991	$112,289	$115,064	$116,617
Operating profit	$ 5,478	$ 5,026	$ 6,078	$ 9,560	$12,254	$15,664	$ 14,495	$ 11,608	$ 14,960

EXHIBIT 1.3 **All snack food sales 1986**

	Sales 1986 (In millions)	Percent
Candy	$7,400	29.9
Cookies/crackers	5,627	22.8
Potato chips	2,977	12.0
Corn/tortilla chips	1,462	5.9
Snack cakes/pies	1,240	5.0
Nuts/meats	1,160	4.7
Frozen pizza	1,063	4.3
Imported and misc.	606	2.4
Dried fruit	508	2.1
Hot snacks	440	1.8
Extruded snacks	456	1.8
Meat snacks	400	1.6
Popcorn	382	1.5
Granola snacks	359	1.4
Pretzels	293	1.2
Other	396	1.6

Source: Snack Food Association, June 1987.

restaurants are estimated to obtain approximately 48 percent of the $112 billion spent for food in the United States.

Potato Chips

Potato chip sales totaled $3.58 billion in 1986, an increase of 9.4 percent over 1985. Barbecue was the most popular flavored potato chip. Several new flavors such

EXHIBIT 1.4 **Salted snack food sales volume by product type**

Product	1985 sales (In millions)	Percent	1986 sales (In millions)	Percent
Potato chips	$3,298.1	46.8	$3,580.0	47.0
Corn/tortilla chips	1,638.8	23.3	1,780.0	23.3
Salted nuts	930.7	13.2	986.8	12.9
Pretzels	341.8	4.8	366.4	4.8
Salted meat snacks	340.8	4.8	348.4	4.8
Extruded snacks	321.1	4.6	342.6	4.5
Popped popcorn	177.6	2.5	221.7	2.7
TOTAL	$7,048.9		$7,625.9	

Source: Snack Food Association Management Report, 1987.

EXHIBIT 1.5 **Industry averages: potato chip sales by flavor and type**		
Flavors	**Percent in 1985**	**Percent in 1986**
Salted/unsalted unflavored chips	70.8	61.0
Barbecue flavored chips	11.5	19.1
Cheddar cheese flavored	6.4	1.8
Sour cream and onion	5.9	3.1
Salt and vinegar	2.2	1.7
Others	3.2	3.3
Types		
Regular chips	60.4	55.6
Rippled/ridged	33.0	33.4
Thick homestyle	6.6	5.3
Kettle-style	n/a	5.7

Source: Snack Food Association 1987 Management Report.

as cajun spiced and jalapeno were introduced but had not achieved much market share. Frito-Lay's "Jalapeno and Cheddar" pushed Lay's brand up 15 percent. (See Exhibit 1.5.)

Corn/Tortilla Chips

Corn/tortilla chip sales were down in 1984 and 1985 but up 8.3 percent in 1986. Double-digit growth rates had occurred from 1980 through 1983. The product category seems to have matured and in spite of introductions of new flavors in 1985, sales grew less than anticipated. However, it is difficult to obtain accurate data for tortilla chip sales due to the number of small producers in California and the Southwest.

The total sales for the category were considered to be $1.78 billion, with tortilla chips accounting for two-thirds of that amount. It appears that corn chips and *not* tortilla chips have been responsible for the declining sales in this product category. (See Exhibit 1.6.)

Extruded Snacks

Extruded snacks are products that have the shape defined as the product is pushed (extruded) through machinery. Although sales were up 6.7 percent in 1986, the extruded snacks share of the overall snack market declined slightly from 4.5 percent in 1985 to 4.4 percent in 1986. (See Exhibit 1.7.)

Salted Meat Snacks (includes Pork Rinds)

Sales of salted meats increased from $340.8 million in 1985 to $348.4 million in 1986. Sales of pork rind products dropped 10 percent while other meat snack

EXHIBIT 1.6 **Industry averages: corn/tortilla chip sales by flavor**

Corn Chips	Percent in 1985	Percent in 1986	Tortilla Chips	Percent in 1985	Percent in 1986
Unflavored (salted)	72.2	65.3	Nacho cheese	58.0	53.0
Barbecue	23.9	27.8	Unflavored (salted)	33.9	37.4
Nacho cheese	3.1	0.4	Other	6.1	3.6
Other	0.6	0.9	Cheddar cheese	2.0	0.2
Unflavored (unsalted)	n/a	5.7	Jalapeno	n/a	3.3
			Unflavored (unsalted)	n/a	2.7
Total Sales $614.0 million			Total Sales $1,170.0 million		

Source: Snack Food Association 1987 Management Report.

sales increased 5.3 percent. Salted meats account for 4.8 percent of the salted snack food market. (See Exhibit 1.8.)

Popped Corn/Pretzels/Nuts

Popped popcorn is a salted snack product that had phenomenal growth in 1981 and has attempted to maintain double-digit increases each year. Sales in 1986 were up 25.7 percent over 1985, to $221.7 million.

Nationally, consumers are concerned about sodium intake which may have affected the sales of pretzels and salted nuts. Sales of these products were up slightly over 4 percent for 1985. In 1986, pretzels were up 7.9 percent to $366.4 million and nuts were up 6.7 percent to $986.8 miliion.

EXHIBIT 1.7 **Extruded flavors**

	Percent of market
Cheddar cheese	61.0
Unflavored	12.7
BBQ	8.2
Nacho cheese	5.1
Sour cream & onion	0.1
Other	12.9

Source: Snack Food Association 1987 Management Report.

EXHIBIT 1.8 **Pork rind flavors**

	Percent of market
Unflavored	55.6
BBQ	29.1
Nacho cheese	1.1
Other	14.2

Source: Snack Food Association 1987 Management Report.

SALTED SNACK FOOD INDUSTRY AVERAGES

Companies with sales over $50 million reported pretax profit margins of 6.14 percent for 1986, down from 9.4 percent in 1985.

In the salted snack food industry, the average has been for cost of goods manufactured to be 55.2 percent of sales, selling and freight have been 23.9 percent, marketing and advertising averaged 9.3 percent of sales, general administrative expenses were 5.5 percent, and pretax income was 6.14 percent of sales.

Within the industry, companies averaged 6.4 percent of gross sales for promotional activities. Advertising accounted for 4.3 percent of gross sales. Promotions, both trade and consumer, accounted for 7.44 percent of gross sales (Exhibit 1.9).

EXHIBIT 1.9 **Average allocation of promotional dollars in snack food industry 1985**

Promotional Activity	Percent of Gross Sales	Percent of Promotional Budget
Advertising	3.1	
Print		45.2
Radio		25.8
Television		19.3
Other		9.7
Promotions	3.3	
Trade		60.6
Consumer		39.4

It appears that most new product development in the industry is left up to Frito-Lay and other large, national manufacturers. Only 24.5 percent of the snack food manufacturers introduced a new product in 1985. However, 48.9 percent introduced line extension products (new size, new flavor of existing product, etc.).

The salted snack food market is growing at a rate of approximately 8.19 percent per year and reached $7.63 billion in total sales in 1986. The major products, such as potato chips and corn chips, have reached the maturity stage of the product life cycle although innovative products like granola balls, and mixed snacks have been recently introduced.

Currently, the snack chip market is about 1.32 percent of the total food industry and is expected to keep growing. Snack chips are projected to make up 1.66 percent of food industry sales by 1995 (according to USDA statistics) as a result of rising per capita income and increasing snack food purchases.

Competition, especially from the large marketing-knowledgeable companies, such as Frito-Lay, Borden, Eagle, is expected to be strong in the future. Consolidation has occurred in the industry and is expected to continue.

Among consumers, health concerns and more meals eaten away from home will reduce the purchases of salted snack food products. Most meals eaten away from home are in fast food restaurants that do not serve chips.

THE COMPETITION

Frito-Lay, a subsidiary of Pepsico, Incorporated, is Golden Flake's major competition throughout the Southeast. Such familiar brands as Fritos, Lay's, Ruffles, O'Grady's, Cheetos, Doritos, and Tostitos are all Frito-Lay products. This formidable competitor owns 50 percent of the salted snack food market. The company has "state-of-the-art" manufacturing facilities in North Carolina, Connecticut, and Indiana, and has an extensive direct retail store delivery distribution system using company-owned, tractor-trailer trucks.

Other competitors have spikes of excellence, producing some very competitive brands for Golden Flake. Some are national in market coverage and others, like Golden Flake, are regionally oriented. A summary of Golden Flake's salted snack food competitors is presented in Exhibit 1.10.

EXHIBIT 1.10 **Competitive summary**

Competitor	Sales (In millions)	Snack Brands	Market
American Brands New York	$ 730	Sunshine, Bell, Bluebell Compadres, Squiggles, Humpty-Dumpty	U.S. and Canada
Anheuser-Busch St. Louis	6,500	Eagle Snacks Cape Cod (Northeast, Florida)	National Roll-out in 1987
Borden, Inc. New York	4,710	Cheez Doodles, Cottage Fries, New York Deli, Wise, Granny Goose	United States

EXHIBIT 1.10 (Continued)

Competitor	Sales (In millions)	Snack Brands	Market
Charles Chips (Mussers Potato Chips) Pennsylvania	*	Charles Chips	38 states and international
Clover Club Foods Vermont	50	Clover Club	Northeastern United States
Adolph Coors Company Colorado	1,280	Coors Chips	7 western states
Culbro Corporation (Snacktime Co.—Indiana) New York	1,090	Tiras, Indian Corn, Chips, Cornies, Pepitos	14 midwestern states
Frito-Lay Texas	2,500	Fritos, Lays, Ruffles, O'Gradys, Muchos, Cheetos, Doritos, Tostitos, Funyuns, Rold Gold	United States
G. Heileman Brewing Co. Wisconsin	1,160	Barrell O'Fun, Red Seal	Southwestern states, Minn. and Maryland
Keebler Company Illinois	876	Krunch Twists, Potato Skins, Cheeblers	United States
Lance, Incorporated North Carolina	355	Lance, Gold-n-Cheese, Lanchos	35 eastern states and D.C.
Mike-Sell's Tennessee	29	Mike-Sell's	Tennessee, Ohio
Moore's, Inc. Virginia	*	Moore's chips	8 Mid-Atlantic states
Nabisco Brands, Inc. New Jersey	6,370	Planters	United States
Procter & Gamble, Inc. Ohio	15,400	Pringles	United States
Ralston-Purina Co. St. Louis	5,860	Chex Snack Mix	United States
Southland Corp. Texas	12,700	Pate, El-Ge, private labels	Northwestern, midwestern states
Zapp's Louisiana	*	Zapp's	Louisiana, Mississippi, Florida
Tom's Georgia	230	Tom's	United States

*Privately held, sales volume not available

GOLDEN FLAKE SNACK FOODS, INCORPORATED

Corporate Goals

While Golden Flake is the market share leader in Alabama, the company knows that being number one in other states is an unrealistic goal given the resources of the industry leader Frito-Lay. Generally, the corporate objective is to be the leader in Alabama and a very strong number two in all other markets.

Golden Flake's number-one-goal is quality. The company believes the quality goal can be achieved by setting the standard for the industry in production, taste, freshness, and productivity.

Another goal is to provide exceptional service and to deliver the freshest products. In spite of its high cost, the direct-delivery distribution system is considered to be the best way to continue to accomplish this goal.

Further, Golden Flake has the objective to double sales dollars every five years. This was an original goal of the company that has been met since it was acquired by the Bashinsky family in 1946.

Finally, Golden Flake wants to attract and retain the best employees in the industry. Although over 1,700 people are employed by Golden Flake, the company has continued to emphasize a family atmosphere by including employees in stock purchase plans and quarterly small group meetings.

Management

Golden Flake's organizational chart illustrates the company's management philosophy. (See Exhibit 1.11.)

Golden Flake 1987 Operating Results

Corporate income was down slightly in 1986 due to the small increase in revenues that were insufficient for the increased costs associated with the greater production capacity acquired over the last two years. Capital expenditures of $30.5 million during 1985 and 1986 were financed out of working capital. The company has no debt resulting from the capital expansion. The results for 1987 have shown improvement over 1986.

No major new products had been introduced in 1986 (although Cheese Puffs were included as a line extension). The company strategy was for market penetration–increased sales in existing markets with existing products. Southern Farms brand Mesquite potato chips were introduced in July 1987, and Ranch-flavored Tortilla Chips in October 1987.

Productivity

In 1985 significant expansion for Golden Flake was completed. A new snack food plant was constructed in Ocala, Florida, a corn tortilla line was added to the

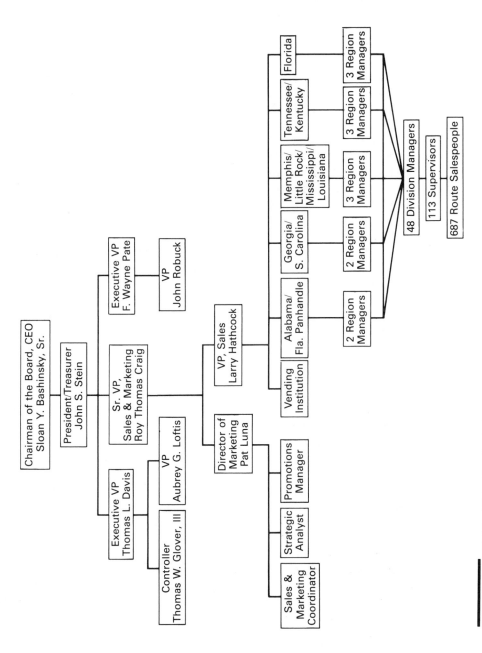

EXHIBIT 1.11 **Golden Flake Snack Foods management**

Nashville plant, and major renovations to conveying and packaging equipment were completed at the Birmingham facility. Three satellite warehouses were built in the Birmingham area. As a result of these expansions and improvements, Golden Flake is now in the strategic position to increase sales volume by up to 50 percent without any significant capital expenditures on plant or equipment.

Golden Flake has "state-of-the-art" processing and packaging equipment that allows for efficient use of raw materials. The new plant in Ocala, Florida, utilizes the latest technologies. These modern facilities enable Golden Flake to compete with Frito-Lay in quality, taste, and freshness.

By establishing manufacturing plants in Ocala, Florida, and Nashville, Tennessee, Golden Flake has been able to provide quick delivery to customers in these areas. (See Exhibit 1.22 for location of manufacturing sites.) The Ocala plant can produce 2,100 pounds per hour of potato chips plus either 1,400 pounds of tortilla chips or 1,000 pounds of corn chips per hour.

A newly constructed potato warehouse in Birmingham will store 20 million pounds of potatoes in an atmosphere that is controlled for temperature and humidity by a computer. The warehouse utilizes hydraulic lifts, conveyer systems, and water flumes for unloading trucks and moving the potatoes to cleaning or storage. Potato warehouses help to ensure that temporary fluctuations in potato supply do not have a significant impact on company operations.

As capacity has increased, expanded markets have been sought. Originally selling only in the Birmingham area, Golden Flake now sells in 13 states in the Southeast.

Marketing Strategy

Golden Flake does not purport to be a leader in the snack food market. The company has been using a follow-the-leader strategy. For example, when Frito-Lay developed "O'Grady's" brand of cheese-flavored potato chip, Golden Flake introduced Au Gratin Potato Chips which was withdrawn in late 1986 and replaced by a cheese-flavored chip.

The company feels that its distribution system will be useful for future growth. Company-owned trucks, driven by company employees, are important in providing outstanding service to customers and controlling distribution costs.

Moreover, the direct distribution system allows for expansion into new territories by what the company calls the "ink blot" method. GF has expanded their market territory gradually outward in every direction from Alabama. They are not willing to skip or jump over a large area of rural population to get to a city. Although GF is nearing Cincinnati and entered Louisville in the fall of 1986, they have not missed the potential customers in northern Kentucky or southern Ohio before reaching for the larger consumer markets.

Market Share   Golden Flake represents only a small part of the total snack food market both in terms of geographical markets and sales volume. Nationally, Frito-Lay is the market leader with a 40-percent share. However, Golden Flake

---

EXHIBIT 1.12 **Golden Flake market share by state**

	Percent in 1986	Percent in 1987		Percent in 1986	Percent in 1987
Alabama			**Tennessee/Kentucky**		
Golden Flake	40	36.3	Frito-Lay	60	57.4
Frito-Lay	35	43.8	Golden Flake	21	10.1
Pringles	7	*	Moores	10	*
Tom's	5	6.2	Tom's	5	1.1
Wise	1	*	Pringles	2	*
Others	12	13.6	Others	2	31.5
Georgia			**Florida**		
Frito-Lay	59	59.0	Frito-Lay	60	62.7
Golden Flake	21	11.2	Golden Flake	10	6.4
Wise	5	*	Tom's	6	8.2
Pringles	5	*	Wise	5	*
Tom's	5	10.9	Pringles	3	*
Moores	2	*	Eagle	2	*
Others	3	18.9	Others	14	22.7
Louisiana/Southern Mississippi****			**Memphis/Little Rock******		
Frito-Lay		62.1	Frito-Lay		70.3
Golden Flake		13.0	Golden Flake		10.5
Tom's		2.9	Tom's		4.2
Others		22.1	Others		15.0

*Share changed, included with "others."

**New markets, 1986 data not available.

Source: Neilson Market Research Data, June 1, 1987.

---

has had the largest market share in Alabama until 1987. (See Exhibit 1.12.) In the recent expansion states of Arkansas, Kentucky, Louisiana, and Ohio, the company's products are increasing in market share.

Positioning Research on consumer perceptions has developed a competitive price-quality positioning map (Exhibit 1.13) that is different from the map that the company believes reflects the actual positions in the marketplace (Exhibit 1.14).

Although Golden Flake's positioning is similar to its competitors, their target market is different. Moore's is the only company with a similar target market, however it appears to be a significant competitor only in Tennessee at this time.

Target Market Demographically Golden Flake has defined the target market as:

- Women aged 20–44
- Families with two or more children
- Upper-lower to middle income

- Blue and gray collar (homemakers, sales, clerical, craftpersons, farmers, manufacturing, service, etc.)
- High school graduate or college graduate
- Rural roots, nontransient

The psychographic characteristics are very traditional:

- Two income, hard working
- Strong work ethic, traditional values such as God, country, family, and home
- Belongers, conformers

Purchases are for a regular use occasion and the dominant buying motive is value. The target customer is interested in quality at a reasonable price. Loyalty has been strong, but is no longer necessarily true as higher discounting has made consumers more price sensitive. Approximately 75 percent of buyers purchase the

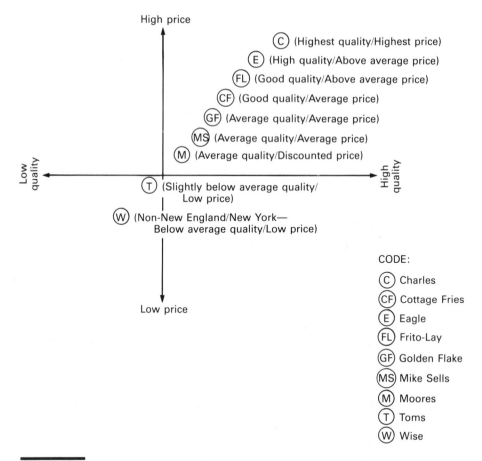

EXHIBIT 1.13 **Competitive positioning price/quality customer perception**

EXHIBIT 1.14 **Positions in the market—company perception**

same brand consistently. Children are purchase influencers. Over 87 percent of purchases are made in grocery stores.

The market potential for this segment is considered to be thirty-five to forty-two percent of the salted snack food market.

Geographically, Golden Flake has followed the "ink blot" strategy from Alabama to the surrounding states. The acquisition of the Tennessee plant and the construction of the Florida plant has enabled the company to increase its geographic market area. Exhibit 1.15 indicates the current geography served by Golden Flake.

Product   Golden Flake's product line is characterized as mature products with low-involvement purchasing. Nearly 85 percent of snack products are impulse purchases.

Potato chips of various types make up over 54 percent of Golden Flake's product line. The next major contributor to sales volume has been tortilla chips, with approximately 9.6 percent of sales. Corn chips, cheese products, pork skins, popcorn, and others contributed lesser percentages to sales volume (Exhibit 1.16). Snack foods in general are in the maturity stage of the product life cycle.

Golden Flake's cash cow is the potato chip. Golden Flake is considered to be an exceptional name by the company because it represents two very desirable attributes of a potato chip—golden in color and flaky in texture.

To make potato chips, a potato is washed, peeled, sliced, and then fried for about two minutes in vegetable oil. While many might consider potato chips to be junk food or "empty" calories, potato chips do offer nutritional value in a diet.

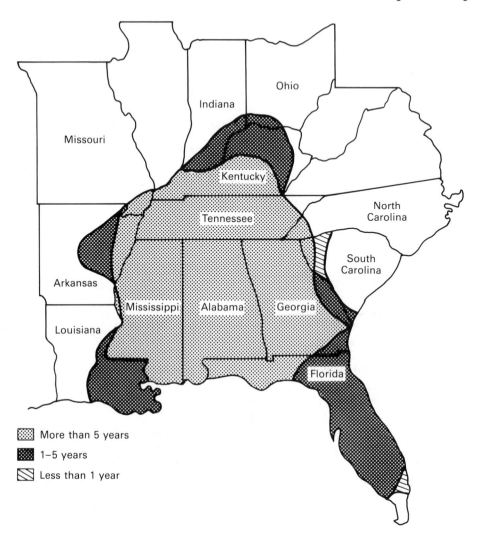

More than 5 years

1–5 years

Less than 1 year

EXHIBIT 1.15 **Golden Flake market area**

Fresh potatoes are approximately 80 percent water. In the quick frying of chips, most of the water is boiled away leaving a dehydrated potato much as a raisin is a dehydrated grape. A one-ounce bag of chips has most of the nutrient value of 3.5 ounces of fresh peeled potato. Specific nutrition information is included in Exhibit 1.17.

In addition, the company distributes a line of cake and cookie items, and pretzels and nuts manufactured by others.

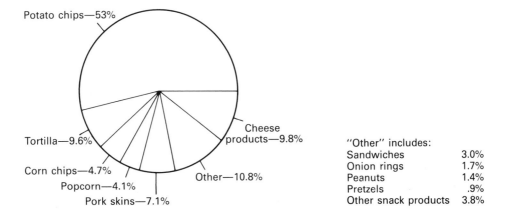

"Other" includes:

Sandwiches	3.0%
Onion rings	1.7%
Peanuts	1.4%
Pretzels	.9%
Other snack products	3.8%

EXHIBIT 1.16 **Golden Flake sales by product—as of June 30, 1987**

Product quality is a major criterion for Golden Flake. Quality testing is continuous. Chips are tested for color, size, amount of salt, oil absorption, and the number of defective chips—those with brown spots or holes. Product testing is done in a very modern quality control lab and through live consumer taste tests.

Golden Flake is perceived to be of high quality and freshness by many customers. However, Frito-Lay is generally perceived to have higher quality. To illustrate, a study in Tennessee indicated that Golden Flake had 97 percent aided awareness but only 20 percent market share. Exhibit 1.18 shows results of a recent consumer study in Tennessee. Using machine-controlled, scientific testing, Golden Flake's product

---

EXHIBIT 1.17 **Potato chip nutrition information**

Nutrition information per serving				Percentage of U.S. recommended daily allowances (U.S. RDA)	
Serving Size	1 ounce	Protein	2	Calcium	*
Calories	150	Vitamin A	*	Iron	2
Protein	2 grams	Vitamin C	10	Vitamin B	4
Carbohydrate	14 grams	Thiamine	2	Phosphorus	4
Fat	10 grams	Riboflavin	*	Magnesium	4
		Niacin	6		

Source: Potato Chip/Snack Food Association, 1986.

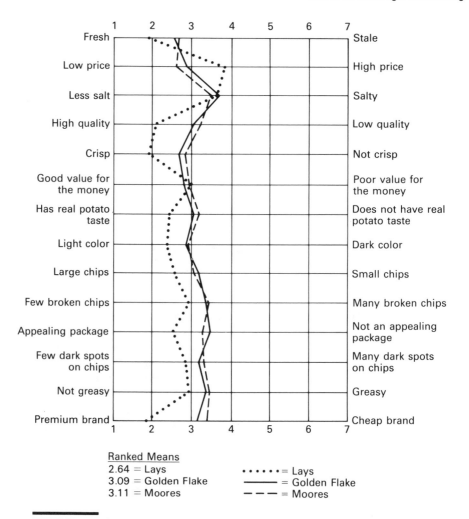

EXHIBIT 1.18 **Average-respondent profile comparisons of Golden Flake, Lays, and Moores—Knoxville, Tennessee 1985**

meets higher standards for color, size, amount of salt, oil absorption, and defective chips than Frito-Lay's Lay's brand yet these factors are not perceived by the market.

New product development is based on customer requests, competitive moves, and salesforce suggestions. Frito-Lay leads the industry in marketing effort and research and development. Recently, Frito-Lay spent $50 million to develop a new potato chip, "O'Grady's." Frito-Lay introduced Delta Gold in 1986–87. It was thought to be aimed directly at Golden Flake, as it was introduced only in the southeast region.

Delta Gold has cannibalized sales of O'Grady's. Frito-Lay Cool Ranch Dorito Chips achieved first year sales of $100 million; General Foods introduced Ranch-Style Tortilla Chips in October 1987.

Acknowledging that Golden Flake cannot and does not expect to make that kind of research and development commitment, the company has elected a "follow the leader" strategy in product development. Golden Flake has introduced "au gratin" potato chips to compete with the O'Grady brand. Almost nothing was spent to develop au gratin chips as Frito-Lay's experience was used. Au Gratin chips were discontinued in 1986 because of poor sales and replaced by cheese chips.

Golden Flake uses a metalized-plastic bag or a foil bag that is heat sealed, providing product freshness for up to eight weeks. Freshness dating is stamped on the bag as a guarantee and to generate customer awareness of the freshness of the product. Packaging costs average approximately 11 percent of manufacturing costs at Golden Flake versus approximately 14 percent for the industry.

Several colors are used to differentiate the various flavors of chips and other snacks. The logo common to all packages is a "cloud" containing the Golden Flake name in block letters (Exhibit 1.19). The type face (style of type) differs for each product category.

EXHIBIT 1.19 **Golden Flake package design**

Pricing Golden Flake prices its products to be competitive. Prices and package sizes are very similar to Frito-Lay and the rest of the industry. Pricing across the industry, especially in potato chips, is very standard. An audit of retail prices in Birmingham for several products indicates that Golden Flake's prices, at least at retail, are in line with competition. Exhibit 1.20 includes prices for selected Golden Flake products. Direct price comparisons by consumers is complicated by the great variety in package size—3 1/2 oz. versus 3 1/8 oz. for example.

Pricing for snack foods is complicated by the fluctuating costs of the commodity products (potatoes and corn) used as ingredients. Golden Flake buys raw materials used in manufacturing on the open market under contract through brokers, and directly from growers. A large part of the raw materials used by the company are farm commodities and are subject to drastic changes in supply and price (Exhibit 1.21).

EXHIBIT 1.20 **Retail prices for selected Golden Flake snack foods in the Birmingham market October 1987**

Product	Golden Flake suggested retail price
1¾ oz. corn chips	.39
7½ oz. corn chips	1.29
8 oz. cheese curls	1.29
1⅛ oz. potato chips	.39
6½ oz. potato chips	1.39
10 oz. potato chips	1.89
16 oz. potato chips	2.49
6½ oz. tortilla chips	1.39
11 oz. nacho chips	2.09
1⅛ oz. peanuts	.39
5 oz. popcorn	1.29
3½ oz. pork skins	1.39
11 oz. pretzels	1.19

The company trades in farm commodity futures to reduce risk and control costs. Company costs and expenses have risen in part due to inflation, but efficient purchasing, increased volume, improvements in production, distribution, administration, and increased sales prices have allowed the company to maintain a profit margin above the industry average.

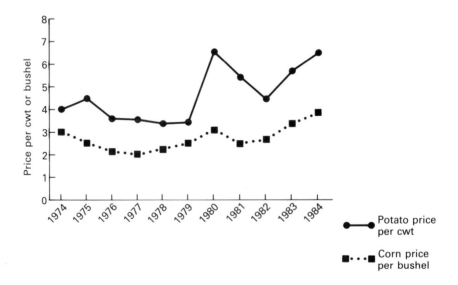

EXHIBIT 1.21 **Raw material price trends—potatoes and corn**

Distribution   Distribution is concentrated in grocery stores and convenience stores with a minimal effort directed to mass merchandisers. Since snack products are perishable with a shelf life of approximately six to eight weeks, Golden Flake uses direct-to-retail-store delivery.

The direct-store-delivery system allows for quicker delivery, which maintains freshness, and less handling, which reduces damage to the product. In addition, the fact that company salespersons stock the racks in the store ensures that the rack looks right, the stock is rotated for freshness, and the display is prepared in a way most conducive to impulse buying by the customer.

Since the primary expense to any grocer is the cost of labor, the direct delivery system provides the store substantial savings in labor cost as well as warehousing cost. In order to provide this service to retailers, the company has a chain of twenty company-owned sales warehouses with several others in various phases of development from planning to construction.

The company warehouses range in size from 2,400 to 8,000 square feet. They are constructed in locations within a marketing area where there is a large enough concentration of routes to make ownership feasible (Exhibit 1.22). The leased warehouses in small areas are unmanned and each salesperson is assigned his or her own secured area. The salesperson is responsible for ordering and inventory control. The larger warehouses have a clerk to handle this function for the sales representatives assigned to the facility.

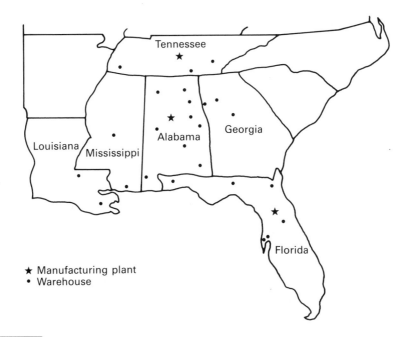

EXHIBIT 1.22 **Location of company-owned warehouses and manufacturing facilities**

A fleet of over 1,000 company-owned and maintained vehicles is used to provide service directly to the retail stores. The direct-store-delivery system is considered to be one of the major strengths of the company because it ensures maximum profits and service for the accounts and maximum control for the company.

A minimum of 87 percent of snack foods are purchased in grocery stores. High volume supermarkets account for the largest portion of sales for all competitors in the industry (Exhibit 1.23).

EXHIBIT 1.23 Dollar sales share by grocery store type/size			
	Golden Flake (In percent)	Frito-Lay (In percent)	Others (In percent)
Supermarkets > $2 million	40.8	41.5	44.9
Chains > $2 million	30.2	34.4	37.5
Independents > $2 million	10.6	7.1	7.5
Chains < $2 million	7.5	4.4	1.1
Independents < $2 million	10.9	12.6	9.0
	100.0	100.0	100.0

Promotion   Each salesperson/driver has an assigned territory and operates from the nearest company warehouse. Sales aids provided include price sheets, plan-o-grams for effective store settings (what the retail shelf should look like), trade promotions (discounts), at least quarterly price "deals" offered for upcoming time periods, copies of ads or storyboards for TV ads to illustrate company advertising and occasionally special "incentives" (gifts) to offer store managers.

Salespeople are formally trained in-house by the regional manager. Following training, a newly hired driver will ride with an experienced driver until the end of the twelve-week training program. Then a territory is assigned.

In Alabama, Golden Flake has high-brand awareness, due primarily to sponsorship with Coca Cola of the old Bear Bryant football program. With the expansion of Golden Flake to other markets, advertising was needed to build awareness and develop the desired image. In 1987, Golden Flake will co-sponsor both Auburn University and University of Alabama football TV programs.

In 1983, advertising expenditures were 6.5 percent of sales; in 1984 advertising increased to 8.4 percent of sales. In 1985, $11,460,000 was spent on advertising, which is approximately 10 percent of sales. While this was above the industry average of 9 percent, it was not sufficient to generate brand awareness in new markets or for new products to meet Golden Flake's growth objective. In 1986 advertising and promotion expenditures were $12,700,000, or 10.88 percent of sales.

Television, radio, and newspaper advertising were budgeted for 1986. The slogan, "Good as Gold" was used. When the advertising did not seem to be achieving desired results, and budgets became tight, the television and radio ads were discontinued. Newspaper and FSIs (free standing inserts) were maintained.

In 1987, advertising expenditures were expected to be $1,332,000, which equals 1.1 percent of projected sales. Babbitt & Reiman Advertising in Atlanta was hired. A new radio campaign "One Taste and You're Stuck—On Golden Flake" began in May 1987. Examples of in-store posters used to support the radio campaign are included in Exhibit 1.24.

Television advertising featured historic figures "with a twist"—Napoleon had his hand inside his jacket because he was eating Golden Flake potato chips. Concept boards for the 1987 campaign are included in Exhibit 1.25.

All products are sold under the family brand of Golden Flake. Due to the regional nature and small advertising budget, the company has not attempted to develop individual brands as Frito-Lay had done with Ruffles, Cheetos, Tostitos, etc. In June 1986 the first attempt at individual branding with "Southern Farms" brand kettle-fried potato chips resulted in Southern Farms generating 1.2 percent of total company sales.

Two-for-one deals are offered to customers in new markets. The customer pays

EXHIBIT 1.24 **Golden Flake in-store posters**

EXHIBIT 1.24 (Continued)

for one bag of Golden Flake potato chips and receives the second similar-sized bag for no additional charge. On-pack cents-off deals are also offered to consumers.

Golden Flake has an adopt-a-school program and provides plant tours for school-aged children where the opportunity to sample a lot of potato chips is present. The company participates in three to eight trade shows each month. In 1986, Golden Flake signed a contract with Associated Film Promotions in Hollywood to place Golden Flake products in movies and on TV programs.

Trade discounts were expected to be over $7 million in 1987 (6 percent of sales). Coupons are planned to be over $1 million (almost 1 percent sales). In 1986, Golden Flake contracted with QUEST USA of Atlanta (consumer promotion firm) to plan and execute consumer promotions. In 1987, Golden Flake expected to spend over $1.2 million on consumer promotions.

Financial Condition

Apparently Golden Flake's good-tasting quality product, priced competitively, has satisfied consumers. Satisfied customers and effective management has enabled

EXHIBIT 1.25 **Golden Flake ad campaign concept boards**

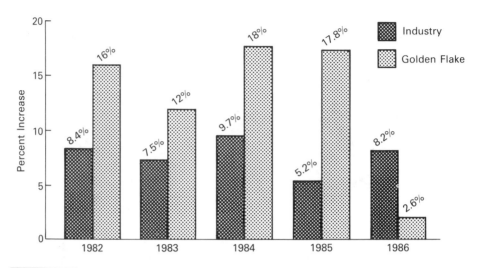

EXHIBIT 1.26 **Golden Flake sales growth compared to industry average**

Source: Snack Food Association, 1987 Management Report; Golden Flake Annual Report

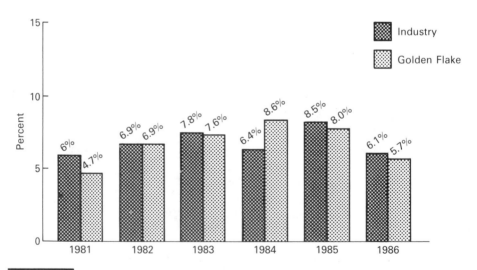

EXHIBIT 1.27 **Golden Flake profit as percentage of sales compared to
                industry average**

Source: Snack Food Association, 1987 Management Report; Golden Flake Annual Report

the company to outperform the industry averages in both sales and profit in the last several years (see Exhibits 1.26 and 1.27).

The conservative management of Golden Flake has kept the company in very good financial condition. Earnings per share has increased more than 25 percent per year over the last five years and the stock price has gone from a high of 4 3/16 in 1981 to a high of 21 in 1985. The 1986 EPS was down slightly as illustrated in Exhibit 1.28 but was improved in 1987.

The consolidated income statement and balance sheets for Golden Flake for 1983 through 1987 are provided in Exhibits 1.29 and 1.30. Exhibits 1.31 and 1.32 are a business segment information summary and financial review.

EXHIBIT 1.28 **Golden Flake Enterprises, Inc.**

Fiscal year	Earnings per share
1981	$.46
1982	.78
1983*	.92
1984**	.67
1985	.73
1986	.53
1987	.61

*In May 1983 the company effected a two-for-one stock split.
**In October 1984 the company effected a four-for-three stock split.

According to the Robinson-Humphrey Investment Report on Golden Enterprises, with the completion of $30.5 million in expansion and renovation, Golden Flake is positioned for growth. Investment income dropped as expansion was funded from working capital. Higher cost of sales and higher sales and administrative expenses were associated with the new facilities start-up and increased promotional efforts. Robinson-Humphrey predicts a return to the company's previous high margins.

EXHIBIT 1.29 **Consolidated statements of income Golden Flake Enterprises, Inc.**
(Years ended May 31, 1985, 1986, and 1987)

	1985	1986	1987
Revenues			
Net sales.........................	$116,632,248	$119,978,611	$122,185,835
Other income, including gain on sale of equipment of $263,791 in 1987, $268,060 in 1986 and $186,766 in 1985	463,297	495,635	685,478
Net investment income............	653,488	288,976	469,404
Total revenues	117,749,033	120,763,222	123,340,717
Costs and expenses			
Cost of sales	51,682,634	53,942,289	53,059,291
Selling, general and administrative expenses	49,618,452	53,185,862	54,237,335
Contributions to employee profit-sharing and employee stock ownership plans.................	1,566,272	1,476,827	1,596,279
Interest	192,458	238,867	88,499
Total costs and expenses	103,059,816	108,843,845	108,981,404
Income before income taxes	14,689,217	11,919,377	14,359,313
Provision for income taxes			
Currently payable			
Federal	3,639,800	4,024,000	4,952,000
State	545,200	530,000	554,000
Deferred taxes	1,061,000	527,000	900,000
Total provision for income taxes	5,246,000	5,081,000	6,406,000
Net income	$ 9,443,217	$ 6,838,377	$ 7,953,313
Per share of common stock			
Net income	$.73	$.53	$.61

EXHIBIT 1.30 **Consolidated balance sheets Golden Flake Enterprises, Inc.**
(May 31, 1986 and 1987)

ASSETS	1986	1987
Current assets		
Cash and certificates of deposit........................	$ 2,071,883	$ 4,763,381
Marketable securities	4,659,433	8,736,912

EXHIBIT 1.30 *(Continued)*

ASSETS	1986	1987
Receivables		
Trade notes and accounts...........................	7,899,290	8,222,608
Other...	188,615	589,061
	8,087,905	8,811,669
Less: Allowance for doubtful accounts...............	20,000	20,000
	8,067,905	8,791,669
Inventories		
Raw materials	2,122,046	2,279,291
Finished goods..................................	3,285,042	2,932,171
	5,407,088	5,211,462
Prepaid expenses	1,088,856	1,312,233
Total current assets	21,295,165	28,815,657
Property, plant and equipment		
Land	4,677,296	4,862,786
Buildings.......................................	17,934,962	18,241,400
Machinery and equipment	22,664,702	23,782,490
Transportation equipment..........................	15,430,144	15,889,970
	60,707,104	62,776,646
Less: Accumulated depreciation	22,112,884	27,477,916
	38,594,220	35,298,730
Other assets	1,585,046	1,336,389
Total	$61,474,431	$65,450,776

LIABILITIES AND STOCKHOLDERS' EQUITY		
Current liabilities		
Checks outstanding in excess of bank balances	$ 829,429	$ 1,087,535
Accounts payable	2,605,232	2,252,639
Accrued income taxes..............................	895,579	—
Other accrued expenses	2,073,657	1,336,960
Deferred income taxes	294,004	324,607
Current installments of long-term debt	113,808	318,808
Total current liabilities	6,811,709	5,320,549
Long-term debt	573,088	254,280

EXHIBIT 1.30 *(Continued)*

	1986	1987
Deferred income taxes	3,361,250	4,230,109
Stockholders' equity		
Common stock—$.66⅔ par value:		
Authorized 35,000,000 shares; issued		
13,828,793 shares	9,219,195	9,219,195
Additional paid-in capital...........................	5,416,498	5,623,673
Retained earnings	36,937,890	41,852,309
	51,573,583	56,695,177
Less: Cost of shares in treasury (757,581 shares in		
1987 and 796,938 shares in 1986)...............	845,199	1,049,339
Total stockholders' equity	50,728,384	55,645,838
Total	$61,474,431	$65,450,776

EXHIBIT 1.31 **Golden Enterprises, Inc. and Subsidiaries**
Summary of business segment information (thousands of dollars)

	Year ended May 31				
	1983	**1984**	**1985**	**1986**	**1987**
Total revenues					
Snack food					
products	$ 81,218	$ 95,991	$112,289	$115,064	$118,810
Bolts and other					
fasteners..........	4,931	4,861	5,388	5,669	4,514
	$ 86,149	$100,852	$117,677	$120,733	$123,324
Operating profit (loss)					
Snack food					
products	$ 12,254	$ 15,664	$ 14,495	$ 11,608	$ 14,228
Bolts and other					
fasteners..........	(107)	68	319	442	21
	12,147	15,732	14,814	12,050	14,249

EXHIBIT 1.31 *(Continued)*

	Year ended May 31				
	1983	**1984**	**1985**	**1986**	**1987**
Elimination of intercompany items..............	(41)	(26)	(28)	(16)	(2)
Investment income of parent company and discontinued business	170	98	100	46	18
Interest expense	(193)	(158)	(192)	(239)	(88)
Parent company expense less than (in excess of) management fees from subsidiaries	(69)	(75)	(5)	78	182
Income before income taxes	$ 12,014	$ 15,571	$ 14,689	$ 11,919	$ 14,359
Assets					
Snack food products	$ 38,089	$ 43,939	$ 54,192	$ 57,982	$ 62,201
Bolts and other fasteners	2,642	2,927	2,941	2,960	2,409
Elimination of intercompany items.............	(290)	(320)	(265)	(150)	—
Corporate assets	1,887	1,859	1,063	682	841
Total assets at May 31	$ 42,328	$ 48,405	$ 57,931	$ 61,474	$ 65,451
Depreciation and amortization					
Snack food products	$ 2,652	$ 2,990	$ 4,828	$ 6,414	$ 7,490
Bolts and other fasteners	$ 111	$ 101	$ 89	$ 92	$ 92
Consolidated	$ 2,780	$ 3,119	$ 4,922	$ 6,509	$ 7,586
Additions to property, plant and equipment					
Snack food products	$ 3,935	$ 7,958	$ 21,680	$ 10,066	$ 3,462
Bolts and other fasteners	$ 86	$ 67	$ 18	$ 57	$ 71
Consolidated	$ 4,073	$ 8,025	$ 21,698	$ 10,123	$ 3,546

EXHIBIT 1.32 **Golden Enterprises, Inc. and Subsidiaries**
Financial review (Dollar amounts in thousands, except per share data)

	Year ended May 31				
	1983	**1984**	**1985**	**1986**	**1987**
Operations					
Net sales and other operating income.......	$ 85,322	$ 99,692	$117,096	$120,474	$122,871
Investment income	956	1,232	653	289	469
Total revenues ...	86,278	100,924	117,749	120,763	123,340
Cost of sales	39,035	43,638	51,683	53,942	53,059
Selling, general and administrative expenses	35,036	41,557	51,185	54,663	55,834
Interest	193	158	192	239	88
Income before income taxes	12,014	15,571	14,689	11,919	14,359
Federal and state income taxes	5,449	6,904	5,246	5,081	6,406
Net income	6,565	8,667	9,443	6,838	7,953
Financial data					
Depreciation and amortization...........	$ 2,780	$ 3,119	$ 4,922	$ 6,509	$ 7,586
Cash flow (net income plus depreciation and amortization)	9,345	11,786	14,365	13,347	15,539
Capital expenditures......	3,981	7,881	20,891	9,569	3,867
Working capital..........	17,277	19,943	12,317	14,483	23,495
Long-term debt	1,318	779	687	573	254
Stockholders' equity	32,358	39,246	46,481	50,728	55,646
Total assets	42,328	48,405	57,931	61,474	65,451
Common stock data*					
Net income	$ .52	$ .67	$ .73	$ .53	$ .61
Dividends	.11	.14	.17	.20	.23
Book Value	2.48	3.01	3.57	3.89	4.26
Price range (high and low bid)	10¼–3¾	11¹¹⁄₁₆–8⁹⁄₁₆	15¾–8⁷⁄₁₆	16½–10¼	15½–11¾
Financial statistics					
Current ratio	3.20	3.78	2.45	3.13	5.42
Net income as percent of total revenues..........	7.6%	8.6%	8.0%	5.7%	6.4%
Net income as percent of stockholders' equity**..............	23.3%	24.2%	22.0%	14.1%	15.0%

* Adjusted for stock splits in years ended May 31, 1983, 1985 and 1986.
** Average amounts at beginning and end of fiscal year.

EXHIBIT 1.32 *(Continued)*

	Year ended May 31				
	1983	**1984**	**1985**	**1986**	**1987**
Other data					
Weighted average common shares outstanding*	12,649,333	13,020,436	13,017,135	13,024,078	13,066,054
Common shares outstanding at year-end*	13,021,397	13,017,397	13,023,082	13,031,855	13,071,212
Approximate number of stockholders	1,600	1,600	1,700	2,100	2,100

*Adjusted for stock splits in years ended May 31, 1983, 1985 and 1986.

CASE 2

The Chevrolet Corvette

In mid-1983 Chevrolet introduced a new, redesigned, version of the Corvette. Simultaneously the price was increased and an advertising campaign comparing Corvette to imported sports cars, primarily Porsche, was begun. Initial sales were strong, but by early 1986 sales were down 25 percent from the same period in 1985. The April 14, 1986, issue of *Autoweek* (p.3) reported, "Corvette and Fiero production will be cut significantly this month to stem a stockpile of sports cars, which are selling slower than predicted according to General Motors. Second-shift production at the Bowling Green, Kentucky Corvette plant will be eliminated . . . ." The Corvette's advertising support appeared to have been reduced from 1983–84 levels, but special lease rates and financing plans were offered in late 1985 and early 1986.

This case was written from public sources by Frank Conley and Nancy Trap under the supervision of Paul Farris, as a basis for classroom discussion rather than to illustrate either effective or ineffective handling of an administrative situation. Copyright © 1986 by The Colgate Darden Graduate Business School Sponsors, University of Virginia, Charlottesville, Virginia.

The time was appropriate for addressing several important questions. What was the proper strategic role for Corvette within G.M. and Chevrolet? How important was advertising in fulfilling that role? What kind of advertising and promotion program would be appropriate? How useful would price promotions be? Finally, what kind of advertising program should be used?

GENERAL MOTORS AND THE AUTOMOTIVE INDUSTRY

In 1985, it was estimated that 16 percent of private, nonagricultural workers in the United States was employed in the manufacture, distribution, maintenance, and commercial use of motor vehicles.[1] Some 52.8 percent of all households owned two or more cars. In households with incomes of $40,000 or more, 87 percent owned two or more cars and 43 percent owned three or more cars.[2] The net sales of G.M., Ford, Chrysler, and American Motors accounted for 3.9 percent of the 1983 Gross National Product.[3] Of the U. S. auto manufacturers, G.M. was by far the largest, dominating the 1985 new-car market with six of the top ten selling cars in the country.

In recent years the U. S. auto industry had faced major market competition from foreign manufacturers. "Voluntary" quotas slowed import penetration in 1984, but imports still accounted for 23.5 percent of total U. S.-market automobile sales.

Recent Developments at G.M.

In response to an increasingly competitive environment, G.M. had recently reorganized five former autonomous car divisions into two groups, the Oldsmobile-Buick-Cadillac group and the Chevrolet-Pontiac-G.M. group. This reorganization reflected a concern of G.M. that historic divisional distinctions between Chevrolet, Pontiac, Oldsmobile, Buick, and Cadillac had become blurred. The problem was compounded by the fact that many of G.M.'s cars looked alike.

Two acquisitions, Hughes Aircraft Company and Electronic Data Systems, provided access to leading-edge technologies as G.M. began to design its auto lines for the twenty-first century. The hope was that the aerospace technology would be adapted in automotive areas ranging from computer-integrated manufacturing to futuristic car dashboard displays. In 1986, G.M. also bought Group Lotus Cars, a British automobile engineering and production firm known for state-of-the-art automotive technology in racing cars.

New ventures for G.M. included a G.M.-Toyota joint venture that produced the new Chevrolet Nova, and the Saturn project that would produce G.M.'s first new

[1] Public Affairs Division of Motor Vehicle Manufacturers' Association of the United States, Inc., *Facts and Figures '85*.

[2] U. S. Department of Transportation, Federal Highway Administration, *Highway Statistics 1984*.

[3] *Ward's Automotive Yearbook*, 46th ed., Harry A. Stark, ed. (1984).

EXHIBIT 2.1 Corvette production data for selected years

Year*	Total Corvette production (In thousands)	Total Chevrolet production (In thousands)	Corvette percent of Chevrolet	Chevrolet percent of domestic production
1953	0.315	1,447	.02	24
1958	9.300	2,367	.39	40
1963	21.500	2,303	.93	30
1968	28.300	2,148	1.31	24
1973	34.500	2,334	1.47	24
1978	46.800	2,347	1.99	26
1982	25.400	1,004	2.52	20
1984	28.200	1,294	2.18	19
1985	46.300	1,626	2.85	19

*No 1983 Model was produced.
Source: Ward's Automotive Yearbook, 46th ed., Harry A. Stark, ed. (1984).

make since the 1930s. Additionally, GM imported and marketed cars from three foreign companies.

Chevrolet

Chevrolet sold several different models of passenger cars (Exhibit 2.2) and a line of trucks. Each model came in a variety of options and prices. In 1985, the Cavalier was the number one selling car in America, and the Celebrity and Caprice

EXHIBIT 2.2 Chevrolet model line sales

Model	1984 Units	1985 Units
Cavalier	377,446	431,031
Chevette	164,917	129,927
Camaro	202,172	199,985
Celebrity	322,198	363,619
Citation	92,174	43,667
Monte Carlo	115,930	112,585
Corvette	34,024	37,956
Other Chevrolet	258,902	280,800
Total Chevrolet	1,565,143	1,600,200
Total G.M. Sales	4,587,508	4,607,458

were third and seventh, respectively. (See Appendix A for a brief description of these models.)

Chevrolet sales were especially subject to swings in the economy, perhaps because the cars were priced lower than other G.M. cars of the same body type. In 1983 Chevrolet Motor Division General Manager Robert Stempel commented, "The last people who stop buying new cars are rich people, and the last people out of work are rich people. That 10 percent unemployment is a helluva lot more important to me at Chevrolet than it is at a lot of upscale car companies."[4]

SEGMENTATION OF THE SPORTS CAR MARKET

Segmentation of the automobile market was complex. Individuals considered economic, status/image, comfort, and performance factors in making a purchase decision and segments often overlapped. Product features and price varied considerably (Exhibit 2.3). See Exhibit 2.4 for an example of a market map depicting the position of various models. Even the sports car market could be further segmented.

EXHIBIT 2.3 **Product and price data for selected sports car models**

Model	Wheel base	Length	Weight	Horse-power	Price	U.S. sales (In units)	U.S. sales percent of production	Number of U.S. dealers
Corvette	96.2	176.5	3280	230	$24,891	37,956	81.0	5,050
Ferrari 308 GTBi	92.1	174.2	3250	230	54,300	n/a	n/a	42
Mazda RX7 Turbo	95.7	168.9	2850	182	14,145	53,810	n/a	767
Nissan 300ZX Turbo	99.2	178.7	3255	228	17,699	67,409	n/a	1,101
Jaguar XJ SC	102.0	187.6	4025	295	32,250	3,784	n/a	167
Porsche 944	94.5	168.9	2900	147	21,440	16,705	n/a	317
Porsche 911	89.5	168.9	2750	200	31,950	5,882	n/a	317
Porsche 928S	98.4	175.7	3540	288	50,000	2,586	n/a	317

Source: Road & Track and *Motor Trend* magazines, 1986 issues and *Automotive News Market Data Book,* 1985, 1986.

Economy sports cars were mass-produced and generally constructed from sub-assemblies taken from the manufacturer's parts bin and then modified and assembled to increase the overall performance of the final product. The *Grand Turismo* (GT) class of sports cars seated four people and had superior performance and handling characteristics. The *high-performance* sports cars were usually produced in relatively small numbers and often had a racing heritage. These cars generally had much higher

---

[4] Daniel F. McCosh, "Marketing the '83s," *Wards Auto World*, October 1982.

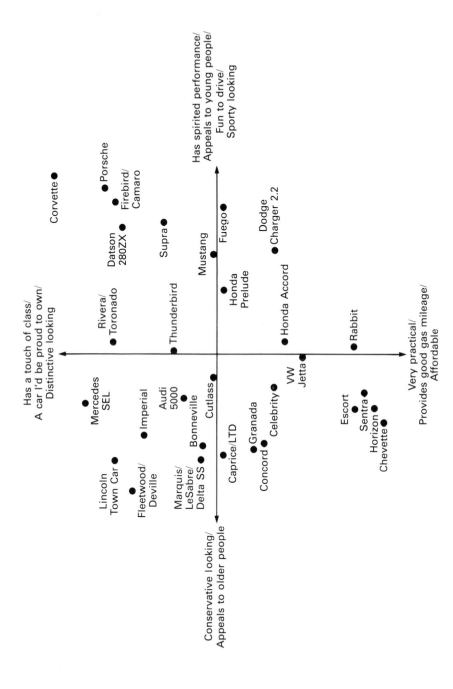

EXHIBIT 2.4 **Sports Car segmentation map**

Source: Modified version of the Opinion Survey Center, Inc., using sampling of 12,000 responses as printed in "Marketing the '83's," *Ward's Auto World*, October 1982.

resale values than others and were looked at by some as investments.[5] (Peter Shutz, CEO of Porsche, paid $8,500 for a 1976 Corvette, and three years later sold it for the same price when he moved to Europe.) High-performance sports cars also could be viewed as a subset of the *luxury-car* market. (Exhibit 2.5 gives demographics for buyers of selected models.)

EXHIBIT 2.5 **1984 new-car buyer demographics**

Car make	Percent male	Median age (Years)	Percent married	Medium household income	Median price paid
Chevrolet	56	41	65	$ 33,400	$10,466
Corvette*	85	38	59	59,200	26,000
BMW	65	35	58	61,000	17,800
Jaguar	64	44	80	100,000+	33,520
Mercedes-Benz	68	46	76	87,500	28,904
Porsche	78	36	62	81,200	26,118

Note: Price could vary on a Corvette depending on the time of year the car was purchased, whether the car was bought off the lot or ordered, and purchaser's negotiating skill. Other car prices were believed to be *relatively* firm.
*In 1981, "median age" and "income" for Corvette owners were 33 years and $33,000, respectively.
Source: *Automotive News,* "New Car Buyer Demographics," April 1984.

G.M. was expected to launch its ultra-luxury two-seat convertible, the Cadillac Allante, in the beginning of 1987. The Allante, designed by Pininfarina, the Italian firm responsible for many Ferrari models, was scheduled for low-volume production and a price tag of $50,000. Industry analysts believed that G.M. was hoping the Allante would provide a "halo" effect for Cadillac, helping to update and differentiate its product image. The car had been premiered on the television series "Dallas," in Fall 1986, replacing a Mercedes Benz 450SEL that had been driven by J. R. Ewing the previous season.

HISTORY OF THE CORVETTE MODELS

1953-1955

Years ago this land knew cars that were fabricated out of sheer excitement. Magnificent cars that uttered flame and rolling thunder from exhaust pipes as big around as your forearm, and came towering down through the white summer dust of American roads like the Day of Judgement . . . today, they have an inheritor—the Chevrolet Corvette.

1955 Corvette ad copy.

[5] David E. Gumpert, "Porsche on Nichemanship," *Harvard Business Review*, March/April 1986.

The Corvette "dream" car was introduced to the public at the 1952 Motorama Show, and the fiberglass-bodied, two-seat convertible was the hit of the show. Chevrolet began regular production of the car in 1953, and limited the production run to 300 cars that were sold to people who qualified as "V.I.P.s"—political figures, movie stars, business executives, and preferred customers. Unfortunately, the V.I.P.s weren't impressed by a sports car that had pop-in plastic windows, leaked in rainstorms, had an anemic six-cylinder engine with an uncivilized two-speed Powerglide automatic transmission, and was slower than a well-tuned Cadillac or Oldsmobile.[6]

The production run in 1954 of 3,640 cars ended with a surplus of 1,500 new Corvettes. Rumors circulated that the car would be scrapped, but the Corvette's salvation occured in two forms: first, Ford, Chevrolet's major competition, came out with the Thunderbird, a two-seat "personal" car that brought out G.M.'s competitive spirit. Second, a 45-year-old German-trained enthusiast, race driver, and designer named Zora Arkus-Duntov began his 20-year association with the Corvette as its head of engineering. For 1955, the production run was 674 cars with a new V-8 engine that improved the Corvette's performance.

1956–1962

Even in Turin [Italy] no one has fuel injection! Si, e'vero'. But the really fantastic item about the new Corvette is not the fuel injection engine, the new four-speed gearbox, the slingshot acceleration or the pasted to the road stability. It is the fact that the Corvette, above all other high performance sports cars in the world, is a true dual-natured vehicle. It is a genuine luxury car and a sports car, both wrapped in one sleek skin. . . .

1957 Corvette ad copy.

The second generation of Corvettes received a major body change, but Chevrolet had to determine if the Corvette was to remain a sports car or forge into Ford Thunderbird territory as a "personal" luxury car. The 1956–1957 Corvettes seemed to appeal to both markets. In 1956, Corvettes took the Sports Car Club of America (SCCA) "C" Production Championship, and in 1960 four Corvettes were entered in the international Le Mans Twenty-Four-Hour Endurance Race. The car was continually refined both mechanically and stylistically. By 1962, *Motor Trend* was saying, "This is an exciting high-performance automobile with real hair on its chest—the type of car that only true enthusiasts will appreciate."

1963–1967

Corvette is America's one true sports car—has been for years. But Corvette is also two body styles. Five engines and three transmissions available. Plus enough other equipment you can order to make any kind of sports car you want. For afficianados, there's the snarly Corvette. Ordered with a 375 horsepower Ramjet, fuel injected V8. . . .

[6] Auto Editors of Consumers Guide, *Corvette, America's Sports Car* (New York: Beekman House, 1984).

> For boulevardiers, there's the plush Corvette, ordered with power brakes, steering and
> windows, tinted glass. . . .
>
>   1965 Corvette ad copy.

The third-generation Corvette was derived from a G.M. styling exercise and
was dubbed the Corvette "Stingray." It came in convertible and fastback coupe
configurations and had many optional features. The car was available with a variety
of engines, the most powerful approaching 500 hp. Lasting only five years, this model
was the most short-lived of the Corvette body styles, but its timeless styling has made
it the most popular model with car collectors and enthusiasts.

1968–1979

> Here it is. It's not really a whole lot different looking. But in 17 years we've never
> changed it just to change it. . . . It's still a car that's built for the person who drives for
> the sheer excitement of it . . . . No, it isn't a hard-core sports car. There are too many
> nice things about it. No, it isn't the smoothest riding car you'll find. But then again it
> won't rattle your bones. What it is is a new Corvette. It's refined for 1970.
>
>   1970 Corvette ad copy.

The fourth-generation Corvette was introduced in 1968, and the "Vette" had
gone through some drastic changes. Corvette production was reduced to 21,801
units in 1971 from the 1969 high of 38,762, which allowed Chevrolet Division
General Manager John DeLorean to place emphasis on improving the car's slipping
quality control. The 1970s ushered in the era of government regulation. Corvette's
performance steadily declined with the addition of catalytic converters and the
unleaded-gasoline mandate. Its horsepower reached a low of 165 in 1975. A T-Top
removable roof was introduced in 1968, offering "top down" motoring without the
hassles. Subsequently, Corvette convertible models waned in popularity and were
discontinued. In spite of these changes and the oil shortages and economic downturns
of the 1970s, Corvette sold well. The entire 1975 Corvette production of 38,465 cars
was sold out by March, and 1976 production jumped to 46,558. Because 1978 was
the Corvette's 25th anniversary, it was chosen as the pace car for the Indy 500; 6,502
replicas of the pace car were made and sold at a handsome premium over the base
list price of $13,653.

1980–1982

> In this ever-changing world some things endure. A find red wine, soft smoke on an
> autumn evening. A walk along the seashore. And Chevrolet Corvette. Now 26 years
> young. And still America's only true production sports car. . . . But beyond the machinery,
> there is the dream—Corvette and the open road.
>
>   1980 Corvette ad copy.

In 1980 Chevrolet sent the Corvette to the fat farm so it wouldn't suffer an
Environmental Protection Agency "gas guzzler" tax. The car lost 280 lbs., and aero-
dynamic styling changes were added to improve fuel economy. The only engine
available was a 305 cu. in. V-8, and the option of manual transmission was dis-

continued. All models sold were automatics. One industry observer commented that the Corvette had become a car for upwardly mobile secretaries. Even though the Corvette had lost much of its performance, it remained popular with the public and the motoring press. *Road & Track* pointed out in its November 1982 issue, that the Corvette remained a car whose function was on par with its form: "No matter how much luxury, electric seats, remote mirrors, or teddy bear hide velour interior you pack into a Corvette, the basic honesty of the car rises above its own image."

THE "NEW" CORVETTE

Now that the skeptics have been silenced, we can get down to business. The most important piece of business concerning the new Corvette. Performance. And in tests on G.M.'s proving grounds, conducted by professional drivers, the new Corvette performs beautifully.

1984 Introductory Corvette ad copy.

There was no 1983 Corvette, as production was shifted to a plant built specifically for producing the new Corvette model (it had 50 percent more production capacity than the old plant). The fifth-generation Corvette was a radical change and showcased G.M.'s latest developments in suspension, braking, and electronic engine control while still remaining true to the basic Corvette layout: front engine/rear-wheel drive and fiberglass body, a two-seat, high-performance sports car.

The new Corvette had a pop-off targa roof and a 350 cu. in. V-8 engine. It featured new technology in the use of fiberglass springs and alloy castings in the suspension system, digital and LED display instrumentation, and electronically controlled fuel injection and overdrive. For 1985, improvements to the fuel-injection system increased power, and in 1986 an Anti-Lock Braking System (ABS) and an improved Anti-Theft System were added. The ride was substantially softened through adjustments to the shock absorbers, and torsional steering shake was reduced with the addition of restrictors in the power steering lines. The convertible model was reintroduced in 1986, at a $4,518 premium over the base sticker price of $27,502. (See Exhibits 2.6 and 2.7 for prices and estimates of maintenance costs, respectively,

---

EXHIBIT 2.6 **1986 dealer's sticker price information (In thousands)**

	Corvette	Porsche 944	Porsche 944 Turbo	Porsche 928S	Datsun 300ZX Turbo
Base Car	$27.5	$24.5	$29.8	$52.0	$20.8
Average Price Paid	23.4	24.1	n/a	n/a	n/a

Source: Casewriter's survey of Charlottesville, Virginia, car dealers, April 1986 and N.A.D.A. Official Used Car Guide.

EXHIBIT 2.7 **Maintenance-and-repair cost comparison**

Cost of maintenance parts	Average replacement time*	Corvette	Porsche 944T	Nissan 300ZX	Mazda RX7
Exhaust System	70,000	$413	$425	$164	$180
Engine Tuneup Cost		$ 90	$160	$160	$100
Clutch	n/a	$270	$892	$117	$160
Sport Shocks	60,000	$360	$517	$685	$344
Factory Engine	100,000	$3,900** (New)	$5,246 (New)	$5,153 (New)	$1,000 (New)
Car Warranty (Months/Miles)	—	36/36,000	24/unlimited	12/12,000	12/12,000

*Longevity of parts depends greatly on driver use and maintenance. The average vehicle was driven 10,300 miles per year.
**With multiport fuel injection.
Source: Casewriter's survey of dealers.

for selected models.) A *New York Times* article of July 26, 1983, wondered "whether the new Corvette has not been priced out of its traditional strength, the youth-oriented market, and into one of older professionals. . . . " The article went on to say, "For G.M., the Corvette represents only a small part of the company's auto output . . . but the Corvette's real value, analysts say, is its ability to lure curious customers into showrooms."

Corvette Advertising

The advertising campaign that introduced the 1984 Corvette was lavish and technically oriented. Chevrolet ran multipage spreads in magazines touting the advanced technology and engineering that were incorporated in the newest generation of Corvettes and stressing its high-performance characteristics. The advertising budget was the highest in the car's history. Chevrolet spent $7,778,900 on the 1984 Corvette—compared to a previous high of $285,300 in 1977. (See Exhibits 2.8 and 2.9 for data on advertising budgets and magazine media respectively.)

The comparison campaign was launched with TV and print ads (see Exhibits 2.10 and 2.11). The cars compared to the 1985 Corvette ($26,703 price as tested) were the Lamborghini Countach, Porsche 944, Porsche 928S, Ferrari 308 GTSi, and Lotus Turbo Esprit. They ranged in price from $26,121 to $103,700 and were tested on 0–60 mph acceleration, braking from 60–0 mph, time through a slalom course, and lateral acceleration on a skid pad. The United States Auto Club (USAC) certified the testing, and the Corvette scored first in two of the tests and second and third

EXHIBIT 2.8 Advertising dollars spent by Corvette and competition (In millions)				
Car make	**1981**	**1982**	**1983**	**1984**
Corvette	—	—	$ 7.8	$ 2.2
Jaguar XJS	—	$ 1.3	3.9	2.0
Nissan 280/300 ZX	$ 6.7	7.0	11.9	15.5
Nissan Total	36.3	48.9	54.7	60.1
Mazda RX7	3.1	9.7	6.1	13.1
Porsche (Total)	6.0	8.0	6.4	2.8

Source: Leading National Advertisers, 1985.

in the remaining two tests. The scoring system that was used allotted six points for first place, five for second, etc. The Corvette was declared the overall winner in the comparison with a score of 21 points. The $103,700 Lamborghini placed second with 18 points.

> . . . Corvette. Ferrari, Porsche, Lotus, Lamborghini. They're Europe's exotic few. And they don't let just anyone into their club. But in the case of the Chevrolet Corvette, they really didn't have a choice. In independent tests conducted by the United States Automobile Club, Corvette was the overall winner.
>
> 1985 Corvette Comparison ad copy.

The comparison campaign was continued in 1986, when Corvette made the Bosch ABS II anti-braking system a standard feature on the car and then compared the braking characteristics of the Lamborghini Countach, Ferrari 308 GTSi, Porsche 944, Lotus Turbo Esprit, and Corvette on a rain-slick curve. The Corvette was the only car to demonstrate the ability simultaneously to stop and steer the curve under maximum braking conditions. Once again it was proclaimed "Corvette, A World Class Champion" against a collection of European exotic cars.

Promotion and Racing Activities

The Chevrolet Division of G.M. published *Corvette News* quarterly and sent it free to purchasers of new Corvettes for three years (thereafter $18 for three years). The 30-page, full-color, glossy magazine kept Corvette owners informed on new Corvette model developments, news of Corvettes on the race track, and do-it-yourself repairs. *Vette Magazine, Vette Vues, Corvette Fever,* and *Keep'in Track* were the titles of four independently published monthly magazines devoted exclusively to Corvette enthusiasts.

There were over 700 organized Corvette clubs in the United States and Canada and a few in Europe. These clubs were federated under the National Council of Corvette Clubs. Club activities included car shows, rallies, slalom races, drag races, and social gatherings. A separate Corvette organization was the National Corvette

EXHIBIT 2.9 Selected sports car magazine advertising, 1983*

Magazines	Corvette dollars (In thousands)	Datsun 280ZX dollars (In thousands)	Porsche 911 dollars (In thousands)	Porsche 928S dollars (In thousands)	Porsche 944 dollars (In thousands)	Median age	Readership Percent median income	Percent college graduates
Architect's Digest	$133.5			$ 56.8	$ 78.1	n/a	n/a	n/a
Business Week	350.0	$162.6	$156.1	117.1	26.7	39.4	25.2	46.9
Car & Driver	31.4	115.6	57.3	111.5	71.4	29.6	18.3	19.9
Food & Wine	62.3			129.3		39.4	16.3	32.2
Fortune	300.9		207.7			37.7	28.8	55.2
Newsweek	925.8	55.8	151.1	226.7	151.1	36.4	18.3	34.0
Road & Track	67.2	95.6	47.8	95.6	75.0	29.4	19.9	29.8
Science Digest	79.2					36.4	17.6	31.0
Science 83	110.0					36.2	17.7	44.5
Smithsonian	265.5			64.7		43.4	20.1	45.3
Sports Illustrated	913.6	60.2	60.2			32.8	18.6	24.8
Time	382.2		451.4	334.3	255.7	36.0	18.3	31.8
Travel & Leisure	142.1					45.7	25.1	36.8
Esquire		86.4	83.4	90.1	64.6	35.2	17.6	39.1
Golf		32.5				42.6	22.3	37.4

Los Angeles	19.6					n/a	n/a	n/a
Money	69.0			67.0		37.3	22.8	41.9
New Yorker	69.9	40.6		40.6	40.6	41.7	23.2	51.7
Playboy	118.6	118.6		118.6		31.1	17.9	19.6
Sports News	32.7					33.7	18.9	27.5
TV Cable	3.6					n/a	n/a	n/a
Inc.				85.3		36.4	25.2	58.4
Forbes		40.1		142.8	42.6	42.1	27.8	57.7
Signature		64.6		22.5		n/a	n/a	n/a
U.S. News and World Report		22.5	103.8	196.1	103.8	42.1	21.2	32.6
Duns Business				25.6	22.5	n/a	n/a	n/a
Gourmet				46.9		n/a	n/a	n/a
Penthouse				37.0	34.0	29.4	17.6	15.6
Sunset				54.3		44.2	20.3	34.5
Tennis				32.7		29.7	16.5	32.4
Texas Monthly				47.4		n/a	n/a	n/a
Town & Country				41.7	11.3	40.2	17.5	34.7
Venture				43.4	24.6			
Total**	$4,084.6	$944.1	$1,605.3	$2,298.9	$1,031.6			

* Higher dollars per ad usually indicate multipage layouts were used.

** Not all magazines are listed, therefore totals and individual entries may not agree.

Source: The PIB/LNA Magazine Advertising Analysis for 1983 and Simmons 1983 Study of Media & Markets In Home Audiences.

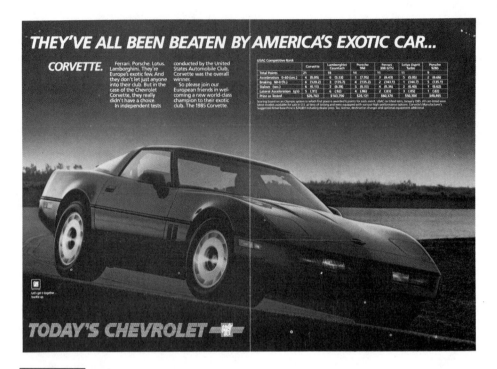

EXHIBIT 2.10 **Ad campaign for the 1985 Corvette**

Restorers Society, organized for people dedicated to restoring older Corvettes to "original" condition.

John Pierce, a member of Chevrolet's Special Products Group explained in the Summer 1985 issue of *Corvette News*, "Our policy is to develop the hardware and technology necessary to win and make sure it's properly represented in competition. We [Chevrolet] figure if we can put together a winner, then there'll be a demand for a better mousetrap." The group's efforts resulted in privately owned Corvette GTPs (Grand Touring Prototypes) participating in the IMSA (International Motor Sports Association) GT's circuit that visited 17 U.S. cities in the 1985 racing season.

For the second race of the 1986 season, the Corvette GTP car qualified but retired early due to mechanical failure. At the fourth race, Road Atlanta, the Corvette's second appearance was greated with skepticism: "if they last. . . . " (from the Ford folk); "if they live. . . . " (the Porsche persons); "They can't run that fast in the race. . . . " (Jaguarists).[7] The Corvette's first victory in the Road Atlanta race broke Porsche's string of 16 consecutive IMSA wins.

In another race series, Showroom Stock, Corvettes dominated. These races pit stock production cars against machines of similar performance capability. The

---

[7] Sylvia Wilkinson, "Hand Grenades One and Two," *Autoweek*, April 14, 1986.

You're driving 55 MPH on a rain-slick curve. Suddenly the unexpected: You stand on the brake pedal and steer to stay in your lane. You might expect Europe's most exotic cars to handle such a crisis effortlessly. Yet for all its awesome straight-line braking ability, Ferrari 308 GTSi failed to negotiate a 150-foot radius curve at maximum braking in USAC-certified testing. Lamborghini Countach failed. Lotus Esprit Turbo failed. Porsche 944 failed. Only the 1986 Corvette demonstrated the ability to steer and stop in these conditions at the same time. Only Corvette made the turn while coming to a controlled stop. When conditions turn foul, Corvette's new computerized Bosch ABS II anti-lock braking system is designed to help improve a driver's ability to simultaneously brake and steer out of trouble. Why does the Corvette feature the world's most advanced braking technology? Because a world-class champion should give you the edge in an emergency. **Corvette. A world-class champion.**

EXHIBIT 2.11 **Corvette comparative advertisement**

Chevrolet Camaro was also promoted in a series of races in which professional drivers competed in modified Camaros capable of 200 MPH speeds.

In 1986, the new Corvette roadster was chosen to be the Indianapolis 500 Pace Car. Chevrolet also developed a futuristic car, the Corvette Indy, that was shown on the 1986 Automobile Show circuit. Built by Lotus, the Indy was a showcase of technology to be used in the next generation Corvette—mid-engine, four-wheel drive, and four-wheel steering.[8]

The value of racing to an automobile's image was difficult to assess. Many sports cars, including Corvette, were featured in ads for tires, auto stereo systems, other accessories and unrelated products. For example, a Corvette was the grand prize in a toothpaste coupon sweepstakes and in numerous other promotions and contests.

Distribution

The Corvette was sold by the Chevrolet network of over 5,000 Chevrolet dealers in the United States. (Porsche, for example, had only 330 authorized dealers.) Some dealers, especially those near large population centers, were known for selling many Corvettes. However most small dealers rarely stocked Corvettes and sold only for special orders. To help those dealers with less experience learn to sell the "new" Corvette, Chevrolet implemented a special dealer training program for 1986. Corvette mechanics also received special training.

Often the Corvette occupied a prominent place on the showroom floor and "Register-to-win a Corvette" campaigns were used by Chevrolet to increase dealer traffic.

THE COMPETITION

Porsche

Porsche was a family-owned European company known for its product quality. In recent years Porsche had introduced new models aimed at new segments. Notable successes were the 944 and 928. Standard company policy was to keep production levels just below the demand level.[9] From 1980 to 1985, Porsche sales grew 56 percent.

Shutz, CEO of Porsche, stated in the 1986 March/April issue of the *Harvard Business Review* that "Our customers are people who place high expectations on themselves. And they expect no less from the companies and people with whom they associate. . . . As a result, in positioning our company we have to strive to be what these people are as individuals. That means, among car companies, we have very high goals. And we have to pursue those goals virtually without compromise." He considered Porsche competition to come from two sectors: luxury discretionary items, such as sailboats and airplanes, and other automobile manufacturers. He believed the Porsche 944's competition included Corvette, Pontiac Fiero, and certain Japanese cars; the 928's competition came from Jaguars, Ferraris, Mercedes Benz large coupes, and the Cadillac Allante; that the 911 had no competition; "It drives like no other car and sounds like no other car."

[8] George Damon Levy, "Corvette Indy," *Autoweek*, January 20, 1986.

[9] op. cit.

EXHIBIT 2.12 **Porsche magazine spread—1986 campaign**

EXHIBIT 2.12 (Continued)

In its advertising, Porsche concentrated on the thoroughness and competence of its cars. The ads appeared to be aimed at people who weren't familiar with Porsche and told a story about the company's engineers, the cars they had designed, and the constant development of Porsche cars being done on the world's most demanding race tracks. Early in 1986 Porsche began a series of lavish magazine spreads, some as many as 12 pages each (see example in Exhibit 2.12). Magazines in the campaign included *Business Week, Time,* and *Newsweek.*

Shutz said Porsche supported cars in international sports car racing for three reasons: "First, it is probably the single most effective way to do our advertising and public relations. It gets us free space in the auto enthusiasts' magazines. The second factor is the contribution that it makes to our technical development . . . the most important . . . is the contribution that racing makes to our corporate culture. The racing activity is highly visible, and it has a couple of characteristics that I find extremely valuable in achieving the kind of quality we want." He added, ". . . racing is an opportunity for us to demonstrate our competence, to demonstrate the state of technology with which we're building their [the public's] automobile."[10]

Porsche's bi-monthly magazine, *Christophorus,* continued articles on Porsche race activities and recent developments, art, travel, and books. The "They Drive Porsche" section read like a "Who's Who" and carried pictures of world-class athletes, royalty, V.I.P.s, and race car drivers with their Porsches. Among those featured in the August 1985 issue were Olympic swimming champion Michael Gross, King Carl Gustaf XVI of Sweden, and a prominent West German physician. Typical advertisers in the magazine were high-quality clothing and accessory manufacturers, jewelers, and European airlines.

In August 1984, as Porsche's distribution contract with Volkswagen of America was about to expire, Peter Shutz, chief executive of Porsche AG, created a new distribution plan to abolish dealers and replace them with agents who would order the cars as they were sold. Instead of keeping inventories, the agents would be supplied by 40 company centers. Two Porsche warehouses would operate in the United States—one in Reno, Nevada, and one on the East Coast. Three weeks after the announcement of the new distribution system, Shutz abandoned it; he stayed committed only to severing Porsche's U.S. link to Volkswagen.[11]

Nissan

In recent years Nissan's (originally Datsun) 240Z model had increased in size, weight, and price. During this time it had evolved from an "economy" sports car to something more like a GT car. A change in image resulted.

> Those in marketing who ply their trade with demographics describe the 300ZX purchaser as one who is not as concerned with ultimate performance as with the "image" of performance. To the Nissan engineers this means a suspension system whose main priority is ride comfort, not cornering power or balance. Under the hood it means a priority on smooth, docile power characteristics rather than serious horses—which might

[10] Gumpert, "Porsche on Nichemanship."

[11] David B. Tinnin, "Porsche's Civil War with Its Dealers," *Fortune,* April 16, 1984.

EXHIBIT 2.13 **Nissan 1986 advertisement**

require too much driver attention, detracting from image-enhancement time. To paraphrase Nissan television advertising: "You may never need this kind of performance, but knowing it's there is awesome."

Motor Trend, January 1986.

Nissan advertising for the 300ZX stressed that it was the best "Z" car ever, technically advanced with a plethora of functional electronic wizardry. The ads did not mention any performance statistics or measurements for the car (see Exhibit 2.13).

Mazda

With the second generation of the very successful RX-7 introduced in 1986, Mazda continued to emphasize the advanced technology and engineering of its sports car model. The ads were dominated by written copy and had technical drawings of components as well as a cut-away view of the car's mechanicals. Mazda also ran ads in car-enthusiast magazines concerning the RX-7's successful racing career. Mazda's evolution was somewhat similar to that of the Datsun (now Nissan) "Z" series. It was initially built and priced to compete in the "economy" sports car segment, but successive generations became heavier and more expensive with more "standard" options. Recent models were thought by some to resemble the Porsche 944 in appearance.

PRESS REACTIONS TO THE NEW CORVETTE

May 1983—Motor Trend tested the Ferrari 308 GTSi, Porsche 928S, Jaguar XJS, and the 1984 Corvette on a race track to determine the best-handling production car available in America. The Corvette was "markedly superior in every handling category and stands alone at the top of the heap . . . the Vette is now something it has never been; a world class performer." *Motor Trend* also voted the Ferrari the most sexually appealing car and the Jaguar "one to live with day in and day out." (See Exhibit 2-14 for a Jaguar ad.) Corvette's appeal as a "daily runner" was diluted by its harsh riding characteristics,[12] but it was the choice for "the hardest-charging backroad burner money can buy." The Porsche 928S "by any clear-headed standard, maybe the best car in the world."

August 1983—Road & Track did a "comparison test" of the Corvette, Ferrari 308GTBi Quattrovalve, Porsche 944, and Porsche 928S. They saw the new Corvette as G.M.'s effort "to build sophistication and high technology into a package that still embodies traditional Corvette values . . . the car is still the bargain leader in its high-roller performance class." In performance tests the Corvette was on par with the competition and best in the lateral acceleration and slalom course speed tests. In "Cumulative Ratings—Subjective Evaluations" (points awarded for performance, comfort/controls and design/styling), the Corvette scored 420 points, Ferrari 451 points, Porsche 928 482 points, and Porsche 944 482 points. The staff's price-independent choice was Ferrari, and the price-dependent choice was the Porsche 944.

November 1985—Motor Trend compared the improved 1986 Corvette to the just-released Porsche 944 Turbo. The Corvette was fastest from 0–70 mph; the Porsche was faster from 70–90 mph in covering the quarter mile and in top speed. The Corvette won the braking, skidpad, slalom, and road course portions of the testing. In conclusion, the testers stated, "Pressed to make a choice between these two exceptional GT's, we'd probably opt for the Corvette. But the final choice lies in individual tastes and driving habits. There's a lot of hot rod in the Vette. A lot of flash and American brashness. The turbo Porsche is understated elegance. Quiet, confident, and subtle. Whichever approach reflects your individual driving habits and ego is the one you'll swear is the hands-down winner and the only logical choice. Just make sure you bring plenty of green stuff."

[12] The ride was substantially softened in subsequent model years.

THE BEST JAGUAR EVER BUILT

An exhilarating 4.2 double overhead cam six with electronic ignition and fuel injection. Perfected year after year, it is probably the most thoroughly proven luxury car engine in the world.

On the Jaguar family tree can be found some of the most famous high performance engines that ever powered a car across a finish line. The engine that moves Jaguar's 1984 XJ6 sedan is a sophisticated descendant of this proud heritage. It is 4.2 liters of purebred Jaguar and you have only to turn the key to discover what that means.

Ignition is almost instantaneous, even in very cold weather, for the car is equipped with an electronic cold start fuel enrichment system as well as advanced electronic ignition and fuel injection. The engine is very strong. Its crankshaft is supported by seven bearings. It is an in-line six with the simplicity of twin overhead camshafts designed to enhance the precision of valve timing and eliminate the wear of push rods and rocker

arms. The aluminum cylinder head contains hemispherical combustion chambers to speed the flow of the fuel/air mixture and the exhaust. The result is a smooth, unflagging and unflappable power plant that has proven its capabilities in literally millions of miles of testing, racing and pleasure driving.

The XJ6 engine is backed up by equally strong and well proven handling and suspension technology. Precise power rack and pinion steering guides the car. Four wheel independent suspension and front antidive geometry insure that the car is surefooted and balanced in turns, level in braking. The car's brakes are power assisted discs on all four wheels, for Jaguars must stop as confidently as they go.

Outstanding performance, ride

and handling are only a part of the many pleasures available to Jaguar owners. While writing its name in many a track record book, Jaguar has also set standards for automotive luxury. The leather is supple. The walnut is hand matched for graining. Conveniences pamper you: power sunroof; cruise control; trip computer; power windows and doorlocks; four speaker stereo radio and cassette player are all standard.

The best Jaguar ever built might just be the best car you've ever driven. Discover that for yourself. Call this toll-free number for the Jaguar dealer nearest you: (800) 447-4700. JAGUAR CARS INC., LEONIA, NJ 07605.

JAGUAR
A BLENDING OF ART AND MACHINE

EXHIBIT 2.14 **Jaguar 1986 advertisement**

EXHIBIT 2.15 **1986 Performance comparison of selected sports cars**

Manufacturer and model	0–60 mph (sec)	1/4 mile (sec)	Top speed (mph)	Braking 80 mph (ft)	Slalom (mph)	Skidpad (G's)	Interior noise 70 mph (DBA)	MPG
Corvette Coupe	5.8	14.4	154	243	58.9	.91	77	19.0
Alfa Romeo Spider	10.4	17.6	103	288	58.4	.77	93	23.8
Ferrari 308 GTBi	6.8	15.2	142	262	58.0	.81	80	16.0
Jaguar XJS HE	7.8	15.6	148	276	56.6	.73	72	13.5
Mercedes Benz 380SL	10.9	18.4	110	277	54.2	.70	74	19.0
Mazda RX7 GXL	8.5	16.5	119	267	62.0	.83	n/a	n/a
Nissan 300ZX Turbo	7.4	15.7	133	249	62.8	.80	73	17.0
Porsche 944	8.9	16.6	123	256	62.5	.86	72	22.1
Porsche 944 Turbo	6.0	14.6	155	255	62.8	.90	72	19.4
Porsche 911 Cabriolet	5.7	14.3	130	266	59.8	.80	79	18.6
Porsche 928S	6.3	14.5	162	247	57.9	.83	71	16.3

Source: Motor Trend's Performance Summary, 1986 issue.

APPENDIX A **The 1986 Chevrolet line**

Chevette: An inexpensive subcompact with standard four-speed manual transmission, rack-and-pinion steering, fully reclining bucket seats, and rear hatch with fold-down rear seat. Available in two models: two-door coupe and four-door sedan. Price $5,280.

Cavalier: America's best selling compact for three years running. Standard features included front wheel drive with rack-and-pinion steering, four-speed manual transmission, and V-6 engine. Options included sunroof, choice of Delco Bose music systems, and rear luggage carrier. Thirteen models available including convertible sedan and wagon. Price: $7,600.

Celebrity: America's best selling mid-size car. Standard features were front-wheel drive with rack-and-pinion steering, V-6 engine with electronic fuel injection, and cloth interior. Models included coupe, sedan, and wagon body types. Wide variety of options allowed for personally "customized" car. Price: $15,000.

Camaro: America's best selling 2+2 sports coupe came standard with V-6 multiport fuel-injection engine, five-speed manual transmission, power steering, sports suspension, rally wheels, and rear hatch. Available options included: Delco Bose wrap-around music system, electric rearview mirror controls, and rear window louvers. Camaro had long received "hand-me-down" Corvette technology, and the Iroc Z28 was available with a Corvette engine option. Camaro races were becoming increasingly popular. Four models to choose from. Price: $10,400.

Caprice: Full-size car offered standard V-6 engine with electronic fuel injection and three-speed automatic transmission, rear-drive power steering, and 20.9 cubic feet of luggage space. Model selection included Brougham and Classic series in sedan and wagon body types. Many options available for personalized customizing. Price: $11,400.

Monte Carlo: Full-size rear-drive automobile with full coil suspension, power steering, and brakes. Standard features included three-speed automatic transmission, electronically fuel-injected V-6 engine, and cloth bench seat with center arm rest. Available in luxury sport and super sport models. Price: $11,700.

Corvette: Performance sports car with standard features including a V-8 engine with tuned-port fuel injection in a choice of four-speed manual with overdrive or four-speed automatic transmissions, vehicle anti-theft system, Bosch ABS II anti-lock brake system, corrosion-resistant fiberglass body, targa roof, air conditioning, and electronic instrument cluster. Options available included leather seats, Delco Bose stereo system, and performance handling package. Also available in convertible model. Price: $28,500.

April 1986—Road & Track's latest testing of the Corvette involved taking it to Italy and running it over a 1000-mile course of autostradas, city streets, and country roads that once made up the famous Mille Miglia Race, competed on in 1927–1957. Other cars included in the test were European versions of the Alfa Romeo GTV 6/2.5, Jaguar XJS Cabriolet, Nissan 300ZX Turbo, and the Porsche 944 Turbo. In this test of cars driven by a group of famous ex-race car drivers, the questions posed were: "If the Mille Miglia were held today, in what order would the cars finish?" and "Which car would you choose for a vacation tour of the Mille Miglia route?" The drivers scored the first question: Corvette 23, Porsche 22, Alfa 13, Nissan 12, and Jaguar 5. They scored the second question: Porsche 25, Corvette 17, Alfa 13, Nissan 11, Jaguar 9.

A summary of *Motor Trend* performance data is contained in Exhibit 2.15. See the appendix B to this case for definitions of technical terms used in the industry.

APPENDIX B **Technical terms**

Tests used in performance comparisons

Skidpad Test—Measured the cornering ability of a car in a steady state. Cars that generated numbers of greater than .8 g force had a stiff suspension and harsh riding characteristics on surfaces rougher than a smooth race track.

Slalom Test—Measured a car's cornering ability in transient maneuvers as it wove through a course of eight pylons spaced at 100-ft. intervals.

Braking Test—Measured the minimal distance required to come to a full stop from a stated speed. Typically tested from 60 and 80 mph.

Innovations in automobile technology
Braking

Anti-Lock Breaking System (ABS)—Disc brake calipers had an electronic sensor that prevent brake lock up in panic stops. This innovation resulted in better stopping power and eliminated loss of control (skidding).

Suspension

Dynamic Suspensions—Being developed so that electronic sensors can detect road conditions, allowing a car's suspension components to react.

Active Suspensions—Sensors monitoring load-induced flex in the rear suspension to adjust the rear wheel suspension automatically.

Driver Adjustable Suspensions—Allowed the driver to alter the stiffness of a car's shock absorber to increase a car's handling performance or ride characteristics.

Engine

Turbocharging—A method of increasing a car's horsepower output by increasing the air flow into the engine's combustion chambers.

Intercooling—Creating a denser charge and increasing the horsepower of a turbo-charged engine by cooling the air charge of a turbo-charger.

Fuel Injection—A system, usually electronic, that controlled and injected fuel directly into the combustion chamber.

CASE 3

BB Gunds

> The success of new concepts, as rare as it is, is largely a matter of good fortune rather than any special prescience on the part of their founders.
>
> —Robert L. Emerson, *Fast Food: The Endless Shakeout,* Lebhar-Friedman Books, 1979, p. 72.

By May 1985, the BB Gunds restaurant chain was up to 17 locations, with an 18th due to open shortly. It was not yet, however, proving to be the strong foundation for further growth and profitability that the senior managment at MM Restaurant Corporation had hoped it would be.

Michael Farmar, concept manager for BB Gunds, knew that the concept had yet to prove itself in the eyes of some. His current task, among others, was to determine whether the concept could be turned around in time to allow it to compete successfully against such competitive restaurant chains as Pepper's, Spoons, Moxie's and J.R. Clements. MM Restaurant Corporation already had two big winners in Maguire's and McElhaney's. Many had hoped that BB Gunds would be the third leg on the stool.

COMPANY BACKGROUND

The BB Gunds chain of restaurants was operated by the MM Restaurant Corporation, based in Phoenix, Arizona. MM was a subsidiary of Universal Brands Corporation (UBC), a diversified food company headquartered in Chicago.

UBC earned $67 million on $1.6 billion in net sales in 1985 (year end May 31). Sales and earnings had both shown consistent, steady growth over the past decade. UBC currently operated with two primary divisions—consumer foods and restaurants.

The consumer foods division, with $935 million in sales in 1985, produced and marketed a variety of products, primarily in the categories of prepared meals and snacks, vegetables and side dishes, milk and dairy products, and coffee and tea. With an impressive stable of brand names, nearly 70 percent of the division's domestic volume came from businesses in which it had the number one or two market share position. The division also marketed food products internationally, and had major sales operations in Europe, Canada, and Latin America.

This case was written by Robert R. Gardner, Administrative Director, Executive Programs, and M. Edgar Barrett, Professor of Accounting at the Edwin L. Cox School of Business of Southern Methodist University. It has been prepared with the cooperation of a firm that wishes to remain anonymous. It is intended as a basis for classroom discussion rather than to illustrate either effective or ineffective handling of an administrative situation. The data in this case are disguised but are based on real data.

UBC's restaurant operation was said to be the largest multiconcept restaurant organization in the world. This division's 1985 operating profit amounted to $77 million on net sales of $670 million. In 1985, the overall restaurant segment represented 42 percent of overall corporate net sales and 53 percent of corporate operating profit. The sales volume growth seemed to indicate that the restaurant operation would become the parent firm's largest division within the next several years. (UBC financial and operating data is provided in Exhibits 3.1 and 3.2.)

EXHIBIT 3.1 **Five year summary of UBC financial statistics**

Annual growth rate							
(In percent)			**Year ended May 31**				
5 Year 1980– 1985	**1 Year 1984– 1985**		**1981**	**1982**	**1983**	**1984**	**1985**
				(In millions, except per-share data)			
		Operating results					
9	12	Net sales	$1155.6	$1184.8	$1290.0	$1460.3	$1634.7
16	13	Gross margin	320.0	348.4	383.7	426.9	482.3
12	12	Earnings before tax	70.7	79.8	80.6	106.3	119.1
13	13	Net earnings	41.9	47.7	48.6	59.4	67.1
11	13	Earnings per share	$ 2.98	$ 3.14	$ 3.20	$ 3.91	$ 4.42
		Changes in financial position					
15	15	Funds from operations	$ 79.4	$ 86.7	$ 85.2	$ 109.4	$ 126.2
5	16	Capital expenditures	79.3	73.0	85.4	98.8	114.5
—	—	Acquisitions	8.8	7.9	—	29.7	54.0
13	12	Cash dividends per share	$ 0.96	$ 1.09	$ 1.21	$ 1.36	$ 1.52
		Financial position					
7	7	Total assets	$ 761.1	$ 849.9	$ 828.3	$ 912.9	$ 972.5
12	11	Stockholders' equity	261.5	311.5	334.7	366.2	407.9
		Statistics and ratios					
		Gross margin to net sales	27.7%	29.4%	29.7%	29.2%	29.5%
		Net earnings to net sales	3.6%	4.0%	3.8%	4.1%	4.1%
		LTD to total capital	42.4%	37.0%	34.4%	29.2%	31.8%
		Dividend payout	32.4%	34.6%	37.8%	34.7%	34.3%
		Return on average equity	16.9%	16.6%	15.0%	17.0%	17.3%
		Market price of common stock					
		High	$ 26	$ 26	$ 33	$ 43	$ 57
		Low	14	15	17	26	32
		Close	23	24	31	39	56

Source: 1985 UBC Annual Report.

The restaurant division was composed of two segments—fast food and full service. The La Fiesta restaurant chain was the primary contributor to the fast food segment. Between franchises and company-owned locations, there were 1,225 La Fiesta restaurants by 1985. System wide, La Fiesta's sales in 1985 (including sales by franchised units) were about $1 billion. Some 35 percent of La Fiesta's domestic units were company-operated.

EXHIBIT 3.2 **Summary of UBC restaurant operating statistics**

	Year ended May 31			
Restaurants	**1982**	**1983**	**1984**	**1985**
Systemwide Sales (Billions)	$ 1.0	$ 1.1	$ 1.4	$ 1.6
(Including sales by franchisees)				
Average Unit Sales (Thousands)				
Fast Food				
La Fiesta	$ 751	$ 838	$ 944	$1,009
Full Service				
Maguire's	1,169	1,312	1,484	1,518
McElhaney's	2,276	2,364	2,323	2,206
Number of Units				
Fast Food				
La Fiesta	865	942	1,027	1,225
Full Service				
Maguire's	199	181	179	181
McElhaney's	66	109	148	177
Other (BB Gunds)		2	5	17
Total	$1,130	$1,234	$1,359	$1,600
Store Operating Profit (Company Stores)				
La Fiesta	13.3%	15.2%	16.7%	15.2%
Full-Service Restaurants	20.4%	21.1%	19.9%	20.1%

Source: 1986 UBC Annual Report.

The full-service component of the restaurant division was operated by MM, which ran a total of 376 restaurant units at year end 1985. In addition to the new BB Gunds gourmet hamburger restaurant, MM's two primary restaurant concepts were McElhaney's and Maguire's. McElhaney's operated 177 units in 1985, which, while located in a wide variety of states, tended to be concentrated in fast-growth states such as Arizona, Florida, Georgia, and Texas. These four states alone accounted for approximately 50 percent of both McElhaney's and Maguire's locations. Average sales per McElhaney's unit in 1985 were $2.2 million. Maguire's operation spanned much the same territory as McElhaney's, with 181 units averaging sales of $1.5 million in 1985.

The Maguire's concept was the older of the two major restaurant chains operated by MM. The concept had been originally designed and developed by John R. Maguire. In 1978, he sold out to UBC. Maguire's, a dinnerhouse chain, was the base on which the full service restaurant division had been built.

McElhaney's, effectively a product of the last ten years, had been the restaurant division's more recent success story. Starting with fewer than a dozen locations in the mid to late 1970s, this casual dining chain had grown dramatically in the early and mid-1980s. (See Exhibit 3.2 for more data on both Maguire's and McElhaney's.)

FORMAL PLANNING AND CONTROL AT MM

The planning and budgeting process in UBC's full-service restaurant operation consisted of the annual preparation of two sets of comprehensive plans, as well as a number of supporting documents and analyses. The two sets of plans, the Annual Plan and the five-year Strategic Plan, were prepared during different times of the year. Annual plans were normally written during the early part of the calendar year (January through March), while strategic plans were drawn up and finalized during the summer months (July through September). The firm's fiscal year ran from June 1 to May 31.

The Annual Plan document for the MM Restaurant Corporation ran to well over 100 pages. Included in the document were narrative and financial data on each of the major concepts (e.g., Maguire's, McElhaney's, BB Gunds, etc.), data on planned capital expenditures for the year, and other data such as the opening schedule for new units.

The Strategic Plan document, which ran several hundred pages in total, tended to include more narrative and more nonfinancial data than was true for the Annual Plan. In addition to the more traditional financial and operating data, this document also included for each concept a discussion of the following items:

- Business profile
- Industry and competitive analysis
- Objectives
- Strategies
- Human resources
- Key assumptions
- History and objectives

At the inception of the BB Gunds concept (fiscal 1983), planning at MM was performed centrally by the firm's Strategic Planning Group. These plans were not assembled in a vacuum, however, as input from concept management was often sought. By 1984, this process had been altered, and planning for a given concept was primarily done by that concept's management.

The general idea behind the development of the annual plan called for data to be built from the foundation of a unit-by-unit data base, with successive consolidations at the concept (BB Gunds), full-service restaurant division (MM), and corporate (UBC) levels. The strategic plan was envisioned as being constructed from a somewhat broader base (i.e., the concept level), but it also went through a series of successive consolidations.

Annual and strategic plans were both approved by MM's senior management before being sent on to the parent company level for approval. Approval of these two plans, including the capital expenditure portions, plus the right to select the top two managers were the only "rights" formally retained by UBC (corporate) management with respect to the MM Restaurant Corporation. UBC executives believed in the concept of a decentralized organization, and the focus on these few "rights" was a specific example of those beliefs in action.

The internal financial reporting process in UBC's full service restaurant operation also consisted of a hierarchy of reports and reporting levels. Monthly profit and loss reports were prepared at the store (unit) level. (An example of a store-level report is shown in Exhibit 3.3). These reports became part of the concept (e.g., McElhaney's or BB Gunds) monthly report which, in turn, was incorporated into the MM monthly report. MM's monthly reports were sent on to the parent company (UBC) level, where they were consolidated into the parent's monthly statements.

Although individual restaurant units had specific annual plans, their performance was not formally compared to the Annual Plan on a monthly basis. At the concept level, however, the monthly consolidated income statement report had separate columns for prior year, annual plan, and actual data—both for the current month and the year to date. (Examples of concept-level reports are shown in Exhibits 3.4 through 3.6).

THE SITE SELECTION PROCESS AT MM

MM uses a centralized real estate department to perform its site selection process. The same people who search for McElhaney's and Maguire's sites look for Gunds sites when required. Real estate employees in this way gain familiarity with a given area, thus benefitting all of MM's concepts.

Sites chosen for MM's various concepts often tended to be those that could be moved into quickly and inexpensively. Lead time, the time between commitment to a site and commencement of operations, was frequently an important factor in the decision. Sunbelt states, such as Texas and Florida, generally required less lead time than other regions of the country. Over the years, both McElhaney's and Maguire's had built strong operations throughout the Sunbelt.

The projected sales volume for a particular concept often played an important role in deciding how much to pay for a given site. In the case of the Gunds concept, for instance, MM management thought it unlikely that the concept would generate more than $1.8 million in annual sales per unit. Working backwards from that expectation, they concluded they could pay no more than $1.3 million for the site, construction, and equipment costs and still make their desired return.

NEW CONCEPT DEVELOPMENT AT MM

In 1981, at the time that the gourmet hamburger concept was first under consideration at MM, the new concept development process was formally controlled by MM's chairman and president. In practice, however, ideas for new restaurant concepts generally originated in the New Concepts Group, headed by Charles Curtis. Curtis reported to Bobby Collins, who was MM's Senior Vice President of Marketing.

The composition of the New Concepts Group—as measured by the formal position held by a member—tended to change from year to year. There tended to be fluidity in the actual membership of the New Concepts Group, however, since the

EXHIBIT 3.3 Representative monthly P&L report at store level

Description	Mo last year Amount	Pct	Mo this year Amount	Pct	3-Mo this year Amount	Pct	3-Mo last year Amount	Pct	YTD this year Amount	Pct	YTD last year Amount	Pct
Dinner Sales	59,406	55.3	90,279	55.4	274,449	56.5	189,754	56.2	971,067	55.7	368,766	55.8
Lunch Sales	48,002	44.7	72,618	44.6	210,961	43.5	147,697	43.8	771,726	44.3	292,417	44.2
Total Sales	107,408	100.0	162,897	100.0	485,411	100.0	337,451	100.0	1,742,793	100.0	661,183	100.0
Food:												
Dinner Sales	47,387	44.1	72,754	44.7	222,180	45.8	153,095	45.4	789,866	45.3	296,602	44.9
Lunch Sales	41,808	38.9	64,267	39.5	186,866	38.5	130,136	38.6	684,007	39.3	257,570	39.0
Total Food Sales	89,195	83.0	137,021	84.1	409,047	84.3	283,231	83.9	1,473,873	84.6	554,172	83.8
Employee Meal Credit	0	.0	0	.0	0	.0	(15)	.0	0	.0	(15)	.0
Cost of Sales	33,473	37.5	44,998	32.9	141,374	34.6	105,973	37.4	523,030	35.5	202,130	36.5
Gross Profit-Food	55,722	62.5	92,023	67.2	267,673	65.4	177,272	62.6	950,843	64.5	352,056	63.5
Liquor:												
Dinner Sales	12,019	11.2	17,525	10.8	52,269	10.8	36,659	10.9	181,201	10.4	72,164	10.9
Lunch Sales	6,194	5.8	8,351	5.1	24,095	5.0	17,561	5.2	87,719	5.0	34,848	5.3
Total Liquor Sales	18,213	17.0	25,876	15.9	76,364	15.7	54,220	16.1	268,920	15.4	107,011	16.2
Cost of Sales	3,697	20.3	5,864	22.7	16,628	21.8	10,897	20.1	55,957	20.8	21,684	20.3
Gross Profit-Liquor	14,516	79.7	20,013	77.3	59,736	78.2	43,323	79.9	212,963	79.2	85,328	79.7
Total Cost of Sales	37,170	34.6	50,861	31.2	158,002	32.6	116,855	34.6	578,987	33.2	223,799	33.9
Total Gross Profit	70,238	65.4	112,035	68.8	327,408	67.5	220,596	65.4	1,163,806	66.8	437,384	66.2
Controllable Expense:												
Service Labor	11,006	10.3	12,230	7.5	36,378	7.5	31,912	9.5	131,479	7.5	68,712	10.4
Kitchen Labor	10,177	11.4	17,412	12.7	48,963	12.0	36,046	12.7	158,175	10.7	80,377	14.5
Management Labor	4,484	4.2	4,591	2.8	11,811	2.4	12,964	3.8	51,246	2.9	26,810	4.1
Bonuses	5,900	5.5	2,365	1.5	10,642	2.2	14,529	4.3	59,156	3.4	27,962	4.2
Payroll Taxes	3,579	3.3	3,322	2.0	11,890	2.5	9,535	2.8	38,404	2.2	20,409	3.1
Benefits	3,245	3.0	2,246	1.4	8,252	1.7	9,322	2.8	31,421	1.8	17,765	2.7
Total Employee Labor	38,391	35.7	42,166	25.9	127,936	26.4	114,308	33.9	469,881	27.0	242,036	36.6

	$	%	%	$	$	%	%	$	$	%	%	$
Entertainer	0	.0	.0	0	0	.0	.0	0	0	.0	.0	0
Operating Supplies	7,864	4.8	5.3	5,665	22,216	4.6	5.0	16,692	80,574	4.6	5.0	32,920
Repairs and Maintenance	1,381	.9	2.7	2,850	6,519	1.3	2.5	8,348	31,996	1.8	2.1	14,110
Recruiting and Training	70	.0	.0	9	120	.0	.1	417	1,557	.1	.1	667
Public Relations	1,078	.7	1.0	1,121	3,326	.7	1.1	3,648	11,245	.7	.9	6,052
Linen and Laundry	537	.3	.4	469	1,603	.3	.4	1,444	5,907	.3	.5	3,223
Uniforms	289	.2	2.0	2,181	2,133	.4	.7	2,332	4,505	.3	.9	6,063
Discount on Cr-Card Sales	494	.3	.3	290	1,578	.3	.3	899	5,418	.3	.3	1,683
General and Administrative	1,485	.9	1.7	1,818	4,589	1.0	1.3	4,209	16,700	1.0	1.6	10,522
Utilities	6,759	4.2	4.5	4,828	18,869	3.9	3.9	13,073	67,104	3.9	4.2	27,514
Unit Approved Advertising	0	.0	.2	247	0	.0	.1	247	1,389	.1	.1	322
Unit Approved Promo Discounts	0	.0	.0	0	60	.0	.0	0	60	.0	.0	0
Vending Income	(107)	(.1)	(.1)	(104)	(364)	(.1)	(.1)	(328)	(1,501)	(.1)	(.1)	(567)
Total Controllable Expense	62,016	38.1	53.8	57,765	188,585	38.9	49.0	165,289	694,835	39.9	52.1	344,545
Total Controllable Income	50,017	30.7	11.6	12,473	138,824	28.6	16.4	55,307	468,971	26.9	14.0	92,839
Adv/Promo Expense	0	.0	.3	322	0	.0	.3	1,012	10,277	.6	.3	1,984
Promo Discounts	0	.0	.0	0	0	.0	.0	(50)	270	.0	.0	(25)
Total Adv and Promo	0	.0	.3	322	0	.0	.3	962	10,547	.6	.3	1,959
Marginal Income After A & P	50,017	30.7	11.3	12,151	138,824	28.6	16.1	54,345	458,424	26.3	13.8	90,881
Occupancy	8,249	5.1	5.5	5,903	24,582	5.1	5.6	18,876	87,493	5.0	5.4	35,829
Taxes	1,841	1.1	1.2	1,250	10,752	2.2	1.2	4,087	22,209	1.3	1.3	8,521
Insurance	(716)	(.4)	.2	157	1,689	.4	.3	887	7,377	.4	.3	2,219
Total Occupancy Expense	9,374	5.8	6.8	7,310	37,024	7.6	7.1	23,850	117,079	6.7	7.0	46,569
Preopening Expense	0	.0	.0	0	0	.0	.4	1,205	0	0	14.1	93,466
Net Restaurant Contribution	40,644	25.0	4.5	4,841	101,800	21.0	8.7	29,290	341,345	19.6	(7.4)	(49,154)
Associate Expense	8,432	5.2	.0	0	17,896	3.7	.0	0	20,460	1.2	.0	0
Trainee Expense	0	.0	.6	628	0	.0	1.1	3,744	0	.0	1.9	12,658
Concept Management	0	.0	.5	537	0	.0	.5	1,687	0	.0	.5	3,311
Corporate Management	0	.0	3.2	3,437	1	.0	3.2	10,798	1	.0	3.2	21,158
Other Income/Expense	(101)	(.1)	(.1)	(75)	92	.0	(.1)	(221)	(732)	.0	(.1)	(470)
Operating Income	32,312	19.8	.3	314	83,811	17.3	3.9	13,282	321,616	18.5	(13.0)	(85,810)

Unit 1029

63

EXHIBIT 3.4 Concept level consolidated income statement—May 1983

	Current month							Current month					
	Prior year		Plan		Current year		Description	Current year		Plan		Prior year	
	Amount	Percent	Amount	Percent	Amount	Percent		Amount	Percent	Amount	Percent	Amount	Percent
	$ 70	68.6%	$ 234	57.9%	$ 108	58.3%	Dinner sales	$1,040	60.3%	$1,439	60.6%	$ 750	65.9%
	32	31.4	170	42.1	78	41.7	Lunch sales	685	39.7	935	39.4	388	34.1
	—	—	—	—	—	—	Franchise revenue	—	—	—	—	—	—
	102	100.0	404	100.0	186	100.0	Gross revenue	1,725	100.0	2,374	100.0	1,138	100.0
	—	—	—	—	—	—	Franchise revenue	—	—	—	—	—	—
	102	100.0	404	100.0	186	100.0	Total sales	1,725	100.0	2,374	100.0	1,138	100.0
							Food						
	38	37.5	156	38.6	86	46.3	Dinner sales	704	40.8	865	36.4	385	33.8
	26	25.4	125	30.9	67	36.2	Lunch sales	575	33.4	698	29.4	300	26.4
	64	63.0	281	69.6	153	82.5	Total sales	1,279	74.2	1,563	65.8	685	60.2
	24	36.8	95	33.8	59	38.5	Cost of sales-Units	465	36.3	529	33.8	255	37.2
	—	—	—	—	—	—	Cost of sales-Meat Cr.	—	—	—	—	—	—
	—	—	—	—	—	—	Cost of sales-Comm. Pr.	—	—	—	—	—	—
	41	63.2	186	66.2	94	61.5	Gross profit	815	63.7	1,034	66.2	430	62.8
							Liquor						
	32	31.1	77	19.1	22	11.9	Dinner sales	336	19.5	568	23.9	365	32.1
	6	5.9	46	11.4	10	5.5	Lunch sales	109	6.3	243	10.2	83	7.3
	38	37.0	123	30.4	32	17.5	Total sales	446	25.8	811	34.2	448	39.3
	9	23.7	28	22.8	6	19.8	Cost of sales	100	22.4	194	23.9	117	26.2
	29	76.3	95	77.2	26	80.2	Gross profit	346	77.6	617	76.1	330	73.8
	33	31.9	123	30.4	65	35.2	Total cost of sales	564	32.7	723	30.5	372	32.7
	70	68.1	281	69.6	120	64.8	Total gross profit	1,160	67.3	1,651	69.5	766	67.3
							Controllable Expense:						
							Employee Labor						
	19	29.2	64	22.8	52	33.9	Restaurant	371	29.0	402	25.7	241	35.2
	3	8.2	5	4.1	4	10.9	Club	42	9.4	60	7.4	35	7.9
	8	7.8	12	3.0	11	6.0	Management	71	4.1	62	2.6	33	2.9
	3	3.2	6	1.5	15	8.2	Bonuses	61	3.5	31	1.3	38	3.4
	—	—	—	—	—	—	Bonuses-Adjustments	—	—	—	—	—	—
	3	2.5	9	2.2	10	5.2	Payroll taxes	55	3.2	51	2.1	34	3.0
	—	—	—	—	—	(.3)	Payroll taxes adj.	—	—	—	—	—	—
	3	3.4	7	1.7	8	4.4	Benefits	55	3.2	41	1.7	37	3.2
	39	38.3	103	25.5	99	53.5	Total employee labor	656	38.1	647	27.3	419	36.8
	1	.7	—	—	—	—	Entertainer	—	—	—	—	—	1
	6	5.7	21	5.2	10	5.4	Operating supplies	94	5.4	120	5.1	81	7.1
	5	5.0	6	1.5	5	2.5	Repairs & maint.-C.I.P.	36	2.1	49	2.1	27	2.4

Item	$	%	$	%	$	%	$	%	$	%	$	%
Repairs & maintenance-adj.	—	—	—	—	—	—	—	—	—	—	—	—
Recruiting & training	14	.8	9	.4	4	.3	3	.7	—	—	—	.3
Public relations	6	.3	22	.9	12	1.0	4	1.0	2	1.0	—	.7
Linen & laundry	13	.8	14	.6	2	.2	2	.5	1	.5	3	.2
Uniforms	—	—	3	.1	6	.6	1	.2	4	2.4	—	2.9
Uniforms—C.I.P.	10	.6	—	—	—	—	—	—	—	—	—	—
Disc.-credit card sales	31	1.8	22	.9	9	.8	3	.7	1	.3	1	.9
General & admin.	—	—	38	1.6	13	1.1	7	1.7	8	4.1	1	1.2
Foreign exchange	—	—	—	—	—	—	—	—	—	—	—	—
Utilities	84	4.9	87	3.7	52	4.6	14	3.5	10	5.4	5	4.6
Unit approved advertising	3	.2	4	.2	2	.2	—	—	1	.5	2	1.5
Unit approved promo disc	—	—	—	—	(1)	—	—	—	—	—	(1)	(.6)
Vending income	(10)	(.6)	(13)	(.5)	(3)	(.3)	(2)	(.5)	—	(.2)	(1)	(1.0)
Total controllable exp.	939	54.4	1,002	42.2	624	54.9	162	40.1	140	75.4	62	60.4
Advertising/promo. exp	222	12.9	649	27.3	141	12.4	119	29.5	(20)	(10.6)	8	7.7
Factor adjustment	5	.3	98	4.1	9	.8	23	5.7	1	.3	—	.1
Promotional discounts	—	—	—	—	—	—	—	—	—	—	—	—
Total adv. & promo. exp.	5	.3	98	4.1	9	.8	23	5.7	(20)	(10.9)	—	.1
Marginal income	217	12.6	551	23.2	132	11.6	96	23.8	19	10.2	8	7.6
Occupancy-units	130	7.6	156	6.6	86	7.6	23	5.7	23	5.7	8	7.5
Occupancy-other	—	—	—	—	—	—	—	—	—	—	—	—
Rent exclusive of int.	—	—	—	—	—	—	—	—	—	—	—	—
Depreciation	—	—	—	—	—	—	—	—	—	—	—	—
Amortization	—	—	—	—	—	—	—	—	—	—	—	—
Taxes	16	.9	13	.5	7	.6	3	.7	2	1.0	1	.9
Insurance	4	.2	7	.3	2	.2	—	—	—	—	—	.1
Insurance adj.	—	—	—	—	—	—	—	—	(2)	(1.0)	—	—
Total occupancy expense	150	8.7	176	7.4	95	8.3	26	6.4	19	10.4	9	8.4
Preopening	147	8.5	126	5.3	—	—	27	6.7	4	1.9	—	—
Preopening-C.I.P.	—	—	—	—	—	—	—	—	—	—	—	—
Net rest. contribution	(81)	(4.7)	249	10.5	37	3.3	43	10.6	(43)	(23.2)	(1)	(.8)
Associate expense	35	2.0	48	2.0	8	.7	4	1.0	1	.7	—	.1
Trainee expense	207	12.0	—	—	1	.1	—	—	—	—	—	—
Assoc. & trainee-unalloc	9	.5	—	—	—	—	—	—	1	.5	—	—
Concept management	865	50.1	701	29.5	1	.1	54	13.4	77	41.3	—	—
Concept management-adj.	55	3.2	—	—	—	—	—	—	6	3.2	—	—
Corporate mgt	687	39.8	742	31.3	31	2.7	76	18.8	70	37.7	(8)	(7.5)
Corporate mgt.-adj.	—	—	—	—	—	—	—	—	—	—	—	—
Commissary expense	—	—	—	—	—	—	—	—	—	—	—	—
Interest income	—	—	—	—	—	—	—	—	—	—	—	—
Interest expense-other	—	—	—	—	—	—	—	—	—	—	—	—
Other (inc.)/expense	—	—	—	—	(1)	(.1)	1	.4	1	—	—	(.2)
Other (inc.)/exp.-adj.	—	—	—	—	—	—	—	—	—	—	—	—
Operating income	(1,938)	(112.3)	(1,242)	(52.3)	(3)	(.3)	(91)	(22.5)	(199)	(106.9)	7	6.9
Profit on invested capital	$(1,938)	(112.3)%	$(1,242)	(52.3)%	$(3)	(.3)%	$(91)	(22.5)%	$(199)	(106.9)%	$7	6.9%

EXHIBIT 3.5 Concept level consolidated income statement—May 1984

Description	Current month Prior year Amount	Current month Prior year Percent	Current month Plan Amount	Current month Plan Percent	Current month Current year Amount	Current month Current year Percent	Current year Current year Amount	Current year Current year Percent	Current year Plan Amount	Current year Plan Percent	Current year Prior year Amount	Current year Prior year Percent
Dinner sales	$108	58.3%	$782	58.4%	$282	59.8%	$1,869	59.1%	$3,742	58.3%	$1,040	60.3%
Lunch sales	78	41.7	558	41.6	190	40.2	1,296	40.9	2,674	41.7	685	39.7
Franchise revenue	—	—	—	—	—	—	—	—	—	—	—	—
Gross revenue	186	100.0	1,340	100.0	472	100.0	3,164	100.0	6,416	100.0	1,725	100.0
Franchise revenue	—	—	—	—	—	—	—	—	—	—	—	—
Total sales	186	100.0	1,340	100.0	472	100.0	3,164	100.0	6,416	100.0	1,725	100.0
Food												
Dinner sales	86	46.3	549	41.0	228	48.4	1,512	47.8	2,628	41.0	704	40.8
Lunch sales	67	36.2	455	34.0	169	35.8	1,149	36.3	2,176	33.9	575	33.4
Total sales	153	82.5	1,004	74.9	397	84.2	2,661	84.1	4,804	74.9	1,279	74.2
Cost of sales-units	59	38.5	314	31.3	153	38.6	968	36.4	1,498	31.2	465	36.3
Cost of sales-meat cr.	—	—	—	—	—	—	—	—	—	—	—	—
Cost of sales-comm. pr.	—	—	—	—	—	—	—	—	—	—	—	—
Gross profit	94	61.5	690	68.7	244	61.4	1,693	63.6	3,306	68.8	815	63.7
Liquor												
Dinner sales	22	11.9	233	17.4	54	11.4	357	11.3	1,114	17.4	336	19.5
Lunch sales	10	5.5	103	7.7	21	4.4	146	4.6	498	7.8	109	6.3
Total sales	32	17.5	336	25.1	75	15.8	503	15.9	1,612	25.1	446	25.8
Cost of sales	6	19.8	67	19.9	17	22.6	107	21.3	318	19.7	100	22.4
Gross profit	26	80.2	269	80.1	58	77.4	396	78.7	1,294	80.3	346	77.6
Total cost of sales	65	35.2	381	28.4	170	36.1	1,075	34.0	1,816	28.3	564	32.7
Total gross profit	120	64.8	959	71.6	302	63.9	2,089	66.0	4,600	71.7	1,160	67.3
Controllable expense: Employee labor												
Restaurant	52	33.9	212	21.1	46	11.5	266	10.0	1,023	21.3	371	29.0
Club	4	10.9	21	6.3	57	76.0	337	67.1	99	6.1	42	9.4
Management	11	6.0	49	3.7	18	3.7	126	4.0	228	3.6	71	4.1
Bonuses	15	8.2	38	2.8	11	2.2	132	4.2	186	2.9	61	3.5
Bonuses-adjustments	—	—	—	—	—	—	—	—	—	—	—	—
Payroll taxes	10	5.2	26	1.9	15	3.2	92	2.9	124	1.9	55	3.2
Payroll taxes adj.	—	(.3)	—	—	—	—	—	—	—	—	—	—
Benefits	8	4.4	22	1.6	13	2.7	76	2.4	111	1.7	55	3.2
Total employee labor	99	53.5	368	27.5	158	33.5	1,029	32.5	1,771	27.6	656	38.1
Entertainer	—	—	—	—	—	—	—	—	—	—	—	—
Operating supplies	10	5.4	57	4.3	40	8.5	162	5.1	278	4.3	94	5.4
Repairs & maint.-C.I.P.	5	2.5	14	1.0	4	.9	61	1.9	62	1.0	36	2.1

	$	%	$	%	$	%	$	%	$	%	$	%
Repairs & maintenance-adj.	—	—	—	—	—	—	—	—	—	—	—	—
Recruiting & training	—	—	5	.4	2	.3	6	.2	22	.3	1	.1
Public relations	2	1.0	8	.6	6	1.3	24	.8	33	.5	14	.8
Linen & laundry	1	.5	3	.2	2	.3	12	.4	18	.3	6	.3
Uniforms	4	2.4	6	.4	8	1.7	20	.6	28	.4	13	.8
Uniforms-C.I.P.	—	—	—	—	(1)	(.3)	3	.1	—	—	—	—
Disc.-credit card sales	1	.3	6	.4	2	.5	12	.4	34	.5	10	.6
General & admin.	8	4.1	13	1.0	8	1.7	46	1.4	58	.9	31	1.8
Utilities	10	5.4	31	2.3	28	6.0	140	4.4	156	2.4	84	4.9
Unit approved advertising	1	.5	—	—	—	—	5	.2	—	—	3	.2
Unit approved promo disc	—	—	—	—	—	—	—	—	—	—	—	—
Vending income	(2)	(.2)	(3)	(.2)	—	(.1)	(2)	(.1)	(18)	(.3)	(10)	(.6)
Total controllable exp.	140	75.4	508	37.9	257	54.5	1,516	47.9	2,442	38.1	939	54.4
Total controllable inc.	(20)	(10.6)	451	33.7	44	9.4	573	18.1	2,158	33.6	222	12.9
Advertising/promo. exp.	1	.3	41	3.1	—	—	21	.7	196	3.1	5	.3
Factor adjustment	—	—	—	—	—	—	—	—	—	—	—	—
Promotional discounts	—	—	—	—	—	—	—	—	—	—	—	—
Total adv. & promo. exp.	1	.3	41	3.1	—	—	21	.7	196	3.1	5	.3
Marginal income	(20)	(10.9)	410	30.6	44	9.4	552	17.4	1,962	30.6	217	12.6
Occupancy-units	19	10.2	49	3.7	18	3.8	153	4.8	207	3.2	130	7.6
Occupancy-other	—	—	—	—	—	—	—	—	—	—	—	—
Rent exclusive of int.	—	—	—	—	—	—	—	—	—	—	—	—
Depreciation	—	—	—	—	—	—	—	—	—	—	—	—
Amortization	—	—	—	—	—	—	—	—	—	—	—	—
Taxes	2	1.0	10	.7	3	.6	33	1.0	44	.7	16	.9
Insurance	2	.2	2	.1	—	—	14	.4	15	.2	4	.2
Insurance adj.	(2)	(1.0)	—	—	—	(.1)	—	—	—	—	—	—
Total occupancy expense	19	10.4	61	4.6	20	4.2	199	6.3	266	4.1	150	8.7
Preopening	4	1.9	100	7.5	117	24.9	190	6.0	400	6.2	147	8.5
Preopening-C.I.P.	—	—	—	—	(24)	(5.1)	23	.7	—	—	—	—
Net rest. contribution	(43)	(23.2)	249	18.6	(69)	(14.6)	140	4.4	1,296	20.2	(81)	(4.7)
Associate expense	1	.7	36	2.7	42	8.9	75	2.4	178	2.8	35	2.0
Trainee expense	1	.5	—	—	45	9.5	—	—	618	9.6	207	12.0
Assoc. & trainee-unalloc	—	—	42	3.1	—	—	511	16.1	—	—	9	.5
Concept management	77	41.3	—	—	92	19.5	—	—	500	7.8	865	50.1
Concept management-adj.	6	3.2	—	—	1	.2	447	14.1	—	—	55	3.2
Corporate mgt	70	37.7	—	—	—	—	1	—	—	—	687	39.8
Corporate mgt.-adj.	—	—	—	—	—	—	—	—	—	—	—	—
Commissary expense	—	—	—	—	—	—	—	—	—	—	—	—
Interest income	—	—	—	—	—	—	—	—	—	—	—	—
Interest expense-other	—	—	—	—	—	—	—	—	—	—	—	—
Other (inc.)/expense	—	—	—	—	—	—	—	—	—	—	—	—
Other (inc.)/exp.-adj.	—	—	—	—	—	—	—	—	—	—	—	—
Operating income	(199)	(106.9)	171	12.8	(248)	(52.6)	(895)	(28.3)	—	—	(1,938)	(112.3)
Profit on invested capital	$(199)	(106.9)%	$171	12.8%	$(248)	(52.6)%	$(895)	(28.3)%	$ —	%	$(1,938)	(112.3)%

67

EXHIBIT 3.6 **Concept level consolidated income statement—May 1985**

							Current/plan % variance	Current/prior % variance
	Current Month							
Prior year		**Plan**		**Current year**				
Amount	Percent	Amount	Percent	Amount	Percent	Description	F (U)	F (U)
$1,869	59.1%	$11,364	60.8%	$6,661	61.3%	Dinner sales	(41.4)%	256.4%
1,296	40.9	7,325	39.2	4,203	38.7	Lunch sales	(42.6)	224.4
–	–	–	–	–	–	Franchise revenue	–	–
3,164	100.0	18,689	100.0	10,864	100.0	Gross revenue	(41.9)	243.3
–	–	–	–	–	–	Franchise revenue	–	–
3,164	100.0	18,689	100.0	10,864	100.0	Total sales	(41.9)	243.3
						Food		
1,512	47.8	8,597	46.0	5,480	50.4	Dinner sales	(36.3)	262.4
1,149	36.3	6,355	34.0	3,795	34.9	Lunch sales	(40.3)	230.3
2,661	84.1	14,952	80.0	9,275	85.4	Total sales	(38.0)	248.5
968	36.4	5,401	36.1	3,336	36.0	Cost of sales-units	38.3	(244.2)
–	–			(3)	–	Cost of sales-meat cr.		
–	–					Cost of sales-comm. pr.		
1,693	63.6	9,551	63.9	5,943	64.1	Gross profit	(37.8)	251.0
						Liquor		
357	11.3	2,804	15.0	1,181	10.9	Dinner sales	(57.9)	231.0
146	4.6	934	5.0	408	3.8	Lunch sales	(56.3)	178.5
503	15.9	3,738	20.0	1,589	14.6	Total sales	(57.5)	215.8
107	21.3	932	24.9	358	22.5	Cost of sales	61.6	(233.9)
396	78.7	2,806	75.1	1,231	77.5	Gross profit	(56.1)	210.8
1,075	34.0	6,333	33.9	3,690	34.0	Total cost of sales	41.7	(243.1)
2,089	66.0	12,356	66.1	7,174	66.0	Total gross profit	(41.9)	243.4
						Controllable expense:		
						Employee labor		
266	10.0	1,538	10.3	1,140	12.3	Service labor	25.9	(328.5)
337	12.7	1,402	9.4	1,539	16.6	Kitchen labor	9.8	(356.2)
126	4.0	836	3.4	435	4.0	Management	31.5	(246.8)
132	4.2	587	3.1	363	3.3	Bonuses	38.1	(174.7)
–						Bonuses-adjustments		
92	2.9	367	2.0	369	3.4	Payroll taxes	(0.4)	(301.7)
–						Payroll taxes adj.		
76	2.4	326	1.7	339	3.1	Benefits	(4.1)	(348.8)
1,029	32.5	4,856	26.0	4,186	38.5	Total employee labor	13.8	(306.9)
–						Entertainer		
162	5.1	788	4.2	634	5.8	Operating supplies	19.6	(292.1)
61	1.9	185	1.0	296	2.7	Repairs & maint.-C.I.P.	(59.9)	(383.8)

Repairs & maintenance-adj.	—	—	—	—	—	—	(27.6)	(695.1)
Recruiting & training	6	0.2	36	0.2	46	0.4	27.7	(499.0)
Public relations	24	0.9	199	1.1	144	1.3	28.1	(463.8)
Linen & laundry	12	0.4	94	0.5	65	0.6	(111.6)	(524.3)
Uniforms	20	0.6	65	0.3	140	1.3	—	—
Uniforms-C.I.P.	3	0.1	—	—	(3)	—	44.0	(536.3)
Disc.-credit card sales	12	0.4	137	0.7	77	0.7	6.9	(349.5)
General & admin.	46	1.4	221	1.2	206	1.9	30.3	(277.6)
Utilities	140	4.4	760	4.1	530	4.9	—	(45.6)
Unit approved advertising	5	0.2	—	—	7	0.1	(51.7)	(10,152.4)
Unit approved promo disc	—	—	—	—	2	—	13.7	248.5
Vending income	(2)	(0.1)	(17)	(0.1)	(8)	(0.1)	(83.1)	(317.1)
Total controllable exp.	1,516	47.9	7,324	39.2	6,324	58.2	(24.0)	48.4
Total controllable inc.	573	18.1	5,032	26.9	850	7.8	—	(1,105.1)
Advertising/promo. exp.	21	0.7	200	1.1	108	1.0	(24.5)	—
Factor adjustment	—	—	—	—	140	1.3	(87.6)	(1,090.4)
Promotional discounts	—	—	—	—	1	—	—	8.9
Total adv. & promo. exp.	21	0.7	200	1.1	249	2.3	—	(401.2)
Marginal income	552	17.4	4,832	25.9	601	5.5	—	—
Occupancy-units	153	4.8	—	—	765	7.0	—	—
Occupancy-other	—	—	188	1.0	—	—	49.0	—
Rent exclusive of int.	—	—	969	5.2	—	—	48.1	—
Depreciation	—	—	42	0.2	—	—	38.7	(303.4)
Amortization	—	—	—	—	—	—	(27.4)	(308.2)
Taxes	33	1.0	196	1.0	100	0.9	(154.1)	(362.7)
Insurance	14	0.4	108	0.6	56	0.5	(409.9)	(368.0)
Insurance adj.	—	—	—	—	—	—	65.6	—
Total occupancy expense	199	6.3	1,503	8.0	921	8.5	—	(1,072.5)
Preopening	190	6.0	816	4.4	1,044	9.6	(60.1)	—
Preopening-C.I.P.	23	0.7	—	—	(4)	—	—	—
Net rest. contribution	140	4.4	2,513	13.4	(1,360)	(12.5)	—	(126.6)
Associate expense	75	2.4	400	2.1	218	2.0	—	—
Trainee expense	—	—	631	3.4	217	2.0	—	—
Assoc. & trainee-unalloc	511	16.1	—	—	1,822	16.8	—	—
Concept management	—	—	633	3.4	217	2.0	—	—
Concept management-adj.	447	14.1	—	—	796	7.3	—	—
Corporate mgt	1	—	594	3.2	217	2.0	—	—
Corporate mgt.-adj.	—	—	—	—	377	3.5	—	—
Commissary expense	—	—	—	—	—	—	—	—
Interest income	—	—	—	—	—	—	—	—
Interest expense-other	—	—	12	0.1	91	0.8	—	(18,629.8)
Other (inc.)/expense	—	—	—	—	7	0.1	—	—
Other (inc.)/exp.-adj.	—	—	—	—	—	—	—	—
Operating income	(895)	(28.3)	243	1.3	(5,322)	(49.0)	(2,290.2)	(494.8)
Profit on invested capital	(895)	(28.3)%	243	1.3%	(5,322)	(49.0)%	(2,290.2)%	(494.8)%

69

person tended to dominate the *position*—as was exemplified by one manager who had been a group member all the way through a period in which he held a variety of functional titles.

The process was structured such that as new concepts were agreed upon by the New Concepts Group, they were passed on to Collins, and ultimately to the president and chairman, for approval. Thereafter, a positioning statement for the concept was drafted and a manager for the new concept was named.

THE BB GUNDS CONCEPT

By early 1981, it was well understood that high on MM's list of priorities was the development of a viable new concept to position beside the already successful McElhaney's and Maguire's chains. A variety of new concept ideas had been considered by the New Concepts Group, including: gourmet burgers, pasta, health food, and gourmet take-out. The health food concept had been tested in one location in Phoenix. This restaurant, Macrobee's, had undergone several revisions in the testing phase and was ultimately abandoned as a new concept direction.

Though the pasta and gourmet take-out concepts were not seriously considered at the time, the gourmet burger concept was deemed worthy of further study.

One of the strongest proponents of the burger concept was MM's then-current chairman, John R. Maguire. In the summer of 1981, MM held an officer's meeting in Santa Fe as part of the overall strategic planning process. Maguire, who had earlier seen a new, and apparently successful, gourmet hamburger restaurant in nearby Albuquerque, used the occasion to take his management team to Albuquerque to see it.

The restaurant visited by the officers was called Chuggrugger's. At the time, this was the restaurant's only location. Chuggrugger's boasted several unique attributes, including gourmet burgers, a condiments bar, and an on-premises bakery and butcher shop. As the MM managers saw it, however, the Chuggrugger's concept had a major Achilles heel: though the restaurant charged premium prices, patrons had to wait on themselves. They stood in line to order and picked up their meal when their names were called.

A direction considered more viable by MM managers was that taken by the Pepper's restaurant chain, headquartered in Phoenix. In 1981, Pepper's had approximately 12 units in an operating area primarily limited to the Phoenix and Tucson vicinities. Like Chuggrugger's, Pepper's delivered a gourmet hamburger at a comparable premium price. Pepper's, however, also provided table service and more comfortable surroundings. In contrast to Chuggrugger's somewhat stark design, the Pepper's atmosphere was warm and inviting with a southwestern flair. Pepper's also offered a broader menu which included some Mexican entrees.

MM managers, and Maguire in particular, had originally hoped to purchase the Pepper's chain. The two sides, however, were unable to agree on a price. The amount MM managers felt they could afford to pay for goodwill was deemed insufficient by

Pepper's management and owners. Ultimately, a senior manager from a rival firm moved to Pepper's to assist in taking it public. (Operational and financial data for both Pepper's and Chuggrugger's are shown in Exhibit 3.7.)

EXHIBIT 3.7 Operational and financial data for Pepper's and Chuggruggers

	1980	1981	1982	1983	1984
Sales Revenue (In thousands)					
Pepper's*	$12,269	$19,785	$26,281	$17,076	$43,157
Chuggrugger's	318	1,058	3,965	10,122	24,523
Net Income (In thousands)					
Pepper's*	$865	$1,343	$1,998	$1,011	$1,990
Chuggrugger's	(54)	59	195	250	30
Units in Operation—Year End					
Pepper's	9	13	18	23	30
Chuggrugger's	1	2	2	15	51

*Pepper's data is for December 31 year end in 1980, 1981, and 1982, for six months ending June 30, 1983, and for year ending June 30, 1984.

Sources: Annual reports, SEC filings, and prospectuses.

Internal Development: The Pepper's Look-a-Like

The New Concepts Group spent better than a year working through the development of its own gourmet hamburger concept. This new, internally-developed concept was to be positioned in the same market segment as the Pepper's operation. With the resources that MM and its parent UBC possessed, it was seen as both desirable and feasible to mount an operation aggressive and ambitious enough to quickly surpass the size of the Pepper's chain.

The Gourmet Burger Concept. In its first positioning statement in the summer of 1981, the gourmet burger concept was described as "a casual, small town 'burger joint' with big town appeal." The modestly priced menu was to feature "the best burgers and fries in town," along with barbequed ribs and salads. Service was to be "fast and efficient with table turns averaging 25 to 30 minutes." The overall atmosphere would be inviting, warm, and colorful. With quality food, efficient service, reasonable prices, and inviting atmosphere, the restaurants would be places that were "fun to go to over and over again."

The concept was to be aimed primarily at the 18–44 age group, ". . . with a broad base appeal among the active, upscale, dual-working and upwardly mobile household." It was to capitalize on popular, high-consumption categories like burgers, ribs, Mexican food, and salads "that will generate high sales volumes and ROIC (return on invested capital) on a capital investment base lower than the corporate average." The menu and overall operation was to be simple in order to maximize productivity, construction, and building size. The targeted food/liquor mix was 70/30.

According to MM's fiscal 1983 Annual Plan, prepared in early 1982, the new concept's primary emphasis was to be on "high labor productivity, limited menu, low food cost, and attractive liquor mix." The technology necessary for the new concept was already available through the company's McElhaney's concept. MM's association with the parent company's La Fiesta operation was also seen as a useful resource.

In the summer of 1983, MM management performed a situation analysis of the gourmet burger concept, evaluating its potential in terms of strengths, weaknesses, opportunities, and threats. The concept was determined to have considerably more strengths than weaknesses. (A summary of this analysis appears in Exhibit 3.8.)

EXHIBIT 3.8 **MM situation analysis of gourmet burger concept**

Strengths	Weaknesses
Low construction costs	Depth of management team
Perceived price value	Timeliness of acquiring sites
Broad-based appeal	Market research
Sales & ROIC performance	Look alike
Daypart spread	Maintaining consistent food
Shorter hours of operation	quality
Cluster distribution	
Productivity	
Training time/cost	
Speed of service	
Parking requirements	
Conversion opportunities	
Quality food	
Growth of targeted audience	
Advertising ability	
Management needed	
Minimal liquor influence	
Opportunity for downtown sites	
Simple and clean concept	
Opportunity for innovation	

Opportunities	Threats
Targeting and evolving with the baby-boom consumer	Capital constraints
	Energy costs
Leveraging a highly fragmented center	Government regulations
As concept evolves analysis of strengths/weaknesses	Growth/expansion of competition
Ability to roll-out 50 units by 1987	Loss of concept management to competition
Opportunity to reduce roll-out time and preopening costs	Work force reduced

Source: MM F83–87 Strategic Plan.

Meanwhile, MM's marketing research showed that the hamburger segment of the restaurant industry achieved revenues of $21.8 billion in 1981, or 1.4 percent of total food service industry sales. Although often viewed as a mature segment, hamburgers still had gained 10 percent in customer traffic in the spring of 1982 versus the prior year.

A relatively untapped market was seen to exist for the gourmet hamburger. This type of hamburger service was characterized by large, high-quality hamburgers priced for good value; a limited menu drawing from popular, high-consumption categories; fast, seated or counter service; full bar service to accompany the meal; and a casual atmosphere (in terms of dress, occasion, and usage) that was more personalized than the typical fast-food hamburger experience. In recent years, several small regional chains had emerged to take advantage of the lack of gourmet hamburger competitors. Though Pepper's and the Red Robin chain, headquartered in Seattle, were attempting to expand, there were as yet no national competitors. (Exhibit 3.9 contains a summary of MM's analysis of the segment's primary competitors.)

Defining the Concept: The First Prototypes.   By mid-1982, MM management had defined a gourmet burger concept and laid plans to open two prototype units. The company's entry into the gourmet hamburger category was to be named BB Gunds. Within the category, Gunds was to be positioned as casual and upbeat, providing a light-hearted and enjoyable eating experience. Service would be fast but not rushed, provided by casually dressed, friendly, and fun-loving employees.

West Palm Beach was chosen as the site of the first Gunds prototype unit. Maguire knew that the Sambo's restaurant chain was failing and directed his real estate department to look into possible conversions of Sambo's units located in the Palm Beach area. Palm Beach was selected for several reasons: Florida was a rapidly growing market, several successful McElhaney's units were located nearby, the lead time between commitment and opening would be relatively short, and Maguire visited the area several times a year for both business and personal reasons.

A site was chosen on a "restaurant row" area of West Palm Beach. A Sambo's restaurant on the site was converted and put into operation in November 1982. The conversion was designed, as one MM officer put it, "to look like the more successful competitors, with clutter on the walls and a Pepper's and Chuggrugger's-like menu."

MM management felt they made a "good deal" for the site and were encouraged by the high restaurant traffic the area received. A McElhaney's unit located across the street from the site was one of the highest volume units in the entire chain. Further, most of the other restaurants surrounding the site were doing quite well.

The West Palm Beach prototype performed superbly in the early going, and, in fact, continued to perform well in future years. Good management at the unit level was put in place early on, and labor costs were held to relatively low levels. In slightly more than a year, the unit had exceeded projections of $1.8 million annually, reaching nearly $2 million in sales on an annualized basis. The unit transformed a favorable impression with the public into a high gross volume and proceeded to maintain its local market position.

MM had also committed to a second site in the Palm Beach area—this one a

EXHIBIT 3.9 ▪ MM's primary competitors in the gourmet burger (with liquor) category—1982

Category: Burgers w/Liquor

Restaurant Name	Parent Company	# Units (Owned/ Fran.)	Additional Units/ Period	Current Annualized Sales (In millions)	Sales $/Unit (In millions)	Reported Date	Comments
Red Robin	—	10 (7/3)	8-9/1982; 50/1987	18.0	1.80	3/82	Average check $6.30 Food cost 33%; Labor 28% Aggressive franchising plans, Western U.S. and Canada 35% liquor mix 11.0% net income
Round the Corner	—	20 (13/7)	8/1982 50/1986	15.0	.75	5/82	Average seating 165 $4.00 check average TV support utilized Actively pursuing franchising; in or near mall locations, business centers 20 varieties of burgers; wine, beer
Hamburger Hamlet	—	22 (co-owned)	—	30.0	1.40	3/82	Haute cuisine burgers; average check $10-15 Began on West Coast, expanded to East (D.C., Atlanta, Chicago)
Max & Erma's	Investor's Spectrum, Inc.	10 (co-owned)	1/1982	10.7	1.40	4/82	Midwest location Average check $10 Added pasta and raw bars to some units 50% liquor mix
Boll Weevil	—	15	5-6/Year	6.0	.43	5/82	Liquor mix 15% Plan to expand out of state
Charlie's Hamburger Joint	Walden Enterprises	4	—	2.0	.50	6/82	Counter service only, 5 burger varieties, pkg. snacks Average check $2.75
Pepper's	—	13	—	25.0	1.90	4/82	Expansion 6-8/year will require outside capital

Source: MM F83-87 Strategic Plan.

former Sizzler Steakhouse located in North Palm Beach. This site was located on the north end of the local trading area and historically had not proved to be a high traffic area. Following a conversion of the Sizzler site, the second Gunds unit opened in April 1983. This Gunds looked very different from the Gunds in West Palm Beach. The North Palm Beach location had more of a McElhaney's look to it, with ferns, ceiling fans, and A-frame ceiling. In contrast to its successful counterpart, this unit failed to meet its projections of $1.7–1.8 million in annual sales, and reached only about $1 million in sales in fiscal 1984.

Concept Manager Turnover.   BB Gunds experienced a succession of concept managers during the period from its inception to its first few years of operation. The first concept manager, put in place during the planning stages, left his position before the West Palm Beach unit was opened. Charles Curtis, who had earlier headed the New Concepts Group, took over as concept manager in 1982. He stayed with the Gunds operation until October 1983, when he was transferred to the West Coast to head McElhaney's California operation.

Vicki Campos was appointed as the third Gunds concept manager in little more than a year's time. Surveying the operation, Campos found there were as yet no clear signs of success. One of her units appeared to be a winner and the other a loser.

Assessment and Expansion: The 1983–1984 Period

In the latter part of 1983, Campos arranged for further market research on the two prototype Palm Beach units. Consumer focus groups were shown the Palm Beach Gunds units and asked to compare them with a Pepper's unit in nearby Boca Raton. Interviews with these focus groups led to the conclusion that Gunds had no strong points of uniqueness. Though this was a relatively minor issue while Pepper's and Gunds operated in different trading areas, it was felt that it was likely to become more significant as the two chains grew.

This latter point was now of more than casual interest to MM's management group, as the chairman of a rival (and successful) restaurant chain had recently moved over to Pepper's. Following the withdrawal by MM from the bidding process, this rival firm's chairman concluded negotiations that would lead to his becoming a significant owner as well as senior executive of the Phoenix-based competitor.

Nonetheless, the immediate issue at hand was still the lack of some point of uniqueness in the Gunds prototype. Campos and other MM managers concluded that what was lacking was an on-premises bakery. A bakery, they reasoned, would convey a sense of freshness and wholesomeness, while adding a degree of theater to the concept. In so doing, however, they determined not to go overboard as they felt Chuggrugger's had done, by having patrons standing in line next to suspended sides of beef.

Refining the Concept: The 1984–1988 Strategic Plan.   In its Fiscal 1984–1988 Strategic Plan, MM managers began to refine their BB Gunds concept. As they readied for expansion, the bakery idea was incorporated into the plans for future units. An exhibition baking area, in fact, was expected to serve as a visual focal point in future restaurants, as a source of fresh buns and desserts, as a "to go" area, and as an ongoing reminder to the customer of the "fresh quality products of BB Gunds."

The plan set two primary objectives for the concept to attain within the subsequent five years: (1) position the concept for rapid growth by firmly establishing it as the premier quality entrant in the gourmet hamburger category, and (2) meet the operational goals (listed in Exhibit 3.10).

EXHIBIT 3.10 **BB Gunds operational goals—1984**

	F'84	F'85	F'86	F'87	F'88
		(Dollars in millions)			
New units	6	10	15	20	25
Total units	8	18	33	53	78
Total sales	$3.9	$23.2	$48.5	$86.8	$140.3
Total PIC*	$ .2	$ .1	$ 4.7	$11.4	$ 20.9
ROIC percent**	(2.8%)	.6%	12.6%	18.1%	21.3%

*PIC is an abbreviation for profit on invested capital, a pretax and pre-interest number.

**ROIC is an abbreviation for return on invested capital.

The plan also called for achieving premier quality status in its category by offering the customer such elements of difference as trendy menu items, "quality to go," baked goods, and a commitment to freshness. Testing of the concept positioning was planned in a number of different markets in order to identify critical success factors. Future test markets were to include college markets, mall locations, large markets with heavy gourmet hamburger competition, and large markets with little gourmet hamburger competition.

Gunds would attempt to gain market presence in key markets by opening two or three units to establish an early concept identity. Media and promotion vehicles would then be evaluated to determine the extent to which the concept was marketing driven. Later, the key markets would be filled in to achieve media efficiency and better market coverage. Target markets for later in the planning period would be selected based on early unit and marketing experience.

MM management planned to use Maguire's management personnel to assist in running the Gunds concept until the 1985 fiscal year. Thereafter, the concept would have its own recruiting and training programs in place.

Expectations for the success of the Gunds concept were relatively high at this point. Once the prototype had been altered and refined, an aggressive roll-out campaign was planned. A popular company slogan at the time, "Lead, Follow, or Get the Hell Out of the Way," seemed particularly appropriate in the context of this spirited new venture.

Expanding the Concept: A New Prototype.   At the beginning of 1984, Campos was put in charge of the McElhaney's concept when its general manager moved elsewhere. Replacing Campos at the helm of Gunds was Jay Hemphill. Hemphill had been a supervisor for Maguire's and had been responsible for some ten of the chain's restaurants. Hemphill inherited the two Palm Beach restaurants along with five new units in varying stages of completion. He instituted several operational changes, primarily in areas of service.

In March 1984, the third Gunds unit opened in Pasadena, Texas (near Houston). The unit's plans were redesigned at the last minute, reducing the bar area in order to incorporate a bakery exhibition area. The Pasadena location was in an area said to be in transition from a primarily blue-collar area to a mix of blue-collar and white-collar residents. The unit had some difficulty with its signage and was not easily visible from the freeway.

Four additional Gunds units then opened in rapid succession, bringing the concept to a total of seven restaurants by the summer of 1984. In May 1984, the chain's fourth unit opened in Mesquite, Texas, a blue-collar/middle-class suburb of Dallas. The fifth unit also opened in May and was located in Kissimmee, Florida, a blue-collar suburb south of Orlando. The sixth unit, again placed in a blue-collar/middle-class neighborhood, opened on Jones Road in Houston in June. The last in this series, the seventh unit, opened in August 1984 in College Station, Texas, the home of Texas A&M University.

Each of the five new units had bakeries. All except the Pasadena location were of the same prototype, a design described by one MM officer as a "functional, coffee shop look." Each of the five most recent units was located on a site believed to be a good buy in light of the $1.3 million informal lid on capital expenditures per unit. Though there ultimately were attempts to select sites in more expensive, high-traffic areas such as the Scottsdale suburb northeast of Phoenix, no one at MM had been willing to sign off on a price tag that could run as high as $2 million.

Evaluating the Expansion Effort

As a research and development effort, BB Gunds had evolved quickly. Two prototypes and various menu items and types of locations were tested during its first two years of development. Evaluation of these various tests led to the formation of a third prototype which was scheduled to be put into operation in early 1985.

The new prototype was to bring together the best elements of previous prototype tests. It would have a warm, comfortable, quality, and upbeat feel. This was to be accomplished through the use of natural and warm materials like brick, rough-hewn wood, and tile that would give a rustic, yet modern look; a variety of fixtures; music at moderate sound levels; plants; attractive lighting; and an active, energetic staff. The new prototype would also make a greater liquor statement with an expanded lounge area.

The revised Gunds Business Profile stated that the new design "should give BB Gunds a definitive position relative to the theme or gimmick competitors in the category." Further, it would "appeal to a broad range of adults, with or without children, across the country. By leveraging its ability to execute on fresh, high-quality food served quickly by a friendly staff, BB Gunds will be able to build a strong price/value relationship."

Industry Analysis. An industry and competitive analysis performed by MM in 1984 as part of the strategic planning process noted that the gourmet hamburger category had reached a $500 million annual sales level as part of the $11 billion casual dining market. The rapid growth of the category was primarily attributed to the aging of the baby-boom generation and their continued fascination with the fast-food experience. The gourmet hamburger category was perceived to offer the desirable elements of fast food (speedy service, price/value) with upgraded food quality, service, and ambience.

A different approach to service and liquor was seen by MM management as splitting the overall gourmet hamburger category into three distinct niches. The three niches identified by MM were adult fast-food, classic gourmet hamburger, and fern burger. (Exhibit 3.11 provides more detail on these niches.)

EXHIBIT 3.11 **Competitors and selected categories displayed by concept elements**

		Gourmet Hamburger			
	Fast Food	**Adult Fast Food**	**Classic Gourmet Burger**	**Fern Burger**	**Fern Bar**
	Burger King McDonalds Wendy's	Chuggrugger's Flakey Jake's Joe Willy's Bonkers Purdy's Round the Corner	BB Gunds Pepper's Spoons Cheddar's Moxies Daly's Dandelion	Red Robin J. R. Clements Hamburger Hamlet T. J. Applebee's	McElhaney's TGI Friday's Bombay Bicycle Club Penrod's
Menu	Limited	Limited	Some non-burger variety	Much non-burger variety	Eclectic
Service	Self and Drive Thru	Self	Table	Table	Table
Liquor	None	15–25%	15–25%	20–35%	35%+
Entree price range	Low	Middle	Middle	Middle	Middle + Upper
Ambience	Basic	Cleverly basic	Casual	Casual	Casual
Extras	Salad bar Breakfast Playgrounds	Produce bar Bakery Butcher shop	Special value, High end entree	?	Entertainment

Source: MM F85–89 Strategic Plan.

The adult fast-food niche was characterized by an extremely limited menu, counter service, and some alcoholic beverages. The ambience was basic and functional. Chuggrugger's, Flakey Jake's, and Joe Willy's were said to fall within this category.

The classic gourmet hamburger niche had been made popular by Pepper's in 1975. It offered table service, full liquor service, and a slightly broader menu of both burger and nonburger items. As noted earlier, MM positioned BB Gunds in this category, against such entrants as Pepper's, Spoons, and Moxie's.

The fern burger niche was defined as a hybrid of both the classic gourmet hamburger and fern bar. While similar to the classic gourmet hamburger, fern burger concepts shared two key factors with fern bar concepts—a much more varied menu and emphasis on some drinking-only usage. Competitors within this category were said to include Red Robin, J. R. Clemens, and Hamburger Hamlet. There had been indications from recent changes in the Pepper's prototype and menu that it was moving directionally toward a fern burger positioning.

MM management viewed the classic gourmet hamburger positioning as having the best potential for long-term growth and viability. According to an internal analysis, its positioning occupied the most distinctive niche, a middle ground between fast food and fern bars that provided consumers with a unique set of benefits.

BB Gunds, according to MM management, was developing in a category where there was a scramble underway by more than 15 major competitors to establish a positioning and gain market share during the category's early development. While there was a tremendous amount of expansion, no one had yet established a preemptive position of leadership. The category was seen to be still new enough in its development and large enough in its scope to allow a new concept like BB Gunds to become the dominant leader within three to five years. It was anticipated that several of the weaker chains would fall victim to an industry shakeout by 1986. Category leaders capable of supporting advertising were expected to survive any such shakeout.

Company Objectives. As a result of its analysis, MM management set its objectives for the Gunds concept for the fiscal 1985–1989 period. These objectives were to position the concept for rapid growth as the premier quality entrant in its category; expand the concept and establish it as the dominant leader in its category; and achieve the goals listed in Exhibit 3.12.

Gunds management expected to achieve the desired positioning through a strategy composed of five primary components:

Target Audience.   The primary target audience was to be adults aged 25–44 with a household income greater than $20,000 and in an equal male/female split. Gunds would possess sufficiently broad appeal to be attractive to individuals both above and below the age and income of the primary target audience. While attracting more of the college educated, white-collar individuals, those with less education and non-professional jobs would also feel comfortable. Though Gunds would be an adult-oriented experience, families with children would have an important role in the customer base.

EXHIBIT 3.12 **BB Gunds operational goals—1985**					
	F'85	**F'86**	**F'87**	**F'88**	**F'89**
		(Dollars in millions)			
New units	13	20	35	40	40
Total units	18	38	73	113	153
Total sales	$14.2	$48.4	$103.9	$194.4	$307.8
Total PIC	$(2.2)	$ 2.7	$ 9.6	$ 25.3	$ 51.1
ROIC percent	(12.2%)	5.7%	10.1%	16.6%	24.0%

*PIC is an abbreviation for profit on invested capital, a pretax and pre-interest number.

**ROIC is an abbreviation for return on invested capital.

Quality Menu.   Gunds was to serve premium quality foods in generous portions and at moderate prices. It would have a high perceived price/value relationship. Items would be prepared fresh, from scratch. The menu would include items with broad appeal. Gunds would produce the best food in the category, though the menu would be limited to items having relatively simple preparation steps and that could be cooked within 6 to 8 minutes.

Each restaurant would offer full bar service. The focus was to be on selling liquor with the meal, instead of building nonmeal liquor sales. Bottled beer and specialty drinks would be the primary liquor offerings. A good price/value relationship on liquor would be built by pricing below the market average.

Quick Quality Eating.   Customers' orders would be taken quickly and food would be delivered to the table within a short time after being ordered. An average table turn of 30–35 minutes would meet the needs of Gunds' on-the-go customers. All food items would be marketed on a to-go basis, as well.

Ambience.   The feel of BB Gunds would be one of a friendly, casual, and upbeat restaurant. It would be a place to go by yourself, to meet friends for a quick quality meal, or for the whole family to enjoy an informal meal away from home.

Customer Touch.   The service staff would be friendly and outgoing, making the customers feel welcome and appreciated. Staff members would be youthful (20-25 years of age) and have an energetic, upbeat attitude consistent with the fast-paced atmosphere of the restaurant.

Signs of Trouble: The 1984–1985 Period

By the summer of 1984, with seven Gunds units in operation, several of the concept's performance objectives appeared to be in jeopardy. Neither Gunds' Profit on Invested Capital (PIC) nor its Return on Invested Capital (ROIC) had yet turned positive. (See Exhibit 3.13 for a summary of the concept's financial data.) The liquor mix, which had originally been projected at 30 percent, had recently fallen as low as 16 percent. Both labor and food costs as a percentage of sales were exceptionally

EXHIBIT 3.13 **BB Gunds financial summary—May 1985**

	June	July	Aug.	1st Qtr.	Sept.	Oct.	Nov.	2nd Qtr.	Dec.	Jan.	Feb.	3rd Qtr.	Mar.	Apr.	May	4th Qtr.	Total
Sales ($000)																	
F'85	657	633	731	**2,021**	681	681	725	**2,087**	744	757	946	**2,447**	1,255	1,349	1,706	**4,310**	**10,684**
Plan	729	998	1,267	**2,994**	1,349	1,456	1,377	**4,182**	1,577	1,583	1,917	**5,077**	2,284	1,990	2,162	**6,436**	**18,689**
F'84	191	224	225	**640**	208	210	212	**630**	250	242	253	**745**	324	354	472	**1,150**	**3,164**
F'83							59	**59**	86	86	94	**266**	118	149	186	**453**	**778**
Liquor Mix (%)																	
F'85	15.1	14.4	14.6	**14.7**	14.9	14.9	13.7	**14.5**	13.3	13.3	14.9	**13.9**	14.7	14.9	15.5	**15.1**	**14.6**
Plan	19.9	20.0	20.0	**20.0**	19.9	20.0	20.0	**20.0**	20.0	20.0	20.0	**20.0**	20.0	20.1	20.0	**20.0**	**20.0**
F'84	16.8	16.7	16.0	**16.4**	15.9	16.2	16.0	**16.0**	15.8	15.3	15.4	**15.6**	13.9	15.0	15.8	**15.7**	**15.9**
F'83							18.6	**18.6**	16.3	16.3	14.9	**15.8**	15.3	16.1	17.2	**16.3**	**16.3**
Food Cost (%)																	
F'85	37.8	38.6	39.4	**38.6**	38.4	36.1	32.7	**35.7**	32.3	33.6	33.8	**33.2**	35.5	36.1	37.1	**36.3**	**36.0**
Plan	37.6	37.0	36.5	**36.9**	36.4	36.2	36.3	**36.3**	36.1	36.0	35.9	**36.0**	35.7	35.8	35.7	**35.7**	**36.1**
F'84	36.0	36.2	37.0	**36.4**	35.8	37.0	34.8	**35.9**	35.5	36.2	34.9	**35.5**	35.2	37.2	38.6	**37.2**	**36.4**
F'83							36.4	**36.4**	29.1	35.8	35.3	**33.5**	36.6	38.1	38.5	**37.8**	**36.2**
Labor Cost (%)																	
F'85	42.4	38.4	34.9	**38.4**	38.3	39.0	35.9	**37.8**	34.8	39.6	35.8	**36.7**	37.0	41.7	40.9	**40.0**	**38.5**
Plan	27.8	25.6	25.5	**26.1**	25.6	24.5	29.9	**26.6**	24.4	25.5	26.3	**25.5**	26.6	26.1	25.1	**25.9**	**26.0**
F'84	34.4	32.1	32.1	**32.0**	35.0	33.8	33.1	**33.9**	31.3	33.0	26.8	**30.3**	28.8	36.6	33.5	**32.8**	**32.5**
F'83							55.3	**55.3**	37.9	34.8	34.7	**35.8**	32.5	36.2	41.7	**37.5**	**38.3**
Total Controllable Income (%)																	
F'85	3.7	5.9	9.0	**6.3**	7.3	8.7	15.3	**10.5**	16.9	5.7	11.7	**11.4**	11.6	2.4	2.7	**5.2**	**7.8**
Plan	23.7	27.1	27.4	**26.3**	27.7	29.0	20.6	**25.8**	29.9	28.2	26.3	**28.0**	25.8	27.0	28.4	**27.0**	**26.9**
F'84	14.1	21.1	16.9	**17.5**	16.0	18.3	20.9	**18.4**	24.9	20.1	26.6	**23.9**	23.1	13.4	9.4	**14.5**	**18.1**
F'83							(11.3)	**(11.3)**	17.6	18.8	19.0	**18.5**	20.2	8.2	3.4	**9.4**	**10.9**
Profit on Invested Capital ($000)																	
F'85	(247)	(254)	(224)	**(725)**	(243)	(267)	(271)	**(781)**	(361)	(540)	(424)	**(1,325)**	(849)	(710)	(932)	**(2,491)**	**(5,322)**
Plan	(163)	(63)	(32)	**(258)**	13	85	(129)	**(31)**	62	79	58	**199**	130	99	102	**331**	**241**
F'84	(15)	(2)	(43)	**(60)**	(4)	(41)	15	**(30)**	27	(54)	(108)	**(135)**	(274)	(149)	(248)	**(671)**	**(895)**
F'83							(178)	**(178)**	(47)	(167)	(187)	**(401)**	(190)	(146)	(181)	**(517)**	**(1,096)**

high. Average sales per unit, which had initially been projected at $1.8 million, had only reached $1.39 million by the end of fiscal 1984. Success of the concept, MM managers agreed, had not yet been proven in multiple markets.

At about this time, UBC executives were beginning to question the viability of the Gunds concept. John Maguire was said to have gone before the UBC board to lend some reassurance and to ask for more time for the concept to prove itself.

Meanwhile, competition within the gourmet hamburger segment appeared to be stiffening. SAGA Corporation had recently acquired the Spoons chain and was in the process of opening several more units. Chuggrugger's had recently gone public and planned to open 187 new units during the next four years, primarily through franchising. Pepper's, Gunds' closest competitor, had also recently gone public and was in the process of opening more than a dozen new units.

In response to Gunds recent and somewhat disappointing results, MM management resolved to set new objectives for the Gunds concept. Operationally, the concept was charged with raising the liquor mix to 25 percent by year end, maintaining the price/quality perception, and reducing the start-up costs of the prototype. Other target ratios for the fiscal 1985 year included a food cost of 36.1 percent and total controllable income of 26.9 percent.

Financially, the concept was asked to improve existing unit margins, control new unit margins during concept expansion, and generate acceptable investment turnover in new units. The concept was to achieve sales objectives of $18.7 million and operating income of $200,000.

The general feeling of management at the time, said company insiders, was that although problems with the concept certainly existed, MM had the money to fix them along the way. Growth, however—and growth early on—was a significant determinant in the concept's overall success. Pepper's was growing and Gunds management was determined to keep pace.

Further Expansion/Continuing Problems. Long before the College Station unit opened in August 1984, MM management had known the concept still wasn't working. The recently opened locations were showing signs that they would fail to meet annual projections. An insider offered the explanation that though food and service were both good, the concept package just wasn't clicking.

To shore up the continued problems, MM top management moved Michael Farmar into the Gunds concept manager position in the summer of 1984. Farmar had been a regional manager for Maguire's, where he had several supervising managers reporting to him. Farmar was told to take a completely fresh look at the Gunds concept and attempt to give it "focus, continuity, and the single vision that makes for a successful concept."

Farmar rallied his employees together, urging them to take control of their futures. "He said the success of this restaurant was up to us, and we could do it," recalled an MM employee. Farmar, however, had little time to make substantive changes in the Gunds operation. The third prototype was scheduled to come on line as 10 new units were rolled out between January and May 1985. The new units were located primarily in the Mountain Southwest and Southeast (Exhibit 3.14).

EXHIBIT 3.14 **Summary of BB Gunds opening dates and locations**		
Unit #1	Nov. 1982	West Palm Beach, FL
Unit #2	Apr. 1983	North Palm Beach, FL
Unit #3	Mar. 1984	Pasadena, TX (near Houston)
Unit #4	May 1984	Mesquite, TX (near Dallas)
Unit #5	May 1984	Kissimmee, FL (near Orlando)
Unit #6	Jun. 1984	Houston, TX (Jones Rd.)
Unit #7	Aug. 1984	College Station, TX
Unit #8	Jan. 1985	Tempe, AZ (near Phoenix)
Unit #9	Jan. 1985	Albuquerque, NM
Unit #10	Feb. 1985	Casselberry, FL (north of Orlando)
Unit #11	Feb. 1985	Oklahoma City, OK
Unit #12	Mar. 1985	Miami, FL
Unit #13	Apr. 1985	Mesa, AZ (near Phoenix)
Unit #14	Apr. 1985	Ann Arbor, MI
Unit #15	Apr. 1985	Bedford, TX (near Dallas)
Unit #16	May 1985	Clearwater, FL (near Tampa)
Unit #17	May 1985	Tucson, AZ

Unmet Objectives. In the spring of 1985, with the last of the series of new units in place and ready to open, MM management saw that the Gunds concept would again fail to meet annual objectives. In fact, the situation appeared to be becoming more grave. Projections for the upcoming fiscal year end showed sales for the Gunds concept would likely reach just $11.9 million. PIC was projected to be a $4 million loss, while ROIC would likely end up a negative 24.9%. To make matters worse, average sales per unit had dropped by 2% to $1.36 million.

The fiscal 1986 annual plan was just being completed and its analysis of the Gunds operating environment was none too optimistic. Though the gourmet hamburger category had undergone explosive growth of late, the competition from 15 major competitors in the category remained stiff. A highly competitive job market existed for quality management and employees, making it difficult to meet ambitious growth plans. Furthermore, a recent forecast predicted a 12 percent increase in the price of ground beef by January 1986.

Though the report cited a number of strengths in the Gunds concept operation, the list of weaknesses was beginning to grow. Operationally, the chain faced a lack of stability caused by rapid expansion. Limited management depth and experience was available at the unit level.

Financially, the sales and earnings figures noted above were not encouraging. Labor costs remained high and the current liquor mix had fallen below 14 percent. Moreover, the concept expansion was boosting general and administrative expenses.

Things looked no brighter on the marketing side. Competition in the segment was increasing, while consumer awareness level of the Gunds concept remained low.

Delivery of consistent food quality was specified as the number one priority for the next fiscal year. Menu and kitchen operations were to be simplified in order to reduce labor costs and to insure consistency. A recent menu redesign produced nine new items and a major upgrade to the burger (ground chuck vs. ground beef). New emphasis was to be placed on quality training, floor management skills, and the maintenance of operating standards. To assist, 15 general managers and managers were to be transferred into the Gunds operation from McElhaney's and Maguire's.

By this time, too, MM was experiencing significant upper management turnover. Within the past couple of years, a number of top managers had left the firm, including John Maguire, CEO; Jeff Kerr, CEO (and successor to Maguire); Bobby Collins, Senior Vice President of Marketing; Dick Haskins, CEO (and successor to Jeff Kerr); and Tom Horton, COO.

TIME FOR A DECISION

Despite the continued problems the Annual Plan set some heady objectives for the concept to meet in the upcoming fiscal year. The plan called for achieving sales of $31.9 million, a PIC of $.4 million, and an ROIC of 1.3%. Sales per unit were projected to reach $1.58 million. Furthermore, 11 new units were scheduled to open at an average cost of $1.5 million.

In addition to the above financial objectives, the plan also called for meeting the following key ratios: food cost—34.5 percent, liquor mix—18.4 percent, liquor cost—22.5 percent, labor cost—28.3 percent, and TCI (total controllable income)—24.9 percent.

Michael Farmar knew that recent improvements to the concept were likely to make the Gunds' picture look a bit brighter. Looking at the objectives that had just been set for his operation, however, he wondered whether these improvements would be significant enough to allow him to meet his objectives. He wondered, too, how the Gunds operation might have been handled differently were MM able to start the whole process over again.

CASE 4

Golden Hybrids Inc.

Golden Hybrids seed company, a medium size family business in Indiana, began operations in 1935. The years following 1935 were years of rapid growth for Golden Hybrids. In 1936, a modest research program was established and a dealer organization was set up consisting of many farm store accounts. In 1939,

This case was prepared by Thomas F. Funk of the University of Guelph, Guelph, Ontario, Canada. It is intended as a basis for classroom discussion rather than to illustrate effective or ineffective handling of an administrative situation. The data in this case are disguised but are based on real data. Copyright © 1988 by Thomas F. Funk. Used by permission from Thomas F. Funk.

Golden Hybrids experienced a serious setback. The industry was changing and this change was not immediately recognized by the management of Golden Hybrids. Farm stores, the traditional retail agent for seed corn, were passing out of the picture in favor of farmer dealers. Since Golden Hybrids had not established a farmer-dealer organization, they realized a substantial decline in sales. Work was immediately started on a farmer-dealer organization and sales picked up again the next year.

In the early 1960s, Golden Hybrids embarked upon an expansion program. A new plant was constructed to have an eventual annual capacity of over 300,000 bushels of processed seed. This is the present facility utilized by the firm.

Sales of seed corn in 1986 amounted to $7.13 million for 110,983 bushels of seed (Exhibits 4.1 and 4.2). Of this total, approximately 70 percent were single-cross varieties and the remaining 30 percent were special-crosses. Although pretax profits had been declining since 1983, management became concerned about this situation only after it learned that profits in 1986 were $52,000 below those of 1985. In attempting to isolate the problem, management observed that all of its costs had been increasing over the period 1982 to 1986. Cost of sales per unit sold had increased from approximately $28 a bushel in 1982 to over $36 a bushel in 1986. This, however, was to be expected because the proportion of single-crosses was increasing and the cost of producing single-crosses was known to be considerably higher than special-crosses.[1] Administrative costs also had increased since 1982, both in terms of absolute dollars and dollars per bushel sold. In 1982, total selling costs were $14.24 per bushel compared with $18.36 in 1986. The current financial position of the company is described in Exhibit 4.3.

EXHIBIT 4.1 **Statement of income and expenses 1982–1986**

	1982	1983	(In thousands) 1984	1985	1986
Sales of seed corn	$4,844	$5,168	$5,468	$6,432	$7,128
Cost of sales	2,472	2,540	2,764	3,332	3,992
Gross margin	2,372	2,628	2,704	3,100	3,136
Selling expenses	1,260	1,232	1,656	1,988	2,036
Administrative expenses	652	648	452	740	780
Net Profit	$ 460	$ 748	$ 596	$ 372	$ 320

On the basis of this analysis, management felt that the real problem it faced was in marketing. It thought that it was simply spending too much money on a marketing program that wasn't effective. To remedy this situation, management felt

---

[1]Single- and special-cross varieties are the major classifications of hybrid seed corn. Single-cross hybrids result from the combination of two inbred lines. They offer the highest yield potential to the farmer, but may have a great deal of performance variability under different environmental conditions. Special-crosses arise from the combination of three or four relatively unrelated inbred lines. They have a wider genetic base and, therefore, have less performance variability and are adaptable to varying environmental conditions. Special-crosses tend to have slightly lower yield potential than single-crosses.

EXHIBIT 4.2 **Unit sales of seed corn**

Year	Total sales (In bushels)
1986	110,983
1985	104,143
1984	92,180
1983	90,701
1982	88,342

EXHIBIT 4.3 **Golden Hybrids balance sheet, August 31, 1986**

Assets		Liabilities and net worth	
Current Assets		Current Liabilities	
Cash	$ 761,800	Accounts payable	$ 328,000
Accounts receivable	1,490,000	Obligations due within	
Inventories	622,400	the year	$1,520,000
Work in process	198,800	Accrued expenses	208,000
	$3,073,000		$2,056,000
Investments		Long-term Liabilities	
Common stock	$ 742,400	Mortgages payable	$ 318,400
Fixed Assets		Net Worth	
Cost	$4,550,000	Capital stock	$ 960,000
Less reserve for depreciation	2,690,400	Earned surplus	2,340,600
Total	$1,859,600	Total	$3,300,600
		Total Liabilities	
Total Assets	$5,675,000	and Net Worth	$5,675,000

---

that a major change was needed. As a result, it immediately began to search for a new marketing manager. In October 1986, Peter Jenkins was hired to direct the company's marketing program.

Jenkins came to Golden Hybrids from Topco, a regional feed manufacturing firm in Illinois, where he was sales manager. He had been in this position for the past six years. As sales manager for Topco, he was responsible for supervising the activities of 25 salespeople selling feed direct to farmers. In addition, he had worked closely with the marketing manager in the development of the total feed marketing program. Management at Golden Hybrids was delighted to obtain his services and felt that he was just the right person to get their marketing program moving again.

Because Jenkins arrived at Golden Hybrids in October, it was too late to make major changes in the marketing program for 1986/87. The program for 1986/87 had been developed months earlier and was in full swing in October. Jenkins thus decided that the best thing he could do would be to spend his time becoming familiar with the seed industry in general, and the situation at Golden Hybrids in particular. Once he had done this, he felt he would be in a position to develop a new marketing approach for 1987/88.

PRODUCT LINE

Golden Hybrids sold 25 different varieties of seed corn, of which 18 were special-crosses and 7 were single-crosses (Exhibit 4.4). The varieties were grouped into three categories—short season, medium season and full season, depending upon their relative maturities. The short-season varieties were well adapted and most popular in the northern corn belt, the medium season in the central corn belt, and the full season in the southern corn belt. However, many farmers would schedule their planting dates in such a manner that they could plant some varieties in each of the three maturity categories.

EXHIBIT 4.4 **Current product line**

	Short season			Medium season			Full season	
Variety	Type of cross	Days to maturity	Variety	Type of cross	Days to maturity	Variety	Type of cross	Days to maturity
263	SPX	87	S33	SX	105	8535	SPX	116
22	SPX	88	S35	SX	105	678	SPX	116
31A	SPX	91	2570	SPX	106	5907	SPX	117
S19	SX	93	S30A	SX	107	603	SPX	117
201	SPX	95	3340	SPX	111	S69	SX	117
2610	SPX	97	593	SPX	113	S75	SX	118
224	SPX	99	5900	SPX	114	706	SPX	119
233	SPX	101				891	SPX	121
S27	SX	103						
214	SPX	104						

The product line of Golden Hybrids was similar to that of many other seed corn firms. Of the 25 varieties in the product line, only two were considered by management as being truly outstanding. These were S27 and 5900. For the past three years, they had shown up extremely well in state yield trials and in commercial applications. Most farmers who had tried them were anxious to use them again.

PRICING POLICY

The overall pricing policy at Golden Hybrids had been to price special-cross varieties substantially lower than competition. In 1986, the price of special-crosses was set at $54.00 a bushel for the medium flat kernal size. This was slightly lower than the average price charged by major competitors (see Exhibit 4.5). Single-cross varieties were sold at $79.00 a bushel in 1986. This represented the lowest price for single-cross varieties in the industry in 1986.

Several seed corn firms recently adopted the practice of grouping varieties for pricing purposes. The idea was to develop a group of outstanding varieties for which

EXHIBIT 4.5 **Current prices**

Company	Special-cross price	Single-cross price
P.A.G.	$55.20	$104.00
Pride	54.80	79.20
Jacques	54.80	80.00
Weathermaster	54.80	79.20
Haapala	54.80	80.00
N.K.	55.00	94.00
Trojan	55.60	88.00
Acco	54.40	84.00
United	55.00	100.00
Pioneer	54.80	96.00
Moews	54.00	84.00
Dekalb	55.60	79.20
Pfister	52.80	103.60
Golden Hybrids	54.00	79.00
Lowe	51.80	101.00

demand was high, and to sell these at a premium over other varieties. Usually the premium was from $4 to $12 per bushel. Golden Hybrids was aware of this practice, but decided not to follow it. It felt that farmers would not buy the higher price varieties in sufficient volume.

RESEARCH AND DEVELOPMENT

Research and development is an important function for Golden Hybrids. Since its founding, Golden Hybrids has been actively engaged in seed research. Beginning in 1980, Golden Hybrids also began some basic genetic research. The primary focus of the company's research program is the development of new and improved varieties. The policy of Golden Hybrids in this respect is to develop as many new varieties as possible for further testing in the 20 test plots maintained by the company throughout the corn belt.

In addition to its research and testing responsibilities, the research department also has primary responsibility for quality control. This involves checking on the performance of all other departments involved in producing and processing the seed to insure that quality standards are continually maintained. At the present time, the research department employs four full-time professional plant breeders.

SALES AREA

In 1986, Golden Hybrids sold seed in 13 states (Exhibit 4.6). Although seed corn is used to some extent in all 48 continental states, over 80 percent is used in the 13 states comprising Golden Hybrids' marketing area. In total, Golden Hybrids

EXHIBIT 4.6 **Golden Hybrids market area**

	Seeding rate (bushels/acre)	Acres planted to corn	Industry sales	Company sales	Market share
Eastern States	0.19	2,018,000	383,420	4,908	1.3
Wisconsin	0.22	2,726,000	599,720	4,822	0.8
Indiana	0.20	5,134,000	1,026,800	20,513	2.0
Missouri	0.18	3,379,000	608,220	1,522	0.2
Ohio	0.21	3,185,000	668,850	16,822	2.5
Michigan	0.20	2,024,000	404,800	18,987	4.7
Iowa	0.20	10,467,000	2,093,400	11,170	0.5
Illinois	0.20	9,993,000	1,998,600	32,239	1.6
Total	0.20	38,926,000	7,783,810	110,983	1.4

seed accounts for approximately 1.4 percent of the total market in the 13-state area. This varies from a high of nearly 5 percent in Michigan to a low of only 0.2 percent in Missouri. The Missouri market was opened in 1985.

MARKETING PROGRAM

The marketing program of Golden Hybrids is similar to that of other seed companies its size. The basic philosophy is to build up a large farmer-dealer organization and push as much seed through these dealers as possible. Thus, major emphasis is placed on personal selling. The total marketing expenditures of Golden Hybrids over the period 1982–1986 are shown in Exhibit 4.7.

EXHIBIT 4.7 **Marketing expenditures**

	1982	1983	1984	1985	1986
Advertising					
Publications	$ 21,600	$ 15,200	$ 41,600	$ 34,400	$ 10,800
Signs	62,000	65,200	45,600	99,200	59,200
Literature	12,800	10,400	25,200	22,000	42,000
Total	$ 96,400	$ 90,800	$ 112,400	$ 155,600	$ 112,000
Promotion					
Exhibits	$ 11,600	$ 10,800	$ 15,600	$ 44,400	$ 56,400
Premiums	195,600	136,000	80,800	133,600	88,800
Discounts	280,400	307,600	365,600	504,000	688,000
Free seed	—	—	144,000	79,200	68,000
Total	$ 487,600	$ 454,400	$ 606,000	$ 761,200	$ 901,200
Salespeople	$ 644,400	$ 650,800	$ 887,200	$1,033,200	$ 981,600
Sales Training	34,000	35,600	50,400	37,600	42,000
Total	$1,262,400	$1,231,600	$1,656,000	$1,987,600	$2,036,800

ADVERTISING

Golden Hybrids has never relied heavily on advertising. In 1986, total advertising expenditures amounted to only $112,000. Of this total, approximately one-half was spent on roadside signs and field markers. The other half was devoted to company literature and advertising in farm magazines. Company literature, for the most part, consisted of a seed catalog describing all of the varieties the company offered for sale and a monthly newletter sent to all the company's dealers. The expenditure of $10,800 for publications advertising represented the cost of a one-half page ad in the July issue of the Indiana and Illinois edition of the *Prairie Farmer* plus other miscellaneous ads in local newspapers.

PROMOTION

Promotional expenditures accounted for approximately 40 percent of Golden Hybrids' marketing expenses in 1986. A total of $56,400 was spent on exhibits at farm shows, county fairs, etc. An additional $88,800 was spent on various types of sales premiums. These premiums varied from year to year and, in 1986, consisted of jackets and caps with the company emblem, ball point pens, and electric frying pans. The jackets and caps were given to all dealers selling in excess of 25 bushels of seed corn. The electric frying pans were given to dealers selling 50 or more bushels. It was felt that these frying pans would appeal to the dealers' wives and that they would encourage their husbands to sell more so they could receive one.

The largest promotional expense was discounts. The most significant were quantity discounts, early-order discounts, and cash discounts. The quantity discount used by Golden Hybrids was similar to that used by most other seed companies. The discount schedule is shown in Exhibit 4.8. In addition to discounts, the company also had a policy of giving away free seed. In most cases, this seed was viewed as payment to dealers for erecting and maintaining field signs.

EXHIBIT 4.8 **Quantity discounts**

Total bushels customer orders	Number of bushels customer pays for
1–4	All
5–9	1/2 bushel less than ordered
10–18	1 bushel less than ordered
19–27	2 bushels less than ordered
28–36	3 bushels less than ordered
37–45	4 bushels less than ordered
46–54	5 bushels less than ordered
55–63	6 bushels less than ordered

PERSONAL SELLING

The largest marketing expenditure incurred by Golden Hybrids was for sales-people or, as they are called in the seed industry, district sales managers. In 1986, Golden Hybrids employed 15 full-time district sales managers in eight sales regions. In some cases, these salespeople would hire part-time assistants to help with delivery prior to planting.

Exhibit 4.9 provides some information on the sales force in 1986. The average age of Golden Hybrids' salespeople was 44 years. Many of the salespeople above the average age were retired farmers who had previously been successful seed corn dealers. A few of the younger salespeople were university-trained agronomists. The number of years with Golden Hybrids varied from a high of 18 to a low of 1, with

---

EXHIBIT 4.9 **Sales force data**

Area/Sales manager	Age	Years with company	Number of dealers	Total sales (In bushels)	Total salary bonus and expenses*	Salesperson cost per bushel
Eastern States						
Dietrich	41	4	110	4,908	$59,512	$12.12
Wisconsin						
Thedens	32	5	103	4,822	54,596	11.32
Indiana						
Williams	43	1	128	9,445	80,004	8.44
Briggs	45	13	160	7,604	85,512	11.24
Findlay	42	16	160	3,464	36,024	10.40
Missouri						
Vanderkamp	58	2	85	1,522	28,980	19.04
Ohio						
Heiserman	48	4	135	8,294	71,784	8.64
Hanusik	36	9	122	8,528	84,788	9.92
Michigan						
Smith	60	18	250	18,987	153,840	8.08
Iowa						
Pieper	33	9	200	8,142	77,540	9.52
Larson	25	2	71	3,028	47,060	15.52
Illinois						
East	33	9	210	9,046	88,608	9.92
Brown	56	2	100	3,763	36,472	9.68
Mefford	58	1	125	3,927	63,672	16.20
Rieker	52	12	250	15,503	110,736	7.12
Average	44	7	147	7,398	$71,564	$9.68

*The average salary for a Golden Hybrid's salesperson was approximately $32,000. This data in this column include the cost of part-time people hired by the salesperson to help out during certain times of the year.

an average number of 7. The average cost per salesperson, including salary, bonus and expenses, was $71,564 in 1986, or $9.68 per bushel sold.

The major job of district sales managers was to service their existing dealer organization. This involved several calls each year to insure that dealers were properly equipped and informed to carry out their selling function. It also involved arranging and conducting dealer meetings in local areas at least once each selling season. Whenever time permitted, district sales managers were instructed to accompany dealers on sales calls. The purpose of this activity was to give the district sales manager the opportunity to observe the sales approach used by the dealer and to make suggestions for improvement. It was also intended to get the dealer started making sales calls. Management felt that most of its dealers were not aggressive enough.

Another task performed by district sales managers was establishing new dealerships. Because dealer turnover was high (10 to 20 percent each year), it was necessary to get at least this many new dealers each year to avoid losing sales.

Although most seed was shipped directly from the main processing plant to the dealers following receipt of farmer signed orders, a certain amount of each variety was also shipped to area warehouses. The additional seed was intended to meet last minute orders when it would be impossible to fill these orders from the main warehouse. The area warehouses were operated by the district sales managers who would attempt to fill these orders from their available inventory. If this were not possible, they would check with other dealers who, because of cancelled orders, might have a surplus of the variety needed elsewhere. In addition to handling the paperwork involved in these transfers, the district sales manager would also handle the actual movement of the seed.

Because all dealers handled Golden Hybrids seed on a consignment basis, frequently it was necessary for the district sales managers to pick up unsold seed at the conclusion of the selling season. This seed would be returned to area warehouses where it was assembled and returned to the main company warehouse to be re-bagged or sold as commercial corn. All district sales managers at Golden Hybrids were required to account for their activities by filling out daily activity summaries and sending these to the sales manager every week. A summary of the activities of each district manager in 1986 is shown in Exhibit 4.10.

DEALER ORGANIZATION

All seed was sold through the company's dealer organization. Golden Hybrids employed two basic types of dealers—farmer dealers and store dealers. The farmer dealers were farmers who agreed to sell Golden Hybrids seed to their neighbors. For their efforts they received a commission based upon the number of bushels sold. The 1986 commission schedule is shown in Exhibit 4.11.

Store dealers were local farm supply outlets, such as feed stores and grain elevators, which operated on the same commission as the farmer dealers. In 1986, Golden Hybrids had 2,029 farmer dealers and 180 store dealers. Some key dealer statistics are shown in Exhibit 4.12.

EXHIBIT 4.10 **Activities of district sales managers**

Area/Sales manager	Setting up new dealers (In weeks)	Servicing old dealers (In weeks)	Selling with dealers (In weeks)	Direct selling (In weeks)	Seed delivery (In weeks)	Seed pick-up (In weeks)	Collections (In weeks)
Eastern States							
Dietrich	7.5	12.5	2.5	2.5	12.5	5.0	7.5
Wisconsin							
Thedens	6.0	24.0	4.0	4.0	5.0	5.0	2.0
Indiana							
Williams	15.0	20.0	10.0	0.0	2.5	1.5	1.0
Briggs	2.5	25.0	5.0	7.5	7.5	1.0	1.5
Findlay	7.5	19.5	0.5	2.5	7.5	5.0	7.5
Missouri							
Vanderkamp	17.5	10.0	5.0	2.5	7.5	5.0	2.5
Ohio							
Heiserman	6.0	24.0	4.0	4.0	5.0	5.0	2.0
Hanusik	2.5	31.5	2.5	0.5	5.0	4.0	4.0
Michigan							
Smith	5.0	20.0	1.0	1.5	10.0	2.5	10.0
Iowa							
Pieper	5.0	35.0	1.0	1.0	4.0	2.5	1.5
Larson	6.0	24.0	4.0	4.0	5.0	5.0	2.0
Illinois							
East	3.5	27.5	2.5	5.0	7.5	1.5	2.5
Brown	12.5	17.5	2.5	2.5	7.5	5.0	2.5
Mefford	15.0	17.5	2.5	0.0	2.5	5.0	5.0
Rieker	5.0	35.0	1.5	1.0	4.0	2.5	1.0
Average	7.7	22.9	3.2	2.6	6.2	3.7	3.5

A breakdown of dealers by size is shown in Exhibit 4.13. This information shows that approximately one-half of Golden Hybrid dealers sell less than 25 bushels per year. Management suspects that most of these small dealers do not in fact sell seed, but rather become dealers so that they can get a larger discount for their own requirements. This may be true to some extent for the 26–50 bushel dealers also. Probably only 51-bushel-and-greater dealers actually sell to their neighbors

---

EXHIBIT 4.11 **Dealer commission schedule**

Type of seed	Number of bushels	Commission
Special-Cross	1–99	$6.00
	100–249	8.00
	250 or more	10.00
Single-Cross	1–99	8.00
	100–249	10.00
	250 or more	14.40

EXHIBIT 4.12 Location and size of current dealers

Sales territory	Number of farmer dealers	Bushels sold by farmer dealers	Average farmer dealer size (In bushels)	Number of store dealers	Bushels sold by store dealers	Average store dealer size (In bushels)
Eastern states	101	4,315	42.7	9	593	65.8
Wisconsin	96	4,758	49.6	7	64	9.1
Indiana	376	18,450	49.7	72	2,063	28.6
Missouri	85	1,522	17.9	—	—	—
Ohio	219	14,799	67.7	38	2,023	53.2
Michigan	236	17,919	75.9	14	1,068	76.2
Iowa	266	10,954	41.2	5	211	42.2
Illinois	650	31,291	48.1	35	948	27.1
Total	2,029	104,008	51.2	180	6,970	38.7

EXHIBIT 4.13 Dealer size distribution, 1980

Bushels sold	Number of dealers
0–25	1,012
26–50	530
51–100	417
101–200	227
200 and greater	60
Total	2,246

and friends. Some recent statistics showed that many larger companies in the seed corn industry had average dealer sizes of 400 bushels per year.

DIRECT SELLING

Because of his background with a company using the direct-selling approach to farmers, and because of his firm conviction that Golden Hybrids was in need of a new marketing approach, Jenkins was seriously thinking about initiating a direct-selling program for 1987/88. Since he was not aware of any instance where this kind of a program had been used by a major seed corn company, he thought it prudent to experiment for a few years before changing over to this method. Through limited initial use, the program could be thoroughly evaluated without risking too many of the company's resources on an untried idea. Jenkins suspected that if such a program caught on, it could be a major breakthrough for Golden Hybrids.

His basic idea was to choose a small geographical area, say a county in a high-potential region of Illinois where Golden Hybrids had poor representation at the present time. In this area he would place the best person he could possibly find to sell direct to large farmers in this county. Jenkins deemed it absolutely necessary that the person selected for this position be a highly trained agronomist capable of adequately conversing with intelligent farmers and making the proper recommendations relating to variety selections, planting rates, planting dates, insecticide program, weed control program, fertilization program, etc. In short, Jenkins wanted to find a person who could be a corn management consultant as well as a seed salesperson. He felt that selling this combination of information, advice, and seed was crucial to the success of the direct-selling program.

To support the efforts of the salesperson, Jenkins planned a concentrated promotional program in the local area. Prior to being called on by the salesperson, each farmer would receive a personal letter from Golden Hybrids informing him or her of this new program and introducing the sales representative. At the same time, the program would be introduced in the area through local newspaper ads and radio spots. A leading farmer in the community would be approached to provide a test plot that the salesperson could use for demonstration purposes. Jenkins estimated that such a program would cost Golden Hybrids roughly $75,000 for promotion, administration, and the salesperson's salary and expenses.

JENKIN'S TASK

In addition to the above information, Jenkins had access to a market research study that had been conducted with 700 corn farmers in the Midwestern United States (Appendix A). He also found some figures in a university publication showing recent trends in the seed corn industry (Appendix B). After reviewing all the available data, Jenkins began preparing a report to present to the Executive Committee of the company. Jenkins knew he would be in for some sharp questions from the committee and he wanted to be sure to cover all elements of the marketing mix in his new program for the 1987/88 year.

APPENDIX A—RESULTS OF MARKETING RESEARCH SURVEY

How many acres of corn did you have this past year?

Acres	Number of farmers	Percent
A. 1–100	64	9.1
B. 101–250	210	30.0
C. 251–500	249	35.6
D. Over 500	177	25.3
	700	100.0

How many different varieties of corn did you plant last year?

	A (1-100)	B (101-250)	C (251-500)	D (500+)	Total
No answer	0.0%	0.4%	1.0%	1.6%	0.6%
One	15.8	4.4	6.2	0.0	7.4
Two	18.6	14.9	6.7	6.3	12.6
Three	27.1	19.7	9.5	4.7	17.1
Four	14.7	21.3	12.4	23.4	17.1
Five	10.2	14.1	21.9	17.2	15.7
Six or more	13.6	25.3	42.4	46.9	29.4

How many different companies did you buy seed from last year?

	A (1-100)	B (101-250)	C (251-500)	D (500+)	Total
No answer	12.4%	12.0%	12.4%	12.5%	12.3%
One	28.8	16.5	11.4	18.8	18.3
Two	23.2	24.1	17.1	15.6	21.0
Three	20.9	27.3	23.3	20.3	23.9
Four	10.7	12.4	18.6	14.1	14.0
Five	2.3	5.6	9.5	7.8	6.1
Six or more	1.7	2.0	7.6	10.9	4.4

Where did you purchase seed corn last year?

	A (1-100)	B (101-250)	C (251-500)	D (500+)	Total
No answer	0.0%	0.8%	0.0%	0.0%	0.3%
Seed store	11.3	9.2	9.0	10.9	9.9
Farmer dealer	79.7	81.1	83.3	76.6	81.0
Company salesman	19.2	25.3	29.0	29.7	25.3
Combined order	0.0	2.4	2.4	6.3	2.1
Elevator	4.5	3.6	3.3	3.1	3.7
Co-op	2.8	5.6	3.3	3.1	4.0
I am a dealer	9.0	7.2	7.6	20.3	9.0

When you want more information about seed corn, where do you get this information?

	A (1-100)	B (101-250)	C (251-500)	D (500+)	Total
No answer	5.1%	5.6%	6.2%	7.8%	5.9%
Retail store	2.8	3.2	1.9	1.6	2.6
Farmer dealer	61.6	61.0	67.1	57.8	62.7
Ag. college	11.9	19.3	21.0	25.0	18.4
Mag. articles	26.6	24.1	21.0	25.0	23.9
Seed corn ads	16.4	18.1	12.4	15.6	15.7
County agent	6.8	11.2	17.1	14.1	12.1

Where have you seen the seed corn advertised that you planted last year?

	A (1–100)	B (101–250)	C (251–500)	D (500+)	Total
No answer	5.6%	7.6%	3.3%	9.4%	6.0%
Billboards	20.3	14.5	18.6	26.6	18.3
Field signs	61.0	63.1	70.0	75.0	65.7
Newspaper ads	26.6	22.5	29.5	37.5	27.0
Farm mag. ads	79.7	74.3	81.4	75.0	77.9
Radio program	27.7	30.9	33.3	28.1	30.6
T.V. commercials	14.7	15.7	16.2	4.7	14.6

How would you rank the following reasons in deciding on the seed you planted last fall?

A. Used this variety before.

Ranking	A (1–100)	B (101–250)	C (251–500)	D (500+)	Total
First	15.8%	23.3%	25.2%	20.6%	22.3%
Second	4.5	4.0	5.7	4.7	4.7
Third	1.1	1.6	1.4	3.1	1.6
Fourth	0.6	1.6	2.4	0.0	1.4
Fifth	0.0	0.8	0.0	0.0	0.3
Sixth	0.0	0.0	0.0	0.0	0.0
Seventh	0.6	0.0	0.0	0.0	0.1

B. A neighbor used this brand and recommended to me.

Ranking	A (1–100)	B (101–250)	C (251–500)	D (500+)	Total
First	0.6%	2.8%	2.4%	1.6%	2.0%
Second	7.3	9.6	7.6	9.4	8.4
Third	5.1	6.4	6.7	9.4	6.4
Fourth	1.7	3.6	3.8	1.6	3.0
Fifth	0.6	1.2	1.9	1.6	1.3
Sixth	0.6	2.0	0.0	0.0	0.9
Seventh	0.6	0.0	0.0	0.0	0.1

C. A salesperson or dealer called on me and wrote my order.

Ranking	A (1–100)	B (101–250)	C (251–500)	D (500+)	Total
First	5.6%	6.4%	5.2%	4.7%	5.7%
Second	4.5	7.2	6.7	3.1	6.0
Third	2.3	6.4	10.8	6.3	6.4
Fourth	3.4	2.8	3.8	4.7	3.4
Fifth	0.0	1.2	1.9	0.0	1.0
Sixth	1.7	1.6	1.0	3.1	1.6
Seventh	0.6	0.8	0.0	0.0	0.4

D. I saw official state yield test results.

Ranking	A (1–100)	B (101–250)	C (251–500)	D (500+)	Total
First	1.1%	2.0%	3.3%	3.1%	2.3%
Second	3.4	4.4	6.7	10.9	5.4
Third	3.4	3.6	5.7	4.7	4.3
Fourth	4.5	4.4	3.3	1.6	3.9
Fifth	0.0	2.0	1.9	3.1	1.6
Sixth	1.1	0.0	1.0	3.1	0.9
Seventh	0.0	1.2	1.0	0.0	0.7

E. I saw a field marked by a seed corn company sign.

Ranking	A (1–100)	B (101–250)	C (251–500)	D (500+)	Total
First	0.0%	0.8%	1.4%	1.6%	0.9%
Second	1.7	4.0	3.3	3.1	3.1
Third	2.8	4.4	5.2	4.7	4.3
Fourth	2.3	5.2	3.3	6.3	4.0
Fifth	3.4	0.8	1.0	1.6	1.6
Sixth	0.0	3.2	2.9	0.0	2.0
Seventh	0.0	1.6	0.0	0.0	0.6

F. I saw or heard an advertisement.

Ranking	A (1–100)	B (101–250)	C (251–500)	D (500+)	Total
First	0.6%	0.0%	0.0%	0.0%	0.1%
Second	0.6	2.4	1.0	0.0	1.3
Third	1.7	2.4	2.4	1.6	2.1
Fourth	0.6	2.4	3.8	1.6	2.3
Fifth	1.7	2.8	2.4	1.6	2.3
Sixth	0.6	2.8	2.4	1.6	2.0
Seventh	1.7	2.8	1.9	3.1	2.3

Which company's seed produces the best yields?

	A (1–100)	B (101–250)	C (251–500)	D (500+)	Total
No answer	42.9%	34.5%	34.3%	23.4%	35.6%
Cargill	0.6	0.8	1.4	1.6	1.0
Dekalb	13.0	13.7	17.6	17.2	15.0
Trojan	0.6	0.4	0.0	0.0	0.3
Funk's	9.6	6.8	8.1	9.4	8.1
Lowes	0.0	0.0	0.0	0.0	0.0
Moews	1.7	1.6	0.0	0.0	1.0

Best yields (continued)

	A (1–100)	B (101–250)	C (251–500)	D (500+)	Total
N.K.	1.7%	1.2%	0.5%	1.6%	1.1%
P.A.G.	2.3	2.4	5.2	6.3	3.6
Pioneer	10.7	19.7	16.2	23.4	16.7
Golden Hybrids	1.1	0.8	0.0	0.0	0.6
Tomco	10.2	11.2	9.5	9.4	10.3
United	0.6	0.8	1.0	0.0	0.7
Others	5.1	6.0	6.2	7.8	6.0

Which company provides the best service, or is most helpful to their customers?

	A (1–100)	B (101–250)	C (251–500)	D (500+)	Total
No answer	58.8%	48.6%	43.8%	31.3%	48.1%
Cargill	1.1	0.0	0.5	1.6	0.6
Dekalb	4.0	10.0	11.0	10.9	8.9
Trojan	0.0	0.4	0.0	0.0	0.1
Funk's	7.9	5.6	7.6	9.4	7.1
Lowes	0.0	0.4	0.0	0.0	0.1
Moews	0.0	1.2	0.0	0.0	0.4
N.K.	1.7	2.4	0.5	4.7	1.9
P.A.G.	1.7	2.0	5.2	4.7	3.1
Pioneer	13.6	16.9	16.7	18.8	16.1
Golden Hybrids	0.6	0.8	0.5	0.0	0.6
Tomco	5.6	4.8	6.7	6.3	5.7
United	0.0	0.0	0.0	0.0	0.0
Others	5.1	6.8	7.6	12.8	7.1

Which company is largest—sells the most?

	A (1–100)	B (101–250)	C (251–500)	D (500+)	Total
No answer	46.3%	37.8%	36.7%	31.3%	39.0%
Cargill	0.6	0.0	1.0	0.0	0.4
Dekalb	18.6	21.3	23.8	17.2	21.0
Trojan	0.0	0.0	0.0	0.0	0.0
Funk's	5.6	3.2	6.7	14.1	5.9
Lowes	0.0	0.0	0.0	0.0	0.0
Moews	1.1	0.8	0.0	0.0	0.6
N.K.	1.1	0.0	0.0	1.6	0.4
P.A.G.	0.6	0.8	1.9	1.6	1.1
Pioneer	23.7	31.3	27.6	29.7	28.1
Golden Hybrids	0.0	0.4	0.0	0.0	0.1
Tomco	1.7	1.6	0.5	3.1	1.4
United	0.0	0.4	0.0	0.0	0.1
Others	0.6	2.0	1.9	1.8	1.6

Which company seems to have the best dealers?

	A (1–100)	B (101–250)	C (251–500)	D (500+)	Total
No answer	64.4%	57.8%	54.3%	51.6%	57.9%
Cargill	1.1	0.0	1.0	0.0	0.6
Dekalb	6.2	11.2	10.5	12.5	9.9
Trojan	0.0	0.0	0.0	0.0	0.0
Funk's	5.6	3.2	3.8	7.8	4.4
Lowes	0.0	0.0	0.0	0.0	0.0
Moews	0.6	1.2	0.0	1.6	0.7
N.K.	1.1	1.2	0.5	1.6	1.0
P.A.G.	2.3	2.0	4.3	1.6	2.7
Pioneer	9.9	15.7	19.0	15.6	15.0
Golden Hybrids	0.0	1.2	0.0	0.0	0.4
Tomco	5.6	3.6	3.3	3.1	4.0
United	0.6	0.0	0.0	0.0	0.1
Others	3.4	2.8	3.3	4.7	3.3

Which company's salespersons are the most aggressive?

	A (1–100)	B (101–250)	C (251–500)	D (500+)	Total
No answer	63.3%	62.2%	51.0%	55.4%	58.5%
Cargill	1.7	0.4	1.4	0.0	1.0
Dekalb	8.5	8.8	13.3	9.2	10.1
Trojan	0.6	0.0	0.5	0.0	0.3
Funk's	4.5	5.2	4.3	7.7	5.0
Lowes	0.0	0.4	0.0	0.0	0.1
Moews	1.7	0.8	0.0	0.0	0.7
N.K.	2.3	0.8	1.4	3.1	1.6
P.A.G.	1.1	1.6	4.8	0.0	2.3
Pioneer	9.0	13.3	17.1	10.8	13.1
Golden Hybrids	0.0	0.8	0.0	0.0	0.3
Tomco	2.3	1.6	1.9	7.7	2.4
United	0.0	0.4	0.0	0.0	0.1
Others	5.1	3.6	4.3	3.1	4.1

Which brands of seed corn did you plant this past year?

	A (1–100)	B (101–250)	C (251–500)	D (500+)	Total
No answer	19.8%	18.1%	16.7%	9.4%	17.3%
Cargill	4.0	3.2	4.8	3.1	3.9
Dekalb	25.4	33.3	38.6	32.8	32.9
Trojan	1.1	0.8	1.0	0.0	0.9
Funk's	16.4	22.9	24.8	29.7	22.4
Lowes	0.6	2.4	0.5	1.6	1.3

Brands of sweet corn planted (continued)

	A (1–100)	B (101–250)	C (251–500)	D (500+)	Total
Moews	4.0%	2.4%	2.9%	4.7%	3.1%
N.K.	6.2	6.0	2.4	4.7	4.9
P.A.G.	9.6	10.0	12.9	14.1	11.1
Pioneer	33.9	42.2	47.1	48.4	42.1
Golden Hybrids	1.7	2.0	1.0	0.0	1.4
Tomco	31.6	27.7	26.7	29.7	28.6
United	1.7	2.0	2.4	0.0	1.9
Others	26.0	31.3	33.8	39.1	31.4

APPENDIX B—TRENDS IN SEED CORN MARKETING

The data in this appendix are taken from a university publication showing marketing mix allocations and detailed advertising and promotion breakdowns for seed corn firms. The principal retailing agent of hybrid seed corn is the farmer dealer. In 1985, farmer dealers handled 76 percent of the seed corn sold, and the other channels—store dealers, direct sales, and farm supply centers—accounted for the remainder.

Marketing expenditures for seed corn firms

	Small			Medium			Large		
	1975	1980	1985	1975	1980	1985	1975	1980	1985
Advertising									
$000	36	52	84	228	348	400	1,180	1,396	1,716
Percent	12	9	11	27	22	21	41	31	28
Promotion									
$000	12	28	36	164	284	300	696	792	1,416
Percent	5	5	5	20	18	16	24	17	23
Personal Selling									
$000	208	436	592	352	744	868	292	1,268	1,776
Percent	66	76	73	42	48	47	10	28	28
Research									
$000	52	52	88	100	176	292	708	1,104	1,356
Percent	17	9	11	12	11	16	25	24	21
Total	312	576	808	852	1,556	1,886	2,884	4,564	6,272

Advertising and promotional allocations for seed corn firms

	Small			Medium			Large		
	1975	1980	1985	1975	1980	1985	1975	1980	1985
Advertising expenditures for seed (as percent of total advertising)									
Outdoor signs	33	14	12	28	32	16	22	21	17
Store displays	—	—	—	1	—	—	—	—	—
Farm magazines	25	22	33	26	39	48	29	28	32
Newspapers	10	5	5	4	2	1	7	7	8
Radio and TV	4	40	35	23	15	8	13	14	14
Direct mail	19	11	12	4	1	10	16	18	17
Other	9	8	3	14	11	17	13	12	12
Total	100%	100%	100%	100%	100%	100%	100%	100%	100%
Promotional expenditures for seed (as percent of total promotion)									
Fair and farm shows	5	4	6	6	4	7	7	6	5
Dealer meetings	3	8	14	14	12	16	28	30	19
Company field days	—	5	8	3	4	4	2	2	1
Dealer incentives	74	53	45	73	62	63	60	58	37
Customer incentives	18	23	23	1	4	3	1	1	35
Other	—	7	4	3	14	7	2	3	3
Total	100%	100%	100%	100%	100%	100%	100%	100%	100%

CASE 5

Baldor Electric Company

In September 1984, Gregory C. Kowert, Baldor's Vice-President for Strategic Planning was reflecting on Baldor's distinctive position in the electric motor market. He listed the following comparative advantages achieved by Baldor:

- Concentration on Industrial Electric Motors—By manufacturing only electric motors for industrial markets, Baldor has been able to focus its resources on a highly specialized market.

This case was prepared by Peter M. Ginter, Andrew C. Rucks, and Linda E. Swayne as a basis for classroom discussion rather than to illustrate either effective or ineffective handling of an administrative situation. Used by permission from Peter M. Ginter.

- Energy-efficient Motors—Through the years, the company has followed the strategy of providing better products at competitive prices. For Baldor, this has translated into better materials and superior engineering directed at durability and energy efficiency.
- Availability—Baldor attempts to sell as many items as possible as stock products and carries heavy inventories of these items positioned close to customers in 28 warehouses around the country. This inventory policy is unique in the industry.
- Independent Representative Sales Organization—The company sells all of its products through independent representatives. Many representatives derive most of their income from Baldor and thus the selling task is accomplished by a group of semiautonomous entrepreneurs compensated by direct incentives.
- Backward Integration—Baldor manufactures more of its component parts than the competition.
- Most Committed to the Industry—Baldor has the largest percentage of its sales in electric motors. Many of the competitors are divisions of larger companies and most compete with other divisions for allocations of resources.

Kowert felt that past strategies, particularly the emphasis on energy efficiency, had brought rapid growth to the company. Baldor appeared to be making the transition from a small- to medium-sized company. However the slight sales decline in 1982 was causing Kowert and the entire marketing team to closely monitor the 1983 plan and to carefully prepare the company's 1984 plan.

BALDOR ELECTRIC COMPANY PROFILE

Edwin C. Ballman founded Baldor Electric Company in St. Louis, Missouri, in 1920. The company opened a plant in Ft. Smith, Arkansas, in 1957, and subsequently moved the corporate headquarters to Ft. Smith. Today there are plants in six states, employing over 2,200 people.

From the very beginning, Baldor's emphasis was on motors that deliver maximum output while consuming a minimum of energy. Kowert thought that the energy crisis in the early 1970s increased the interest in energy efficiency, which led to rapid growth for the company.

Baldor has been the fastest growing company in the electric motor industry. During the period between 1971 and 1981, Baldor's growth rate was approximately 22 percent annually, almost 80 percent faster than the industry as a whole. As illustrated in Exhibit 5.1, Baldor's market share increased about 15 percent during the 1975 recession, by 20 percent during the 1982 business contraction, and doubled during the period between 1973 and 1982.

Product Line

In 1982 Baldor Electric vigorously expanded its new-product development program. The program greatly increased the depth and breadth of the company's

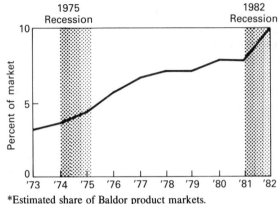

*Estimated share of Baldor product markets.

EXHIBIT 5.1 **Baldor's market share 1973–1982***

product line. With the exception of 1976, more new motors were added to Baldor's product line in 1982 than during any previous period. All Baldor's motors are manufactured in accordance with industry standards supplied by NEMA (National Electrical Manufacturers Association).

Baldor reacted to the increased popularity of permanent-magnet direct-current motors used in a broad variety of adjustable-speed applications by expanding the line to a total of fifteen stock models. In addition, Baldor supplies a broad variety of direct-current shunt wound motors, which also are used in adjustable-speed and torque applications. Baldor's line of such control motors includes models ranging from 1/50 to 15 HP and is among the broadest in the motor industry. Exhibit 5.2 identifies the major product lines produced by the company.

EXHIBIT 5.2 **Baldor product lines**

Explosion-proof motors—The company supplies explosion-proof motors ranging to 100 HP, including models with all performance characteristics required for service on offshore drill rigs.

Agribusiness—Baldor's line of agri-duty motors traditionally has been considered one of the industry's broadest and most diversified. In order to further strengthen their position in this market, Baldor added a series of specialized models such as centrifugal fan motors, confinement house motors, vacuum pump motors, aeration fan motors, and grain stirring motors.

Small motors—Baldor had been active in the development of "small" motors as well. The Baldor/Boehm line includes more than 70 different models in the subfractional horsepower range, along with a newly designed mounting allowing for greater versatility. In addition, the Baldor/Boehm line includes permanent split capacitor AC motors in 18 different ratings and an expanded selection of permanent magnet motors.

Heavy-duty motors—The company also markets a variety of heavy-duty cast-iron motors ranging in size from 1 1/2 through 15 HP in their 300 and corrosion-protected lines.

Super-E-Series—The Super-E line (super energy efficient) is designed primarily for applications where energy consumption is unusually high and motors are operated continuously for extended periods.

Additional lines—Other product lines include close-coupled pump motors and motors specifically designed for use with six-step and pulsewidth-modulated inverters.

During 1983, Baldor introduced a new super-efficient line called the Baldor SUPER-E. As shown in Exhibit 5.3, the efficiency of the new SUPER-E line is considerably higher than the average "premium motor." The new line not only had higher efficiency than other manufactured super-efficient models but also cost less.

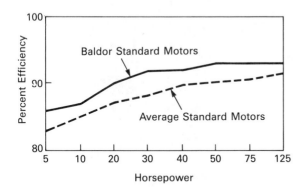

EXHIBIT 5.3 **SUPER-E efficiency comparison—Baldor Standard vs. "average standard" motors***

*Efficiencies of "average standard" motors as shown in U.S. Department of Energy, November 1980 report: "Classification and Evaluation of Electric Motors and Pumps."

The introduction of the SUPER-E motors places Baldor in a unique competitive position. Baldor is the only motor manufacturer capable of offering a choice between competitively priced standard motors, or competitively priced premium motors—both higher in efficiency than other manufacturers' comparable lines.

Promotion

Advertising and trade promotion traditionally have been important elements in Baldor's marketing mix, serving as direct lines of communication to an extremely broad and growing audience of customer and sales prospects. In addition, these efforts directly support the selling activities of Baldor representatives and distributors.

Advertising objectives are to develop brand recognition and brand preference. The investment in advertising and promotion during 1982 was over 20 percent higher than in 1981. The reason for the increase was the introduction of many new products and continued penetration of new markets. Much of the 1983 advertising has been directed toward promotion of the new SUPER-E motors. The efficiency savings is prominent in Baldor advertising to the trade (Exhibit 5.4).

Channels of Distribution

Baldor's products are marketed through a well-established network of distributors as well as direct to OEM's. Exhibit 5.5 depicts these channels.

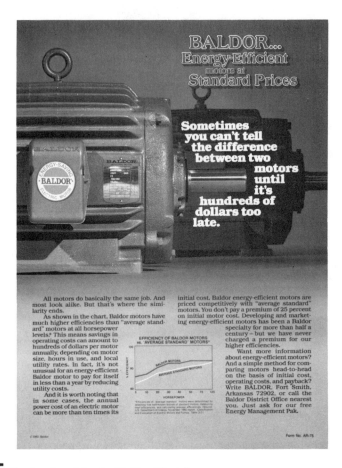

EXHIBIT 5.4 **Trade advertising by Baldor Electric**

Motors flow through 34 District Offices in the United States and Canada. Factory stocks of more than 1,800 different types of motors are maintained at 28 geographical points (Exhibit 5.6). Baldor maintains a sophisticated computer-based communication system which links sales offices, plants and corporate headquarters. The system makes it possible for the sales team to quickly determine the product status of motors and locate products needed to correct a temporary out-of-stock condition.

The industrial distributor is becoming more important in the motor industry. Better design, increased applications, higher speeds, and greater reliability have broadened the use of electric motors to various new industries. Distributors have greater familiarity with these new markets than Baldor's sales force.

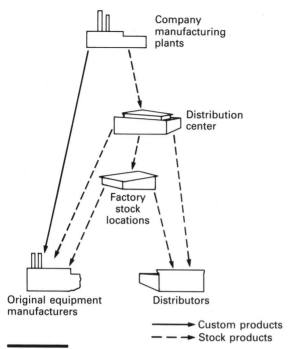

Company manufacturing plants

Distribution center

Factory stock locations

Original equipment manufacturers

Distributors

———▶ Custom products
— — –▶ Stock products

EXHIBIT 5.5 **Baldor's channels of distribution**

Financial Position

While sales declined 6.3 percent in 1982 from 1981, the company has maintained a strong financial position and liquidity. Exhibit 5.7 shows Baldor's consolidated earnings for the years 1980 through 1982 and Exhibit 5.8 presents Baldor's consolidated balance sheet.

Baldor's dollar and unit sales declined in 1982 for the first time in 22 years. However, during this period Baldor continued to gain market share. The cost of doing business increased in 1982 due to the rise in manufacturing expenses and a lower volume of sales. The increase in manufacturing expense results from increases in compensation, other manufacturing expenses including depreciation expense on new machinery acquired to improve quality and productivity, and engineering expenses due to the company's commitment to research and development. Cost of goods sold, as a percentage of sales, was lower for 1981 than 1980, due primarily to lower raw material costs.

The company has maintained a conservative capital position. Long-term obligations were 15 percent of total capitalization on December 31, 1982 (stockholders' equity plus long-term obligations) compared to 18 percent on December 31, 1981. Four and a half million dollars of industrial revenue bond financing was received in 1981. No new long-term financing was sought in 1982. Exhibit 5.9 presents a ten-year summary of important financial data for Baldor Company. Exhibit 5.10

EXHIBIT 5.6 **Locations of Baldor's plants, district offices, and warehouses (United States and Canada)**

shows the changes in Baldor's financial position from 1980 through 1982 and Exhibit 5.11 provides a statement of stockholder's equity.

Penetration of International Markets

During 1982, Baldor completely changed their method of marketing to foreign countries. For many years at Baldor, international sales were handled by an export management company. Recently, Baldor brought this function "in house." Each international market is studied individually, rather than collectively as in the past, to determine the best method of distribution. As a result, Baldor established representatives in many targeted countries and is seeking representation in others. Representatives recently have been established in such markets as Latin America, Australia, the United Kingdom, West Germany, the Middle East, and Singapore.

EXHIBIT 5.7 **Consolidated earnings of Baldor Electric (1980–1982)**

	Year ended December 31		
	1980	1981	1982
	(In thousands except share data)		
Net sales	$ 146,454	$ 160,162	$ 150,031
Other income—net........................	270	1,546	1,405
	$ 146,724	$ 161,708	$ 151,436
Cost and expenses			
Cost of goods sold	102,286	110,556	108,373
Selling and administrative.................	23,812	25,382	25,201
Profit sharing	2,399	3,024	2,067
Interest................................	868	843	927
	$ 129,365	$ 139,805	$ 136,568
Earnings Before Income Taxes...........	17,359	21,903	14,868
Income taxes............................	7,950	10,170	6,350
Net Earnings........................	$ 9,409	$ 11,733	$ 8,518
Earnings per common share	$1.50	$1.84	$1.33
Weighted average common shares outstanding	6,284,229	6,376,052	6,426,256

Baldor has also increased its product capability in the international markets by introducing motors with standards interchangeable with those outside the United States. In addition, Baldor is increasing international advertising and participation in foreign trade shows.

CURRENT SITUATION

The company has been extremely successful in differentiating its products from competitors by offering energy-efficient motors at competitive prices. However, sales were down 8.2 percent in 1982 and Greg Kowert knew he had to make a recommendation to increase sales.

Several options were easy to identify. The electric motor market continued to offer opportunities since there were many small companies that had not been able to completely serve the market. New products could be developed to meet the needs of new markets which have been projected to grow rapidly and international markets presented good opportunities. The lines between motors, controls, and the devices they control have blurred, thus, Baldor could diversify into related areas of computers and/or robots.

Greg Kowert wondered which one or combination of opportunities he should recommend to continue the growth of Baldor. He supposed he should start with a thorough situation analysis of the electric motor industry.

EXHIBIT 5.8 Consolidated balance sheet for Baldor Electric (1982)

Assets	December 31 1981 (In thousands)	December 31 1982 (In thousands)
Current Assets		
Cash and temporary investments	$ 15,322	$ 17,252
Receivables, less allowances of $560,000 in 1982 and $490,000 in 1981	25,945	24,598
Inventories		
Finished products	17,758	20,901
Work-in-process	10,731	8,762
Raw material	18,950	17,212
	47,439	46,875
LIFO valuation adjustment (deduction)	(16,406)	(16,712)
	31,033	30,163
Deferred income taxes	1,550	1,107
Other current assets	1,414	
Total Current Assets	75,264	73,120
Other Assets	2,767	2,663
Property, Plant and Equipment		
Land and improvements	1,289	1,316
Buildings and improvements	9,425	10,073
Machinery and equipment	26,624	34,889
Allowances for depreciation and amortization (deduction)	(13,093)	(15,996)
	24,245	30,282
	$102,276	$106,065

Liabilities and stockholders' equity	December 31 1981 (In thousands)	December 31 1982 (In thousands)
Current Liabilities		
Accounts payable	$ 10,021	$ 8,043
Employee compensation	2,388	2,035
Profit sharing	3,022	2,041
Anticipated warranty costs	2,850	2,950
Other accrued expenses	1,603	1,978
Income taxes	1,958	1,436
Current portion of long-term obligations	1,205	998
Total Current Liabilities	23,047	19,481
Long-term Obligations	13,497	12,610
Deferred Income Taxes	2,262	3,130
Stockholders' Equity		
Preferred stock, $.10 par value Authorized shares: 5,000,000 Issued and outstanding shares: none		
Common stock, $.10 par value Authorized shares: $25,000,000 Issued and outstanding shares: 1982—6,427,570; 1981—6,378,645 (less shares held in treasury: 1982—90,535; 1981—123,665)	638	643
Additional capital	10,340	11,243
Retained earnings	52,492	58,958
	63,470	70,844
	$102,276	$106,065

EXHIBIT 5.9 **Ten-year summary of selected financial data for Baldor Electric (In thousands, except percents and per share data)**

	Net sales	Cost of goods sold	Net earnings	Per share data		Percent return on average equity	Stockholders' equity	Total assets	Long-term obligations	Working capital
				Net earnings	Dividends					
1982	$150,031	$108,373	$ 8,518	$1.33	$.320	13%	$70,844	$106,065	$12,610	$53,639
1981	160,162	110,556	11,733	1.84	.290	20	63,470	102,276	13,497	52,217
1980	146,454	102,286	9,409	1.50	.240	20	52,448	81,973	10,318	43,733
1979	140,018	98,304	9,331	1.50	.193	24	42,985	74,112	11,210	36,310
1978	120,105	81,251	8,642	1.40	.140	29	33,929	60,466	7,427	28,462
1977	94,277	66,149	5,741	.95	.093	25	25,582	48,466	6,106	20,983
1976	70,832	49,405	4,043	.69	.070	24	20,258	36,348	4,458	17,769
1975	56,081	41,095	2,418	.50	.050	21	12,951	27,628	4,688	11,854
1974	51,123	39,651	1,285*	.26*	.033	13	10,632	25,214	5,041	9,826
1973	41,736	30,649	1,800	.37	.033	21	9,488	19,670	2,910	7,702

Compound Annual Growth Rate (From 1972 Base)
10 Yr.   17%   22%   18%   27%

*After decrease of $891,000 ($.19 per share) in 1974 resulting from 1974 change to last-in, first-out and full absorption method of inventory valuation.

EXHIBIT 5.10 Changes in Baldor Electric's financial position (1980-1982)

| | Year ended December 31 | | |
| | 1980 | 1981 | 1982 |
	(In thousands)		
Funds Provided			
Net earnings	$ 9,409	$11,733	$ 8,518
Expenses not requiring outlay of working capital:			
Depreciation and amortization..................	2,732	3,410	4,113
Deferred income taxes	767	436	868
From Operations	12,908	15,579	13,499
Issuance of treasury stock to			
employee profit sharing plan	1,233	559	642
Additions to long-term obligations			
(less $1,500,000 unexpended proceeds			
included in other assets)		3,000	
Utilization of unexpended debt proceeds	1,733		377
Stock option plans	319	572	266
Total Funds Provided	16,193	19,710	14,784
Funds Used			
Dividends	1,498	1,843	2,052
Additions to property, plant and			
equipment (including assets acquired			
in purchase of Nupar Manufacturing			
Company of $3,399,000 in 1981)...............	6,504	7,771	10,139
Reduction of long-term obligations...............	891	1,321	887
Other	(123)	291	284
Total Funds Used	8,770	11,226	13,362
Increase in Working Capital	7,423	8,484	1,422
Working capital at beginning of period	36,310	43,733	52,217
Working Capital at End of Period	$43,733	$52,217	$53,639
Changes in Components of Working Capital			
Increase (decrease) in current assets:			
Cash	$ 4,045	$ 9,513	$ 1,930
Receivables.................................	1,006	1,103	(1,347)
Inventories	676	2,776	(870)
Deferred income taxes	263	269	(1,550)
Other current assets.........................	(45)	489	(307)
Increase (Decrease) in Current Assets	5,945	14,150	(2,144)
Increase (decrease) in current liabilities:			
Accounts payable............................	(1,381)	3,563	(1,978)
Accrued employee compensation			
and other liabilities	(1,114)	1,572	(859)
Income taxes................................	867	241	(522)
Current portion of long-term obligations	150	290	(207)
Increase (Decrease) in Current Liabilities	(1,478)	5,666	(3,566)
Increase in Working Capital	$ 7,423	$ 8,484	$ 1,422

EXHIBIT 5.11 **Statement of Baldor Electric's stockholder equity**

	Common stock Shares	Amount	Additional capital (In thousands)	Retained earnings	Total
Balance at January 1, 1980	6,167	$617	$ 7,678	$34,691	$42,986
Employee profit sharing plan	71	7	1,226		1,233
Stock option plans	47	5	314		319
Net earnings				9,409	9,409
Common stock dividends—					
$.24 per share				(1,498)	(1,498)
Balance at December 31, 1980...	6,285	629	9,218	42,602	52,449
Employee profit sharing plan	31	3	556		559
Stock option plans	63	6	566		572
Net earnings				11,733	11,733
Common stock dividends—					
$.29 per share				(1,843)	(1,843)
Balance at December 31, 1981...	6,379	638	10,340	52,492	63,470
Employee profit sharing plan	33	3	639		642
Stock option plans	16	2	264		266
Net earnings				8,518	8,518
Common stock dividends—					
$.32 per share				(2,052)	(2,052)
Balance at December 31, 1982...	6,428	$643	$11,243	$58,958	$70,844

INDUSTRY NOTE:

Electric Motors

The United States electric motor industry can be divided into two primary segments—industrial motors and consumer, or appliance, motors. A few of the big manufacturers, like General Electric and Westinghouse, supply both markets. Some producers like Baldor make only industrial motors. Still others specialize in consumer motors.

The industrial/consumer distinction is ordinarily used to identify the difference between motors made in extremely high volume (usually fractional HP consumer market motors) and those usually manufactured in lower volume (higher HP motors

This industry note was prepared by Peter M. Ginter and Linda E. Swayne and is intended as a basis for classroom discussion rather than to illustrate effective or ineffective handling of an administrative situation. Used by permission from Peter M. Ginter.

designed for special and heavy usage). Generally, consumer motors are made with less durable, lower quality parts, while industrial motors are manufactured for greater durability and more rugged conditions.

KEY COMPETITORS

There are approximately 340 companies in the United States involved in the production of motors. In a 1981 company study, the top three companies in the industry accounted for over 50 percent of the industry's sales, while the top eleven companies accounted for approximately 80 percent of the industry's sales. Exhibit 1 illustrates electric motor sales comparisons for the top eleven companies.

	1969		1981		
Company	Sales (Mtr. only)	Rank	Sales (Mtr. only)	Rank	Percent to total sale
General Electric	519	1	1200	1	4
Emerson (Incl. USEM)	285	3	700	2	20
Westinghouse	353	2	450	3	5
Exxon (Reliance)	122	4	290	4	n/a
W. W. Grainger	75	5	265	5	25
Baldor	18	11	151	6	94
Franklin Electric	30	9	150	7	94
Siemens-Allis (A-C)	70	6	125	8	n/a
Gould (Century)	60	7	120	9	7
Litton Industries (L/A)	40	8	100	10	n/a
Marathon Electric	25	10	80	11	n/a

EXHIBIT 1 Estimated electric motor sales for the industry's leading firms

Source: Baldor Electric Company.

The electric motor industry is a growing industry with strong competitors including many of the best known companies in America (such as GE and Westinghouse). To a great degree, the relative strengths of competitors help maintain high quality products. One measure of this quality has been the industry's ability to export four times as many motors as is currently imported. The financial position and operating results of most of the top companies in the industry are very strong (Exhibit 2).

General Electric—General Electric (GE) is the industry leader and the only company manufacturing a full line of electric motors. The company is also the single

EXHIBIT 2 1981 Operating results for selected electric motor firms

	Total assets	Total net worth	Current ratio	Long-term debt to total capital	Net earnings to total sales	Return on average total assets	Return on average equity
General Electric	$20,942	$ 9,128	1.2	.104	.061	.083	.19
Emerson	2,201	1,386	2.4	.106	.080	.130	.21
Westinghouse	8,316	2,837	1.03	.180	.047	.058	.163
Exxon	62,931	28,517	1.3	.153	.049	.093	.206
W. W. Grainger	472	335	2.2	.041	.065	.119	.180
Franklin Electric	98	53	2.3	.263	.041	.074	.141
Baldor Electric	103	63	3.3	.175	.073	.127	.202
Siemens-Allis (A-C)	1,594	656	1.5	.305	—	—	—
Gould (Century)	1,597	810	2.3	.299	.052	.061	.119

largest exporter of motors and generators, although its motor sales account for less than 10 percent of GE's total sales. General Electric is respected in the industry as a very well-managed company producing quality products.

Emerson Electric—Emerson Electric is second in terms of motor sales and has maintained a rapid growth rate over the last five years. Emerson's sales comprise approximately two-thirds consumer motors distributed through Emerson Motor division and one-third industrial motors sold through U.S. Electrical Motors.

Westinghouse—Westinghouse, third in sales among the motor manufacturers, has a broad line of electric motors. However, its growth rate has been below the average of other leaders in the industry. Baldor's management speculated that the lack of growth is likely due to a number of other concerns that have diverted management attention from motor sales in the last few years.

Reliance Electric—Reliance, a subsidiary of Exxon since 1979, has maintained a good reputation regarding the quality of their electric motors, and continues to be a well-respected manufacturer of industrial motors and a tough competitor in the industry.

W. W. Grainger—Grainger's expertise has been as a distributor of products to industry through its stores; its catalog the "Blue Book"; and direct to original equipment manufacturers (OEMs). Motors represent about 25 percent of Grainger's sales.

Baldor Electric Company—Baldor focuses on energy-efficient industrial electric motors and sells to distributors and OEMs. Since 94 percent of its sales are electric motors, Baldor is committed to the electric motor industry.

ELECTRIC MOTORS

Rather than being used for one purpose by a single market, electric motors are used in many types of machinery and equipment by both consumers and industrial users throughout the world. The electric motor markets can be segmented into five major product categories. These categories include:

- fractional horsepower motors—motors under one horsepower
- integral horsepower motors and generators
- prime mover sets—internal combustion engine/generator combinations
- motor generator sets—electric motor/generator combinations
- other equipment (servos, synchros, resolvers, parts, and accessories)

The electric motor is a rotating machine used for the conversion of electrical energy to mechanical power. Motors can meet a variety of service requirements such as running, starting, holding, or stopping a load.

Electric motors are the sole method of converting electrical energy to mechanical power. No matter what the source of energy, coal, oil, gas, or nuclear, an electric motor is utilized for conversion of the electric energy to mechanical power. Advantages of electrical power are ease of transportation over great distances, and ease of control compared to other forms of energy. Currently 30 percent of all energy is converted to electrical power and 64 percent of that generated electricity is used to power motor-driven equipment.

The basic science used in operation of the electric motor has remained the same since its invention early in the nineteenth century. There have, however, been substantial refinements in manufacturing processes and size of the components. Exhibit 3 summarizes the different types of AC- and DC-powered motors and indicates the many possible market-niche strategies available to manufacturers of electric motors.

Induction motors account for approximately 90 percent of the sales in the fractional and integral horsepower ratings. This type of motor is the simplest and most rugged. The stator "induces" an electric current in the rotor, which has no wiring resulting in a motor that is less expensive and less subject to failure than other types of motors.

The major variations for induction motors relate to the construction of the rotor (squirrel cage or wound rotor) and the operating current (single-phase or poly-phase). Most industrial systems use 3-phase AC current while most consumer applications use single phase. However, the motor can be designed to run on either single- or poly-phase current.

Squirrel cage rotors utilize a laminated steel core fitted with slots into which conductors are placed as the rotor. Wound rotor units employ a copper winding in the rotor assembly. Wound rotor units are more expensive and usually limited to variable speed applications (electronic control devices).

Synchronous motors are used in applications where constant operating speed is required—the AC motor operates in perfect synchronization with the frequency of the line current. They can be constructed to run on single-phase or poly-phase current. Integral horsepower synchronous motors are constructed with a rotor that must be supplied with DC current from an external source.

Commutator motors produce rotary motion through the interaction of two stationary electromagnetic fields. The commutator functions as a rotating switch that reverses the direction of current flow to the armature coil (or rotor) every half revolution of the motor. Commutator motors can be run on either AC or DC current, although most are of the DC type.

DC motors have quick signal response, can be easily operated at different speeds, and can be given precise speed-torque relationships. Applications using DC motors include those that have precise control characteristics, such as instrumentation, material handling and automation equipment, computer output devices, and word processing equipment.

ELECTRIC MOTOR MARKET GROWTH

Electric motors are fundamental to a modern industrialized society. The 1980s appear to hold many changes for the United States as well as all the world economies. Specifically, there will be increased emphasis on factory automation, electronics,

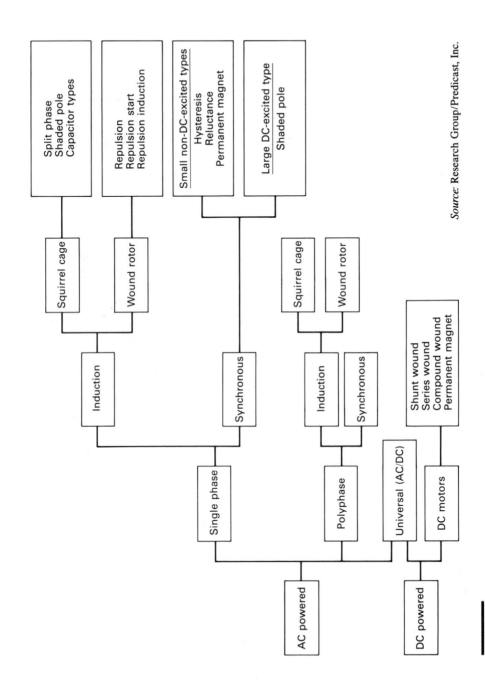

EXHIBIT 3 **Summary of motor types**

and conservation of resources, which suggests greater demand for efficient electric motors. Thus it appears that the pace of change in the electric motor industry will accelerate.

Sales of motors increased from 107 million units in 1963 to over 300 million in 1978—an annual growth rate of over 7 percent. This growth exceeded the less than 5 percent growth in U.S. production of motors because of expanding mechanization and use of motorized equipment in all sectors of the economy. While the prices of electric motors declined due to improved designs, materials, and manufacturing processes during this period, price increases have been rapid since the mid 1970s primarily because of higher rates of inflation. Growth patterns by motor type and by selected industries for electric motors are summarized in Exhibits 4 and 5.

EXHIBIT 4 **Market growth by motor type (In percent)**

Motor type	Average annual growth 1970–1975	Average annual growth 1975–1980	Average annual growth 1970–1980
Fractional horsepower motors	5.7	16.1	10.8
Integral horsepower motors, excluding land transportation	11.5	9.6	10.5
Land transportation motors	12.1	10.3	11.2
Prime mover generator sets, except steam or hydraulic turbine	16.3	12.2	14.2
Motor generator sets and other rotating equipment	−0.4	12.5	5.9

Source: Business Trend Analysts.

Projected growth by motor type indicates that projected real growth is largest for integral horsepower motors (approximately 10 percent annual growth), while growth for fractional horsepower is projected to be flat, and other motor type segments are expected to have moderate growth (Exhibit 6). While currently small markets, servo motors and other motors used in factory automation are expected to grow to approximately $200–$400 million in the 1980s.

Demand for electric motors is projected to increase across all categories. Relative growth for selected electric motor markets is illustrated in Exhibit 7.

INDUSTRY DYNAMICS

The electric motor industry is capital intensive with substantial investments required in facilities, machinery, and tooling. The required high investments create formidable entry barriers. In addition, the industry is of a technical nature requiring sophisticated engineering skills. As a result, only one new company has entered the

EXHIBIT 5 **Growth in the purchase of motors by selected industries (In millions)**

Industry	1972	1977*
Refrigeration and heating equipment	$344.5	$593.9
Household laundry equipment	94.1	141.8
Household refrigerators and freezers	76.8	98.7
Construction machinery	29.2	88.5
Electric housewares and fans	40.8	58.6
Electric computing equipment	34.1	55.2
Motor vehicle parts and accessories	9.0	41.3
Blowers and fans	23.4	37.9
Special industry machinery	25.1	37.4
Mining machinery	12.4	35.4
Machine tools, metal cutting types	20.6	33.3
Household appliances	20.5	31.0
Household vacuum cleaners	7.6	28.3
Office machinery and typewriters	6.0	28.2
Shipbuilding and repair	9.8	26.0
General industrial machinery	12.5	23.5
Conveyors and conveying equipment	9.2	22.1
Industrial trucks and tractors	10.6	19.3
Printing trades machinery	8.0	16.5
Woodworking machinery	8.6	16.1
Household cooking equipment	6.5	15.9
Machine tools, metal forming types	7.1	15.3
Measuring and controlling devices	2.2	14.6
Hoists, cranes, and monorails	8.4	13.6
Lawn and garden equipment	1.6	12.2
Elevators and moving stairways	11.7	12.0
Radio and TV sets	13.0	11.7
Power driven hand tools	10.3	11.6
Engineering and scientific instruments	5.1	11.0
Food products machinery	11.2	10.6
Metal working machinery	4.0	10.1

*Preliminary figures.

Source: Business Trend Analysts, Census of Manufacturers.

EXHIBIT 6 **Projected growth in motor sales by motor type 1980–1990* (In percent)**

Fractional horsepower motors	9.9
Integral horsepower motors, excluding land transportation	19.3
Land transportation motors	17.2
Prime mover generator sets, except steam or hydraulic turbine	15.0
Motor generator sets and other rotating equipment	7.8

*Includes estimated 10 percent annual inflation.

Source: Business Trend Analysts.

EXHIBIT 7 **Relative growth for selected electric motor markets**

Item	1978	1985	1990
Mfg Production Index	147	193	230
mil motors/index pt	1.82	1.99	2.12
Motor, Generator Sales (mil units)	267.2	383.5	488.0
Fabricated Metals	4.5	5.8	6.6
Machinery & Equipment	34.5	40.5	45.9
Electrical & Electronics	42.0	62.7	73.3
Transport Equipment	34.4	40.7	46.2
Instruments	5.6	8.1	10.1
Toys, Games, Other Mfg.	43.3	64.0	76.4
Interplant Transfers	102.8	161.7	229.5
$/unit	16.5	26.5	42.6
Motor, Generator Sales (mil$)	4403.9	10,170	20,780
Fabricated Metals	101.9	203	290
Machinery & Equipment	1,823.1	3,864	5,856
Electrical & Electronics	620.5	1,427	2,250
Transport Equipment	455.7	1,266	6,772
Instruments	158.2	320	485
Toys, Games, Other Mfg.	145.6	270	392
Interplant Transfers	1,098.9	2,820	4,735

top eleven companies in the industry over the last fifteen years. (This company was founded by a past owner of another one of the top companies.) Finally, the sunk costs of electric motor production also make it difficult for a company to exit the market.

Major factors currently affecting the electric motor industry include rising energy costs, electric vehicles, factory automation, and technological evolution. Rising energy costs have resulted in an increased emphasis by customers for product quality and energy efficiency. Energy cost increases are projected by the federal government to continue for the foreseeable future. Many manufacturers are offering higher efficiency electric motors at premium prices to meet this demand. It is estimated that energy-efficient motors now account for 11 percent of the 5–20 horsepower market, compared to 1 percent in 1977.

The difference of a few percentage points in energy efficiency can result in a complete payback of the motor's purchase cost within the first year for larger horsepower units. Exhibit 8 illustrates the possible savings with an energy-efficient 50-horsepower motor versus an average standard motor based on different hours of operation. Because of such cost savings, many users are considering replacing their less efficient motors with new, energy-efficient electric motors.

Forecasts are for electric vehicles to be used increasingly for consumer and industrial transportation. Increased usage will result from rising costs of fossil fuel, improved battery technology, and operating efficiencies of electric vehicles.

EXHIBIT 8 **Possible savings through energy-efficient motors**

Power cost per KWH	Annual Savings 50 HP motor		
	40 hour week (1 Shift)	**80 hour week (2 Shifts)**	**168 hour week (Continuous)**
.02	$ 72.07	$144.15	$ 302.71
.04	144.15	288.30	605.42
.07	216.22	432.45	908.14
.08	288.30	576.60	1,210.85
.10	360.37	720.74	1,513.56

50 Weeks per year

Factory automation is creating a whole new market for electric motors. This new field, electronic motors, includes the servo motors and controls used for the movement and precise positioning of robots, machine tools, and factory vehicles. This particular portion of the industry is in its infancy and includes many small companies. The most successful of these small electric motor companies will be subject to acquisition by the larger firms in the industry.

Technological evolution has become important not only to the markets served but also to the individual companies within the motor industry. Automation of the electric motor manufacturer's factories, thus taking advantage of the newer production technologies, will be critical to the companies' abilities to compete as low-cost producers.

KEY FACTORS FOR SUCCESS IN THE ELECTRIC MOTOR INDUSTRY

Several factors are essential if a firm is to have long-term success in the electric motor industry. The key factors appear to include:

- Market share
- Product differentiation
- Product quality and reliability
- Price/low cost production
- Distribution
- Research and development
- Financial strength

Market Share

Market share is an important factor for success in the electric motor industry because the industry is maturing and consolidation is quite likely. Firms that do not command significant share of the total market or are not firmly entrenched in a particular segment of the market may be subject to acquisition as competition becomes more intense.

Product Differentiation

Many of the larger firms attempt to compete in a number of distinct markets, while the smaller firms generally tend to concentrate on developing a special niche. Most of the highly successful firms in the industry have segmented the market and have developed different products to serve as many of the segments as possible. Examples of successful market segmentation include the Franklin Electric—submersible pump motors; W. W. Grainger—unique distribution through catalog and company owned stores; and Baldor—product availability and energy-efficient motors.

While it is possible and perhaps even essential to be successful in the short run by serving specialized markets, broad market coverage may better assure long-term success as the company is not dependent upon the contingencies of a single market.

Product Quality and Reliability

Because much of the industry produces motors for the industrial market, durability and reliability are quite important. Quality issues include the mechanical and electrical functions, raw materials used, durability, efficiency, and care of manufacturing. Company image concerning quality is important in the consumer market as well.

Price/Low Cost Production

In a mature industry, the low cost producers are usually the most successful. As an industry matures, competition increases (the electric motor industry has 340 companies) and it becomes more difficult to provide a unique product. Therefore as the technology of market segments stabilizes and products become relatively standardized, price becomes a major consideration. In order to offer low prices, manufacturers must be low-cost producers.

Distribution

The electric motor producer must have well-established distribution systems in order to meet customer needs. Important factors in electric motor distribution are:

- Availability—the ability to deliver immediately from stock
- Delivery reliability—the ability to consistently meet delivery lead times
- Service—a close, friendly relationship with customers (primarily OEMs).

Research and Development

In today's environment, modernized manufacturing methods and technical product developments will be needed to remain competitive. Therefore, firms in the industry will have to seriously engage in both process and product research and development.

Financial Strength

Adequate financial strength is required for companies in the industry to remain competitive and respond to possible strategic moves by other companies. Financial support is necessary for quality assurance programs, distribution system needs, and research and development requirements.

CASE 6

Peter Piper Pizza (B)

INTRODUCTION

"C'mon over to Peter Piper Pizza," waves the rotund pizza cook whose face is familiar to most of us. This familiar chef that appears in his striped apron and chef's hat, is Anthony Cavolo, chairman and chief executive officer of Peter Piper Pizza. It was in November 1973, when Cavolo and his son-in-law, Steven Herrgesell, opened the first Peter Piper Pizza restaurant in Glendale, Arizona. Currently, there are 90 restaurants throughout eight southwestern states, of which 32 are company owned and 58 are franchised.

Upon retirement from the restaurant business in New York, Cavolo moved to the Phoenix area in 1973 and went to work for a pizza company there. By November of that same year, Cavolo decided to take his many years of restaurant experience and open a pizza restaurant of his own.

In 1974, Cavolo began to experience some difficulties. Faced with limited financial resources, he changed his concept to "lower prices and quality pizza." With this new concept, Cavolo invested his final $3,000 and went before the public on television. "Good pizza at low, low prices," was all Cavolo had to say in order to turn his pizza business into the success that it is today!

Peter Piper Pizza is one of the fastest growing restaurant chains in the nation, selling approximately 7 million pizzas a year. In 1985, sales were $42 million with 1986 sales expected to reach $60 million.

This case was prepared by Richard F. Beltramini, Associate Professor of Marketing and Advertising at Arizona State University, as a basis for classroom discussion rather than to illustrate effective or ineffective handling of an administration situation. Copyright © 1986 Richard F. Beltramini. Used by permission from Richard F. Beltramini.

Due to the success of the first Peter Piper Pizza restaurant in Glendale, Cavolo decided to open a second in the East Valley. This was the first franchised restaurant and it opened in Tempe in 1977. Currently, 64 percent of all Peter Piper Pizza restaurants are franchised. This seems to be fairly consistent with the franchising activity of the restaurant industry as a whole.

Franchising has become the "wave of the future" for the restaurant industry.[1] The number of franchisee-owned restaurants has increased from 47,544 in 1984, to 56,259 in 1986. The corresponding sales have also increased from $27 million to $33.5 million. Among the top franchised restaurants in the United States, four are pizza chains (see Exhibit 6.1). The estimated total number of pizza restaurants is 16,259, of which 10,959, or 67 percent, are franchisee-owned.[2] Pizza sales commanded 11.4 percent of the total industry's sales in 1984 (see Exhibit 6.2).

UNITED STATES RESTAURANT INDUSTRY TRENDS

Americans have less time to prepare meals, but they have more money to spend. About half of all American households consist of one or two persons, and 50 percent of all households have two wage earners. All of this, coupled with the fact that about 60 percent of women age 20 to 44 work outside of the home, explains the increase in disposable income and the decrease in leisure time. In 1984, Americans allocated 15.1 percent, or $390.1 billion of their disposable income to food purchases. The amount of money that was spent on food purchases away from home was 29 percent, of which 40 percent was generated by the fast-food segment. The remaining 71 percent of Americans' food dollars were spent in grocery stores.[3] These trends seem to indicate that Americans will continue spending more of their disposable income for the consumption of food away from home.

Convenience stores are beginning to compete in the fast-food segment. Food-service volumes at convenience stores have risen from four percent in 1980 to about 10 percent in 1984. This area has become a great opportunity and a big competitor of the restaurant industry, and is projected to reach 15 percent in the next few years. The advantage of convenience stores is the variety of products that they have available. One can not go to a fast-food restaurant and purchase a meal along with beer, cigarettes, gas and diapers for example. Also, fast-food restaurants have become more restaurant-oriented by placing more emphasis on menu variety than fast service.[4]

The issues of nutrition and calories are continuing to be of concern to those eating out, influencing their eating decisions. Those who are nutrition and calorie

---

[1] John Naisbitt, "2001: A Franchising Odyssey," *Nation's Restaurant News,* March 3, 1986, pp. F13.

[2] Jacque White Kochak, "New products deliver quality and freshness," *Restaurant Business,* September 20, 1985, pp. 101–114.

[3] "Food industry is steady as she goes," *Standard and Poor's/Industry Surveys,* pp. F13–17.

[4] Howard Schlossberg, "Time on their side: Convenience stores have groceries, gas, banking machines—and a quick meal," *Restaurants & Institutions,* April 2, 1986, pp. 13.

EXHIBIT 6.1 **Systemwide sales by company and franchise***

Franchise system	Sales 1984 (In thousands)	Sales 1985 (In thousands)	1984–1985 Percent change
McDonalds	$10,000	$11,000	10
Burger King	3,420	3,990	17
Kentucky Fried Chicken	2,850	3,100	9
Wendy's	2,420	2,700**	12
Hardee's	1,900	2,200	16
Pizza Hut	1,700**	2,100	24
Dairy Queen	1,390	1,572	13
Taco Bell	925**	1,140**	23
Big Boy	1,000**	1,135**	14
Domino's Pizza	626	1,097**	75
Arby's	757	814	8
Church's	634	739**	17
Ponderosa	585	681	16
Long John Silver's	602	637	6
Jack in the Box	588**	612**	4
Dunkin' Donuts	532	577	8
Shoney's	516	576	12
Roy Rogers	443**	507**	14
Sizzler	384	443	15
Baskin-Robbins	389**	423**	9
Bonanza	401	421	5
Western Sizzlin'	428**	420**	(2)
Popeyes	304	355**	17
Chi-Chi's	273	334	22
Little Caesar's	227	300	32
Sonic Drive-In	283	292	3
Rax Restaurants	216	280	29
Perkins	281	274	(3)
Captain D's	239	270	13
Godfather's Pizza	304	268	(12)
Total	$34,390	$39,258	

*Includes international operations.
**Estimated.
Source: Restaurant Business, March 20, 1986, pp. 182.

conscious, tend to eat those foods that they believe are nutritious and low in calories.[5] However, although consumers are asking for nutritious, low calorie foods, restaurants tell us that what consumers order are "perceived" healthy foods: high quality, light, fresh foods. The fast-food industry is responding to these trends and offering "lite" menus. For example, McDonalds has introduced the McDLT hamburger that has

[5]"Continued growth likely for restaurant industry," *Standard and Poor's/Industry Surveys,* pp. R139–141.

fresh lettuce, tomatoes and onions, and Wendy's has added mulit-grain buns and a "Light Side" menu featuring baked potatoes and salads.[6]

Also of concern, especially to the "Yuppie" segment, is a trend toward preferring comfort, service, and status. These concerns have brought about a new trend featuring the "gourmet" eating experience. This new trend is evidenced by gourmet hamburgers on freshly baked rolls, croissants, and even gourmet pizza.[7]

Finally the trend toward ethnic foods has grown within the restaurant industry. Mexican food has been among the most successful, with the popularity of Japanese, Chinese, and Indian foods growing.[8] Exhibits 6.2–6.4 illustrate the growing competition in the restaurant industry, and the trends in consumer preferences. Exhibit 6.4 also illustrates influences in selecting a restaurant.

EXHIBIT 6.2 **Sales by product group**

Product group	Number of companies	Sales (In thousands)		Percent total industry	
		1984	1985*	1984	1985
Hamburgers, franks roast beef, etc.	105	$22,043,955	$24,058,881	50.1	50.0
Steak, full menu	111	7,767,393	8,413,997	17.9	17.5
Pizza	104	4,932,329	5,721,265	11.4	11.9
Chicken	33	3,891,165	4,402,558	9.0	9.2
Mexican	36	2,113,104	2,403,653	4.8	5.0
Seafood	12	1,074,426	1,202,950	2.5	2.5
Pancakes, waffles	13	985,350	1,065,430	2.3	2.2
Sandwich and other	51	626,060	739,839	1.4	1.5
Total	465	$43,433,782	$48,008,573	99.4	99.8

*Data estimated by respondents.

Source: Restaurant Business, March 20, 1986, pp. 174–175.

THE PHOENIX PIZZA MARKET

In general, Peter Piper regards all fast-food restaurants as competitors. Peter Piper Pizza is geared towards getting the order out fast, and they can have a pizza ready in 15 minutes or less. Also regarded as competition are a number of "ma and

[6] Rona Gindin, "The healthy food phenomenon," *Restaurant Business,* February 10, 1986, pp. 127–142.

[7] Andrew Kostecka, "Restaurant franchising in the economy," *Restaurant Business,* March 20, 1986, pp. 172–182.

[8] Ibid.

EXHIBIT 6.3 **Most patronized pizza restaurants**

| | Rank | |
Pizza restaurant	1983*	1984
Godfather's	1	1
Pizza Hut	2	2
Pizza Inn	4	3
Shakey's	5	4
Pizza Time Theatre	7	5
Straw Hat Pizza	6	6
ShowBiz Pizza	3	7

*Adjusted to reflect the deletion of chains with less than a 100-person patronage base.

Source: Restaurants & Institutions, December 19, 1984, p. 111.

EXHIBIT 6.4 **How Americans decide where to eat**

Source/influence	Ranking of influence
Recommendation of a friend	65.0
Reputation of the restaurant	39.8
Suggestion of a family member	39.0
Price discount	24.6
Coupons	23.9
Newspaper advertisement	21.3
Restaurant review in newspaper	19.9
Advertisement on TV	10.3
Advertisement on radio	6.7
Magazine dining guide	5.9
Restaurant review on radio	3.9

Source: Restaurants & Institutions, December 5, 1984, pp. 105.

pa stores." These are the single- or double-unit pizza restaurants that are often small and family owned. However, Peter Piper's most direct competition are the various other pizza chains that compete within the same markets in which Peter Piper's does. Among these chains within the Phoenix market are: Domino's (32 units), Pizza Hut (30 units), Little Ceasar's (14 units), Godfather's (10 units), Pizza Inn (10 units), Gino's (10 units), Village Inn (5 units), Round Table (3 units), and ShowBiz Pizza Place (2 units). On a national level, Pizza Hut has continued to be the market leader with Domino's at the number two spot (see Exhibit 6.5).

Of all of these leading pizza chains, Pizza Hut and Domino's are considered most threatening to Peter Piper Pizza. These two chains are considered to be Peter Piper's top competitors because they are the two top selling pizza chains. However, in the Phoenix market, Peter Piper Pizza is the market leader, holding a 33 percent market share, with Pizza Hut and Domino's trailing close behind.

EXHIBIT 6.5 **National pizza leaders**

Restaurant	Units	1984 Sales	Market share	Avg. unit volume
Pizza Hut	4,332	$1.9 billion	19.4	$450,000
Domino's	2,300	625 million	6.4	416,000
Godfather's	900	312 million	3.2	450,000
ShowBiz Pizza Place	364	n/a**	—	950,000
Pizza Inn	720	252 million	2.6	415,000
Little Caesar's	600	230 million	2.3	383,000*
Shakey's	318	200 million	2.0	520,000
Round Table	430	162 million	1.7	440,000
Mr. Gatti's	350	135 million	1.4	450,000
Ken's Restaurant Systems	240	130 million	1.3	Mazzio's—936,000 Ken's—500,000

*Estimated by Restaurant Business.

**The merger of ShowBiz and Pizza Time Theater created a much larger chain than in 1984.

Source: Restaurant Business, September 20, 1985, p. 104.

A recent study by the Gilmore Research Group revealed that Phoenix residents are more likely to be experienced with Peter Piper Pizza or Pizza Hut than any other pizza restaurant in the area (see Exhibit 6.6). This study also revealed pizza restaurant preferences among Phoenix residents. Overall, once pizza diners try Peter Piper Pizza, they are most likely to prefer it. However, approximately three out of ten pizza diners visit Peter Piper Pizza most often, and almost twice as many visit its major competitor, Pizza Hut.[9]

EXHIBIT 6.6 **Pizza restaurant experience among Phoenix residents**

Percent of residents	Dining experience
60	Peter Piper Pizza or Pizza Hut
33 1/3	Village Inn, Pizza Inn, and Godfather's
25	Gino's, Domino's, and Chuck E. Cheese's

Source: Gilmore Research Group, 1984, pp. 28.

The same study conducted by the Gilmore Research Group found that Phoenix residents enjoy a variety of restaurants when dining out. Closely following the national trend, Mexican restaurants have shown to be the most popular. Approximately nine out of ten Phoenix residents will dine at a Mexican restaurant. Eight out of ten

[9]Gilmore Research Group, 1984, pp. 9–38.

Phoenix residents will eat at either a hamburger or pizza restaurant, and seven out of ten will dine at seafood restaurants.[10]

PETER PIPER PIZZA'S MARKETING COMMUNICATIONS APPROACH

"Coupons, coupons, coupons!!! At Peter Piper's you don't need any coupons," quips Mr. Cavolo. Since Cavolo opened his first Peter Piper Pizza restaurant, coupons and promotions such as those used by the competition (see Exhibit 6.7), have been against his philosophy. Cavolo keeps his prices low so that consumers do not have to wait for a coupon to come out before going out for pizza. However, there are exceptions. Occasionally, Cavolo will run a back-to-school coupon to help attract students at the start of the school year. Also, coupons are used when entering into new markets to encourage trial. Cavolo has found that consumers sometimes tend to equate his low price with low quality. By using the coupons, Cavolo hopes to get the consumer that is unfamiliar with Peter Piper Pizza into the restaurant to try his high quality pizza. Then, consumers tend to return on their own, because they like the pizza.

EXHIBIT 6.7 **Competitors' promotions**

Competitor	Promotion
Restaurant A	A large pizza for the price of a medium.
Restaurant B	Buy a pizza at regular price and get a second pizza of equal or lesser value free.
Restaurant C	A 12 inch one-item pizza for $5.99 and two free cokes.
Restaurant D	Buy one pizza and get another pizza of the same size, free.
Restaurant E	$3.00 off any large thin crust pizza or $2.00 off any large original crust pizza.
Restaurant F	$2.00 off any large pizza or $1.00 off any medium pizza.
Restaurant G	Free quart of Coke with the purchase of a large or medium pizza.

Peter Piper's recently tested their first store promotion. For every large Coke that was bought, the consumer received a plastic tumbler with the Peter Piper Pizza logo on it. The objective of this promotion was to thank the customer for supporting Peter Piper Pizza and to differentiate Peter Piper Pizza from the competition. Cavolo believes that it is not enough to offer quality pizza for a low price anymore. To

[10] Gilmore Research Group, pp. 9–38.

compete successfully with the competition, restaurants need to get their names into the consumer's households.

Cavolo believes that community awareness is what has made Peter Piper's Pizza a strong competitor. Therefore, he wants Peter Piper's to get out into the community and work with it. Participating in a number of charitable promotions has been a positive way for Peter Piper's to accomplish this. The majority of these promotions included donating 50 cents on every pizza purchased to various nonprofit organizations, including for example, the Special Olympics, Phoenix Children's Hospital, and the Epilepsy Foundation. Also adding to these successes was the Bowl-A-Thon that Peter Piper Pizza sponsored to benefit the Muscular Dystrophy Foundation. All of these promotional activities represent Peter Piper's public relations work. They have proven to be great opportunities to add to Peter Piper Pizza's positive image within the Phoenix community.

"No coupons. No gimmicks. No Tuesday night specials. Just good pizza at a low, low price," continues Cavolo. Price and quality pizza are the major themes in Peter Piper Pizza's advertising campaigns. As a matter of fact, Cavolo will give any customer their money back if they are not fully satisfied with their pizza at Peter Piper's.

Cavolo feels he can guarantee quality and low price for a number of reasons. By taking advantage of all volume discounts, Peter Piper Pizza can pass these savings on to the consumer. Peter Piper's employs high-volume production techniques that allow for greater efficiency than if skilled labor were employed. This minimizes the extra labor costs that would be incurred if skilled labor were to be used. Also, by limiting the menu selection to pizza, salad, beer, and soft drinks, Peter Piper's minimizes paid labor costs that would be required if the menu were expanded. Most Peter Piper Pizza restaurants are located along main streets or strip malls where rent costs are lower. Finally, all management at Peter Piper Pizza restaurants is well trained and closely supervised in regards to cost and production controls. Cavolo believes that this is vital in order to minimize unnecessary spending. All of the above are employed in order to keep Peter Piper's costs low, passing the savings on to the consumer by way of lower prices.

Cavolo believes in using nothing but fresh, quality ingredients in his pizza. Therefore, he only uses 100 percent mozzarella cheese, the finest California tomatoes, dough made fresh daily with the finest grade of flour, and quality toppings.

Selling prices at Peter Piper Pizza are up to 50 percent less than what the competitors normally charge. By continuing to keep the menu selection to pizza, salad, beer, and soft drinks, Peter Piper's is able to keep the prices low. By adding more variety to the menu, additional labor costs would be incurred. Although 60 percent of Peter Piper's business is take-out, delivery will not be added to Cavolo's concept due to the added insurance costs involved. All of these extras would mean added costs to Peter Piper's, and ultimately added costs to the consumer too. Cavolo would like to continue his quality pizza/low-price concept.

During Peter Piper's first year in business, approximately $7,000 was spent on advertising. Currently, $800,000 was allocated toward the 1986 advertising budget for the Phoenix market alone. Typically, the budget totals approximately five percent of sales (see Exhibit 6.8). According to Cavolo, this is what has worked best for Peter Piper's, and there have been no thoughts regarding any changes in this area.

EXHIBIT 6.8 **Peter Piper Pizza's advertising budget, company owned stores**

Year	Sales (In thousands)	Advertising budget
1986 (est)	$16,000	$800,000
1985	14,200	710,000
1984	11,100	555,000
1983	7,900	395,000
1982	5,700	285,000
1981	3,400	170,000
1980	2,300	115,000
1979	1,600	80,000

Source: Company records.

In the past, Cavolo believed in handling all advertising in-house. During this time, Peter Piper Pizza was not as big, or as competitive as it is today. Therefore, Cavolo has felt that Peter Piper's advertising did not need the creative talents, production technology, or planning expertise that an agency would provide. In addition, Cavolo did not feel that the extra finances involved in hiring an agency would have been justified. However, Peter Piper Pizza has recently hired an agency to work on creative and production. Cavolo felt that to continue to be competitive, better quality commercials were needed. The production quality of the commercials can be upgraded substantially through the use of an agency. Cavolo and his in-house personnel work side by side with the agency to continue the same general flavor in Peter Piper Pizza's advertising.

Currently, Peter Piper's is utilizing four media: spot television, spot radio, newspaper, and outdoor. The majority of the budget (90 percent), is devoted to television. Cavolo believes that Peter Piper's success in the beginning was a result of advertising on television, and therefore, he remains loyal to it. Also, Cavolo's friendly face has become familiar to many through the use of television and adds a personal touch. The remaining portion of the budget is allocated to radio, newspaper, and outdoor (Exhibit 6.9).

As mentioned earlier, newspaper is utilized only rarely, capturing about two percent of the budget. It was not until recently that radio was introduced into the media schedule. Therefore, Cavolo is currently observing how radio will affect his level of sales. This medium currently only commands three percent of the budget. Two outdoor billboards rotate throughout the Phoenix area, which account for the remaining five percent of the budget. This overall media mix used by Peter Piper's is fairly consistent with some of the top pizza chains in the nation (see Exhibit 6.10).

EXHIBIT 6.9 **Sample advertisement**

EXHIBIT 6.10 **Competitors' advertising budget**

Competitor	Ad budget (In thousands)	Media used
Pizza Hut	$64,456.7	NSOC
Domino's	18,205.4	NSOC
Godfather's	8,749.8	SO
Round Table	2,821.5	SO
Little Caesar's	2,174.9	SO
Pizza Inn	2,126.2	SO
ShowBiz Pizza	2,108.0	SO
Shakey's	1,294.4	SO
Gino's	18.5	O

Note: N = Network T.V.
    S = Spot T.V.
    O = Outdoor
    C = Cable T.V. Networks
Source: *LNA AD $ Summary*, 1985, pp. 111–347.

Peter Piper's radio and television advertising runs for three weeks each month. By doing so, Peter Piper's can achieve the high level of frequency that is desired. As a company representative remarked, "We want to blast them for GRPs (gross rating points)." The television spots are run during the first and third weeks of each month, with the radio spots also running every third week of each month. The advertising appears all through the year, with the heaviest periods corresponding with the heaviest monthly sales (see Exhibit 6.11).

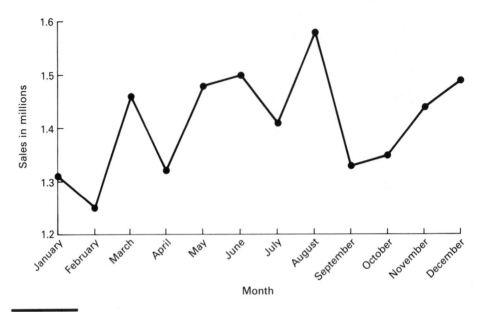

EXHIBIT 6.11 **Peter Piper Pizza—Phoenix ADI sales**

With the production needs for Cavolo's commercials being minimal, five or six television commercials are produced in an hour. This schedule enables Cavolo to keep his production costs down to about $200 per commercial, or $1,000 per hour as compared to the thousands spent by Peter Piper Pizza's competitors.

Cavolo as the main attraction in Peter Piper's commercials is what has worked best. Each 30-second spot features Cavolo as the spokesperson. In front of the camera stands Cavolo with his chef's hat, white shirt, striped apron, and that all-familiar friendly smile, telling his viewers of his good quality pizza at low, low prices. For each flight, the copy for the commercials changes, but Cavolo remains in the spotlight.

The 30-second radio spots also feature Cavolo as the spokesperson. As in the television spots, the radio spots emphasize Cavolo's two main benefits—price and quality (see Exhibit 6.12). Cavolo's approach is simple and straightforward, but it has helped make Peter Piper's the success that it is today.

Cavolo attributes the majority of his success to the believability of his simple and straightforward approach. Several years ago, Peter Piper's tested a cartoon character of Cavolo, but this was very unsuccessful. This experience proved to Cavolo that there was no substitute for the real "him." He believes that he creates a postive image for Peter Piper Pizza, and that is what has made it a success.

EXHIBIT 6.12 **Peter Piper Pizza television and radio spots**

Television spot

"You see alot of commercials for pizza: this one tastes great, that one looks delicious, but there's one thing they keep leaving out. . .the price. Peter Piper Pizza tastes great, looks delicious and costs less than the others. Our large special six-item pizza is only $5.95; all our others are even less. Try a great combination. . .Peter Piper Pizza with an icy cold Coke. So come on over to Peter Piper Pizza."

Radio spot

"Can we talk? I'm Tony from Peter Piper Pizza, and I know that most of you are pizza lovers. And I also know that some of you are paying as much as $9 or $10 for a pizza! Now that's silly. At Peter Piper Pizza our large six-item special is only $5.95. All our others are even less. Try your next Peter Piper Pizza with an icy cold Coke. So for all the pizza lovers, stop paying those high prices. For a good pizza at low, low prices, come on over to Peter Piper Pizza."

CHALLENGE FOR THE FUTURE

Cavolo is very confident in his concept of quality pizza at a low price. Although trends will come and go, Cavolo has no plans for adjusting his concept to meet these new demands. He feels that pizza will always be a favorite among Americans, and that his concept will always be attractive to a good many of these pizza lovers.

Cavolo will always keep his pizza top quality. However, there is no way that he can get around price increases when there are increases in the price of his ingredients. The fact that the economy may change, leaving even more disposable income available in the hands of the consumers, would not influence Cavolo to increase his prices, he claims.

Cavolo has two main advertising objectives for the future that he would like his advertising to accomplish: to sell the quality product at a low price, and to serve as a reminder to consumers. As the yearly sales continue to rise, so will the advertising budget. However, he seems adamant that the budget will always remain at five percent of sales.

The recent hiring of an advertising agency may be the beginning of a long-term plan. As Peter Piper's becomes more competitive, Cavolo believes that a better quality commercial will have to be produced. He feels that this will be achieved best through the use of an agency. Therefore, the agency will become part of the picture more and more. Currently there are no plans to change the creative with Tony under the spotlight. It is a concept that has worked well and Cavolo plans to keep it unless the concept proves otherwise.

Unlike various other pizza chains, Cavolo does not believe in setting specific goals toward expansion activities. "We're a one-step-at-a-time business, not 127 stores by 1987," remarks a company representative. Peter Piper's seems to stand alone on this philosophy. Exhibit 6.13 indicates that many of the other pizza chains

EXHIBIT 6.13 **Competitors' outlooks**

Competitor	Outlook
Domino's	Beginning international expansion with units planned in Germany and other European countries.
Godfather's	"Wait-and-see" strategy following acquisition of parent Diversifoods by Pillsbury.
Pizza Hut	200 units a year for next five years. Emphasis on urban areas such as New York, Chicago, Los Angeles.
Pizza Inn	Expansion resumed after four years of retrenchment. Expanding on military bases and overseas, among other places.
Round Table	Planning to build 60 new units this calendar year, with majority in Southern California.
Shakey's	With revamping, expansion picking up. Close to 100 new franchised locations now under contract.
ShowBiz	Concept revamping could give ShowBiz a shot in the arm. Marginal units have been closed but owner Brock Hotels Corporation remains confident.

Source: Restaurant Business, September 20, 1985, p. 104.

include plans to expand greatly in the future. Currently, Cavolo would like to limit expansion in the Phoenix market to company stores only. In other markets however, there are no specific plans for the future. Currently, Peter Piper's has just penetrated the California market. To enter big markets such as this, Cavolo has learned that one must have a number of stores to open at once to be successful. This means that where there are future expansion plans, there must also be those interested in franchising to open enough units to be successful. This further challenges Peter Piper Pizza's marketing communications programs for the future.

CASE 7

British Airways

On Sunday, April 10, 1983, a six-minute commerical for British Airways (BA) was aired in the middle of a weekend talk show. The commercial included a statement by Lord King, BA's chairman, and highlighted BA's achievements during the previous two years. The commercial also included the inaugural showing of a ninety-second advertisement known as Manhattan Landing. This advertisement and three others formed the basis of an unprecendented £31 million advertising campaign designed to promote BA's brand name and corporate image worldwide.[1]

BRITISH AIRWAYS

By many criteria, BA was the largest international airline in the world. In 1982–83, BA carried 11.7 million passengers on 130,728 international departures, well ahead of Air France which carried 9.6 million international passengers. In terms of international passenger miles, BA's 37 billion a year comfortably surpassed Pan Am. BA flew to 89 cities in 62 countries outside the United Kingdom during 1982–83. Forty-two percent of BA sales were made in the United Kingdom, 25 percent in the rest of Europe, and 33 percent in the rest of the world.

BA was a state-owned enterprise, formed as a result of the 1972 merger of British European Airways and British Overseas Airways Corporation. The economies of scale in the work force which many expected from the merger were slow to materialize. Partly as a result, BA continued to record annual losses throughout the 1970s. BA's financial performance was aggravated by increases in the price of fuel oil stemming from the 1973–74 energy crisis. In addition, greater price competition, especially on transatlantic routes, resulted from the deregulation of international air fares. An example of this trend was the advent of the low-price, no-frills Laker Airways Skytrain service on the lucrative transatlantic route in 1979.

The election of a Conservative government in the United Kingdom in 1979 prompted a change in approach towards the management of BA. The new adminis-tration was determined to reduce the losses that almost all state enterprises showed

---

Copyright © 1984 by the President and Fellows of Harvard College. This case was written by Professor John A. Quelch as a basis for classroom discussion rather than to illustrate effective or ineffective handling of an administrative situation. Reprinted by permission of the Harvard Business School.

[1] BA's fiscal year ran from April 1 to March 30. At the time of the case, £1 was equivalent to about $1.50.

each year and, in many cases, to restore these enterprises to private ownership. A new chairman, Sir John (later Lord) King, was appointed to head BA in 1980. He initiated programs to improve BA's products and services along with a hiring freeze and an early retirement program to reduce the size of the work force. By March 1983, BA's work force had been reduced to 37,500 people from 59,000 just three years earlier. In addition, BA showed a profit in 1982–83 for the first time in ten years, compared to a £500 million loss in 1981–82 (see Exhibit 7.1).

EXHIBIT 7.1 **British Airways income statement, April 1, 1982–March 31, 1983**

Sales revenues (In millions)

Passengers on scheduled services	£1,771
Passengers on charter services	86
Freight	151
Mail	36
Ground arrangements for package tours	100
	£2,144
Expenses	
Staff	£ 593
Aircraft	101
Engineering	107
Operations	863
Marketing	205
Accommodation, ground transport and administration	159
Recoveries	(158)
Ground arrangements for package tours	102
	£1,972
Operating surplus	£ 172
Plus Operating surplus from nonairline activities*	18
Plus Other income**	20
	£ 210
Less Cost of capital borrowings and tax	£ 149
Profit before extraordinary items	51
Plus Profit on sale of subsidiaries	26
Profit	£ 77

*Including BA helicopters, BAAC, and IAC.

**Investments in other companies, interest earned on cash deposits, and surplus from disposal of assets.

Industry observers believed that BA would have to sustain this improved performance if stock was to be offered to private investors by the end of 1984. So the programs of product and service improvement continued, together with further labor cutbacks. Recently introduced Boeing 757s were added to the fleet in 1983, a quality contol division was established, and the U.K. Super Shuttle was introduced.[2]

The turnaround in performance was recognized when BA received the 1983 Airline of the Year award, based on a survey of business travelers. However, although costs were reduced and the quality of service improved, BA's public image remained weak. Along with other nationalized industries, BA continued to share a reputation for inefficiency and incompetence. Accordingly, Lord King stated that one of his main objectives was "to make the airline proud again."

ADVERTISING DURING THE 1970s

During the 1970s, BA country managers had revenue responsibility for BA's marketing and operations in their individual markets. The advertising agencies with which they dealt were appointed by BA headquarters. Foote, Cone & Belding (FCB) had held the BA account in the U.K. since 1947, and as a result, many country managers outside the U.K. also used FCB subsidiaries or affiliates.

In 1978, British Airways appointed FCB as its worldwide agency, meaning that all country managers *had to* deal with the FCB subsidiaries or affiliates in their countries. The purpose was to achieve a more favorable commission rate from FCB rather than to increase centralized control of advertising content around the world. Indeed, in the United States, where the BA account moved from Campbell Ewald to FCB, the BA advertising theme built around Robert Morley and the slogan, "We'll take good care of you" was retained intact since it had only recently been launched (see Exhibit 7.2). Although the Morley campaign was considered a success, building as it did on Britian's favorable reputation in the United States for old-fashioned hospitality, the campaign nevertheless caused problems for BA executives in the United States. In the words of one, "It overpromised on customer service; every time something went wrong, my phone would ring off the hook."

Prior to the appointment of FCB as the worldwide agency, BA country managers were not required to submit their proposed advertising copy to headquarters for approval. There were certain loosely defined guidelines governing the presentation of the BA logo, but beyond that, local country managers and their agencies were free to determine their own advertising copy. Major advertising campaign concepts did, however, require headquarters approval. Following the appointment of FCB as the worldwide agency, this procedure changed. Each December, BA country managers would submit to headquarters requests for advertising funds for the following fiscal year as part of the annual planning process. Once the commercial director at headquarters had allocated these funds, each country manager would then brief the local FCB agency or affiliate, and develop the advertising copy for the coming year. Country managers in the larger markets would submit their advertising copy to the commercial director in London more as a courtesy, while the smaller countries were

---

[2]Four shuttles operated between London and Manchester, Glasgow, Edinburgh, and Belfast. Tickets could be purchased in advance or on board and flights typically left every hour during the day.

"We're up in the air
before most airlines
even wake up!"

We can beat the experience

British Airways beats Pan Am's experience five times a day. After all, we have more business seats to London than Pan Am and TWA combined.

You'd like a 10 a.m. flight? Of course we have it...we've had it for years. And British Airways offers something really special on it. First Class and Super Club® passengers receive a voucher worth £20 (about $33) for dinner in any one of four exclusive restaurants. Tourist passengers receive a voucher for a choice of one of five evenings of cabaret entertainment with dinner.*

British Airways has the very first flight out daily (9:30 a.m. Concorde). So we're up in the air before most airlines even wake up. We also have the last daily flight out (10:00 p.m.) and three

flights in between. And British Airways Super Club seats are by far the world's widest business class seats.

Need we go on? We could mention our free helicopter service,** or our preferred hotel and car rental rates for business travelers, or our longstanding commitment to our 10 a.m. flight. And you'll be pleased to note that your flight miles between the U.S. and London will count as credit toward the A Advantage® travel award plan.

So you see, British Airways has no trouble beating the experience. It's experience like ours that makes us the world's favourite airline. That's why British Airways flies more people to more countries than anyone else. See your travel agent or corporate travel department.

*Offer valid April 15-October 31, 1983 and subject to government approval. For full fare USA originating passengers only. See vouchers for details.
**Helicopter service free for Concorde, First Class and Super Club passengers.

DEPARTURE	AIRCRAFT	FREQUENCY
9:30AM	Concorde	Daily
10:00AM	TriStar/747	Daily
1:45PM	Concorde	Daily
7:00PM	747	Daily
10:00PM	747	Daily

British airways
The World's Favourite Airline™

EXHIBIT 7.2 **Robert Morley campaign magazine advertisement**

required to submit their proposed copy for approval. Headquarters required changes in about 5 percent of cases, typically on the grounds that the advertising overstated claims or was inconsistent with the image BA wished to project.

Whatever the intent, the result of this process was inconsistent advertising from one country to another. First, campaigns varied across markets. The Robert Morley campaign was only considered suitable for the United States. And a recently developed U.K. campaign in which a flight attendant emphasized the patriotism of flying the national flag carrier could likewise not be extended to other countries. Second, commercials and advertising copy promoting the same service or concept were developed in different markets. There were limited procedures within BA and the agency for ensuring that the best ideas developed in one market were transferred to other markets. Finally, the quality of FCB's subsidiaries and affiliates varied significantly from one country to another, aggravating the problem of inconsistency.

BA advertising during this period, like the advertising for most other major airlines, tried to persuade consumers to choose BA on the basis of product feature advantages. Rather than attempting to build the corporate image, BA advertising emphasized superiority and differentiation in scheduling, punctuality, equipment, pricing, seating, catering, and/or in-flight entertainment. Advertising typically focused on particular products such as the air shuttle, BA tour packages, route schedules, and classes of service, such as Club service.[3] The impact on sales of many of these product-specific and tactical advertising efforts could be directly measured. In addition, the commercial director responsible for BA advertising worldwide insisted that a price appear in all advertisements in all media. Frequently, BA advertisements compared the prices of BA services to those of competitors. The commercial director's insistence on including price information in each advertisement frequently caused problems. For example, in the United States, the APEX fare[4] to London from New York differed from that from Boston or Chicago, so different commercials had to be aired in each city.

The 1982-83 advertising budget of £19 million was allocated almost entirely to advertising of a tactical or promotional nature. Only the patriotic "Looking Up" campaign in the U.K. made any effort to develop BA's corporate image. About 65 percent of the 1982-83 budget was allocated by the commercial director to the International Services Division (ISD); about 30 percent to the European Services Division (ESD), and about 5 percent to the Gatwick Division, which handled BA air tours, package holidays, and cargo business in the United Kingdom.[5] BA advertising expenditures during 1982-83 for fourteen representative countries are listed in Exhibit 7.3 together with other comparative market information.

---

[3]The BA equivalent of Business Class.

[4]Advance purchase excursion fare.

[5]The geographical coverage of the ISD and ESD mirrored that of the old BOAC and BEA.

EXHIBIT 7.3 Comparative data for fourteen markets

	BA 1982–83 worldwide passenger revenues (Percent)	1982–83 advertising expenditures (In thousands of £)	Principal BA competitors	BA's market share versus principal competitor	Business/pleasure BA passengers (Percent)
United Kingdom	42	6,223	British Caledonian* Pan American	Similar	42/58
United States	14	5,773	Pan American TWA	Lower	26/74
Germany	5	228	Lufthansa British Caledonian	Lower	50/50
Australia	3	967	Qantas Singapore Airlines	Similar	6/94
France	3	325	Air France British Caledonian	Lower	52/48
Japan	3	393	Japan Airlines Cathay Pacific Airways	Lower	30/70
Gulf States	2	134	Gulf Air Kuwait Airlines	Lower	12/88
Canada	2	991	Air Canada Wardair	Lower	11/89
South Africa	2	331	South African Airways TAP (Air Portugal)	Lower	15/85
Italy	2	145	Alitalia Dan Air	Lower	50/50
New Zealand	1	125	Air New Zealand Singapore Airlines	Similar	3/97
Egypt	.5	53	Egyptair Air France	Similar	26/74
Zimbabwe	.4	41	Air Zimbabwe KLM	Higher	8/92
Trinidad	.3	77	BWIA	Higher	7/93

*These are BA's principal competitors on international routes. BA's main competitors on domestic U.K. routes were British Midland Airways and Dan Air.

SAATCHI & SAATCHI APPOINTED

In October 1982, the Saatchi & Saatchi (S&S) advertising agency was asked by Lord King to explore the possibility of developing an advertising campaign that would bolster BA's image and that could be used on a worldwide basis. S&S was one of the first agencies to espouse the concept of global brands. In newspaper advertisements such as that shown in Exhibit 7.4, S&S argued that demographic and cultural trends, and, therefore, the basic factors underlying consumer tastes and preferences, were converging. In addition, S&S noted a growing spillover of media across national borders, fueled by the development of satellite television. Given these trends and the increasing level of international travel, S&S viewed the concept of global brands employing the same advertising themes worldwide as increasingly plausible.

Following its appointment, S&S set up a Central Policy Unit (CPU) to plan and coordinate work on the worldwide BA account. This unit included a director aided by specialists in research, planning, and budgeting. Over a two-month period, the CPU developed into a complete account team; one section handled advertising in the U.K. and Europe while the second handled advertising in the rest of the world. The account team included a creative group and a senior media director who had international experience.

After winning the BA account, S&S had to resign its business with British Caledonian, Britain's principal private airline. This business amounted to £3.5 million in media billings in 1982. Three S&S offices in other countries had to resign competitive airline accounts. Of the 62 countries in which BA had country managers, S&S had wholly owned agencies in 20 and partly owned agencies in 17. In the remaining countries, S&S retained a local agency, in some cases an FCB affiliate, to continue handling the BA account. S&S did not permit its overseas affiliates to collect commissions on locally placed media billings as compensation for working on the local BA account. Rather, each affiliate received a fee or share of the commission for the services it performed from S&S headquarters in London. S&S billed BA headquarters for all of its services worldwide, except in the case of markets such as India where legal restrictions inhibited currency transactions of this nature.

The relationship between S&S affiliates and headquarters was closer than it had been when FCB handled the BA account. A BA country manager would work with the local S&S agency to develop an advertising copy proposal which would be submitted to BA headquarters in London on a standard briefing form. The BA headquarters advertising manager would then decide whether to approach the S&S account team in London to develop a finished advertisement to be sent back to the BA country manager. Under this system, neither BA country managers nor their local agencies were involved in the design of advertising copy except in terms of working requests, stating objectives, and suggesting content. According to S&S executives, the frequency with which certain types of advertisements were requested meant that it might, in the future, be possible to develop standard "ad mats." BA country managers and their local agencies would simply fill in the relevant destination and fare information on these ad mats and would not have to submit them to London for approval.

THE OPPORTUNITY FOR WORLD BRANDS.

Nowadays, life for branded goods manufacturers is not as straightforward as it once was.

Many years ago manufacturers first recognised that advertising could provide a key foundation for their business growth.

They realised that while their customer was the retailer, the actual 'consumer' was the public; that advertising could enable them to build a solid position in their market by building the goodwill of their real customer – the 'consumer'.

They also saw that if they, the manufacturers, did something to move their goods from retailers' shelves as quickly as they arrived on them, trade would be brisk and everyone would be satisfied.

Thus the manufacturer became the advertiser of 'branded' products, the retailer became the purveyor of 'brands' and advertising became a conspicuous feature of the age.

This happy cycle produced 'brands' of startling endurance and longevity, as the table below shows.

Brand Character

Nowadays, when probed deeply, consumers describe the products they call brands in terms that we would normally expect to be used to describe people. They tell us that brands can be warm or friendly; cold or modern; old-fashioned; romantic; practical; sophisticated; stylish and so on.

They talk about a brand's persona, its image and its reputation – and this 'aura' or 'ethos' is what characterises a brand.

It follows that all brands, like all people, have a 'personality' of one kind or another. But like the strongest individuals, the strongest brands have more than mere personality – they have 'character' – more depth, more integrity, they stand out from the crowd.

Note the importance that one major marketer attaches to this concept.

"My acid test on the issue is whether a housewife intending to buy Heinz Tomato Ketchup in a store, finding it to be out of stock, will walk out of the store to buy it elsewhere or switch to an alternative product."

A J O'REILLY
PRESIDENT & CEO, H J HEINZ

This explains why the best marketers try to develop powerful brand characters. They make them less vulnerable in the market-place. They help a higher quality product to be perceived as such by consumers.

Today, the establishment of such strong and enduring brands is rather more difficult.

☐ Static populations mean static markets which means increased competition for market share.

☐ Product quality is converging, with increasing technological parity among major marketers.

☐ The influence of the retailer and retailers' own store brands is growing in many parts of the world.

☐ Marketing expenses are growing, as manufacturers respond to the ever-higher cost of reaching the consumer.

All in all, the pressures on manufacturers' brands are immense.

Superior Product Quality

Serious marketers know that in the face of these pressures the success of their brands can only rest on superior product quality.

They know that as the consumer views more products as commodities, it becomes harder to

establish a meaningful point of difference for their products. They know that clever marketing and promotion of cosmetic differences cannot paper over this.

They know that the longevity of their brands is helped by good marketing, but is founded on superior product performance and this in turn is founded on their ability to produce a *higher quality product at a lower cost.*

Which is why market leaders' priorities are now focusing on a common objective which was not among their priorities in previous decades – to work diligently to be the *low-cost producer* in their market.

Low costs provide the means to achieve that happiest of all situations – higher product quality ... fewer price increases ... and more advertising.

Low costs are the priority as a sound base for all the other steps needed to build growth.

Thus, the competitive intensity of maturing packaged goods markets around the world has brought to the fore the economic logic of world brands – *the opportunity for international economies of scale as the basis of long-term strategic security.*

Today, the most thoughtful companies are adopting a new approach to international marketing.

And as they pass through the five basic stages in the life of a multinational corporation as seen in the chart below.

And as they pass through stages 4 and 5 the need for pan-regional and world marketing is emerging at the heart of their business strategy.

"The globalization of markets is at hand. With that, the multinational commercial world nears its end, and so does the multinational corporation.

The global corporation operates as if the entire world (or major regions of it) were a single entity; it sells the same things in the same way everywhere.

Corporations geared to this new reality can derive competitive strengths that still live in the disabling grip of old assumptions about how the world works."

PROFESSOR THEODORE LEVITT
HARVARD UNIVERSITY

A New Approach

After the vicissitudes of the 1950s and 1960s, more companies are now reaching the status of having acquired 'critical mass' in various regions of the world. They are now starting to turn from primary concern about 'return on acquisition investment' and 'overhead recovery' towards getting to grips with long term franchise building across each world region.

At the same time the progressive harmonization of 'headquarters' and 'local' management culture and style, evolving from more frequent two-way movement of personnel, is enhancing the likelihood of successful adoption and execution of pan-regional business strategies.

And meanwhile in Europe, management's strategic thinking is beginning to broaden to match the dimensions of the Common Market as legislative harmonization focuses attention on pan-European issues.

International Growth Priority

Companies have passed through the bygone age when many of them treated 'Overseas Division' as the poor cousin of the organisation, struggling to compete in foreign markets with strongly established indigenous competitors.

The international divisions of many companies are now beginning to 'come of age' and receive their rightful allocation of corporate resource, if only for the practical reason that corporate earnings growth in many multinationals is today often provided by non-domestic markets.

Business System Economics

The strategic value of pan-regional branding lies in the scale economies it affords across the company's business system – to help make the company the low-cost producer.

Where the economies arise will vary by product category, and may include research and development, materials purchasing, manufacturing, distribution and advertising.

The optimum business system for a European beer, for example, is markedly different to that for chewing gum, but the principle is the same. Secure, franchise-protected volumes at the regional scale can allow a company to *build a preemptive cost structure which will eventually put it out of reach* of competition.

All these factors set the conceptual framework within which a truly pan-regional brand can exist in the years ahead. The international need is to look for market similarities between countries, not to seek out differences. Similarities will be the new fuel for growth.

The creative process will still be as vital as ever; marketers in each location will still be dependent on the intuitive creative judgement of locally based creative management, but this effort will be marshalled to a single-minded overall advertising strategy.

Marketing Learning Curve

There is then a real marketing learning curve that allows the progressive refinement of a success formula, as the pan-regional brands broaden their experience country by country.

The best creative brains are given an opportunity to develop advertising for an entire region of the world, and not simply for one market – to find a real advertising idea *so deep in its appeal* that it can transcend national borders previously thought inviolate.

Consumer Convergence

In the past, the successes in world branding have been few, and have been achieved by virtue of the sheer will and far-sighted commitment of managements who stayed consistently with a long-term vision for the business. Procter & Gamble is a company in this category that comes to mind.

In the future, the only winners in cross-country branding will be companies who have seen that social developments are making redundant the old idea that differences between nations are decisive in framing marketing strategy.

The most advanced manufacturers are recognising that there are probably more social differences between Midtown Manhattan and the Bronx, two sectors of the same city, than between Midtown Manhattan and the 7th Arrondissement of Paris. This means that when a manufacturer contemplates expansion of his business, consumer similarities in demography and habits rather than geographic proximity will increasingly affect his decisions.

Demographic Convergence

Trends of vast significance to consumer marketing, such as ageing populations, falling birth rates, and increased female employment are common to large segments of the modern industrial world.

Consumer convergence in demography, habits and culture is increasingly leading manufacturers to a consumer-driven rather than a geography-driven view of their marketing territory.

Decline of the Nuclear Family

Some of the most telling developments spring from the same source – the decline of the nuclear family. Observers have attributed this to various causes – the rapid pace of technological development; higher labour productivity which reduces hours of work; and other more metaphysical notions such as the emergence of a 'liberal' philosophy, which increasingly recognizes that a woman's role can exist outside the home.

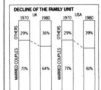
Whatever the causes, the effects in terms of household composition have been dramatic. There are now less children per household, and a declining proportion of households which conform to the two-adult-two-children pattern.

The result is the erosion of the traditional family unit and its clarity of role and relationship. The effects have been illustrated by the decline of formal meal-taking and the corresponding increase in the sales of 'instant' and 'convenience' foods. The multinational expansion of fast-food franchises like McDonalds is another manifestation of the same trend.

Changing Role of Women

The table below shows the change in the role of women in the working population over the past decade. The fact that the majority of women in most modern societies now have a job requires a major adjustment to current ideas on communicating with a consumer group that no longer conforms to the home-centred stereotype of yesteryear.

Associated with this change, there has been a well documented trend to lower marriage rates and higher divorce rates. This trend has led one group of social scientists to invent the phrase 'serial monogamy' to describe what they forecast to be the nature of relationships in the 1980s and beyond. They suggest that there will be an increasing tendency for couples to live together for a number of years, then to change their partners and set up home afresh, changing again after a few years, and so on. This discontinuity in formal relationships, especially where children are involved and re-marriages occur, will have profound effects on family relationships.

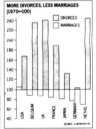
Static Populations

Population growth is now almost zero in the western world. All modern industrial countries are forecast to produce population growth of much less than 1% per annum over the next 20 years. It is hardly surprising that within this static population, the age structure is undergoing a transformation. The over 65s are a growing group relative to the 25–65s, and that group is growing relative to the fourteen and unders.

EXHIBIT 7.4 **Saatchi & Saatchi newspaper advertisement**

Higher Living Standards

In most western countries, improvements in the material standard of life have resulted in a growing demand for consumer durables and for more leisure. This is reinforced by shorter working weeks that accompany technological progress and productivity growth.

The entry of women into the labour market itself creates a demand for consumer durables to ease the strain of 'keeping house'.

HIGHER LIVING STANDARDS

	GROWTH IN REAL PERSONAL CONSUMPTION 1970–82
USA	+ 42%
UK	+ 26%
FRANCE	+ 60%
GERMANY	+ 34%
JAPAN	+ 65%

SOURCE: HENLEY CENTRE

Cultural Convergence

At the same time as demography is converging, television and motion pictures are creating elements of shared culture. And this cultural convergence is facilitating the establishment of multinational brand characters. The worldwide proliferation of the Marlboro brand would not have been possible without TV and motion picture education about the virile rugged character of the American West and the American cowboy – helped by increasing colour TV penetration in all countries.

Observers believe that cultural convergence will proceed at an accelerated rate through the next decade – particularly with the deployment of L-SAT high-power TV satellites throughout Europe.

EUROPE'S NEW SUPER STATIONS

These developments will reduce cultural barriers as countries exchange their media output through satellite networks – for the first time allowing viewers freer access to international television without the barrier of language.

Marketing Timetables

Analysis of all these demographic, cultural, and media trends is allowing manufacturers to define market expansion timetables. Essentially, marketers will be tracking trends which indicate when a region is ready for attack via programmes they have tested elsewhere.

For example, current changes in European laundry practices were foreshadowed by similar trends in the US during the late '60s and early '70s. Thus a US manufacturer of low-suds detergent would examine the growth in the penetration of front-loading washing machines in the UK to assess the ripening potential for his own product.

MARKET EXPANSION TIMETABLES

% OF HOUSEHOLDS OWNING FRONT LOADING WASHING MACHINES

SOURCE: COMPANY RESEARCH

Consider also Europe's soap powder manufacturers. Driven by improved washing machine technology and the increased popularity of relatively fragile synthetic and coloured fabrics, European laundry habits have converged. Every major nation now washes a majority of its wash loads in under 60°C water. This has created a common need for a product which performs well under these circumstances.

The result has been the marketing of single brands with a common brand name, product formulation, and positioning across the whole of Europe.

In the future, the only winners in cross-country branding will be companies who do a lot of things right and synthesise their efforts effectively around three golden rules:

1. To market clearly differentiated products that either drive, or capitalise on, real convergences in consumer habits and tastes.

2. To create a dedicated management value system that mirrors the vision of a pan-regional branded business.

3. To monitor their brands' character on a consistent, continuous, comparable basis across geography and over time.

The opportunity for world brands is there to be seized but only for those companies with the long-term determination to meet these stringent requirements.

Here are two other examples of the global approach in action – for British Airways and Procter & Gamble's Pampers. The Pampers brand was introduced in the US in the late 1960s. Pampers created the disposable diaper market by providing a product that was more convenient and more absorbent than cloth diapers at a price consumers were willing to pay. Pampers is now Procter & Gamble's largest brand and is sold on a similar strategy almost all over the world. If the Pampers business was a separate company, it would rank in the top one-third of the 'Fortune 500' list.

Does a global advertising campaign have to be bland? Not according to the South China Morning Post which described B.A.'s new worldwide campaign as *"unique and imaginative"*, or the Sydney Morning Herald – *"a radical departure from the usual formula"*, or Newsweek – *"a tour de force"*, or the Wall Street Journal – *"the most audacious attempt ever ... to run a new world campaign"* or the London Sunday Times – *"a flash of inspiration."*

The Agency is now working on a similar exercise on Silk Cut for American Brands/Gallaher – a Company whose marketing was recently described by the Financial Times as *"an object lesson for its competitors on the economics of brand discipline".*

65 OFFICES IN 38 COUNTRIES.

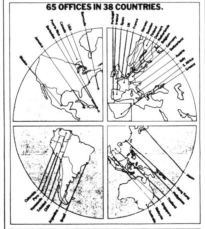

THE UK AGENCY WORKS WITH 6 OF BRITAIN'S TOP 10 ADVERTISERS.

THE US AGENCY HANDLES MORE No. 1 BRANDS THAN ANY OTHER AGENCY IN AMERICA.

THE INTERNATIONAL NETWORK WORKS WITH 44 OF THE WORLD'S TOP 200 ADVERTISERS.

Impact on Agency Structure

What are the implications of these trends for the advertising industry?

Business service companies, such as agencies, benefit from the increasing complexity of problems in their areas of expertise. Knowledge has value, and there is a greater 'value-added' during periods of turmoil and change in the business environment.

Most observers believe that the trend to pan regional or global marketing will have a marked impact on the structure of advertising agencies because world brands require world agencies.

A HANDFUL OF WORLDWIDE AGENCY NETWORKS WILL HANDLE THE BULK OF $125 bn WORLD ADVERTISING EXPENDITURE FOR MAJOR MULTINATIONALS.

Many expect to see the advertising industry moving in the same direction as accounting, banking, financial services, etc. – a polarization between worldwide networks servicing global corporations, and strong local firms handling domestic clients in their own country.

SOME OF THE AGENCY'S CLIENTS IN 3 OR MORE COUNTRIES

ALLIED LYONS	IBM
AMERICAN BRANDS	JOHNSON & JOHNSON
AMERICAN MOTORS	NABISCO BRANDS
AVIS	NESTLÉ
BLACK & DECKER	PEPSICO
BRITISH AIRWAYS	PROCTER & GAMBLE
BSN GERVAIS DANONE	PLAYTEX
CADBURY SCHWEPPES	ROWNTREE MACKINTOSH
CHESEBROUGH POND'S	TIMEX
DU PONT	UNITED BISCUITS

This is pleasant for the business prospects of those agencies who can serve this global requirement, but leaves open one important question – whether this trend will result in *better* advertising. On this question opinions differ.

Some agency managers are fond of saying that they would rather operate a solid, disciplined international network than run the best creative agency in the world.

Meantime, others declare that they would rather have high creative standards than succumb to the arthritis of international management structures.

Both these viewpoints ignore the possibility of combining discipline and creativity in one international organisation. This is because is it hard to do.

IN 1982, OUR UK AGENCY WON MORE TOP UK ADVERTISING AWARDS THAN ALL THE OTHER MAJOR MULTINATIONAL AGENCIES PUT TOGETHER.

SOURCE: GOLD AND SILVER AWARDS IN THE CAMPAIGN PRESS AWARDS, D&AD AND BRITISH TELEVISION ADVERTISING AWARDS.

The Company has always aimed to create the one type of agency which has somehow eluded the grasp of those few men and women who have tried to achieve it – a large agency, certainly, with all the stability that gives to employees, and all the backup that provides for clients – but one which at the same time also succeeds in being progressive, youthful and innovative in approach.

The fact that this combination has so rarely been achieved in our industry increases the sense of purpose with which we continue to pursue it as our goal.

This has been the fundamental spur to our growth over the years.

HIGH CREATIVITY ACROSS A DISCIPLINED WORLD NETWORK. THE COMPANY'S CONSISTENT STRATEGIC GOAL.

Last month Saatchi & Saatchi Company PLC, the parent company of the worldwide agency network, announced its results for the year ended September 30th 1983. It was the Company's 13th successive year of profit growth. In the year pre-tax profits rose by 103%, earnings per share by 40%, dividends per share by 45%.

Over the last five years the Company has shown a compound average growth of 43% in pre-tax profits, 33% for earnings per share, and 37% for dividends per share.

If you would like a copy of the Chairman's Statement on these results please write to the Company Secretary, Saatchi & Saatchi Company PLC, at 80 Charlotte Street, London W1A 1AQ, or 625 Madison Avenue, New York, New York 10022.

SAATCHI & SAATCHI
COMPTON WORLDWIDE.

The system described above varied somewhat from one country to another. BA country managers and their local agencies in the five most important long-haul markets (United States, Canada, Australia, South Africa, and Japan) had slightly more autonomy than their counterparts in less important markets. Although all advertising had to be approved in London prior to use, finished copy could be developed in the local market by the local agency in conjunction with the BA country manager.

An early example of how commercials might be developed for use in more than one country under the S&S approach occurred at the end of 1982. The U.S. country manager developed an advertising proposal for the "Inbound" line of package tours from the U.S. to the United Kingdom. Members of the agency creative team in the United States and BA executives from New York came to London to develop proposed scripts for the commercials. These were then approved by the U.S. country manager, but the commercials were shot in the United Kingdom so that British scenery could be included. These same commercials were subsequently used in South Africa and the Caribbean with different voiceovers; these countries' budgets could not be stretched to fund their independent production of television commercials of this quality.

Meanwhile, organization changes occurred at BA. Following the appointment of Mr. Colin Marshall as managing director in February 1983, the three divisions were replaced by eight geographic market centers that handled BA's basic passenger business and three additional business units handling cargo, air charter services, and package tours. These eleven profit centers reported to Mr. Marshall through Mr. Jim Harris, marketing director.[6] Mr. Harris also supervised a central marketing services staff involved with strategic planning, advertising, market analysis, and market research. An advertising manager who reported to the general manager for marketing services was responsible for agency relations and for the review and implementation of advertising by BA country managers. One of his assistants handled relations with the United Kingdom and European country managers; a second handled relations with the remaining country managers.

Under this new organization, BA country managers submitted their annual marketing plans, including proposed advertising and promotion budgets, to the appropriate market center manager in London. The country managers were informed in 1983 that their future budget proposals would have to provide detailed objectives and research support. In particular, country managers would have to forecast how their overall sales and profits would be impacted by particular advertising and promotion programs. The total advertising budget would be allocated among the country managers according to the quality of the proposals and according to which markets were designated for maintenance or development spending levels.

If a country manager required additional advertising funds during the fiscal year or wished to offer special consumer price deals and travel agency commissions above the norm applicable to the countries in his or her market center, he or she could apply to the market center manager in London. The marketing director held a reserve fund to deal with such contingencies and reserved the right to reallocate

[6]The marketing director performed the tasks previously undertaken by the commercial director. The latter title was no longer used.

funds designated for one market to another during the fiscal year if, for example, foreign currency fluctuations altered the attractiveness of one market versus another as a holiday destination.

Development of the Concept Campaign

The S&S creative team was charged with developing an advertising campaign that would restore BA's image and prestige, and not necessarily by focusing on specific BA products, services, and price promotions. The agency described the qualities of the ideal advertising concept for the campaign: "It had to be simple and single-minded, dramatic and break new ground, instantly understood throughout the world, visual rather than verbal, long-lasting, likeable, and confident." S&S executives believed that the type of product-feature-based advertising used by BA and traditional in the airline industry could not satisfy these objectives. First, an airline competitor could easily match any product-based claim BA might make. Second, such advertising only impacted that portion of the target market who viewed the benefit on which superiority was claimed (e.g., seat width) to be particularly important. The agency believed that only a brand concept campaign could focus consumers on the permanent and essential characteristics of BA that transcended changes in product, competitive activity, and other market variables.

The agency established the following five objectives for the worldwide BA concept campaign:

- To project BA as the worldwide leader in air travel.
- To establish BA as the world's most successful airline.
- To demonstrate the superiority of BA products.
- To add value in the eyes of passengers across the whole range of BA products.
- To develop a distinctive, contemporary, and fashionable style for this airline.

The account team had the benefit of consumer research that S&S had conducted in July 1982 with business and pleasure travelers in the U.K., United States, France, Germany, and Hong Kong to better understand attitudes towards and preferences for particular airlines. Based on these data, S&S executives concluded that consumers perceived most major airlines as similar on a wide array of dimensions. To the extent differences existed, BA was viewed as a large, experienced airline using modern equipment. However, BA was rated poorly on friendliness, in-flight service, value for money, and punctuality. In addition, BA's image varied widely among markets; it was good in the United States, neutral in Germany, but weak in France and Hong Kong. The name of the airline and the lack of a strong image meant that consumer perceptions of its characteristics were often a reflection of their perceptions of Britain as a country.[7] BA was often the carrier of second choice after a consumer's national flag airline, particularly among consumers taking a vacation trip to the United Kingdom.

[7]In addition, some BA executives believed that BA was perceived more favorably in countries that had previously been served by BOAC than those previously served by BEA.

By November 1982, BA had developed in rough form a series of eleven television commercials around the theme "The world's favorite airline." The lead commercial of the concept campaign, known as "Manhattan Landing,"[8] was to be ninety-seconds long with no voiceover during the first 40 seconds and with a total of only 35 words of announcer copy. It would show the island of Manhattan rotating slowly through the sky across the Atlantic to London accompanied after 70 seconds by the statement that "every year, we fly more people across the Atlantic than the entire population of Manhattan."[9] Ten other commercials known as the "preference" series showed individuals (from an Ingrid Bergman look-alike in Casablanca to members of a U.S. football team) receiving airline tickets and being disappointed to find that they were not booked on BA. International celebrities such as Peter O'Toole, Omar Sharif, and Joan Collins were shown at the end of each commercial checking in for a BA flight. The announcer copy for all the preference commercials was identical. Storyboards for Manhattan Landing and one of the preference commercials are presented as Exhibits 7.5 and 7.6. The intention was to air these commercials in all BA markets worldwide with changes only in the voiceovers.

EXHIBIT 7.5 **Manhattan landing storyboard**

In November, the BA board of directors approved production of Manhattan Landing and three of the preference commercials. Production costs for these four commercials were estimated at £1 million.[10] S&S executives were asked to have the

---

[8]The Manhattan Landing commercial was originally conceived as a corporate advertisement to be shown exclusively in the United Kingdom to support BA's privatization effort. When it became clear that the offering of BA stock to the public would be delayed until at least the end of 1984, it was decided to include it in the worldwide concept campaign.

[9]BA flew 1.5 million passengers across the Atlantic to the United Kingdom in 1982–83, more than Pan Am and TWA combined. The population of Manhattan was 1.4 million.

[10]Recent BA television commercials had cost about £75,000 to produce.

MUSIC: "AS TIME GOES BY".

V.O.
Oh the disappointment when you find you're not booked on your favourite airline.

British Airways fly more people to more countries than anyone else.

It's the world's favourite airline.

British airways

EXHIBIT 7.6 **Casablanca preference campaign storyboard**

finished commercials ready for launch by April 1983, a very tight schedule given the complexity of the executions.

While the commercials were being produced, members of the S&S account team and BA headquarters advertising executives traveled to each BA market. Their purpose was to introduce and explain the worldwide concept campaign at meetings attended by each BA country manager and his or her staff along with representatives of the local BA advertising agency. These visits occurred during January and February 1983 and involved the presentation of storyboards rather than finished commercials.

Reactions to the Concept Campaign

Reactions varied. The concept campaign was well received in the United States, although the BA country manager was concerned about its dissimilarity from the existing Robert Morley campaign, which emphasized traditional British values. In India, there was some questions as to whether Manhattan would hold any significance for the local audience. In other countries, including former British colonies, the claim "the world's favorite airline" was met with reactions such as "you must be joking!" The claim seemed to lack credibility particularly in those markets where BA was in a relatively weak share position versus the national flag carrier. In other markets, such as France and Kuwait, only the state-owned airline was allowed to advertise on television, so the BA concept commercials could only be used in cinema advertising.

Questions about the proposed campaign were also raised by S&S affiliates. Since the parent agency had built its reputation on the importance of developing clear-cut positioning concepts, the proposed commercials seemed inconsistent with the philosophy of the agency. Even though the preference commercials were each planned to be 60-seconds long, some agency executives argued that they were too cluttered and tried to achieve too many objectives.

In particular, the 90-second Manhattan Landing commercial was greeted by some with amazement. One agency executive commented: "The net impact of three 30-second commercials would surely be greater?" The South African agency requested a 60-second version of the commercial because the South African Broadcasting Company would not sell a 90-second piece of commercial time. S&S management had to decide whether to accommodate this request.

Other BA country managers were concerned that the concept campaign would reduce the funds available for local tactical advertising presenting fare and schedule information specific to their particular markets. One BA manager, after seeing the proposed campaign commented, "Where are the smiling girls, the free cocktails, and the planes taking off into the sunset?" Another asked, "Will this campaign sell seats?" The BA proposal to spend half of the worldwide 1983–84 advertising budget of £26 million on the concept campaign meant that the amount available for local tactical advertising would fall from £19 million to £12 million. Preliminary BA concept and tactical advertising budgets for fourteen representatives countries are presented in Exhibit 7.7. Partly in response to the country managers' concerns, the total budget was raised to £31 million in April when BA's 1982–83 operating results were known. Forty percent of the new budget was allocated to the worldwide concept campaign, 60 percent to tactical local market advertising.

EXHIBIT 7.7 British Airways concept and tactical advertising budgets: Initial 1983–84 plan (In thousands)

	Concept campaign			Tactical campaigns	Row total
	Apr.–Sep.	Oct.–Mar.	Total		
United Kingdom	£ 4,700	£1,200	£ 5,900	£ 3,200	£ 9,100
United States	2,600	750	3,350	2,450	5,800
Germany	450	450	900	607	1,507
Australia	500	100	600	350	950
France	150	200	350	269	619
Japan/Korea	200	70	270	400	670
Gulf States	0	35	35	190	225
Canada	900	200	1,100	400	1,500
South Africa	300	75	375	250	625
Italy	150	100	250	225	475
New Zealand	100	0	100	100	200
Egypt	50	0	50	30	80
Zimbabwe	32	0	32	25	57
Trinidad	18	0	18	27	45
Other	n/a	n/a	860	3,220*	4,080
Total	£10,150	£3,180	£14,190	£11,740	£25,930

*Includes contingency fund.

Some country managers complained that their control over advertising would be reduced and that a corporate advertising expenditure in which they had no say would be charged against their profits. BA headquarters executives responded that while the country managers were required in 1983-84 to spend 40 percent of their budgets against the concept campaign, they were free to determine the media allocation of concept campaign expenditures in their markets and the weight of exposures given to each of the four executions. They were also free to spend more than 40 percent of their budgets on the concept campaign if they wished.

Despite such concessions, the Japanese country manager remained adamantly opposed to adopting the concept campaign. On the London-Tokyo route, Japan Air Lines held a 60 percent market share compared to BA's 40 percent. Of the traffic on the route, 80 percent originated in Japan, and 80 percent of those on board BA flights were tourists on package tours. The Japanese country manager rejected the concept campaign as inappropriate. He presented market research evidence showing that his main challenge was selling Britain as a destination rather than developing consumer preference for BA.

The April 10 Launch

Some S&S executives had hoped that BA would commit almost all of its 1983-84 advertising budget to the concept campaign. However, local marketing requirements highlighted by the country managers necessitated the continuation of tactical advertising, albeit at a reduced rate. The logo and slogan from the concept campaign were, however, to be incorporated in BA tactical advertising and the requirement that tactical creative copy be developed by S&S in London ensured that this would be the case.

Despite all the reservations they had encountered, BA and S&S executives in London felt that they had sold the campaign effectively to most of the BA country managers. Thus, an invitation was mailed by Lord King to all BA employees in the United Kingdom to view the introductory television commercial on April 10. Videocassette copies of this six-minute commercial were mailed to BA offices around the world. BA country managers invited representatives of the travel industry to attend preview parties timed to coincide with the launch of the new concept campaign in their respective countries.

The campaign was launched in the United Kingdom on April 10 as planned and, within two weeks, was being aired in twenty countries. For two reasons, a few country managers adopted a "wait and see" attitude. First, the marketing of package tours for the summer season had already started in the northern hemisphere. Second, many country managers had exhausted their 1982-83 advertising budgets by the end of January, with the result that consumers had not been exposed to any BA advertising for several months.

The Concept Campaign in the United States

The United States was one of the countries in which the concept campaign was launched on April 10. The BA country manager welcomed the campaign since consumer research indicated that BA's size was not recognized by most consumers in a country where, for many, bigger meant better. When asked to name the airline that carried the most passengers to the United Kingdom, more respondents cited Pan Am and TWA than BA. The results of the survey, conducted in New York and Los Angeles in March 1983 showed the following:

- Unaided awareness of BA as a leading international carrier was 41 percent in New York (Pan Am—85 percent; TWA—74 percent) and 33 percent in Los Angeles (Pan Am—76 percent; TWA—74 percent).
- Unaided recall of BA advertising was 21 percent in New York and 17 percent in Los Angeles.
- BA was mentioned as one of the three largest airlines in the world by 15 percent of New York respondents and by 13 percent of Los Angeles respondents.
- BA was mentioned as one of the three best international carriers by 11 percent of New York respondents and by 9 percent of Los Angeles respondents.

The BA country manager viewed the concept campaign as a means of addressing some of these deficiencies. Since the claim "the world's favorite airline"

EXHIBIT 7.8 **Media budget and schedule of British Airways U.S. concept/brand campaign**

	April–June 1983		Sept.–Oct. 1983	
	Number spots	**Expenditures (In thousands)**	**Number spots**	**Expenditures (In thousands)**
Spot television (in 6 gateway markets)*	686	$2,900	175	$572
Newtwork television**	4	1,040	—	—
Cable television	40	104	25	58
Total	730	$4,044	200	$630
Reach/Frequency				
Gateway cities	86%/8.7 times		63%/3.3 times	
Remainder of U.S.	45%/1.2 times		—	

Audience composition	**Percent reached**	**Index***
Adult men	48	102
Adult women	52	99
Age 25–54	73	137
Household income $30,000+	47	169

*New York, Washington, Boston, Miami, Chicago and Los Angeles.

**Only the Manhattan Landing execution was shown on network television. It was targeted at the 78% of U.S. households not reached by the spot television advertising.

***Each index figure represents the percentage degree to which the audience reached included more or fewer people than the U.S. population at large.

was well-documented, the U. S. country manager did not anticipate a legal challenge from Eastern Airlines that used the slogan "America's favorite way to fly."

The media plan for the concept campaign (Exhibit 7.8) called for a combination of spot television in BA's six key gateway cities, national network television, and commercials on Cable News Network. The Manhattan Landing commercial was scheduled to be shown four times on national network television. Management argued that this would provide BA with exposure in important markets near gateway cities and would also excite the BA sales force and the travel industry. Four exposures were deemed sufficient given the commercial's creative originality. They would reach 45 percent of the U. S. adult population an average of 1.2 times.

The budget for the concept campaign from April to June was $4 million. Nevertheless, during this period, the BA country manager expected to be outspent by Pan Am and TWA in BA gateway cities. In 1982-83, Pan Am and TWA advertising expenditures for domestic and international routes combined approximated $65 million and $50 million respectively.

In addition to the concept campaign, the BA country manager had also developed a business campaign and a leisure campaign for 1983-84.

Business Campaign. Recent consumer research indicated that Pan Am and TWA were perceived as superior to BA on attributes important to business flyers. BA advertising directed at business people had not significantly improved these perceptions (BA and TWA advertisements targeting the business traveler are presented in Exhibits 7.9 and 7.10). However, the perceptions of BA among its business passengers were much more positive than those of non-BA passengers, indicating significant customer satisfaction. BA's U.S. marketing director concluded that BA had a substantial opportunity to increase its share of the transatlantic business travel market.

The following three objectives were established for the 1983-84 business advertising campaign:

1. Increase awareness of the name "Super Club" as a service comparable to or better than TWA's Ambassador Class and Pan Am's Clipper Class.
2. Increase the business traveler's awareness and knowledge of the features of all three BA business travel services—Concorde, First Class, and Super Club.
3. Maximize the "halo" benefits of BA's Concorde in marketing efforts directed at First Class and Super Club consumers.

The media schedule for the business campaign (Exhibit 7.11) emphasized national magazines and both national and local newspapers. Magazines were selected which had higher than average percentages of readers in BA's gateway cities. Newspapers with strong business sections were given preference.

Leisure Campaign. BA advertising targeting the leisure traveler had traditionally focused on BA's hotel, car rental, and package tour bargains. Despite high

CUT HERE for Pan Am's 18½"
Clipper Class seat.

CUT HERE for TWA's 20⅞"
Ambassador Class seat.

WORLD'S WIDEST AIRLINE SEAT CUTS OTHER AIRLINES DOWN TO SIZE.

British Airways Super Clubˣ
When you're travelling on business, we offer you the widest seats in the air. We give you 24 inches between armrests — more room than TWA or Pan Am!* You'll always be next to an aisle or a window, and you have almost a foot of work space between you and the next passenger.

American Airlines AAdvantageˣ **Program**
Show us your number at check-in and your flight miles on British Airways between the U.S. and London will count towards your AAdvantage travel award plan.

First Class Comfort
Lean back in luxury in our sumptuous First Class, with its sleeperseats and impeccable British service.

The Ultimate: Concorde
If you want to reach London in half the usual time, there's only one way — our Supersonic Concorde.

It's no wonder that British Airways fly more people to more countries than anyone else. After all, we're the World's Favourite Airline. Call your travel agent or corporate travel department.

British airways
The World's Favourite Airline™

*Measurements are inside armrest to inside armrest. British Airways has a few Super Club seats only 22" wide due to structural requirements. However, all Super Club seats are wider than our competitors'

EXHIBIT 7.9 **British Airways business campaign magazine advertisement**

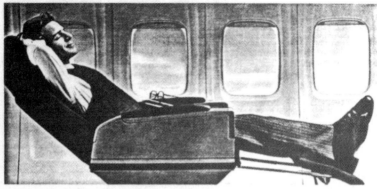

EXHIBIT 7.10 **TWA business segment magazine advertisement**

consumer recall of these "bolt-on" features, consumer perception research indicated that BA lagged its competitors on attributes such as "good value for money" and "good deal for leisure travelers." Accordingly, BA's advertising agency suggested that these bolt-on features be subordinated to the objective of creating a general impression of value for money through advertising an airfare bargain along with BA's expertise in things British.

EXHIBIT 7.11 **Media budget and schedule of British Airways business campaign in the United States**

	Dec. 1982–March 1983*		April–June 1983		Sept.–Oct. 1983	
	Number insertions	Expenditures (In thousands)	Number insertions	Expenditures (In thousands)	Number insertions	Expenditures (In thousands)
22 Magazines	8	$121	30	$745	22	$674
3 Newspapers (Wall Street Journal, New York Times, Los Angeles Times)	9	563	13	371	17	276
	17	$684	43	$1,116	39	$950
Reach/frequency: men 25–54						
Gateway cities			73%/7.4 times**		65%/5.4 times	
Remainder of United States			67%/6.3 times		55%/3.5 times	

Audience composition	Percent reached planning foreign travel for business	Index
Adult men***	72	147
Age 25–54	69	126
Attended/graduated college	64	197
Household income $35,000+	55	284

*No insertions prior to February 1983.
**Figures are for December 1982 through June 1983.
***In 1982–83, about 10% of transatlantic business travelers were women.

The objectives for the 1983 summer campaign were to:

1. Capitalize on BA's reputation as a marketer of good vacation buys, reinforcing consumers' willingness to arrange their European vacations with BA.
2. Promote awareness of and demand for BA's summer transatlantic leisure-oriented fare of $549 round trip.

A BA summer campaign newspaper advertisement and a Pan Am advertisement targeting the leisure traveler are reproduced in Exhibits 7.12 and 7.13. BA executives were planning on developing print advertisements targeting the leisure market that would mirror the commercials in the concept campaign if it proved successful.

The media schedule for the leisure campaign (Exhibit 7.14) emphasized spot television and the travel sections of local newspapers. Their late advertising deadlines meant that fare changes could be quickly communicated to consumers.

EXHIBIT 7.12 **British Airways leisure segment print advertisement**

EXHIBIT 7.13 **Pan Am leisure segment print advertisement**

EXHIBIT 7.14 **Media budget and schedule for British Airways U.S. leisure campaign**

| | Dec. 1982–March 1983 | | April–June 1983 | | Sept.–Oct. 1983 | |
	Number of spots, insertions	Expenditures (In thousands)	Number of spots, insertions	Expenditures (In thousands)	Number of spots, insertions	Expenditures (In thousands)
Spot television (10 markets)	—	—	450	$795	—	—
Local newspapers (11 markets)	3–4/market	$641	3–7/market	$620	4–6/market	$550
Reach/frequency: adults 25–54 Average market	40%/2.0 times		75%/5.0 times		47%/2.9 times	

Audience composition	Reach to those planning foreign vacations (In percent)	Index
Adult men	45	96
Adult women	55	105
Age 25–54	60	114
Household income $30,000+	49	175

CONCLUSION

As BA and S&S executives implemented the worldwide concept campaign and the biggest advertising effort in BA history, they contemplated several issues. First, if awareness, recall, and sales data indicated that the campaign was not having the desired impact in a particular market, would BA headquarters permit the country manager to curtail the concept campaign? Second, if the campaign was successful, how long could it be sustained before becoming "tired?"

A third issue was how competitive airlines would respond to the BA concept campaign. Believing that the major carriers wished to avoid a new worldwide competitive price war, BA executives believed that they would adopt a "wait and see" attitude. However, market share losses would make retaliation inevitable, particularly in markets like the Far East where Singapore Airlines and Cathay Pacific held high market shares and were extremely price-competitive. In such a situation, should BA steadfastly continue to spend 40 percent of its advertising budget on the concept campaign or should some of these funds be diverted to tactical advertising in particular local markets? The probability of such diversion of funds depended partly on the emerging profit picture during the fiscal year and partly on the level of unspent tactical advertising funds. It was, therefore, more likely to become an issue towards the end of the fiscal year.

A further related issue was the appropriate budget split between the concept campaign and tactical advertising in 1984–85. Some BA executives argued that if the concept campaign were successful, it would be possible to reduce expenditures on the campaign to a maintenance level and proportionately restore tactical advertising. They maintained that such a move would shift control of the advertising budget from S&S back to BA. But agency executives argued strongly that the concept campaign should be centrally administered from BA headquarters and that expenditures on the campaign in each country should not, unlike tactical advertising, be regarded as a routine operating cost. They also argued that the concept campaign was essential to BA's long-term effectiveness and should not be sacrificed to short-term operational requirements.

CASE 8

AmSouth Bancorporation: Positioned for Growth

John W. Woods, Chairman of the Board and Chief Executive Officer of AmSouth Bancorporation, reflected upon AmSouth's development and the recent changes in the banking industry as he watched construction of the new thirty-one-story AmSouth/Harbert Plaza from his office window. Woods thought it ironic that the new $140 million AmSouth Bancorporation headquarters building would project stability, yet, the future of banking in Alabama had never before been so volatile. He believed that it was only a matter of time until a number of Alabama banks would be acquired by large regional banks from outside the state.

AmSouth Bancorporation, headquartered in Birmingham, Alabama, was the state's largest banking institution, with assets over $5.9 billion. Its principal subsidiary, AmSouth Bank N.A., served Alabama through more than 140 full-service banking offices. In 1987, AmSouth Bancorporation had nearly 5,000 employees and was the only bank holding company in Alabama to be listed on the New York Stock Exchange.

Over the last fifteen years, CEO Woods had directed AmSouth's aggressive growth within Alabama and had positioned AmSouth to be a buyer of out-of-state banks. In order to continue being a leader in the banking industry, Woods believed that AmSouth had to maintain an aggressive growth position. Yet, Woods realized that AmSouth could not take the position that the bank was not for sale at any price. AmSouth was publicly owned, and management had to listen to any proposition that would benefit the shareholders.

THE DEVELOPMENT OF AMSOUTH

AmSouth traces its history back to 1872, a year after the city of Birmingham (named after the steel city in England), was incorporated. Captain Charles Linn, a Swedish immigrant, recognized the city's growth potential and together with six other locally prominent businessmen, organized the first bank—the National Bank of Birmingham. In 1881, the City Bank of Birmingham and the National Bank of Birmingham merged to become the First National Bank of Birmingham, with combined deposits of $750,000.

This case was prepared by Peter M. Ginter and Linda E. Swayne from materials developed in a student project by Judi Ciza, Scott Crain, Trisha Powell, Robert Rastello, Barney Trammell, and Scott Woods as a basis for classroom discussion rather than to illustrate effective or ineffective handling of an administrative situation. Used by permission from Peter M. Ginter.

Structuring for Growth

During its first 100 years, the First National Bank became the leading bank in Birmingham, the financial and commercial center of Alabama. Additional details concerning First National's development are presented in Exhibit 8.1. In December 1970, revisions of the Alabama Bank Holding Company Act were signed into law and the shareholders of the First National Bank of Birmingham overwhelmingly approved the formation of a holding company to be called Alabama Bancorporation.

With First National as the lead bank, Alabama Bancorporation developed rapidly into the state's largest and strongest multibank holding company. Within ten years, the holding company included 20 affiliate banks which operated more than 100 offices throughout Alabama.

Also during the 1970s, Alabama Bancorporation took steps toward diversification into bank-related areas by acquiring the Engel Mortgage Company and organizing the Alabama Financial Corporation. Both subsidiaries were headquartered in Birmingham and operated throughout the Southeast.

Engel Mortgage Company, a wholly owned subsidiary, specialized in single family, commercial, and income producing properties. This acquisition of a non-banking affiliate supplemented lending activity into five southern states. The newly formed Alabama Financial Corporation provided specialized financial services in real estate lending, equipment leasing, second mortgage loans, and receivables and inventory loans throughout the Southeast.

AmSouth Bancorporation in the 1980s

In 1981, Alabama Bancorporation's shareholders voted to change the institution's name to AmSouth Bancorporation. The new name was adopted in order to imply that the corporation had regional influence rather than just being limited to Alabama. In 1983, the First National Bank of Birmingham (the major bank affiliate of AmSouth Bancorporation) changed its name to AmSouth Bank N.A. and merged all the affiliate banks into one bank. Engle Mortgage Company changed its name to AmSouth Mortgage Company, Inc.

AmSouth's management adopted this centralized philosophy in order to achieve greater operational/managerial efficiency and to develop a more positive image. They further believed this structure would enable AmSouth to be more competitive and to deliver standardized banking products to all of their markets.

MARKETING STRATEGY

AmSouth's marketing is typical of the banking industry as a whole. Few banks have successfully targeted one segment in the marketplace. Most banks try to develop products for all segments in the market. AmSouth's marketing strategy has been to serve the entire market, however, the company has identified three primary

EXHIBIT 8.1 **Summary of AmSouth's history**

1871	The city of Birmingham founded
1872	National Bank of Birmingham formed by Capt. Charles Linn
1873	National Bank opened for business on January 2nd
	Moved into the first permanent home; a three-story building
1884	Merged with two-year-old City Bank of Birmingham to become The First National Bank of Birmingham
1890	First bank in Alabama to reach total deposits of over $1 million
1902	Berney National Bank of Birmingham merged with First National
1904	Moved into new permanent home; a ten-story building
1905	Deposits totaled a record $4 million
	First National represented over 14% of the state's total deposits
1915	Deposits totaled a record $9 million
1929	Crash on Wall Street in October began a nationwide depression
1930	American Traders Bank merged with First National to bring combined deposits to $72 million
1933	Forced to shut doors when President Franklin D. Roosevelt declared a banking holiday
	General Persons, president of First National, instigated a bill to permit branch banking in Jefferson County (Birmingham)
	Six suburban banks merged with First National to form Birmingham's first branch banking system
1946	Introduced the new convenience of drive-in tellers
1960	Computers introduced
1968	First National began to research the idea of establishing a multibank holding company
1970	Bank Holding Company Act signed into law
1971	The First National/Southern Natural Gas Building completed
	Acquired Engel Mortgage Company and organized Alabama Financial Corporation
1972	Formation of Alabama Bancorporation multibank holding company
	First National Bank of Birmingham became the first affiliate, followed by American National Bank, The Trust Company of Mobile, and the First National Bank of Decatur
1981	Legislation passed to allow Alabama banks to merge across county lines
	Alabama Bancorporation consolidated and changed its name to AmSouth Bancorporation
1983	First National Bank of Birmingham became the first affiliate to change its name to AmSouth Bank N.A.
	All affiliates changed their names and merged with AmSouth to become AmSouth bank branches
1984	Total assets reached a record $4 billion
1985	Merger with FirstGulf Bancorporation in Mobile
1986	ALERT system made available to all federally insured Alabama depository institutions
	Alabama passed interstate banking bill
1987	Merged with First Tuskaloosa (Alabama)
	Interstate banking bill becomes effective July 1, 1987
	Merged with First Mutual—the first interstate acquisition

EXHIBIT 8.2 **AmSouth customer segmentation**

Mass Middle Base
Age: 18 to 30
Income: $0–$25,000
Education: Some college

Emerging Affluent
Age: 30 to 45
Income: $25,000–$50,000
Education: College graduate

Affluent Base
Age: 45 to 65
Income: $50,000+
Education: College graduate
some post-graduate work

---

segments—the Mass Middle Base, the Emerging Affluent Base, and the Affluent Base. Demographic profiles of these segments are presented in Exhibit 8.2.

Geographic Markets Served

In 1987, AmSouth Bank had 142 branches located in 23 of Alabama's 67 counties. In 1987, AmSouth ranked first, second, or third in market share in 17 counties. Approximately 75 percent of AmSouth's deposits were in the major markets of Birmingham, Mobile, Huntsville, and Montgomery. These four areas contained 36 percent of the state's population and 42 percent of its total income.

AmSouth's banking network is divided into four geographic regions, with each region headed by a regional executive assisted by various support personnel. The regions, counties served, and major markets are shown in Exhibit 8.3.

Products

In attempting to serve their market segments, AmSouth has developed literally hundreds of products. The products are grouped around consumer checking and commercial checking, savings, and loans. AmSouth categorizes its services into eleven product groups as shown in Exhibit 8.4. Many of these products were targeted for different market segments as shown in Exhibit 8.5.

A major product within several categories was loans. In 1987, approximately 50 percent of the loans had been directed to commercial, financial, and agricultural concerns; while real estate loans (both short-term construction and long-term mortgage) represented approximately 30 percent of the outstanding loan balance; the

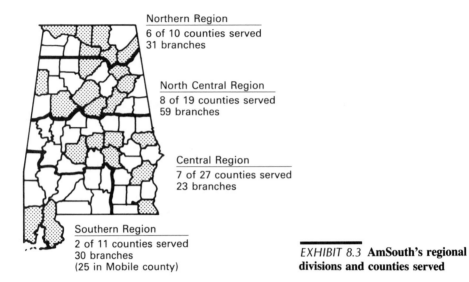

Northern Region
6 of 10 counties served
31 branches

North Central Region
8 of 19 counties served
59 branches

Central Region
7 of 27 counties served
23 branches

Southern Region
2 of 11 counties served
30 branches
(25 in Mobile county)

EXHIBIT 8.3 **AmSouth's regional divisions and counties served**

EXHIBIT 8.4 **Categories of AmSouth's products**

Retail Transaction Services—offers four types of checking accounts, ATM, telephone banking, and direct deposit.

Retail Savings and Investment Services—offers customer savings accounts, money market investment accounts, certificate of deposit accounts, time deposit accounts, safe deposit boxes, individual retirement accounts, and discount brokerage services.

Retail Credit Services—consumer single-payment loans, consumer installment loans, revolving credit services, executive line of credit services, equity line of credit services, educational loans, adjustable-rate first mortgages, and home equity loans.

Personal Financial Services—a package of services containing checking, telephone banking, and others.

Bond Department Services—a broad range of taxable and tax-free investment opportunities for individual, corporate, and correspondent customers.

Business Deposit Services—checking accounts, savings accounts, and investment accounts for businesses.

Commercial Lending Services—tax-free lending, commercial real estate loans, commercial construction loans, residential construction loans, and other commercial services to aid in the smooth operation of a business.

International Banking Services—import and export lines of credit, foreign collections, and foreign exchange for businesses that either import, export, are multinational, or are foreign owned.

Correspondent Banking Services—services performed for other banks such as data processing and item processing.

Cash Management Services—lock box services, direct deposit, and payroll services.

Trust Services—all types of trusts, individual investment management, and natural resource management services.

EXHIBIT 8.5 **Product target markets**

Mass middle	Emerging affluent	Affluent
Regular checking	N.O.W. accounts	Personal financial
Check-for-less	Money market	services
Bonus banking	checking	Retail time deposit
62 and Over	Asset management	investments
Statement savings	account	Individual retirement
Passbook savings	Home equity loans	accounts
Investment savings	Consumer single pay	Executive line of credit
MasterCard	loans	Equity line of credit
VISA	Adjustable rate	AmSouth brokerage
Consumer installment	mortgages	services
loans	American Express	Tax-free agency
Telephone bill payment	Goldcard	account
William Teller Network	Traveler's checks	Safe-deposit box
Money orders		Third-party investments
Cashier's checks		Mutual funds
		Unit trusts
		Financial planning

remaining 20 percent consisted of consumer installment loans. These percentages were similar to the loan composition of AmSouth's major competitors in Alabama.

Promotion

AmSouth's management believed that in the highly competitive banking environment of the 1980s, promotion emerged as the most important element of the marketing mix. AmSouth executives realized that they must become more marketing oriented to be competitive. In 1987, AmSouth spent 43 percent of its promotional budget on newspaper advertising. These advertisements were placed primarily in the business section and were directed toward the affluent market. Copy in the advertisements generally revolved around price competition (interest rates) and image advertising. See Exhibit 8.6 for AmSouth's advertising budget media allocation and an example newspaper advertisement.

Throughout the 1980s, AmSouth was very concerned about the image they conveyed to the public. Thomas M. McCulley, Senior Vice President of Marketing, indicated that AmSouth's competitive advantage was "professionalism, and the way we do business." AmSouth's image in Birmingham was one of a banking leader —secure, courteous, strong, profitable, and convenient. This image, however, was not always the case in other parts of the state. Sometimes others viewed AmSouth as an impersonal "Birmingham" bank.

EXHIBIT 8.6 **Advertising budget media allocation**

Newspaper	43%
Television	37%
Outdoor	11%
Magazine	8%
Radio	1%

Sample Newspaper Ad

Look What We're Up To Now.

Fixed Rate
24-Month Or Longer CD

8%

For A Limited Time.

Now, for a limited time only, AmSouth is offering a
very special rate on our 24-Month Fixed Rate CD. So call today and ask about it.
But hurry. At this rate, we can't keep it up forever.

AMSOUTH®
For Your Growing Needs.

Rate quoted is annual rate of simple interest and is subject to change daily. Please call for current rate information. This CD requires a minimum deposit of $500. A substantial interest penalty is required for early withdrawal and this offer is not available to financial institutions. © 1987 AmSouth Bank N.A. Member FDIC.

Customer Service

Another element of promotion that AmSouth emphasized was customer service. Every employee went through a customer service training program in which they were taught about AmSouth's products and how to be friendly and courteous to the customer. AmSouth followed up this training program by sending people into branches to act as customers to see how well the training worked. In addition, AmSouth gave a customer service award each month that recognized employees who exhibited outstanding customer service. Cash bonuses and vacations accompanied the recognition.

AMSOUTH'S OPERATIONS AND ORGANIZATION

AmSouth's Operation Center served as a central processing unit for all information of the bank. Daily transactions and other data were shipped to the center via various modes of transportation and were processed and redistributed. Stan Bailey, head of the Operations Center, indicated that the company pursued a manufacturing approach in dealing with the large quantities of information. All information was shipped daily to the Operations Center by car, truck, airplane, and in some instances, by telephone lines. When the data arrived, it was treated as raw material. The information was sorted, checked for validity, and captured on file. At the end of each day, the information was converted into a finished product and redistributed.

In order to handle the information—over 2 million items per day—AmSouth initiated a "generation upgrade" in 1987, focusing on building an integrated information processing system. The main component of this upgrade was a newly acquired IBM "Sierra class" mainframe computer, which doubled AmSouth's computing capacity.

Organization

AmSouth was organized on a functional basis that divided the state into regions and the overall responsibilities for the bank's services into specialized divisions. Service delivery systems included those areas of the bank having direct customer contact: Corporate Banking, Retail Banking, and Bond and Trust. Other divisions and departments including Operations, Corporate Services, Personnel, the Comptroller's Group, Marketing, and Regional Banking, provided the planning, manpower, controls, and strategies that supported the product-related divisions and coordinated the bank's overall performance. AmSouth's organization structure is presented in Exhibit 8.7.

AMSOUTH'S FINANCIAL CONDITION

In 1987, AmSouth Bank was the pre-eminent financial institution in Alabama. AmSouth's Statement of Condition and Statement of Income are presented in Exhibits 8.8 and 8.9. AmSouth's net income after tax ranged from $37.4 million in 1984 to $61.0 million in 1986. This increase in net income was achieved on revenues that grew from $391.1 million in 1984 to $431.6 million in 1986. Profits increased at a rate almost double that of the growth experienced in revenue. The majority of the growth occurred after 1985.

Bank profitability is also measured through return on average assets (ROAA) and return on average equity (ROAE). AmSouth Bank's return on average assets increased to 1.17 percent in 1986 from a 1984 low of .95 percent. AmSouth historically performed at or above the average level of performance of this measure relative to other banks operating in the Southeast. The bank's return on average equity also increased to 16.64 percent from a 1983 low of 13.60 percent. The equity-to-asset ratio of AmSouth Bank declined from a high of 7.73 percent at the end of 1982 to 6.49 percent at the end of 1986.

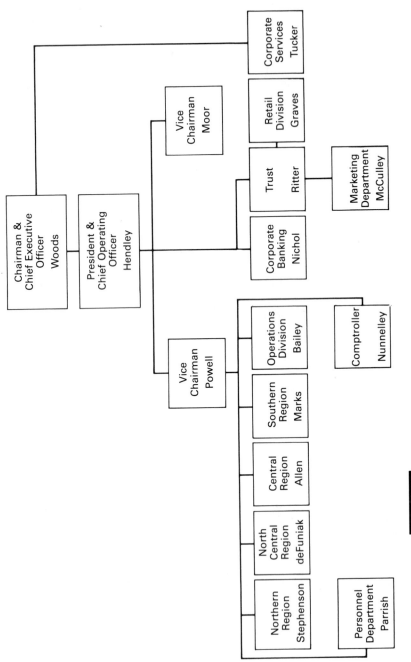

EXHIBIT 8.7 **AmSouth Bancorporation, AmSouth Bank N.A. top management**

EXHIBIT 8.8 **Consolidated statement of condition—AmSouth Bancorporation and subsidiaries**

	1985	1986
	(In thousands)	
Assets		
Cash and due from banks	$ 450,177	$ 442,656
Earning assets:		
Time deposits in other banks	1,203	0
Federal funds sold and securities purchased under agreements to resell	129,875	4,225
Trading account securities	21,915	44,333
Investment securities (market value of $1,224,855,000 and $916,459,000, respectively)	928,173	1,201,914
Loans	3,443,586	3,928,461
Less: Allowance for loan losses	47,135	52,904
Unearned income	67,178	56,855
Net loans	3,329,273	3,818,702
Total earning assets	4,410,439	5,069,174
Premises and equipment, net	111,729	107,761
Customers' acceptance liability	71,293	102,815
Accrued interest receivable and other assets	183,404	220,300
	$5,227,042	$5,942,706
Liabilities and Shareholders' Equity		
Deposits and interest-bearing liabilities:		
Deposits:		
Noninterest-bearing demand	$1,063,791	$1,155,876
Interest-bearing demand	804,119	1,039,412
Savings	296,364	339,185
Time	1,182,509	1,282,643
Certificates of deposit of $100,000 or more	393,571	632,711
Total deposits	3,740,354	4,449,827
Federal funds purchased and securities sold under agreements to repurchase	729,970	792,788
Commercial paper	17,233	15,085
Other borrowed funds	184,407	87,058
Long-term debt	71,873	27,201
Total deposits and interest-bearing liabilities	4,743,837	5,371,959
Acceptances outstanding	71,293	103,803
Accrued expenses and other liabilities	67,298	81,516
Total liabilities	4,882,428	5,557,278
Commitments and contingencies		
Shareholders' equity:		
Preferred stock—no par value:		
Authorized—2,000,000 shares;		
Issued and Outstanding—none	0	0
Common stock—par value $1 a share:		
Authorized—75,000,000 shares and 25,000,000 shares, respectively:		
Issued and Outstanding—19,555,257 shares and 19,411,821 shares, respectively	19,412	19,555
Capital surplus	160,363	163,752
Retained earnings	164,839	204,989
	344,614	388,296
Less deferred compensation on restricted stock	0	2,868
Total shareholders' equity	344,614	385,428
	$5,227,042	$5,942,706

EXHIBIT 8.9 **Consolidated statement of earnings—AmSouth Bancorporation and subsidiaries**

	1984	1985	1986
	(In thousands except per share data)		
Revenue from earning assets			
Interest and fees on loans	$282,585	$319,159	$346,672
Interest on investment securities:			
Taxable securities	57,315	40,530	59,251
Tax-free securities	21,378	21,532	23,017
Interest on time deposits in other banks	9,679	45	102
Interest on federal funds sold and securities purchased under agreements to resell	18,588	8,181	1,060
Interest on trading account securities	1,081	1,370	1,517
Dividends on preferred stock	480	0	0
Total revenue from earning assets	391,106	390,817	431,619
Interest expense			
Interest on interest-bearing demand deposits	40,199	40,863	45,338
Interest on savings deposits	11,715	12,418	15,620
Interest on time deposits	94,412	91,925	85,951
Interest on certificates of deposit of $100,000 or more	42,891	34,464	29,311
Interest on federal funds purchased and securities sold under agreements to repurchase	49,725	28,540	47,382
Interest on commercial paper	1,806	1,336	1,142
Interest on other borrowed funds	16,256	14,777	7,275
Interest on long-term debt	2,639	6,402	6,723
Total interest expense	259,643	230,725	238,742
Gross interest margin	131,463	160,092	192,877
Provision for loan losses	15,741	20,053	18,601
Net interest margin	115,722	140,039	174,276
Noninterest revenues			
Trust Department income	14,450	17,604	22,012
Service changes on deposit accounts	15,176	18,727	21,974
Securities gains	1,150	1,986	5,255
Mortgage administration fees	9,414	9,475	10,122
Other operating revenues	22,169	24,184	33,205
Total noninterest revenues	62,359	71,976	92,568
Noninterest expenses			
Salaries and employee benefits	75,888	85,484	97,134
Net occupancy expense	10,182	11,894	13,487
Equipment expense	15,919	18,621	21,718
Other operating expenses	37,703	44,252	58,566
Total noninterest expenses	139,692	160,251	190,905
Income before applicable income taxes	38,389	51,764	75,939
Applicable income taxes	965	5,255	14,927
Net income	$ 37,424	$ 46,509	$ 61,012
Average common shares outstanding (In thousands)	15,939	16,767	19,483
Earnings per common share	$2.32	$2.77	$3.13

AMSOUTH'S GROWTH STRATEGY

As suggested in Exhibit 8.1, AmSouth has emphasized growth throughout its history. In 1987, AmSouth continued this strategy by merging with First Tuskaloosa Corporation (First Tuskaloosa retained the original spelling of Tuscaloosa). First Tuskaloosa was the largest independent bank in Alabama with a 115-year history. In addition, AmSouth has taken advantage of Alabama's interstate banking legislation by announcing the acquisition of First Mutual Savings Association of Florida, the largest independent financial institution in Northwest Florida. It was the first interstate acquisition announced by an Alabama bank holding company. First Mutual must become a full-service bank before its acquisition under regulations of the Federal Reserve Board. AmSouth has also agreed to acquire Gulf First Holding Corporation, and its subsidiaries, Gulf Coast Holding Corporation, and the $78 million-asset First National Bank of Panama City, Florida.

A MARKETING IMPERATIVE

CEO Woods realized that if AmSouth was to continue to grow, effective marketing would be essential. A new banking era was at hand. Woods had been an advocate of interstate banking. He believed that it was in the best interest of Alabama consumers as well as AmSouth's shareholders. Large banks would bring more competition, which should bring better and cheaper services. Also, larger banks would allow for more efficient uses of capital. Woods wondered what new marketing strategies should be adopted to assure that AmSouth would be one of the "super" banks that could provide better products to the customers.

Industry Note:

The Banking Environment

Banking has operated in a relatively stable environment for many years. However, today the industry is facing a dramatically new operating environment. Deregulation has allowed new forms of competition and new competitors and the passage of interstate banking legislation has widened considerably the "playing field." The

This industry note was prepared by Peter M. Ginter and Linda E. Swayne as a basis for classroom discussion rather than to illustrate effective or ineffective handling of an administrative situation. Used by permission of Peter M. Ginter.

strategies that worked in the past in the banking industry are no longer appropriate and bankers must consider a whole new set of contingencies in managing their banks.

On a national scale, banks continue to fail and write off bad loans at record rates. Through the middle of May 1987, 78 banks had failed, and Federal Deposit Insurance Corporation Chairman L. William Seidman said he expects the number for the full year to reach 200, up from last year's record of 144 failures. The banks with the lowest relative level of loan losses have been the mid-sized, regional banks with assets of between $1 billion and $5 billion. These banks are too small to make extensive foreign loans, but large and diversified enough not to be brought down by heavy dependence on farm or energy loans.[1]

Other factors that have contributed to the declining performance of banks in recent years include:

- The drop in the rate of inflation that undermined farm, energy, and real estate loans that had been extended based on expectations that the double-digit inflation rates of the late 1970s and early 1980s would continue.

- The strength of the dollar overseas for the past two to three years which hurt manufacturers of exported goods, an important part of banks' customer base.

- Competition from Wall Street, as direct issuance of securities has proven to be a less expensive and more efficient form of financing than bank loans for many of the banking industry's prime customers.[2]

The changes that have taken place in the banking industry have been largely beyond the control of the banks. This industry provides a good example where institutions within the market must respond to changes in the external environment in order to survive. Those banks that do not consider the new environmental contingencies and develop explicit strategies directed towards the environment will likely become victims of that environment.

Industry Consolidation

The large banks are being spurred on to acquire competitors by a number of forces, including increasing competition in the industry, aggressive merger practices of rival banks, and the prospect of being a player in interstate banking. Reaction to the acquisitions is split along fairly predictable lines, with bankers involved in the mergers touting increased services and credit to rural communities, small-bank executives bemoaning the loss of venerable, independent institutions, and customers saying they are not sure what to think.

The key players in what most bankers see as inevitable consolidation of banking in Alabama are the five largest bank-holding companies: AmSouth Bancorporation,

---

[1]*The Birmingham News*, June 7, 1987, p. 1D.
[2]Ibid., p. 1D.

SouthTrust Corporation, First Alabama Bancshares, Central Bancshares of the South, and Colonial Bancgroup. The result has been a reduced number of banks in Alabama. From 1981 to 1985, the number of banking organizations in the state dropped five percent, according to the Federal Reserve Bank of Atlanta. At the same time, deposits have become concentrated in fewer organizations, and the big banks generally have seen substantial growth in their assets. A recent survey by Arthur Andersen & Co. found that bankers around the nation expect the total number of banks in the country to shrink about 20 percent by 1990.[3]

The banks being purchased within Alabama are primarily in rural areas, have less than $100 million in assets, and have been owned by the same family for decades. Buyouts of small banks by larger ones have caused discontent in some communities, where a big bank from Birmingham is seen as an abstract institution. The common wisdom when a "big-city" bank comes with an offer to buy a smaller one is that it submerges the independence of the local banking industry. One small town mayor has claimed, "It is more difficult to obtain a small loan at the bank since it was bought out by SouthTrust. Pulpwooders used to go out and get a $100 or $200 loan. Now, the minimum is $750."[4]

Though executives at small and large banks say they respect and are friends with one another, there emerges a resentment of big-bank interests. Many independent bankers believe that the bank-holding companies lost touch with customers in rural communities. "It's not reasonable to expect they would have the same interest in a community where their boards of directors don't live," says Gene Faulkner, president of the Citizens Bank in Prattville, which is 10 miles outside of Montgomery, Alabama.[5] In order to be successful, big banks operating branches that are distant from the corporate office have had to make changes in the way they think about their business and their customer. Small banks have had to change as well in order to survive.

BANK MARKETING

Marketing is relatively new to the banking industry. Previously, those responsible for the marketing function were not referred to as marketers but customer service representatives or public relations representatives. With deregulation and increasing competition not only from banks, but also from nonbanks (such as savings and loans, financial services companies, etc.), the industry has had to develop more of a marketing orientation.

Research has repeatedly shown that the single most important factor in consumers' choosing a bank is convenience. Thus, banks established branches at every available high traffic area. To increase market share, banks simply built more branches. However, since deregulation, the cost of building and operating a branch

[3]*The Birmingham News*, December 8, 1986, p. 8D.
[4]Ibid., p. 8D–9D.
[5]Ibid., p. 8D–9D.

had to be carefully weighed against the revenues that the specific branch would generate. Construction costs had increased and fewer branches were being built. With the slowdown in the number of branches being built, bankers were looking for new ways to grow.

Product Development

One strategy selected by many banks was new product development. There has been a proliferation of new products and old familiar products have been renamed and packaged in new ways. Marketing was needed to identify segments and needs in the market. From the segments and needs identified, specific products were developed to satisfy those needs. By putting a variety of products together such as an interest-bearing checking account, a safe-deposit box, a bankcard, and others, into a "deluxe" package and marketing it to a specific customer, a new product was developed that was then promoted to a specific target market.

In banking the 80-20 principle applies. Twenty percent of a bank's customers generally account for 80 percent of the bank's business. Banks prefer to target the affluent customer because they have larger balances for both loans and money held in accounts. Most new products have been aimed at capturing the affluent segment. However, some banks have recently instituted "no-frills" accounts which are designed for people who write very few checks and do not maintain large balances.

In the last five years, more products have been introduced by banks than in the previous twenty years. Rather than having one or two types of checking accounts and one or two types of savings accounts, banks now have a multitude of products such as brokerage accounts, money market accounts, mortgages, insurance, IRA's, equity line of credit, etc., in addition to the more traditional products.

Banks today generally have a variety of types of checking accounts—some earning interest with a minimum balance, others also earning interest but at a higher rate because of higher minimum balance requirements. Other products such as savings accounts have become less important, especially to the affluent, as money market accounts pay higher interest rates.

Line of credit is a generic product that banks have offered for many years. It is an example of an old familiar product being repositioned and heavily promoted to win new customers. However, with the new tax law, it is being repositioned for the affluent as a way to avoid high taxes. The Cash Reserve Account (the bank covers the customer's check when the account contains insufficient funds) is another new product that is a repositioned line of credit.

Individual Retirement Accounts (IRAs), another product that came into existence due to government law, were generally considered to be loss leaders. The cost to market the product, including heavy investment in advertising, was very high for most banks. Actually many banks lost money in winning these accounts, but IRAs represented stable business (people don't move their IRA's much) and over the long run banks hoped that IRAs would be profitable. With new tax laws in 1986, IRAs became more beneficial to the lower-income segment of the market—one that had been less desirable to banks.

Automatic teller machines (ATMs) have been a real boon and boondoggle for banks. The major advantage of this new product was that customers can be served at any time of the day or night—a real competitive advantage. Also, many customers use the ATM instead of the expensive, labor-intensive teller in the branch bank. However, ATMs are extremely expensive, highly sophisticated machines. They require such a large fixed cost that many transactions have to be handled every day in order for the machine to break even. Most locations don't approach the number required. Thus ATMs are a glamorous product that offered a distinct competitive advantage to the first bank to offer the service, but the advantage did not last very long as other banks quickly installed similar products. Being first with ATMs carried a high price for such a short-term competitive advantage but, developing a network of ATMs was usually profitable as the network developer charges all the other banks for customer usage.

Because banks have been advertising a multitude of new products and attempting to position products for specific market segments, marketing research has become more important. Previously marketing research consisted of asking what the competition is doing, finding out, and then offering something very similar. Because of regulation there was not much difference in products or prices and not much need to advertise. Today, psychographics as well as demographics are being used to develop new products, for positioning, and for advertising.

The early advertising done by banks was promoting premiums to be given to individuals who opened accounts. Consumers were not stupid and they began opening small accounts at many banks to receive the teddy bear, electric blanket, etc., that were being given away. Banks realized that this type of promotion was not accomplishing their objective. Banks advertised friendliness, customer service, and convenience. Most messages were the same and little differentiation was accomplished. With better target market definitions and positioning statements, advertising has begun to play a role in establishing an image for a specific product or for the bank itself.

Bank Rates

In most communities, banks exist as oligopolies. There is a price leader and several relatively large followers, along with a number of smaller banks that may or may not be followers. Depending on how "hungry" they are, some small competitors in the area may choose not to follow the leader. They offer higher rates for deposits and lower rates for loans. The bank that does this generally is desperate for deposits and in effect is "buying" them. Generally, this is not a long-term strategy because the costs involved to increase the bank's revenues are too great.

Bank prices include the price for services that are offered (fee-based services), the rates they charge to customers who borrow money (loan rates), and the rates they pay to use customer's deposits (interest rates). There is not much opportunity to maintain different rates (the oligopolistic element of banking) because the products are similar, location is convenient, and competitive information is readily available. Yet banks have much greater opportunity to set prices since the deregulation of the financial industry.

Rates are set according to the cost of funds from the Federal Reserve and elsewhere, the cost to get the customers, expectations about the economy, the financial needs of the bank, and rates set by competition. When the prime rate goes up, banks generally change their rates. The price leader, usually the largest bank, is closely monitored by the other banks in the area to see the new rate the big bank will set. Then the various banks tend to follow the leader. This conscious parallel action is not illegal as long as the bankers do not get together and discuss what the rates should be.

Because of the narrowing spread of interest rates from deregulation (what they have to pay for deposits versus what they have to earn from loans), banks have had to look to other sources for income. Setting service charges or service fees for bank products has allowed banks to generate needed revenues while they keep rates competitive. When most people open a N.O.W account they make comparisons about the minimum balance and the interest rate paid. Few customers investigate how much it will cost if they want to stop payment on a check or if they overdraw their account. Therefore, the banks tend to put high fees on these services. It usually costs the bank a fraction of the amount charged to stop payment, for example. When interest rates were highly regulated and there was little competition, banks could offer these services for no extra charge. Today, service fees represent important revenue for the bank.

Banks have a marketing opportunity if they are able to capitalize on it. Most branch banks have one or more customer service representatives as well as a branch manager. These employees can make up a sales force for the bank. Since "cross selling" of bank products is the major area of interest in bank marketing today, the challenge is to train customer service representatives so that they can sell the bank's various products while providing customer service at the same time. This means that the service representatives need to learn more than just the products that they service at the branch. Products like mortgages, brokerage activity, life insurance, etc., are not familiar to the typical branch employee who has always been a personable order taker. The idea behind cross selling is to get the customer who has a checking account with the bank to also open a savings account or a money market account or a line of credit, etc.

Some innovative banks have developed a retail sales force whose responsibilities are to identify affluent citizens in the community and market the bank's products to them. Experienced salespersons, not bankers, make these cold calls to attempt to generate more business.

The bank branch is beginning to look more like a retail store. Department store designers are being employed to make the branch look less stodgy and more like a fun, inviting place to be.

SIZING UP COMPETITION

Bank size is measured in terms of assets. Bank assets are the loans that the bank has generated. Loan quality (the likelihood that the loan will be repaid along with interest in a timely manner) is important when looking at assets. The more high-quality loans a bank has (low investment in foreign countries/companies that may default, loans not totally involved with one industry that may have difficulties in times of poor economy—steel, textiles, farming) the more it will receive in interest payments (revenues).

Market share is measured by the total dollar value of consumer deposits held by the bank, compared to competing banks in the area. Consumer deposits generate funds and revenue for the bank, but are less stable than loans. Consumers will change banks rather easily, especially if they use only one of the bank's products, such as a checking account. The more of the bank's products they purchase, the more likely they are to remain with the same bank in spite of any little problems.

THE LEGISLATIVE ENVIRONMENT

Recently, banking-related legislation has affected operations more than any other aspect of the banking environment. Over the last several years there have been a variety of legislative initiatives that have or will affect the banking industry. Some of these initiatives are outlined in Exhibit 1.

Banking Industry Regulation

From 1933 through the 1980s the banking industry was characterized by restrictive governmental regulations. The regulations were the result of the financial crisis of 1929. The structure of the regulatory system of the United States is of a dual nature. Regulation is imposed on the banking industry not only by the Federal Government but also by the various state governments. The principal federal laws are the Federal Reserve Act of 1913, the Federal Deposit Insurance Corporation Act of 1950, the Truth in Lending Act of 1968, and the Fair Credit Reporting Act of 1971. In 1980, the Depository Institution Deregulation and Monetary Control Act was passed which caused significant changes in the competitive environment. This federal legislation had the following effects:

- Provided for identical reserve requirements for Federal Reserve member and nonmember banks, as an incentive for banks to remain a member.
- Established the same reserve requirements for banks, savings and loans, mutual savings banks, and credit unions. These reserve requirements are the percentage of total demand deposits that banks are required to hold in a reserve account at the Federal Reserve Bank. The total reserves are reflective of the loan capabilities of the institution, as the higher the required reserves, the smaller amounts of capital the bank has available to loan.

EXHIBIT 1 **Bank-related legislative initiatives**

---

1. Congress has become more concerned about the safety of the banking industry rather than its structure.

2. Bills are being pushed in Congress and by consumer groups that would cap credit card rates, limit the time banks can hold checks before paying out money, and force banks to offer free accounts to low-income depositors.

3. Current interstate banking laws allow banks to acquire or merge with banks across state lines (where allowed by state law), but not start new banks from "scratch" across state lines.

4. A Supreme Court decision permits dozens of commercial companies to operate limited-service banks.

5. Nonbank banks are permissible under the Bank Holding Company Act of 1956 because they do not meet the complete definition of a bank.

6. Legislation passed by Congress must allow banks to compete with nonbank banks on equal footing.

7. Congress has threatened to close the loophole in the 1956 Bank Holding Company Act by redefining "bank" to include all institutions that are insured by the FDIC.

8. The Supreme Court has ruled that regional interstate banking mergers are legal.

9. Bankers expect legislators to make it easier for commercial banks to acquire thrift institutions in other states.

10. New York banks do not foresee that southeastern state legislators will ease restrictions for them anytime soon.

11. Congress wants to eliminate the reserve method of accounting for bad debts. Only those debts that become worthless could be deducted from taxes.

12. Congress also wants to eliminate the exemption from Federal income tax allowed to banks on interest earned on state and local obligations. The effect would be reduced demand for tax-exempt securities, which would raise states' and municipalities' interest costs.

13. Instead of carrying losses back ten years and forward five, banks may be required to follow the same rules as other corporations; back three years and forward 15.

14. Bankers can expect any tax reform bill to limit deductions for business meals and entertainment.

15. Bankers must be aware of any tax-rate reduction and make certain there is graduation included so smaller banking firms do not bear a disproportionate share of the tax burden.

16. Bankers must urge equal treatment for banks and other financial services companies when tax reform issues are discussed. The proposal on loan loss reserves, for example, would affect banks but not insurance companies.

- Extended the availability of the Federal Reserve System's services to all depository institutions at a fee.
- Eliminated all interest-rate ceilings payable on deposits in depository institutions.
- Authorized all depository institutions to provide checking account services

(previously not available to savings and loans, mutual savings banks, or credit unions).

- Authorized automatic transfer systems (electronic cash transfers—the first step toward a cashless society).
- Authorized interest-bearing checking accounts (N.O.W Accounts).
- Raised F.D.I.C. coverage from $40,000 to $100,000 on individual accounts.
- Empowered savings and loans to issue credit cards and expand their consumer loan business.
- Allowed mutual savings banks to make business loans and accept demand deposits (checking accounts) from their business customers.
- Allowed depository institutions to become competitive in offering a broad range of services.
- Exempted several kinds of loans from state usury laws (mortgages, business, and agricultural loans).

The principal impact of the bill was to increase competition within the banking industry. Savings and loans, mutual savings banks, and credit unions were made direct competitors capable of offering the same kinds of products as traditional banks.

In reaction to the increase in bank-related legislation, Jack Hurley, Chairman of First Alabama, indicated, "We are actually more concerned with the re-regulation that we see happening." The re-regulation is targeted towards interest rates on credit cards, limiting the time banks are allowed to hold unclaimed money, and setting limits on service fees that banks are allowed to charge. A major concern for banking institutions is that the nonbanking financial firms do not have to comply with these regulations.

Interstate Banking Legislation

Perhaps the most significant legislation affecting the industry are the recent laws concerning interstate banking. The Interstate Banking Bill, which became effective July 1, 1987, was passed by the Alabama legislature in February 1986. This bill further opened competitive banking within the southeastern region of the country. As presented in Exhibit 2, states immediately effected by this legislation included the following:

Arkansas	Mississippi
District of Columbia	North Carolina
Florida	South Carolina
Georgia	Tennessee
Kentucky	Virginia
Louisiana	West Virginia
Maryland	

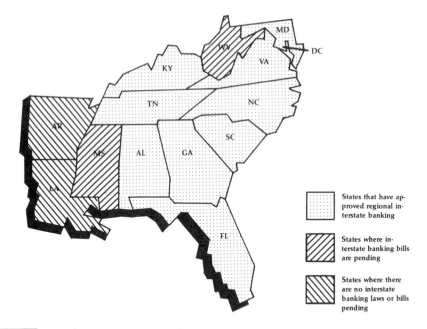

EXHIBIT 2   **Interstate banking in the southeastern region**

The fundamental intent of the law was to allow for reciprocal banking between the states. For the Alabama version of the bill, banks outside the state would be able to purchase Alabama banks and Alabama banks would be able to purchase banks outside of Alabama. Thus far, four of the five largest Alabama banks, (AmSouth, SouthTrust, First Alabama, and Colonial) have made acquisitions outside of Alabama. The law was designed to allow for an increase in the competitive environment. However, bank executives and analysts suggest that the pace of Alabama's bank deals will move fairly slowly. By the end of 1987, no banks from outside the state had purchased any Alabama banks.

Interstate Banking Rationale and Recent Activity

Interstate banking advocates have suggested that in the long run, larger banks could bring more competition, which would mean better and cheaper services. Also, it was believed that larger banks would be more willing to introduce expensive technology, such as sophisticated cash-management systems for business customers. In addition, large regional banks could be powerful forces in fostering economic development of the region.

Most of the interstate banking acquisition activity in the Southeast through 1986 involved Georgia and North Carolina bank companies purchasing South Carolina and Florida bank companies as shown in Exhibit 3. In the South Atlantic states, which Alabama included in its interstate banking region, most deals involved Virginia bank

---

EXHIBIT 3 **Southeastern interstate banking mergers and acquisitions**

James Madison Ltd. (D.C.) and McLean Bank (Va.)

James Madison Ltd. (D.C.) and First Continental Bank (Md.)

Citizens and Southern Georgia Corp. and Landmark Banking Corp. of Florida

Citizens and Southern Georgia Corp. and The Citizens and Southern Corp. (S.C.)

Trust Co. of Georgia and Sun Banks of Florida to Form SunTrust Banks Inc.

Citizens Fidelity Corp. (Ky.) and United Bank of Indiana

Citizens Fidelity Corp. (Ky.) and Indiana Southern Financial Corp.

Citizens Fidelity Corp. (Ky.) and First Midwest Bancorp (Ind.)

Planters Financial Corp. (Ky.) and Williamson County Bancorp Inc. (Tenn.) to form
  Central South Bancorp Inc.

First Union Corp. (N.C.) and Atlantic Bancorporation (Fla.)

First Union Corp. (N.C.) and Central Florida Bancorp

First Union Corp. (N.C.) and Southern Bancorporation (S.C.)

First Union Corp. (N.C.) and Citizens DeKalb Bank (Ga.)

First Union Corp. (N.C.) and First Bankers Corp. of Florida

NCNB Corp. (N.C.) and Bankers Trust of S.C.

NCNB Corp. (N.C.) and Southern National Bancshares Inc. (Ga.)

NCNB Corp. (N.C.) and Pan American Banks Inc. (Fla.)

NCNB Corp. (N.C.) and First National Bank of Lake City (Fla.)

NCNB Corp. (N.C.) and Gulfstream Banks Inc. (Fla.)

NCNB Corp. (N.C.) and Exchange Banks Inc. (Fla.)

NCNB Corp. (N.C.) and Ellis Bancorporation (Fla.)

Southern National Corp. (N.C.) and Horry County National Bank (S.C.)

Wachovia Corp. (N.C.) and First Atlanta Corp. to form First Wachovia Corp.

Banc One Corp. (Ohio) and KYNB Bancshares Inc. (Ky.)

Fifth Third Bancorp (Ohio) and American Bancorp Inc. (Ky.)

Fifth Third Bancorp (Ohio) and First Kentucky Bancshares

Huntington Bancshares Inc. (Ohio) and Commonwealth Trust Inc. (Ky.)

First American Corp. (Tenn.) and First Ashland Corp. (Ky.)

Bank of Virginia Co. and Security National Corp. (D.C.)

Bank of Virginia Co. and Union Trust Bancorp (Md.)

Dominion Bankshares Corp. (Va.) and State National Bank of Maryland

Dominion Bankshares Corp. (Va.) and The National Bank of Commerce (D.C.)

First Virginia Banks Inc. and Commercial Bank of Bel Air (Md.)

Sovran Financial Corp. (Va.) and D.C. National BanCorp Inc.

Sovran Financial Corp. (Va.) and Suburban Bancorp (Md.)

United Virginia Bankshares Inc. and NS&T Bankshares Inc. (D.C.)

United Virginia Bankshares Inc. and Bethesda Bankcorporation (Md.)

companies buying Maryland and Washington, D.C., bank companies. Such purchases in the South have helped boost the size of major bank holding companies, known as super-regionals.

Many of the early interstate acquistions reflected the desire of Georgia and North Carolina banks to expand into the high growth markets of South Carolina and Florida. Most analysts have agreed that Alabama does not represent that kind of growth market and have predicted a slow pace of interstate mergers within Alabama. Furthermore, the analysts have suggested that when mergers occur, they will more likely comprise out-of-state banks buying Alabama companies rather than the other way around. For instance, John Burke, a bank analyst with the Robinson-Humphrey Company securities firm in Atlanta suggested, "In the long term, when you consider the size of the [Alabama] market and the resulting size of the banks, a substantial number of them will probably wind up being acquired or merged into organizations in other states."[6]

Reactions to the Interstate Legislation by Alabama Banks

SouthTrust Chairman Wallace D. Malone Jr., First Alabama Vice-Chairman Richard D. Horsley and Colonial President Ed V. Welch agree that "at least two Alabama banks will sell out within the next several years."[7]

However, SouthTrust's Malone said his bank will not sell. AmSouth Chairman John Woods said his bank has been preparing to be a buyer since 1981, when its stock was listed on the New York Stock exchange. However, "I don't think that a senior officer of a publicly owned company can responsibly take the position that a company is not for sale at any price anytime."[8]

Colonial's Welch said, "We will continue to manage our bank on the survivor route until it would behoove us to listen to a proposition that would be of benefit for our shareholders."[9]

First Alabama's Hurley said that they will not merge with any other large Alabama bank holding company, but will consider nearly any other banking combination.[10] First Alabama Vice Chairman Horsley stated, "We are looking at our options. We haven't committed to any of the various options . . . whatever our decision, it will have to be in the best interest of our stockholders."[11]

[6]*The Birmingham News*, March 3, 1986.

[7]*The Birmingham News*, "New Era to Dawn in July 1987, But Don't Expect a Flurry of Fast-paced Bank Deals," March 3, 1987.

[8]Ibid.

[9]Ibid.

[10]*The Birmingham News*, "First Alabama Would Consider Merger with Holding Companies Outside State," May 1, 1986.

[11]*Ibid.*

Related Legislation

Alabama Governor Guy Hunt recently signed into law a bill that would give Alabama's savings and loan associations the same rights as banks to spread outside the state. The new law will give Alabama savings and loans an opportunity to merge with savings and loans in other Southern states, and will allow out-of-state institutions to buy Alabama S&L's. The law took effect July 1, 1987, the same day as Alabama's new interstate banking law. So far, few business deals have been announced as a result of the new S&L law. However, as a result of the law, Birmingham-based Alabama Federal Savings and Loan Association, the second-largest thrift in the state, roughly doubled its assets with the purchase of the Slidell, Louisiana, First Federal Savings Bank ($55 million) and First Financial Bank of New Orleans ($190 million).

THE COMPETITIVE ENVIRONMENT

The current operating environment within Alabama has been dominated by five major bank-holding companies. Total assets for the largest Alabama banks are presented in Exhibit 4 and performance indicators (earnings per share, dividends per share, and net income) are shown in Exhibit 5.

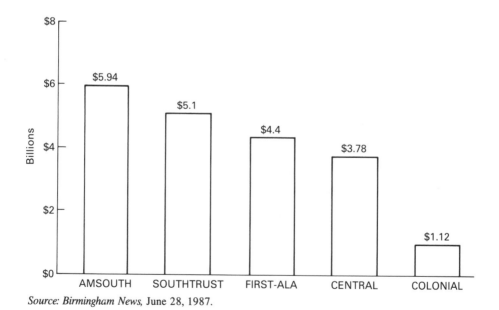

Source: Birmingham News, June 28, 1987.

EXHIBIT 4   **Assets of the largest Alabama bank holding companies**

EXHIBIT 5 Performance indicators for the five largest Alabama banks					
	1982	1983	1984	1985	1986
AmSouth					
EPS[1]	$ 2.81	$ 3.02	$ 2.32	$ 2.77	$ 3.13
DPS[2]	1.70	1.20	1.34	.84	1.07
NI[3]	31,900	33,594	37,424	46,509	61,012
SouthTrust					
EPS	$ 3.14	$ 2.44	$ 2.96	$ 1.98	$ 2.26
DPS	1.06	1.17	.86	.60	.67
NI	22,864	27,861	34,451	44,249	53,737
First Alabama					
EPS	$ 1.06	$ 1.28	$ 1.41	$ 1.64	$ 1.67
DPS	.42	.45	.50	.56	.64
NI	35,026	41,255	45,455	52,887	54,078
Central Bancshares					
EPS	$ 3.45	$ 3.63	$ 3.70	$ 1.46	$ 1.73
DPS	.86	1.18	1.32	.50	.58
NI	23,108	24,752	25,444	30,635	36,461
Colonial					
EPS	$ .84	$ 1.80	$ 1.95	$ 2.05	$ 2.20
DPS	.38	.40	.36	.47	.50
NI	1,210	2,641	5,242	8,094	11,071

[1] EPS = Earnings per share.
[2] DPS = Dividends per share.
[3] NI = Net income reported in thousands (000).

AmSouth Bancorporation

AmSouth Bancorporation is the largest bank-holding company in Alabama and has grown primarily through expansion. Although not quite as aggressive as SouthTrust, they have made the commitment to being an Alabama bank by breaking ground for a new $140-million headquarters building in Birmingham. In addition, AmSouth has recently acquired First Mutual Savings Association, a 16-office Northwest Florida Savings and Loan Association, and has agreed to acquire Gulf First Holding Corporation and its subsidiaries, Gulf Coast Holding Corporation and the $78 million-asset First National Bank of Panama City, Florida. AmSouth currently has over $5.9 billion in assets and 14 percent marketshare.

SouthTrust Corporation

SouthTrust is the most aggressive of the five Alabama banks and has grown primarily through acquisition. Recently SouthTrust acquired four Alabama banks with assets of $228 million and four Florida banks with $234 million in assets. This growth strategy has enabled SouthTrust to add $462 million to its asset base. In 1987, SouthTrust assets totaled over $5.1 billion. SouthTrust currently enjoys the second largest portion of the state marketshare with 9.5 percent.

First Alabama Bancshares

While the third largest bank holding company in the state, First Alabama Bancshares generally has outperformed the Alabama competitors in net income. First Alabama's growth has occurred primarily through acquisition. In 1986, five acquisitions added $400 million to assets and in 1987 plans were announced to acquire banks in Northwest Florida and a mortgage company in Georgia for an additional $900 million in assets. First Alabama has total assets of $4.4 billion and 8.8 percent market share.

Central Bancshares of the South

Central is the only player in Alabama who has not adopted an aggressive acquisition strategy. Central Bankshares has indicated that for the present it will stay on the sidelines and pursue an internal growth strategy. Central Bank's CEO Harry Brock stated, "Most banks go [are sold] to the highest bidder. Now, I'm a private-enterprise kind of guy, and I'm procompetitive. But I can't justify the price." The current assets of Central are over $3.78 billion. Central currently is at a 7.3 percent marketshare in the state.

Colonial Bancgroup

Colonial, the fifth largest bank-holding company in Alabama with assets of $1.12 billion, has used the interstate law to grow. It has announced plans to acquire Liberty Bank at Pensacola, Florida. During 1986, Colonial acquired 17 Alabama banks with assets of nearly $900 million. Colonial's marketshare is relatively small in comparison to the other four major bank holding companies in Alabama.

Major Regional Banks

The ten largest super-regional banks in the Southeast are shown in Exhibit 6. The super-regional bank holding companies have not put the purchase of Alabama banks at the top of the priority lists. NCNB Corporation is the largest banking company in the Southeast with assets of $27.5 billion, which is over five times as large as the largest Alabama bank, AmSouth, which has $5.9 billion in assets. First Union is the second largest bank in the Southeast with assets of $26.8 billion followed by SunTrust Banks with $26.2 billion. The smallest of the Southeast super-regional banks, CenTrust Savings Bank of Miami, has assets of $6.1 billion, which is still larger than the largest Alabama bank.

EXHIBIT 6 **Ten largest banks in the Southeast**

Bank	Headquarters	1986 Assets (In billions)
NCNB Corporation	Charlotte, N.C.	$27.5
First Union	Charlotte, N.C.	26.8
SunTrust Banks	Atlanta, Ga.	26.2
Barnett Banks	Jacksonville, Fl.	20.2
Citizens & Southern Corporation	Atlanta, Ga.	18.8
First Wachovia Corporation	Winston-Salem, N.C.	18.7
Southeast Banking Corporation	Miami, Fl.	12.5
CityFed Financial Corporation	Palm Beach, Fl.	10.7
Florida National Banks	Jacksonville, Fl.	6.9
CenTrust Savings Bank	Miami, Fl.	6.1

Source: The Birmingham News, June 29, 1987.

ECONOMIC OUTLOOK FOR THE SOUTHEASTERN UNITED STATES

It would appear that banking and banking services will continue to prosper in the Southeast. As a whole, the Southeast region has consistently performed above the national average in all major measures of economic growth. For the past quarter century, the region has attracted new people and industry which has kept the area in the forefront of the nation's growth. The Southeast is expected to continue to perform well during the next five to ten years. The continued economic prosperity is attractive to banks and means that many southeastern banking markets are likely targets for acquisitions by large interstate banks.

However, areas within the Southeast are predicted to grow at dramatically different rates. For instance, states on the Atlantic Coast, Florida, Georgia, and the Carolinas, are currently thriving and should continue to do so in the coming decade. Alabama, Kentucky, Louisiana, Mississippi, and Tennessee offer a stark contrast to the Atlantic Coast states. Together, they have contributed less than one fourth of the region's job growth since 1982, versus about 40 percent between 1960 and 1980. The weaker states will improve their share of growth slightly in the next ten years, but they probably will not lead the region.

THE INTERSTATE GAME

In the face of interstate banking and the acquisition mania that has occurred, economists David A. Phillips and Christine A. Pavel conducted a thorough analysis of the banking industry and have determined some characteristics of the players (those banks that become involved either as a buyer or a target) and spectators (banks that do not become involved in interstate banking).

They have identified the following four major criteria that separate the players from the spectators:

1. Market share is a significant factor. Players tend to be the largest organizations within their states.
2. Profitability, as defined by net spread, (the difference between a bank's income from earning assets and its cost of funds expressed as a percent of its average earning assets) is also considered significant. The greater the net spread, the greater the profitability and the greater the likelihood of becoming involved as a player.
3. Primary focus of the bank is different for spectators and players. Spectators tend to concentrate on local markets and have larger percentages of real estate loans.
4. Size is the predominant factor that differentiates players from spectators.[12]

The bank that has a large base of insured deposits and a small commercial loan portfolio has the greatest potential to become a target. Those banks that are acquiring other banks have looked at several criteria before making the acquisition and have used these criteria to determine a fair market price for the bank. The following variables have been utilized to investigate a target:

1. Overhead expenses (defined as salary and occupancy expenses) as a percentage of average earning assets—the average overhead cost for a target firm was 2.9 percent.
2. Net spread—the higher the net spread the higher the offering price.
3. Mid-size business—the target will receive a higher offering price if it has a high percentage of mid-size business in its geographical area.
4. Market size—The price an acquiring bank is willing to pay increases with the size of the metropolitan market where the target is based.[13]

[12]D.A. Phillips and C.A. Pavel, "Interstate Merger-Forces and Forecasts," *The Bankers Magazine*, January–February 1987, pp. 54–59.

[13]*Ibid.*

CASE 9

Anheuser-Busch Company, Inc: Marketing Strategy for the 1990s

On March 15, 1986, August A. Busch III sat in his office reviewing his staff's analysis of his first ten years' strategic plan. He was preparing himself for the next day's staff meeting. Many changes had been made in the company since its founding more than a century ago. He was proud. Anheuser-Busch had come a long way. Diversification strategies had proven successful and continued growth seemed evident. But, where would the company go in the fast paced competitive environment in which it operated? Its primary objective was well-planned and managed growth, and the company's long-term diversification strategies of vertical integration, internal development of new business areas, and acquisitions reflect this commitment. "Beer . . . will remain our top priority, as evidenced by substantial future capital commitments." But the plan, he thought, couldn't stop there.

COMPANY HISTORY—AN ENTREPRENEURIAL SPIRIT

In 1852, George Schneider founded the Bavarian Brewery in St. Louis, Missouri. Five years later, on the brink of bankruptcy, the brewery was sold to a competitor, who renamed it Hammer and Urban. By 1860, the new company defaulted on a loan to Eberhard Anheuser. Anheuser, a successful soap manufacturer, assumed control of Hammer and Urban and four years later asked his son-in-law, Adolphus Busch, to join the brewery as a salesman. Busch, who became the driving force behind the new venture, became a partner in 1873, and the president between 1880 and 1913. In 1879, the name of the brewery was changed to Anheuser-Busch Brewing Company.

Adolphus Busch was a pioneer in the development of a new pasteurization process for beer and became the first American brewer to pasteurize his beer. In 1894, he and Carl Conrad developed a new beer that was lighter in color and body. This new beer, Budweiser, gave Busch a national beer, for which he developed many

This case was prepared by Professor Thomas L. Wheelen, and Janiece L. Gallagher, an MBA student, of the University of South Florida. Research assistance was performed by Kelli Anderson, Kim Hart, and Cathy Lee of the University of South Florida at Sarasota. It is intended as a basis for classroom discussion rather than to illustrate effective or ineffective handling of an administrative situation. Copyright © 1987 by Dr. Thomas L. Wheelen. This case may not be reproduced in any form without written permission of the copyright holder. Used by permission from Thomas L. Wheelen.

marketing techniques to increase sales. By 1901, the annual sales of Anheuser-Busch had surpassed the million-barrel mark.

In 1913, August A. Busch succeeded his father as president of the company, serving as president during the prohibition era between 1920 and 1933. He led the company in many new diversification endeavors such as truck bodies, baker's yeast, ice cream, corn products, commercial refrigeration units, and nonalcoholic beverages. With the passage of the 21st Amendment, Anheuser-Busch returned to the manufacturing and distribution of beer on a national basis, and in 1934 the company went public.

August A. Busch, Jr., succeeded Adolphus Busch III as president and chief executive officer in 1946. He was elected chairman of the board in 1956, a position created in 1949 when Eberhard Anheuser presided as the first chairman. During his tenure, eight new breweries were constructed and sales increased eleven fold, from 3 million barrels in 1946 to 34 million barrels in 1974. He also guided the company as it continued its conglomerate diversification strategies into real estate, family entertainment parks, transportation, the St. Louis Cardinals baseball team, and can manufacturing. Busch was currently serving as honorary chairman of the board of Anheuser-Busch Companies, Inc., and chairman and president of the St. Louis National Baseball Club, Inc. Richard A. Meyer, the only nonfamily president, served from 1971 to 1974.

August A. Busch III born on June 16, 1937, is the fifth generation of the Busch brewing dynasty. He started his career hauling beechwood chips out of 31,000-gallon aging tanks. In his youth "Little Augie" was a hell-raiser, but he has changed to a conservative "workaholic" after attending The University of Arizona and The Siebel Institute of Technology, a Chicago school for brewers. He was elected president in 1974, and chief executive officer in 1975. During his tenure, sales doubled from 34 million barrels in 1974 to 68 million barrels in 1985, the company maintained 11 breweries having a capacity of 75.27 million barrels, and Anheuser-Busch continued its successful conglomerate diversification efforts (Exhibit 9.1).

In his ten years of managing the company, Busch has transformed it from a large, loosely run company into a tightly run organization with an emphasis on the bottom line. Busch is known for his tough-mindedness and intensity, his highly competitive nature, and his attention to detail. As Mr. Dennis Long, president of the company's brewing subsidiary, said, "There is little that goes on that he doesn't know something about." Busch, a brewmaster, is known for making unscheduled visits to the breweries at all hours of the day and night. He compares beers daily from different plants and suggests remedies for any variations in looks and taste. Mr. Long added, "Let there be no doubt. He's at the helm and he sets the tone."

During the summer of 1985, Mr. Busch's 21-year-old son, August A. Busch IV was employed in the Corporate Yeast Culture Center at the St. Louis headquarters. Commenting about the succession of his four children, Mr. Busch says: "If they have the competency to do so, they'll be given the opportunity. You learn from the ground up. Those of us who are in this company started out scrubbing the tanks." So, the younger August Busch began his career with Anheuser-Busch.

EXHIBIT 9.1 **Anheuser-Busch subsidiaries**

Anheuser-Busch, Inc.
Metal Container Corporation
Busch Agricultural Resources
Container Recovery Corporation
Anheuser-Busch International, Inc.
Campbell Taggart, Inc.
Eagle Snacks, Inc.
Busch Industrial Products Corporation
Busch Entertainment Corporation
Busch Properties, Inc.
St. Louis National Baseball Club, Inc.
Civic Center Corporation
St. Louis Refrigerator Car Company
Manufacturers Railway Company

THE ORGANIZATION

On October 1, 1979, Anheuser-Busch Companies, Inc., was formed as a new holding company. The company was organized into three business segments: (1) beer and beer-related companies, (2) food products companies, and (3) diversified operations.

In 1985 the beer and beer-related business segment contributed 77.3 percent of the net sales and 95.8 percent of the operating income. Exhibit 9.2 is a sketch of each of the eighteen companies that comprise the three business segments. Financial information for each of these business segments is shown in Exhibit 9.3.

EXHIBIT 9.2 **Anheuser-Busch Companies, Inc.—business segments**

Beer and beer-related companies

Company	Year founded	Activities
Anheuser-Busch, Inc.	1852	It ranked as the world's largest brewer, selling 68.0 million barrels of beer in 1985, and has been the industry leader since 1957. It distributes 11 naturally brewed products through 960 independent beer wholesalers and 10 company-owned wholesalers.

Busch Agricultural Resources	1962	It processes barley into malt. In 1985, it supplied 32% of the company's malt requirements. It grows and processes rice, and has the capacity to meet 20% of the company's rice needs.
Container Recovery Corporation	1979	It was the country's largest aluminum recycler in 1985.
Metal Container Division	1974	It is expected to produce 5.8 billion lids and 5 billion cans in 1986. This would represent 35% of the company's requirements and 6.4% of all beverage cans and lids in the U.S.
Anheuser-Busch Beverage Group	1985	It is responsible for nonbeer beverages. In 1985, it acquired two mineral water companies—the Saratoga Spring Co. and Sante Mineral Water Co. It offers three wine products—Master Cellars Wines, Baybry's champagne coolers, and Dewey Stevens premium light wine coolers.
Anheuser-Busch International, Inc.	1981	It is the company's international licensing and marketing subsidiary. The world beer market is 3.5 times as large as the domestic market.
Busch Media Group	1985	It is the company's in-house agency to purchase national media time.
Promotional Products Group	n/a	It is responsible for licensing, development, sales, and warehousing of the company's promotional merchandise.

Food products companies

Company	Year founded	Activities
Campbell Taggart	1982	It has 75 plants and approximately 19,000 employees. It consists of bakery operations, refrigerated products, frozen food products, and international subsidiaries.
Eagle Snacks	1978	It produces and distributes a premium line of snack foods and nuts. In 1984 it began self-manufacturing virtually all of its snack products, and in 1985 it purchased Cod Potato Chip Company.
Busch Industrial Products Corporation	1927	It is the leading producer and marketer of compressed yeast and also produces autolyzed yeast extract.

Diversified operations

Company	Year founded	Activities
Busch Entertainment	1959	It is the company family entertainment subsidiary. It consists of The Dark Continent, (Fl.), The Old Country (Va.), Adventure Island (Fl.), Sesame Place (Pa.), and Exploration Cruise Line (7 ships). In 1985, more than 2.9 million people visited the Dark Continent, and 2.05 million visitors came to The Old Country.
Busch Properties	1970	It is the company's real estate development subsidiary with commercial properties in Virginia, Ohio, and California. It continues to develop a planned community in Williamsburg, Va.
St. Louis National Baseball Club, Inc.	1953	St. Louis, Cardinals.
Civic Center Corporation	1981	It owns various downtown St. Louis properties.
Busch Creative Services	1980	It is a full-service business and marketing communications company, selling its services to Anheuser-Busch and other Fortune 500 companies.
St. Louis Refrigerator Car Company	1878	It is one of the company's transportation subsidiaries with three facilities. It provides commercial repair, rebuilding, maintenance, and inspection of railroad cars.
Manufacturers Railway Company	1878	This is the other transportation subsidiary. It operates 42 miles of track in the St. Louis area, 525 insulated railroad cars used to ship beer, 48 hopper cars, and 77 boxcars. It includes a fleet of 200 trailers.

The company's vertical integration strategy has resulted in increased knowledge of the economics of those businesses, assured quantity and quality of supply, and control of both packaging and raw materials.

Anheuser-Busch continues to cultivate internally developed businesses such as Eagle Snacks with the philosophy of maintaining premium quality through self-manufacture, including control of both packaging and raw materials. In 1985 Eagle Snacks added plant capacity through the acquisition of Cape Cod Chip Company and through plant expansion.

EXHIBIT 9.3 **Financial information for business segments (In millions)**

1985	Beer and beer related	Percent	Food products	Percent	Diversified operations	Percent	Eliminations	Consolidated
Net sales	$5,412.6	77.3	$1,416.4	20.9	$189.6	2.8	$ (18.3)	$7,000.3
Operating income	797.0	95.3	28.5	3.4	6.8	0.8		832.3
Depreciation and amortization expense	161.7	—	53.2	—	21.2	—		236.1
Capital expenditures	416.2	—	103.7	—	36.1	—		601.0
Identifiable assets	3,515.6	—	935.9	—	174.6	—		4,626.1
Corporate assets								495.3
Total assets								5,121.4

1984	Beer and beer related	Percent	Food products	Percent	Diversified operations	Percent	Eliminations	Consolidated
Net sales	$5,001.7	76.8	$1,343.9	20.6	$169.5	2.6	$ (13.9)	$6,501.2
Operating income	728.2	96.5	16.5	2.2	10.0	1.3		754.7
Depreciation and amortization expense	141.1	—	42.3	—	20.0	—		203.4
Capital expenditures	393.1	—	106.7	—	19.4	—		519.2
Identifiable assets	3,214.7	—	811.8	—	128.0	—		4,154.5
Corporate assets								370.2
Total assets								4,524.7

1983	Beer and beer related	Percent	Food products	Percent	Diversified operations	Percent	Eliminations	Consolidated
Net sales	$4,586.0	76.0	$1,311.9	21.7	$149.3	2.5	$ (13.0)	$6,034.2
Operating income	649.9	92.7	47.3	6.7	3.6	.5		700.8
Depreciation and amortization expense	129.5	—	40.3	—	17.5	—		187.3
Capital expenditures	348.1	—	54.8	—	25.1	—		428.0
Identifiable assets	2,994.1	—	768.6	—	143.7	—		3,906.4
Corporate assets								423.8
Total assets								4,330.2

Another internally developed diversification, Master Cellars Wines, has become part of the newly created Anheuser-Busch Beverage Group. Two other acquisitions were the Saratoga Spring Co. and Sante Mineral Water Co.

In 1985 the company became an investor in its first venture capital fund, Innoven, an established fund that has been very successful over the years. With this company, Anheuser-Busch gained exposure to new business areas being developed by the small start-up companies in which Innoven invested capital.

Busch Entertainment expanded in 1985, acquiring Exploration Cruise Lines. This six-vessel fleet cruises such areas as Mexico, Tahiti, and Alaska.

The company extended its research and development program with Interferon Sciences, which has been developing and clinically testing both material and recombinant forms of interferon, an antiviral agent found in the human body. The program has been extended for three more years.

Planning for the future, Anheuser-Busch will continue its long-term plans for diversification. These efforts are to be maintained as long as they are consistent with meeting the company's objectives.

THE PRODUCT

Beer uniquely fits comtemporary lifestyles. The five hallmarks of beer as a consumer beverage are convenience, moderation, health, value, and thirst-quenching properties. Each member of the Anheuser-Busch family of eleven beers is positioned to take advantage of this lifestyle. Exhibit 9.4 shows the target market for each of the company's beers.

EXHIBIT 9.4 **Anheuser-Busch beers**

Beer	Class	Target market
Budweiser	Premium	Any demographic or ethnic group and any region of the country
Bud Light	Light	Young to middle-age males
Michelob	Super-premium	Contemporary adults
Michelob Light	Light	Young, active, upscale drinker with high-quality lifestyle
Michelob Classic Dark	Premium Dark	Yuppies
Busch	Premium	Consumers who prefer lighter-tasting beer
Natural Light	Light	Beverage to go with good food
LA	Low Alcohol	Health conscious consumers
King Cobra	Malt Liquor	Contemporary male adults, age 21–24
Carlsberg	Lager	Import market
Elephant Malt Liquor	Malt Liquor	Consumers who enjoy imported beer

EXHIBIT 9.5 **Apparent beer consumption by type**

Type	1975	1980	1982	1983	1984	Percent change 1983–84
		(In millions of barrels)				
Popular	65.4	30.0	29.5	30.5	36.0	+18.0
Premium	71.6	102.3	95.7	94.6	87.0	− 8.0
Super-premium	5.0	11.5	10.6	10.6	9.5	− 5.9
Light	2.8	22.1	32.5	34.1	35.3	+ 3.5
Low alcohol				*	0.8	
Imported	1.7	4.6	5.8	6.3	7.2	+14.3
Malt liquor	3.8	5.5	6.4	6.4	5.6	− 9.4
Ale	n/a	1.9	1.8	1.7	1.4	−17.6
Total	150.3	177.9	182.3	183.7	182.8	− 0.5

n/a—not available. *Less than 50,000 gallons.
Source: Impact Databank.

There has been a major shift in the consumption of beer by type or class (see Exhibit 9.5). It was expected that per capita beer consumption would decline at about 1 percent or less during 1986, and remain flat throughout the balance of the 1980s. This would be accompanied by an expected rise in beer prices by 2 percent in 1986 and 1987. Also, the Census Bureau indicates a drop in the 20-to-39 year age group (see Exhibit 9.6).

EXHIBIT 9.6 **U.S. population projections***

Age group	1986 Number (In thousands)	1986 Percent of total	1990 Number (In thousands)	1990 Percent of total	2000 Number (In thousands)	2000 Percent of total
Under 5 yrs.	18,453	7.7	19,198	7.7	17,826	8.6
5 to 14 yrs.	33,408	14.0	35,384	14.2	38,277	14.3
15 to 19 yrs	18,416	7.7	18,968	6.8	18,943	7.1
20 to 24 yrs.	21,301	8.9	18,560	7.4	17,145	6.4
25 to 29 yrs.	21,838	9.2	21,522	8.6	17,396	6.5
30 to 34 yrs.	19,950	8.4	22,007	8.8	19,019	7.1
35 to 39 yrs.	17,894	7.5	20,001	8.0	21,753	8.1
40 to 44 yrs.	14,110	5.9	17,846	7.2	21,990	8.2
45 to 49 yrs.	11,647	4.9	13,980	5.8	19,763	7.4
50 to 54 yrs.	10,817	4.5	11,422	4.6	17,356	6.5
55 to 64 yrs.	22,188	9.3	21,051	8.4	23,787	8.9
65 yrs. & over	23,609	12.0	31,697	12.7	34,921	13.0
All ages	238,831	100.0	249,656	100.0	267,955	100.0

*Includes Armed Forces abroad.
Source: Department of Commerce, Population Series P-25 as of July 1, 1985.

EXHIBIT 9.7 **U.S. production facilities**

Brewery	Year opened	1986 Capacity (In millions of barrels)	Bud	Bud Light	Michelob Light	Michelob	Busch	Natural Light	LA	Michelob Classic Dark
St. Louis	1880	12.7	X	X	X	X	X	X	X	X
Newark	1951	5.3	X	X	X	X				X
Los Angeles	1954	10.9	X	X	X	X		X	X	X
Tampa	1959	1.8	X	X			X	X		
Houston	1966	9	X	X	X	X		X		
Columbus	1968	6.3	X	X	X	X	X	X		
Jacksonville	1969	6.6	X	X	X	X	X	X		
Merrimack	1970	2.97	X	X	X	X	X	X		
Williamsburg	1972	8.7	X	X	X	X	X	X	X	
Fairfield	1976	3.9	X	X	X	X		X		X
Baldwinsville	1982	7.1	X	X	X	X		X	X	
Total		75.27								

Anheuser-Busch has eleven breweries located in nine states, with an annual capacity of 75.27 million barrels of beer (see Exhibit 9.7). A twelfth brewery at Fort Collins, Colorado, is scheduled to be operational in 1988, and its annual capacity will be 5 million barrels. Only the St. Louis plant brews all nine beers (Carlsberg and Elephant Malt Liquor are imported brands manufactured in Denmark).

In order to meet the increasing demand for its beer, Anheuser-Busch has developed an extensive expansion and modernization program. The expansion of the Houston brewery was completed in 1985, providing an additional 5 million barrels of capacity. The modernization programs for the St. Louis, Newark, and Merrimack plants were also completed.

PROMOTION

Anheuser-Busch, probably the largest sponsor of sporting events, vehicles, and broadcasts, has had its beers affiliated with sports for years (see Exhibit 9.8). In fact, the company sponsored the 1984 Olympics, and spent in excess of $100 million advertising on sports television and radio in 1985. Out of a total $522.9 million spent on advertising in 1985, Anheuser-Busch spent $225.25 million in television advertising (see Exhibit 9.9). The top 15 beer advertisers spent a total of $497,163,000 on television advertising in 1985 (see Exhibit 9.10).

Anheuser-Busch began running advertisements exploiting patriotic fervor, a resurgence in the pride of being an American. Miller followed the same advertising strategy. Budweiser sales increased; Miller sales decreased. Budweiser sales are very important to Anheuser-Busch as Bud accounts for more than two-thirds of the company's beer production and one-quarter of the whole domestic market.

EXHIBIT 9.8 **Anheuser-Busch's sports affiliation**

Budweiser	**Michelob**
Horse racing	Lacrosse
Soccer	Rugby
Boxing	Golf
Boat racing	Sailing

Bud Light	**Michelob Light**
Triathlon	Skiing
Track	Volleyball
Boat racing	Tennis

Busch
NASCAR auto racing
Billiards

Source: Anheuser-Busch 1986 Fact Sheet.

EXHIBIT 9.9 **Anheuser-Busch advertising expenditures in 1985**

Media	**(In thousands)**
Magazines	$13,956
Newspapers	5,611
Newspaper suppliers	327
Business publications	724
Network television	154,503
Sports television	70,747
Network radio	8,929
Sports radio	39,713
Outdoor	5,105
Network cable	16,395
Total Measured Media	$316,011
Total Unmeasured	206,889
Total	$522,900

Source: Advertising Age, Sept. 4, 1986.

Following its new strategy, Anheuser-Busch has fine-tuned the campaign "For All You Do, This Bud's For You" into a very successful "You Make America Work, And This Bud's For You." In 1985, measured media ads and promotions topped $80 million for Bud, the most heavily advertised beer in the United States.

EXHIBIT 9.10 **Top 15 beer advertisers on television**

	1985		
	Network	**Spot**	**Total**
Anheuser-Busch Cos.	$143,235,200	$ 55,820,000	$199,055,200
Phillip Morris Cos. (Miller, et al)	112,541,600	27,337,300	139,978,900
Adolph Coors Co.	18,076,400	33,586,800	51,663,200
Stroh Brewery Co.	31,847,700	8,163,800	40,011,500
G. Heileman Brewing Co.	6,931,300	8,782,700	15,714,000
Braueri Beck & Co.	—	4,160,300	4,160,300
RJR Nabisco, Inc. (Fosters, Moosehead)	90,900	1,198,900	1,289,800
Genesee Brewing Co.	192,000	4,962,500	5,154,500
Van Munching & Co.	6,502,900	9,165,800	15,668,700
S & P Co. (Pabst, Pearl, Hamms)	—	1,847,300	1,847,300
Molson Cos.	99,200	1,800,400	1,899,600
Latrobe Brewing Co.	—	444,500	444,500
Pittsburgh Brewing Co.	—	853,700	853,700
John Labatt, Ltd.	—	567,400	567,400
Masters Brewing Co.	—	929,000	929,000
Category Total	$329,202,500	$167,961,100	$497,163,600

Source: Modern Brewery Age, April 13, 1987, p. 1.

PRICING

Anheuser-Busch's pricing strategy varied somewhat by market. Actually, by offering eleven different types of beer there was a product to satisfy each price point. However in markets were Miller was the number-two brand, pricing was set to be competitive. In markets where Heileman threatened the number-two position, Busch set prices more aggressively.

DISTRIBUTION CHANNELS

The company distributes its beer in the United States and the Caribbean through a network of 10 company-owned wholesale operations employing approximately 1,600 people and about 960 independently owned wholesale companies (see Exhibit 9.11). The independent wholesalers employ approximately 30,000 people. Canadian and European distribution is achieved through special arrangements with foreign brewing companies.

Sales volume at the wholesale level ranges from 870 barrels to 1.1 million barrels annually. However, the LA (low alcohol) and Busch brands are presently available only in selected markets around the country.

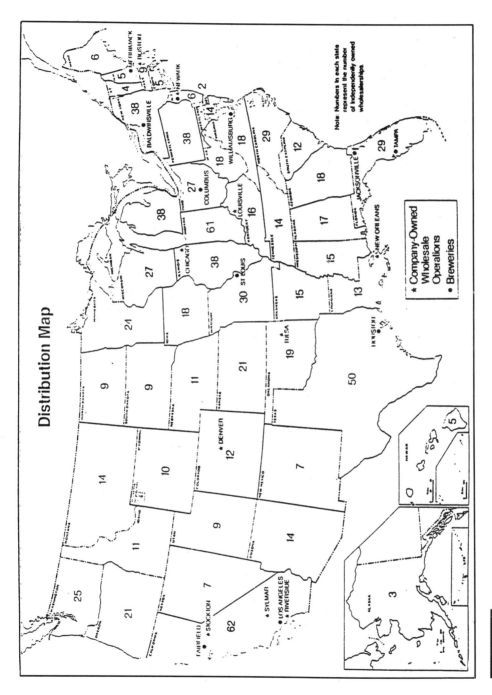

EXHIBIT 9.11 **Distribution map**

THE EXTERNAL ENVIRONMENT

Competition

In 1984, there were 92 domestic brewery plants with a total capacity of 232.7 million barrels of beer. Operating at 78.7 percent of capacity, shipments were 178.4 million barrels (see Exhibit 9.12). This was quite a contrast to the 430 brewers in 1850 who produced 750,000 barrels per year. By the end of the century, there were 1,169 brewers producing over 1 million barrels per year. In 1954 there were 310 plants and 263 brewers, and by 1963 this number shrunk to 211 plants and 171 brewers. This concentration of the industry continued through the next decade resulting in a total of 88 plants and 41 brewers in 1980.

Anheuser-Busch has set a corporate objective of 40 percent market share by the late 1980s. As Mr. Long, President and CEO, said, "We have always seen yesterday's success not as our ending point or a conclusion, but as a springboard into tomorrow's challenges." The challenging objective for the 1990s will be a 50 percent market share. In 1985, the company's market share was 37.1 percent, compared with 35 percent share in the previous year, and 23.4 percent a decade ago. The sales and market share figures of Anheuser-Busch's competitors are shown in Exhibit 9.13.

Miller Brewing has been Anheuser-Busch's prime competitor since Philip Morris Company acquired Miller in 1970. Its market share in 1970 was 4.2 percent (5.1

EXHIBIT 9.12 **U.S. brewing industry capacity and usage in 1984**

Brewer	Number of plants	Total capacity (In millions of barrels)	Shipments	Percent of capacity
Anheuser-Busch	11	66.5	64.0	96.2
Miller Brewing (Philip Morris)	7	54.0	37.5	69.4
The Stroh Brewery	7	32.6	23.9	73.3
G. Heileman Brewing	12	26.5	16.7	63.4
Adolph Coors	1	15.5	13.1	85.2
Pabst Brewing	4	15.0	11.6	77.3
Genesee Brewing	1	4.0	3.0	75.0
Christian Schmidt[1,2]	2	5.0	2.1	42.0
Falstaff Brewing[3]	5	5.0	2.3	46.0
Pittsburgh Brewing	1	1.2	1.0	83.3
All others	41	7.4	3.2	43.2
Domestic total	92	232.7	178.4	78.7

[1] Includes 2.8 million barrels which are tax-free exports and military shipments.

[2] Includes Ohio plant which closed Nov. 1984.

[3] Includes Pearl Brewing Co. and General Brewing Co.

Sources: Company Annual Reports; *Modern Brewery Age Blue Book* and *Impact* Databank.

EXHIBIT 9.13 Sales of leading U.S. brewers (In thousands of barrels)

Company	1970		1980		1984		1985		Percent change in volume 1984-85
	Volume	Market share	Volume	Market share	Volume	Market share	Volume	Market share	
Anheuser-Busch	22,202	18.1	50,160	28.2	64,000	35.0	68,000	37.1	+ 6.3
Miller Brewing	5,150	4.2	37,300	21.0	37,520	20.5	37,100	20.3	− 1.1
The Stroh Brewery	3,276	2.7	6,161	3.5	23,900	13.1	23,400	12.8	− 2.1
G. Heileman Brewing	3,000	2.4	13,270	7.4	16,760	9.2	16,200	8.8	− 3.3
Adolph Coors Co.	7,277	5.9	13,779	7.7	13,187	7.2	14,738	8.1	+11.8
Top 5, total	40,905	33.3	120,670	67.8	155,367	85.0	159,438	87.1	+ 2.8
Other domestic	80,995	66.0	52,830	29.6	20,133	11.1	15,662	8.6	−22.1
Total domestic	121,900	99.3	173,300	97.4	175,500	96.1	175,100	95.7	− 0.2
Imports	900	0.7	4,600	2.5	7,200	3.9	7,900	4.3	+ 9.7
Grand total	122,700	100.0	177,900	100.0	182,700	100.0	183,000	100.0	+ 0.2

million barrels), ranking it as seventh in the industry. The company experienced rapid growth in the 1970s due to the successful introduction of "Lite" beer. Anheuser-Busch countered with two separate strategies. First, the company increased its advertising budgets, taking on Miller in head-to-head competition. Then, Anheuser-Busch developed a strategy of flanking each of Miller's products in every beer category with two Anheuser-Busch beer products (e.g. premium beers—Budweiser and Busch flanked Miller High Life).

Over the past three years, Miller has introduced eight new brands of beer. Although the company had to mothball its Trenton, Ohio, brewery in 1984, its market share grew to 20.3 percent (37.1 million barrels) by 1985, and the company now ranks second in the industry. Miller's sales volume did decline by 1.1 percent in 1985. This was attributed to Miller High Life's continued sales weaknesses. Miller's other premium beer, Lowenbrau, was also competing poorly at this time. However, Miller's profits were up by approximately 17 percent in 1985 over the depressed profit in 1984.

In 1981, the Stroh Brewery purchased F&M Schaefer and closed their Detroit brewery (7.2 million barrel capacity). On April 27, 1982, the Joseph Schlitz Brewing Company was merged into The Stroh Brewery, resulting in Stroh becoming the third largest brewer. The company shipped 13.1 million barrels of beer in 1985, representing 12.8 percent market share and 2.1 percent decline in sales volume over the previous year.

G. Heileman Brewing, the United States' fourth largest brewer, has been very effective in competing against Anheuser-Busch in regional markets. It has successfully developed and implemented a strategy of acquiring struggling local brewers at low cost. After acquiring the new brewery, Heileman reintroduced its brands with an aggressive marketing plan. Anheuser-Busch countered with a strategy focused on heavy price competition from its Busch brand. Although G. Heileman halted its planned expansion into the southwest market, the company's market share grew from 2.4 percent (3.0 million barrels) in 1970 to 8.8 percent (16.2 million barrels) in 1985. The company's earnings from the brewing industry declined by 11 percent in 1985, and it closed its small Phoenix plant (500,000 barrels).

The fifth largest brewer, Adolph Coors Company, had a 13-percent volume increase in sales in 1985. This increase was the result of an aggressive expansion in the New England and Illinois markets. Coors' profits from beer increased by 77 percent over its poor 1984 performance.

The top five brewers in the nation accounted for 87.1 percent of sales in 1985, a 2.6 percent increase over the previous year. Pabst Brewing, the sixth largest brewer, experienced a decline in market share from 6.5 percent in 1984 to 5.0 percent in 1985. The company's new owners aggressively increased prices in 1985.

Social Values and Beer

Anheuser-Busch ". . . is deeply concerned about the abuse of alcohol and the problem of driving while intoxicated. It supports the proposition that anything less than responsible consumption of alcoholic beverages is detrimental to the individual, to society, and to the brewing industry." The company has been a leader in developing programs that support this position.

The TIPS program was developed in 1985 by Heath Communications Corporation, Anheuser-Busch, and the Miller Brewing Company to train retail personnel to deal effectively with patrons who overindulge. Approximately 1,500 Anheuser-Busch wholesaler employees are now certified trainers. Their goal is to train 10,000 retail servers nationwide.

Anheuser-Busch was the first major brewer to run alcohol abuse messages on network television. The company is an active sponsor of SADD (Students Against Drunk Driving), and it developed Operation ALERT (Action, Leadership, Education, Responsibility, and Training) which serves as an umbrella covering a variety of different educational and awareness programs.

Legislation and Litigation

In recent years, Anheuser-Busch has become more active in monitoring and taking positions on issues that could have a major impact on the company.

Trademark Protection.   Recently, a lawsuit has been filed by G. Heileman Brewing and joined by Miller Brewing Company against Anheuser-Busch's use of "LA" (low alcohol) as a brand name. As did a previous suit by the Stroh Brewery, these breweries claim LA is a generic term. Anheuser-Busch won the Stroh Brewery suit with their claim that LA is a trademark and not a generic term.

Exclusive Distribution.   The Malt Beverage Interbrand Competition Act of 1985 deals with the exclusive wholesale distribution rights for distributors within their territories. The state of Indiana is the only state to forbid exclusive distribution contracts, and 27 states require the contracts.

In 1977, a Supreme Court decision ruled such exclusive contracts can be legal if the contracts don't hamper competition, but that a decision would be made on a case-by-case basis. Distributors and brewers say that this court decision has created lawsuits by inviting competitors, both wholesalers and retailers, to challenge the competitor's exclusive distribution contracts.

This new bill, which has been cleared by the Senate Judiciary Committee, would preserve the right to sue for antitrust violations. The 140-member U.S. Brewers Association and the 2,000-member National Beer Wholesaler Association have lobbied for the bill, since they feel it would clarify the existing antitrust law. Opponents to the bill, including the Federal Trade Commission, Senator Strom Thurmond, Senator Howard Metzenbaum, and numerous consumer groups, feel that exempting the beer industry from the antitrust laws would increase prices and reduce competition. In fact, the New York Attorney General has filed a class action lawsuit against Miller, Stroh, Heileman, and Anheuser-Busch claiming that their exclusive agreements with distributors have caused price increases and decreased competition.

Minimum Drinking Age.   The National Minimum Drinking Age Act of 1984 granted the federal government the authority to withhold federal highway funds from states that failed to raise their legal drinking age to 21 by 1986. Currently, there are some 40 states that mandate or have approved a 21-year-old minimum drinking age.

Anheuser-Busch and Minorities.   In 1983, The Reverend Jesse Jackson's campaign PUSH, directed against Anheuser-Busch Companies, Inc., accused the company of discriminating against blacks and encouraged minorities to boycott Anheuser-Busch's products. Using the battle cry "Bud is a Dud," Jackson claimed the company did not do business with enough minorities, did not hire and promote black employees, did not patronize black-oriented community organizations, and did not have enough black wholesalers in the distribution system. Eventually, Mr. Wayman Smith, Vice President of Corporate Affairs, was able to make the Reverend Jackson aware of the company's minority hiring and promotion practices, their support to minorities throughout the country, and the role of minority suppliers. As a result of Jesse Jackson's campaign, Anheuser-Busch agreed to:

1. Spend $23 million in procurements from minority businesses.
2. Spend $8 million on advertising in minority media.
3. Spend $10 million in construction performed by minority firms.
4. Hold $2 million in certificates of deposit in 41 minority-owned banks.
5. Establish lines of credit for $6 million with 25 of these banks and $6 million in payroll deposits.

EXHIBIT 9.14 **Consolidated balance sheet**

Assets	1984	1985
	(In millions of dollars)	
Current Assets		
Cash and marketable securities (marketable securities of $119.9 in 1985 and $69.3 in 1984 at cost, which approximates market)	$ 78.6	$ 169.6
Accounts and notes receivable, less allowance for doubtful accounts of $3.1 in 1985 and $2.8 in 1984	275.6	301.7
Inventories—		
Raw materials and supplies	212.7	225.4
Work in process	65.7	73.5
Finished goods	37.5	38.8
Total inventories	315.9	337.7
Other current assets	106.2	156.5
Total current assets	776.3	965.5

Investments And Other Assets

Investments in and advances to unconsolidated subsidiaries	42.9	56.7
Investment properties.....................................	18.1	16.5
Deferred charges and other non-current assets	87.1	97.5
Excess of cost over net assets of acquired businesses, net	85.3	99.3
	233.4	270.0

Plant And Equipment

Land..	85.4	91.8
Buildings	1,399.3	1,578.7
Machinery and equipment.................................	2,920.6	3,381.4
Construction in progress	395.3	288.9
	4,800.6	5,340.8
Less accumulated depreciation............................	1,285.6	1,454.9
	3,515.0	3,885.9
Total Assets	$4,524.7	$5,121.4

Liabilities and Shareholders Equity

Current Liabilities

Accounts payable......................................	$ 338.2	$ 425.3
Accrued salaries, wages and benefits	150.3	177.1
Accrued interest payable.................................	26.8	30.1
Due to customers for returnable containers	31.8	33.1
Accrued taxes, other than income taxes	43.6	56.9
Estimated income taxes..................................	39.0	31.3
Other current liabilities	66.3	84.0
Total current liabilities	696.0	837.8

Long-term Debt	835.8	861.3
Deferred Income Taxes...................................	755.0	961.7
Convertible Redeemable Preferred Stock (Liquidation Value $300.0)................................	286.9	287.6

Common Stock And Other Shareholders Equity

Preferred stock, $1.00 par value, authorized 32,498,000 shares in 1985, 1984 and 1983; none issued	—	—
Common stock, $1.00 par value, authorized 200,000,000 shares in 1985, 1984 and 1983; issued 146,633,977, 48,641,869 and 48,514,214 shares, respectively	48.6	146.6
Capital in excess of par value	173.2	90.4
Retained earnings..	1,829.3	2,142.3
Foreign currency translation adjustment	(6.6)	(4.4)
	2,044.5	2,374.9
Less cost of treasury stock (8,114,453, 4,692,456 and 358,656 shares in 1985, 1984 and 1983, respectively)	93.5	201.9
	1,951.0	2,173.0
Commitments And Contingencies	—	—
Total Liabilities and Shareholder's Equity	$4,524.7	$5,121.4

EXHIBIT 9.15 Financial summary—operations

Consolidated Summary of Operations	1975	1976	1977	1978	1979	1980	1981	1982	1983	1984	1985
Barrels sold	35.2	29.1	36.6	41.6	46.2	50.2	54.5	59.1	60.5	64.0	68.0
Sales	$2,036.7	$1,753.0	$2,231.2	$2,701.6	$3,263.7	$3,822.4	$4,409.6	$5,185.7	$6,658.5	$7,158.2	$7,683.3
Federal and state beer taxes	391.7	311.9	393.2	442.0	487.8	527.0	562.4	609.1	624.3	657.0	683.0
Net sales	1,645.0	1,441.1	1,838.0	2,259.6	2,775.9	3,295.4	3,847.2	4,576.6	6,034.2	6,501.2	7,000.3
Cost of products sold	1,343.8	1,175.0	1,462.8	1,762.4	2,172.1	2,553.9	2,975.5	3,331.7	4,113.2	4,414.2	4,676.1
Gross profit	301.2	266.1	375.2	497.2	603.8	741.5	871.7	1,244.9	1,921.0	2,087.0	2,324.2
Marketing, administrative and research expenses	126.1	137.8	190.4	274.9	356.7	428.6	515.0	752.0	1,220.2	1,332.3	1,491.9
Operating income	175.1	128.3	184.8	222.3	247.1	312.9	356.7	492.9	700.8	754.7	832.3
Interest expense	(22.6)	(26.9)	(26.7)	(28.9)	(40.3)	(75.6)	(89.6)	(89.2)	(111.4)	(102.7)	(93.4)
Interest capitalized	10.9	10.3	7.7	11.7	8.4	41.7	64.1	41.2	32.9	46.8	37.2
Interest income						2.4	6.2	17.0	12.5	22.8	21.3
Other income (expense), net	1.9	1.7	4.1	.7	5.4	(9.9)	(12.2)	(8.1)	(18.8)	(31.8)	(16.9)
Loss on partial closing of Los Angeles Busch Gardens		(10.0)									
Gain on sale of Lafayette plant								20.4			

Income before income taxes	165.3	103.4	169.9	205.8	220.6	271.5	325.2	474.2	616.0	689.8	780.5
Income taxes	80.6	48.0	78.0	94.8	76.3	99.7	107.8	186.9	268.0	298.3	336.8
Income before cumulative effect of an accounting change	84.7	55.4	91.9	111.0	144.3	171.8	217.4	287.3	348.0	391.5	443.7
Cumulative effect of change to the flow-through method of accounting for the investment tax credit					52.1						
Net income	84.7	55.4	91.9	111.0	196.4	171.8	217.4	287.3	348.0	391.5	443.7
Per share—Primary											
Income before cumulative effect of an accounting change	.63	.41	.68	.82	1.07	1.27	1.60	1.99	2.17	2.47	2.84
Cumulative effect of change to the flow-through method of accounting for the investment tax credit					.38						
Net income	.63	.41	.68	.82	1.45	1.27	1.60	1.99	2.17	2.47	2.84
Per share—Fully diluted	.63	.41	.68	.82	1.45	1.27	1.54	1.96	2.17	2.47	2.84
Cash dividends paid											
Common stock	28.8	30.6	32.0	37.0	40.7	44.8	51.2	65.8	78.3	89.7	102.7
Per share	.21$\frac{1}{3}$	.22$\frac{2}{3}$	.23$\frac{2}{3}$	.27$\frac{1}{3}$	.30	.33	.37$\frac{2}{3}$	.46	.54	.62$\frac{2}{3}$	.73$\frac{1}{3}$
Preferred stock									29.7	27.0	27.0
Per share									3.60	3.60	3.60
Average number of common shares	135.3	135.3	135.3	135.3	135.6	135.6	136.2	144.3	160.5	158.7	156.3

FINANCIAL CONDITION

Financial data for the company can be found in Exhibits 9.14 and 9.15. For the next five years, the company has planned for extensive capital expenditure programs to take advantage of growth opportunities in its three business segments. The company is not opposed to long-term financing for some of its capital programs, but cash flow from operations will be the principal source of funds to support these programs. For short-term capital requirements, the company has access to a maximum of $500 million from a bank credit-line agreement.

CASE 10

Sit 'n Pick Essential Products, Inc.

Ray Campbell sat back and admired his work. After months of redesigning he finally had the Sit 'n Pick to his satisfaction. The combination stool and pail looked good and was sturdy enough to hold a 300-pound person. The production problems were resolved. Now it was really up to his sister Carolyn to market his invention.

Ray had studied drafting in college before being persuaded to quit and go to work for his uncle in a family business. When embezzlement by the uncle caused the business to fail, Ray began working for Plastic Formers Company as the production plant manager. He frequently designed and constructed the plastic molds used in the company's production processes.

A dentist asked Ray to design a dome that could be used by dentists for protection when they were working with dangerous chemicals. Water accessibility and ventilation inside the dome were required. Ray designed a product that he demonstrated at a national dental association meeting. The product was instantly successful and was very profitable for the dentist; however, Ray's salary at Plastic Formers did not change. He vowed to design a product that he could patent: something essential.

When Plastic Formers became erratic in paying him, Ray quit, bought a farm, and went to work as a quality control manager for a major electronics company. It was the farm that provided the impetus to develop Sit 'n Pick.

Ray's wife was plagued by a bad back and had difficulty picking the vegetables in their large garden on the farm. She asked Ray to build a bucket she could sit on.

This case was prepared by Linda E. Swayne. It is intended as a basis for classroom discussion rather than to illustrate effective or ineffective handling of an administrative situation. Used by permission of Linda E. Swayne.

EXHIBIT 10.1 **Sit 'n Pick in use**

The result, after a number of modifications, was Ray's useful product that could be patented—Sit 'n Pick.

The product is manufactured in a rotational mold. Four pounds of hot polyethelene are poured into the mold which is then rotated to coat the inside. When the polyethelene is cooled, the mold is removed. One mold produces four Sit 'n Picks every twenty minutes.

Because the plastic is hard, Ray's wife suggested a pad be added to the seat. The center reinforcing bar acts as a built-in handle. Most people who saw it suggested that the only thing missing was a handle. Ray decided to add a label that identified the handle and also provided an address for the company.

HANDLE
Essential Products, Inc.
P.O. Box 519
Newell, North Carolina
28126

Ray's sister, Carolyn Ward, was willing to take on the task of marketing Sit 'n Pick. She had experience in sales, first as a real estate agent, and then with a producer of custom business magazines where she was responsible for selling advertising space.

Now that the product was ready, Ray and Carolyn were trying to decide on a price. Ray spent his own money to incorporate, obtain the patent, and develop the product (Exhibit 10.2).

EXHIBIT 10.2 **Start-up costs**

Incorporation fees and taxes	$ 552.00
Patent fees	650.00
Injection mold (additional molds $1000 each)	1,621.00
Die to stamp pads (seat cushion)	80.00
Jigsaw to cut out pail piece	125.00
R & D	5,382.00
Prototype production	400.00
	$8,810.00

Ray wanted to manufacture Sit 'n Picks in his garage workshop but it appeared that he would have to pay $5,500 yearly in insurance. A local manufacturer had the capability of producing Sit 'n Picks. Using one mold the cost per unit would be $7.65. By purchasing additional molds at a cost of $1,000 each, the cost could be reduced to the amounts shown in Exhibit 10.3.

EXHIBIT 10.3 **Cost to produce**

Number of molds	Cost per unit
1 mold	$7.65
7 molds	6.25
10 molds	5.00
12 molds	4.16

Each Sit 'n Pick was made of four pounds of plastic at a cost of $.60 per pound. Quantity discounts for the plastic were at such high levels that Ray didn't think they would ever buy enough to qualify. Therefore, the minimum raw material cost was $2.40 per unit.

At lower levels of production, the machine re-tooling charge and labor were relatively high per unit, resulting in the $7.65 cost. If sales were good, Ray planned to buy more molds. Other costs would be incurred to complete the product (Exhibit 10.4).

EXHIBIT 10.4 **Sit 'n Pick manufacturing costs**

Unit to be picked up at plant	$7.65
Seat pad	0.551
Glue to attach pad to seat	0.20
Label to identify handle, manufacturer	0.075
Mailing label	0.02
Box for shipping	0.67
Tape to close box	0.03
Instruction sheet (includes disclaimers)	0.126
Labor (pack, prepare; 100/hour)	0.05
Transportation	0.09
Actual product cost, ready to ship	$9.462

The seat pad was being cut out of polyurethane foam that was firm and tear resistent. If the density of the pad was reduced by one pound the seat would be a little softer and slightly cheaper. The pad costs $.49 in material, $.011 in shipping to Newell, North Carolina, and $.05 tooling charge (actual charge, $15.00 per set-up) for a total of $.551. The cost for glue, boxes, and instruction sheets would also decline if larger orders were placed. Costs were based on an initial production run of 250 units.

Other operating costs that were incurred include a warehousing charge, telephone, and product liability insurance (Exhibit 10.5). Ray and Carolyn were very concerned about product liability. Ray designed the Sit 'n Pick to hold a 300-pound person in hot weather with the sun directly hitting it. The insurance company recommended that the instruction sheet (disclaimer statement) indicate that Sit 'n Pick was not to be used by those weighing more than 300 pounds and it was not to be used as a step stool. Actually the Sit 'n Pick was a pretty handy stool as long as all weight was kept on the stool portion. Any shift of weight to the pail portion, because of its design, would cause the climber to fall (Exhibit 10.6).

After figuring cost information, Ray and Carolyn had to determine the price they thought consumers would be willing to pay. A skimming strategy had definite appeal since Ray was interested in re-couping his investment as quickly as possible. However, a plastic stool was selling for $3.79 at a typical discount store and plastic buckets could be purchased for as little as $.88. A stool and bucket could cost $4.67

EXHIBIT 10.5 **Operating costs per month**

Warehouse	$200.00
Telephone	65.00
Insurance	17.50
Office supplies	10.00
	$292.50

EXHIBIT 10.6 **Sit 'n Pick instability**

which is significantly *less* than Ray's production costs for a Sit 'n Pick. How much more would customers be willing to pay for the novel combination of a stool and bucket?

The critical decision in determining price was based on the target market. Will Sit 'n Pick be purchased by serious home gardeners and DIY's (do-it-yourselfers) for their own use or will it be purchased as a gift? The individual buying the product for his or her own use would likely compare the cost of purchasing a stool plus a pail against the cost of Sit 'n Pick. A gift item, on the other hand, is more subject to specific price points—the customer is looking for a $10 gift, a $20 gift, or a $25 gift. The target market selected would directly affect distribution and promotion decisions that had to be made, as well.

Ray was certain that patent infringement could be easily avoided by simple modifications to his idea. He estimated that Essential Products would only have one season without direct competition. Mass producers of plastic products (such as Rubbermaid) would have significantly better marketing opportunities. The company needed to move quickly to get the product to the marketplace. Carolyn knew that if they sold through retailers, they would be able to speed up distribution. There were over 7,000 farm/garden supply stores in 1982 and many more garden supply departments in discount and department stores (Exhibit 10.7). A variety of merchant wholesalers, agents, brokers, commission merchants, and manufacturers respresevatives were available to service the retailers.

If Essential Products were to use a channel of distribution rather than direct marketing, more decisions had to be made. Transportation charges, quantity discounts, cash discounts, functional or trade discounts, and promotional allowances had to be computed in the analysis to determine the price for Sit 'n Pick.

Postage and handling fees would be an additional cost to final consumers who purchased directly from Essential Products. This is a common practice in direct

---

EXHIBIT 10.7 **Retail farm/garden supply stores by size**

Annual store sales	Number retail stores	Total sales
Less than $50,000	1,029	$ 27,557,000
$50,000 to less than $100,000	931	66,305,000
$100,000 to less than $250,000	2,076	343,804,000
$250,000 to less than $500,000	1,593	565,501,000
$500,000 to less than $1,000,000	1,083	739,839,000
Over $1,000,000	605	989,013,000
	7,317	$2,732,019,000

Source: Statistical Abstract, 1985.

---

marketing and customer resistence was not expected to the typical $2.00 postage and handling fee. However, transportation charges to channel members would vary considerably according to the distance shipped. If they used delivered pricing (F.O.B. destination) they had to consider a single-zone or multiple-zone pricing policy. An individual Sit 'n Pick weighed six pounds and a four-pack box weighed 27 pounds. The shipping charges from Newell, North Carolina, are illustrated in Exhibit 10.8 and Exhibit 10.9.

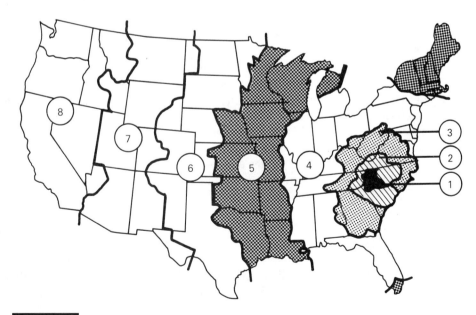

EXHIBIT 10.8 **Shipping charge zones from Newell, N.C.**

EXHIBIT 10.9 Shipping charges for zones

| | Cost | | | |
| | 6 lb. | | 27 lb. | |
Zone	Parcel post	Pvt. carrier	Parcel post	Pvt. carrier
1	$1.58	$1.57	$ 2.45	$ 3.30
2	1.74	1.57	2.92	3.30
3	2.04	1.89	3.85	4.54
4	2.50	2.30	5.18	5.83
5	3.18	2.59	7.20	7.08
6	3.92	2.98	9.38	8.82
7	4.74	3.39	11.60	10.64
8	6.49	3.82	16.99	12.56

Regarding a quantity discount, Carolyn knew the following questions had to be answered:

1. What would be the minimum quantity required before the discount would be applied?
2. How many quantity categories should be established for additional discounts on larger purchases?
3. What is the maximum quantity to qualify for additional discounts (maximum discount allowed)?
4. What should be the amount of discount for each category?

In the nursery/garden supply industry, functional discounts are typically offered and vary from 8 percent to 15 percent for wholesalers and 33 percent to 50 percent for retailers. Wholesalers and retailers demand the larger discounts from smaller, lesser-known manufacturers. Cash discounts of 2/10 net 30 are commonplace in the nursery/garden supply industry. Carolyn thought Essential Products would probably have to match that discount.

Rather than using a longer distribution channel, Carolyn favored direct marketing to consumers, either by direct mail or by the shopping section of *Southern Living* or similar magazines.

According to Simmons Market Research Bureau, in 1984 four percent of the adult population purchased gardening-related products by mail or phone. *Southern Living* readers have a slightly higher usage of mail or phone. Six percent of *Southern Living* readers purchased gardening products by mail or phone over the last twelve months. Total adult subscribers were 2,253,000 in 1985, however 6,488,000 adults were reached by the Southern food- and garden-oriented publication. *Southern Living* charged $1,700 for a 2 1/4-x-2 inch ad, inserted one time. Camera-ready copy was required.

Recently, information was received from another publication, *Organic Gardening*, that seemed like a better, less expensive alternative to *Southern Living*. Circulation

---

EXHIBIT 10.10 **Magazine circulation and cost comparisons for garden-oriented publications**

Magazine	Circulation	Cost classified (1/12 pg. BW)	Cost display (1/3 pg. 4C)
Better Homes & Gardens	8,058,839	$5,604.20	$35,221.00
Country Living	1,183,916	2,180.00	14,290.00
Family Handyman	1,204,148	1,305.50	8,950.00
House Beautiful	867,736	1,190.00	12,940.00
Mother Earth News	857,010	1,190.00	6,760.00
Organic Gardening	1,378,628	1,620.00	n/a
Outdoor Life	1,514,660	1,500.00	12,210.00
Popular Science	1,803,994	2,205.00	13,675.00
Southern Living	2,253,569	1,700.00	15,920.00
Sunset	1,387,855	1,103.50	n/a

Source: *Consumer Magazine and Agri-Media Rates and Data*, July 27, 1985.

---

and costs for selected magazines indicate that *Organic Gardening* could be a good choice (Exhibits 10.10 and 10.11).

Carolyn felt that a national list of adults with gardening interests could be purchased from one of the many mail list suppliers for about $40 per thousand. The direct mail piece could be very simple and inexpensive or very "slick" with color photos and special offers at a higher price. The price that was determined for the product would affect the kind of direct mail piece that should be developed.

Everything seemed to revolve around the price for Sit 'n Pick. Carolyn favored a direct marketing strategy using classified sections of magazines and direct mail. She thought those customers would be willing to pay $19.95 for a Sit 'n Pick. Ray preferred using a longer channel of distribution (W-R-C) because Essential Products would sell in quantity to a few buyers and Ray could use the cash flow to begin other products. Many issues had to be resolved, and quickly, if the product was going to be available for the spring start of the gardening season.

EXHIBIT 10.11 **Magazine readers gardening activities**

Did outdoor gardening as a leisure activity in last 12 months	Bought vegetable seeds in last 12 months	Bought $10+ vegetable seeds in last 12 months	Bought $20+ vegetable seeds in last 12 months	Bought $20+ vegetable garden fertilizer in last 12 months	Bought flower seeds in last 12 months	Bought $10+ flower seeds in last 12 months	Bought $20+ flower seeds in last 12 months	Bought trees, plants, seeds by mail in last 12 months
ORGANIC GARDENING 187	ORGANIC GARDENING 137	ORGANIC GARDENING 210	ORGANIC GARDENING 251	ORGANIC GARDENING 166	ORGANIC GARDENING 120	Country Living 167	Country Living 215	ORGANIC GARDENING 336
Sunset 171	Mother Earth News 109	Country Living 149	Mother Earth News 158	Popular Science 115	Sports Afield 108	ORGANIC GARDENING 162	ORGANIC GARDENING 155	Mother Earth News 314
Mother Earth News 154	Field & Stream 107	Mother Earth News 130	Country Living 139	Popular Mechanics 110	Country Living 106	Better Homes & Gardens 122	Popular Science 147	Country Living 257
Country Living 138	Sports Afield 103	Family Handyman 130	Popular Science 125	Country Living 110	Popular Science 106	Popular Mechanics 122	Popular Mechanics 146	Popular Mechanics 189
Popular Mechanics 128	Popular Mechanics 102	Field & Stream 118	Popular Mechanics 119	Family Handyman 105	Better Homes & Gardens 106	Popular Science 119	Family Handyman 140	Family Handyman 175
Better Homes & Gardens 125	Family Handyman 102	Popular Mechanics 111	Field & Stream 108	Mother Earth News 105	Mother Earth News 105	Family Handyman 117	Mother Earth News 133	Southern Living 149

Family Handyman	Mechanix Illustrated	Better Homes & Gardens	Family Handyman	Field & Stream	Popular Mechanics	Mother Earth News	Mechanix Illustrated	Better Homes & Gardens
Family Handyman 123	Mechanix Illustrated 102	Better Homes & Gardens 107	Family Handyman 101	Field & Stream 104	Popular Mechanics 102	Mother Earth News 109	Mechanix Illustrated 124	Better Homes & Gardens 148
Popular Science 119	Popular Science 102	Popular Science 106	Better Homes & Gardens 96	Better Homes & Gardens 95	Field & Stream 101	Mechanix Illustrated 108	Better Homes & Gardens 115	Mechanix Illustrated 124
Outdoor Life 118	Outdoor Life 101	Sports Afield 105	Mechanix Illustrated 84	House Beautiful 95	Sunset 100	House Beautiful 95	Field & Stream 104	House Beautiful 121
Field & Stream 118	Country Living 99	Outdoor Life 104	Southern Living 80	Sunset 99	Outdoor Life 99	Field & Stream 95	House Beautiful 101	Outdoor Life 114
Southern Living 118	Better Homes & Gardens 97	Mechanix Illustrated 97	Sports Afield 76	Southern Living 88	Family Handyman 95	Sports Afield 91	Sports Afield 101	Popular Science 110
House Beautiful 116	Sunset 91	House Beautiful 82	House Beautiful 72	Sports Afield 88	House Beautiful 93	Southern Living 83	Southern Living 95	Sports Afield 109
Mechanix Illustrated 112	Southern Living 88	Southern Living 75	Outdoor Life 62	Mechanix Illustrated 85	Mechanix Illustrated 91	Outdoor Life 74	Outdoor Life 91	Field & Stream 100
Sports Afield 101	House Beautiful 77	Sunset 50	Sunset 11	Outdoor Life 81	Southern Living 90	Sunset 54	Sunset 43	Sunset 56
Index of 100 = composition of: 32.6%	46.3%	14.9%	5.6%	6.7%	43.4%	8.6%	3.8%	4.0%

Source: 1984 SMRB Study.

CASE 11

The Home Baking Company: Reaching a Crossroad

It was unfortunate that McDonald's had put the decision for a bakery dedicated to producing exclusively for the fast-food leader on hold, thought Ernest Stevens, President of Home Baking Company. He had advocated developing the proposal to build the bakery because it would free capacity at the present plant and provide a significant amount of demand from the southeastern McDonald's fast-food restaurants. However, the news from the fast-food industry for 1986 was not great. Stevens wondered if he should tie Home Baking's future so closely to the success of the fast-food giant.

Home Baking Company operated under the philosphy that a high level of service and quality would result in continued growth for the company. Growth had always been an important objective for Home Baking. However Mr. Stevens believed that if Home Baking Company was to continue to grow in 1987, some difficult decisions had to be made. Home Baking was at a crossroads and these decisions would dramatically influence the character of the company for many years. These decisions concerned Home Baking's future position as a supplier to the fast-food industry, alternatives for new product and market development, alternatives for expanding production capacity, and methods for financing additional growth.

Home Baking Company, a family-owned bakery located in Birmingham, Alabama, offered over forty products in three main categories—hamburger buns, hot dog buns, and brown 'n serve rolls. Home Baking marketed bread products primarily to the fast-food industry throughout the state of Alabama and in defined markets in Georgia, South Carolina, and the Florida panhandle. In addition, the company distributed to restaurants, hotels, schools, and hospitals in Birmingham and surrounding areas. All of the company's products were packaged and labeled under the "Tasty" brand and were not available at the retail level.

Since its founding, Home Baking enjoyed steady growth. The company's growth paralleled the growth of the fast-food industry during the 1970s and 1980s. However, Stevens was concerned that the fast-food industry had reached "maturity" and the growth of the industry would taper off. In order to maintain the growth of Home Baking, Stevens believed that the company must re-evaluate their market position and range of products.

This case was prepared by Peter M. Ginter and Linda E. Swayne from materials developed in an M.B.A. student project by Janice Boatwright, Dennis Bobo, Renee Gafford, Jacqueline Garner, Marlene McCain, and Mike Rugh. It is intended as a basis for classroom discussion rather than to illustrate effective or ineffective handling of an administrative situation. Used by permission from Peter M. Ginter.

THE DEVELOPMENT OF HOME BAKING COMPANY

Home Baking Company opened its doors in 1920 as a general full-line bakery. Three horse-and-buggy routes were used originally to distribute the company's full line of bakery foods house-to-house and to retail outlets. The full line of goods initially included pies and pastries, as well as loaf bread, french bread, and other bread products. High labor and distribution costs soon put an end to home deliveries and steered the company into the restaurant segment of the market.

Operations ran smoothly until 1971 when the company faced an important decision. Increasing labor costs and renegotiated union contracts forced the company to specialize their services and automate their operations in order to remain competitive. Stevens redirected the business to providing hamburger buns to the fast-food industry and adopted drop shipment distribution (direct delivery in truck or van load quantity). The repositioning established Home Baking as strictly a manufacturing company and concentrated its production in roll products such as hamburger buns, hot dog buns, and brown 'n serve rolls.

From a modest start of one delivery route serving twelve McDonald's restaurants, Home Baking Company's "bulk sales" department grew to 28 routes serving over 500 customers. In 1987, fast-food chains accounted for the majority of the company's business. In addition to the bulk sales department, a "route sales" department was created. Route sales included sales to restaurants, hotels, schools, hospitals, etc., in metropolitan Birmingham and Jefferson County. This department grew to 12 metropolitan routes serving almost 500 customers.

In 1975, Home Baking installed new bun-line processing equipment to replace outdated ovens and floor cooling racks. This investment resulted in major improvements in efficiency for the company. With the addition of a second bun-line in 1979, the company's automated equipment provided a competitive edge over other bakeries. Although newer and improved equipment became available, Home Baking continued to rely on the two bun-line processing equipment purchased in the 1970s, with modifications made in the equipment.

Since its early years, the company's net sales increased dramatically from approximately $3 million in 1977 to $12 million in 1986. Home Baking Company acquired a leadership position in its market area by relying on an image of quality and service.

THE BAKING INDUSTRY

The baking of bread and bread products constitutes a large portion of the food industry. In 1986, bakeries produced over $22 billion dollars worth of goods and provided employment for over 164,000 workers. The shipment of breads and cakes represented about 68 percent of the baking industry, while cookies and crackers provided the remainder. Of this total, slightly over 25 percent of the dollar volume was attributed to the single-shop retail bakery selling directly to the consumer.

In 1986, large baking plants did exist, but most production was handled by relatively small plants scattered across the country. Over the years, the optimum size plant for bakeries had been established at about 150 to 250 employees. Due to excessive transportation cost and the highly perishable nature of baked foods, optimum distribution was within a limited area around the point of manufacture. Although many bakeries produced in only one location, large companies controlled most of the industry. Several food conglomerates operated twenty to sixty bakeries across the country located primarily near large population centers.

In 1986, several firms had embarked upon major capital improvements at the same time that excess capacity led to plant closings in other parts of the country. Confronting overcapacity, Keebler shut down its Philadelphia operation. Campbell Taggart closed its Kansas City plant and now supplies that market from other facilities. Continental Bakeries ceased production at two bread facilities and halted output of sweet goods at two others. Between July 1985 and January 1987, Continental closed six bread plants.

Planned 1986 capital expenditures of some major bread and cake manufacturers includes, Campbell Taggart, $100 million; Pepperidge Farm, a unit of Campbell Soup, $33 million including $25 million for a new plant in Florida; and Flowers Industries, $24 million.

Technology

The baking industry has made tremendous strides from the time of mom and pop bakeries. In the early years, the baking industry was labor intensive, however because of increasing labor costs, mechanization was introduced. Initially, only baking equipment was motorized, allowing for increased batch sizes. Then the assembly line was introduced. Soon the entire process was automated which reduced the number of workers to strategic points in the baking process. In order to remain profitable, most of the industry has adopted automated processes.

The industry trend in the 1980s is towards even more mechanization and less labor. Computers and programmable controls are being integrated into the baking process. Personal computers and information management have helped the industry gain better control of inventories and have expedited the movement of finished goods.

The future of the industry may prove even more exciting as bakery engineers utilize the computer. It is only a matter of time before a total robotic bread production facility replaces the present system. In addition, biogenetic engineers are on the verge of producing ingredients that will revolutionize the baking industry. Higher protein, disease-resistant wheat is winning favor with farmers. Experiments with the crystalline structure of sweeteners also have proven very successful. New yeast products are being studied in order to reduce the fermentation process time and improve the taste of existing products.

Competition

In 1987, Home Baking Company had four major competitors—Interstate Brands Corporation, Flowers Industries, Campbell Taggart, and Golden State Bakery.

Interstate Brands Corporation, headquartered in Kansas City, marketed its products nationally. Interstate's markets were primarily retail, offering brands such as Millbrook, Dutch Hearth, Butternut, and Dolly Madison. Although Interstate Brands had a bakery in Birmingham, it had low market share in Home Baking Company's non-consumer market. One reason was that Interstate's ingredients and processes were designed as supermarket products, while Home Baking's products were better suited for restaurants. In addition, Home Baking had better service and a shorter lead time for delivery. In order to provide a wider product line to its restaurant customers, Home Baking purchased certain bread products for resale.

Flowers Industries, Inc., was a national company headquartered in Thomasville, Georgia. It produced a diverse retail product line including Holsom, Cobblestone Mill, Sunbeam, Roman Meal, and Nature's Own brands of bakery products. Flowers closed its bakery in Birmingham and sold its area distribution routes to its drivers. Subsequent servicing problems resulted in Home Baking's acquiring several of Flower's customers. Recently however, Flowers opened a specialty plant in Opelika, Alabama, producing hamburger buns, and recaptured some of its previous business. Flowers has had low market share in Home Baking's non-consumer market because Home Baking was viewed as having better quality and service.

Flowers also owned a subsidiary in Orlando, Florida, called Continental Food Service. This subsidiary produced fresh and frozen products and was the primary competitor of Home Baking's frozen products in the Florida panhandle.

Campbell Taggart, a subsidiary of Anheuser-Busch, was a national retail producer of branded baked goods such as Colonial, Rainbow, and Earthgrain. It distributed products in the retail market in Birmingham, but had no local bakery. It had a low market share in non-consumer markets due to Home Baking's high quality and service.

Golden State Bakery made hamburger buns and other food products solely for McDonald's. In 1987, Golden State and Home Baking were the only approved McDonald's bakeries in the Atlanta region. Golden State had six production facilities including a bakery in Atlanta. At one time, its hamburger buns were all frozen, but Home Baking began taking its market share in Georgia with fresh products, so Golden State switched to fresh. However, Home Baking still had a slight competitive edge in quality and a significant edge in service. Exhibit 11.1 provides a comparison of key financial highlights for Home Baking Company and their major competitors.

HOME BAKING'S MARKETING MIX STRATEGIES

Product

Home Baking's product line consisted of over forty fresh items including hamburger buns, hot dog buns, brown 'n serve rolls, and breads. They also produced frozen hamburger buns. Exhibit 11.2 shows Home Baking's products by percent of total sales. Hamburger and hot dog buns were produced in a variety of sizes and specifications such as seeded, coloring, whole wheat, etc., according to the requirements specified by high volume buyers.

EXHIBIT 11.1 Financial highlights comparison

	Home Baking			Flowers			Interstate Bakeries	
	1984	1985	1986	1984	1985	1986	1984	1985
Return on assets	13.2%	11.4%	10.0%	8.4%	7.6%	7.8%	8.9%	4.2%
Return on equity	30.4%	23.6%	18.3%	19.1%	20.0%	20.5%	29.9%	10.7%
Net income/sales	3.2%	2.8%	2.4%	3.7%	4.1%	4.2%	2.7%	1.1%
Current ratio	1.4	1.3	1.6	1.5	1.4	1.5	1.0	1.0
Total assets								
(In thousands)	$2,168	$2,563	$2,888	$262,915	$336,639	$377,849	$210,476	$177,009
Asset growth	18.1%	18.2%	12.7%	12.8%	28.0%	11.2%	n/a	15.9%
Net income								
(In thousands)	$286	$291	$288	$22,140	$25,645	$29,531	$18,632	$7,534
Income growth	142.4%	1.7%	(1.0%)	15.2%	15.8%	15.2%	84.3%	(60.0%)
Sales revenue								
(In thousands)	$8,962	$10,365	$11,825	$602,995	$626,274	$698,394	$685,604	$703,578
Sales growth	20.9%	15.7%	14.1%	15.5%	3.9%	11.5%	2.9%	2.6%

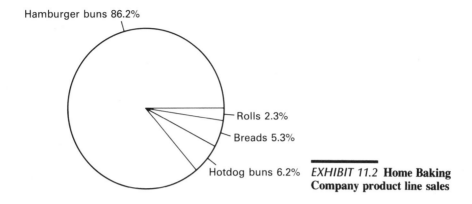

EXHIBIT 11.2 **Home Baking Company product line sales**

Because Tasty products were made especially for restaurant and fast-food distribution, they were of higher quality than products distributed to the retail sector by competitors. Home Baking was committed to providing a quality product by using only the best ingredients and paying close attention to detail. Strong spring flour with a high protein content and high-fructose corn sweetener were used in all buns and rolls. In an effort to produce only the best product, the conventional sponge-dough process was used instead of the much faster continuous breadmaking process. Each step in the process was timed and adjusted to assure the highest quality product.

High quality and good service are the primary reasons customers buy from Home Baking. Many of the competition's products, while adequate for supermarket consumers, are not well-suited for eateries that may serve hundreds of hamburgers and hot dogs daily. For example, hamburger buns that are not cut at the proper depth will roll up going through a conveyor. Hot dog buns that are cut too deep will fall apart. Such problems pose too much inconvenience for most fast-food restaurants.

Production Method. Most bread products have the same basic components in approximately the same portions. As shown in Exhibit 11.3, flour is the main

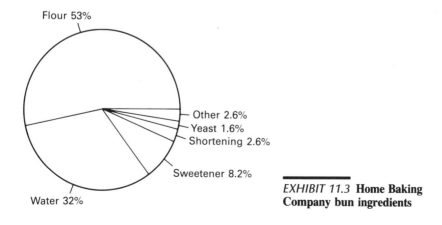

EXHIBIT 11.3 **Home Baking Company bun ingredients**

ingredient, followed in descending order by water, sweetener, shortening, yeast, salt, and other ingredients. Home Baking used the same ingredients in their buns and rolls, but the specific percentages and special additives specified by clients were a closely held secret.

Home Baking used the conventional sponge-dough process to produce bread. Exhibit 11.4 presents the basic steps in bread production. In the sponge-dough process, about 60 percent of the flour required for a batch was automatically weighed into the mixing bowl. Yeast, the enrichment ingredients, and the yeast foods were added on top of the flour; the proper amount of water was metered in, and these ingredients were mixed into a doughy mass called a sponge. The sponge was dumped into greased troughs that were wheeled into a temperature- and humidity-controlled room to ferment for approximately four hours. After the sponge was properly fermented, it was remixed, then the remaining flour, water, nonfat dry milk, salt, sweetener, and other minor ingredients were added. The remix was carefully timed because mixing too little or too much harmed bread quality.

The dough was then pumped into the divider where it was forced out of the chamber onto a traveling belt. The moving belt carried the dough to the rounder where it was converted to smooth, spherical shapes. The rounded dough was transferred to an overhead proofer where the dough relaxes and becomes pliable. Then, each dough piece was conveyed to the molder where it passed through rollers and dropped into the baking pans.

The panned dough passed through a temperature- and humidity-controlled area where it rises and expands to about six times its original volume. The dough then moved to the oven where it baked for approximately twenty minutes. The baked bread was depanned automatically and conveyed continuously until it cooled. Once the bread cooled, it passed razor-sharp blades that made uniform slices. The bread was then automatically covered by a transparent film, heat sealed or twist tied, and placed in racks for shipment. The process took about six hours.

Price

Tasty products were priced slightly higher than those of the competition, but this factor had not significantly hurt sales. Historically, Home Baking had been a price follower, but in 1986 it initiated a price increase with no affect on sales. Home Baking offered the same prices to all their customers in route sales, but in bulk sales, Home Baking gave quantity discounts. Exhibit 11.5 shows Home Baking's price list.

Home Baking's sales managers agreed that $.10 per-dozen price cut by a competitor would seriously damage Home Baking's sales. However, there was disagreement among management concerning the probability of aggressive price competition in the industry as all the firms would experience decreased profits.

Promotion

Because Home Baking sold to channel members, they did little advertising except for a single billboard located at company headquarters and delivery vans

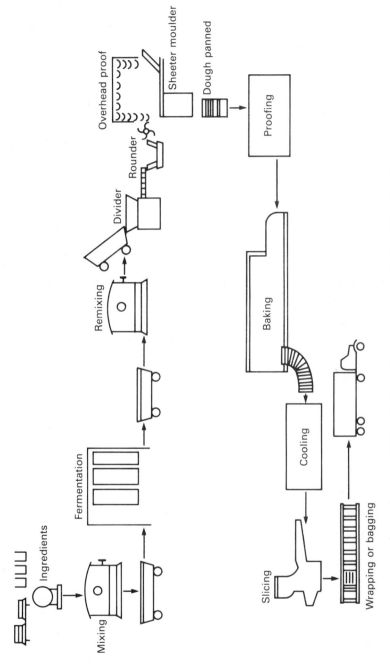

Source: Courtesy of Union Machinery Division, American Machine & Foundry Company.

EXHIBIT 11.4 **Conventional sponge dough-process**

EXHIBIT 11.5 **Home Baking price list**

Item	Wholesale Price
1-1/2" Pullman	$ .92
2" Pullman	1.00
1# Wheat	.87
1-1/2# Wheat	1.05
2# International Rye	1.45
2# Pumpernickel	1.45
Texas Toast	.92
1-1/2" Round Top	.92
Bar-B-Q Bread	.87
Grecian Bread	3.00
Squaw Bread	2.30
Stick Bread	.90
English Muffins (Pkg. 6)	.90
Onion Buns (12)	1.89
8" Poor Boy Sour Dough (Pkg. 4)	.97
6" Poor Boy Sour Dough (Pkg. 6)	1.05
8" Poor Boy (8)	1.08
3-3/4" Bun (12)	.84
3-3/4" Bun (60)	4.00
4" Bun Seeded (60)	4.35
4" Bun Plain (60)	4.10
4" Bun Seeded (12)	.91
4" Bun (12)	.86
4" Double Decker (30)	2.52
4" Double Decker (6)	.72
4" R. B. (60)	4.50
4" R. B. (12)	.94
4-1/2" Bun Seeded (40)	3.73
4-1/2" Kaiser Bun Seeded (40)	3.83
5" Bun (8)	.95
5" Bun (20)	2.00
5" Seeded (8)	.99
5" Seeded (20)	2.08
Hot Dog (12)	.84
Foot Long (6)	.91
7" Seeded Hot Dog (12)	.96
5" Steak Bread Seeded (8)	.77
5" Steak Bread Seeded (40)	3.85
6" Steak Bread (40)	3.57
6" Specialty Bun (24)	2.86
Parker House (12)	.52
Chicken Roll (36)	1.16
B & S Seeded (16)	.86

painted with the Tasty logo. Promotion primarily consisted of personal selling. The division sales manager typically would pay a call to the owner or manager of a restaurant or fast-food outlet and provide them with information about Tasty products and supply product samples. Route sales salesperson/drivers were compensated with a small salary plus 10 percent commission. Bulk and frozen salespersons were paid salaries but no commission. In addition, the company participated in trade shows that acquainted suppliers and customers with Home Baking's products and service.

A percentage breakdown of Home Baking's operating expenses for 1986 are presented in Exhibit 11.6. This comparison shows the significance of selling expenses as a percent of the total operating budget.

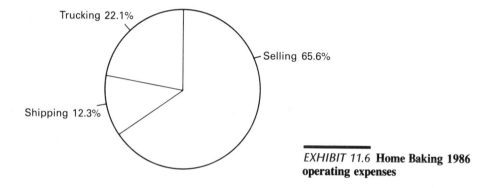

EXHIBIT 11.6 **Home Baking 1986 operating expenses**

Distribution System

Home Baking organized four company-owned channels to distribute its products, each managed as a sales division. All products were delivered by truck directly to the buyer. Exhibit 11.7 shows the percentage of total sales for each sales division.

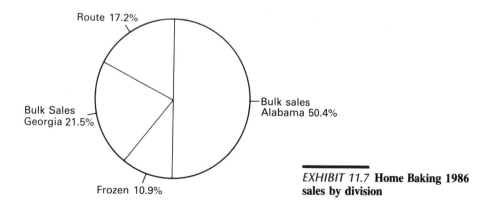

EXHIBIT 11.7 **Home Baking 1986 sales by division**

Route Sales Division.   This department sold and delivered to local restaurants, schools, nursing homes, and hospitals in and around the Birmingham metropolitan area. Deliveries were made during the daytime hours on Monday, Tuesday, Thursday, Friday, and Saturday. A high level of personalized service including specific delivery times and custom product size and ingredients was maintained.

With $2 million in net sales in 1986, route sales constituted approximately 17 percent of the company's sales. In 1986, route sales maintained 85 percent of the market share in its geographic market. However, management viewed route sales as having low potential for growth unless there was expansion to other large cities.

Bulk Sales—Alabama.   This division drop-shipped products to fast-food restaurants in Alabama. Most deliveries were made to McDonald's, Burger King, Hardee's, Wendy's, and Jack's. Deliveries were made every other night. This division's net sales were $6 million in 1986, representing slightly over 50 percent of total sales for the company. In the Alabama geographic area Home Baking had 70 percent market share.

Bulk Sales—Georgia.   The Bulk Sales—Georgia division operated similarly to the Alabama bulk department except products were distributed from the Atlanta warehouse. The distribution area was metropolitan Atlanta and east to Athens, Georgia. With $2.5 million in net sales in 1986, this division contributed just over 21 percent of the net sales of Home Baking. The division maintained a 20 to 25 percent market share in Atlanta and 40 percent market share in the area east to Athens. The business growth-rate potential for this geographical area was considered to be high by Home Baking's management.

Frozen Sales.   Distribution areas for Frozen Sales included south Georgia, the Florida panhandle, coastal Mississippi, southern South Carolina, and Alabama. Deliveries were made every seven days. Customers included Wendy's and four Burger King restaurants. This department also offered leases on freezers to fast-food outlets for $.05 per dozen buns. This division provided $1.2 million or about 11 percent of net sales. The potential for this division was considered quite high as frozen product could be shipped anywhere in the country.

Physical Distribution

Home Baking maintained separate truck fleets for bulk and route sales. Ten van-type trucks delivered Alabama bulk sales, and one refrigerated tractor trailer was used for frozen bun delivery. In Atlanta, four van-type trucks made local bulk deliveries, and one tractor trailer shuttled products from the Birmingham production facility.

Local Birmingham route sales were serviced by fourteen step-type vans. Two regular vans were used in Birmingham and one in Atlanta to provide quick "special deliveries" for customers who ran low on products.

Home Baking's distribution expenses were divided into three main categories—shipping, selling, and trucking expenses. A comparison of these expenses as a percent of sales for the last six years is included in Exhibit 11.8. This exhibit shows that operating expenses remained relatively stable over the six-year period.

EXHIBIT 11.8 **Operating expense comparison for Home Baking Company**

Operating expenses	1982	1983	1984 (Percent of sales)	1985	1986
Shipping	2.45	2.63	2.99	3.55	3.55
Selling	16.54	16.61	17.28	17.67	18.93
Trucking	6.41	6.00	5.65	5.89	6.37
Total	25.40	25.24	25.92	27.11	28.85

HOME BAKING'S PRODUCTION FACILITY

Home Baking's headquarters facility consisted of a 30,000-square-foot building that housed offices, production operations, and storage. A separate off-site leased building of 11,000 square feet provided storage for frozen buns. The company also leased a dry warehouse of 4,000 square feet for bulk distribution in Atlanta. In 1986 the company purchased land adjoining the headquarters property for future expansion.

Plant Capacity

Production in the plant was accomplished by two independent automated lines capable of producing at maximum capacity 700,000 pounds of bread products per week. With scheduled down time required for cleaning and maintenance, efficient operating capacity was between 600,000 and 650,000 pounds per week. If the facility was operated at peak capacity for prolonged periods of time, maintenance and cleanliness problems would occur.

Home Baking operated the plant 24 hours per day, seven days a week. The only down time was twelve hours on Tuesday and Saturday for cleaning and maintenance. Production at the facility followed the trend in sales and was expected to increase through 1987. Exhibit 11.9 shows production volumes for 1985, 1986, and through June 1987. The maximum output to date was 613,019 pounds for the week ending April 25th. The average production for the year was approximately 550,800 pounds. With a maximum output of 700,000 pounds per week, the plant was running at an average of 73 percent capacity with a peak of 85 percent capacity. Management had estimated that if sales continued to increase in 1988 as they had over the past five years, daily output requirements would exceed capacity in June 1988.

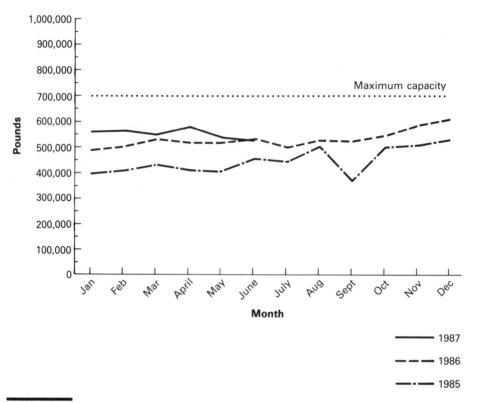

EXHIBIT 11.9 **Home Baking production**

Dedicated Bakery

Golden State and Home Baking submitted proposals in 1986 to build an exclusive bakery in the Atlanta region for McDonald's. As the end of 1987, uncertainty existed as to which firm would build the bakery. The dedicated bakery would produce at least 13.5 million buns per year for exclusive distribution to 348 McDonald's restaurants in the Southeast. The proposal temporarily had been put on hold by McDonald's.

MANAGEMENT

Home Baking Company maintained the philosophy that a high level of service and quality would result in reaching their goal of continued growth. An "open" management style was employed, providing each department full autonomy. Exhibit 11.10 shows Home Baking's organizational structure.

Ernest Stevens had been the president and general manager of Home Baking since 1971 and provided the planning, organization, direction, and control in the

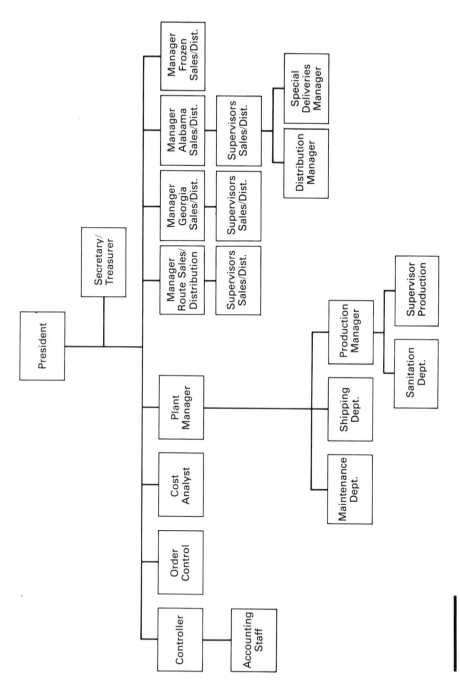

EXHIBIT 11.10 **Organization chart for Home Baking Company**

company. Also, he was responsible for policy decisions affecting day-to-day operations. Major line positions reporting to Stevens were the controller, director of sales, and plant manager. However, the director of sales had retired in December 1986 and was never replaced. The responsibilities of the director of sales were assumed by the president.

Jerry King, the plant manager, made the day-to-day operating decisions. He was a graduate of Alabama University and the American Institute of Baking. King, who was very capable and experienced, often worked seven days a week. As Home Baking grew, so did his responsibilities. King negotiated labor contracts, handled grievances, hired plant personnel, and was responsible for training. Since there was no personnel or labor relations department at Home Baking, King was also responsible for many of these functions.

Of the 170 employees at Home Baking Company, ninety were union members (the Retailers, Wholesalers, and Department Store Union). Union jobs consisted of manufacturing, engineering, and maintenance while distribution employees filled the nonunion positions.

FINANCIAL CONDITION

Throughout the 1970s and 1980s, Home Baking was a financially sound company. On December 31, 1986, total assets were $2.9 million, including $1.6 million of equity. Total revenues for 1986 were $12 million resulting in net income of $288,171. The sales growth is displayed in a bar chart in Exhibit 11.11. Sales have grown from $4,742,000 in 1980 to $11,825,000 in 1986 for a six-year growth rate of 150 percent.

Capital Structure

Home Baking was limited in the amount of capital resources available. Total stockholder's equity was $1,578,000 as of December 31, 1986, consisting of $68,000 in capital stock and $1,519,000 of accumulated retained earnings. The corporate capital structure was very simple with five stockholders, all members of the Stevens family, holding all 955 outstanding shares of common stock. The company had paid few dividends to its stockholders as earnings were retained and reinvested in the company. In addition, the family was quite reluctant to relinquish control of the stock through an equity offering.

THE FAST-FOOD INDUSTRY

In the middle 1980s, the fast-food industry in the United States experienced a slow down in growth rate. Signs of distribution saturation, increasingly intense competition, and a growing number of business failures accounted for much of the

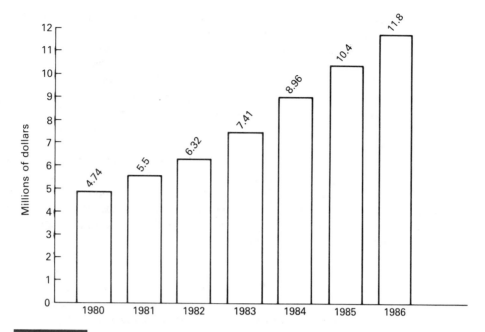

EXHIBIT 11.11 **Home Baking Company net sales, 1980–1986**

decline. During this period, the success of individual fast-food chains hinged on quick response to consumer tastes and effective marketing.

Of the top fast-food hamburger chains, the market leader, McDonald's, continued to defy industry trends with 14 to 15 percent earnings growth per year. With a 20 percent market share in the United States and a new store opening somewhere in the world every seventeen hours, McDonald's continued its steady growth.[1] Mid-1980 additions to its menu included the McDLT and salads. McDonald's has responded to the health conscious trend by emphasizing the nutritional value of its hamburgers in its advertising.[2]

Burger King, second in market share with about 7 percent of fast-food industry sales, opens a new store on the average of once a day.[3] Burger King, a subsidiary of Pillsbury, introduced the "Burger Bundle"—three small hamburgers in one package with different condiments on each in 1986.

Wendy's International has had a number of problems in the 1980s. Wendy's had to trim back management, buy some of its franchises, and close some stores. Furthermore, it experienced three unsuccessful product introductions: whole-grain

[1]E.S. Ely, "America Loses its Appetite for Fast Foods," *Financial World*, 155, January 22–February 4, 1986, pp. 18–26.

[2]Scott Hume, "McDonald's Heavy in Print for Nutrition," *Advertising Age*, January 19, 1987, p. 90.

[3]E.S. Ely, "American Loses its Appetite for Fast Foods," *Financial World*, 155, Janaury 22–February 4, 1986, pp. 18–26.

buns, breakfast foods, and "lite" menus. In 1986, average sales dropped 9.6 percent partly due to its cutback in breakfast sales.[4]

Hardee's, the market challenger of the 1980s, has gained market share on the industry leaders. With advertising that ridiculed Burger King's Whopper and the McDLT, Hardee's marketing goal was to force their competition to reposition.[5]

In the 1980s, regional chains and upstarts were vulnerable in the fast-food market because of the marketing strength of the industry leaders. These chains were hoping the giants would continue to fight among themselves and leave the "little guys" alone.[6]

A trend in the fast-food industry was the use of dedicated bakeries to provide all the buns for a major chain in a specified region. In exchange for the vendor establishing such a dedicated bakery where the sole customer could closely control product specifications and monitor quality, the bakery received exclusive distribution rights to the customer's stores throughout the region. Such an arrangement guaranteed a high level and long-term demand.

REACHING A CROSSROADS

Ernest Stevens wondered what kind of company Home Baking would be in ten years. The industry was changing and Stevens believed that Home Baking would have to change with the industry. Stevens knew that the decisions he was facing would shape the future character of the company and would play a large part in Home Baking's success or failure. Stevens wondered if the company, in the long term, should be so dependent upon the growth of the fast-food industry. Would the growth of this industry continue to support the growth of Home Baking?

Stevens also knew that his conclusions regarding the future of the fast-food industry would have an impact on a more immediate problem. Plant production was rapidly approaching full capacity. Should he expand at the present location; build an additional plant at a new location; or wait for the McDonald's decision on the dedicated bakery? In addition, how should he finance the new growth? These decisions were so important and Stevens felt as if he had little guidance.

[4]"Restaurants Face Difficult Future," *Standard and Poor's Industrial Survey*, (Standard and Poor's Company: New York) April, 1987, L36.

[5]Scott Hume, "Hardee's Sized Up Burger King's Whopper," *Advertising Age*, January 19, 1987, p. 90.

[6]Rona Gindin, "Challenging the Giants," *Restaurant Business*, 85, October 10, 1986, pp. 221-31.

CASE 12

Three Bond Company, Ltd.: Serving The Customer

Three Bond had come a long way since it offered its first product in 1955. However, after experiencing growth rates of over 25 percent per year for decades, Three Bond's growth had been growing at about 15 percent per year for the past several years. The sales goal for 1986 was 25 billion yen (about $170 million), as compared to 22 billion yen for 1983, with an expected eight percent before-tax profit. While research and development currently averaged about three percent of sales, Three Bond's goal was to raise that expense to between 8 and 10 percent. Tadasu Nonaka, President of Three Bond Co., Ltd., commmented on the firm's basic strategy:

> More than a quarter of a century (33 years) has passed since Three Bond came into being, and today we are on the road to new and exciting horizons. Today we are expanding our scope to include an ever broader range of fields, and to bring benefit to ever more people, not only in Japan, but worldwide.
>
> Three Bond has already come a long way from the days of its first product, "Liquid Gasket No. 1." Our current offerings run the gamut from bonds and lubricants to labor-saving machinery and even full-scale work project contracting. Our products are used in a kaleidoscopic variety of industries, including everything from transportation, architecture, and civil engineering, to today's most sophisticated electronics. And thanks to the limitless research and development capabilities of our dedicated staff, Three Bond looks forward with confidence to providing an even wider range of customer services in the future.
>
> We are also taking steps to develop our overseas bases of operation in order to bring Three Bond's highly acclaimed products and services to more people in more nations around the world. We presently maintain subsidiary offices in the United States, France, and Brazil, as well as a representative office in Singapore. In addition to supplying products directly to world markets, we also aim to establish indigenous production centers designed to spur local economies. A major staff of Three Bond technicians and sales personnel are on hand to offer full assistance in these efforts.
>
> Three Bond also plays an active and aggressive role in seeking out and introducing high-quality foreign products and advanced technologies to meet user needs in Japan. In this way, we contribute to mutual development and mutual prosperity, for a happier, harmonious world.

This case was written by Dr. William R. Boulton, Professor of Management, University of Georgia. It is intended as a basis for classroom discussion rather than to illustrate effective or ineffective handling of an administrative situation. Copyright © 1988 by Dr. William R. Boulton. All rights reserved. Used by permission from William R. Boulton.

Our utmost goal, of course, is to serve. To serve better, faster, and more widely. For the benefit of our customers, wherever they might be.

Three Bond's sealing products and technologies were used by every automobile manufacturer in Japan. They were well respected by anyone who utilized their services.

Three Bond's commitment to customer service was described in early 1986 by Masashi Mizushima, manager of planning and administration:

> We now guarantee 30-minute service and we want to give that service 24 hours per day. We need flex-time for our employees in order to do that. We need to have some people here by 8:00 a.m., and some here until 6:00 p.m. or later. We will need some people to be available all night long. We are considering four-day work weeks so that we can accomplish this. We would then use some job rotation system to cover our customer's needs. We tell our customers that we have no holidays as far as they are concerned.

Three Bond's management were confident that strong loyalty from their growing legions of customers around the world would achieve ever greater accomplishments in the years ahead.

BACKGROUND

It was in May 1955 that Chairman Osamu Ukumori founded Three Bond. His founding objective was to eliminate the tremendous waste of precious energy owing to "unavoidable" leaks—leaks which were robbing Japan of approximately one trillion yen each year. Mr. Ukumori explained:

> In 1954, in the days long before Japan even dared to dream of its forthcoming economic miracles, I was stopped at a traffic light at a major intersection in Tokyo. As the light turned green and the car in front of mine pulled away, I noticed two small puddles on the spot where it had been idling. One was oil, the other was water. "Such a waste," I thought. "Why doesn't someone do something about such wasteful leaks?" Then I thought again: "No, why don't I do something about such wasteful leaks?" But words alone are meaningless, and it is actions that speak. Indeed, I decided, I will do something about it. And I did. I invented Three Bond's first liquid gasket. It provided Three Bond with its start—and led to a history of dedication to produce the products needed to improve man's everyday life. Service to mankind: It's a Three Bond tradition.

Three Bond's first contribution to curbing such national waste was an all new concept in gaskets; a liquid gasket known as "Three Bond No.1." Subsequently Three Bond proceeded to develop other grades of liquid gasket as well. By preventing leakages and promoting longer machine service life, these products contributed substantially to the legendary growth of the Japanese industrial infrastructure.

THREE BOND'S PRODUCT LINE

Three Bond has escalated its accomplishments in the liquid gasket field towards the ultimate goal of eliminating the need for solid gaskets. Their gasket elimination process was calling the OLG System—the On-Line Gasket System. With the OLG System, liquid gasket application was performed by application robots that attained unprecedented time and labor savings, enhanced productivity, and improved cost performance. The original robot had been developed in cooperation with Fanuc. The OLG System also claimed to provide higher sealing quality and accuracy, and allowed the use of lighter and less expensive parts. Three Bond was selling about ten of these sealing robot systems per month.

Three Bond's OLG System had become only one of many products and applications used to improve customer's production processes. These labor-saving, automatic dispensing units were developed to enable the user to more efficiently apply Three Bond's liquid gaskets, locking agents, adhesives, and sealants automatically to a fixed place, in fixed quantities, for specified periods of time. Mizushima commented further on Three Bond's move to improve customers' production processes:

> We didn't start out by looking at factory problems. We did look for ways in which different businesses could use our products. We would attempt to sell them value added by showing them how they could reduce their costs or improve productivity and quality by using our products. We then had to develop new application equipment to help them use our products.

Liquid gasket technology was developed on the concept that the application of sealent to the seal surface would better prevent leaks. Its success has made it an industrial material that was indispensable to all sorts of industries to improve product performance, extend product life, and reduce costs.

Beyond the liquid gasket business, Three Bond also engaged in the development and marketing of a complete variety of adhesives and sealing agents, including anaerobic, cyanoacrylate and structural adhesives, silicone sealants, ultraviolet curing resins, and single- and double-component epoxy compounds. Anaerobic adhesives and sealants, for example, did not harden as long as it had air contact, but when shielded from air in a sealing application it hardened to achieve powerful binding without any contraction. By contrast, cyanocrylate monomer provided firm adhesion when moisture from the air caused instantaneous reaction. Epoxy adhesives would harden or provide protection under a wide variety of conditions where water, humidity, or other liquids caused hardening problems, corrosion, or slipping. These fine-chemical materials were used in such industries as transportation, electrical engineering, civil engineering, and architecture. Three Bond also sold products that were marketed through distributors worldwide for the general consumer.

Mizushima explained further about the focus of Three Bond's products:

> Three Bond has stuck to its basic technologies in sealers, adhesives, rust preventions, and lubrications. These are our basic technologies. Sealer applications in the

automobile, electrical, and manufacturing industries represent about 50 percent of sales. Bonding applications are concentrated in manufacturing industries. Construction industries use sealing technologies to prevent water leakage, especially in underground tunnel applications. We sell maintenance products to the after markets and compact and easy-to-use products to the "do it yourself" markets.

These technologies have a variety of applications for R&D to develop specific products. Capsules are made in a variety of sizes for anything from seeds that have their own nutrients to adhesives. There are a wide variety of applications for the automobile industry and for after service related products. We also can apply ultraviolet radiation to various products to improve bonding speeds. Applications such as these represent about half of our sales. Somewhere between 15 to 20 percent of our applications are for electrical machinery, around 10 to 12 percent for the construction industry, and about 20 to 30 percent for industrial materials.

In planning for the future, Three Bond was striving to develop new fine-chemical and engineering materials to meet the stringent demands for high quality and accuracy in the age of electronics, mechatronics, and optronics. Three Bond's research and development staff maintained close contact with research centers both in Japan and abroad, an arrangement that not only permitted Three Bond to develop and offer its own new product technologies to the world, but also allowed newly developed techniques and products from abroad to be introduced into Japan.

THREE BOND'S MARKETS

Three Bond had a wide range of customers. Mizushima, manager of planning and administration, explained:

> We sell direct to about 50,000 customers. With such a wide variety of customers, there is no risk from cyclical or seasonal variations and sales are stable by selling to all industries. As a result, we now segment our customers by industry. Our growth reflects the basic industry structure. As sectors begin to grow, we try to spot them and grow with them. The fastest growing segments have rapidly developing needs and we can find ways to help them with those needs.

The Transportation Industry

With nearly 120 million people living in an area the size of California, Japan had developed elaborate networks of transportation to move its people. The legendary super-high-speed bullet train, of course, provided but one thread in the nationwide rail system. As metropolitian areas grew ever more congested, subway construction proceeded at a rapid pace. Nearly 200 kilometers of underground lines crisscrossed Tokyo and its suburbs by the mid-1980s. Automobiles, trucks, construction and farm machinery, and aircraft provide the power and means for Japan's mobility and growth. These various transport machines used Three Bond's products daily. For example, manufacturers of transportation equipment frequently specified Three Bond products for use on their production lines and, in the automobile industry, designated Three Bond products as Genuine Products.

Applications in the transportation industry of Three Bond gaskets, adhesives, lubricants, and paints included oil pan sealing, sealing of parts on cylinder blocks, fixing of differential ring gear bolts, fixing of bearings, lubrication of crank shaft journals, cleaning brake drums, lubrications and sealing of disk brake cylinder boots, and bonding of weather stripping. Products included liquid and solid gaskets, locking agents, anaerobic adhesives, cleaners, rust-proofing agents and lubricants, antiseizing lubricants, chassis paints, etc.

Electricity and Electronics Industries

Consumerism in Japan had forced consumer products to become ever more sophisticated in their technology. Electric appliances such as televisions or audio and video equipment had to meet the high quality demands not only of Japanese buyers, but of users around the world. The typical Japanese television had achieved an average life of nearly eight years by the mid-1980s. Of course, such items now incorporated the latest in electronics technologies, permitting convenience, accuracy, and reliability on a level unimaginable even a decade ago. In all of these products, Three Bond played an important role as producer of sealants, adhesives, and other products critical to the production and maintenance of electronic products.

Applications in the electronics industry included bonding of electrical tips to printed circuit boards, encapsulating diodes, molding insulation coils, protecting electrical contact points, fixing parts in place, sealing switching terminals, and heat pressing bonded calculator covers during production. Products included insulation sealants, moisture-proof coating materials, conductive adhesives, cyanoacrylate adhesives, anaerobic adhesives, ultra-violet curing adhesives, silicone sealants, heat-press film adhesives, electrical contact point protectors, etc.

Engineering and Construction Industries

Due to land limitations, Japan had to take maximum advantage of all available space. Firm's had to bore tunnels through mountains, excavate subways far beneath city streets, create ports on land reclaimed from the sea, and generally undertake immense engineering and construction projects. As a highly industrialized country, Japan also had to constantly expand its plant capacity, and build even newer manufacturing centers requiring increased integration of engineering and construction technologies.

These construction projects typically required the latest developments in humidity and water sealing technologies. Thus demand for Three Bond's products that provide watertight sealing of tunnels or greater adhesive strengths for construction projects had been growing. In addition to providing such products, Three Bond also engaged in a wide range of construction services on a direct contract basis.

Applications in the construction and engineering industries included anticorrosive lining of water treatment tanks, lined pipes at power stations, underground wall segments sealing, floor surfaces for factories, finished and weather-proofed external walls and wall sections. Products included water-proofing materials, lining and coating materials, flooring materials, adhesives, sealants, and related construction services.

General Industries

Three Bond also contributed to the development of numerous other industries. Its products were vital in the production process of a wide range of precision instruments: cameras, watches, measuring equipment, etc. They were also used in medical equipment, e.g. as sealing agents for syringe needles. In fact, it was rather difficult to find an industry that did not rely to some degree on Three Bond's product support. General applications included precision solid gaskets, bonded watch glass, sealed and bonded syringe needles, lamination bonding of camera lenses, anticorrosive lubrication for fishing reels, sealed gas stove cylinders, and antiseizing bonding for shoe spikes.

THREE BOND'S ORGANIZATION

Three Bond Company, Ltd. was primarily a holding company for its wholly owned subsidiaries. The Three Bond parent had about 380 personnel with almost 1,200 personnel in its subsidiaries. It had primary responsibility for financial controls, personnel, administration, and research and development. As a basic philosophy of personnel distribution, Three Bond's goal was to have a proportion of 7-1-1-1. Sales would have 70 percent, manufacturing 10 percent, R&D 10 percent, and administration 10 percent. Of the 380 corporate personnel, about 200 were engineers and about 30 percent were actually involved in research and development activities. The subsidiaries included the majority of sales personnel.

Management Philosophy

Three Bond described its style of management as "management by philosophy." As Osamu Ukumori, chairman of Three Bond explained:

> At Three Bond, we frequently speak of our corporate "heart"—the driving spirit that beats the pulse of our everyday actions. Like the human heart, our corporate heart survives on the power of love and the joy of loving others. Without its constant pulsation, Three Bond would be but an empty shell, a robot of industrial enterprise, an unneeded appendage to the body of mankind.
>
> Love is an emotion that corporate hearts at times have difficulty expressing. For no matter how righteous the founding principles of a corporation may be—and Japanese businesses are widely known for their fondness of slogans and philosophical creeds—it is only when the emotion of love is received and acknowledged that its existence has

any meaning. Words alone are but platitudes; it is actions that signal sincerity and truth. For Three Bond, love is manifested in numerous ways. In the contribution we make to the betterment of human society. In the efforts we make to create new products to serve man's needs. In the appreciation we show to those who give of themselves in our behalf. Love and concern are what set Three Bond apart. They are the reasons why Three Bond is so often introduced in the media, and they are the reaons why Three Bond succeeds where others fail.

Mr. Ukumori expressed special concern for his employees. He continued:

> Three Bond believes in the need to show loving appreciation for work well done. Our employees are respected as individuals, and they are rewarded with the pride of accomplishment. The conventional timecard system was abolished as early as 1964, for we at Three Bond seek to inspire dedication and enthusiasm, not commitment to a clock and a mechanical attitude of serving one's time. We also operate on a five-day work schedule—a policy implemented way back in 1961, at a time when other Japanese corporations were just beginning to make the heaviest demands on workers to accomplish economic success. Why this break with Japanese "tradition"? Because Three Bond is different. We know that creativity is the greatest gift that our employees have to offer. And creativity requires time to rid the mind of pressures. Time to relax and enjoy the pleasures of life. Time to be human, to love and be loved.
>
> Three Bond. Some might say that we're un-Japanese. We just like to think of ourselves as different. Because we care. We really do.

Mr. Mizushima also commented on Three Bond's philosophy:

> We like to enjoy doing our work, so we make things fun. For example, TQC (total quality control) has been a serious business for most Japanese companies. At Three Bond, we have made it a game. There are lots of symbolic prizes and money given for improvements. At headquarters, we have a swimming pool and restaurant for employees. There is a golf club across the street.
>
> We also believe in letting the individual have some choice in doing what he likes. You can choose your own career path. We encourage employees to challenge anything they see that is wrong. The company will lend them money to set up a business and allow them to use the company brand name.

Distribution and Sales

To meet the needs of its Japanese customers, Three Bond had created an expansive direct sales network reaching to every corner of Japan. Sales subsidiaries were divided into several geographic regions. According to Mr. Mizushima:

> We presently operate 46 major sales centers as well as 82 local sales outlets. We also have a route sales network embracing numerous wholesale distributors, plus seven construction material centers specializing in direct construction contracting and material sales. The Three Bond sales network is unique in that it is highly diversified according to industrial specialization and regional location—a system that assures precise matching of product offerings with specific customer needs. Sales engineers get salaries and a rebate from the corporate office for sales made.

The local sales outlets are organized into 3B [Three Bond] shops, jobber shops, and companion shops. The 3B shops handle the large, national clients. Jobbers handle medium-sized companies. Companion shops handle small clients. Each shop has its own list of assigned customers to visit and serve. Each shop is a wholly owned subsidiary that has its own president. A 3B shop will typically have a president, secretary, and from two to four sales engineers. This structure allows for a feeling of independence and personal accomplishment for employees. They develop and present proposals to their customers for cost reduction, process changes, and new applications. They also send information on customer inquiries and problems back to headquarters and the research and development department.

The Three Bond distribution and service network was initially designed to bring Three Bond products and services to Japanese customers. The same network, however, has now become an effective route for introduction of foreign products and technologies into Japan. A broad range of overseas goods and services reached Japanese customers through Three Bond as they continued development of this channel.

Three Bond also had its own concept of sales management as described by Mr. Mizushima:

Another of the more unusual features of our domestic sales network is our sales staff. Sales representatives are referred to as "sales engineers" in recognition of their achievements in the technical aspects of their job. At Three Bond we believe that a salesman should be more than just a good seller of goods and services; he must also be thoroughly familiar with the technical applications of our goods and services in order to understand customer requirements and offer pertinent advice in product selection and utilization. More than 650 such "sales engineers" are on duty nationwide. We have a lot of internal competition for trips, awards, and money. We also allow sales engineers to buy cars and lease them back to the company.

Sales engineers must study books on their customers' products and equipment and on Three Bond's products and must take exams twice per year. As they pass the exams, they can move into a higher sales classification level which gives them more responsibility and freedom. There are three levels of sales classification that vary in salary by about 10,000 yen per level per month.

To ensure strong support for Three Bond's customers, a special service system was also established. Mr. Mizushima explained:

Selling, of course, is but one facet of customer service, and after-sale care is equally important. For this purpose, we have created an on-line computerized system to handle customer service needs from any point in the nation. With this system, we can guarantee a response to any customer inquiry or request within 30 minutes. It's just one example of Three Bond's commitment to work in harmony with the customer—even long after the product has been sold.

Pricing of Three Bond's services was not necessarily cheap. Three Bond priced according to the value added to their customers. Mr. Mizushima explained:

We believe that we must add value to our customers to continue to grow. In doing so, and providing the kind of service that we do, we must price according to the value we contribute to the customer. For example, we try to price at about one percent of what the customer saves from our applications. A second way is to price 100 times the raw material cost. By looking at the pricing from these two direction, we come to a pricing decision.

Three Bond Production

Three Bond produced and sold chemical products such as sealants, adhesives, lubicating agents, anaerobic sealants and adhesives, anticorrosive agents and epoxy compounds, and labor-saving equipment. It also carried out molding and processing operations by using these products in combination with special techniques and accumulated know-how.

In addition, Three Bond provided a broad range of production services to its customers. Many services were add-on or value-added products such as microencapsulation processing. By this process, the thread section of such parts as screws, bolts and pipes were given sealing and locking capability. The screw, for example, was subjected to the sealing/locking agent that, when tightened, breaks the microcapsules to cause instant polymerization. Instant locking then occured while leaks were also prevented. The user could select from seven different coating liquids to best meet the temperature, pressure, contact fluids, and screw dimensions of the application. The process lowered cost by reducing working time, rationalizing stock control, saving on parts, relaxing tolerance values, reducing the number of claims due to improved machine performance, and retaining such improved performance and stability for workers. This service was provided through Three Bond's own production facilities.

To ensure that Three Bond could meet the tight production schedules that had become a standard requirement for parts suppliers in Japan, the company's production facilities had been distributed throughout Japan. Mr. Mizushima explained:

> Three Bond's nationwide production system is also representative of our deep concern for outstanding service. By dispersing production facilities throughout the country, not only do we achieve more stable distribution of Three Bond products and services in all local areas but we also enhance indigenous production to meet the needs of local customers.

Administration

Having a diversified sales organization spread across the country made the integration of activities difficult. This required significant communication as Mr. Mizushima described:

> We require reports to let us know the activities of the subsidiary companies and to get suggestions for products and applications. We also have lots of meetings, the number of which we are trying to reduce. There are also a lot of telephone calls and FAX communications going to and from headquarters. There is a lot of give and take. We believe that the subsidiaries should be free to do and take action, but they must report the details of their actions.

Technology Orientation

Mr. Mizushima emphasized that Three Bond's distinctive competence was in the company's ability to meet its customers' technical needs. He explained:

> Our biggest strength is the fact that we are close to our customer. To encourage this, we have an internal patent system for our sales engineers. There are two types of patents that we reward with rebates. One is for marketing innovations—where an employee comes up with a new application for an old product. For example, one employee recognized that we could use our sealing technology for coating TV towers and power line towers to save maintenance personnel from tearing clothing and getting hurt. That is a large potential market and the employee gets a sales rebate of 50,000 yen per tower. The second kind of patent is for new technology.
>
> We have a lot of know-how for reducing user's costs, for chip bonding applications, in materials like printed circuit tape, and in software programming for robot applications. We don't have any product strategies. We only work to support our users' needs.
>
> Three Bond also uses its sales room and application room effectively to help educate the user. The sales room shows applications for the variety of technologies that Three Bond has. By taking the customers' personnel through the show room, they get ideas for innovations within their own companies. The application room is open to customers so they can come to Three Bond and develop their own applications in secret or with help from Three Bond's sales engineers.

Automatic Robot Application Systems

To improve customer efficiency in using its products, Three Bond produced a broad selection of unique, sophisticated application systems and equipment. Automatic applicators, for example, had been developed for application of liquid gaskets, locking agents, adhesives and sealants. This equipment permitted automatic application of precise amounts where needed. Through the application of such equipment and systems, Three Bond helped to improve performance and rationalization of the production processes used for customer products. Such equipment and services not only saved labor through automation but also added to the cleanliness of the work environment and to improved quality of their customers' final products. Three Bond's objective was described by Mr. Mizushima as follows:

> Three Bond's sales objective is to bring process innovation to the customer's factory. For example, we helped Casio change its calculator production to a lamination process that eliminated all assembly requirements. They were able to cut their cost and produce the thinnest calculator on the market. Our primary innovation, however, is to integrate liquid gasket equipment onto our customers' production line. We also can help them combine the lock and seal process into a single process. We want to do things for the customer that other companies can't do for them.

Equipment sales included fully automated sealing robots, handy liquid gasket applicators, precision liquid dispensers, and extrusion pumping application equipment. Equipment applications also included the microencapsulation of bolts, plugs and nipples, insulation molding of electrical parts, precoating of mating parts with dried liquid gaskets, and color-coded water faucet screws and dry cells.

One of Three Bond's most successful production automation processes was its robot for liquid gasket applications. According to Mr. Mizushima:

> We sold our first three units to Toyo Kogyo (Mazda) in 1978. We worked with Fanuc to develop the robot and had six or seven subcontractors provide components for the robot. We now have a teaching playback unit and we sell about 10 per month. They sell from 4 million yen for the cheapest one to as high as 40 million yen for the most expensive. Typically they sell for 5 to 10 million yen. Three Bond only sells their sealing equipment as systems using their robot. We have sold several thousand robots now. The use of robots helps our customer reduce costs, improve productivity, improve quality, and eliminate the need for gasket inventories.

Mr. Mizushima also commented on Three Bond's competition:

> In the U.S., Locktight is our number-one competitor. 3M is a competitor, but not as significant. We have 95 percent of the microencapsulated screw business. In Japan, Toa Gosei and Nitto Denko are our primary competitors. In fine-chemicals, we also compete with the chemical companies like Sumitomo Chemicals. Those firms dominate the chemical distribution channels.

> Dow, Corning, and General Electric also make bonding materials similar to ours, but they use our old-type systems. We have made proposals to a number of companies in the United States to use our robot system. G.M. Pontiac is now testing it. Ford is bench-testing it. International Harvester and Cummings plan to use it. On-line sealing applications require continuous speed in three-dimensional tracking, which is quite difficult.

Diversification

Three Bond was looking at new areas of business that were not so heavily dependent on the petroleum industry. Mr. Mizushima explained:

> We have tried to diversify away from oil derivative products. We have developed encapulated seeds for agriculture, but there is no need for them in Japan where farm plots are so small. They would work best where the seeds can be spread by mechanical means or by air. We are looking at the United States, Canada, and Brazil as likely markets for this product.

> We also got into producing fish food and producing prepackaged eel. The eel uses a special container that will keep it hot once it is warmed. It is quite good and since seven out of 10 Japanese consider eel one of their favorite foods we feel it has a good market potential.

> We have also opened three restaurants in which we sell our eel. These are experiments to find new areas of business that don't rely so heavily on petroleum-based products. We are also trying to reformulate our products without the petroleum base.

In describing some of the continued development of products within Three Bond's current product line, Mr. Mitzushima noted:

> We have developed adhesives using ultraviolet curing for fiber optics connectors. We are also looking at electromagnetic field curing. Mattel is a competitor in this area.

CASE 13

Dakotah, Inc.

In May 1987, Dakotah, Inc. appeared to be on the brink of a new era of growth and profitability. The South Dakota–based manufacturer of bedcoverings and associated textile home furnishings had enjoyed record sales of over $13 million in 1986 and record after-tax profits of nearly $400,000. It's products, marketed from a posh showroom in New York City, were widely recognized by department store buyers and consumers alike as the top-of-the-line in textile home furnishings.

Dakotah was an employee-owned company headquartered in the small town of Webster, South Dakota (population, 2,400). It had seven plants located in small towns in three counties in the northeastern corner of South Dakota that had a combined population of 24,448 (see Exhibit 13.1).

HISTORY OF DAKOTAH, INC.

In 1970, George Whyte was 21, an age when many of his peers were thinking about finishing college and finding a job, but Whyte was worried about pigs. As a VISTA (Volunteers in Service to America) volunteer, Whyte had encouraged the farm families of rural northeastern South Dakota to participate in an economic development program called, "Pigs for Pork." Farmers were given bred sows by the federal government to raise and eventually sell at market. When the price of pork plummeted the program failed. The pigs cost more to raise than their market value. The program had done nothing to improve the distressed economic condition of farmers in this depressed region.

Undaunted, Whyte hit upon another idea. He had noticed the farm wives making beautiful handcrafted quilts. His grandmother had made quilts and he knew something of their value. He turned his attention to the talent and skill of the women of the families who were participating in the "Pigs for Pork" program and realized this might be the opportunity he was looking for. Whyte convinced the wives

This case was prepared by Diane Hoadley and Philip C. Fisher of the University of South Dakota, Vermillion, South Dakota. It is intended as a basis for classroom discussion rather than to illustrate effective or ineffective handling of an administrative situation. This case was presented at the Midwest Society for Case Research Workshop, 1987. Used by permission from Philip C. Fisher.

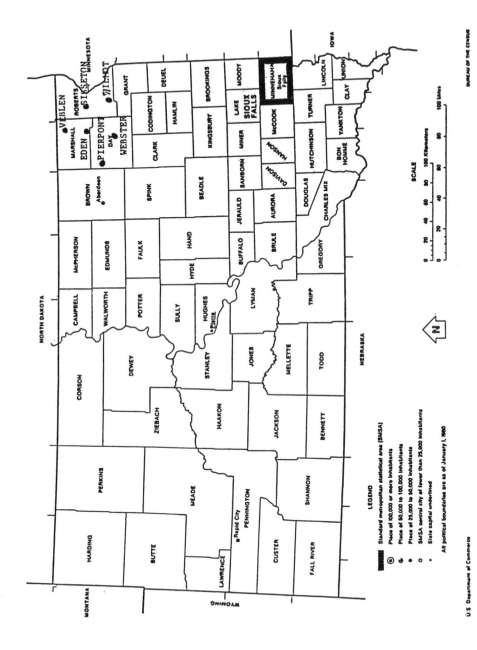

EXHIBIT 13.1 **South Dakota Metropolitan Statistical Area, counties, and selected places**

and daughters of these farmers that they could successfully produce and sell their handcrafted items. Whyte and Bob Pierce, who headed the Northeast South Dakota Community Action Program, collected hand-sewn quilts, afghans, pillows, shawls, and a variety of other items from the women in a three-county region of northeastern South Dakota. Armed with these samples, Whyte and Pierce flew to the East Coast in an attempt to market the products to department store buyers.

They failed miserably. They flew first to Washington, D. C., engaged a hotel suite, got out the telephone book, and contacted the department stores listed in the Yellow Pages. "Oh God, it was awful!" exclaimed Whyte recounting the events. No one even came to look at the products. Whyte and Pierce then flew to New York City and repeated the process with the same discouraging results. They knew the circumstances required more aggressive tactics, so they put their samples in a trunk and marched unannounced into the office of the quilt buyer for one of New York's leading department stores. They were promptly removed by the store's security guards.

On their way back to South Dakota, discouraged but still hopeful, they stopped at Dayton's, a department store chain based in Minneapolis. There they saw the assistant buyer for the drapery and bedspread department. He, too, was not interested in the handcrafted products being shown, but he put Whyte in contact with a leading independent manufacturers' representative in New York City, Park B. Smith.

Smith flew to South Dakota in September 1971, liked what he saw, made some suggestions for design changes, and negotiated a contract with Whyte to produce a line of samples to show in the November home furnishings market in New York. Twice a year, in November and May, buyers gather on Fifth Avenue in New York City to preview new home furnishings merchandise and to place orders for the products that will appear in their stores.

The South Dakota farm women had from Labor Day to November 5th to style and produce their first product line. The women focused on quilts and pillow shams and succeeded in having a line of samples ready for the market. This time the products received a better reception from the department store buyers. *Home Furnishings Daily*, the home furnishings industry trade journal, ran a front page article stating that "Dakotah has the freshest design ideas in the last 100 years in bed covers." Over $50,000 in orders were placed at that first show.

Back in South Dakota, a $54,000 Small Business Administration loan provided the capital to purchase sewing machines and enough fabric to fill the orders, but working capital was still inadequate. The Webster, South Dakota, Junior Chamber of Commerce raised $1,600 to buy fuel oil; the local Isaac Walton League donated the use of their building; and Whyte and the women worked for six months without pay until they delivered their first shipments to the buyers. They organized as the Tract Handicraft Industries Cooperative, and the firm was off and sewing.

In 1986 this employees' cooperative, reorganized as an employee-owned corporation in 1976, had sales of almost $14 million, had over 400 employees, and was considered to be the Mercedes Benz of the bed covering industry.

MARKETING

Dakotah manufactured and sold textile home furnishings products in four major categories, bed coverings (bedspreads, comforters, etc.) which accounted for 50 percent of sales, pillows (including decorator pillows) which made up 40 percent of sales, window treatments (curtains, draperies, etc.) which were 5 percent of sales, and miscellaneous items (shower curtains, napkins, placemats, wall hangings, etc.) which accounted for the remaining 5 percent of sales. Approximately 50 percent of these items were sold in department stores, 40 percent to mass- and catalog merchants (Spiegels was the largest single customer), 5 percent to bed and bath specialty stores, and 5 percent to the hotel and motel industry. Dakotah also operated its own factory outlet store in Webster. Dakotah products were distributed in all 50 states and the company had a small amount of export sales.

Dakotah was a very small producer in a large industry. Manufacturer's sales in the textile home furnishings industry were estimated at $3.9 billion in 1985; of this amount, sales of bedspreads and bed sets were $375.7 million (this did not include sheets and pillowcases for which sales were estimated at $813.5 million). The largest competitor was Spring Mills with total sales of $1.5 billion, 64 percent of which were in textile home furnishings. Another major competitor was Fieldcrest Cannon with sales of $1.1 billion. The industry was becoming increasingly concentrated in the face of pressure from foreign competitors. Major developments had been the acquisition of Burlington Industry's sheet and towel division by J. P. Stevens, Fieldcrest's purchase of Cannon, and West Point Pepperell's purchase of Cluett Peabody. Firms chose acquisitions as a means of expanding product lines to avoid the risk and cost of establishing new brand names. Well-established brand names were considered important in succeeding against imports. Another industry response to foreign competition was the increased use of automated production techniques. All large producers used a relatively high degree of automation to produce both fabrics and finished goods. In spite of these developments, the textile industry averaged net profits of only .32 percent of sales in 1986.

In the face of such competitive pressures, Dakotah had succeeded in establishing strong brand identification. George Whyte explained how this was done. "Dakotah sells a lot of sizzle. Once you create the image, the product sells itself. So we have invested a great deal of time and money in creating the image." Dakotah's major thrust to create an image began in 1976 when the newly incorporated company contracted with a consulting firm that specialized in the development of corporate identities. The consulting firms's first recommendation was to change the name of the products from Dakotah Handcrafts by Tract, and the name of the organization from Tract Handcraft Industries Cooperative, Inc. to just Dakotah. The company and its products are now identified by the name, Dakotah, written in distinctive script (Exhibit 13.2 includes the company identification logo).

The next step in creating the Dakotah image was to develop a magnificent company showroom in the midst of the home furnishings market in New York

City. Much time and money were spent in finding the right location and creating a suitable ambience. Finally a space became available on the ground floor of the textile market building, located on Fifth Avenue between 30th and 31st Streets. The building houses offices for several textile and home furnishing manufacturers. Whyte created a spacious and dramatic office that rivals the office of any chief executive officer for a Fortune 500 company.

The New York showroom and offices were owned by a Dakotah subsidiary, Dakotah USA. Employees there were technically employees of the subsidiary. Sales were under the management of Neil Zuber, Vice President of Sales. Zuber ran the

EXHIBIT 13.2 **Bird of Paradise**

New York showroom and coordinated the selling activities of 11 independent sales representatives, each assigned an exclusive geographical area. John Panarello, the Vice President of National Accounts, sold to the large department stores and catalog merchants.

Great care was taken so that the Dakotah name written in its characteristic script was the only trademark to appear before the public. Whyte also insisted that the Dakotah name be featured in any catalog layout of the products, a practice ordinarily reserved for a few select designers such as Bill Blass and Ralph Lauren.

Whyte believed that Dakotah's principal strength was its ability to create high-fashion, uniquely designed items (Exhibit 13.2). Dakotah focused on designs that created an up-scale contemporary look. The first designs came from Whyte and other staff members. By 1982, Whyte recognized the need to hire a professional designer and asked one of Park Smith's former employees, Belinda Ballash, to join the Dakotah company. Ballash worked out of her office in Pacific Palisades, California, supplying Dakotah with designs reflecting the most up-to-date trends from the West Coast. In May 1987, Whyte hired another designer housed on the East Coast to provide designs reflecting East Coast trends. The designers were employees of Dakotah USA.

Although Dakotah products were styled to reflect current fashion taste which, in 1987, was returning to a "country" look, Whyte believed that Dakotah's emphasis would remain on products with contemporary styling. Whyte's attention to creating a unique look for the Dakotah products had been successful. Dakotah had always had difficulty filling its orders, sometimes running months behind and occasionally not allowing its sales representatives to take new orders for periods of up to two months. In 1987, Whyte negotiated a licensing agreement with The Spring Mills Company, the leading manufacturer of sheets and pillow cases, for use of Dakotah designs for a new line that would feature the Dakotah name. Whyte believed that similar licensing agreements would be negotiated with manufacturers of other home furnishings products.

In 1986, Whyte decided to move Dakotah into the hospitality market. The company had previously sold furnishings to hotels and motels on a limited scale, decorating some suites for the Hyatt Corporation. Whyte was convinced that more appealing interior furnishings would improve occupancy rates. His first major deal was with the Super 8 Motel Company. The Super 8 Company, headquartered in Aberdeen, South Dakota, fifty miles from Webster, was a motel franchise chain with over 400 budget motels in the United States and Canada. After testing guest responses to some of the products, Super 8 agreed to purchase bedspreads, wall hangings, and pillow ensembles. Dakotah became the exclusive supplier of bedcoverings to the corporate-owned motels, and a recommended supplier for the franchises.

With this success, Whyte planned to pursue the hospitality industry vigorously. In 1987, these sales were being handled by a two-person telemarketing effort located at the Webster headquarters. Initial results had been very encouraging. Company plans were for hospitality to be 15 percent of total sales by 1988, 30 percent in 1989, 40 percent in 1990, and 50 percent of sales by 1991.

MANUFACTURING

Dakotah bedcoverings were unique in that they were made with a technique called applique. In appliqueing, decorations are created by cutting pieces of one material and applying them to the surface of another. Manufacturing processes at Dakotah were a mixture of skilled hand work and highly automated processes. The decorative pieces of fabric were bound to the surface of the background material with adhesive then outlined with zigzag stitching which was done by manually guiding the fabric through a sewing machine. This process was labor intensive and required considerable skill. Other manufacturing processes, such as the decorative stitching at the edges of the bedcoverings, were performed by computer-controlled machines.

Dakotah operated seven plants in six small towns, all in northeastern South Dakota. Two plants were located in Webster—Webster 1 and Webster 2. Webster 1 employed 45 people who were engaged in the initial measurement and cutting of all fabric used in the other plants. Webster 1 also produced the batting or fiberfill used to give bulk to the bedspreads. Batting production was highly automated. It was made from bales of purchased fiber that were fed into hoppers. These fibers were then woven into rolls of batting 40-yards long in one continuous automated process that could be adjusted as to width and thickness of the batting.

Dakotah had recently acquired a computer-controlled laser fabric cutter that would be used to cut the pieces of cloth used in appliqueing. Patterns would be fed into the computer that would lay out the pieces on the fabric so as to minimize waste. Additional benefits from the laser cutter would be reduced labor and increased capacity. The laser cutting also would bind the edges to eliminate the ravelling that sometimes occurred with the current method which employed a hand guided, power driven, circular blade.

Webster 2 was located a block away from Webster 1 and included the company's administrative offices. This plant did the finishing and shipping for all products except pillows. In the final step of the manufacturing process, the decorated top of the bedspread and the underside fabric were placed on large frames with the batting in between. Large computer-controlled quilting machines sewed the three layers together. These machines also could be programmed to sew decorative designs on the bedspreads. Some bedspreads without applique were decorated entirely with the quilting machines. Appliqued coverings were then outlined and embellished with stitching, a process in which the coverings were again manually guided through a sewing machine. The operators of this process were the most highly skilled in the plant. The process not only required manual dexterity, but the operators sewed the designs from memory. Webster 2 employed 80 people in manufacturing.

Other Dakotah plants were located in Veblen, South Dakota (population 322), where 93 people produced and shipped pillows; Wilmot, South Dakota (population 492), which produced shams, or decorative pillow coverings, and employed 43 people; Eden, South Dakota (population 126), where draperies and bedskirts were made and 36 people were employed; Pierpont, South Dakota (population 165), where appliques were bound to the coverings and 30 people were employed; and Sisseton, South Dakota (population 2,717), where hanging samples used as point-of-purchase displays were made. Thirteen people were employed there. Several of these plants had the versatility to perform skilled hand-stitching operations used in making bedspreads and other products. Approximately 90 percent of the employees in manufacturing were women.

Company executives believed that Dakotah had an important competitive edge in manufacturing skills. While design changes were important to retain the distinctive look of the Dakotah products, protection from copying came largely from the fact that the appliqued designs were difficult to manufacture and Dakotah had more expertise in the appliqueing processes than any one else. It was also a difficult process to automate or mechanize. Only one competitor made appliqued products. As one manager put it, "We have an edge in marketing and design. Survival depends on success in manufacturing."

Manufacturing operations were under the management of Ed Johnson. Company executives gave him credit for solving the production problems which had previously given the company a reputation for not being able to meet promised delivery dates. One company executive estimated that in 1986 the company had turned away from two to four million in sales and company sales representatives were quoting delivery dates of six months. He said, "People can build a house faster than they can get the bedspreads." Continued automation was constrained by capital requirements. For example, the new laser cutter had cost $300,000. Dakotah had invested over $3 million in plant and equipment during the five years prior to 1987 and planned to invest well over $1 million in 1987.

Manufacturing workers at Dakotah were paid an average of $4.51 an hour. Skilled workers such as fabric cutters or applique stitchers could make as much as $4.92. The base wage was 20 to 30 percent below the manufacturing wages paid in larger eastern South Dakota cities such as Watertown or Sioux Falls, but well above the $1.50-an-hour labor costs of Korean and Taiwanese textile manufacturers. The clerical staff was paid at rates similar to those paid in Sioux Falls. Top managers at Dakotah were paid salaries substantially below industry averages.

"The concept of this company is to make jobs," stated Richard Engel, the chief financial officer. "So we try to control the cost of the product through mechanization, experimentation, and heavy investment." Engel saw the employee-ownership concept as being of mixed benefit. It gave employees a sense of commitment, but it severely limited its access to capital. Dakotah had $1.25 million in outstanding long-term notes. This included approximately $65,000 in a revolving working-capital loan financed at one percent above the prime rate and the rest in the form of a six-year loan secured by machinery and equipment at one-and-a-half percent above the prime rate. At one time the company had paid 4 1/2 to 5 points over prime. (For financial statements, see Exhibits 13.3 and 13.4.)

When asked about the company's improved performance in 1986, Engel attributed it to several factors. The recruitment of more experienced middle managers, significant investments in machinery and equipment, better cost controls, and the development of new markets such as the hotel and motel industry were all judged to have been significant. Some of these initiatives began as early as 1983 and the results began showing up in the financial statements in 1986.

EXHIBIT 13.3 **Balance sheets for Dakotah, Inc.**

	1980	1981	1982	1983	1984	1985	1986
Assets							
Current assets							
Cash	$ 12,162	$ 81,447	$ 81,629	$ 3,207	$ 25,558	$ 16,372	$ 18,171
Accounts receivable less allowance for doubtable accounts	1,325,765	1,289,537	1,278,584	1,912,920	1,635,032	1,337,006	1,718,731
Merchandise inventory	1,207,482	1,448,964	1,769,199	3,103,208	2,405,746	2,352,272	1,994,279
Prepaid income tax	35,915	29,398	12,880	115,392	80,114	66,441	
Other current assets	19,413	3,831	17,587	25,142	7,239	12,686	16,094
Total current assets	2,600,737	2,853,177	3,159,879	5,159,869	4,153,689	3,784,777	3,747,275
Property, plant and equipment—less accumulated depreciation	775,438	904,634	1,325,579	1,780,827	1,640,582	1,415,983	1,732,239
Other assets	19,420	19,420	22,770	11,830	11,010	9,190	9,270
Total assets	$3,395,595	$3,777,231	$4,508,228	$6,952,526	$5,805,281	$5,209,950	$5,488,784
Liabilities and Stockholder's Equity							
Current liabilities							
Notes payable—Bank	$ 839,111	$ 927,856	$ 511,720	$1,849,604	$1,487,241	$1,124,104	$ 264,537

Capital lease obligations	21,700	21,700	14,868	16,336	17,718	19,140	20,886
Notes payable—other	101,385	92,654	49,593	31,153			
Accounts payable	632,650	632,225	853,646	1,394,598	747,876	632,589	828,303
Income tax payable	8,891	16,607					
Other current liabilities	122,278	86,174	174,971	277,395	199,188	286,303	408,935
Total current liabilities	1,726,015	1,777,216	1,604,798	3,569,086	2,452,023	2,062,136	1,522,661
Long-term debt							
Notes payable—bank			880,000	1,210,000	1,140,000	870,000	1,250,000
Capital lease obligations	496,347	475,398	465,364	448,337	430,821	412,154	391,088
Notes payable—other	89,930	70,541					
Total long-term debt	586,277	545,939	1,345,364	1,658,337	1,570,821	1,282,154	1,641,088
Stockholder's equity							
Common stock	679,448	928,999	927,948	927,435	926,434	936,382	1,159,383
Contributed capital	13,207	13,207	13,207	13,207	13,207	13,207	13,207
Retained earnings	390,648	511,870	616,911	784,461	842,796	916,071	1,152,445
Total stockholders' equity	1,083,303	1,454,076	1,558,066	1,725,103	1,782,437	1,865,660	2,325,035
Total liabilities and stockholders' equity	$3,395,595	$3,777,231	$4,508,228	$6,952,526	$5,805,281	$5,209,950	$5,488,784

EXHIBIT 13.4 Income statements for Dakotah, Inc.

	1980	1981	1982	1983	1984	1985	1986
Sales	$9,628,706	$10,721,784	$9,124,241	$12,300,726	$13,729,250	$11,708,748	$14,085,870
Less returns and allowances	487,616	472,897	344,014	479,567	605,621	645,166	410,329
Net sales before discounts	9,141,090	10,248,887	8,780,227	11,821,159	13,123,629	11,063,582	
Less discounts	17,912	14,473	8,647	7,908	7,928	2,659	
Net sales	9,123,178	10,234,414	8,771,580	11,813,251	13,115,701	11,060,923	13,675,541
Cost of goods sold							
Merchandise inventory	1,251,553	1,207,482	1,448,964	1,769,199	3,103,208	2,405,746	2,352,272
Purchases	3,576,734	4,227,009	3,532,998	5,326,805	4,551,872	3,642,072	4,721,640
Freight in	195,760	191,943	207,934	238,175	164,711	123,026	141,341
Direct labor	1,615,935	1,820,766	1,591,026	2,769,484	2,478,520	2,206,586	2,350,930
Employee fringe benefits	98,877						
Payroll taxes	119,257	155,466	140,935	330,376	213,148	197,406	228,861
Cost of goods available for sale	6,858,116	7,602,666	6,921,857	10,434,039	10,511,459	8,574,836	9,795,044

Less merchandise inventory—end of year	1,207,482	1,448,964	1,769,199	3,103,208	2,405,746	2,352,272	1,994,279
Cost of goods sold		6,153,702	5,152,658	7,330,831	8,105,713	6,222,564	7,800,765
Gross profit	3,472,544	4,080,712	3,618,922	4,482,420	5,009,988	4,838,359	5,874,776
Operating expenses							
Manufacturing	462,506	601,535	729,888	1,023,828	1,276,410	1,349,893	1,574,785
Selling	1,254,170	1,772,059	1,393,449	1,788,532	1,831,548	1,656,810	1,844,953
Shipping	312,128	275,127	340,730	336,820	379,414	323,299	371,997
Financial	311,236	216,027	218,372	308,677	480,412	326,000	254,921
General and administrative	617,110	722,736	758,941	920,559	937,439	1,060,443	1,148,188
Total operating expenses	2,957,150	3,587,484	3,441,380	4,378,416	4,905,223	4,716,445	5,194,844
Income from operations	515,394	493,228	177,542	104,004	104,765	121,914	679,932
Royalty income, net	4,330						
Provision for income taxes	34,299	52,607	40,949	(83,951)	7,328	25,966	40,423
Contribution to employee stock bonus plan	371,213	250,000					250,000
Net income	114,212	190,621	136,593	187,955	97,437	95,948	389,509

Dakotah had formal five-year goals for profit and growth. These included sales growth of 15 percent, net pretax earnings on sales of 4 percent in 1987 rising to 12 percent by 1991, and achievement of an average rate of return on stockholders equity of 15 percent. "If we want to grow," Engel said, "we have to look to external equity. We can support 10 percent growth but 25 percent will require more. We have reached the limit of debt financing." Engel recognized that going outside the limits of employee ownership for equity capital was a departure from an important company policy. "One thing I have learned is that some things are sacred." Employee ownership was one of those things.

DAKOTAH'S FUTURE

Dakotah had begun as a manufacturing company established to create jobs in northeastern South Dakota. Over the years the focus of the company had shifted from manufacturing to marketing. "It is our forte," explained Whyte. He believed that marketing opportunities through licensing and franchising could allow Dakotah to grow to a $100-million company over the next ten years.

Licensing possibilities included such products as wall and floor coverings, a more extensive line of window treatments, as well as other textile products. A franchised chain of Dakotah stores would allow the company greater access to a larger number of consumers. Both of these alternatives would allow the company to increase its revenues with a relatively small capital investment.

Dakotah was beginning to consider other markets. In 1986, Dakotah quietly began selling pillows to Wal-Mart, a large discount chain. Sales were $1.5 million with $2.5 million expected in 1987. The possibilities for increased sales through discount outlets raised the possibility that overseas manufacturing of Dakotah designs might be considered.

Finally, the capital limitation of confining equity ownership to employees was recognized as an obstacle to growth. Perhaps employee ownership was no longer "sacred". However, it was a decision with far-reaching consequences. "The intent is still to create jobs," Whyte said. "The concept of employee ownership has not changed yet."

CASE 14

Atlanta Cyclorama

The director of the Atlanta Cyclorama was sitting in his Grant Park office speculating over his greatest challenge, namely devising the 1987 promotional plan for the Cyclorama and long-range strategies for the attraction for future years. Attendance will have to be increased from an estimated 342,000 in 1986 to 500,000 in 1989, and sales will have to exceed one million dollars per year by 1990. Attendance in 1982 was 195,000 and in 1983 it reached 300,000. Attendance figures for 1984 through 1986, broken down by ticket class, are shown in Exhibit 14.1.

EXHIBIT 14.1 **Breakdown of Cyclorama attendance and revenue by ticket class**

	1984		1985		1986	
Ticket class	**Attendance**	**Revenue**	**Attendance**	**Revenue**	**Attendance**	**Revenue**
Adult ($3.00)	117,000	$351,000	129,005	$387,015	146,789	$440,367
Adult Group & Senior Citizens ($2.50)	82,463	$206,158	77,030	$192,575	82,325	$205,813
Children ($1.50)	20,446	$ 30,669	22,465	$ 33,698	25,840	$ 38,760
Child Group ($1)	7,096	$ 7,096	6,637	$ 6,637	6,122	$ 6,122
Free	41,217	—	37,578	—	42,120	—
Tour Groups	30,000	$ 57,483	29,315	$ 67,891	38,900	$ 90,098
Total	298,222	$652,406	279,000	$687,816	342,096	$781,160

THE ATLANTA CYCLORAMA

Before the invention of motion pictures, opportunities for the general public to view past events were definitely limited. One vehicle for accomplishing this desire was the cyclorama which is defined as "a 360 degree circular painting which when viewed from its interior gives the illusion that the viewer is in the scene." A cyclorama is also sometimes referred to as a panorama. Hundreds of these cycloramas were painted and shown in American cities in the latter half of the nineteenth century; however, today only fourteen survive throughout the world. In the United States, in addition to the Atlanta Cyclorama, a panorama is on exhibit at the Gettysburg Battlefield in Pennsylvania, and another is in the Metropolitan Museum of Art in New York.

The Atlanta Cyclorama was created in 1885 and depicts the 1864 Battle of Atlanta which is familiar to all who have seen the movie "Gone With The Wind." The masterpiece is a 50-foot-high, 400-foot circumference painting in the round, with a three-dimensional diorama complete with figures added by the W.P.A. in the 1930s. The Cyclorama was first displayed in a frame building in Grant Park in 1912. In 1921, the painting was moved to its present building. After years of use and limited maintenance, the attraction had fallen into an advanced state of disrepair so serious that by 1979 the Cyclorama had to be closed. Extensive restoration ensued at a cost of $11 million. For two and a half years, workers repaired the tears and flaws in the painting and revamped the three-dimensional diorama that serves as the paintings foreground. The restoration effort also included the installation of a revolving viewing platform as well as the refurbishing of the building that houses the painting. The exhibit reopened to the public in 1982. In addition to the famous painting, visitors can also admire other exhibits related to the Civil War: for instance, the famous locomotive "Texas," winner of the "great locomotive chase." It is the same train that a group of Confederates drove to Ringgold to chase Union raiders who had stolen the locomotive "General." Thus, the Atlanta Cyclorama is part historical museum, part artwork and part Confederate memorial. The Cyclorama shares its Grant Park location with the Atlanta Zoo, thus providing a combination sight-seeing opportunity.

Grant Park is located three miles south of the downtown hotel district. In past years, the zoo had exerted a negative influence on attendance at the Cyclorama because local media stories highlighted the fact that the zoo had fallen into a state of disrepair and that animals had been poorly treated. Fortunately, civic pride had lead to a revitalization program for the zoo in 1985, and a major renovation similar to that experienced by the Cyclorama had been completed by late 1986. Zoo attendance had increased steadily with the renovation efforts, growing from 280,000 in 1984 to almost 570,000 in 1986 (Exhibit 14.2).

The Cyclorama is owned and operated by the Atlanta City Government. Exhibit 14.3 is an organization chart for this operation. In addition to a director and an

EXHIBIT 14.2 Attendance figures for the Atlanta Zoo	
Year	**Attendance**
1986	567,269
1985	344,087
1984	279,805
1983	448,397
1982	402,118
1981	347,828
1980	363,433
1979	388,832
1978	452,051

EXHIBIT 14.3 **Cyclorama organization chart**

associate director, there is a staff of seventeen persons. The director is a professional, chosen by civil service procedures. The City Council authorizes the budget and exercises control over the other activities.

THE PRODUCT AND ITS MARKET

Every year, a very diversified crowd visits the Cyclorama. The admission price is very reasonable: $3.00 for adults ($2.50 if in groups of ten or more), $2.50 for senior citizens, $1.50 for children ($1 if in groups of ten or more), and children under six are admitted free. School groups are also admitted free. Furthermore, there is no charge for parking.

Different groups of people flock to this attraction. The attendance can be segmented into four categories: tour groups (consisting mainly of senior citizens and school groups), conventioneers, visitors and tourists, and finally local residents. These market segments all exhibit particular characteristics.

Tour groups. This segment tends to visit the Cyclorama on weekdays. For both segments (school children and senior citizens), the visit usually occurs once a year.

Conventioneers. Atlanta is the third largest convention city in the United States in terms of numbers of conventions hosted. In 1985, 1.5 million conventioneers

EXHIBIT 14.4 **Atlanta conventioneers' attendance, per year**

Year	Conventions hosted	Attendance
1985	1400	1,500,000
1984	1200	1,110,000
1983	1100	1,300,000
1982	1000	1,150,000
1981	1150	1,128,000
1980	1090	1,002,900
1979	970	876,800
1978	800	850,000
1977	760	760,000
1976	725	635,000

came to Atlanta. Mostly, they stayed in the downtown area and remained in Atlanta about 3 days. Exhibit 14.4 and Exhibit 14.5 present the conventioneers' attendance growth, and their average daily expenditure and length of stay, from 1976 to 1985. The main problem they encounter is the lack of activity and entertainment close to downtown. At the heart of the convention area in Atlanta is the Georgia World Congress Center. The Georgia World Congress Center started its operations in Atlanta in September 1976. At that time, it offered 350,000 square feet of exhibition space. But with the convention market booming, it soon proved to be insufficient. In April 1985, the Georgia World Congress Center officially celebrated its expanded opening: 650,000 square feet of exhibition space, and over one million square feet of floor space. The center is one of the world's top meeting/exhibit facilities, with its ballroom, auditorium, corporate conference center, and seventy meeting rooms.

Expanded exhibition space is, of course, only one dimension of the convention business opportunity. To host large meetings requires a sufficient quantity of con-

EXHIBIT 14.5 **Atlanta conventioneers' daily expenditure and length of stay, per year**

Year	Average daily expenditure	Length of stay
1985	$141.00	3.0 days
1984	$141.00	3.0 days
1983	$135.00	3.0 days
1982	$126.00	3.5 days
1981	$110.00	4.0 days
1980	$ 99.00	4.0 days
1979	$ 81.00	4.0 days
1978	$ 77.00	3.5 days
1977	$ 73.50	3.5 days
1976	$ 70.00	3.2 days

venient hotel facilities. Atlanta has also experienced a dramatic increase in the number of downtown hotel rooms, from 9,065 in 1979 to 12,596 in 1985.

The combination of exhibition space and large number of hotel rooms has placed a marketing challenge before the Atlanta Convention and Visitors Bureau. This organization has spearheaded an aggressive program designed to persuade groups to hold their conventions in the city. Atlanta is expected to host even more conventions, thus endowing this market segment with growth potential.

Tourists and Sightseers. This market is more than twice the size of the conventioneer market. Summer is the favorite season to visit Atlanta because 43 percent of the yearly tourists come to visit during June, July, and August. Exhibit 14.6 presents Cyclorama percentage attendance by month. Many Atlanta visitors come to meet with family (45%); others (39%) come to sightsee, with 14 percent specifically mentioning tourist sites and 3.5 percent mentioning cultural sites. Their stay is shorter; one to two days, but many of them enjoy two or three attractions during their visit.

EXHIBIT 14.6 Cyclorama average attendance by month	
	Percent of total
January	5
February	5
March	7
April	7
May	6
June	13
July	14
August	16
September	10
October	8
November	6
December	3

Mention should be made of another tourist group, namely the people who flow through Atlanta as they travel to and from the state of Florida. Atlanta is located on two interstate highways, I-75 and I-85, which provide corridors for traffic to and from the Northeast and Midwest sections of the United States. Large numbers of tourists living in these regions spend their vacations in Florida, and the state of Georgia has tried for many years to convince these persons to "Stay and See" Georgia. For example, a number of welcome centers were set up at the state borders where information about tourist attractions in the state is distributed. Exhibit 14.7 gives some indication of the magnitude of this opportunity. Sporadically, the state has done media advertising in such areas of origin as Ohio and Michigan. In 1985, the state of Georgia tripled its tourist advertising budget to $2.1 million, using "Adventures in the great unknown—Georgia" as a campaign theme.

EXHIBIT 14.7 **Number of visitors to the Atlanta Welcome Center**	
Year	**Number of visitors**
1985	11,600
1984	10,995
1983	7,638
1982	2,035
1981	5,119
1980	4,763
1979	3,498
1978	5,229
1977	6,219
1976	6,605

Local Residents and Their Out-of-Town Guests. Atlanta and its metropolitan area encompassing eighteen counties contained an estimated population of 2,326,000 at the end of 1984. This figure can be contrasted with the 1980 population figure of 2,138,231 people, and the 1970 and 1960 figures of 1,684,200 and 1,247,649 respectively. The city is growing rapidly but the expansion is taking place mostly at the northern perimeter of the city, far from downtown. However, the population in Atlanta is very mobile: most Atlantans are from other states and many have only been in Atlanta for a short period of time.

CONSUMPTION PATTERNS AND ATTITUDES

Visitors to the Cyclorama seek to fulfill four different types of needs: education, enjoyment of art, history, and entertainment. But each segment exhibits specific trends which affect the attractiveness of the Cyclorama.

Conventioneers. One major pattern observed is that Atlanta conventioneers very seldom bring their spouses with them, and only 18 percent bring their children. When planning tours, convention planners seek attractions with overall appeal, uniqueness, ability to accommodate large groups, and accessible parking. The Cyclorama fits all these needs remarkably well, plus it has that "Old South" charm that is so appealing to conventioneers. Furthermore, the Cyclorama can be rented to a private group. It will accommodate up to 180 people at a time on its rotating platform.

Tourists and Sightseers. Tourists almost always have access to a car and they are looking for a day-long entertainment schedule. Attributes that are salient in their choice of attractions are: accessible from freeway, parking, fun for the whole family, near other attractions, and uniqueness. Once again, the Cyclorama fares well on all.

Residents and Guests. This segment is looking for a full day experience offering a good time/value ratio. The closeness to the zoo and the low admission price play in the Cyclorama's favor. However, it should be remembered that the guests' host will likely influence their choice. Thus, since the Cyclorama is visited at most once a year by local residents, this can have a negative impact on the Cyclorama.

The Cyclorama is a product that is unique. But, it also has many competitors because it belongs in the generic category of tourist and cultural, attractions. In the past, the Cyclorama had cooperated with other historical/cultural attractions by the use of cross-promotion techniques such as distributing each others brochures. Additional Atlanta attractions include: (1) Stone Mountain Park, with over 5.6 million visitors (2) Six Flags Over Georgia, an amusement park that admitted over 2.5 million visitors (3) Fernbank Science Center which attracted 700,000 visitors and (4) The Martin Luther King, Jr. Center with its 500,000 visitors. In 1986, the Carter Presidential Library opened to the public and proved to be a popular attraction. Other competing activities in which visitors can participate are shopping, theatre, and nightlife.

TRADE

The Cyclorama is a product that does not lend itself easily to trade activities. However, the Cyclorama is a stop on the tour lists of six different Atlanta operators: Atlanta Tours, Arnell Tours, Brewster Motor Coach, Gray Line of Atlanta (a picture of the diorama is featured in their promotional brochure), Metro Tours and Southeastern Stages. Furthermore, many school groups and senior citizen groups visit the Cyclorama.

PAST EXPERIENCE WITH COMMUNICATIONS ELEMENTS

Advertising

In 1986, most of the Cyclorama's promotional budget was allocated to advertising. Ads were run for three months in *Southern Living* and for seven months in the weekly "Saturday Leisure Guide" of the *Atlanta Journal-Constitution*. In addition, advertising in connection with special events was scheduled. In 1986, $40,000 was budgeted for routine advertising, plus $6,000 for special advertising. Advertising for the Cyclorama tends to be simple, staid, and dignified. Print ads are of the reminder type, treating it as a presold product. Exhibit 14.8 is an example of the print ad that ran in the local newspaper.

Personal Selling

Up to now, the product itself and the budgetary restrictions have prevented the use of this communication tool for the Cyclorama.

Exhibit 14.8 **Sample newspaper ad, 1984**

Sales Promotion

Sales promotion tools used in 1986 were information brochures and cents-off coupons. The brochures are mostly distributed at welcome centers and at Atlanta Convention and Visitors Bureau booths.

The brochures are factual and focus on the historical appeal. They too, possess the dignity and seriousness of tone generally associated with cultural and historical attractions. Couponing has been directed primarily at conventioneers and $2,000 of the 1986 budget was spent on media for this purpose. Effectiveness studies have yet to be undertaken.

Publicity/Public Relations

The Cyclorama has been the subject of many articles in local magazines and newspapers. It has also been featured in public service announcements on radio and television. The Cyclorama is also doing cross-publicity with other national attractions such as the Gettysburg Cyclorama, the Boston Fine Arts Building, the Milwaukee Historical Society, and the Atlanta Historical Society.

MEDIA COST AND AUDIENCE INFORMATION

The Atlanta area is served by a variety of print and broadcast media. Exhibit 14.9 shows some cost and audience data for the major print vehicles in the Atlanta

---

EXHIBIT 14.9 **Atlanta area print media cost and audience data**

Cost and audience data for black and white print ads

Newspaper; 3 inch ad	Costs		Number of readers (000's)		
	1 time	52 times	All adults	Women	Men
Atlanta Journal-Constitution	$ 277	$14,404	963	475	488

Magazines; 1/3 page ad	1 time	6 times	All adults	Women	Men
Southern Living, Georgia edition	$2,090	$12,540	190	133	57
Atlanta edition, full page ad only	3,930	21,240	100	70	30
Atlanta Magazine	1,025	5,670	33		
Business Atlanta	755	4,110	24	3	21
Georgia Trends	850	4,530	27		
Where/Atlanta	850	4,260	60		
Key/Atlanta	115	690	10		

---

area. The major newspaper is the *Atlanta Journal-Constitution* which publishes a morning and evening edition. A single 3 inch ad costs $277 and runs in both the morning and evening papers. In terms of magazines *Southern Living* is very popular, containing articles on travel, cooking, and history. An advertiser can place a full or fractional page ad in a statewide edition or a full page ad in a metro Atlanta edition. The three magazines, *Atlanta Magazine, Business Atlanta,* and *Georgia Trends,* are slick periodicals that reach an upscale suburban family or business audience. The two magazines *Where* and *Key* are "What to do in Atlanta" periodicals and are distributed free to hotel guests.

Exhibit 14.10 shows the cost and audience data for broadcast media. The data for a thirty second television spot on the networks' morning news programs are shown. Also, data for Atlanta's five biggest radio stations are shown for the morning drive-time period. The radio stations have different creative formats in addition to different costs and audiences.

A serious constraint facing the director of the Cyclorama as he sets about designing the 1987 promotional plan for the Cyclorama is in the area of budget. The Atlanta City Council has authorized an expenditure of $50,000 for a publicity fund. The amount is available for media advertising and sales promotion efforts. Personal selling and publicity activities are carried out by the director and associate director as part of their overall duties. A separate printing budget of $25,000 pays for brochures and similar forms of direct advertising.

The director realizes that the budget allocated to the Cyclorama is not sufficient given the task of generating an appreciable increase in attendance. Therefore, he is fully aware of the importance of making the right decisions as he designs the Cyclorama's 1987 promotional plan.

EXHIBIT 14.10 **Atlanta area broadcast media cost and audience data**

Cost and audience data for 7:00 am to 9:00 am, weekdays

Television 30-second spot	Cost	Rating*	Number of viewers/listeners (In thousands) All adults	Women	Men
WSB (ABC, Good Morning America)	$350	4.0	108	64	44
WAGA (CBS, Morning News)	125	1.3	36	22	14
WXIA (NBC, Today Show)	375	3.4	92	56	36
Radio 60-second spot					
WZGC (Top 40)	250	1.3	36	19	17
WQXI (Adult Rock)	350	1.9	51	27	24
WSB (Contemporary)	200	1.4	38	20	18
WFOX (Rock Oldies)	150	.9	24	13	11
WKHX (Country)	250	1.9	51	26	25

*Rating is a measure of audience size expressed as a percentage of 2,699,800 adults, the survey area's population base for 1987.

CASE 15

Saunders Leasing System, Inc.: Coping with the 1980s

"The business has changed so significantly. It requires a whole new terminology, a whole new outlook, new management and new thinking. I think we're from the old school," observed Harris Saunders, Jr., co-chairman of the family-owned Saunders Leasing System, Inc. His younger brother and co-chairman, Bob Saunders, agreed. Affectionately referred to as "the boys," 61-year old Harris and 53-year old Bob had been involved in the operations of the company for nearly 40 years.

This case was prepared by Peter M. Ginter, Linda E. Swayne, and John D. Leonard. It is intended as a basis for classroom discussion rather than to illustrate effective or ineffective handling of an administrative situation. Used by permission from Peter M. Ginter.

SAUNDERS LEASING SYSTEM, INC.: BEFORE DEREGULATION

The Saunders Company was founded in 1916 by Warwick Saunders and his four sons; Warwick, Jr., Joe, Ellis, and Harris. It is credited as being the first car and truck rental business in the United States. Twenty-seven-year old Joe Saunders got the idea when the family and business car (a Moline Knight Dreadnaught touring car made by the Moline Automobile Company) broke down one evening in 1915 and he borrowed a Model T Ford. Joe realized that if he could use a temporary vehicle, plenty of other people might also.

Joe, like other members of the family, had tried various businesses and sold various products. He felt that in car rental he had at last found a need that was so great, the service would sell itself. Thus, in August 1916, Joe placed a seven-line classified advertisement in the *Omaha World Herald* offering a five-passenger Ford for rent. Joe is often credited with giving birth to the vehicle-renting industry. The ad that created an industry is shown in Exhibit 15.1.

The fledging Saunders Company soon owned a whole fleet of cars and had offices in major cities around the nation. The car-rental company grew, but truck leasing grew even faster and became the company's main line of business. By the 1950s, automobile rentals were phased out in order to concentrate on leasing and renting heavy-duty vehicles.

Saunders Leasing System, Inc., like many other companies, had over its long history changed its name and corporate organization several times. However, the

---

Automobiles for Hire.

Five-passenger Ford for rent: perfect running condition, nearly new: will rent to reliable party by hour, day, week *or* month. You may drive the car or I will furnish the driver. My charges are per mile, the only reasonable arrangement. Douglas 3622. Evenings and Sundays, Douglas 3676.

Source: Harris Saunders, Sr., *Top Up or Down?: The Origin and Development of the Automobile and Truck Renting and Leasing Industry—Since 1916.* Birmingham: Birmingham Printing and Publishing Company, 1985, 22–25.

EXHIBIT 15.1 **First vehicle leasing advertisement**

Saunders family operated the business continuously. In the beginning the name was Ford Livery Company. In 1918, it was changed to Drive It Yourself Company and then, in order to personalize the business, it was changed to Saunders Drive It Yourself System. During the depression of the 1930s for a while, the corporate names were Central States Car Rental Company, Midwest Drive It Yourself Co., Saunders System Washington Co., and Baltimore Drive It Yourself Co. All four corporations used the same service mark and trade names. All rental stations were known by one name, Saunders System. In 1955 the name was changed to The Saunders System Corporation and finally in 1966, on the advice of stock underwriters, the name Saunders Leasing System, Inc. was adopted. Examples of Saunders' logos are shown in Exhibit 15.2.

Source: Harris Saunders, Sr., *Top Up or Down?: The Origin and Development of the Automobile and Truck Renting and Leasing Industry—Since 1916.* Birmingham: Birmingham Printing and Publishing Company, 1985, 22–25.

EXHIBIT 15.2 **Saunders' logos**

Early Challenges

Throughout the 70 years of Saunder System's existence, several significant events challenged or changed the course of the company's development. The firm had to respond to the demands of World War I, The Great Depression, the post-World War II recovery, the inflation of the 1970s, and trucking deregulation.

Very few firms were prepared for the crash of 1929 and the depression that followed. Saunders System was essentially wiped out and the Saunders family lost their business. The Saunders brothers were able to buy some rental facilities at auction when they could assume the mortgages, pay for the equipment, and negotiate an equitable lease with the owner of the building. Some operations, and the Saunders name, were able to continue in this fashion.

The Growth Era

The business was restructured in the 1930s. Four geographical divisions were formed and a new, smaller company prevailed. It was during this time that the family realized that in addition to selling their service they needed to develop stronger balance sheet ratios and a better working capital position.

The post-World War II era was a time of economic boom. It was during this time that Saunders System deemphasized car leasing and concentrated on truck leasing. The truck leasing segment of the business grew more rapidly and became their major focus.

During the 1960s, the Saunders family considered the option of making Saunders System a public firm. The advantages of increased prestige, increased equity capital, and increased ability to use stock versus cash for other financial transactions weighed heavily in the decision. The costs of going public for Saunders included reduced managerial freedom, increased cost of accounting methods and reporting, increased time and money spent with underwriters, analysts, etc., and pressure to show improvements on a quarterly basis.

Finally in 1967, Saunders Leasing System made their first public stock offering. Additional offerings were made in 1972 and 1982. The family retained over 51 percent of the ownership of the firm with a French firm building a 21 percent share. The balance of the outstanding shares were not consolidated in any other large holding.

Energy Crisis

The 1970s were a time of great pressure on costs. The emergence of OPEC created tremendous problems for the fuel industry. Subsequently, the trucking industry and related services suffered. High inflation also contributed to the economic pressures faced by business. Pressure on the trucking industry was lessened somewhat by industry regulation. Escalating prices were passed on to customers and price competition was dampened. Performance within the industry was generally maintained at status quo. Regulated prices were essentially the same, but firms were able to differentiate themselves by their service record and image. Saunders Leasing System continued to build a strong image of service during this time.

SAUNDERS LEASING SYSTEM INC.: AFTER DEREGULATION

The decade of the 1980s brought a new era for the trucking industry and Saunders Leasing System. Deregulation contributed to overcapacity within the industry and new methods of competition, which were formerly banned, became prevalent. Weaker firms were acquired or went bankrupt, while stronger firms became larger and stronger.

By the mid-1980s, Saunders had become one of the largest of the nation's full-service leasing companies with 141 service centers and freight terminals located across the United States and Canada. Saunders competed with such billion dollar giants as Ryder, Hertz, and Leaseway truck rental companies. As of 1986, Saunders had over 2,000 employees, a fleet of over 8,000 vehicles, and served more than 5,700 truck transportation clients. Saunders offered a full line of transportation services tailored to each client's needs.

The deregulation of the early eighties forced the industry to address a freer, more competitive market. While Saunders Leasing System remained competitive, the company did not show the strength of the industry leaders such as Ryder.

Organization and Reorientation

Prior to deregulation, the company's management, as with most trucking firms, was oriented toward trucking operations rather than marketing or company strategy. In 1985, Gordon Shelfer, Jr. became the first nonfamily member to become President and Chief Executive Officer in the history of Saunders. The competitive pressures of the market, the effects of trucking deregulation, and the company's attempt to focus on marketing and cost reduction contributed to his nomination as CEO.

Shelfer reorganized Saunders on a functional basis with four primary departments—marketing, operations, human resources, and finance and administration. The resulting organization of Saunders Leasing System, Inc. is illustrated in Exhibit 15.3. In this organization the Executive Vice President of Marketing was responsible for Carrier Services, advertising, research and planning, and sales and field marketing. The Vice President for Operations directed the Driver Central Operations, the tire remanufacturing operation, and maintained all company equipment. The Executive Vice President of Finance and Administration was responsible for the management information system, budgeting, legal matters, and accounting. The Senior Vice President of Human Resources maintained labor relations, safety of facilities and vehicles, training, the in-house newspaper, and employee support.

Two additional directors reported to Mr. Shelfer—the Director of Properties and the Director of Internal Audit. The Director of Properties was responsible for negotiating leases, buildings and facilities, and complying with EPA regulations. The

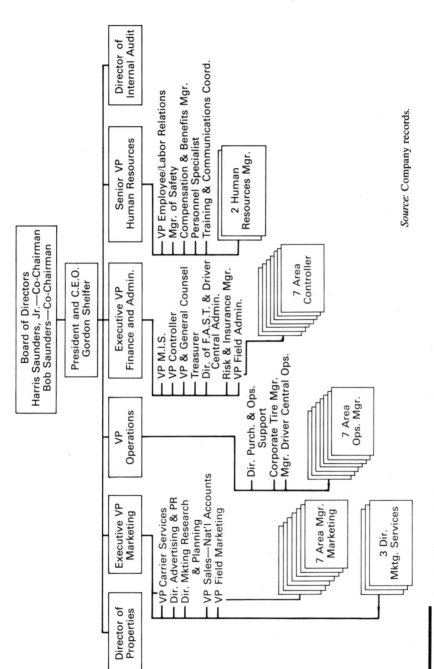

Board of Directors
Harris Saunders, Jr.—Co-Chairman
Bob Saunders—Co-Chairman

President and C.E.O.
Gordon Shelfer

Director of Properties

Executive VP Marketing
- VP Carrier Services
- Dir. Advertising & PR
- Dir. Mkting Research & Planning
- VP Sales—Nat'l Accounts
- VP Field Marketing

7 Area Mgr. Marketing

3 Dir. Mktg. Services

VP Operations
- Dir. Purch. & Ops. Support
- Corporate Tire Mgr.
- Mgr. Driver Central Ops.

7 Area Ops. Mgr.

Executive VP Finance and Admin.
- VP M.I.S.
- VP Controller
- VP & General Counsel
- Treasurer
- Dir. of F.A.S.T. & Driver Central Admin.
- Risk & Insurance Mgr.
- VP Field Admin.

7 Area Controller

Senior VP Human Resources
- VP Employee/Labor Relations
- Mgr. of Safety
- Compensation & Benefits Mgr.
- Personnel Specialist
- Training & Communications Coord.

2 Human Resources Mgr.

Director of Internal Audit

Source: Company records.

EXHIBIT 15.3 **Organization of Saunders Leasing System, Inc.**

Director of Internal Audit examined the four primary functions to make sure they were following procedures and regulations.

In an attempt to make the company more competitive and reduce costs, Shelfer streamlined management and increased management's span of control. Shelfer felt that overhead had been allowed to grow too rapidly. In the past, the firm added staff and enlarged budgets in order to meet projected sales volume, but would not cut back responsively when revenues fell short of expectations. The result was excessive overhead costs that increased each year. Not enough attention was paid to costs in a market that had become very cost competitive.

The reorganization of company operations reduced eleven area offices to seven, enabling management to improve coordination and to somewhat reduce overhead costs. The seven area offices and cities with facilities/terminals are shown in Exhibit 15.4.

In addition to the reorganization, Shelfer reinforced "Client Tailored Services" in which a client's individual needs were identified, then services were tailored to meet those needs. In conjunction with tailored services, Mr. Shelfer encouraged top management to get out into the field to interact with customers and field personnel. Top management exposure strengthened client relations, Saunders' internal communications network, and increased employee loyalty and understanding of the business. Further, Mr. Shelfer managed the company with an emphasis upon performance, cost reduction, maintenance of quality standards, and market segmentation.

Product Line

With deregulation of the trucking industry, Saunders had developed a wide line of products for its clients. Saunders' array of products are discussed below.

Full-Service Leasing.   As the company evolved, full-service leasing accounted for less and less of the Saunders business. In 1985 (illustrated in Exhibit 15.5), leasing comprised approximately 50 percent of the total revenue of Saunders. A full-service lease with Saunders included all parts, tires, maintenance, fleet driver, safety training, substitute vehicles, optional full tax services, fuel, and insurance. In addition, the vehicle leased by Saunders was painted the colors desired by the client company.

The service was tailored primarily toward the client who wanted to control his or her distribution system but did not want to handle daily operational and maintenance problems. Depending upon the needs of the client, lease terms typically ranged from six months to three years. Two major clients with full-service leasing arrangements were Nabisco and K-Mart Corporation.

Truck Rental.   Truck rental is the short-term use of tractors, trailers, and trucks. Short-term vehicle rental is often used for rush loads and during peak seasons. In the past, truck rental was the mainstay of Saunders System. While truck rental diminished in relative importance in Saunders' revenue mix, as indicated in Exhibit 15.5, it still made up almost 15 percent of 1985 revenues. Two clients that used truck rental were Texas Instruments and Sears, Roebuck Company.

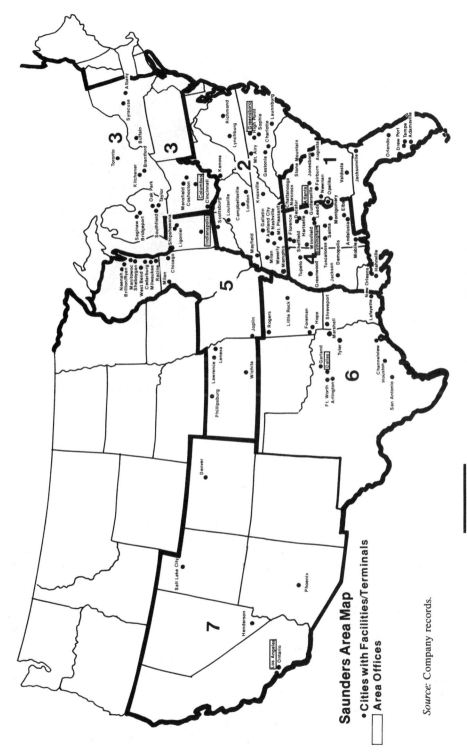

Saunders Area Map

- **Cities with Facilities/Terminals**
- ☐ **Area Offices**

Source: Company records.

EXHIBIT 15.4 **Saunders' area offices and facility locations**

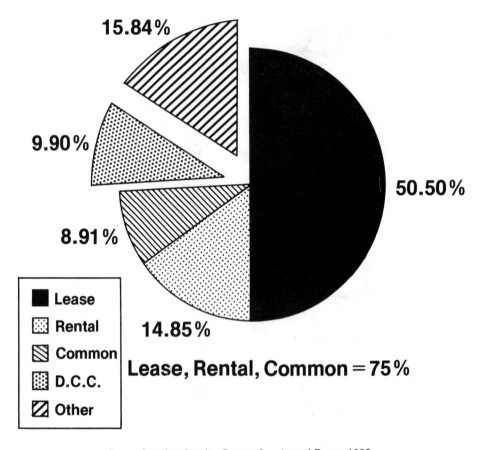

Source: Saunders Leasing System, Inc. Annual Report 1985.

EXHIBIT 15.5 **Revenue mix in 1985**

Common Carriage.   Another important product in the Saunders line was common carriage, comprising approximately nine percent of total revenue. Common carriage provided shipping services including the shipping of general and specific commodities on flatbed trailers, vans, and dump and tank trailers.

Saunders Carriers, Inc., a part of the common carriage business, was organized as a subsidiary of Saunders System after its acquisition in 1980. This subsidiary specialized in the safe handling of bulk liquids and was recognized nationally for its safety record. Emergency response teams, trained to handle tank accidents, were stationed at each Saunders' terminal. Special emphasis was given to preventing or reducing potentially harmful environmental consequences. In 1985, Saunders Carriers, Inc. built the nation's most technologically advanced terminal dedicated to the cleaning of bulk liquid trailers and the proper treatment of the resulting waste water. Two clients that used this service were Monsanto Company and Du Pont.

Dedicated Contract Carriage (DCC). Although it began operations in 1984, dedicated contract carriage comprised almost 10 percent of Saunders' revenue in 1985. Saunders DCC handled all the transportation needs of a client, including in-depth analysis of the client's service needs. DCC provided all required vehicles, a fully equipped truck maintenance facility, quality drivers, supervisors, mechanics, delivery scheduling, and all related paperwork. Saunders assumed total responsibility for the management and operation of the client's distribution system. In addition, Saunders' vehicles were painted with the client's corporate colors and logo. Two importat clients for this service included AT&T and Goodyear Tire and Rubber Company.

Truck Maintenance. Saunders offered truck maintenance to companies that owned their fleet but did not want to service their vehicles. Under this program, Saunders' personnel performed the same preventive maintenance, service, and repairs for a client's vehicles as they did for Saunders' vehicles. Two clients using this service were Weyerhaeuser and Royal Cup, Inc.

Driver Central (Road Breakdown and Driver Assistance). Driver Central was an emergency assistance system providing drivers with prompt road assistance any hour of the day, any day of the year. A computerized records system and a specialized communications system were used to access more than 19,000 service facilities in the United States and Canada. The facilities were no more than 30 miles apart, allowing for prompt service.

The communication system allowed for up to a six-way phone conference. Driver Central documented all actions taken so the client would know exactly what happened and how long it took to remedy the situation. This service was started in 1976 as a means to cut "down time" for leased fleets. In 1976, it reduced down time by 40 percent. Two clients using this service were W. R. Grace and Co. and Hammermill Paper Company.

Fuel and State Tax (FAST). FAST was designed to help fleet operators with the complex task of state fuel and mileage tax reporting. FAST helped customers get the best prices and services for fuel wherever they go. Because fuel is one of the largest cost factors in truck fleet operation, this was important.

Fuel taxes vary from state to state, not only in amount but in requirements regarding paying taxes on fuel used within a state although bought in another state. Some states allow tax refunds for over-purchases; some charge a tax on fuel used in the state even though tax was paid in the state of purchase. There are almost as many different fuel tax regulations as there are states. Customers of the FAST program did not have to keep up with the frequent changes in state laws; nor did they have to handle the complicated and time-consuming state fuel tax reports nor the annual audits made by the states. In addition, a client's fuel purchasing and use patterns could be analyzed periodically in order to make recommendations concerning the minimization of tax liabilities and other costs. Two clients for this service included Beatrice and Tom's Foods, Inc.

Fuel Management. The Fuel Management System provided assistance in the management of over-the-road fleet fueling. Clients could choose between two types of credit cards that were computer linked to fuel stops and service centers in the United States and Canada. The "Electronic Fuel Card" enabled a client's drivers to obtain fuel and service at over 500 fueling centers nationwide. The "Cash Card" enabled a client's drivers to select from over 1,500 fuel stops and 100 service centers in the United States and Canada. Both services provided a client with consolidated fuel billings and fleet management reports. Two clients using this service included Burger King, and the Ship-N-Shore Division of General Mills.

Consulting and Safety Programs. The consulting and safety programs assisted clients in the analysis and improvement of client distribution systems. The program included investigation and recommendations concerning intercorporate hauling, intermodel alternatives and distribution routes, driver training, and freight brokerage services. Transportation Industry Consultants, Inc., another Saunders' subsidiary, specialized in helping companies analyze and streamline their distribution methods. The safety program offered audiovisual aids designed to instruct drivers to anticipate and handle all types of road problems. Two clients using this service included Coca-Cola Bottling Company and South Central Bell.

Remanufactured and New Tires. Saunders operated its own facility for the remanufacture of long-lasting radial truck tires. Saunders' remanufactured brand was called the Long Rider. Truck Central, Inc., the tire-supply subsidiary of Saunders, sold more than 100 types and sizes of new major-brand truck tires. In addition, Saunders would custom remanufacture a client's worn tire casings using state of the art tire remolding equipment. Truck Central offered professional advice on the uses of radial and remanufactured tires. Two clients for this service were Avondale Mills and West Point Pepperell.

Used Vehicles. Late model Saunders' trucks, tractors and trailers were available for sale at the end of their respective lease periods. These vehicles were sold by area rental account managers from strategically located centers across the nation.

Financial Condition

Revenues for 1985 were a record, surpassing 1984 revenues, the previous record year. As indicated in Exhibit 15.6, total revenues for 1985 increased by $6.2 million or 2.3 percent over those of 1984. This increase was due to a larger fleet size, a greater volume of used revenue equipment sales, and the company's successful expansion in dedicated contract carriage. Operating expenses for 1985, exclusive of depreciation, decreased by $850,000 from 1984; however, 1985 depreciation and interest expenses were higher than 1984.

Exhibit 15.7 shows Saunders' consolidated balance sheet. In 1985, total assets increased to approximately $274.9 million from $260.1 million in 1984 and $208

EXHIBIT 15.6 **Consolidated statement of income**

	1983	1984	1985
	(Dollars in thousands, except per share)		
Revenues			
Vehicle lease	$138,622	$146,092	$147,610
Vehicle rental	27,367	33,215	29,528
Common carrier	34,198	29,744	18,809
Contract carrier		4,818	20,102
Other services..............................	40,912	51,094	55,120
	241,099	264,963	271,169
Cost and expenses			
Operating expenses, exclusive of depreciation.....	192,793	210,764	209,914
Depreciation (net of gain on sale of revenue equipment, $4,422 in 1985; $5,003 in 1984; $2,793 in 1983)...........................	27,054	28,584	33,989
	219,847	239,348	243,903
	21,252	25,615	27,266
Interest expense	16,207	18,755	21,234
Income before provision for income taxes	5,045	6,860	6,032
Provision for income taxes	790	1,125	895
Net income	$ 4,255	$ 5,735	$ 5,137
Net income per common and common equivalent share	$ .61	$ .85	$ .58

Source: Saunders System, Inc. Annual Report 1985.

million in 1983. Long-term debt also increased to $157.6 million in 1985 from $153 million in 1984 and $116.1 million in 1983.

DEREGULATION OF THE TRUCKING INDUSTRY

One of the more significant events in the history of the trucking industry was the deregulation legislation passed in the early 1980s. Three recent pieces of legislation had great influence on the Industry—the 1980 Motor Carriers Act, the 1982 Surface Transportation Assistance Act, and the 1982 Staggers Rail Act. (See Industry Note: Motor Carrier Transportation for details. It appears after this case.)

The Impact of Deregulation on the Industry

Deregulation directly affected the number of competitors entering the market, and eased operating restrictions for those already in service. The free market envi-

EXHIBIT 15.7 **Consolidated balance sheet**

Assets	1983	1984	1985
Current Assets			
Cash	$ 2,759	$ 2,850	$ 5,187
Accounts receivable			
Trade	23,670	25,772	29,927
Other	3,850	2,972	2,590
Inventories	6,547	5,288	5,448
Prepaid vehicle licenses and taxes.................	2,321	2,610	4,054
Other prepaid expenses..........................	1,198	1,696	2,401
	40,345	41,188	49,607
Revenue equipment, at cost	241,061	292,413	289,739
Less accumulated depreciation	88,229	91,867	87,638
	152,832	200,546	202,101
Operating facilities, at cost......................	16,915	17,969	19,565
Less accumulated depreciation	7,198	7,735	8,323
	9,717	10,234	11,242
Unamortized leasehold improvements	1,847	2,330	3,464
	164,396	213,110	216,807
Deferred charges	648	3,110	5,902
Costs in excess of net assets of businesses			
acquired	2,378	2,437	2,392
Other assets	235	210	225
Total assets.................................	$208,002	$260,055	$274,933

Liabilities & stockholders' equity

Current Liabilities			
Current portion of long-term notes payable	$ 648	$ 612	$ 724
Notes payable—bank	3,500	2,400	3,400
Accounts payable, trade	8,494	8,722	8,325
Accrued liabilities	4,726	6,426	5,410
	17,368	18,160	17,859
Revenue equipment obligations due within			
one year	21,578	30,830	26,637
Long-term Debt			
Revenue equipment obligations due beyond			
one year	112,864	149,925	155,226
Notes payable, net of current portion above	3,214	3,076	2,346
	116,078	153,001	157,572
Deferred income taxes	7,021	8,084	8,797
Other liabilities................................	434	449	459
Preference Stock—Redeemable, par value $1.00 per share, Series C, Cumulative Nonvoting.			
Liquidation value $2,920,000	4	3	3
Capital in excess of par value	3,636	3,277	2,917
	3,640	3,280	2,920

Common Stock, Preference Stock— Nonredeemable and Other Stockholders' Equity Common stock, par value $1.00 per share			
Class A, authorized 15,000,000 shares	3,222	3,248	3,353
Class B, authorized 6,500,000 shares............	3,029	3,037	2,948
Preference stock, par value $1.00 per share, Series A, Convertible Voting. Involuntary liquidation value $231,000....................................	18	18	18
$1.20 Convertible Exchangeable Preference stock, par value $1.00 per share, Cumulative Nonvoting. Involuntary liquidation value $12,995,000			1,300
Capital in excess of par value	92	142	10,728
Retained earnings, as annexed	35,769	40,045	42,581
	42,130	46,490	60,928
Less common stock in treasury, at cost, 95,308 shares, 1985 and 1984; 98,028 shares, 1983 ...	247	239	239
	41,883	46,251	60,689
Total liabilities and stockholders' equity	$208,002	$260,055	$274,933

Source: Saunders System, Inc. Annual Report 1985.

ronment created a "buyer's market" where shippers were able to demand lower rates and improved service. While it appears that the increased competiton held down shipping costs, the failure rate of trucking firms escalted rapidly. In addition to business failures, acquisition and intermodal mergers increased.

New Market Entries.　The deregulation of the trucking industry facilitated ease of entry which resulted in overcapacity and subsequently price (rate) erosion. The American Trucking Association reported that from 1980 to 1982, some 43,000 new operating certificates were issued. Approximately 80 percent of these were issued to existing firms.[1] Between 1980 and 1984, the number of regulated motor carriers jumped 70 percent to over 30,000.[2] Additionally, private carriers were allowed generous back-haul options which reduced the available demand for existing firms and added to industry capacity.

In addition to new firms, many existing carriers moved swiftly to accelerate their long-term growth strategies. Five- and ten-year-plans were executed in two years or less. Many trucking firms were overly optimistic concerning geographical expansion. Moreover, many firms had inadequate capital to support an expansion strategy, especially at the same time that margins were being squeezed because of falling prices.

Most new firms entered the truckload (TL) segment of the market. A single operator could secure a route with dedicated tonnage from a single source and

[1]Standard and Poors Industrial Surveys, February 20, 1986, R–30.
[2]Ibid., R–29.

operate profitably. Expanding into the less than truckload (LTL) segment required substantial capital (terminals, equipment, etc.) and was an alternative for only the larger, stronger firms in the industry.

Industry Consolidation.   The trucking industry's responses to the new environment had both economic and social ramifications. Dun & Bradstreet indicated that in 1978 there were 162 trucking business failures, in 1984 there were 1,409, and in 1985 there were 1,533. An American Trucking Association official stated that 20 percent of all for-hire motor carriers (6,000 firms) could be forced out of business.[3] In addition, society had shown increasing concern for the actions of the trucking industry. Safety records were under scrutiny and trucking firms were required to take costly remedial action for spills, accidents, etc.

As a result of low operating margins and acquisition strategies by the large firms, consolidation in the industry had occurred. Mr. Powell, CEO of Yellow Freight System stated that "deregulation makes the big firms stronger, forces the smaller firms into niches, and allows the medium-sized firms to get squeezed."[4]

Saunders' CEO, Gordon Shelfer, cautioned however that deregulation was more of an indirect force in the leasing segment of the business. He stated "it may have quickened the inevitable, but the real issue facing the industry is cost control. Companies have to realize that approaching a more competitive environment without having cost in line will tend to highlight weaknesses."

Increasing Environmental Complexity.   In addition to deregulation, the turbulent economy of the 1980s contributed to a more complex industry. Adding to the difficulty of management were the rise and fall of interest rates, the declining cost of new equipment and fuel, and the unpredicability of the used truck market.

During the era of double-digit interest rates, leasing had become an attractive alternative to ownership. As a result, Saunders' leasing business did well. However, when interest rates declined, many companies, both trucking and nontrucking were able to finance purchases of equipment at rates competitive to Saunders' 12.5 percent cost of capital.

In the late 1970s to the early 1980s there had been undercapacity in the trucking industry which enabled used vehicles to be sold at premium prices. The used truck segment was an important part of Saunders' business. As a result of the high used vehicle prices, Saunders raised the salvage value (and reduced the amount of depreciation) of its vehicles. Most of the used equipment inventory was "cab over" type trucks due to federal length laws. Subsequently, two events had a substantial impact on the profitablity of Saunders. First, federal legislation was enacted allowing longer vehicles on the highways (drivers tend to prefer the longer conventional cabs for safety and ride). Secondly, overcapacity occurred in the trucking industry. The selling price of new trucks fell significantly which made ownership more attractive.

[3]Standard and Poors Industrial Surveys, May 29, 1986, R-3.
[4]New York Times, December 22, 1985, F17.

Furthermore, fuel prices began to fall. Cheaper equipment, lower interest rates, and lower fuel costs caused more manufacturers to opt for ownership rather than leasing to meet their transportation needs. Used equipment became more difficult to sell. Seemingly without warning, the bottom fell out of the used truck market and Saunders had a lot of under-depreciated and idle "iron."

The result of factors such as these made planning in the leasing segment of the industry extremely difficult. Consequently, planning tended to have a shorter and shorter focus. Mr. Shelfer indicated that "changes were taking place in the industry which had a tremendous impact on the business but were impossible to predict and thus, by the mid-1980s, we were reacting rather than planning."

SAUNDERS STRATEGY

In 1986 Saunders Leasing System was in the final year of a five-year plan that focused primarily on geographic and product expansion. Through the strategy, Saunders had continued to be a national truck leasing firm with a wide variety of related services. Implementation of the strategy included the replacement of approximately 70 percent of the sales force with more aggressive, better trained people to meet the challenges of the new marketplace.

Changes to the management structure allowed for better communications and market assessment. Saunders had an advanced computer system and terminal network. They routinely replaced trucks on a set schedule. They kept up with the latest in new trucking technology and kept the fleet new and clean looking. Management felt they had laid the necessary groundwork for making the firm viable, at least into the 1990s.

Commenting on the strategy, Gordon Shelfer, president of Saunders, stated, "The current strategy, which has been in place for about four years, allowed us to hold our own in the industry. But we're not going to meet our objective of 16 percent rate of return." Mr. Shelfer continued, "We have a hard time competing against the big guys in the industry. They have a tremendous cost advantage because of their size. They can get better prices on fuel, parts, and capital through volume buying and the way they secure additional capital."

The president further reflected, "Saunders had the opportunity to grow. In the early 1970s, the leasing portion of Ryder and Saunders were approximately the same size. Ryder went aggressively to the equity markets for financing and Saunders did not. Saunders had grown rapidly in the 1960s but we needed additional equity capital in order to continue the same course. The 'boys,' however, have made it clear that the dividend policy would not change and our operating results and capital structure probably aren't good enough to support a more aggressive growth objective. Moreover, equity financing is not desirable because the market for Saunders stock was weak. However, if we don't expand, I don't know how much longer we can compete given the nature of this business."

INDUSTRY NOTE

Motor Carrier Transportation

Few industries in this decade have had as much change as the transportation industry. Deregulation, fluctuating prices for fuel and new vehicles, and escalating costs have contributed to making transportation much more competitive. Adaptations have had to occur in methods of operation and management philosophy. In many ways, transportation is very different from the industry it was in the 1970s.

Tranportation is the movement of people or goods from one location to another. A number of distinct types of transportation can be identified:

- Passenger transportation—movement of human beings.
- Cargo transportation—movement of anything other than people by any of the five modes of transportation.
- Intracity (urban) transportation—movement between two points within a metropolitan area.
- Intercity transportation—movement beginning in one city and ending in another city.
- Intrastate transportation—movement between points in the same state.
- Interstate transportation—movement where the origin and destination are in two different states.
- Domestic transportation—movement between points within the United States and its territories.
- International transportation—movement between the United States or its territories and another country; or movement between two non-U.S. points.

Traffic or transportation managers are responsible for inbound and outbound transportation decisions for an organization. Specifically mode and carrier decisions are used to meet company objectives.

TRANSPORTATION MODES

The five modes of transportation include rail, water, pipeline, highway, and air. However, seldom does a shipper have the choice among all of the modes. For example, little water shipping occurs in Kansas. The nature of the cargo,

This industry note was prepared by Peter M. Ginter and Linda E. Swayne. It is intended as a basis for classroom discussion rather than to illustrate effective or ineffective handling of an administrative situation. Used by permission of Peter M. Ginter.

characteristics of the mode (speed, cost, etc.), and availablity of service are important in mode selection.

Transportation of cargo is measured in ton miles—one ton of cargo moved one mile. Although declining, railroads still are the dominant mode of transportation accounting for 30 percent of ton miles (Exhibit 1).

EXHIBIT 1 **U.S. transportation by mode**

Mode	1975 (Ton-miles)	1975 (In percent)	1984 (Ton-miles)	1984 (In percent)
Rail	759,000	36.74	936,000	36.65
Motor carrier	454,000	21.97	602,000	23.57
Water	342,000	16.55	404,000	15.82
Pipeline	507,000	24.54	605,000	23.69
Air	3,700	00.19	6,600	00.26

Source: U.S. Bureau of the Census, *Statistical Abstract of the United States: 1986*, p. 591.

Specific modes are selected based on accessibility, reliability, speed, flexibility, control, and liability. Some carriers offer specialized equipment for products, such as flammable liquids or oversized construction materials, that provide access to a market that otherwise would be less accessible.

Reliability is often a major consideration in mode selection. Companies schedule a carrier to deliver at specific times in order to maintain supplies so that sales are not lost. However, too early delivery can be equally dissatisfying because the companies do not have excess warehouse space to store product delivered ahead of schedule. Shippers want reliable methods of transportation with delivery at the agreed upon time.

With time-sensitive goods, speed is the most important factor in determining mode selection. Control, or knowing where a shipment is at any point in time, is an important consideration for some shippers. Accuracy and timeliness in locating goods has become increasingly important as shippers attempt to maximize their customer service and minimize costs by diverting goods in transit. Moreover, the extent of damage and the loss record (liability) is a service consideration for mode and carrier selection.

Flexibility is a service variable important to some shippers. Meeting unusual needs such as unscheduled pick-ups or deliveries, "rush" deliveries, etc., are important mode-selection factors to the traffic manager in order to meet company objectives.

After determining the appropriate mode of transportation, carrier selection is determined by service and rate consideration. Carriers supply transportation services and can be private or for-hire carriers.

MOTOR CARRIER TRANSPORTATION

Motor carrier transportation provides a lifeline for our economy by fulfilling needs that are critical to any industrialized nation. Without trucking, shippers could not compete effectively in the marketplace and customers would not enjoy the magnitude of choice. As shown in Exhibit 1, trucking accounts for approximately 24 percent of total cargo ton miles in interstate movement of goods. Furthermore, trucking has the largest portion of intracity movement of goods.

The motor carrier industry is segmented by the type of goods transported, the geography covered, and the nature of service offered. Exhibit 2 outlines the major segments in the U.S. trucking industry.

There are four legal forms of carriage—common, contract, exempt, and private. Common carriers are for-hire transportation companies that are required to charge reasonable rates, to avoid undue or unjust discrimination, to serve the public, and to deliver. Common carriers are expected to serve all customers who request their services provided they have the equipment and operating authority to haul the commodity.

Contract carriers are for-hire carriers bound only by the agreement that they negotiate with the shipper that contracts for their service. Exempt carriers are for-hire carriers but are exempt from economic regulations. Private carriers are company owned/managed fleets of trucks to transport company products and are not required to follow economic regulations.

There are an estimated 150,000 private fleets in trucking.[1] Some firms by necessity acquire their own fleet because of specialized equipment needs. Others own their own fleets because of perceived rate or service advantages.

Motor Carrier Regulation

Historically the freight transportation industry was the first regulated sector of our economy beginning with the Interstate Commerce Act of 1887. The U.S. trucking industry has been regulated by the federal government since the enactment of the Motor Carrier Act of 1935.

The Motor Carrier Act was modeled after railroad regulation. Carriers were granted operating authority between cities. Since this system treated trucks identically to trains, the capability of trucks to travel anywhere that roads existed was not acknowledged.

The Motor Carrier Act required truckers to obtain federal "certificates of public conveniency and necessity" before offering their services to the public. The Act required approval of the routes truckers were to take (sometimes even specific roads to travel) and approval of the rates or tariffs to be charged. Proposed tariffs differing from the rest of the industry were rarely granted and truckers were penalized if the prices they charged were lower or higher than those approved. Free of competition

---

[1]J. V. Strickland, "Private Carriage Boosted by Deregulation," *Distribution*, September 1980, p. 30.

EXHIBIT 2 **Motor carrier segments for cargo**

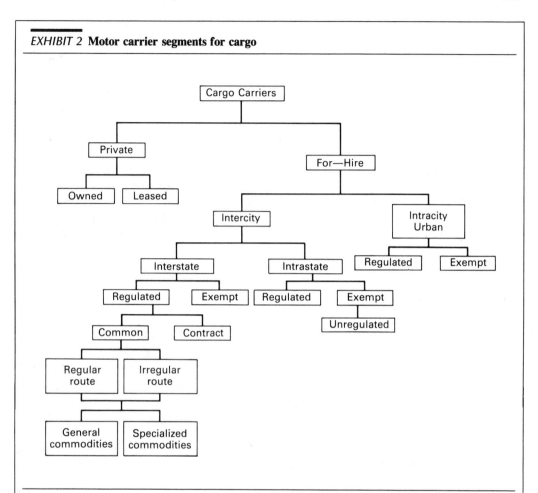

- Regulated refers to economic regulation either by the Interstate Commerce Commission (ICC) or by a specific state or city.
- Exempt refers to specifically identified commodities not subject to regulation (usually agricultural products such as livestock, grains, etc.).
- Unregulated means that a state has no economic regulation or has completely deregulated trucking.
- Contract carrier negotiates service levels and rates with a shipper.
- Regular route means regularly scheduled service over designated roads.
- Irregular route allows a carrier to service between points by any route cleared for safe operation.
- General commodities usually refers to packaged freight.
- Specialized commodities include heavy machinery, liquids, refrigerated products, forestry products, explosives, etc.

Source: Adapted from F.A. Stephenson, *Transportation USA,* Reading, MA: Addison-Wesley, 1987.

and protected by the ICC, the industry kept rates high. Consequently, truckers competed on the basis of service and not rates.

ICC approval was required for any mergers involving trucking companies. Additionally, the ICC prohibited two-way operating rights that resulted in trucks returning from their destination with an empty trailer (backhauling).

During this period, the only way for companies in interstate commerce to expand was to gain additional operating rights from other carriers who were ceasing operations. Excessive costs were associated with the purchasing of operating authority and the protection of rates.

Dramatic changes occurred with the passage of the Motor Carrier Act of 1980. The two major areas of change were the lessening of control over pricing and reduction in ICC interference in granting operating authority. No longer were truckers required to demonstrate public need in order to obtain operating rights. With additional carriers entering the industry and less rate restriction, price competition became a major factor in the market.

Specifically, the purpose of the Motor Carrier Act of 1980 was to reduce unnecessary government regulation of motor carriers. The major provisions of the Act include:

- Lifting the burden of proof from the applicant for an operating permit. Now a person objecting to the permit would have to prove that the service would be inconsistent with the public convenience and necessity.
- Granting truckers a "zone of rate-making freedom." Carriers were permitted to raise or lower rates by ten percent a year without having to obtain ICC approval.
- Directing the ICC to repeal rules requiring truckers to take circuitous routes or to stop at designated intermediate points.
- Directing the ICC to reduce restrictions on the commodities that could be carried by a trucking firm and the territory that could be served.[2]

The 1980 Motor Carrier Act left much to the discretion of the ICC, and the members of the deregulation-minded commission went further than the law required.[3] They began to routinely approve applications for operating authority recognizing that new, competitive services are almost never inconsistent with the "public convenience and necessity." New rates (tariffs) have also been routinely approved resulting in intense price competition.

The results of the deregulation have been an increase in the number of carriers, lower prices and better service, including service to smaller communities. However, the large firms have grown larger and some predict that greater concentration in the industry will eventually lead to higher prices.

[2]"Summary of Provisions of the Motor Carrier Act of 1980," Report of the National Motor Freight Traffic Association, Incorporated, June 20, 1980.

[3]"Time to Complete Trucking Deregulation," *Backgrounder,* The Heritage Foundation, Washington, D. C., January 16, 1986, p. 3.

Certainly those companies that can achieve economies of scale will be able to offer a lower price to customers and could eventually eliminate the inefficient producers from the industry. Industry statistics for selected motor carrier companies are included in Exhibits 3 to 5.

In 1980 there were 18,945 general freight carriers in the United States. With deregulation, there were 30,481 general freight carriers by the end of 1984.[4] At the same time, there has been a significant increase in the number of failures in the industry. In 1979 there were 67 intercity trucking companies that ceased operations. In 1980 there were 125, in 1984 there were 549, and in 1986 the number of failures reached 1,533. The failures had been predicted as deregulation eliminated the inefficient and inept from the industry.

Individual firms have been affected by deregulation differently as each company chose strategies of expansion or contraction. For instance, RLC Corporation with over 50 percent of their revenues from bulk chemical shippers, and Leaseway who had over 50 percent of their revenue from two customers (General Motors and Sears), had distinct areas of specialization. In contrast, management at Gelco decided to make the company smaller. They sold their European trailer division and attempted to sell a Puerto Rican trucking subsidiary.[5]

Ryder, on the other hand, had been rapidly expanding by acquisition and continued an expansionary strategy after deregulation. Other firms, overly optimistic concerning geographical expansion, had inadequate capital to support expansionary strategies, especially at the same time that margins were being squeezed because of falling prices.

While no uniform tracking of trucking industry rates is collected on a national scale, people involved either as shippers or as companies in the industry agree that the cost of moving goods has declined. One industry executive estimated the total savings to the economy from deregulation to be $50 billion annually.[6]

The savings have been a result of the truckers' abilities to institute cost reductions. For example, less paperwork (red tape) is involved, which reduces costs and trucks no longer have to travel empty on backhauls, the return trip after a delivery. More efficient use of resources is accomplished when tariffs can be earned in both directions.

Increased competition has led to many companies offering discounts to shippers and negotiating lower-priced individual contracts with shippers. Most shippers reported better service since deregulation because shippers and truckers are free to determine the level and type of service to be provided.[7] More frequent service, delivery at specific locations, special care for certain fragile items, or merely faster service can be negotiated.

[4]Ibid.

[5]Value Line Investment Survey, July 1986.

[6]Robert V. Delaney, "Managerial and Financial Challenges Facing Transport Leaders." *Transportation Quarterly*, January 1986.

[7]David K. Lifschultz, "Some Deregulation Myths," *Traffic World*, August 26, 1985.

EXHIBIT 3 Selected trucking company revenue and net income

	1984		1985		1986	
	Operating revenues (In millions)	Net income	Operating revenues (In millions)	Net income	Operating revenues (In millions)	Net income
General Commodity Motor Carriers						
Arkansas Best Corporation	$ 630.2	$ 12.3	$ 633.58	$ 18.29	$ 665.39	$ 20.31
Carolina Freight Corporation	468.8	12.1	554.90	16.89	572.11	17.42
Consolidated Freightways, Inc.	1,704.9	74.5	1,999.62	87.96	2,063.24	88.59
IU International Corporation	2,514.8	7.9	1,630.08	38.23	1,594.40	1.35
Overnite Transportation	415.0	33.9	507.63	44.55	523.66	46.75
Roadway Services, Inc.	1,461.5	100.0	1,688.73	79.04	1,709.01	75.39
Transcon, Inc.-/Calif.	326.0	5.4	336.49	1.74	344.26	2.04
Yellow Freight System-Del.	1,380.0	44.1	1,616.43	68.37	1,665.52	70.09
Contract Motor Carriers/Leasing						
Gelco Corporation	$ 929.0	$ 13.1	$1,016.39	$ (2.67)	$ 794.77	$(15.10)
Leaseway Transportation Corp.	1,348.5	42.3	1,440.66	32.25	1,451.90	33.10
RLC Corporation	374.5	15.2	406.58	7.85	419.52	13.37
Ryder System, Inc.	2,485.9	117.6	3,328.25	139.70	3,609.91	152.80
Saunders System, Inc.	265.0	5.7	271.17	5.10	n/a	n/a

Source: Standard and Poor's Industry Surveys, January 15, 1987.

EXHIBIT 4 **Trucking industry selected financial information—contract motor carriers/leasing**

Price-Earnings Ratio (high-low)	1983	1984
Gelco Corp.	*	25–14
Leaseway Transportation Corp.	15–12	11– 7
RLC Corp.	36–17	15– 8
Ryder System Inc.	14–10	12– 8
Saunders System Inc.	13– 7	7– 5

*not meaningful

Source: Standard and Poor's Industry Surveys, Feb. 20, 1986.

The fear that small communities would lose trucking service has not been realized. An ICC study indicated that only 2 percent of all shippers responding considered their service to be worse since deregulation and a majority of shippers reported that the number of carriers serving them had increased or remained the same.[8]

Even with the reforms of the Motor Carrier Act of 1980, trucking companies are still required to file applications and forms with the ICC before offering a new service, discontinuing a service, raising or reducing their rates, and merging with another company. The paperwork is costly. In 1985 the ICC received almost 1.4 million tariff or rate filings.[9] Some in the industry argue that rate filings are necessary to enable customers and competitors to contest changes in rates. Others argue that in the competitive situation in today's market, dissatisfied customers can easily find another motor carrier that will satisfy their price and service needs.

Federal legislation has changed trucking regulation for interstate operations, however, approximately 40 states still heavily regulate intrastate trucking. There are substantial costs to customers. For example, it cost $612 to ship a truckload of detergent from Dallas to Houston—a 243 mile trip. The same truckload from Dallas to Tulsa, Oklahoma—a 275 mile trip, cost $375.[10]

Other Legislation Affecting Trucking

The 1982 Surface Transportation Assistance Act gave firms the authority to operate multiple trailer vehicles and wider and heavier trucks on designated federal highways. In addition, the act raised both federal and state road-use taxes.

---

[8]"ICC Says Deregulation Has Not Reduced Truck Service to Small Towns," *Traffic World*, September 20, 1982, p. 28.

[9]"Secretary Dole Pushes Deregulation as Beneficial to Trucking Industry," *Daily Traffic World*, September 30, 1985, p. 1.

[10]"Time to Complete Trucking Deregulation," p. 7.

▬▬▬
EXHIBIT 5 **Trucking industry selected financial information—contract motor carriers/leasing**

Return on equity (%)	1980	1981	1982	1983	1984
Gelco Corp.	29.0	28.6	14.5	*	6.3
Leaseway Transportation Corp.	19.5	17.8	9.9	13.3	14.3
RLC Corp.	22.3	13.5	6.1	6.8	15.1
Ryder System, Inc.	17.1	17.5	15.8	16.8	16.6
Saunders System, Inc.	11.0	13.4	4.7	9.6	12.2

Return on assets (%)	1980	1981	1982	1983	1984
Gelco Corp.	2.7	2.5	1.3	*	0.5
Leaseway Transportation Corp.	5.5	5.6	3.2	4.2	4.3
RLC Corp.	6.1	3.9	1.6	1.6	3.5
Ryder System, Inc.	3.6	4.3	4.4	4.8	4.6
Saunder System, Inc.	2.2	2.5	1.1	2.1	2.5

Return on revenues (%)	1980	1981	1982	1983	1984
Gelco Corp.	6.2	6.0	3.1	*	1.4
Leaseway Transportation Corp.	4.6	4.5	2.5	2.9	3.1
RLC Corp.	6.3	4.0	2.0	2.1	4.0
Ryder System, Inc.	3.3	3.8	4.0	4.2	4.7
Saunders System, Inc.	1.8	2.0	0.9	1.8	2.2

Debt/capital ratio (%)	1980	1981	1982	1983	1984
Gelco Corp.	78	81	82	83	84
Leaseway Transportation Corp.	43	42	46	39	48
RLC Corp.	49	50	56	58	61
Ryder System, Inc.	58	49	49	47	49
Saunders System, Inc.	74	71	70	69	73

Earnings per share ($)	1980	1981	1982	1983	1984
Gelco Corp.	3.65	4.67	2.51	(2.38)	0.94
Leaseway Transportation Corp.	3.63	3.70	2.22	3.12	3.54
RLC Corp.	1.24	0.80	0.34	0.34	0.83
Ryder System, Inc.	1.47	1.76	1.81	2.15	2.47
Saunders System, Inc.	0.58	0.77	0.29	0.61	0.85

Book value per share ($)	1980	1981	1982	1983	1984
Gelco Corp.	(8.84)	0.27	2.88	1.86	3.37
Leaseway Transportation Corp.	19.15	21.44	21.19	22.40	23.41
RLC Corp.	5.51	5.81	4.73	4.95	5.61
Ryder System, Inc.	8.64	10.54	11.61	12.73	14.80
Saunders Leasing System, Inc.	4.72	5.25	5.30	5.79	6.51

*not meaningful

Source: Standard and Poors Industry Surveys, Feb. 20, 1986.

The 1982 Staggers Rail Act allowed existing railroads the opportunity to consolidate and to compete with one another on pricing. Newly designed rail cars and greater efficiency in route scheduling increased carrying capacity. These efficiencies led to faster delivery and favorable rates for shippers, thus narrowing the price/service differential between rail and trucks.

An appropriate area of regulation for the ICC appears to be trucking safety. Competitive pressures may be causing companies to cut corners on maintenance and to keep their drivers on the road for extended time periods (regulations specify that one person cannot drive for more than ten hours in a day followed by eight consecutive off-duty hours, no more than 60 hours in a consecutive seven-day period and no more than 70 hours in a consecutive eight-day period). Either or both factors may account for the increase in the number of truck accidents - up 18 percent in 1984.[11] The Motor Carrier Safety Act of 1984 provided the ICC with specific powers to regulate safety.

PRIVATE TRUCKING

Deregulation has caused major changes within the industry. Private carriers have been given intercorporate operating rights that allow them to carry property of other subsidiaries of the parent company on backhauls. They can also apply for and be granted for-hire common carrier and contract carrier authority to haul goods for fees. Low start-up costs and deregulation have induced many companies to enter private trucking.

Advantages of private trucking include flexibility, control, speed, reduced loss and damage, and lower transportation costs. However, a company may not have the capital to invest in equipment or the management expertise in transportation. Added problems in scheduling and burdensome paperwork are required to seek and obtain the backhaul traffic necessary to keep private fleets working to desired levels of profitability. Furthermore, for-hire transportation costs seem to be falling rapidly, making private fleets less advantageous.

Successful use of a private fleet appears to be based on productive use of the equipment and cost efficiencies. Private carriers exist to haul the goods of the parent company. Therefore, less backhaul opportunity and seasonal variations may result in poor equipment utilization. Additionally, private fleets are required to pay state fuel taxes for fuel consumed by vehicles operating on each state's highways.

Furthermore, private carriers have to be concerned with liability for cargo and equipment, and injury to operators and bystanders. Unknown environmental factors can also have a detrimental effect on private carriage. Fuel costs may escalate rapidly or the demand for the company's product may decline making private trucking far from being risk free.

[11]Ibid, p. 8.

Truck Leasing

Truck leasing has emerged as a way to obtain the advantages of private trucking while reducing some of the risks. Full-service leasing permits a shipper to utilize a fleet of trucks with minimal up-front capital and to avoid maintenance responsibilities. Skilled transportation managers employed by the leasing company operate the fleet. Risk is minimized since the company can easily exit from private trucking if cost/service objectives are not achieved.

With leasing, the company does not have to worry about mechanical failures, as the lessor totally maintains the fleet including routine maintenance and emergency repairs. Fuel costs are typically lower because of the quantity discounts for bulk purchasing by the lessor. One-way trips become more cost efficient as the lessor handles backhaul requirements.

Each service utilized is charged to the company and, over time, may mean that the cost of leasing is more than the cost of owning a fleet. However, the reduction in risk seems to be a determining factor and many companies who otherwise would not have entered into private trucking are doing so through the lease option.

Single-Source Leasing

Since 1982, the ICC has allowed owner-operators to lease equipment and drivers to private carriers. Single-source leasing has increased the private carrier's ability to meet increased temporary demand for hauling at minimum cost and risk. Leases can be as short as 30 days and provide equipment and drivers. The private carrier has complete control over the equipment and driver for the period of the lease, but has no maintenance or labor responsibilities.

COMMON CARRIAGE

To become a common carrier in today's deregulated environment applicants must prove they are fit, willing, and able and establish that the proposed service will fulfill a public purpose. Consequently, entry into common carriage has been eased substantially. With financial responsibility and a shipper that indicates the need for the carriage proposed, a new common carrier can enter the industry. And they have. In 1980 there were 18,045 carriers. That number increased to 30,481 in 1984, an increase of 69 percent.[12]

Regular-route common carriage is characterized by national, regional and local networks of terminals linked by longhaul operations. This business is primarily built around less-than-truckload (LTL) shipments. Scheduled departures, preplanned stops and destinations, and published rate schedules are common in the regular-route common carriage.

[12]Ibid, p. 3.

Less-than-truckload carriers have not been affected as much by deregulation, although the segment continues toward greater concentration. Because of the capital-intensive network of terminals required to bring small lots together and mix them into larger lots with the same destination, a natural barrier to entry exists. Small regional carriers used to supply service for short hauls to larger LTL carriers. Now the larger firms are buying out the regional supplier or expanding to develop their company into a national full-service carrier. The top five companies in LTL have increased their share of the business to 40 percent in 1984 (29 percent in 1978).[13]

Irregular-route-service companies have broad operating authority and freedom to use any routes to deliver goods. Irregular-route companies have concentrated on truck load (TL) shipping needs. Thus, they avoid small shippers, high variable costs, and capital intensive terminals required of the LTL shippers.

Irregular-route carriage is characterized by a large number of firms, reliance on owner-operators (independents who own and drive their own trucking equipment), demand-activated schedules and many nonunionized firms. The major area of turmoil in the trucking industry appears to be in the TL sector.

Private carriers, both owned and leased operations, and contract carriers have attempted to capture market share in this profitable segment from the common carriers. TL shipping is less capital intensive. Only a rig and a driver are needed as compared to the many terminals required in the LTL segment. The specific carrier types are blending and today irregular route carriage is more like contract carriage than a form of common carriage.

CONTRACT CARRIAGE

Contract trucking is truckload (TL) oriented, door-to-door hauling. Entry has been facilitated because only a permit is required. A permit is granted when the applicant proves that they are fit, willing, and able, and the service would be consistent with the public interest.

Contract carriers have become more aggressive marketers since deregulation. Due to their lower labor costs, they have been able to favorably compete on a price basis with the more unionized common carriers. A large portion of truckload traffic that used to be moved by common carriage is now being moved by contract carriage.

INDUSTRY PROBLEMS

Deregulation has caused many carriers to redefine the business they are in. Lifting of restrictions has allowed many companies to expand from truckload and common carriage to less-than-truckload and contract carriage.

[13]Charles R. Enis and Edward A. Morash, "Some Aspects of Motor Carrier Size, Concentration Tendencies and Performance After Deregulation," *Akron Economic and Business Review*, 18 (Spring 1987), p. 91.

While many new carriers have entered the industry in every segment, many have also left the industry. It seems that the larger companies have become larger and the smallest companies have left the industry.

Rapidly rising fuel costs, federal and state user's taxes, insurance expense, and labor expense have caused the collapse of many motor carriers—and not all of them are small. McLean Trucking, fifth largest carrier in 1984, filed for bankruptcy in January 1985.[14]

Escalation of Insurance Premiums

Carriers are responsible for the property they move. The ICC requires insurance for property loss/damage, as well as injury to bystanders and the environment. In 1985 alone, insurance premiums for carriers jumped 300 to 500 percent.[15] These significant jumps in the cost of insurance were due to falling interest rates, poor insurance company investments of premiums, and high jury awards.

Lower premiums had been available to carriers as the insurance industry aggressively competed for market share. When the insurers finally realized that market share gains were coming at the loss of profits, they weren't terribly concerned because they could easily invest premiums at higher interest rates. But when the prime rate fell, the insurance industry suffered billions of dollars in losses. Although it was an insurance industry problem, it became a trucking problem as liability insurance is required by the ICC and higher premiums had to be paid.

In addition, the national trend of juries to award high settlements to victims has affected all insurance premiums and trucking is no exception.

If a carrier prefers the alternative of self insurance, the ICC requires the posting of a $1 million line of credit for payment of claims. In 1986, approximately 90 percent of the industry could not meet this requirement.[16]

Price Competition

Competition, and in particular price competition and discounting, has caused carriers to manage their resources better. Equipment, labor and capital all have to be efficiently utilized. Greater cost control practices have been instituted throughout the industry. Shippers have benefitted by lower costs and more tailored services.

Intermodal Competition

Containerization by other modes of transportation, including air, water and rail, and the use of private trucking to handle the containers after reaching the destination

[14]John Cleghorn, "Fuel Prices, Economy to Keep Trucking Industry Rolling," *The Charlotte Observer*, January 18, 1987, p. 7K.

[15]F. A. Stephenson, Jr., *Transportation USA*, Reading, Massachusetts, Addison-Wesley Publishing Company, 1987, p. 330.

[16]Standard and Poor's Industry Surveys, May 29, 1986, R–3.

point is allowing other modes to be more competitive with trucking. Some of these competitors are purchasing or merging with trucking companies developing large, intermodal carriers.

Piggyback, fishyback, and airtruck are being offered to speed service and cut costs for shippers. Shippers are interested in dealing with a single carrier as deregulation makes it more difficult for the transportation manager to monitor the activities and rates of many carriers.

Knowledgeable Shippers

Traffic managers are searching for and finding ways to reduce transportation costs. They are shipping larger quantities to take advantage of volume discounts, taking advantage of backhaul rates, shipping items in concentrated form to reduce cargo weight, using off-peak periods, redesigning containers to permit more units to be loaded in a transport vehicle, shipping items in disassembled form to reduce volume, and negotiating multiple shipments at one time to generate quantity discounts.

Lack of Marketing Orientation

Before deregulation, marketing was relatively nonexistent in the trucking industry. Motor carriers had sales departments and traffic departments. Traffic departments determined routes and rates and the sales department attemped to convince shippers to use the company's services at the rate established. There was little or no price competition because all rates were approved by the ICC.

With deregulation, truckers are attempting to determine what customers want and to provide that level of service at a price that customers are willing to pay. Frequently however, truckers find that they cannot afford to supply service at the price customers are willing to pay . With many competitors and an emphasis on price, clearly new and innovative strategies were needed. Many firms, grasping for survival, have turned to marketing.

Pricing appears to be a major marketing variable in the trucking industry. Prices set too high will lose business and prices set too low may mean that a carrier cannot cover variable costs. Market research has been used to find what services and prices customers are seeking. Market segmentation has highlighted some specific types of industries with unique service requirements. Segmenting variables used have included commodities shipped, customer type, size of shipment, speed of delivery, and length of haul.

Target marketing can help the carriers understand the necessity of focusing their efforts on profitable business. Targeting encourages companies to service those kinds of customers where the firm has a comparative price or service advantage.

Higher-priced companies have the opportunity to differentiate their service and convince customers that the service is worth the additional cost. More reliable service, better pick-up and delivery schedules, better credit terms, better-than-average loss and damage records, better tracing and control, faster delivery times, and simplified paperwork are ways that trucking firms can differentiate their transportation service.

George G. Morris, a finance analyst specializing in trucking firms, indicated three strategies for success in the industry: national distribution with a full line of differentiated products and emphasis on attractive service/price trade-offs, low cost producers, and specialty firms with services targeted toward profitable industry segments.[17]

[17]George G. Morris, "Deregulation Benefits Shippers, the Public and Well-Run Truckers," *Investor News*, May 1983, p. 1.

CASE 16

The Roxy Dinner Theatre

Tom Thayer sat alone in the dark of the empty stage. "I really love this business," he thought, "but some changes have to be made if we are to survive." Tom was President of South Stage Theatre Corporation, owners of the Roxy Dinner Theatre. He had just left the cast party that clebrated the first full month of operation at the Roxy. The cast was still celebrating its artistic success when Tom left. Now he must consider the business side of the Roxy's first month.

The Roxy Theatre is located in downtown Clarksville, Tennessee. Constructed in the 1930s, the Roxy enjoyed many years of profitable operation as a motion picture theatre showing first run cinema classics like "Casablanca," "Gone With The Wind," and Roy Rogers Westerns. In 1974, the Roxy was forced to close its doors due to lack of business. Shopping center cinemas had taken most of the old theatre's patrons. The Roxy lay dormant and fell into a state of disrepair until June 1980, when a minor renovation was attempted by a community theatre group. This attempt failed and the Roxy once again closed its doors in January 1981. It seemed there was little hope for the Roxy, and it was slated for demolition to make room for parking in the downtown area. It was then that a group of young entrepreneurs decided to establish a theatre in Clarksville, saving the old building in the historic downtown location.

This case was prepared by Steven J. Anderson, Christoph Nussbaumer, John E. Oliver, Albert J. Taylor and Jeanne Whitehead. It is intended as a basis for classroom discussion rather than to illustrate effective or ineffective handling of an administrative situation. Used by permission from John E. Oliver.

EXHIBIT 16.1 **Roxy Dinner Theatre**

SOUTH STAGE THEATRE CORPORATION

In July 1981, a group of five young people from varied theatrical backgrounds formed the South Stage Theatre Corporation and leased the Roxy building. Each of the five owners held an equal $2,000 share in the corporation and occupied a seat on the board of directors. Each had unique qualifications and played a personal role in the operation of the Roxy.

Tom Thayer, age 27, was the President of the corporation. He was selected to serve in this role by his colleagues only because officers were necessitated by the articles of incorporation. Tom graduated from Clarksville Northwest High School in 1975, attended the American Musical and Dramatic Academy in New York on scholarship, and studied acting with Sally Welch, a protege of Lee Strasberg. He had been in the theatre since age 12 both locally and in New York. Tom taught dramatic arts at the Rhodes School in Maine. He functioned as primary director, choreographer, designer, writer, coach, carpenter, and general business manager.

Carmello Roman, age 27, also graduated from Clarksville Northwest High School in 1975, attended Austin Peay State University briefly, then studied graphic arts at Stephens College, Missouri, on scholarship. Like Tom, Carmello studied acting with Sally Welch and performed extensively in local area productions. When not working in New York as a graphic artist, Roman designed make-up and costumes for the Roxy and assisted in direction, acting techniques, and choreography. Roman did all the graphics, brochures, and posters for the Roxy.

Ginger Mulvey, age 28, was Vice President for Marketing and General House Manager. Ginger graduated from Clarksville High School in 1974. She had extensive acting experience in the Clarksville area and worked as an actress sporadically for five years in New York. Ginger returned to Clarksville to open the Roxy. Her duties included hiring staff, inventory, serving as hostess, reservations, some accounting and marketing, and publicity photos.

Tom Griffin, age 26, was the technician. A native Clarksvillian, Tom graduated from Clarksville High School in the mid 1970s. He was the son of a long-time theatre professional who taught at the local state university. Tom did a stint in the U.S. Air Force in Germany where he handled lighting for the oldest English-speaking theatre in that country. Griffin was in charge of all the technical aspects of the Roxy, including the design of lighting for plots and sets, construction of sets, lighting of performances, inventory and procurement of set materials, directing, and performing.

John McDonald, age 38, was a native of Memphis, Tennessee. John had acting experience in soap operas and off-Broadway shows. He taught acting at the American Academy of Performing Arts and at the Rhodes School in Maine where he met Tom Thayer. McDonald was primary director of the children's theatre and workshops, selected plays, helped design sets and directed about one-third of the shows.

The Roxy owners were a tightly knit group that had great cumulative drive to make the Roxy a success. The group's primary objective, as evidenced by the Statement of Purpose in Exhibit 16.2, was to bring the performing arts to Clarksville and the surrounding community. Profit was necessary, but was not the primary motivation of the group.

PERFORMING ARTS IN THE MIDDLE-TENNESSEE AREA

Clarksville, Tennessee, is a town of about 60,000 people located in Montgomery County, which adds another 30,000 people to the available market population. The primary employer in the area is Fort Campbell, the home of the U.S. Army's 101st Airborne Division where 20,000 military personnel plus additional civilian support personnel work bringing the total area market population to 110,000. Austin Peay State University has approximately 5,000 students, faculty, and staff. Forty different plants employ approximately 5,000 people in manufacturing. Agriculture is a major contributor to the economy with beef and dairy cattle, dark-fired tobacco, corn, wheat, and soybeans leading the list of commodities produced in the area. The rest of the population is employed in either government or retail establishments serv-

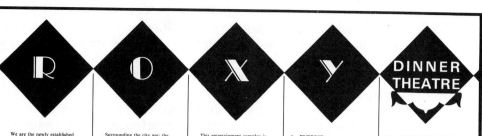

We are the newly established South Stage Theatre Corporation composed of Clarksville residents who have been working throughout the country in professional theatres and related industries. We have decided to return to Clarksville to establish a professional dinner theatre company in our home town.

Before we go any further, let us give you some information about the Clarksville area.

Clarksville is located in Middle Tennessee on the scenic Cumberland River with a population of over a quarter of a million people within a 50 mile radius.

Its residents are active in civic, religious, athletic and cultural organizations with a strong interest in visual and performing arts.

Clarksville is the home of Austin Peay State University with a student/faculty population of approximately 5000. There are 4 high schools, 3 junior high schools and various elementary and private schools.

Surrounding the city are: the Fort Campbell Military Reservation, home of the 101st Airborne Division; Hopkinsville, Kentucky; Nashville, the state capital, home of the Grand Ole Opry and recording capital of the world, and a well-populated rural community.

The presence of the Fort Campbell Military Reservation and neighboring colleges, as well as a strong tourist industry, provides a large influx of people from surrounding states and the nation as a whole.

We, the South Stage Theatre Corporation, are proposing to bring a new concept in theatre and entertainment to this active area.

The growing populus can support and deserves to have in its boundaries this professional theatre. The community has always been very supportive of The Arts and will welcome this addition to its cultural outlets.

This entertainment complex is located near the public square in Clarksville's historic downtown district, across from the new First National Bank and the proposed Rodeway Inn. This centrally-located site has convenient parking and access to all major thoroughfares.

We intend to renovate and restore the old Roxy Movie Theatre at 100 Franklin Street into a new and exciting entertainment complex augmented by interested community members and artists from around the country.

With the support and cooperation of the Clarksville community, we know this endeavor will provide a much needed entertainment service, while being a community-oriented force and integral business partner.

The following outlines our intentions and beliefs for establishing the new Roxy Dinner Theatre.

I. PURPOSE
(a) To provide the community with an entertainment facility that incorporates an evening of sophisticated dining and theatrical enjoyment at a reasonable price.
(b) To provide local artists with the opportunity to showcase their talents.
(c) To incorporate the professional standards developed by many successful theatres around the nation. Professional artists will be hired to work with this theatre in cooperation with the Actors' Equity Association and the resident staff.

II. ARTISTIC DESIRE
(a) To serve the community by providing professional productions of American plays and musicals.
(b) The season will encompass a revolving showcase of mediums including:
   1. Musical Plays
   2. Revues
   3. Dramas
   4. Comedies
   5. Local talent: i.e., orchestras, cararet bands and supper club style entertainment.

III. DINNER
(a) Each ticket includes a complete dinner, with a choice of cuisines.
(b) Alcoholic beverages will be available at an additional charge.

IV. ADDITIONAL SERVICES
We plan to expand in the future into the following areas:
(a) Gallery space for the visual arts
(b) Daytime Aerobics classes
(c) Children's Theatre
(d) Theatrical program directed toward the elderly and disabled
(e) "The Lillian," a members club upstairs at the Roxy. Members will be invited to preview openings, select seating, hold membership in the "Reel Club," a club devoted to films of a bygone era, and other special attractions.

We hope that the Clarksville community will be as excited about the South Stage Theatre Corporation at the Roxy as we are.

The possibilities of this new endeavor are boundless. The community is important in the success of this theatre, and we hope that our cooperation will create an atmosphere of high artistic values and lively community involvement.

Once established, this union of local talent and professional involvement will surely heighten the cultural experience of all who become involved.

Join us in the creation and celebration of the opening of the new Roxy, Clarksville's first professional dinner theatre.

EXHIBIT 16.2 **Statement of purpose**

ing the military, education, manufacturing, and agricultural communities. Nashville, Tennessee is forty miles away.

The Roxy faced competition from primary as well as secondary competitors. The following is a list of their competitors:

1. The Barn Dinner Theatre was located in Nashville, Tennessee, 40 miles from Clarksville. For $17.25, patrons were provided with a catered meal similar to those offered by the Roxy. The schedule was similar to the Roxy's, but nationally known talent was sometimes featured.

2. The Fort Campbell Dinner Theatre charged $11 for a ticket that included a meal. They were open year round on Friday and Saturday nights and showcased local Fort Campbell talent in modern plays similar to the Roxy's fare.

3. The Soldier Show Theatre at Fort Campbell was a motion picture cinema that charged $2 per ticket.

4. The Tennessee Performing Arts Center in Nashville was usually open on Friday and Saturday evenings, featuring Broadway shows with the original casts like Mickey Rooney in "Sugar Babies." Five shows per year-round season were usually offered at prices that varied from $10 to $25. No meals were served, but cocktails and other beverages were offered during intermissions.

5. The Austin Peay State University Theatre and Music Department offered free performances with no meals or refreshments. Shows were offered year-round and usually featured student talent, but occasionally featured a professional Shakespearean group or other special talent.

6. The Kiwanis Club Community Theatre offered four performances each of three different plays per year at a cost of $8–$10 per ticket. No meals or beverages were available.

7. The high school drama club offered three free performances of two modern plays each year.

8. The Capri Twin and Martin 4 motion picture theatres charged $3.75 per ticket.

THE ROXY OPENS

Before the Roxy could be opened, an extensive physical renovation of the building was necessary. In fact, the doors could not be opened until they were replaced by fire doors. The proscenium (the area located between the curtain and the orchestra) of the original stage was struck, the theatre seats were removed, and platforms for new seating were built. The neon green and red interior was repainted and a projected stage was built. After much work, planning, and training, the Roxy opened its doors on November 3, 1981, as a fully operational dinner theatre.

OPERATING THE ROXY

The Roxy staff established a production schedule of 144 performances per year based on 12 performances per month of 12 different shows per year. Six of the 12 shows were to be musicals. Each show would run three weeks with four performances per week. This left one week per month between shows to prepare for the next show's three-week run.

A Thursday night show was available without dinner for $8 a person. On Friday and Saturday nights, patrons could see the show with or without dinner. The price was $8 without a meal and $13, $15, or $17 with a meal, depending upon seating. On Sundays, a brunch performance was featured for $11. Dinners were catered by a local restaurant. Waiters were hired to serve all meals. While the Roxy had a bar and maintained a bartender, it did not have a liquor license and sold only beer and soft drinks. "Brownbagging" by patrons was permitted. Seating was highly flexible, consisting of small tables and chairs that could be clustered to create many different seating arrangements.

Open auditions were held and performers, selected from the community, donated their time and talents. The supply of talent was entirely dependent upon those persons in the area willing to volunteer their time for rehearsals and performances. This would limit the types of performances the Roxy could present in the future, especially musicals.

The primary promotional tool for the Roxy was advertising in the entertainment section of the local newspaper. This advertising was "donated" in exchange for tickets. There was no other charge if the finished copy was provided. Very little additional advertising was available or sought by the staff. Limited funds were a major constraint. An example of an ad is shown in Exhibit 16.3. *Fund Raisers*

The five members of the Roxy staff performed a variety of tasks that were often rotated and shared. Specialization was not possible due to the mercurial

EXHIBIT 16.3 **Example of Roxy advertisement**

nature of theatre operations. One day might require intensive work on costumes or choreography, while another day might require greater attention to sets or rehearsal. The flexibility of the members was a plus, and the feelings of cohesiveness and comraderie were strong within the group. Members worked in the cold of winter to save on utility bills and often relied on "happy hour" at a nearby hotel for food.

The freewheeling, flexible style of the group, while positive in most respects, caused problems in some areas of operations. For instance, there was often confusion concerning reservations, advertising, and cash disbursements. In fact, accounting records for purchases, bills to be paid, receipts, and disbursements were not kept on a regular basis. Check stubs often showed amounts with no explanations, or explanations with no amounts. The Roxy operated on a shoestring. Often, when bills were due, funds were not available to pay them. The Roxy staff discovered, by accident, that it was less expensive to bounce a check at the bank than to pay a reconnection fee for utilities. It became their unwritten policy to write checks on insufficient funds to pay bills. This allowed the Roxy to continue operations while they scrambled to produce funds to cover the check. Funds were provided from several sources—the sale of tickets, meals, and beverages; cash donations of patrons, who were noted in the programs as angels and saints according to the size of the donation; and donations of old clothes, furniture, rugs, etc., by concerned friends.

Expenses for a performance consisted of costumes, sets, script rentals, royalty payments, advertising, printing, food, labor costs, musicians (for musicals), and overhead items such as utilities. Cash was limited so expenditures were made only for the most necessary items. Often, old sets were cannibalized to create new ones. Additional props or parts were sometimes borrowed from local businesses in exchange for tickets, sometimes donated by concerned patrons, or, if absolutely necessary, purchased at the lowest possible cost often with tickets proffered to sweeten the deal.

For musicals, the Roxy staff made a verbal agreement with a pianist to provide music for $600 per show. Royalties for musicals were expected to average $975 per show while royalties for a play averaged $250. The first production was a play, not a musical.

Labor expense included the cost of a bartender at $75 per week and four waiters who worked approximately 16 hours a week at $2.05/hour plus tips during the three-week run of the show. The cost of a catered meal was $6.50 per plate.

The fixed costs associated with operating the Roxy included a $910 monthly lease payment, $540 per month to repay a renovation loan (half of which was interest), and $150 per month for insurance. The principals paid themselves a total of $1,175 per month. This included the $235 rent for two of the members' apartment. In addition, they retained an attorney to keep track of royalties, entertainment taxes, and other required recordkeeping and reporting. Entertainment taxes were 6.75 percent of ticket sales.

Utilities expenses included telephone, gas for heating, and electricity for lighting. The telephone bill was expected to average $220 per month. Gas expense would probably average $1,000 per month during the four months of winter and $50 per month during the warmer months. Electricity averaged $400 per month.

Because of the informality of the Roxy staff, two of the owners elected to have the corporation pay their rent of $235 per month rather than draw salaries.

THE FIRST MONTH

November 1981 had been an exciting time for the members of the Roxy group. Ticket sales amounted to $10,734, even though an average of only 118 of the 200 available seats were filled at most performances. However, Tom was concerned about a number of things. He could not tell how many of the seats at a performance were filled by holders of free tickets. He also had no record of how many meals were sold, given away, or spoiled. He also did not know how many tickets of each price had been sold.

He had a cigar box filled with notes, receipts, bills, and canceled checks. Upon examination of the contents, Tom found the following information:

1. A bill for $303.33 for graphic design of advertising and programs.
2. A bill for $460.00 for the printing of programs.
3. A paid receipt from the U.S. Post Office for $88.
4. A bank statement indicating monthly service and NSF (not sufficient funds) charges of $57.75.
5. A note from Tom that the corporation owed him $33.37 for the use of his personal auto for business trips.
6. Paid receipts totaling $331.74 for props.
7. A laundry paid receipt for $300.28 for cleaning costumes.
8. Several bills from plumbers and electricians for repairs to the old building totaling $893.45. Tom wasn't sure whether such expenses might be incurred every month.
9. Canceled checks indicating several purchases of supplies (napkins, cleaning supplies, etc.) totaling $391.82.
10. Other miscellaneous paid items totaling $312.50.
11. Canceled checks to the caterer totaling $4,722.92.
12. A bill for $115 for attorney fees.

Tom believed that he could construct an income and expense statement and that he could find out the number of tickets the Roxy must sell to break even. But he was more concerned about how to control disbursements, free tickets, meals, and other operational problems. More importantly, Tom was concerned about filling the house with a paying audience. When audiences didn't just appear, Tom had begun questioning whether the market for the Roxy's productions was as rosy as the group imagined in its Statement of Purpose (Exhibit 16.2).

An economics professor from the university had mentioned something about regional node theory to Tom. According to the professor, people from small towns would travel to larger regional population centers for shopping and entertainment, but it was questionable whether people from the larger city would travel to the smaller town for the same purposes. Since the Roxy had not advertised outside Clarksville, it was difficult for Tom to know whether audiences would travel from Nashville to the Roxy.

In his discussions with friends, Tom found that many believed that the majority of area residents were apathetic toward the arts and support of the arts, especially the performing arts. The statement that, "If it's in Clarksville, it can't be very good," was expressed by more than one acquaintance. One person responded that there was a limited audience for anything more intellectually stirring than a tractor pull and an inherent distrust of any form of entertainment out of the norm. Others expressed a hesitancy to spend more than the price of a movie ticket for any form of entertainment. Some thought the transient population with wide cultural backgrounds afforded by Fort Campbell was unaware of cultural events in the local community.

Tom wondered whether serving meals was a good idea, and whether serving alcoholic beverages might increase the audience size. He had obtained information from the State Alchoholic Beverage Commission indicating that, following an inspection of a business's premises, a liquor license could be granted. This required businesses seating 75–125 persons a minimum fee per year of $600, paid to the Alcoholic Beverage Commission. The business must procure business tax licenses from the city and county that would equal the fee paid to the Alcoholic Beverage Commission ($600) and put up a $10,000 bond. The fee for a business seating 126–175 persons was $750 in addition to the $10,000 bond.

Once the liquor license was secured, an outlay of up to $5,000 would be necessary to stock liquor and mixers. An experienced bartender would be required at a wage of $5 an hour.

A study of some local restaurants that served both dinner and liquor showed 25–30 percent of their total profits came from business at the bar. Bars usually earned a 70-percent profit per dollar on liquor sales. This was an after-tax profit estimate.

Tom was perplexed as he wondered what needed to be done to operate the Roxy profitably, fill the house, solve the money problems, and keep the group together. One thing was certain though. The Roxy team had never enjoyed life as much as they had in the last thirty days. They all agreed that they were willing to continue their poor but fulfilled lifestyle even if the Roxy didn't return a profit.

CASE 17

Ozark Glass Company

Ozark Glass, a division of Ozark-Mercantile, Inc., is a manufacturer of colored sheet glass located in a medium-sized city in the Southwest. The company was founded in 1974 by Dr. Steven Connors and originally operated as an antique shop specializing in merry-go-round horses. The objective of the firm was simply to provide a hobby for Dr. Connors and his wife, Arlene.

By 1976, the company had expanded into a stained glass studio teaching interested consumers stained glass as a hobby. At this time, a stained glass artist joined the firm as a partner. The company then started to actively pursue the profitable do-it-yourself market. Classes were started to teach hobbyists how to work with stained glass. The classes increased the public's knowledge of uses for stained glass. One of the students became particularly interested in opening a store in Tulsa, Oklahoma, patterned after Ozark Glass. Thus, the concept of franchising stained glass products was developed. Six additional stores were soon opened.

The rapid expansion of the company led to an inability to purchase enough glass to satisfy the demands of the franchise stores. When the firm was unable to reach an agreement with its present supplier to open an additional facility under a joint agreement, Ozark Glass started its own 16,700 square-foot manufacturing facility in April 1978.

The plant is one of only 15 stained glass manufacturing facilities in the United States. The plant employs 62 people and has a capacity to produce 250,000 pounds of glass a month. Since opening the plant, Ozark Glass has grown to the third largest producer of stained glass in this country.

The plant is equipped with five furnaces that produce a product line consisting of 150 colors of glass. The product lines include three types of transparent glass: cathedral—a single-colored glass; streaky—a glass containing two or more colors mixed together; and wispy—glass that is streaked with white glass. In addition, the company produces two types of glass: semilescent—glass that transmits light but little or no image; and opalescent—a dense glass that transmits light in reduced amounts.

This case was prepared by Professor C.P. Rao and James DeConinck of the University of Arkansas. It is intended as a basis for classroom discussion rather than to illustrate effective or ineffective handling of an administrative situation. All names of individuals and the company have been disguised. This case was made possible by the cooperation of a business firm that remains anonymous. Presented at the Case Research Association Case Workshop, Atlanta, November 1986. All rights reserved by the authors. Used by permission from C.P. Rao.

GROWTH STRATEGY

The company has experienced impressive growth since opening its manufacturing facility in 1978. In that year, total sales were $30,000, all domestically generated. By 1981, total sales had expanded to slightly more than $2 million, and in 1985 total sales topped the $3 million level. Of particular importance has been the growth of the export market. Since 1979, export sales have shown a five-fold increase from $198,000 to slightly more than $1 million in 1985. The export market has accounted for approximately 35 percent of sales since 1981 (see Exhibit 17.1).

EXHIBIT 17.1 Ozark Glass Company gross sales for 1978–1985			
Year	**Gross sales**	**Domestic sales**	**Export sales**
1985	$3,180,869	$2,058,023	$1,122,846
1984	2,824,928	1,844,678	980,250
1983	2,565,784	1,683,155	882,629
1982	2,324,080	1,508,328	815,752
1981	2,090,000	1,448,365	641,635
1980	1,859,668	1,364,431	495,237
1979	1,413,978	1,215,556	198,422
1978	30,000	30,000	none

THE EXPORT MARKET

Ozark Glass Company's exporting began when the company received inquiries from overseas readers of advertisements placed in U.S. trade publications. Although the company's advertising was not specifically directed at overseas readers, management aggressively pursued these inquiries by first sending a letter to each inquiry and second by phoning each prospect. The transoceanic phone call was especially impressive to the prospects.

These inquiries led to the company's first international sales to an Australian firm, Yencken Sandy Glass Industries, in December 1978. After a visit to Ozark Glass Company's manufacturing facility, the Australian firm purchased $20,000 of merchandise.

The Australian firm invited the President of Ozark Glass to Australia to conduct a series of seminars to six retail stores handling glass supplies on how to market and display stained glass. The seminars led to orders being placed from each of the six stores.

Ozark Glass was able to enter the New Zealand market after Yencken Sandy Glass Industries sold glass products to several New Zealand firms. Inquiries were soon received from these firms in New Zealand. Following a strategy similar to the one employed in Australia, a representative of Ozark Glass made a personal visit to explain how to display glass products and set up instructional classes to generate interest among hobbyists in working with stained glass. Despite intense competition from European manufacturers, Ozark Glass became the largest seller of stained glass in both Australia and New Zealand.

The success of Ozark Glass was attributed to a willingness to compete against European stained glass firms. Since the art of manufacturing stained glass had orginated in Europe, many people in Australia and New Zealand believed European glass was superior. This had caused American manufacturers to avoid competing in this market. Ozark Glass was able to successfully sell in this market because of its personal sales visits to potential clients and its willingness to assist customers in all aspects of the stained glass business. In addition, the use of a telex machine allowed the firm to communicate with international clients.

During 1980, the firm started to receive a small number of orders from Japan. These Japanese firms had also become familiar with Ozark Glass Company's product line through advertisements in U.S. trade publications. The firm pursued these leads through the use of the telephone. Although some problems resulted because of the language barrier, the company concluded the Japanese firms did not understand what stained glass was, but purchased the product because it was considered "Western."

The company contacted the Japanese firm from whom they had received orders and requested permission to conduct a lecture on the uses of stained glass. Most of the stores agreed to allow Ozark Glass to visit their stores. An interpreter was provided by each store. Additional prospects were obtained from the U.S. Commerce Department. The lectures enabled the company to convert many small clients into large customers and to also gain new prospects for future sales. The success in the Japanese market reinforced to the company the value of personal visits to increase sales.

Although both the Japanese and Korean markets appeared profitable, Ozark Glass lost both markets to a West Coast competitor whose cost was $.79 per square foot compared to $.90 per square foot for Ozark Glass. No effort was made to compete directly with the competitor. A once-promising market was simply abandoned.

Perhaps Ozark Glass was willing to abandon the Far Eastern market because of increased activity in Europe. Even while the Far Eastern market had been expanding, the company had become interested in pursuing the difficult but lucrative European market. The company viewed the European market as attractive because of the lack of competition from other American firms. In addition, Ozark Glass was targeting the hobby market and anticipated no direct competiton from European glass manufacturers. The difficulty in competing against European manufacturers was because of a perceived notion on the part of European customers about the inferiority of American glass.

In an effort to pursue the European market, Ozark Glass contacted the European office of the State Industrial Commission. The Commission provided the company with a list of potential customers. The company aggressively pursued these leads through the use of telephone calls and letters. As anticipated, the pursuit of the European market was a difficult process because of the perceived superiority of European glass. As a way of convincing Europeans of the quality of American glass, the company adopted the following slogan, "European Quality From the Heart of America." Although penetrating the European market was difficult, Ozark Glass eventually obtained a German distributor for its glass products. The German client placed five orders for stained glass over the next 18 months. This company is Ozark Glass Company's largest customer in Europe. The success in Europe was considered a "coup" for the company since it was believed in industry circles that an American firm could not successfully compete in Europe.

The success in Europe was attributed to a difference in European glass, which is similar to window glass, compared to the glass sold by Ozark Glass, which is stained glass. This is important because Ozark Glass is targeting the hobby market which uses stained glass and thus has no direct competitor in Europe.

The firm's success in exporting earned it a Presidential "E" award in 1981 (see Exhibit 17.2). This award is given to firms that have shown excellence in acquiring international sales. The award further enhanced the company's belief in its motto of "people sell people."

Ozark Glass has relied on informality in developing its export marketing strategy. From an organizational structure perspective, both domestic and international sales are the responsibility of the national sales manager. This individual reports to the vice president of the company who in turn reports to the president. All three individuals have responsibility in developing plans for the overseas markets. The company has adopted a policy of flexibility instead of establishing a formal set of export objectives.

In the early 1980s, Ozark Glass pursued the export market as the primary means of generating continued growth. The reason for this decision was that the company encountered few U.S. competitors in overseas markets. In fact, no other domestic manufacturer had international sales exceeding 5 percent of their gross sales. Because of the lack of European or American competition in the European market and the past success in international markets, Ozark Glass has high expectations for continued growth abroad.

PRODUCT STRATEGY

The company offers three sheet sizes of glass—10"x10", 21"x25", and 25"x42"—for both domestic and international clients. The company does not offer special metric measurements for the international market.

Because of the perceived superiority of European glass, Ozark Glass placed special emphasis on manufacturing a high-quality product. As mentioned earlier, Ozark Glass has adopted the following slogan as a method of emphasizing the quality of its products when selling overseas, "European Quality From the Heart of America."

An important characteristic of high-quality stained glass is the ease with which it can be cut. According to industry experts, Ozark Glass products are among the industry's softest.

EXHIBIT 17.2 **Recognition for exporting success**

Firm Wins Exporting Award

Ozark Glass company's growth in export sales has earned the firm a Presidential "E" award from the U.S. Department of Commerce.

The award was presented August 25 to Dr. Steven Connors, President of Ozark Glass, and Ron Miller, Vice President and General Manager.

Ozark Glass rolls about 2.9 million pounds of stained glasses annually from its plant at 4915 Briar Road. One-third of its annual production is shipped to Germany, Switzerland, Italy, Scandinavia, Australia, New Zealand, Japan, Taiwan, Korea, South America, Mexico, and Canada.

The plant supplies 27 Ozark Glass retail franchises, a number of foreign and domestic retail customers, and four foreign manufacturers of ready-made, Tiffany-style lamps and lighting fixtures.

United States hobbyists make up the fastest-growing market, according to Miller. There are about 500,000 do-it-yourself glass-craft workers, and per capita spending on their hobby averages $200 a year.

Most stained glass stores offer classes in glass techniques. Ozark Glass stores also sell works by accomplished students on consignment. "We are especially proud of our shipment to Europe. We were told there was no market there since stained glass originated in Europe," said Miller.

Other advice that since Europeans consider stained glass a trade, they would not be receptive to it as a craft, was also mistaken, said Miller. The agent for Ozark Glass in Germany is succeeding in a market historically dominated by European glassmakers.

The Australian market, however, is primarily made up of professional stained glass workers, possibly because of the strong British influence of trade unions and apprenticeships.

Ozark Glass has opened a franchise in Osaka, Japan, and is considering a second store in Japan, where the stained glass hobby is catching on rapidly.

"The Japanese do very meticulous, exacting work. They tend to try difficult projects and they relish going to school. Typically, a Japanese student attends classes at least a year. Most U.S. students go six weeks to learn the two basic techniques, lead and copper foil," said Miller.

The factory produces 150 colors and combinations of glass. Cathedral glass is the transparent jewel tones. Opalescent is a milky, translucent glass. Streakies combine cathedral and opalescent glasses. Ozark Glass is one of the few makers of iridescent glass, which has a light-reflecting surface.

Last July, Connors brought in English glass engineer Michael Chambers as a technical consultant. Chambers is a graduate of Sheffield University, a leading school for glassmaking.

His expertise has meant "tremendous differences in the quality of our production and cost efficiency," said Miller.

Chambers' father and brother have applied for immigration permits, and their arrival will allow Ozark Glass to begin production of antique glass, now exclusively manufactured in Europe.

Molten stained glass is rolled into flat sheets, while antique glass is first blown into a cylinder. The process requires cutting away the top and bottom of the cylinder, slitting the sides, then reheating the piece and flattening it.

The result is a heavy, transparent glass containing irregular bubbles. Antique glass is used mainly in doors and furniture pieces such as China cabinets.

Ozark Glass began as an antique shop opened by Connors' wife, Arlene in 1974. Mrs. Connors studied stained glass techniques in order to restore antique glass pieces she offered in the shop.

When she branched into stained glass classes, the Connors' found that materials were often scarce and shipments delayed.

They opened the office-warehouse factory complex in 1978 and launched their first four franchises by 1979.

Mrs. Connors now designs windows and trains new franchises. She is assisted by Miller's wife, Penny, who also manages the local store at 714 N. Sterling.

Ozark Glass has now become the fourth largest stained glass manufacturer in the United States. It is one of the youngest and smallest firms to receive the Presidental citation for exporting.

Selected by the U.S. Department of Commerce, award-winning firms much achieve export sales growth equal to or exceeding their domestic sales growth.

PROMOTION STRATEGY

Ozark Glass spends almost no money conducting market research and only about one percent of sales on advertising. Demographics or economic indicators are not used as part of management's strategy to obtain potential clientele. Instead the company relies on inquiries from advertisements in various trade publications followed by a personal visit from a management representative to generate sales abroad.

The company believes that the best way to generate long-term growth in international markets is to develop a strong franchise network. The company currently has three international franchises and anticipates opening two additional franchises in London and Mexico City.

The company has also been generating sales through exhibits at international trade shows in Germany, England, Mexico, Puerto Rico, and South America. In the past, trade shows have generated several small orders and new contacts. The company plans to increase participation at trade shows with special emphasis being placed on penetrating the South American market.

PRICING POLICY

Ozark Glass follows a cost-plus pricing strategy. Two different price lists are used—one for franchise outlets and the other for wholesale accounts (see Exhibit 17.3). Both price lists contain seven levels of pricing ranging from the lowest priced items (A) to the highest priced items (G).

The franchise price list contains prices that are 5 to 100 percent higher than the wholesale price list depending on the size of the order. Because of the higher profit margin on franchise sales, the company is actively attempting to expand its franchise network. Although franchise outlets generally are subjected to higher costs, no minimum order is required. In addition, on orders of $1,000 or more, franchise pricing is similar to the wholesale price list. For example, the following volume discounts are allowed:

Glass Weight	Discount
150 pounds	15%
200 pounds	20%
500 pounds	33%
1,000 pounds—33% and no freight charges	

A minimum order of 1,000 pounds is required to qualify for the wholesale price list.

Ozark Glass prices its products by the pound. This has created a problem in both domestic and international markets. For example, several competitors price by the square foot and a conversion factor must be used when submitting quotes. By

EXHIBIT 17.3 **Wholesale per-pound price list**							
Price code	A	B	C	D	E	F	G
Full sheets	$1.80	$1.89	$2.15	$2.33	$2.60	$2.55	$3.30
Half sheets	2.20	2.30	2.60	2.80	3.35	3.10	3.90
10 by 10's	2.79	2.92	3.33	3.60	4.20	3.95	5.10

dividing the square-foot price by 1.5, a comparison can be made to pound prices as quoted by Ozark Glass and prices by the square-foot as quoted by many of the company's competitors. A similar problem exists when negotiating prices with an international account where pounds must be converted to square meters. The company has adopted a similar conversion equation to alleviate this problem.

FOREIGN EXCHANGE RATES

Export sales have suffered during the past several years because of the strength of the dollar. Ozark Glass Company's competitive pricing advantage in Europe has been reduced. The company has had to cut its profit margin to maintain a slight pricing advantage over European competitors.

The fluctuating exchange rates have forced management to pay greater attention to day-to-day rates. For example, sales to Germany are evaluated on a daily basis. The company allows an additional 3 percent discount if the trading rate of the German mark is 2.7 times greater than the dollar.

The company employs no systematic strategy in evaluating the international market regarding currency fluctuations. The firm does not employ a finance specialist to aid in rate forecasting or engage in advance negotiations regarding fluctuating exchange rates when marketing to overseas accounts.

The company is anticipating greater international sales due to the decline in the value of the dollar. Ozark Glass believes that with the decrease in the value of the dollar, international sales and profits should both increase. The firm is especially optimistic concerning sales to Europe.

MANUFACTURING PHILOSOPHY

All of the company's products are produced in one manufacturing facility. Sales are currently not exceeding the capacity of the facility although the plant does have room for increased expansion if it becomes necessary. Management does not anticipate the need for an additional manufacturing facility in the near future.

Although having only one manufacturing facility has some cost disadvantages when supplying certain markets, management believes that maintaining one facility allows it to maintain greater quality control over the product line. The company has achieved success in large part because of the quality of its glass in comparison to other manufacturers. Because of this, the company is reluctant to enter into any joint ventures or licensing agreements as a way of expansion.

The company's present location also allows for an abundant supply of sand, the most important raw material in the production of stained glass. The region also provides Ozark Glass with inexpensive natural gas to operate its glass furnaces. Because of the inexpensive price of natural gas in the area, the company is often able to sell its products to European accounts at a price below that of European competitors.

DISTRIBUTION CHANNELS

A telex and long distance watts lines are the primary means of conducting sales internationally. However, the company does employ sales agents in Germany and Canada to assist in direct sales to these two countries. The sales agents are used because many potential clients are unfamiliar in the use of stained glass and other related products. Management attributes the unfamiliarity with stained glass products to immaturity of the market. As the market matures, management anticipates the continued use of sales agents to generate business in remote areas.

A freight forwarder is employed to handle transportation of products to international accounts. The forewarder is responsible for coordinating both sea and land carriers and for handling all necessary paperwork such as obtaining permits and authenticating bills of lading.

CASE 18

Springfield Remanufacturing Corporation

Salespeople desperately tried to generate new orders. Company President John Stack stated that he had enough work for the remaining employees through August, but that he needed a "big play" by September. Stack considered whether to lay off employees (Springfield Remanufacturing Corporation had never had a layoff) or to

This case was prepared by Professors Charles W. Boyd and D. Keith Denton of Southwest Missouri State University. It is intended as a basis for classroom discussion rather than to illustrate effective or ineffective handling of an administrative situation. Copyright © 1987 by Charles W. Boyd and D. Keith Denton. Used by permission from Charles W. Boyd.

avoid the layoff and risk the financial stability of the corporation. A dejected Stack noted, "I guess we will find out if we mean what we say—we'll show them the numbers—we'll see."

FORMATION OF THE COMPANY

On February 1, 1983, after nearly three years of rumors and frustration, the financially troubled International Harvester (IH) sold one of its last remaining diesel engine and engine component remanufacturing operations as part of its turnaround strategy. IH needed to do something because of its $4 billion debt load and $1.6 billion in operating losses. During a depressed truck and farm economy, the corporation was seeking answers to its troubles. Therefore, they decided to sell the Springfield plant and four other parts-remanufacturing centers. IH's sale of their Springfield, Missouri, facility marked the end of IH's remanufacturing activities but not the end of their troubles. IH later sold its Farm Division in order to save the Truck Division, and later reorganized as NAVISTAR.

The Springfield Remanufacturing Corporation (SRC) facility employed 171 workers at the time of the sale. It was originally meant to be sold to Dresser Industries, a major customer of the plant, despite the fact that SRC's employees had had a bid on the table to purchase the company. When negotiations with Dresser broke down in December 1982, employees of the firm began to consider forming their own company. Springfield Remanufacturing Corporation was the result of these discussions when two months later employees obtained financing from the Bank of America in San Francisco. The company and the 68,000-square-foot plant was bought from IH by a group of 13 employees for approximately $7 million at three percentage points above the prime rate. The plant's assets provided enough collateral so that the employees did not have to give the lender any of the equity in the firm.

Twelve of these new owners were former employees and managers of IH at the plant. The thirteenth was Don McCoy, the controller of the IH Division of which the Springfield plant was part. President of the new corporation was John P. (Jack) Stack who had previously been plant manager. Stack and the other twelve owners decided to broaden the ownership of the new corporation through an employee stock ownership program. As former employees were rehired, they decided to set aside each year a portion of the corporate earnings to buy some of the company's unissued stock. This stock would then go into a trust fund for workers. The employee stock ownership plan (ESOP) was greeted with enthusiasm. Foreman Joe Loeber noted, "It added a little incentive to know you're working for your own future and not just the other guy's. Everybody's excited." The managers owned shares of stock and signed an agreement that the corporation would issue shares of stock directly into the ESOP. Thus the ESOP became the vehicle for employee ownership of the firm.

Stack and other management realized the plant's future lay outside of IH. He noted, "We were really different. IH employees were normally represented by United Auto Workers and the Springfield plant wasn't." As early as two years before the actual sale, local management at the Springfield plant submitted a bid for the plant that was not given serious consideration by IH. A year later a more detailed plan was submitted but again was rejected. In five weeks they closed the deal.

The day after the sale, SRC brought back 30 of their former IH employees and increased their employment by 30 a day until most of the original employees were back. When SRC started business they had signed up 60 percent of their old customers. Before the sale, they had $10 million in sales of parts for construction equipment, another $7 million for farm equipment, and $3 million for trucks.

On February 1, 1983, Jack Stack, President of SRC, issued a news release stating that the new firm would remain in Springfield and would continue to be a major rebuilder of diesel engines, injection pumps, water pumps, and other engine components. The news release noted that SRC would be a supplier of remanufactured engines and engine components to IH's agricultural equipment and truck dealers.

The news release, like the news about the IH sale of the Springfield facility, did not tell the whole story about this unique situation. It was no secret that many of IH's manufacturing facilities had suffered from abrasive employee-management relations. When Jack Stack arrived at the facility four years before the eventual sale, the employees were on the verge of forming a union and the company was running behind production schedule. Stack was sent from IH headquarters and given six months to straighten out the problem at the plant or close it.

Stack called a meeting with all employees and "begged" them to give him and his team a chance to change things. He promised to listen, and he promised change. The employees agreed to give him a chance. The union election was scheduled for March 10; this gave Stack two months to win over the employees. Stack won the election as over 75 percent of the employees voted in favor of management over the union.

Management's relations with employees began to change. There were better human relations, better communications, and better cooperation. Three topics were emphasized to the employees: safety, housekeeping, and quality. Statistical measures for these three activities were developed by management and taught to the employees. Eventually the employees were taught about cost and profits. Data were graphed, kept updated, and posted in prominent places within the plant. As a result, employees became very goal oriented. Stack commented: "You've got to have an enemy to have a team. If you can set that enemy outside your organization and declare what that enemy is, that's the unifying factor behind the whole organization." So such things as safety problems and quality rejects became the enemy, and improving performance in these areas became the employees' goals. As a result, the organization's efficiency and effectiveness improved dramatically.

One year later production was up 30 percent. By June 1984, the facility had become the "best" of the outside firms performing remanufacturing work for IH. They had remained profitable during the time that similar facilities had been losing money.

Several programs that Stack and others started during this time were given credit for helping turn things around. One of these is the Quality of Work Life

(QWL) program in which employees analyze and propose solutions to organizational problems. They had also formed small employee groups, known as quality circles, that were used to make the plant more efficient and productive. Innovative approaches were also used. For example, when IH imposed a wage freeze, the QWL group decided to go to a flex-time, four, 10-hour/day week. This saved employees money on transportation and lunches and reduced absenteeism by giving workers a day off so they could take care of personal business.

METEORIC RISE

The rise of SRC from the ashes of IH was almost immediate and profound. Their success did not go unnoticed by the news media. Several articles on their success were written, and the firm was featured in an issue of *INC.* magazine. A television documentary by PBS was aired during the Fall of 1987.

During 1984, SRC increased sales by 20 percent to $15.5 million. A year later business increased by 40 percent to $23 million in sales, and 100 employees were added to the payroll to bring total employment to 225.

In one year they remanufactured 2,500 engines, and in two years of operation the firm had warranty returns averaging less than one percent. SRC's customers included Ingersoll-Rand, J.I. Case, Dresser Industries, and International Harvester.

A red-letter day for SRC came in April 1985, two years after their formation, when SRC announced that they had received a contract from General Motors (GM) to remanufacture 15,400 5.7 liter V–8 diesel engines for GM's Oldsmobile Division. There are about 1.5 million GM cars in service powered by the 5.7 liter engine. GM decided to subcontract the remanufacturing of these engines because daily demand had stabilized at a level that GM management no longer considered justifying the plant space it had devoted to the remanufacturing. GM ceased production of the 5.7 liter diesel engine a week prior to signing the contract with SRC. The volume of SRC's work was expected to slowly decrease as the cars powered by the 5.7 are taken out of service over time.

Lee Shroyer, marketing manager, said the contract could mean 40 new jobs in Springfield and 60 new jobs at a satellite operation in the nearby community of Willow Springs. With this contract SRC became the first company to be named as an authorized engine rebuilder for GM. The three-year contract was expected to be worth $40 million to SRC. An SRC manager stated, "We should continue to work with GM as long as we can maintain their quality and safety requirements and I don't see any problem with that." With this new business, 1985 sales were expected to exceed $30 million.

Because of this new business, additional fixtures, tooling, jet sprays, and new arrangements were made in the Springfield plant to improve the flow of materials. To accommodate increased business, SRC needed a new building. In May 1985, they secured an additional building in Willow Springs, a small town 70 miles away. Stack expected to be turning out five engines per day by mid-May and 125 per day by

November. By November they expected to employ 75 people and eventually employ 150 after 2 years.

REASONS FOR SUCCESS

SRC's 40-percent growth rate did not come by accident. They would not have received the GM contract if they did not turn out extremely high-quality products. Stack noted that a remanufacturing or recycled assembly is 30- to 40-percent the price of a new one, which means lower inventory carrying cost for the original equipment manufacturer (OEM) customer. SRC warranties are as good or better than those of a new product. Less than 1 percent of their products are returned for any reason—the industry average is 6 percent. Some of their products are guaranteed to be delivered within 48 hours. Within the industry they have some of the best warranties, lowest cost and highest reliability. During recent years, SRC experienced almost a 400 percent growth in business, and a 5 percent decrease in overhead cost. This growth occurred despite the depressed agriculture and construction industries.

Their success is built on at least four ingredients: Jack Stack, the charismatic and thoughtful president; a very capable management team; a positive philosophy toward employees; and employee ownership. Stack is the visionary who keeps the company focused on its objectives and clearly believes in his management style. Stack is complemented by those around him. Mike Carrigan, Vice President of production, is a self-confessed "pack rat" who totally understands the production process. He is always looking to improve methods of operation and reduce waste. He would much rather fix what he has rather than buy something new. He seems ideally suited to this recycling work. Gary Brown, the Human Resources Manager, likewise knows the personnel function and knows what kind of people SRC is looking for. Both Brown and Carrigan say there are two types of people—competitive and noncompetitive. They look for the competitive "hungry" ones. The ones who like to win, who like to compete, and who are interested in self-improvement.

SRC tries to maximize their people. They spend a great deal of time trying to cultivate an air of trust and openness between people. Stack noted, "There's not a financial number our employees don't know or have access to." They conduct weekly meetings with employees where they go over the business, including financial statements, operating income, profits, losses, assets, liabilities and other financial figures. All employees may not know or understand all the financial figures, but they know the figures are available. They do know what each department contributes and costs the company. Stack has been quoted as saying, "We teach them about finance and accounting before we teach them how to turn a wrench."

Management at SRC also tries to make work fun. They are constantly setting standards for direct and indirect labor and then try to make games out of achieving results. These games are set up so employees understand what is needed and have incentives and rewards given. A popular phrase around SRC is STP—GUTR (Stop The Praise—Give Us The Raise). SRC pays employees a sizable bonus if quarterly financial goals are met. Winning at the "game" is based on an employee's ability to save labor and/or material cost. Some employees at the plant receive as much as 12 percent of their salary in bonus money. Employees also receive cash payments for suggestions that save the company money. When safety goals are met, insurance money is refunded to SRC and is used to purchase gifts of appreciation.

SRC also practices a decentralized-participative style of management where they try to push decision making down to the lowest level. Employees and first-line supervisors are encouraged to take on new tasks. For example, most supervisors "adopt" an area outside their supervisory area. One supervisor may be in charge of controlling chemical costs ranging from solvents to "white out" correction fluid. Another supervisor may be in charge of all plant abrasives. Management at SRC believes it teaches everyone the value of cooperation and makes them better at communicating and persuading since they must convince others outside their area to control costs in their "adopted" area. Of course all of these programs are enhanced because of ESOP. It is not someone else's business, it's theirs.

MARKETING CONCEPT

SRC fills a market niche with the OEM being the customer. The marketing concept is simple and straightforward. Diesel engines are usually employed in trucks, earth-moving equipment, and other types of "workhorse" applications in which these engines labor daily under heavy strain. Because of this heavy usage, vital engine parts eventually break down, and the user must either purchase an entirely new piece of equipment, have the engine repaired, or have the engine or its major components rebuilt. The first option is often passed up due to the very high expense of purchasing an entirely new piece of equipment. Each of the other options requires the services of a firm that either builds or repairs engine components. This is known as the aftermarket.

Most firms in the engine or automotive aftermarket compete against the OEM company that originally built a particular engine component by offering their own repair service or replacement part. As a result, the OEM loses market share in the aftermarket. The distinctive difference of SRC is that the company seeks to restore a portion of this lost market share to the OEM by serving as the OEM's contracted provider of aftermarket engine components by providing the OEM with a replacement engine or engine component. As a result, the OEM is spared the tremendous costs of real estate, plant, and equipment investment that would be necessary to do their own remanufacturing work. SRC incurs these expenses for the OEM and sells a quality remanufactured product built to exacting specifications that will cost the OEM customer less than if it produced its own new component. In addition, new engines or components are available when needed because they are produced in quantity rather than individually prepared upon demand. This means that the end-user can get a failed piece of equipment up and running again much quicker and at a lower cost than might otherwise by possible.

An example will help illustrate the advantages SRC can offer an OEM customer. Suppose a truck operated by a commercial carrier is put out of commission by the failure of the fuel injection pump. The trucking company will likely inquire to the OEM regarding the problem. The OEM may be able to offer a new replacement pump for $580. The trucking company may instead buy a new or rebuilt pump at a lower price from a competing company in the aftermarket. Another alternative would be to have the failed pump repaired, but this would entail more downtime for the truck and thus lost revenue to the trucking company. If the OEM had a contract with SRC, however, the OEM would have a high-quality remanufactured fuel injection pump that had the same warranty as a new pump to sell to the trucking company for $300.

As a result of its remanufacturing operations, SRC is able to add value to its OEM customers in a number of ways:

1. Preserving part of the OEM's market share in the automotive aftermarket.
2. Providing the OEM more total profitability over the entire life of the engine.
3. Preventing costly investment in plant and equipment for remanufacturing operations (these operations cannot be performed on an OEM's existing production lines). These savings become even more important when the OEM must continue to supply components for an engine that has gone out of production.
4. Since SRC uses an efficient job-shop operation, it is able to sell its products to its OEM customers at a relatively low price. This saves the OEM customer money and lowers its inventory carrying cost.

SRC sales personnel visit OEM engine and equipment builders around the country and try to explain to their management teams how SRC can add value to their operations in the above-listed ways. They try to make them aware of all the costs they must still incur *after* they have sold their products. These costs include warranties, return parts, labor, and inventory carrying costs. They try to explain how SRC can minimize these costs and increase the OEM's total profitability and their share of the aftermarket.

SHORT-TERM FORECASTS FOR THE AUTOMOTIVE AFTERMARKET

The success of the automotive aftermarket is highly dependent upon the rate of new car sales and the number of older vehicles in service. This gives them knowledge of the size of the "pipeline" of new-to-aging cars that represent the size of their market.

The 1987 outlook for the U.S. automobile industry has been summarized as follows:

For 1987, U.S. car and truck output is projected to decline about five percent from the 11.5 million units estimated for 1986, even if no lengthy strikes occur when UAW contracts expire next fall. Following an estimated 12 percent decline in 1986, profits for 1987 may recede another 20 percent or so, despite efficiency gains. This relatively unfavorable outlook reflects lower unit volume, mounting competition, a less favorable sales mix, costly sales incentive programs, and plant closing costs.[1]

While 1987 sales are projected to be five percent lower than 1986 sales, it should be remembered that 1984–1986 sales were well above the long-term U.S. sales trend for this industry.

The average age of vehicles on the road is particularly important to SRC and other firms in the automotive aftermarket since their business comes from the wearout of vehicle parts and components. Exhibit 18.1 reveals that the average age of American-produced cars and trucks in use has increased during recent years.

EXHIBIT 18.1 **Average age of American-produced cars and trucks**

Year	Passenger cars	Motor trucks
1985	7.6	8.1
1984	7.5	8.2
1983	7.4	8.1
1982	7.2	7.8
1981	6.9	7.5
1980	6.6	7.1
1979	6.4	6.9
1978	6.3	6.9
1977	6.2	6.9

Major replacement parts supplier Federal-Mogul Corporation estimates that sales of automotive aftermarket parts will grow approximately 2.6 percent in real terms over the next few years. GM estimates a 2.5–3.0 percent real growth rate. The Motor and Equipment Manufacturers Association (MEMA) estimates a 3.3 percent average compound growth rate in the number of vehicles in operation through 1990.

A TURNING POINT

Four years after their initial formation, SRC was enjoying their success. The firm was by now sufficiently diversified into the industry's market niches, which Stack referred to as the "four cyclinders": construction equipment, agricultural equipment, trucks, and automobiles. Customers had been added so rapidly to each "cylinder" during the four-year period that Stack decided it was time to consolidate the company's gains. The 1987 financial plan was prepared in August 1986, completed in October, and approved in November. The strategy for 1987 would be to seek no new customers. Instead, the sales and marketing operation would be reorganized and would concentrate on enhancing service to SRC's present customers. There had

---

[1]The data reported in this subsection of the case were obtained from Standard & Poor's *Industry Surveys*, April 1987, pp. 75, 80, and 85.

not seemed to be time to do that during the four previous years of rapid growth; this year the company would take the time. See Exhibits 18.2, 18.3 and 18.4 for summary financial data.

EXHIBIT 18.2 **Springfield Remanufacturing Corporation and Subsidiary—consolidated balance sheets**

Assets	January 29, 1984	January 27, 1985	January 26, 1986	January 25, 1987
Current Assets				
Cash	$ 316,688	$ 20,597	$ 13,584	$ 50,082
Trade accounts receivable, less allowances for doubtful accounts	2,547,771	2,098,321	3,184,409	2,237,471
Inventories	9,514,189	8,055,556	10,451,968	9,230,828
Prepaid income taxes	298,200	—	—	—
Prepaid expenses and other current assets	48,645	39,826	37,875	32,637
Total Current Assets	12,725,493	10,214,300	13,687,836	11,551,018
Property, Buildings and Equipment	291,043	669,177	1,905,348	2,244,519
	$13,016,536	$10,883,477	$15,593,184	$13,795,537
Liabilities and Stockholders' Equity				
Current Liabilities				
Notes payable	$ 7,141,616	$ 2,526,557	$ 2,677,195	$ 383,658
Accounts payable	1,907,233	2,661,636	5,825,521	3,867,352
Accrued contribution to employee stock ownership trust	—	413,510	521,011	—
Income taxes payable	—	—	47,000	363,340
Other current liabilities	727,954	771,721	900,450	1,211,717
Current portion of long-term debt	10,006	297,280	309,002	358,533
Total Current Liabilities	9,786,809	6,670,704	10,280,179	6,184,600
Excess of Net Assets Acquired Over Cost	3,146,838	2,360,129	1,573,420	786,710
Long-term Debt	43,377	1,126,922	1,317,522	2,537,874
Deferred Income Taxes	—	—	34,000	10,000
	12,977,024	10,157,755	13,205,121	9,519,184
Stockholders' Equity				
Class A Common Stock, voting, par value $.10 per share, 1,500,000 and 500,000 shares authorized, 1,140,000 and 500,000 issued and outstanding	50,000	50,000	50,000	114,000

Class B Common Stock, nonvoting, par value $.10 per share, 10,000,000 and 1,000,000 shares authorized, 1,984,500 and 541,500 shares issued and outstanding	50,000	51,000	54,150	198,450
Additional paid-in capital	—	5,100	124,365	603,300
Retained earnings	(60,488)	619,622	2,159,548	3,688,114
Treasury stock, at cost	—	—	—	(327,511)
	39,512	725,722	2,388,063	4,276,353
	$13,016,536	$10,883,477	$15,593,184	$13,795,537

EXHIBIT 18.3 Springfield Remanufacturing Corporation and Subsidiary—consolidated statements of earnings

	January 29, 1984	January 27, 1985	January 26, 1986	January 25, 1987
Net sales	$16,347,600	$23,976,808	$27,818,322	$37,937,498
Cost of goods sold	13,420,229	20,696,029	23,766,826	30,864,793
	2,927,371	3,280,779	4,051,496	7,072,705
Gain (loss) on disposal of inventory	—	—	115,138	(2,229,765)
	2,927,371	3,280,779	4,166,634	4,842,940
Operating expenses Selling, general and administrative	2,826,165	2,158,463	2,570,828	2,850,189
Contribution to employee stock ownership trust	—	419,610	521,011	706,216
Interest	948,403	798,305	597,462	442,039
	3,774,568	3,376,378	3,689,301	3,998,444
	(847,197)	(95,599)	477,333	844,496
Nonoperating income Amortization of excess of net assets acquired over cost	786,709	786,709	786,709	786,710
Other, net	—	—	351,884	331,295
	786,709	786,709	1,138,593	1,118,005
Earnings (or loss) before income taxes	(60,488)	691,110	1,615,926	1,962,501
Income taxes	—	103,000	76,000	350,000
Earnings (or loss) before extraordinary item	(60,488)	588,110	1,539,926	1,612,501
Extraordinary item—tax benefit from utilization of loss carryforward	—	92,000	—	—
Net earnings (or loss)	$ (60,488)	$ 680,110	$ 1,539,926	$ 1,612,501

EXHIBIT 18.4 **Springfield Remanufacturing Corporation and Subsidiary—consolidated statements of changes in financial position**

	January 29, 1984	January 27, 1985	January 26, 1986	January 25, 1987
Source of Funds				
Operations				
Earnings (loss) before extraordinary item	$ (60,488)	$ 588,110	$ 1,539,926	$ 1,612,501
Charges (credits) to operations, not requiring outlay of working capital—				
Amortization of excess net assets acquired over cost	(786,709)	(786,709)	(786,709)	(786,710)
Depreciation	30,349	97,057	247,408	499,901
Increase (decrease) in deferred income taxes	—	—	34,000	(24,000)
Funds provided by (used in) operations	816,848	(101,542)	1,034,625	1,301,692
Additions to long-term debt	60,275	1,500,000	489,500	2,688,500
Extraordinary item—tax benefit from utilization of loss carryforward	—	92,000	—	—
Contribution of common stock to employee stock ownership trust	—	6,100	121,500	706,216
Excess of net assets acquired over cost	3,933,547	—	—	—
Sale of treasury stock	—	—	—	258,073
Disposals of property, buildings and equipment	—	—	51,495	—
Proceeds from sale of common stock	100,000	—	915	—
Decrease in working capital	—	—	135,939	—
	$ 4,093,822	$ 1,496,558	$ 1,833,974	$ 4,954,481
Application of Funds				
Reduction and current maturities of long-term debt	16,898	$ 416,455	$ 298,900	$ 1,468,148
Additions to property, buildings and equipment	321,392	475,191	1,535,074	839,072
Purchase of treasury stock		—	—	688,500
Increase in working capital	2,938,684	604,912	—	1,958,761
	$ 3,276,974	$ 1,496,558	$ 1,833,974	$ 4,954,481

Analysis of Working Capital Changes				
Increase (decrease) in current assets				
Cash	$ 316,688	$ (296,091)	$ (7,013)	$ 36,498
Trade accounts receivable	2,547,771	(449,450)	1,086,088	(946,938)
Inventories	9,514,189	(1,458,633)	2,396,412	(1,221,140)
Prepaid income taxes	298,200	(298,200)	—	—
Prepaid expenses and other current assets	48,645	(8,819)	(1,951)	(5,238)
	12,725,493	(2,511,193)	3,473,536	(2,136,818)
Increase (decrease) in current liabilities				
Notes payable	7,141,616	(4,615,059)	150,638	(2,293,537)
Accounts payable	1,907,233	754,403	3,163,885	(1,958,169)
Accrued contribution to employee stock ownership trust	—	413,510	107,501	(521,011)
Income taxes payable	—	—	36,000	316,340
Other current liabilities	727,954	43,767	139,729	311,267
Current portion of long-term debt	10,006	287,274	11,722	49,531
	9,786,809	(3,116,105)	3,609,475	(4,095,579)
Increase (Decrease) in Working Capital	$ 2,938,684	$ 604,912	$ (135,939)	$ 1,958,761

But during the period from November 1986 to February 1987, several significant changes occurred at General Motors: the $700 million payoff to Ross Perot, a huge stock buyback, and continued competitive problems in the automobile market. And what happened to GM was important to SRC, since 50 percent of SRC's business was with GM during 1986. In April 1987, GM notified SRC that they would need 5,000 fewer engines from the firm during 1987 than previously planned. To SRC, this meant 50,000 manhours, or 25 percent of its 1987 business.

Fortunately, SRC moved six months previously from remanufacturing diesel engines exclusively to also remanufacturing gasoline engines. The firm began remanufacturing 30 gasoline engines per day for Chrysler in February 1987, and later began remanufacturing them for GM too. This new business helped cushion the blow from the loss of GM's diesels, but not nearly enough. It was clear that SRC will have to work hard for new business during 1987; it would not be the year of concentrating on customer enhancement which Stack had hoped it would be.

By early June 1987, Springfield Remanufacturing Company had responded to the situation with an increased attrition rate from its 400-person work force. During the next six months, 43 employees had been terminated: 20 for performance reasons, the rest voluntarily. Still no layoff program was instituted, but time was running out. Stacks "big play" has to come soon. He wondered what options were available, what would be the effect of his actions?

CASE 19

3M Enters the People's Republic of China: Environment and Conditions in Negotiating Within the PRC, 1980–85

"I think we should begin an investigation and evaluation of the desirability of establishing a 3M company in China," 3M's President for International Operations observed one day early in 1980. He was conferring with John Marshall, longtime 3Mer recently designated as 3M's representative for the People's Republic of China (PRC).

"Indeed, this looks like the time to get our investigation started," responded Mr. Marshall. "The changes over the past few years have certainly been favorable. But there will be many questions to find answers to and decisions to make before we're done."

"That's true," rejoined the executive. "But I think we can lay down some guidelines now. For one thing, I believe we should try for a wholly owned subsidiary as we usually have elsewhere. Let's avoid the joint venture with a Chinese government firm, that other foreign firms have used. But we must bring to the Chinese the products they want. Probably we should manufacture there, and reinvest earnings for a number of years."

On the basis of these instructions, Mr. Marshall set about obtaining permission for 3M to set up a wholly-owned subsidiary in the People's Republic of China, and getting the manufacturing operations underway. More than four years later, in November 1984, after extended and sometimes delayed negotiations, 3M announced that the PRC had issued 3M a license for such a subsidiary and that 3M was set to begin manufacturing in Shanghai in 1985.

A significant feature of 3M's subsidiary in China was that it was the first to be wholly owned by a foreign firm. Previously, China had permitted foreign firms to enter only in joint ventures with a Chinese firm, or merely to have a sales office or third-party sales representative there.

This case was prepared by Delbert C. Hastings with the assistance of Esra Gencturk. It is intended as a basis for classroom discussion rather than to illustrate appropriate or inappropriate handling of an administrative situation. The U. S. Department of Education funded the preparation of this case under Grant #G00877027. Copyright © 1985 by the Case Development Center, University of Minnesota, School of Management, 271 19th Avenue South, Minneapolis, MN 55455. No part of this publication may be reproduced, stored in a retrieval system, or transmitted in any form or by any means—electronic, mechanical, photocopying, recording, or other—without the permission of the University of Minnesota. Used by permission from the Case Development Center.

China observers had mixed reactions to 3M's announcement. Robert Perito, Director of the Office of China Affairs, U.S. Department of Commerce, viewed it as a "very exciting thing in the history of China and U.S.-Chinese economic relations." Others pointed to the ambiguity surrounding the 3M-China agreement and dangers for future misunderstandings between the two parties. China was accustomed to joint ventures, but had had no experience with 100 percent foreign-owned subsidiaries. Indeed, the agreement was silent on significant points: taxes, repatriation of earnings, and 3M's potential expansions to other products and areas of China. 3M had not committed itself to export from China, but had agreed to balance its foreign exchange expenditures with foreign exchange earnings. Significantly, the PRC itself had not yet resolved numerous internal and external problems created by its recent "open door" to external (chiefly Western) economic relationships.

Was the timing appropriate in 1980 for 3M to seek entry into China? Even the quest for entry can be time consuming and expensive. While China was a major country with one billion people and significant resources, by 1980 its economic development and personal income levels were still very low and its markets undeveloped. Its new leader Deng Xaoping had, during the years just after Mao's death in 1976, shifted the country's course substantially away from the Maoist version of Marxist-Leninist socialism, toward individual capitalism. But as late as 1985 the permanence of that drastic change was still in question.

On the other hand, would anything be gained by waiting? If entry was to be difficult, the sooner started the better. And the shift toward capitalism in China was likely not only to make entry easier, but also to spark a period of industrial and economic growth and perhaps also of consumption spending.

Thus by early 1985, 3M had achieved its goal of entering the People's Republic of China under the conditions it had established and was beginning manufacturing in Shanghai. 3M's situation and its experiences up to that point represent a chronicle of strategy and decision making in international business that is interesting for analysis and evaluation.

THE 3M COMPANY

Headquartered in Maplewood, an eastern suburb of St. Paul, Minnesota, 3M had been a multinational since 1951 when it made its first direct investments abroad. 3M had achieved much experience in the complex process of entering foreign countries, setting up manufacturing and laboratory facilities, and developing markets. In 1985, the firm had subsidiaries in 52 principal locations outside the United States, 35 of which included manufacturing. As a measure of 3M's emphasis on research, product development, and modification and process development, 19 of these subsidiaries had laboratories. In 1985, 3M products were being marketed in more than 135 countries, including the 52 just mentioned.

The firm's worldwide sales revenues rose from $7.0 billion in 1983 to $7.7 billion in 1984, pushing 3M up from 47th to 45th among Fortune 500 firms. In 1984,

34 percent ($2.633 billion) of 3M's revenues were generated by its international subsidiaries. These international sales figures did not include sales of joint venture companies or exports direct from the United States to countries where 3M did not have subsidiaries. 3M's $530 million direct exports from the United States made the firm the 33rd largest U.S. industrial exporter, according to the August 6, 1984 issue of *Fortune* magazine.

At the end of 1984, 3M had 86,707 employees, 36,468 of them in consolidated and nonconsolidated subsidiaries outside the United States. Following a standing 3M policy, fewer than 100 employees outside the United States were U.S. citizens. An international staff of approximately 800 at 3M headquarters in Maplewood and in Brussels, Belgium, provided support to the subsidiary operations in other countries. Common among publicly held corporations, 3M had in 1985 many more stockholders (113,675) than employees.

The firm's 1984 annual report presented the information given in Exhibit 19.1 on 3M's operations by major geographic areas for the years ended December 31, 1982, 1983, and 1984.

EXHIBIT 19.1 **3M performance by geographic areas***
(Millions of U.S. dollars)

		United States	Europe	Other countries	Total company
Net sales to customers,	1984	$5,190	$1,599	$916	$7,705
including exports	1983	4,595	1,573	871	7,039
	1982	4,074	1,618	909	6,601
Operating income	1984	$ 946	$ 183	$157	$1,286
	1983	838	170	131	1,139
	1982	695	213	140	1,048

*The data include export sales and certain income and expense items which are reported in the geographic area where they originate.

During these years worldwide recession and the strong dollar affected 3M's sales and earnings outside the United States both directly and via the currency translation effect.

3M'S PRODUCTS, TECHNOLOGY, AND ORGANIZATION

3M was founded in 1902, making sandpaper, broadening to masking tape (both for painting automobiles), then to cellulose ("Scotch") tapes, and from there to an array of more than 55,000 products. 3M considered its main corporate expertise to be coatings technology, but its developments in that field produced many extensions. As of 1985, 3M specialized in adhesives and abrasives, electronic products, photographic films, and medical products. Research and development were considered vital to 3M's continued profitability and growth.

3M stated its long-term goals as follows:

- Unit-volume growth of 10 percent a year, on average.
- Pretax profit margins of 20 percent or better.
- Return on stockholders' equity of between 20 and 25 percent.
- At least 25 percent of annual sales from products introduced within five years.

The firm takes these goals as serious guidelines.

3M was organized into four main sectors, each headed by an executive vice president: industrial and consumer; electronic and information technologies; life sciences; and graphic technologies. International operations was set up as a fifth sector, though product-dependent on the previous four. International operations was subdivided into four areas, each headed by an area executive: Europe, Latin America, Australia-Asia-Canada, and Africa and Middle East. These area executives reported to an executive vice president for International Operations. The area executive for Australia-Asia-Canada had responsibility for 3M's operations in China.

HOW 3M GOT INTERESTED IN CHINA

The United States and the People's Republic of China had no diplomatic relations and hence no economic relations from Mao's takeover in 1949 until President Nixon's 1972 initiatives. At that juncture China's size and potential attracted 3M, as it did many other world firms.

Responsibility for exploring opportunities in China was first assigned to 3M East, a wholly owned subsidiary headquartered in Zug, Switzerland, responsible for 3M's Eastern bloc dealings. 3M East was familiar with centrally planned economies and the continuing U.S. export licensing restrictions affecting them. Until 1978, 3M's business with China was small—modest sales of finished products and purchases of a few raw materials for 3M's use. During those years China's foreign business was handled largely through the biennial Canton Trade Fairs (the Chinese Export Commodities Fairs). On a government-to-government level (e.g. China-Rumania or China-USSR), business was accomplished through bilateral trade agreements. Private firms operated mostly through on-the-spot negotiations.

In 1978, China began its current modernization and industrialization campaign. In January 1979, full U.S.-Chinese diplomatic relations were restored. 3M then saw the possibility of reaching the largely untapped Chinese market. Mr. Marshall's assignment followed early in 1980.

Those responsible for the 3M decision recognized that knowledge of the history and culture of China and of the founding of the People's Republic of China was required in order to select and set the firm's proper course of action.

THE PEOPLE'S REPUBLIC OF CHINA

Background

The People's Republic of China, occupying a major portion of east and south-east Asia is, after the Soviet Union and Canada, the third largest country in the world. (See Exhibit 19.2.) Its 3.7 million square miles place it just below Canada's 3.85 million and just above the United States' 3.6 million. Situated on the west edge

EXHIBIT 19.2 **Map of China**

of "the Pacific Rim," the PRC borders North Korea, the USSR, the Mongolian People's Republic, Afghanistan, Pakistan, India, Nepal, Sikkim, Bhutan, Burma, Laos, and Vietnam. Its near neighbors include South Korea, Japan, India, Hong Kong, and Taiwan, the latter considered by the PRC to be a separated but not independent province of China.

According to its official 1982 census, the PRC had a population of 1,008,175,288 (an unofficial 1984 estimate was 1,031,600,000), making China the world's most populous country as well as its only billion-person country, with 22 percent of the world's people.* In its official 1953 census, China's population was counted at 582,603,417, yielding a compounded annual intercensal growth rate of 1.9 percent. Recognizing that it could not achieve increasing standards of living levels for its people while population growth continues even at that rate, China instituted a strict program of family planning, with a goal of one child per family. Even if that were successful, China's population would still increase for the next twenty years because of the large number of women of child-bearing age and the relatively low death rate.

Almost all the people live in the fertile eastern third of the country. China has a number of large cities, topped by Shanghai with an estimated 12 million in 1984. The capital, Beijing (formerly known as Peking or Peiping), has 9.2 million, Tianjin (Tientsin) 7.77 million; other major cities include Harbin, Xian, Wuhan, Hankow, Canton, Changchun, Shenyang, and Nanking.

Regardless of the number and size of these cities, China was one of the least urban countries in the world (between 13 and 21 percent, depending on source consulted; the United States was 74 percent urban). In its more fertile areas, population per square mile was among the highest in the world. By contrast, China's western half consists of arid plateaus and mountains whose sparse population includes several minority groups, most of them nomadic.

Religion did not hold a high place in contemporary Chinese social practice. Ancestor worship was formerly the basis of Chinese religious thought. The ancient philosophy of Confucius still influenced Chinese attitudes. (Chinese Communist discourse equated Confucian belief to "feudalism.") Buddhism, Taoism, and Christianity also claimed a number of members, and some western tribes were Moslem. Communist dogma required atheism, but the PRC was less vigorous than the Soviet Union in opposing organized religious practice.

Shortly after World War II China came under Communist rule. The Chinese Communist Party, founded in 1921, struggled for 28 years under the leadership of Mao Tse-tung against the Manchu dynasty and later the Kuomintang (or Nationalist) forces. The Nationalist forces were headed, during World War II and for years thereafter, by Chiang Kai-shek, a close ally of the United States in its war against Japan.

With Soviet support, Mao's troops finally achieved victory in 1949. Nationalist forces and supporters retreated to Taiwan, established there the Republic of China,

---

*Taiwan's 12,456 square miles, its 18 million people, and its independent economy are not included in any totals in this case.

and promised to return as the rightful ruler of all China. On October 1, 1949 the People's Republic of China was formally proclaimed by Mao Tse-tung from the rostrum of the Gate of Heavenly Peace in Peking, with the ringing declaration that "The Chinese people have stood up." The socialist management of China had begun.

BRIEF HISTORICAL SKETCH OF CHINA

China is regarded as having the world's oldest continuous civilization, with a recorded history of nearly 4,000 years. China was ruled by imperial dynasties from about 1500 B.C. until the early 20th century. China had achieved an advanced civilization by 1200 B.C. Philosophers Confucius, Lao-tse, and Mencius adorned the Chou dynasty which ruled from 1122 to 249 B.C. Warring factions divided the country until Emperor Ch'in Shih Huang Ti reunited the country in 246 B.C. During his reign the Great Wall was begun to hold out the Tartar tribes who had been pushed to the north by the Chinese. Overland traders created contact between China and Europe, and trade flowed between China and Rome during the prosperous Han dynasty, 206 B.C. to 220 A.D. During this long ancient period the territory under the rule of successive dynasties shifted in location and size. Despite occasional setbacks, the area ruled expanded greatly to encompass much of present-day China.

During its early history, China contributed much to world technology. Paper was invented in China about 105 A.D. The Chinese also originated printing with blocks and movable type, and invented gunpowder, the crossbow, suspension bridge, canal lock, watertight compartments for ships, and the magnetized needle that became the compass; all later facilitated the Renaissance of Europe. The T'ang dynasty (618 to 809 A.D.) ruled over the golden age of China, with outstanding painting, sculpture and poetry. At that time Canton was opened as a trading port, and numerous foreign business people were attracted to that city.

Because of its advanced civilization, China became known as "The Middle Kingdom" (the center of the world). All the world, it was said, eventually came to China to pay obeisance to the Emperor. The emperor knew only an empire and subjects, never any equals. Westerners, and outsiders in general, were regarded as barbarians, an attitude that persisted into recent times. A visitor to the court of Kublai Khan in the year 1275 was Marco Polo. Genghis and Kublai Khan conquered China and the latter set up the Mongol or Yuan dynasty (1280–1368). The Mongols were overthrown by the native Chinese Ming dynasty (now known mainly for their prized ceramics), who were in turn replaced by the Manchus from the North in 1644. Thus the Chinese were ruled for considerable periods by the foreign Mongol (or Yuan) and Manchu (or Ch'ing) dynasties.

China came under European influence in the 1500s, during the Ming dynasty, with the explorations of the Portugese (who founded their trading city of Macao), the Dutch, and the British. These traders saw China, just as it has been seen ever since, as a large market for their goods and a source of goods for sale in the rest of the world. In the late 1700s, further pushes toward trade with China were made. Traders developed a substantial market in China for opium. The Manchus, seeing its destructive effects, prohibited its importation but smuggling and other means were used, leading to the Chinese "opium den," a literary symbol of the depravity of the times.

The Chinese attempted to restrict foreign entry and operations but were forced by the British during the Anglo-Chinese (or Opium) War of 1839–42 to sign the first of what the Chinese call the "unequal treaties." These unilaterally imposed pacts opened five treaty ports, required the Chinese to repay the British for a large supply of opium burned by a Manchu official who sought to free the Chinese from its addiction, and to cede the island of Hong Kong. France, Russia, and the United States demanded privileges similar to Britain's. At this time large parts of Shanghai were taken as an enclave of "international concessions" by the European countries, who claimed and achieved extraterritorial rights. Shanghai's industrialization and modern development date from that period.

In the Treaties of Tientsin in 1858, signed during a second foreign war (1856–1860), China yielded more concessions, exempted nationals of these countries from Chinese law, guaranteed safe traveling and trading in the interior of China, permitted foreign diplomats to live in Peking, legalized buying and selling of opium, and permitted free entry of missionaries. The Russians took all Chinese territory north of the Amur River and adjacent lands to the east, including the site of Vladivostok. The Chinese still lay claim to all lands surrendered at that time, leading to Soviet nervousness and defensive postures along the current border. The British also supported the Manchu emperor in the Taiping peasant rebellion against the emperor; an American and later a British officer ("Chinese" Gordon) led troops suppressing the revolt.

The obvious weakness of the Manchu empire, militarily and otherwise, permitted foreigners to enforce their demands and operations on China. Interferences with Chinese sovereignty were numerous. On occasion the Chinese, with or without the action of the Emperor, sought to resist these humiliations but proved powerless to prevent them. Nevertheless, this period of Chinese history understandably left a deep resentment in the Chinese psyche, a feeling that has significantly affected all dealings with the European countries, the United States, and Japan ever since, and crops up in current concerns over Hong Kong, Macao, and Taiwan. But during this 19th-century concessions, period western powers did build a railroad network, a telegraph system, and a mining industry, giving China the basics for industrialization and modernization.

In 1899, the United States supported the "Open Door Policy" under which all nations would have equal access to trade with China, and secured its acceptance by other nations. The Sino-Japanese war of 1894–95 was followed by more Chinese concessions as European powers took advantage of Chinese weakness. The Russians moved into Manchuria. The antiforeigner Boxer Rebellion of 1900, initiated by a secret Chinese patriotic society, was suppressed by joint European action. The imperial form of government was obviously inadequate to the times.

One force for change, not deeply rooted but attractive to some educated Chinese, was democracy. A leader arose in the person of Dr. Sun Yat-sen, who led a nationwide rebellion of the Kuomintang (or Nationalist) Party. Dr. Sun was declared president of the Provisional Chinese Republic in 1911, and the last Manchu emperor was forced to abdicate the following year. But the Chinese masses knew little of democracy and the movement floundered. Internal strife continued and Dr. Sun's death in 1925 brought a combined Kuomintang-Communist government, led by the Kuomintang's Chiang Kai-shek who soon broke with the Communists and tried to suppress them. (The movie "Sand Pebbles," the story of a U.S. Navy patrol craft on the Yangtze, illustrates well the tenor of the times from the American point of view.) However, the Chinese Communists managed to maintain their existence and continued building their party and military force, fighting off persistent Nationalist army attacks.

Though resisted by China and the Nationalist government, Japan invaded Manchuria in 1931 and soon seized China's northern provinces. Chiang was forced to set up a new capital far to the west in Chungking, which he occupied throughout World War II. The United States and British supported Chiang throughout World War II, first by rail and later by trucks over the famed "Burma Road." In 1945, Japan surrendered and was forced out of the Chinese mainland.

The Early PRC (Socialist) Era

Owing to loyalties to war-time ally Chiang Kai-shek as well as post-World War II resistance to Communist expansion, much of the Western world cut off relationships with the newly founded People's Republic of China. The United States adopted a "containment" policy against the likelihood of a worldwide spread of communism during the 1950s Cold War period. From 1950 to 1960, China was thus dependent on Soviet aid to launch its "socialist reconstruction." That program called for massive infusion of capital and technology, following the pattern the Soviets had installed in the USSR 30 years earlier. The Leninist-Stalinist model was oriented toward heavy industry, and hence was capital intensive and urban oriented, deemphasizing agriculture and the rural areas.

After a surprise attack by North Korea in June 1950, the United Nations came to the support of South Korea. China intervened late in 1950 on the side of fellow-socialist North Korea, battling U.N. forces (of which the bulk were U.S. troops). A stalemated settlement in 1953 left a residue of bad feelings between the PRC and the United States.

Despite China's 30-year friendship treaty and the USSR's aid to the PRC in industrialization, China felt itself an equal with and not a satellite of the USSR. Arguing that post-Stalinist USSR had "gone revisionist," Mao claimed sole rights to the Marxist-Leninist mantle of ideological purity. By 1958 the friendship treaty was abrogated. The Soviets removed their technicians and equipment, leaving China to progress as best it could. Though left in some economic and social disarray, the Chinese were undaunted and were determined to continue building a modern nation. But owing to its ideological stance, Maoist China continued to urge "people's wars" in underdeveloped countries around the world.

Although the PRC's development strategy attained impressive growth rates during the 1950s, its social and political costs sparked a debate at top levels of the Chinese Communist Party and the government. Mao's first priority was ideological purity and strict avoidance of "the capitalist road." A leading alternate faction wanted more pragmatism to speed economic betterment of the country. But the Maoists asked whether the basic goals of the revolution (egalitarian society, mass participation, and the "new communist man") should be discarded or relegated to a poor second place in favor of economic growth. This schism of belief became fixed. After Mao's death it was the basis of the "second revolution" discussed later in this case. Both sides, however, agreed on China's need to modernize and its goal of overtaking and eventually passing the world's industrial leaders. However, rooting out the bourgeois (independent and capitalist) tendencies of the Chinese people, and settling internal party struggles resulted in numerous fatalities during the decades following establishment of the PRC.

The first decade of socialist operation of the economy (the 1950s) taught the Chinese that the Leninist-Soviet model, concentrating on heavy industry and an urban economy, did not fit China. China's agriculture was perceived to be the base of the economy, requiring adequate attention and investment by the central planners. But industry was still to be "the leading factor."

Despite Mao's stature, two of his initiatives engendered opposition and weakened his political position. One was the "Great Leap Forward" program begun in 1958, combining the formation of communes in the rural areas with "backyard industry." Though reversed within three years, the results were disastrous, setting back China's industrial progress and bringing social upsets not overcome by the mid-1980s.

The second, the Cultural Revolution, was initiated in 1966. It was partly an attempt by Mao and his collaborators to regain lost political power and partly (referring to the basic schism above) Mao's final attempt to implant permanently his views of human nature and of proper social and economic organization into the Chinese culture. In his view, all too many people and even his corevolutionist Marxist comrades were giving way to pragmatism rather than socialist principle, embracing "the capitalist road" of private gain and private property. Mao sought a "permanent revolution" to weed out these tendencies continuously. Mao and his co-believers formed and unleashed on the country the teenaged Red Guards, who denounced hundreds of political and party officials in meetings and on wall posters. Schools and universities were closed and the Red Guards spread throughout China; no area was exempt. Mao's "learn from the peasants" campaign drove intellectuals, professionals, and bureaucrats from their posts to live in communes throughout China.

The Cultural Revolution, though eminently sensible to Mao and to his Red Guards who lived by Mao's "little red book" inflicted heavy damage. It engendered a backlash of anger and ill will toward Mao and his faction that was expressed openly and vehemently once Mao had fallen. (Deng Xiaoping shortly took advantage of this backlash.)

Ironically this antilearning, antitechnology movement was proposed in 1964, the same year that China exploded its first nuclear (fission) bomb at Lop Nor; the fusion bomb followed in 1967. An orbiting satellite was launched by Chinese engineers in 1970. And somehow the Chinese economy continued to function during the Cultural Revolution, even if at impaired efficiency. During the Cultural Revolution, "red" was preferred to "expert" in managers of factories and economic units. Such managers largely remained after the Cultural Revolution, a legacy yielding persistent industrial inefficiency.

In 1971, the People's Republic of China was admitted to the United Nations. The U.N. had voted to expel Nationalist China (Taiwan or Formosa) from the "China" position dating from the U.N.'s founding and to put the PRC in its place. In February 1972 President Nixon visited Peking (now Beijing), met with Mao and Chou En-lai, and the U.S.-Chinese rapprochement began. The United States continued its economic and military support of the nationalist government of Taiwan. But in deference to the PRC, a representative of nondiplomatic status was substituted for its former ambassador.

A revised national constitution was adopted by the Fourth National People's Congress on January 17, 1975 replacing the one promulgated in 1954. The new constitution defined the PRC in strict Marxist terms as a "socialist state of the dictatorship of the proletariat"; the previous constitution had sanctioned a multiclass and multiparty framework. The new constitution also solidified the Communist Party's Leadership role over the state's organizations, immensely strengthening the Party's power over the state.

The year 1976 brought the PRC to its greatest historical divide to date. Chou En-lai, Mao's long-time colleague and top government official, died early in the year. Mao himself succumbed on September 7. A power struggle for succession followed. The radical leftist "Gang of Four," Mao's aids in his "Cultural Revolution" (one was Mao's widow, Chiang Ching), failed in a power bid. With their ousting and trials, the rule of Deng Xiaoping and his associates swung the pendulum away from strict Marxist-Maoist ideology and toward political and economic pragmatism. Increasingly in the 1980s the swing was in the direction of "the capitalist road." Mao's attempted ideological solidification became a surprisingly quick casualty after his death.

The rise of Deng Xiaoping led to significant changes in the PRC's domestic, political, economic, and foreign affairs. Deng's group was dedicated to national economic and technological advancement. Their changes were sufficiently great to be labeled a "second revolution." Acceptance of the changes revealed that economic accomplishment was more attractive than socialist ideological purity. Even the top official newspaper, *The People's Daily*, editorialized that the views of Marx and Lenin were outmoded and would no longer aid in solving China's problems.

The "Second Revolution"

In October 1978 Chinese Communist Party Chairman Hua Guofeng announced the PRC's "open door" policy and outlined the 10-year plan (1976–1985) that the Chinese called "The Four Modernizations." The four areas targeted for modernization were agriculture, industry, defense (especially military weaponry), and science and technology. The entire program was to be accomplished by the year 2000.

According to China-watchers, the new measures were "more far-reaching than anything yet attempted in the Communist world." The Four Modernizations attempted to merge Communism with market forces, including policies to free centrally set industrial prices, slashing subsidies, and allowing inefficient enterprises to fail, giving factory production managers more freedom and attracting foreign investment.

By any standard the Four Modernizations plan was ambitious. It called for a 10 percent average annual growth in industrial output. Agricultural output was to rise at four or five percent per year through 1985. The Plan's industrial development component set the goal of completing 120 key projects, including 10 new steel plants, nine nonferrous metal complexes, 10 new oil and gas developments, eight coal mines, 30 electric power generating facilities, as well as development of five harbors and six railway extensions.

Closely related to the growth priority were new attitudes toward science and technology, and toward integrating China into the international economy. Chairman Hua stated that:

> We should learn from foreign countries now, but should we [not also] do so when we overcome our backwardness and become advanced? Yes, because even then other countries will still have points worth learning, and we should still learn from them. What is wrong with that? After 10,000 years, we must still learn from others.

The drastic attitudinal reversals of 1978 and later gave China a more outward-looking world view. Major post-Mao diplomatic achievements included a peace and friendship treaty with Japan and normalization of relations (i.e. exchange of ambassadors) with the United States, followed by Vice Premier Deng Xiaoping's visits to those countries. The 1978 PRC-Japan treaty officially smoothed the aftermath of Japan's pre-World War II invasion and occupation of large parts of north China. Similarly, the foundation for the January 1979 full normalization of United States-China relations was laid during President Nixon's visit to China in February 1972.

These diplomatic developments led to expanded economic and trade relations between China and Japan, the United States, and the countries of western Europe. Foreign trade missions to China and Chinese scientific and commercial delegations visiting abroad increased sharply. Commercial negotiations, agreements, and contacts reached an unprecedented pace. Though some hitches occurred, China became increasingly flexible in its trading practices. Ideological opposition to the use of foreign borrowing and credit declined, and the PRC chose to enter joint ventures, some with private foreign firms.

The PRC shortly found the Four Modernizations program overly ambitious and scaled it down. But the directional shift was permanent. The drastic contrast to Mao's methods and goals became apparent only as the new policies created changes in Chinese society and economy.

China's policies of "opening doors to the West" stemmed from PRC leaders' recognition that modernization "by the year 2000" could not succeed (certainly not within an acceptable time) without major involvement of foreign businesses, science, and technology. For geopolitical reasons and because of the USSR's backwardness, China avoided Soviet involvement, looking only to the West, especially to the United States, for assistance. Given China's traditional aversion to involvement with foreigners as well as the risks and negatives of consorting with Western capitalism, China would have preferred to modernize by its own efforts. But that course was impractical and unrealistic. The opening of China and acceptance of close business and trade links with the West indicated the importance China's leaders placed on modernization; they were ready to accept the risks of links with the West in order to achieve their goals.

Economic Growth: The PRC's Gross National Product

Considerable turmoil followed the deaths of Chou En-lai (Zhou Enlai) and Mao Tse-tung (Mao Zedong) and the Gang of Four controversy. One spokesman said that at the end of Mao's Cultural Revolution in 1976, "China was adrift." But when Deng succeeded in taking control, China's economic situation stabilized. Exhibit 19.3 sets forth China's Gross National Product (GNP) growth from 1970 to 1982.

Even though approximate, Exhibit 19.3 reveals that the PRC's economy grew substantially under central direction. At compounded annual average rates, from 1970 to 1982 GNP in current dollars grew 14 percent per year, GNP in constant dollars 6.6 percent, and real GNP per capita 5 percent. Per capita real product rose by nearly 80 percent during the 12-year period. Though some of this product went into capital formation, Chinese living standards apparently rose markedly during the period (1976 and 1981 were problem years, showing lower accomplishment). To the business firm, increasing consumer incomes translated into increasing market size.

Production growth apparently accelerated; China in the mid-80s was in the midst of an economic boom. United States CIA estimates show China with a 13 percent real GNP increase in 1984, and an average of 8 percent from 1981 through 1984, well above the U.S. average of 2.7 percent.

The boom set off a consumer spending spree. Chinese consumers bought not only the usual bicycles, radios and watches, but also TV sets and motorbikes. The effect on imports and the trade balance concerned central government authorities.

Capital Investment and Capital Formation

As in most developing countries, particularly those seeking self-sufficiency, capital investment represented China's most difficult problem. Efforts to increase construction and capital formation had limited success. The PRC's capital formation in 1981 totaled 42.8 billion yuan ($25.0 billion), still above the 38.0 billion yuan ($22.2 billion) plan target. In 1982, investment spending rose markedly to 55.6 billion yuan, 22 billion over the target.

EXHIBIT 19.3 **Gross national product of the People's Republic of China 1970–1982, with percent change from previous year (In billions of U.S. dollars, except for per capita)***

	Current dollars Total		Constant (1981) Dollars Total		Per capita	
	Dollars	**% Change**	**Dollars**	**% Change**	**Dollars**	**% Change**
1970	$144.0		$306.8		$362	
. .	. .		. .		. .	
1975	271.0	13.5**	420.8	6.5**	462	5.0**
1976	293.0	8.1	—		—	
1977	338.0	15.3	—		—	
1978	400.0	18.3	—		—	
1979	471.0	17.8	564.2	7.6**	584	6.1**
1980	552.0	17.2	603.5	7.0	616	5.4
1981	622.0	12.7	622.0	3.1	626	1.6
1982	698.0	12.2	658.4	5.9	653	4.3

*Estimation of any country's GNP is notoriously difficult, and international comparisons are especially so because of lack of data, differences of definition, changes in exchange rates, etc. The figures in this exhibit must be taken as rough approximations.

**Average annual compounded rate from previous given year.

Source: Total and Constant Dollar GNP: U.S. Statistical Abstracts, 1982–83 and 1985 editions; data from the International Bank for Reconstruction and Development and the U.S. Central Intelligence Agency. Percentage changes and per capita figures calculated by the writer from constant GNP, the latter assuming a constant population growth rate from 1970 to 1982.

Students of China have cited their tendency to have too many projects underway at one time; the Four Modernizations program illustrated the point. During the Seventh Plan (1986–1990) the policy line was to proceed more slowly and rationally.

Major investment needs were in electric power (exacerbated by rising consumer demand) and the transportation system. With the rail network overused, developing coastal cities turned to water transportation. But that action merely created overuse of port facilities, docks, and warehouses, with concomitant delays and some spoilage. Enormous capital needs thus existed for factory, power, and transportation modernization.

As noted earlier, the 1949–1976 era emphasis was on heavy industry. The Deng reforms shifted toward light industry and agriculture, and increases in consumer goods. By 1983 a balance had been achieved by reducing growth in heavy industry and increasing growth of light industry. During 1979–1981 a total industrial capacity annual growth rate of 14 percent was achieved though heavy industry output fell by 4.7 percent. In 1984 both light and heavy industry achieved growth rates of over 11 percent. Thus the mid-1980s saw rapid progress toward both increased industrial capacity and balanced light and heavy industry.

Foreign Trade

Though all developing countries must import large quantities of equipment and materials, China's sheer size made its import needs proportionately greater. Hence, it was forced to push exporting to earn hard currencies but with due regard for its own needs for those materials. Consumer goods imports were of secondary importance. China required foreign firms to cover their import exchange needs by their exports. Since goods suitable for the U.S. market were limited, China sought diversification into suitable products. The PRC also sought to balance its trade with each trading partner, (country).

In modernizing, China occasionally used the turnkey method, importing complete plants and equipment incorporating desired technology. An example was petroleum exploration and process technology. To conserve foreign exchange China also purchased "bare technology," and only that which could not be produced in China. The first enterprises selected for upgrading included textiles, electronics, telecommunications, food processing, machinery, building materials, chemicals, coal, and electric power.

Much of China's trade was with Japan, which supplied both consumer goods—TVs and radios—and industrial and capital goods. The United States was a relatively small supplier because of its 1949-1972 embargo, as well as United States' textile policy, protecting its textile and clothing producers, with China strongly objecting. European countries were also major suppliers to the PRC.

Total exports of China stood at U.S. $23.3 billion in 1983, $24.6 in 1984. Imports were $19.8 and $23.8 billion for these years, yielding a positive (but declining) overall trade balance.

China's trade balance with the United States had been negative ($2.68 billion in 1980, $.63 in 1982) on U.S. exports to China of $3.75 billion in 1980 and $2.91 billion in 1982. Reversal occurred in 1983; United States exports to China dropped sharply to $2.16 billion, and recovered only to $2.7 billion in 1984. China's shipments to the United States were $2.22 and $3.2 billion, giving China a positive trade balance with the United States. Major U.S. exports were (in descending order of value) wheat, synthetic resins, logs, corn, cotton, fertilizer, yarns and thread of polyester and nylon, polyester fibers, and measuring and controlling instruments. China shipped gasoline, crude petroleum, and a variety of clothing and textile products to the United States.

Financial Condition

In contrast to many developing countries, China maintained good international financial condition, with a relatively small external debt (estimated at U.S. $4.7 billion at the end of 1983 and $6.0 billion a year later) and with total gold and foreign exchange reserves in late 1983 of U.S. $19.8 billion. However, China's foreign exchange reserves ($14.8-$15 billion at the end of 1984) were small in relation to the enormous number and scope of the new projects needed in a country as economically and industrially underdeveloped as China. Thus, the PRC's late 1980s development program had to be based on foreign credits, with resulting increases in external debt. And, as noted above, high consumer import elasticity required controls to prevent ill effects on the PRC's balance of payments and foreign reserves.

In the 1980s, China initiated limited use of foreign bank loans. The PRC held membership in the World Bank and its subsidiaries and the International Monetary Fund, and also received United States Export-Import Bank credits. Thus, its institutional arrangements were proceeding along desired lines.

ECONOMIC CHANGES UNDER THE SECOND REVOLUTION

3M continued its analysis of China by examining economic changes brought about under Deng. In furtherance of the "second revolution" China had established economic modernization and development as its highest priority. This modernization goal was implemented by a number of new and pragmatic policies coupled with increased flexibility of others. The open-door policy encouraged foreign investment as part of the process, with inflow of foreign capital, technology and management skills, and increased Chinese export capabilities.

Problems to be Overcome

A major problem faced China's capability for industrial growth in 1980. As the decade opened, much of the country's physical plant, equipment, and technology predated the PRC's founding in 1949. A light truck plant observed by the writer in 1980 in Shenyang was vintage 1938. And Factory 428 in Datung, built by the Russians in 1954, was still producing one coal-burning locomotive a day with its original technology—the only coal-burners still being produced in the world. The problem encompassed all PRC industries, but was most critical in energy, especially coal and electric power, railways and telecommunications, which were therefore assigned highest priority for investment. The immensity of the modernization task underlay the commitment of China's economic leaders to the use of foreign capital, firms, and technology in modernizing.

A second problem was low quality of output coupled with low worker productivity. Chinese authorities hoped that along with foreign technology would come knowledge of management methods capable of boosting output quality and output per worker.

Another desired change was to continue the shift away from the Soviet-imposed heavy industrial model that had dominated for 30 years, toward more consumption and light industrial production. Planners believed that small investment in light industry would sharply increase consumer goods output, create new employment, and increase exportable output. Such shifts could also release agricultural acreage for inputs to light industries, with their export earnings used to import grain. The shift away from heavy industry would also lessen the strain on China's limited energy resources. (But note a contradiction: basic lack of capacity still existed in the heavy industries.)

Still another problem was that of distribution. Soviet socialist dogma held distribution to be unproductive. The Cultural Revolution brought havoc to that industry because it was too private for Mao's tastes. In 1979, that private sector had nearly disappeared. In a population of one billion, only some 150,000 people were engaged in private trade.

In the 1980s, Deng's shifts to enterprise autonomy and private ownership brought problems of coordination of the economy, perhaps only transitional but nevertheless difficult. The absence of a free price system and of developed markets in products made good production decisions difficult. In most cases prices continued to be controlled by the central planners rather than reflecting true economic forces of supply and demand. Duplication of private and government facilities also appeared, since planners ignored the existence of private operations.

Methods and Policies

The early reforms in 1979 and 1980 reversed the policy of blind pursuit of production without regard for real costs, overhead, market demand, or national needs, and instituted experiments in economic and industrial management. Pay was to be linked more directly to output levels, and bonus systems were introduced. Experiments were run with a central tax policy to encourage economic efficiency, and the old policy of profit remittances to factory staffs was dropped. These experiments were deemed sufficiently promising that the program was introduced nationwide in June 1983, and the policies were formalized in law and regulations.

The major policy changes and innovations resulting from these experiments included:

- Reform of industrial management.
- Dropping of state budget allocations to enterprises in favor of bank loans.
- Substitution of taxes for direct profit remittances to the state.
- Use of bonus incentives in industrial establishments, but also permitting discharge of managers and employees for incompetence and malingering.
- Permitting private firms and private enterprise to exist in the economy.
- Reintroduction of free markets in the cities.
- Liberalization of the distribution system.
- Closing of some inefficient factories.
- Removing Communist Party unit secretaries for incompetence.

In addition, the following techniques and organizational forms new to China were permitted to encourage foreign investment, trade, and fast growth areas with special privileges: joint ventures, compensation trade arrangements, barter, and special economic zones.

A leading feature of the Deng-era industrial output was the shift to the enterprise profit system. Instead of turning all earnings over to the central government, managers simply began paying "taxes," keeping the excess for reinvestment and improvements. The list of price-controlled commodities was slashed. Price and consumer motivations directed more of the output, with consequent improvements in economic efficiency.

A major socio-economic reform intended to enliven the economy, especially the rural areas, was the discontinuance of Mao's commune system. Moves away from the commune system had started shortly after the failure of the Great Leap Forward. In September 1982, the Twelfth Congress of the Chinese Communist Party officially approved the dismantling of the communes and the return to the pre-Mao township and village structure. By October 1983, nearly 20 percent of China's communes had been replaced by the township system. Dismantling was followed by what was called the "household responsibility system," a shift in contrast to central government responsibility. In that system, land was contracted from the government to individual operators, who paid a fixed amount of their output to the local authorities and agreed to meet government procurement targets for grain, cotton, or other key commodities. The land contracts ran from five to 15 years, with farm operators obtaining the right to sell privately their excess output, and even to transfer the land to another family.

Commune dismantling, the shift to "household responsibility" and the contract system soon affected agricultural output. Alert farm producers shifted from the basic products emphasized by the central planners to varied outputs appealing to consumer tastes. Yet a grain surplus was produced in 1984, exceeding 1983's 387 million tons by a comfortable margin, and cotton and oilseeds output was also higher. One estimate was that some 75 percent of agricultural labor in China had been excess, given reasonable use of available technology.

Rural fairs were resurrected, and supply and marketing cooperatives were formed, to increase the supply and availability of consumer goods in rural areas. These efforts expanded peasants' individual decision-making power, giving them a freer hand in marketing over-quota production and in purchasing previously unavailable consumer goods.

Another post-1979 reform was the introduction of private participation in city markets. By the end of 1982, almost 1.5 million people or about 1.3 percent of the urban work force was engaged in private activities, running their own businesses, or working for private employers. By the third quarter of 1983, the urban private sector numbered two million workers. About one-half of the private growth was, as might be expected, in retail sales, and about 15 to 20 percent each in restaurants and foodservice, and repair services. Manufacturing and processing accounted for only a small portion of privately owned firms. And in most industries the private portion was small, overshadowed by the large government commercial systems.

Of importance to 3M, distribution problems, especially of the wholesale and industrial supplier variety, remained to be solved. Producers were accustomed only to producing for shipment to government warehouses rather than actively selling their products, or directly filling orders from or needs of other enterprises. And transportation inadequacies compounded the problem.

Special Economic Zones

In 1979, the PRC designated four Special Economic Zones (SEZs), each containing a central city. In 1984, fourteen coastal city Economic Development Zones

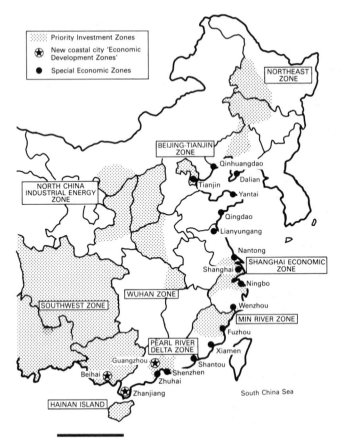

EXHIBIT 19.4 **Economic development zones**

(EDZ) were added (see Exhibit 19.4). These special zones/cities were given more freedom and autonomy to attract foreign investment and to speed modernization via Western capital, technology, and business knowhow. The SEZs were permitted to offer potent incentives to outside investment, including a lower income tax of 15 percent and provisions for tax holidays of from one to five years, simplified entry and exit procedures, and certain duty-free imports. Native Chinese free enterprises were given more latitude than elsewhere in China. Firms were given the right to hire and fire. Early results in growth and development were startling. Most of the initial outside investment came from overseas Chinese, especially from Hong Kong, but other foreign inquiries were being received.

These SEZs and EDZs broadened immensely the favorable location options for foreign firms entering or planning to enter the PRC. The cities stretched from Dalian in the north to Shanghai and Guangzhou and on to Zhanjiang in the southwest. Tentative plans called for incorporating Hong Kong into the SEZ system in 1997 when it was, by treaty, to be returned by Britain to PRC jurisdiction. Starting in 1984 minimal restrictions applied to traffic between Hong Kong and the nearby SEZs.

Development of the Legal System

Historically, China has had a scanty legal system, with interpersonal differences often settled by mediation with passersby. A modern economy obviously required more. This lengthy legislative process got underway in 1979.

An important development was the 1983 implementation of the 1979 joint-venture law. The implementing regulations codified Chinese contracting practices and policies, a significant encouragement of foreign investment in China. No law with respect to wholly-owned foreign subsidiaries was available, however, before 3M's approach.

Between 1980 and 1985, China developed legislation supporting its open-door policy for trade and commerce with the West. This legislation covered the following areas: a) company registration, b) labor management, c) special economic zones, d) foreign enterprise taxation, e) exchange controls, f) offshore petroleum, g) marine environment protection, h) trademarks, and i) a patent law. The legislation was then supplemented by detailed regulations in specific areas.

Negotiations toward a China-United States Investment Treaty were held during 1983 and 1984. The completed treaty would cover investment, compensation in event of expropriation, dispute settlement, and transfers of capital and earnings (i.e. exchange, convertibility, and repatriation).

Foreign Investment in the PRC in the 1980s

Deng's reforms and initiatives stimulated foreign investment in China. From 1979 to 1983 the foreign component of approved investment in China (including joint ventures, processing and co-production) amounted to more than $1 billion, with ten percent in joint ventures. The overall total of United States investment in China was unknown but a large number of U.S. firms were known to have invested or signed agreements. U.S. companies operating in China in 1985 included IBM, Alcoa, Coca Cola, McDonnell Douglas, Pepsico, Bethlehem Steel, Union Carbide, and Texaco. Japanese companies included Hitachi, Mitsubishi, Nippon, Sumitomo and Toyo Engineering. Western European companies included British National Coal Board, Pilkington, and Davy Powergas from the United Kingdom, as well as Volkswagon, Belgian Bell, and Peugeot.

Foreign investment projects underway in 1984 included railway building and port modernization with Japan, nuclear power projects in planning or underway with Great Britain, France, and Germany; coal and offshore oil exploration with a number of countries, and hydropower with the United States. Additional coal and petroleum projects were under consideration.

PROBLEMS AND PROSPECTS FOR FOREIGN INVESTMENT IN CHINA

Generally, foreign companies were permitted to do business with China through joint ventures or sales officers or representatives. As noted above, Chinese law was amended to permit foreign companies to set up limited liability companies (i.e.

corporations) under joint ownership with Chinese enterprises. These joint ventures had to be authorized by the Foreign Investment Control Commission. The China International Trust Investment Company was set up in 1983 to coordinate use of foreign investment and technology. A foreign partner was permitted to hold not less than 25 percent of the equity ownership but could hold more. The foreign technology or equipment was required to be "genuinely advanced and appropriate to China's needs."

The joint venture law required that foreign equipment and technology be provided with minimal drawing on China's limited supply of foreign currencies. The PRC favored what it called "consignment" arrangements: the foreign company supplied raw materials or capital equipment and was paid in goods manufactured from those materials or with that equipment (a form of countertrade).

Despite these favorable developments, several uncertainties remained. First was the political climate. Although appearing to be opening up, China did not abandon its tradition of self-reliance. Deng's reforms were resented by some powerful Chinese, including Communist Party secretaries and the army, where senior generals were retired so as to change the army's outlook and replaced by officers more amenable to Deng's policies. Given the deeply entrenched personal and political interests and the feudal tradition, China-watchers were only cautiously optimistic about the possibility of real and enduring change. A further risk lay in Deng's advanced age; he was born in 1904. *The Financial Times* of October 29, 1984 reported that since 1978 Deng had had to fight every inch of the way to introduce reform. The sheer size and diversity of the country was also an impediment. People in tradition-bound Yunnan in the southwest resented change imposed from Peking far to the northeast. Party secretaries felt threatened by reforms that removed their power. The army feared losing its grip over the country. Followers of Mao saw no reason that the Long March should give way to greedy foreigners who wanted only to enrich themselves.

Deng's chief lieutenants, Prime Minister Zhao Ziyang and Party Secretary Hu Yaobang, were nowhere near his equal in political stature. News stories during 1985 pointed out that Deng was rapidly putting younger men into both Chinese Communist Party and government posts, and was grooming successors to both Hu and Zhao. But the residual strength of ideological Marxism-Maoism was difficult to judge. Party functionaries who subscribed to Mao's ideas still held key government jobs throughout China; many of them had a constitutional dislike for Deng's "capitalist road" strategy. Thus another wrenching realignment could not be ruled out. However, observers in mid-1980 believed the likelihood of realignment would decrease the longer Deng remained in power and the more his policies paid off in a better way of life and standard of living for the people, as seemed to be occurring.

A second uncertainty was the multilayered bureaucracy, which slowed progress and raised business costs. Duplication of responsibilities at the state, province, and city levels left foreign firms confused as to which level, organization, or ministry, to contract. Low-level functionaries avoided risk by not making decisions, letting matters stagnate or, under pressure, passing the matter to the level above without recommendation. High officials avoided decisions for self-protection and because they were unfamiliar with the details of local situations. As Finance Minister Zhang Jingfu complained, "Where there should be centralization there isn't, and where there should be decentralization, it's missing." The central government sought to overcome the problem by decentralizing decisions to the provinces, and allowing state enterprises more management independence and greater control over funds. But the problem remained.

Finally, the arbitrary and noneconomic price system arising in central planning remained a major problem. Prices in China reflected neither costs of production, relative scarcities, nor the strength of demand. Raw materials tended to be undervalued, finished products overvalued. Rather than guiding producer and consumer decisions and providing economic coordination, the arbitrarily set prices impeded and misled. Reformers in Deng's administration expected to address the pricing problem systematically during 1985. But the majority of the PRC's economy would still be centrally planned, with a periphery of free market prices. Problems related to price were expected to continue.

Given uncertainties on the one hand and opportunities for entry into the potentially vast Chinese market on the other, the current situation was aptly summed up by one foreign contractor: "Don't imagine that China is going to be a bonanza. It's a demanding market, and it's only worth going into if your technology is strong and you are prepared for the long haul."

3M'S EFFORTS TO ENTER THE CHINA MARKET

The story of 3M's entry into China began in 1972, when President Nixon began normalizing relations with the country, visiting China in person and lifting the long-standing U.S. embargo on trade. Full diplomatic relations, with exchange of ambassadors, were not effected until 1979. It was at the time of the 1972 opening, ("Not wide open, just a crack," according to Mr. Marshall) that 3M decided to take a look. China was then an unknown to 3M as well as to most Americans. But 3M was an experienced world producer and marketer, doing about a third of its business abroad, including some at the spring and fall Canton Trade Fairs. Officials at the top held the firm conviction that 3M should have manufacturing facilities in China as soon as conditions permitted.

The times were not auspicious for such initiatives. Mao's Cultural Revolution (1966 to 1976) though abating after 1969 was still a threat. Always somewhat xenophobic, China did not welcome foreign intrusion even after the Nixon visit, preferring foreign trade through bilateral agreements with selected foreign governments, notably the USSR and India. China then exported nontechnological commodities—metals and minerals, feathers, teacups and linens—and bought limited amounts of commodities such as fertilizers. Trade was unsophisticated and handled substantially through the biennial Trade Fairs.

Believing that China was entering a new era, in 1976, 3M decided that its China office should be shifted from Zug to the main Maplewood headquarters. The shift was based on the following reasoning:

- 3M's business opportunities in China were worth increased attention and development at that time.

- 3M's moves and proposals would be more credible to the Chinese if initiated from headquarters rather than from a remote branch.
- Entry would require a coordinated effort potentially involving all 3M divisions and subsidiaries that would be best achieved through the firm's headquarters.
- Access to senior management and corporate resources could be more readily provided in Maplewood.
- Potentially valuable in-house expertise could be developed by enlarging contacts in China to include all personnel with any involvement.

In practical terms, the "China function" was shifted from Zug to Maplewood by transferring John Marshall, who handled that responsibility for 3M East. Mr. Marshall was well acquainted with the firm's dealings with the centrally planned economies of the USSR, Eastern Europe, and China.

3M had established a Hong Kong office, 3M Far East Limited, in the early 1960s. Its main function was to serve the Hong Kong market. A position was established in 3M Far East Limited about 1975 to service Hong Kong customers who were reselling 3M products to China. This position subsequently developed into the China Trade Division, which remained a division of 3M Far East Limited in Hong Kong.

Mr. Marshall and other 3M officials at headquarters observed Deng's major policy changes in 1976 and later and pondered how best to organize for business in China. Would an agent or a representative office, or direct 3M presence work best? This question was answered from 3M's experience as well as its assessment of China at that time: "If we are serious, we must build our own expertise and contacts. Our understanding is that the Chinese like direct dealing with the head office rather than agents or sales representatives; it is a matter of face. Also, outsiders can't tell the firm's story and sell its products with the same conviction and dedication." But a successor to Mao had not yet appeared; the time did not seem ripe. 3M continued its sales efforts and by the late 1970s had a modest selling and export business in China.

In 1980, 3M's top international executive attended a conference of top business executives that was addressed by an American expert on China. By this time Deng and his group were more firmly in power. This speaker described the Four Modernizations economic plan, and closed with this advice, "Consider getting into China now, even if you are flying blind. You can help shape the future, get palatable solutions for entry problems before they are set by the Chinese. Also you will have status as a founder instead of a latecomer or follower; this status is important to the Chinese."

It was at this point that Mr. Marshall was assigned the task set forth at the beginning of this case, including the requirements of full ownership of a Chinese subsidiary, production for the local market rather than exporting, and low beginning investment.

Knowing the historic Chinese reluctance to admit foreign firms as well as the socialist rejection of private enterprise, Mr. Marshall had his doubts that full ownership of a Chinese subsidiary was possible. But he knew that if he expressed his doubt, he would be told, "How will we know until we try?"

On Mr. Marshall's asking where the facility ought to be located, he was told: "You decide."

From the beginning, 3M's efforts and negotiations to "get into China" were low-keyed and informal. There were no consultants, no major investigations, no company conferences, no presentations to and votes by the board of directors—just a key executive's convictions and general instructions to Mr. Marshall. And so Mr. Marshall began his five-year task. He made or obtained the necessary decisions as he went along, after discussions with many people, conferences with 3M international executives, a lot of reading, and as Mr. Marshall says, "talks with people in airports, on planes, and in a lot of other places!" In the process Marshall became convinced that the decision to get into China was correct, and he began to concentrate on the manufacturing option, and choice of products and location.

Mr. Marshall followed the injunction to bring the Chinese what they wanted. Mr. Marshall did no formal product investigations but decided by reading and discussion at 3M, in China, and elsewhere. His investigations led Marshall to electrical and telecommunications products as the top choices, primarily because:

- Managers of this 3M product group had international orientation since its products were already distributed globally.
- Manufacturing facilities for these products already existed elsewhere in the Far East and their experience could provide guidance.
- Small front-end investment would be required.
- Depth of this product line presented opportunities for future product introductions in China; the line was good for startup and for scale up.
- These products would match two of China's pressing needs—electrical generation and distribution, and telecommunications products.*
- These products could be designed for China's needs rather than for export.

Making the products in China would require few workers. However, 3M was capital and manufacturing intensive, not labor intensive. 3M was not seeking entry into China for cheap labor, but rather to serve the Chinese market.

To select a plant location, Mr. Marshall again did no formal study. But his trips to China, reading, discussion, and observation convinced him that Shanghai was best, for the following reasons:

- Shanghai was China's most industrialized area, producing about one-sixth of its GNP. Guangzhou (Canton), a high second choice, was close to Hong Kong but had by contrast a small industrial area.
- Shanghai city officials were familiar with Western corporations.
- Shanghai had strong historical links with the outside world.

---

*In 1981 China had, per thousand people, 4 telephone sets, 5 TV receivers, and 60 radio receivers. (Comparable figures for the United States were 789, 631, and 2110.) Japan and Germany had been leaders in serving these Chinese markets.

- Shanghai was open to new ideas and business ways, setting the pace for other cities in China.
- Shanghai was the most Westernized Chinese city in social environment and in its business and economic infrastructure.
- Shanghai had good railway connections to all parts of China, a well-equipped port, and good internal and foreign communications.

Shanghai was also one of the 14 coastal port city Economic Development Zones mentioned earlier. The new 3M firm in China might qualify for the EDZ's special privileges.

Negotiations with Chinese Officials

Based on these decisions, in 1980 Mr. Marshall prepared a proposal setting forth 3M's ideas, including 100 percent ownership and production for sale in China only.

After arranging the necessary entry visa, which was complex in itself, Mr. Marshall took the proposal to China and opened negotiations. This was the first trip of 50. Though he initially doubted the possibility of full-ownership, he had confidence arising from 3M's entry and achievements in many other countries.

Mr. Marshall started, as directed, with the Ministry of Foreign Economics and Trade in Beijing.* Having located the proper officials, Mr. Marshall presented his proposal, with explanation and discussion. The Economic and Trade Ministry accepted the proposal for study and consideration. To his surprise the Ministry did not summarily reject 3M's proposal for 100 percent ownership. Rather, officials were interested and open to the idea. However, they lacked rules and experience to deal with the ownership status.

Mr. Marshall left the proposal with the Ministry. But he soon began to learn the inevitable lesson: one must push to get anything done in the PRC. Yet one must always be polite and diplomatic. With experience Mr. Marshall developed the following technique. After a meeting he would summarize the discussion and say, "Here's what we have agreed. Please discuss it with your people. I'll be back in three months for your decision." This technique set a time schedule, one that would mildly embarrass the Chinese officials if they failed to meet it. Mr. Marshall would return as promised and pick up where he had left off. Between visits he conferred with his superiors and other 3M departments concerning product and market possibilities in China, and of course the tactics of negotiation.

After the Ministry had taken his proposal, Mr. Marshall made several trips to China without achievement. But after some urging, the Economics and Trade Ministry passed the proposal up the government hierarchy. It finally reached the State Council level.

---

*In the government of the People's Republic of China, the top agency is the State Council. Just below is the State Planning Council, and under it the State Economic Committee. Below that comes the Ministry of Foreign Economic Relations and Trade.

Early negotiations dealt in hypotheticals: this is the kind of organization and structure we could put in place. If you permitted us to do this, we would do that, and it would have the following outcomes and advantages. Hypothetical discussion had its disadvantages; Mr. Marshall could not be definite with the Chinese officials or with 3M's departments. He pointed out to the Chinese that 100 percent ownership would relieve them by assigning 3M full responsibility and risk for success. 3M was prepared to accept this risk, which they judged to be small, based on their experience in similar situations. 3M's goal was to grow in China, with China. Mr. Marshall also pointed out that 3M's full-ownership firm would be an initial example, permitting the PRC to formulate regulations for such subsequent firms. He stated 3M's position thus: "We want this type of firm because we know the business well and can accept the total risk. We can react quickly. We are good corporate citizens, experienced in many countries. We can and will develop local Chinese managers."

Finally, initial Ministry approval was given by an official: "OK, get in touch with Shanghai Electrical Machinery Company. Make a deal through them." This was a major step forward, since approval in concept of the fully owned status permitted 3M to move from hypothetical into definite plans.

But this approval also presented a problem. 3M wanted to establish from the outset its preferred conditions in China. The Shanghai location and the tie to a firm in Shanghai would provide a good base, but 3M wanted the Chinese to recognize that that would be only a start. Mr. Marshall said, for example, "We don't want to be in China to make a given product or even a few electrical products. We want to be in as a national concept, as a way of serving the entire country, getting eventually into many products. So we don't want just a parochial approval or a tie to a small Chinese firm." 3M wanted long-range approval and permission sooner or later to broaden to more product lines and locations.

In Shanghai, 3M also dealt with an appointed representative of SITCO, the Shanghai Investment and Trust Company, a government corporation under the city of Shanghai. Shanghai is a municipality governed directly from Beijing, possessing status equal to a province. (China's governmental organization includes two other such municipalities—Beijing itself and Nanjing—plus 23 provinces. A municipality's government structure is much like that of the top level, though with Bureaus rather than Ministries.) Shanghai's First Bureau of Management and Economics came directly under the Shanghai Municipal Government. In the 3M situation, the First Bureau dealt with policy matters, giving coordination, liaison and continuity. Under the First Bureau came government corporations, 14 in all. One of these was the Shanghai Electrical Machinery Company. In 3M's case, this company (SEMC) handled the business aspects of 3M's project. Shanghai Electrical in turn operated 40 plants. One of these was the Shanghai Insulating Materials Plant, or SIMP, with which 3M later dealt at length.

At the Shanghai Electrical Company, Mr. Marshall found acceptance and helpfulness, but also the feeling that 3M's presence was a good deal of work and trouble without much payoff for Shanghai Electrical, which had its own business to run and quotas to meet. Sometimes Mr. Marshall felt they were saying to themselves, "We wish you had never come."

An early problem in negotiating with Shanghai Electrical was that there was no format under which they could deal with 3M's proposal; no law or regulations existed for fully owned status. But joint-venture law and regulations did exist. Mr. Marshall responded, "You had to create initial regulations for joint ventures since you didn't have them before either. So why not try the same early development method for wholly owned foreign firms? 3M has a wide range of products that will meet requirements and needs of China and of your firm. With respect to the wholly owned status, you needn't let anyone else in to China on that basis until our case is developed and evaluated."

Mr. Marshall characterized negotiations as follows: negotiations were at times like two people leaning out the windows of two skyscrapers separated by an alley and shouting across. They may eventually agree at that level, but then the Chinese would say, "But now you must see Charlie down on the ground floor." The Chinese are not good on hypotheticals and the abstract. They have been geared to simple business arrangements and concrete events. They don't see breadth and possibilities—they aren't 'big picture' people.

It was now Spring 1981. After 3M's initial proposal, Mr. Marshall always sent his next proposal or elaboration to the appropriate staff before his visit, giving them opportunity for study and consultations with superiors. As in all bureaucracies, the Chinese always covered themselves. Dialogue on the next visit might go as follows:

Mr. Marshall: "What is your view of our proposal?"
Chinese official: "We sent it to Beijing."
Mr. Marshall: "What recommendations did you make to Beijing about our proposal?"
Chinese official: "None."
Mr. Marshall: "Is it OK with you if we contact our friends in Beijing?" (It is good to do some discreet name dropping. Thus "I can go to him if you don't shape up.")
Chinese official: "OK." (To himself, "That gets the monkey off my back.")

As Mr. Marshall observed, "You must, of course, deal very diplomatically with the Chinese in all aspects of the negotiations. But if you get to know a man well, as we did with a number of officials over this period, you can speak more frankly."

So 3M went to Beijing, to its Ministry contacts. Thus 3M was selling its project at two levels: in Beijing at the national policy level and in Shanghai at the level of business operations. 3M developed a push in Shanghai, a pull in Beijing. At the Beijing level, 3M obviously had to deal in political context and specifically in the ideology of socialism. The Chinese regarded the idea of independent free enterprise as ideologically suspect. Any bureaucrat would have had to be bold to accept it. To overcome this problem, Mr. Marshall sold 3M's ideas on the basis of its corporate experience, its being in China as a guest but operating as a good citizen of the country meeting the country's needs. Mr. Marshall pointed out that "In Italy we are Italian," to emphasize the point that 3M adapts to and fits into each country in which it operates. Also, 3M would bring in very few Americans; worldwide, 3M has only about one per subsidiary.

An impediment in the negotiations was China's desire to have 3M commit itself to exporting from China, and 3M's desire not to be so committed. In negotiations the Chinese repeatedly pressed for such a commitment. In the late stages of negotiation the Chinese officials said, "Put a general commitment to export in. We won't hold you to it." But Mr. Marshall responded, "In three years both of us will be gone, and your successors will give such a commitment a strict interpretation."

The Chinese then objected that 3M would not earn foreign exchange to pay for their own needed imports for a Shanghai plant. But Mr. Marshall responded, "You do need foreign exchange. But you sell, for example, ash trays to Hong Kong, then use the earnings to import technology from Japan. 3M brings its technology directly, in machinery and methods. So we are saving you foreign exchange."

As another negotiating technique, Mr. Marshall brought out objections he thought his Chinese counterparts might feel but be embarrassed to express. Then he tried to counter or explain such possibilities. He used a two-column list with China's advantages on the left and 3M's advantages on the right. The list of China's advantages was always longer!

To show openness and good will, and to inform the Chinese about 3M's wholly owned subsidiaries, 3M offered a tour of the firm's installations in the United States and elsewhere. The Chinese could observe how 3M and the specific plants operated, and talk with 3M officers and workers. As Mr. Marshall pointed out, such a trip would show up any 3M misrepresentations or deceptions.

The offer was accepted. In 1982, 3M hosted a tour of four officials from the Ministry of Foreign Affairs in Beijing, and two from the city of Shanghai's Investment and Trust Company (SITCO). The tour included 3M subsidiaries or plants in Canada; Hutchinson and New Ulm, Minnesota; Silicon Valley, Mexico; the Philippines; and Hong Kong. In Washington, D.C., the Chinese discussed 3M's proposal at their own embassy and at the U.S. Department of Commerce. The guests saw all plant operations, worker training, and sales of products, and conferred at length with managers and workers. In Hong Kong, all the personnel were Chinese.

The Mexican plant was especially instructive. In 1982, Mexico saw oil prices dropping, budget cuts, devaluation of the peso, and freezing of foreign exchange. The majority of multinationals in Mexico either withdrew, or reduced operations and employment to a minimum. But 3M's wholly owned subsidiary continued as before. The parent company extended credit so 3M Mexico could continue to import needed components and materials from the United States, even when dollar exchange was unavailable. 3M Mexico's self-sustaining business serving the needs of the local market precisely paralleled 3M's proposal to China. And the parent company had supported the subsidiary during crisis.

At the end of the tour, Mr. Marshall expected some response, perhaps a favorable recommendation or promise of a report to superiors. Instead, to Mr. Marshall's surprise, the officials gave immediate verbal approval of 3M's wholly-owned subsidiary. But the promised written approval was delayed. In October 1984, 3M received a formal written license to operate in China.

In later negotiations, terms desired by both sides took definite form. Insight into these late topics of discussion came when an official of the Shanghai Investment and

Trust Company, Mr. Zhou Li, stated his view to a reporter of the *Asian Wall Street Journal*:

> The license should give 3M the right to operate in two product areas only: electrical tapes and electrical connectors. The products were to be designed for use in the Chinese telecommunications, electrical power, and electrical machinery industries. The 3M project would be approved on a trial basis—or as a "transition stage"—for three to five years. After that, if China decided to go ahead with foreign sole proprietorships, the project would be ratified as such. Otherwise, he said, the initial license would have to be terminated or turned into a joint venture. If extension of the agreement were desired, the products that would be manufactured by 3M in China would be decided on the basis of local conditions and business environment.

These terms were, however, more restrictive than 3M would have accepted and were apparently not submitted to 3M for discussion.

Then, unexpectedly, a hitch developed from an outside source. A story in the *Wall Street Journal*, written by Hong Kong-based Frank Ching, raised questions about 3M's proposed operations. Ching reported that a SITCO man, a friend of 3M, told Ching that 3M was a good company, but "we call them the 3 No Company: No joint ventures, No exports, No technology transfers." The story was repeated in a foreign press summary that circulated among Chinese officials. Mr. Marshall's counterparts were understandably upset. Six months of explaining, going over reasons for 3M's stands and values to China, were required to re-establish progress.

By 1984, the preliminary approval in hand, 3M began the detailed tasks of forming a work force and a distribution system, finalizing all necessary arrangements with SITCO, SEMC and its SIMP plant. The Chinese were helpful but inertia remained. The Chinese would say, at lower levels, "It is pointless to do these things. We don't know when you will be permitted to start." And at the top levels, "We can't approve these things until we know the details." So Mr. Marshall just had to push, as he had from the beginning.

On the operational phases, substantial help came from others in 3M: engineering, trade, training, finance and banking, taxes, and customs. An eight-person 3M task force provided needed expertise. It spent a week in Shanghai and "performed a lot of arranging in a short time."

Mr. Marshall visited China in the Spring of 1984 to tidy up final details. Another visit was planned for June 1984 to finalize the required four agreements with appropriate Chinese bodies. Preliminary work took a week. The final documents were to be signed on Friday afternoon. Government officials, lawyers, and other dignitaries were present. However, an impasse developed over the name to be used. 3M wanted the name 3M China so as to be prepared for expanding its operations throughout the country. But the Chinese officials said they could not approve that name. Mr. Marshall asked why the Chinese had not objected earlier since 3M's proposal had set forth the desired name. No response was forthcoming. So the signing ceremony was called off and 3M's officials returned to the United States.

3M's executive vice president for international operations wrote to the Chinese officials setting forth 3M's reasons for its desired name, but received no response.

On a later trip to China, Mr. Marshall was told that use of the word China in a name required top-level approval and could not be achieved quickly.

So Mr. Marshall went to Beijing to negotiate use of the desired name. He argued, "In Taiwan, we are 3M Taiwan. So in China we need a higher-level name than, say, 3M Shanghai." But the Chinese countered, "That would make Taiwan equal to the People's Republic of China, and you know we could not stand for that."

Later, the Beijing authorities, without explanation, gave approval to 3M's name choice. 3M valued highly this approval since, as Mr. Marshall noted, use of the word China in the name carried the implication of a national and nationwide license, a strong point for 3M. Receiving approval from Beijing had a favorable effect on getting approval from the officials of the Shanghai government.

Earlier 3M had also submitted a bound collection of documents and letters from the United States Department of State, the Minnesota Secretary of State, and others, endorsing 3M and its proposal.

By the end of September 1984 everything seemed to be in order again. The Chinese authorities said, "If you have everything submitted by the end of September, final approval can come in November." This deadline was met, and the signing was duly carried out.

On November 10, 1984 the People's Republic of China gave the Minnesota Mining and Manufacturing company a formal license to operate in Shanghai a wholly owned subsidiary bearing the name 3M China. The license was valid for a period of 15 years, from November 9, 1984 to November 8, 1999. 3M had wanted a 30-year license but settled for 15.

Early Stages of 3M China's Operations

3M China's Shanghai plant was officially opened March 7, 1985. The 3M board of directors met in Shanghai for the occasion. Production of electrical tape and electrical connectors began late in July 1985. Ronald G. Harber, an experienced 3Mer, was appointed manager. His work force comprised six people; the equipment comprised eight machines. Initial production included cutting long rolls of tape into narrower widths. The 11,000-square-foot factory building was on the grounds of and rented from the Shanghai Insulating Materials Plant. 3M had dealt at length with SIMP, and had developed helpful personal relationships. SIMP was also the channel for 3M's Chinese labor. Initial selection was made by the Shanghai Foreign Service Company, a government facility set up to assist foreign companies operating in Shanghai. 3M China's local manager could release workers by making a written report on the individual and giving 30 days notice. But he could not use some ordinary U.S. methods: raises or other incentives required negotiation through the Shanghai Foreign Service Company.

3M China's initial investment amounted to about $3 million, a small sum as foreign investments go. For this investment, 3M China had achieved several goals: access to a mammoth market; a situation permitting study of and familiarity with Chinese markets and methods; initial products tailored to fit China's needs; and possibilities of gradual expansion to other products and to additional plants, provided Chinese permission could be achieved.

The negotiations had brought out several points reinforcing 3M's insistence on the fully owned subsidiary rather than a joint venture with a Chinese partner. The great diversity and broad spectrum of 3M's products made the firm unique; no Chinese firm sufficiently matched 3M to permit a joint venture. And as might be expected, foreign firms operating in joint ventures in Shanghai were running into difficulties. Resistance to change, and ingrained Chinese work habits and expectations were leading problems. Furthermore, common advantages of indigenous joint-venture partners in other countries—a developed marketing structure within the native firm, an existing customer base, and broad familiarity with the needs and wants of customers and with marketing methods, practices and laws in the country—all these were missing in China since, under the centrally planned economy, Chinese manufacturers had carried on no marketing activities at all.

Benefits to China were expected to include not only the 3M products, but also basic information on organizing an inventory system, minimizing waste, controlling pollution, and improving productivity. As the operation expanded, Chinese managers and technical workers were expected to be trained in China by 3M technicians from the United States and elsewhere. Chinese employees might also be trained at 3M facilities elsewhere.

Raw and semifinished materials as well as the capital equipment needed by the venture were imported for the initial startup, but 3M believed that later production facilities would be at least partially equipped from local sources.

Initially, marketing was to be wholly within China. Export opportunities could not be ignored, although as noted no firm commitment to export existed. Sales within China were to be in renminbi, the Chinese currency. Counter to some views, 3M saw this as a competitive opportunity. Foreign firms exporting to China needed to sell for dollars or other hard currency in order to take proceeds out. But China's need to conserve hard-currency foreign exchange limited such sales of importers, while all Chinese firms (such as 3M China) could sell in Chinese currency. In the longer run, 3M needed, of course, to find some way to repatriate earnings. But for some years, 3M's renminbi earnings were to be reinvested in their expansion in China.

3M also set up a joint-venture trading company with a Chinese firm independent of 3M China. The joint venture was to export Chinese products. The foreign exchange so earned would give 3M flexibility for earnings repatriation and help 3M meet its commitment to match its foreign exchange expenditures with earnings.

3M expected its prices in China to be established under its standard formula—evaluating costs, and pricing for a fair return. However, 3M had to remember China's price maintenance and review board, with which 3M China was required to clear its prices.

Obviously, the PRC retained overriding control over all of 3M's activities in the country, both because of its sovereign rights and because 3M's agreements with the PRC had not settled all details. But influence was expected to be two sided. The Chinese had agreed to 3M's proposal because they expected 3M's favorable influence on their production technology and efficiency. Indeed, through the negotiations, 3M had assisted the PRC's development of a legal structure for fully owned foreign subsidiaries. 3M China would also be a demonstration model for independent Chinese firms, should the PRC broadly extend such privileges to its own citizens.

CASE 20 ───────────────────────────────────

┌──┐
│   │
│   **TenderCare Disposable Diapers**   │
│   │
└──┘

Tom Cagan watched as his secretary poured six ounces of water onto each of the two disposable diapers laying on his desk. The diaper on the left was a new, improved Pampers, introduced in the summer of 1985 by Procter & Gamble. The new, improved design was supposed to be drier than the preceding Pampers. It was the most recent development in a sequence of designs that traced back to the original Pampers, introduced to the market in 1965. The diaper on his right was a TenderCare diaper, manufactured by a potential supplier for testing and approval by Cagan's company, Rocky Mountain Medical Corporation (RMM). The outward appearance of both diapers was identical.

Yet the TenderCare diaper was different. Just under its liner (the surface next to the baby's skin) was a wicking fabric that drew moisture from the surface around a soft, waterproof shield to an absorbent reservoir of filler. Pampers and all other disposable diapers on the market kept moisture nearer to the liner and, consequently, the baby's skin. A patent attorney had examined the TenderCare design, concluding that the wicking fabric and shield arrangement should be granted a patent. However, it would be many months before results of the patent application process could be known.

As soon as the empty beakers were placed back on the desk, Cagan and his secretary touched the liners of both diapers. They agreed that there was no noticeable difference, and Cagan noted the time. They repeated their "touch test" after one minute and again noted no difference. However, after two minutes, both thought the TenderCare diaper to be drier. At three minutes, they were certain. By five minutes, the TenderCare diaper surface seemed almost dry to the touch, even when a finger was pressed deep into the diaper. In contrast, the Pampers diaper showed little improvement in dryness from three to five minutes and tended to produce a puddle when pressed.

These results were not unexpected. Over the past three months, Cagan and other RMM executives had compared TenderCare's performance with ten brands of disposable diapers available in the Denver market. TenderCare diapers had always felt drier within a two- to four-minute interval after wetting. However, these results were considered tentative because all tests had used TenderCare diapers made by RMM personnel by hand. Today's test was the first made with diapers produced by a supplier under mass manufacturing conditions.

ROCKY MOUNTAIN MEDICAL CORPORATION

RMM was incorporated in Denver, Colorado, in late 1982 by Robert Morrison, M.D. Sales had grown from about $400,000 in 1983 to $2.4 million in 1984 and were expected to reach $3.4 million in 1985. The firm would show a small profit for 1985, as it had each previous year.

Management personnel as of September 1985 included six executives. Cagan served as President and Director, positions he had held since joining RMM in April 1984. Prior to that time he had worked for several high-technology companies in the areas of product design and development, production management, sales management, and general management. His undergraduate studies were in engineering and psychology; he took an M.B.A. in 1981. Dr. Morrison currently served as Chairman of the Board and Vice-president for Research and Development. He had completed his M.D. in 1976 and was board certified to practice pediatrics in the state of Colorado since 1978. John Bosch served as Vice-president of Manufacturing, a position held since joining the firm in late 1983. Lawrence Bennett was Vice-president of Marketing, having primary responsibilities for marketing TenderCare and RMM's two lines of phototherapy products since joining the firm in 1984. Bennett's background included an M.B.A. received in 1981 and three years' experience in grocery product management at General Mills. Two other executives, both also joining RMM in 1984, served as Vice-president of Personnel and as Controller.

Phototherapy Products

RMM's two lines of phototherapy products were used to treat infant jaundice, a condition experienced by some 5 to 10 percent of all newborn babies. One line was marketed to hospitals under the trademark Alpha-Lite. Bennett felt that the Alpha-Lite phototherapy unit was superior to competing products because it gave the baby 360-degree exposure to the therapeutic light. Competing products gave less than complete exposure, with the result that the Alpha-Lite unit treated more severe cases and produced quicker recoveries. Apart from the Alpha-Lite unit itself, the hospital line of phototherapy products included a light meter, a photo-mask that protected the baby's eyes while undergoing treatment, and a "baby bikini" that diapered the baby and yet facilitated exposure to the light.

The home phototherapy line of products was marketed under the trademark Baby-Lite.™ The phototherapy unit was portable, weighing about 40 pounds, and was foldable for easy transport. The unit when assembled was 33 inches long, 20 inches wide, and 24 inches high (see Exhibit 20.1). The line also included photo-masks, a thermometer, and a short booklet telling parents about home phototherapy. Parents could rent the unit and purchase related products from a local pharmacy or durable medical equipment dealer for about $75 per day. This was considerably less than the cost of hospital treatment. Another company, Acquitron, Inc., had entered the home phototherapy market in early 1985 and was expected to offer stiff competition. A third competitor was rumored to be entering the market in 1986.

EXHIBIT 20.1 **Print advertisement for home phototherapy unit**

Bennett's responsibilities for all phototherapy products included developing marketing plans and making final decisions about product design, promotion, pricing, and distribution. He directly supervised two product managers, one responsible for Alpha-Lite and the other for Baby-Lite. He occasionally made sales calls with the product managers, visiting hospitals, health maintenance organizations, and insurers.

TenderCare Marketing

Right now most of Bennett's time was spent on TenderCare. Bennett recognized that TenderCare would be marketed much differently than the phototherapy products. TenderCare would be sold to wholesalers, who in turn would sell to supermarkets, drugstores, and mass merchandisers. TenderCare would compete either directly or indirectly with two giant consumer goods manufacturers, Procter & Gamble and Kimberly-Clark. TenderCare represented considerable risk to RMM.

Because of the uncertainty surrounding the marketing of TenderCare, Bennett and Cagan had recently sought the advice of several marketing consultants. They reached formal agreement with one, a Los Angeles consultant named Alan Anderson. Anderson had extensive experience in advertising at J. Walter Thompson. He also had responsibility for marketing and sales at Mattel and Teledyne, specifically for the marketing of such products as IntelliVision,™ the Shower Massage,™ and the Water Pik.™ Anderson currently worked as an independent marketing consultant to several firms. His contract with RMM specified that he would devote 25 percent of his time to TenderCare the first year and about 12 percent the following two years. During this time, RMM would hire, train, and place their own marketing personnel. One of these people would be a product manager for TenderCare.

Bennett and Cagan also could employ the services of a local marketing consultant who served on RMM's advisory board. The board consisted of twelve business and medical experts who were available to answer questions and provide direction. The consultant had spent over twenty-five years in marketing consumer products at several large corporations. His specialty was developing and launching new products, particularly health and beauty aids. He had worked closely with RMM in selecting the name TenderCare,™ and had done a great deal of work summarizing market characteristics and analyzing competitors.

MARKET CHARACTERISTICS

The market for babies' disposable diapers could be identified as children, primarily below age three, who use the diapers and their mothers, primarily between ages eighteen and forty-nine, who decide on the brand and usually make the purchase. Bennett estimated there were about 11 million such children in 1985, living in about 9 million households. The average number of disposable diapers consumed daily in these households was thought to range from 0 to 15 and to average about 5.

The consumption of disposable diapers is tied closely to birth rates and population. However, two prominent trends also influence consumption. One is the disposable diaper's steadily increasing share of total diaper usage by babies. Bennett estimated that disposable diapers would increase their share of total diaper usage from 75 percent currently to 90 percent by 1990. The other trend is toward the purchase of higher-quality disposable diapers. Bennett thought the average retail price of disposable diapers would rise about twice as fast as the price of materials used in their construction. Total dollar sales of disposable diapers at retail in 1985 were expected to be about $3 billion, or about 15 billion units. Growth rates were thought to be about 14 percent per year for dollar sales and about 8 percent for units.

Foreign markets for disposable diapers would add to these figures. Canada, for example, currently consumed about $250 million at retail, with an expected growth rate of 20 percent per year until 1990. The U.K. market was about twice this size and growing at the same rate.

The U.S. market for disposable diapers was clearly quite large and growing. However, Bennett felt that domestic growth rates could not be maintained much longer because fewer and fewer consumers were available to switch from cloth to disposable diapers. In fact, by 1995, growth rates for disposable diapers would begin to approach growth rates for births, and unit sales of disposable diapers would become directly proportional to numbers of infants using diapers. A consequence of this pronounced slowing of growth would be increased competition.

COMPETITION

Competition between manufacturers of disposable diapers was already intense. Two well-managed giants—Procter & Gamble and Kimberly-Clark—accounted for about 80 percent of the market in 1984 and 1985. Bennett had estimated market shares at:

	1984	1985
Pampers	32%	28%
Huggies	24	28
Luvs	20	20
Other brands	24	24
	100%	100%

Procter & Gamble was clearly the dominant competitor with its Pampers and Luvs brands. However, Procter & Gamble's market share had been declining, from 70 percent in 1981 to about 50 percent. The company had introduced its thicker Blue Ribbon™ Pampers in an effort to halt the share decline. It had invested over $500 million in new equipment to produce the product. Procter & Gamble spent approximately $40 million to advertise its two brands in 1984. Kimberly-Clark spent about $19 million to advertise Huggies in 1984.

The 24 percent market share held by other brands was up by some 3 percentage points from 1983. Weyerhaeuser and Johnson & Johnson manufactured most of these diapers, supplying private-label brands for Wards, Penneys, Target, K-Mart, and other retailers. Generic disposable diapers and private brands were also included here, as well as a number of very small, specialized brands that distributed only to local markets. Some of these brands positioned themselves as low-cost alternatives to national brands; others occupied premium ("designer") niches with premium prices. As examples, Universal Converter entered the northern Wisconsin market in 1984 with two brands priced at 78 and 87 percent of Pampers' case price. Riegel Textile Corporation's Cabbage Patch™ diapers illustrated the premium end, with higher prices and attractive print designs. Riegel spent $1 million to introduce Cabbage Patch diapers to the market in late 1984.

Additional evidence of the intense competition in the disposable diaper industry was the major change of strategy by Johnson & Johnson in 1981. The company took its own brand off the U.S. market, opting instead to produce private-label diapers for major retailers. The company had held about 8 percent of the national market at the time and decided that this simply was not enough to compete effectively. Johnson & Johnson's disposable diaper was the first to be positioned in the industry as a premium product. Sales at one point totaled about 12 percent of the market but began to fall when Luvs and Huggies (with similar premium features) were introduced. Johnson & Johnson's advertising expenditures for disposable diapers in 1980 were about $8 million. The company still competed with its own brand in the international market.

MARKETING STRATEGIES FOR TENDERCARE

Over the past month, Bennett and his consultants had spent considerable time formulating potential marketing strategies for TenderCare. One strategy that already had been discarded was simply licensing the design to another firm. Under a license arrangement, RMM would receive a negotiated royalty based on the licensee's sales of RMM's diaper. However, this strategy was unattractive on several grounds. RMM would have no control over resources devoted to the marketing of TenderCare; the licensee would decide on levels of sales and advertising support, prices, and distribution. The licensee would control advertising content, packaging, and even the choice of brand name. Licensing also meant that RMM would develop little marketing expertise, no image or even awareness among consumers, and no experience in dealing with packaged-goods channels of distribution. The net result would be that RMM would be hitching its future with respect to TenderCare (and any related products) to that of the licensee. Three other strategies seemed more appropriate.

The "Diaper Rash" Strategy

The first strategy involved positioning the product as an aid in the treatment of diaper rash. Diaper rash is a common ailment, thought to affect most infants at some point in their diapered lives. The affliction usually lasted two or three weeks before being cured. Some infants are more disposed to diaper rash than others; however, the ailment probably affects a majority of babies. The ailment is caused by "a reaction to prolonged contact with urine and feces, retained soaps and topical preparations, and friction and maceration" (*Nelson's Text of Pediatrics,* 1979, p. 1884). Recommended treatment includes careful washing of the affected areas with warm water and without irritating soaps. Treatment also includes the application of protective ointments and powders (sold either by prescription or over the counter).

The diaper rash strategy would target physicians and nurses in either family or general practice and physicians and nurses specializing either in pediatrics or dermatology. Bennett's estimates of the numbers of general or family practitioners in 1985 was approximately 65,000. He thought that about 45,000 pediatricians and dermatologists were practicing in 1985. The numbers of nurses attending all these physicians was estimated at about 290,000. All 400,000 individuals would be the eventual focus of TenderCare marketing efforts. However, the diaper rash strategy would begin (like the other two strategies) where approximately 11 percent of the target market was located—California. Bennett and his consultants agreed that RMM lacked sufficient resources to begin in any larger market. California would provide a good test for TenderCare because the state often set consumption trends for the rest of the U.S. market. California also showed fairly typical levels of competitive activity.

Promotion activities would emphasize either direct mail and free samples or in-office demonstrations to the target market. Mailing lists of most physicians and some nurses in the target market could be purchased at a cost of about $60 per 1,000 names. The cost to print and mail a brochure, cover letter, and return postcard was about $250 per 1,000. To include a single TenderCare disposable diaper would add another $400 per thousand. In-office demonstrations would use registered nurses (employed on a part-time basis) to show TenderCare's superior dryness. The nurses could be quickly trained and compensated on a per-demonstration basis. The typical demonstration would be given to groups of two or three physicians and nurses and would cost RMM about $6. The California market could be used to investigate the relative performance of direct mail versus demonstrations.

RMM would also advertise in trade journals such as the *Journal of Family Practice, Journal of Pediatrics, Pediatrics*, and *Pediatrics Digest*. However, a problem with such advertisements was waste coverage because none of the trade journals published regional editions. A half-page advertisement (one insertion) would cost about $1,000 for each journal. This cost would be reduced to about $700 if RMM placed several advertisements in the same journal during a one-year period. RMM would also promote TenderCare at local and state medical conventions in California. Costs per convention were thought to be about $3,000. The entire promotion budget as well as amounts allocated to direct mail, free samples, advertisements, and medical conventions had yet to be decided.

Prices were planned to produce a retail price per package of 12 TenderCare diapers at around $3.80. This was some 8 to 10 percent higher than the price for a package of 18 Huggies or Luvs. Bennett thought that consumers would pay the premium price because of TenderCare's position: the pennies-per-day differential simply would not matter if a physician prescribed or recommended TenderCare as part of a treatment for diaper rash. "Besides," he noted, "in-store shelf placement of TenderCare under this strategy would be among diaper rash products, not with standard diapers. This will make price comparisons by consumers even more unlikely." The $3.80 package price for 12 TenderCare diapers would produce a contribution margin for RMM of about 9 cents per diaper. It would give retailers a per-diaper margin some 30 percent higher than that for Huggies or Luvs.

The Special-Occasions Strategy

The second strategy centered around a "special-occasions" position that emphasized TenderCare's use in situations where changing the baby would be difficult.

One such situation was whenever diapered infants traveled for any length of time. Another occurred daily at some ten thousand daycare centers that accepted infants wearing diapers. Yet another came every evening in each of the 9 million market households when babies were diapered at bedtime.

The special-occasions strategy would target mothers in these 9 million households. Initially, of course, the target would be only the estimated one million mothers living in California. Promotion would aim particularly at first-time mothers, using such magazines as *American Baby* and *Baby Talk*. Per-issue insertion costs for one full-color, half-page advertisement in such magazines would average about $20,000. However, most baby magazines published regional editions where single insertion costs averaged about half that amount. Black and white advertisements could also be considered; their costs would be about 75 percent of the full-color rates. Inserting several ads per year in the same magazine would allow quantity discounts and reduce the average insertion cost by about one-third.

Lately Bennett had begun to wonder if direct mail promotion could instead be used to reach mothers of recently born babies. Mailing lists of some 1–3 million names could be obtained at a cost of around $50 per 1,000. Other costs to produce and mail promotional materials would be the same as those for physicians and nurses. "I suppose the real issue is, just how much more effective is direct mail over advertising? We'd spend at least $250,000 in baby magazines to cover California while the cost of direct mail would probably be between $300,000 and $700,000, depending on whether or not we gave away a diaper." Regardless of Bennett's decision on consumer promotion, he knew RMM would also direct some promotion activities toward physicians and nurses as part of the special-occasions strategy. Budget details were yet to be worked out.

Distribution under the special-occasions strategy would have TenderCare stocked on store shelves along with competing diapers. Still at issue was whether the package should contain 12 or 18 diapers (like Huggies and Luvs) and how much of a premium price TenderCare could command. Bennett considered the packaging and pricing decisions interrelated. A package of 12 TenderCare diapers with per-unit retail prices some 40 percent higher than Huggies or Luvs might work just fine. Such a packaging/pricing strategy would produce a contribution margin to RMM of about 6 cents per diaper. However, the same pricing strategy for a package of 18 diapers probably would not work. "Still," he thought, "good things often come in small packages, and most mothers probably associate higher quality with higher price. One thing is for sure—whichever way we go, we'll need a superior package." Physical dimensions for a TenderCare package of either 12 or 18 diapers could be made similar to the size of the Huggies or Luvs package of 18.

The Head-On Strategy

The third strategy under consideration met major competitors in a direct, frontal attack. The strategy would position TenderCare as a noticeably drier diaper that any mother would prefer to use anytime her baby needed changing. Promotion activities would stress mass advertising to mothers using television and magazines. However, at least two magazines would include a dollar-off coupon to stimulate trial of a package of TenderCare diapers during the product's first three months on the market. Some in-store demonstrations to mothers using "touch tests" might also be employed. Although no budget for California had yet been set, Bennett thought the allocation would be roughly 60:30:10 for televison, magazines, and other promotion activities, respectively.

Pricing under this strategy would be competitive with Luvs and Huggies, with the per-diaper price for TenderCare expected to be some 9 percent higher at retail. This differential was needed to cover additional manufacturing costs associated with TenderCare's design. TenderCare's package could contain only 16 diapers and show a lower price than either Huggies or Luvs with their 18-count packages. Alternatively, the package could contain 18 diapers and carry the 9 percent higher price. Bennett wondered if he really wasn't putting too fine a point on the pricing/packaging relationship. "After all," he had said to Anderson, "we've no assurance that retailers or wholesalers would pass along *any* price advantage TenderCare might have due to a smaller package. Either one or both might instead price TenderCare near the package price for our competitors and simply pocket the increased margin!" The only thing that was reasonably certain was TenderCare's package price to the wholesaler. That price was planned to produce about a 3-cent contribution margin to RMM per diaper, regardless of package count.

Summary of the Three Strategies

When viewed together, the three strategies seemed so complex and so diverse as to defy analysis. Partly the problem was one of developing criteria against which the strategies could be compared. Risk was obviously one such criterion; so were company fit and competitive reaction. However, Bennett felt that some additional thought on his part would produce more criteria against which the strategies could be compared. He hoped this effort would produce no more strategies; three were plenty.

The other part of the problem was simply uncertainty. Strengths, weaknesses, and implications of each strategy had yet to be given much thought. Moreover, each strategy seemed likely to have associated with it some surprises. An example illustrating the problem was the recent realization that the Food and Drug Administration (FDA) must approve any direct claims RMM might make about TenderCare's efficacy in treating diaper rash. The chance of receiving this federal agency's approval was thought to be reasonably high; yet it was unclear just what sort of testing and what results were needed. The worst-case scenario would have the FDA requiring lengthy customer tests that eventually would produce inconclusive results. The best case would have the FDA giving permission based on TenderCare's superior dryness and on results of a small-scale field test recently completed by Dr. Morrison. It would probably be a month before the FDA's position could be known.

"The delay was unfortunate—and unnecessary," Bennett thought, "especially if we eventually settle on either of the other two strategies." In fact, FDA approval was not even needed for the diaper rash strategy if RMM simply claimed (1) that TenderCare diapers were drier than competing diapers and (2) that dryness helps treat diaper rash. Still, a single-statement, direct-claim position was thought to be more effective with mothers and more difficult to copy by any other manufacturer. And yet Bennett did want to move quickly on TenderCare. Every month of delay meant deferred revenue and other postponed benefits that would derive from a successful introduction. Delay also meant the chance that an existing (or other) competitor might develop its own drier diaper and effectively block RMM from reaping the fruits of its development efforts. Speed was of the essence.

FINANCIAL IMPLICATIONS

Bennett recognized that each marketing strategy held immediate as well as long-term financial implications. He was particularly concerned with finance requirements for start-up costs associated with the California entry. Cagan and the other RMM executives had agreed that a stock issue represented the best option to meet these requirements. Accordingly, RMM had begun preparation for a sale of common stock through a brokerage firm that would underwrite and market the issue. Management at the firm felt that RMM could generate between $1 and $3 million, depending on the offering price per share and the number of shares issued.

Proceeds from the sale of stock had to be sufficient to fund the California entry and leave a comfortable margin remaining for contingencies. Proceeds would be used for marketing and other operating expenses as well as for investments in cash, inventory, and accounts receivable. It was hoped that TenderCare would generate a profit by the end of the fiscal year in the California market and show a strong contribution to the bottom line thereafter. California profits would contribute to expenses associated with entering additional markets and to the success of any additional stock offerings.

Operating profits and proceeds from the sale of equity would fund additional research and development activities that would extend RMM's diaper technology to other markets. Dr. Morrison and Bennett saw almost immediate application of the technology to the adult incontinent diaper market, currently estimated at about $300 million per year at retail. Underpads for beds constitute at least another $50 million annual market. However, both of these uses were greatly dwarfed by another application, the sanitary napkin market. Finally, the technology could almost certainly be applied to numerous industrial products and processes, many of which promised great potential. All these opportunities made the TenderCare situation that much more crucial to the company. Making a major mistake here would affect the firm for years.

CASE 21 _____

Software Publishing Company

INTRODUCTION

Fred Gibbons, Janelle Bedke, and John D. Page started Software Publishing Company in 1980. All are former employees of Hewlett Packard's marketing division and have been strongly influenced by the Hewlett Packard environment. The effervescent Gibbons is President and Chairman, Bedke is Vice President/General Manager, and Page is Vice President for Research and Development. Initially, the company followed a strategy similar to that of many packaged food distributors striving to develop a complete family of brand name software products that could be advertised widely and sold through retail channels.

The first program produced by Software Publishing Company was developed for the Apple computer system in the early 1980s and was called Personal Filing System or PFS for short. In addition to the file management system, additional programs were added to perform word processing, graphics, communications, proofreading, and spreadsheet functions. All programs in the series have a common interface and structure, which facilitates learning how to operate them and makes it easy to transfer data from one program to another. After the initial success with programs designed to run on Apple computers, in the mid-1980s the PFS series was adapted for use on IBM and IBM-compatible machines. Gibbons remarked that there was a general feeling that expansion was occuring much more rapidly in the IBM software sector than in the Apple area, but development efforts and energies had been so concentrated on Apple products that the company failed to take advantage of the obvious transition.

PFS programs are inexpensive, easy to use, and compatible with each other, but have fewer capabilities than programs marketed by major competitors such as Microsoft, Lotus, and Ashton Tate. Until 1986, Software Publishing had no single program that would perform an integrated series of spreadsheet, word processing, and file management functions on the order of Lotus 1-2-3 or Ashton Tate's Framework. Although the company had been increasing profits and sales during the fourth quarter for every year since 1980, sales volume declined significantly during the last quarter of 1985 due to increasing competition from other software companies and a slowdown in the demand for personal computers.

The research and written case information was prepared by William C. House and Robert D. Hay, University of Arkansas, presented at the Case Research Symposium (New Orleans, 1987), and evaluated by the Case Research Association's Editorial Board. Distributed by Case Research Association with all rights reserved to the authors and Case Research Association. It is intended as a basis for classroom discussion rather than to illustrate effective or ineffective handling of an administrative situation. Used by permission from William C. House and the North American Case Research Association.

In December 1985, while on the ski slopes at Squaw Valley in Nevada, Fred Gibbons suffered a stroke which left him paralyzed on one side. Janelle Bedke took over many of Gibbons functions temporarily, but within one month the hard-charging Gibbons was back in his office with only a slight limp to show for the experience.

PRODUCT LINES: BREADTH, DEPTH, AND PRICING STRATEGIES

Gibbons' initial strategy was to develop a broadly based, widely recognized family of programs that were easy to learn to use and that would be within the price range of the average home computer or office computer user. Programs developed initially for Apple computers were converted to IBM versions and both versions were sold through retail channels. IBM made arrangements with the company to sell the entire PFS line under the IBM assistant series label, further enhancing the company's sales prospects.

While other companies concentrated on larger, more complex programs with greater functionality and carrying prices ranging from $300 to $600, Software Publishing sold its programs for prices ranging from $125 to $140. Several of the more successful software companies (e.g., Lotus and Ashton Tate) obtained the bulk of their revenues from a single product. Software Publishing Company, in contrast, received no more than one third of its revenues from any single product.

By the end of 1985, Software Publishing had sold more programs than any other software developer (i.e., about two million units compared to about 1.6 million for Lotus), but the gross profit per package was about $60 compared to approximately $200 for more sophisticated programs. Many retailers claimed that PFS profit margins were too narrow and program capabilities were too limited to justify full-scale promotion of the PFS line. In addition, the demand for easy to use, limited function programs was decreasing while the demand for more powerful programs with expanded capabilities, to take full advantage of faster operating speeds and larger memories of newer computer hardware, was increasing. The number of first-time computer users appeared to have tapered off during the past two years.

Gibbons ruefully conceded that the company spread itself too thin during the mid-1980s, trying to develop programs for the McIntosh, Apple, IBM private label, and IBM-PC compatible audiences. Despite clearcut indications that the IBM compatible programs were going to have the greatest future growth potential, the company waited almost two years to start phasing out the Apple programs.

Software Publishing was also experiencing competition from unexpected quarters. Apple Computer had switched from being a user of PFS programs to becoming a powerful competitor. Appleworks, a file manager that sold for about $250, competed aggressively with the PFS series for the same customers, resulting in lost sales for the company. Symantec, a software company formed by industry veterans several years ago, had introduced a new program called Q&A which was the equivalent of three combined and upgraded PFS programs. Although not as successful as dBase and Lotus, Q&A, at a price level of about $300, had obtained a number of sales that otherwise might have gone to the PFS family.

NEW PRODUCT DEVELOPMENT AND PRODUCT LINE ACQUISITION

Two new product lines were announced by Software Publishing Company in 1986. File management, report generation, spreadsheet, word processing, and communication capabilities formerly provided by separate programs in the PFS series were combined in a single program called First Choice. This integrated program was designed for novices and first-time users. Software Publishing believed the moderately priced and highly touted First Choice would prove attractive to a new wave of first-time users. Although officially priced at $195 through normal retail channels, the program could be obtained from discount mail order houses for slightly less than $100. The individual PFS programs were also available from the same sources for less than $90 each.

The previous PFS program family did not allow users to upgrade to more sophisticated programs and many industry observers felt that the product development process took too long to complete. The PFS professional Write, File, and Plan packages were developed to provide expanded word processing, file processing, and spreadsheet capabilities to experienced users. These updated, expanded versions of the stand-alone PFS programs were designed to appeal to a growing number of veteran users with a price tag of about $150 per program.

A major disadvantage of the high-end programs was that they faced stiff competition from the more sophisticated software programs offered by other major software suppliers than the lower-level programs would. Many prospective purchasers might think the more expensive programs with greater capabilities such as Lotus 1-2-3, dBase III, RBase$_5$, or Q&A were better buys than a medium-price-range version of the PFS series.

The Professional Write (word processing) program had expanded mail-merge capabilities while the Professional Plan (spreadsheet) could read data and formulas from other worksheets such as Lotus. The professional programs, while menu-based like the simpler and earlier PFS programs, had added pull down menu structures, macros, and quick entry keys to appeal to more experienced users. On-line help facilities had been expanded and manuals upgraded. These programs stressed ease of use but with more powerful capabilities than available previously. The company had slowly moved away from its image of providing programs for beginners only. One drawback was that the change of image and modifications in the familiar-user interface might cause confusion among dealers and users alike as to the level at which the programs were aimed.

Many of the new product decisions were made by employee committees rather than by a few top-level executives. A major decision was to change the familiar-user interface; other product line changes were made on the assumption that a large number of buyers would be purchasing low price PC clones. The product line modifications apparently did not consider the effect that the introduction of the new PS-2 personal computer with its faster, larger capacity, and multiuser capabilities along with 3½ inch disks would have on application software sales. The company has stated that it would continue to sell Apple versions of the PFS series but its primary emphasis in future years would be on its IBM-compatible lines.

Software Publishing Company acquired Harvard Software in 1986 as another means of expanding its existing product lines. This acquisition gave the company access to Harvard Project Manager and Harvard Presentation Graphics programs which were higher priced and more complex than the PFS series. Shortly thereafter, it introduced the Harvard Professional Publisher desktop publishing program for the IBM-PC. This program was developed by an outside software developer to be marketed exclusively by Software Publishing Company. The Clickart Personal Publishing line was also acquired from T-Maker to give the company desktop publishing capabilities in the low-end market.

DISTRIBUTION AND SALES

Software Publishing Company markets the PFS line through distributors, independent sales representatives, and in-house salespersons to more than 3,500 retailers. Sales are also made directly to corporations, although PFS products are not on the approved list of many corporations and many organizations consider the PFS series as designed for home rather than business or office use. Retail sales have typically been highest in the fourth quarter, and lowest in the first quarter. Exhibit 21.1 shows the changing composition of sales revenues for the company.

EXHIBIT 21.1 **Composition of sales revenues**			
	1984	**1985**	**1986**
Retail sales	80%	61%	72%
OEMS/IBM royalties	16%	30%	20%
Direct consumer sales	4%	9%	8%

In order to beef up its marketing efforts, Software Publishing Company hired four brand managers from packaged goods companies (e.g., Proctor & Gamble, Chlorox). This augmented sales staff is trying out a number of new marketing techniques to increase revenues and profits. Free trial diskettes are offered to potential customers. Information on software products is being sent out via direct mail to targeted personnel, and advertisements are frequently carried in personal computer magazines. Selected corporate managers are being sent free copies of some software packages in order to help increase organizational awareness of the PFS family.

SOFTWARE ECONOMICS AND COMPETITION

Software packages developed for large mainframe or minicomputer systems normally have long product life cycles, high user-assumed maintenance costs, and small unit-volume sales. In contrast, software packages for smaller systems tend to have shorter life cycles, larger unit sales, and lower maintenance costs. At least one microcomputer software developer, Lotus Development, had announced its intention to develop and market a minicomputer and mainframe version of its popular spreadsheet package, 1-2-3. However, it was uncommon for a given company to try to establish a position in all three market areas.

According to Ashton Tate spokespersons, the major competitive factors in microcomputer software sales were package, price/performance, marketing efforts/expenditures, ease of maintenance and use, documentation and training, vendor size/reputation, and product line integration. (*Industry Surveys*, November 6, 1986). Brand recognition and new product acquisition or introduction was also becoming more important in the current marketing environment. The software industry was similar in many ways to the book publishing industry where a company could be successful if it could develop and market one or two best sellers.

Site licensing and quantity discounts had become increasingly important as sales to corporate buyers increased. Site licensing allowed unlimited copying of products and availability of multiple copies on a much lower per-unit basis than otherwise possible. Software Publishing permitted site licenses for the PFS series to be purchased for a one-time fee of $75,000, and $100,000 for the Harvard series. The site licensing included rights to duplicate disks and manuals, technical notes, technical support for one year, and sizable discounts on upgrades. Unlimited multiple hard disk installations were also permitted in contrast to previous policies.

Barriers to entry existed in the microcomputer software industry and it is quite possible than only a few of the present leaders would survive without further product line acquisitions or mergers. Extensive research and development outlays by existing companies, ability to market products through multiple distribution channels, and a requirement for adapting existing software to take advantage of technological improvements in computer hardware are likely to inhibit the successful entry of additional software development companies.

Microcomputer software package sales were estimated to be more than $3 billion dollars in 1986. Sales for 1986 increased 26 percent over 1985, compared to

---

EXHIBIT 21.2 **Personal computer sales and microcomputer software sales for years 1983 to 1986**

	1983	1984	1985	1986
Personal computer sales				
Units (in millions)	6.2	7.7	6.4	7.1
Dollars (in billions)	$8.6	$14.3	$16.2	$16.8
Microcomputer software sales				
in millions of units for six largest				
microcomputer software companies	177	400	555	808

Source: DATAQUEST in *USA Today,* May 1987.

more than 50 percent in 1984 and 1983. Software sales have tended to closely follow sales of microcomputer hardware. Although sales of spreadsheet, word processing, and file management/data base systems seemed to be stabilizing, sales of project management, CAD/CAM, and graphics programs are expected to increase much faster in the next several years than sales of other types of application software. Personal computer sales in units and dollars and software sales for the six largest microcomputer software companies for 1983 to 1986 are shown in Exhibit 21.2.

Research and development efforts and expenditures were likely to assume increasing importance in the last half of the 1980s. R&D outlays as a percentage of sales revenues for the major microcomputer firms are given in Exhibit 21.3.

EXHIBIT 21.3 **R&D expenditures as a percentage of sales revenues**		
Company	**1984**	**1985**
Ashton Tate	6.0	9.3
Lotus Development	9.4	9.4
Micropro	14.5	19.6
Microsoft	12.2	10.4
Software Publishing	12.3	16.1

FINANCIAL AND SALES ANALYSIS

After increasing from four million dollars in 1982 to $37.2 million in 1985, software package revenues declined to $23.7 million in 1986. Net income declined to $700,000 in 1986 as compared to $5.8 million in 1985. Exhibit 21.4 presents the sales revenues and market shares for Software Publishing and five of its major competitors for 1983 through 1986.

Exhibit 21.5 shows net income in millions of dollars and net income as a percentage of sales for the six largest microcomputer software companies for the years 1983 to 1986.

Net income as a percent of sales declined from 15.7 percent in 1985 to 2.95 percent in 1986, and return on assets decreased from 35.7 percent in 1982 to 24.0 percent in 1985. Return on equity declined from a high of 132 percent in 1982 to 32.3 percent in 1985. The company has no long-term debt and its current ratio increased from 2.8 in 1983 to 7.2 in 1985. Earnings per share have ranged from $.13 in 1982 to $.83 in 1985. Per-share earnings for the 1985–1986 fiscal year were $.10. The price/earnings ratio of the stock varied from 9-1 to 20-1 in 1984 and 1985.

On November 15, 1984, the company sold 1,840,000 shares of common stock at $7.00 per share in its initial public offering. Company officers and directors hold about 30 percent of the shares outstanding. The stock price ranged from 4 3/4 to

EXHIBIT 21.4 **Sales revenues and market shares for largest microcomputer software companies**

Company	1983		1984		1985		1986	
	In millions	Percent	In millions	Percent	In millions	Percent	In millions	Percent
Lotus	$53	29.9	$157	39.3	$226	40.7	$283	35.0
Ashton-Tate	18	10.2	43	10.8	82	14.8	211	26.1
Microsoft	50	28.2	97	24.3	140	25.2	198	24.5
Micropro	45	25.4	67	16.8	43	7.7	52	6.4
Software Publishing	10	5.7	24	6.0	37	6.7	24	3.0
Borland	1	0.6	12	3.0	27	4.9	41	5.0

EXHIBIT 21.5 **Net income for six largest microcomputer companies**

Company	1983		1984		1985		1986	
	In millions	Percent	In millions	Percent	In millions	Percent	In millions	Percent
Lotus	$13.7	25.9	$36.0	23.0	$38.2	16.9	$48.3	17.1
Ashton-Tate	1.1	5.9	5.3	12.3	6.5	7.9	16.6	13.6
Microsoft	6.5	13.0	15.9	16.3	24.1	17.2	39.3	19.9
Micropro	4.3	9.5	5.8	8.7	0.2	0.5	0.3*	0.6
Software Publishing	1.4	14.0	3.6	15.4	5.8	15.7	0.7*	3.0
Borland	0.1	10.6	1.5	13.0	5.2	19.2	8.4**	20.6

*Preliminary figures for 1986.

**Based on fiscal year ending March 31, 1986.

8 1/2 during 1986. The company has not paid any dividends so far and does not plan any dividend declarations at present, believing that company earnings should be plowed back into company operations.

APPENDIX A **National Economic Indicators for Years 1983–1986**

	1983	1984	1985	1986
		(In billions)		
Personal consumption expenditures	$2,234.5	$2,428.2	$2,600.5	$2,762.5
Durable goods expenditures	289.1	331.2	359.3	388.1
Nondurable goods expenditures	816.7	870.1	905.1	932.7
Expenditures for services	1,128.7	1,227.0	1,336.1	1,441.7
Corporate profits	196.7	230.2	222.6	244.1
New plant/equipment outlays	304.8	354.4	379.3	390.8
Business equipment expenditures	115.4	134.2	139.6	138.6

Source: Department of Commerce, Bureau of Economic Analysis.

CASE 22 —

JJ's—Women's Clothing Store

"I must admit owning JJ's has been fun, Beth, in spite of some of the uncertainties. We've had to work hard, but I think it's been worth it."

"Oh, I agree, Ann," replied Beth Sommers, co-owner of JJ's. "There were times I didn't think we'd make it to our second anniversary. And I know we're not out of the woods yet, but I think we could already write a book!"

Ann Winters and Beth Sommers reflected on their two years of ownership of the women's fashion shop and the ups and downs of retail business in a small, rel-

This case was written by JoAnn K.L. Schwinghammer and Charles Wagner. It is intended as a basis for classroom discussion rather than to illustrate effective or ineffective handling of an administrative situation. The data in this case are disguised but based on real data. Used by permission from JoAnn K.L. Schwinghammer.

atively rural Minnesota community. Their present conversation was directed toward determining how well they had done, and charting a future course of action.

"I just know we can increase traffic here in the store, and sales, Beth. I suppose we could advertise more, but we never seem to know if it's working very well. We want to be sure that whatever we do is cost effective. This isn't exactly the best time to be wasting money on ideas that are chancy."

The women felt that it was their good "business sense" that had helped them survive these past two years in a community basically dependent on agriculture— other businesses there had not been so fortunate. But their concern, for the summer of 1987, was how they could improve sales, how much money they would have to spend on advertising and promotions, and what those programs should be.

BACKGROUND

JJ's was a women's clothing store located in St. Peter, Minnesota, and owned by Ann and Beth since April 1985. Ann, a resident of St. Peter for all of her 20-some years, and Beth, mid-40s, had learned the retail clothing business while working together at another St. Peter women's clothing store, whose owner was somewhat of a matriarch of women's clothiers in town, having been in retail for 54 years. Their dream had been to one day have a store of their own, and when they learned that JJ's was being sold, they decided to take advantage of the opportunity. JJ's had been in existence for three years when Beth and Ann purchased it, although it had another name for part of that time. The previous owner, Jane Johnson, had done most of the work of running the store herself, and was tired of the demands it placed on her. The sale was "sealed with a hug" on April 1, and Beth and Ann energetically set about operating their own store.

THE CITY AND SURROUNDING AREA

St. Peter, Minnesota, a city of approximately 9,000 residents, was located on the Minnesota River 65 miles southwest of Minneapolis-St. Paul, and twelve miles northeast of Mankato. The city enjoyed some recognition in the state, since it was one of the oldest cities in Minnesota, founded in 1853, and had thirteen sites on the National Registry. St. Peter had produced five governors, and may itself have been the state capital, had the bill declaring it as such not been stolen while awaiting the governor's signature.

Minnesota Avenue, (U.S. Highway 169), running the length of the city, was lined with most of St. Peter's retail trade. The central business district could be defined as an area approximately one and one-half blocks on either side of Minnesota Avenue from Walnut Street to midway between Broadway Avenue and Chestnut Street (see Exhibit 22.1). Industries in St. Peter were varied, ranging from a regional treatment center with extensive mental health facilities, education, and electronics, each employing

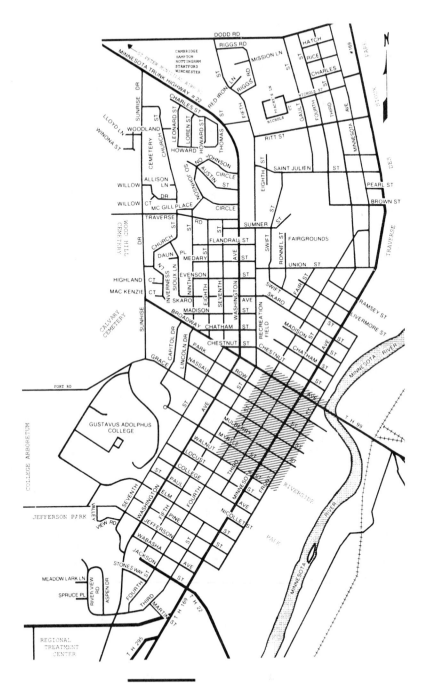

EXHIBIT 22.1 **St. Peter, Minnesota**

several hundred persons, to a woolen mill, to a small organ factory employing eight persons. St. Peter was also the home of Gustavus Adolphus College, a private, four-year, liberal arts school with a sound reputation. Since tuition at Gustavus Adolphus was higher than Minnesota state schools and several other regional private schools, students were likely to be from relatively wealthy families or were likely to work to partially support their college educations. Exhibit 22.2 provides information about St. Peter's population trends, retail sales, industry composition, transportation, community services, and education.

Recently discussions had been held regarding potential downtown renovation. Options ranged from " streetscaping" in the core of downtown, to building a one-block small mall, to building a four-block larger mall. The current sentiment, based on information provided by an outside paid consultant, favored building a mall, although plans were not yet sufficiently developed to detail the size and location. At city meetings, residents and community leaders expressed overwhelming support for keeping retail and entertainment downtown, rather than on some outlying acreage yet to be determined. Of the factors considered in developing a retail area, those most important to the residents included retaining downtown retailing, stopping shopping center competition, and improving the retail mix. Discussions on financial feasibility were expected to narrow the choices, with a decision for action expected nearer to the end of 1987.

Beth and Ann themselves felt that there was a "new fresh attitude" among St. Peter retailers. The Retail Council, a committee of the St. Peter Chamber of Commerce, had undertaken numerous planned activities to encourage and support St. Peter's retail establishments. The retailers believed consumers in this region were quite typical, though sometimes they seemed more prone to bargain hunting.

Much of the concern retailers and residents had for downtown improvement stemmed from growing recognition of the impact of competing market areas. A St. Peter resident could drive to Minneapolis in just over an hour. Large malls built in the south and east suburbs of Minneapolis enticed shoppers from outlying areas. In addition, St. Peter shoppers were attracted to Mankato, which, together with North Mankato, offered many nationally known chain stores, services, and recreational opportunities (See Exhibit 22.3). While the population of Mankato and North Mankato was around 40,000 people, several educational institutions added to this population base: Mankato State University, Bethany Lutheran College, Mankato Technical Institute, and Rasmussen Business College. Many of these students, particularly those attending Mankato State University, lived in the twin cities of Minneapolis-St. Paul and their suburbs, and commuted there to work on the weekends.

THE STORE

JJ's was located on Third Street, one block west of Minnesota Avenue, between Grace and Mulberry Streets, in the Konsbruck Hotel building. Built in 1901, the hotel occupied about two-thirds of the length of Third Street on that block, and

EXHIBIT 22.2 **St. Peter community profile**

Population	1960	1970	1980	1985 (est.)
St. Peter	8,484	8,339	9,056	9,082
Nicollet County	23,196	24,518	26,920	28,190

Industry	Number of employees
Health care	1,025
Education	630
Electronics	245
Total manufacturing	2,900
Total nonmanufacturing	4,960
Total labor force	13,601 (county)
Unemployment: 4.2% annual average	

Transportation

Rail: 2 lines daily, no passenger service
Truck lines: 4
Bus: 1 intercity line
Air: 1 airport; nearest commercial airport: Mankato
Highways: 35 miles to I-35; 69 miles to I-90
    Federal: #169 through city; State: #99, 22, 295, 333

Community services

Motels: 3; units: 50
Hospital beds: 46; Nursing home beds: 150
Doctors: 10; Dentists: 8
Churches: 12
Banks: 2; Deposits: $120 million
Sports: college
News media: Newspaper: 1 weekly; Radio stations: 2 AM, 2 FM; Television: 0
Retail sales: County $70.9 million (1985)
            St. Peter $41.9 million (1985)
Per-capita income: County $11,123 (1984)

Education	Number	Enrollment	Grades
Elementary schools	2	860	K–6
Senior high schools	1	805	7–12
Parochial schools	1	141	K–6
Colleges	1	2,230	Gustavus Adolphus
		(1,252 women, 978 men)	

Source: Minnesota Department of Energy and Economic Development, 1987, St. Paul, MN.

EXHIBIT 22.3 **Mankato and North Mankato community profile**

Population	1960	1970	1980	1985 (special census)
Mankato	23,797	30,895	28,637	28,692
Blue Earth County	44,385	52,322	52,314	52,964 (1985 est.)
North Mankato	5,927	7,347	9,145	9,844
Nicollet County	23,196	24,518	26,920	28,190 (1985 est.)

Industry	Number of employees
Total manufacturing	4,455
Total nonmanufacturing	18,563
Total labor force	23,018 (county)
Unemployment: 5.3% annual average	

Transportation

Rail: 7 lines daily, no passenger service
Truck lines: 6
Bus: 2 intercity lines
Air: 2 commercial airlines; charter and jet service
Highways: 40 miles to I-35; 51 miles to I-90
    Federal: #14, 169; State: #68, 65, 22

Community services

Motels: 12; units: 679
Hospital beds: 272; Nursing home beds: 384
Doctors: 90; Dentists: 34
Churches: 47
Banks: 10; Deposits: $638 million
Sports: college; Professional: fall practice site for Minnesota Vikings
News Media: Newspaper: 1 daily; Radio stations: 2 AM, 4 FM; Television: 1
Retail sales: both counties $434.1 million (1984)
            both cities $326.6 million (1984)
Per-capita income: Blue Earth County $10,945 (1983)
            Nicollet County $ 9,902 (1983)

Education	Number	Enrollment	Grades
Elementary schools	8	3,414	K–6
Senior high schools	2	2,838	7–12
Parochial schools	12	1,493	K–12
Colleges	4	13,105	Mankato State University (6815 women, and 6290 men)
		n/a	Bethany Lutheran College
		n/a	Rasmussen Business College
		930	Mankato Technical Institute (375 women, 555 men)

Source: Minnesota Department of Energy and Economic Development, 1986, St. Paul, MN.

was now divided into five business places on the first floor, with residences for low-income persons on the second floor. The business place closest to Mulberry Street was currently unoccupied. Other businesses in the hotel building included a bar, an art and framing gallery, and a second-hand clothing store. The bar, the oldest tenant of the building, was actually a private club, established in the early 1900s as a men's fraternal organization. While no longer restricted to men, its membership was made up of long-time residents of St. Peter; the bar tended to be patronized by older people. An empty lot lay between the hotel building and a restaurant on the corner of Third and Grace. Across the street from JJ's stretched a parking lot for a relatively large low-cost food store, and a fire station.

The store was typical of buildings of its age: it had high ceilings, narrow doorways, and wooden floors. JJ's occupied approximately 1,500 square feet on the first floor and basement, although the basement was virtually unusable, due to lack of upkeep throughout the years. In fact, the dirt basement floor had been improved with floor covering. The sales area was divided from the work and storage area in the rear by a wall with a doorway on the right (See Exhibit 22.4). Clothing racks lined the walls; a central counter at the back wall and clothing racks left just enough

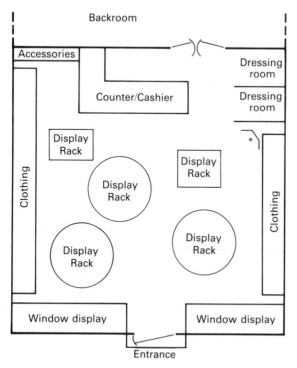

*Three-way mirror

EXHIBIT 22.4 **JJ's store layout**

room for shoppers to maneuver between the displays. The back room contained a desk for record keeping, a chaise and a few chairs, and several additional clothing racks for lay-a-ways and new inventory. The basement was accessible only through a trap door in the floor of this work area.

When Beth and Ann bought the store, they made few changes except the improvements they believed to be necessary, such as adding window film to prevent clothes from fading, shades, carpet in the window display areas, and a decorative border around the doorway. Planned improvements included wallpapering and air conditioning.

JJ's was open Mondays through Thursdays from 9:00 a.m. to 5:30 p.m., even though typical closing time for retail businesses in St. Peter was 5:00. In addition, JJ's was open until 9:00 p.m. on Fridays, and 5:00 p.m. on Saturdays. No retail clothing stores were open on Sundays in St. Peter.

The owners believed Fridays and Saturdays to be their busiest days although sometimes Mondays could be busy. A typical Saturday's sales would range from $500 to $600, while a typical weekday might bring in between $250 and $500, with fluctuations by season. Weather also had an effect on sales. The past winter had been extremely mild, so little fluctuation in sales was apparent. The owners also believed that about 50 percent of the people who entered the store were "just looking." These people were important, however, since they were likely to be good future business. If people came into the store once, the owners felt they were likely to come back. One of their problems at this time was lack of awareness, even in St. Peter. It was a small enough town that people would look elsewhere to find something different.

While the owners did not know exactly what their trade area was, they believed it to be St. Peter, towns to the north such as Le Sueur where store selection was extremely limited, Henderson, and perhaps even as far as Belle Plaine, which was 25 miles away. They were quite sure they drew from other small towns in the near vicinity. JJ's also drew some people from Mankato, on their way to Minneapolis. The owners even had some business from people who lived in towns such as Madelia, 20 miles south of Mankato. Occasionally, they would be visited by Minneapolis shoppers who prefered small retail shopping areas because of the services offered.

Of the other women's clothing stores in St. Peter, none carried clothing appropriate for the "young career" woman. One well-established store appealed to older people who were willing to pay higher prices, another catered to women with children, and carried a mix of women's and children's clothing. A children's clothing store was believed to be going out of business soon. There had been a store, located on the river side of Minnesota Avenue, catering to the college and career woman, but it didn't survive. Businesses located on the east side of the Avenue seemed to have a harder time, perhaps because most of St. Peter was to the west of Minnesota Avenue. In addition, the owners of the unsuccessful store spent about $25,000 in redecorating, perhaps more than could have been recovered in a reasonable amount of time. Another reason that was given for the store's failure was that, "this is a small town and people didn't know the owners."

THE RETAIL MIX

Merchandise

When Ann and Beth purchased JJ's in 1985, the lines of clothing carried by the store were appropriate for young women between twelve to eighteen. Realizing that those ages represented a limited market for long-term business, they chose to keep three vendor-lines, but changed the others. Since they have been in business, they have changed some of the lines for other reasons: some were not the quality the owners were seeking, and some sales representatives were difficult to deal with.

The owners characterized their lines as "young missy" and "young career." In the early phase of their business, they carried lines for which a mother would probably shop with or for her daughter; after their line changes, items were usually selected by the intended wearer. This change in focus was appropriate, the owners believed, because the young college women, and particularly the young career women (women who would be working in or near St. Peter), had the need and the ability to buy.

While JJ's did not carry "Guess?" or "Esprit" brands of clothing, which required a minimum order of $5,000, they did carry other popular brands: D.D. Sloane, Zena, White Stag, and Catalina, for example. The types of merchandise included slacks, skirts, blouses and tops, and casual and a few semi-dressy dresses. They carried several lines of accessories as well.

Of the Zena brand, JJ's carried jeans and denim clothing, some dyed and some twills, priced at retail about $43 to $45, considered to be a moderate price by Ann and Beth. These were available in missy (8–18) and junior (5–13) sizes, and could only be ordered in even dozens. Even so, Ann and Beth had no choice regarding the sizes or sometimes even the colors that were included in each dozen they would receive from Zena. This sometimes created a problem, since the larger sizes were often the first to sell, with little demand for the very small sizes. Zena used a "factor," a representative (often a bank) through which to handle payments from store owners and managers. Dealing with this channel facilitator sometimes added complexity to their communications with Zena, even to the point of holding up orders if there were misunderstandings on payments.

Under the D.D. Sloane label, JJ's stocked sweaters, knit dresses, sportswear, jackets, pants, and shorts, usually retail priced at $40 to $60, somewhat higher than most of JJ's other merchandise. Of this better line, the owners were able to buy pieces in lots of four. Garland was also considered by Beth and Ann to be a good-quality line. Well known for many years as a sweater manufacturer, Garland also manufactured print skirts. These items were priced moderately, $30 to $40; JJ's purchased them in minimum quantities of six items.

White Stag was a widely distributed brand of good-quality knit separates, with tops cut a little fuller, and pants, skirts, and shorts with elastic waist bands. These were available in missy sizes, were usually purchased at JJ's by women over 25, and were moderately priced. This had been a popular brand for JJ's. Catalina knitwear was also sized for the missy figure and included moderately priced swim and sportswear. JJ's could order any amount and size from the manufacturer.

Either Ann or Beth would go to the market five to six times a year, usually to Minneapolis, where they could visit several vendors at a time. While some vendors' offices and showrooms were located in hotels, others sold out of their homes. Occasionally, sales representatives would come to St. Peter. The owners had made an effort to find new lines through visiting with reps in each of these situations. They needed to order merchandise at least four months early. For instance, fall merchandise for July delivery must be ordered during the first week in April. On occasion, Beth and Ann would be able to special-order merchandise if they needed a special size or color, although most vendors did not make this service available to small retailers.

Since the two owners did not employ any other help, they were responsible for all the duties necessary to keep the store operating, including ordering, selling, planning and preparing displays and advertisements, pressing and marking clothing, making payments to vendors, handling customer service, and doing any other tasks that needed to be done. They shared responsibilities flexibly, adapting to each other's personal schedules as the need arose, though it did so infrequently. While they did not have a formal partnership agreement, they had recently discussed the benefits of having one.

Service

Ann and Beth offered many services to their customers that would not be found in larger stores. Perhaps their most important service was the personal attention they were able to offer. For many women shopping for clothing, having assistance in selecting correct sizes and colors was desirable. In addition to accepting Visa and Mastercard, Beth and Ann offered a store charge, with monthly payments and no interest on the unpaid balance. Lay-away was available, with a 30 percent initial payment, and additional payments according to the customer's ability. After a length of time one of the owners would call the lay-away customer to check on their desire, either to keep the product on lay-away or put it back on the floor for sale. Customers could take home an item of clothing for trial, with next-day payment or return. The owners stressed that since this was a small town, they knew people and had a good idea of who could and who could not be trusted. To date, they had only had one bad risk, a woman who charged merchandise worth $250 and didn't make payments.

JJ's also offered to take back unacceptable merchandise. In fact, they sometimes felt that this service was too good, since occasionally customers would take advantage of it. They described one woman who purchased an oversized "balloon" style sweatshirt, with black animals printed on white fabric. Instructions printed on a garment tag, and reiterated verbally to the woman by Ann, cautioned against washing the garment in anything other than cold water. Several weeks later the woman returned the garment, quite worn and faded. It was taken back and replaced with a new, identical garment. The woman returned with the second garment equally worn sometime later. Ann took the garment back and gave the woman credit, even though she suspected that the sweatshirt had been washed in hot water or otherwise treated harshly. No other purchasers of the garmet had similar problems.

They also offered free gift wrapping, and Beth would do alterations, such as hemming, if it was not too involved. If they were aware of a seamstress or tailor locally who desired to do alterations, they would gladly make recommendations; however, they were not aware of someone who could accomodate them.

Pricing

The owners set their margins to be slightly lower, by a dollar or two, than most other area stores. Some items, however, such as White Stag, came preticketed. For accessories, they generally used the standard 100 percent markup.

Their fee for handling Visa and Mastercard was four percent. They had more cash sales than credit. Other than that one bad debt, they had little or no difficulty with offering a store charge. For their lay-away customers, when a payment was received, that amount was rung up as a sale for that day. Terms for payments to their vendors were typically 8/10, net 30.

Promotions

Ann and Beth made their own advertising decisions, and understood the value of advertising in generating customer traffic and sales. They developed the message but usually had a friend who was an artist do the layout and design. They appreciated their friend's help, even though she was sometimes hard to motivate, resulting in insufficient lead time to prepare good ads. Even though they were doing more advertising than the previous owner, they were uncertain if they were doing enough, or if what they were doing was effective. In addition, they wondered if there might be other forms of promotion that they hadn't yet tried that might work for their store.

There were several activities that the Retail Council organized for St. Peter retailers. These events were chosen by a subcommittee of the Council, and voted upon by the full membership. Ann and Beth had participated actively in many of these events. For 1987, the Retail Council's list of suggested events consisted of those activities listed in Exhibit 22.5.

In addition to those events, JJ's participated in a Hospital Auxiliary style show at the beginning of April, held at a local restaurant overlooking the Minnesota River. Attendance was in excess of 350 people. A fall style show was held in November with several other businesses, for students of Gustavus Adolphus, the local university. At this event, gift certificates were distributed, as well as coupons for the following week. This event was felt to be successful in attracting new business.

The fall style show also contributed toward raising funds for another project sponsored by the Retail Council. On the evening after Thanksgiving, the community turned out for "The Big Turn On," lighting the elaborate Christmas lights and decorations on Minnesota Avenue. Fund raising events intending to raise $13,000

EXHIBIT 22.5 **Retail promotions for 1987**

Date	Promotion
February 27th	Library Reserves
April 4th	Style Show
May 15–16th	Clean-Up Sale 8 a.m.–9 p.m. Friday 8 a.m.–5 p.m. Saturday
June 10th	Sunrise Sale 6 a.m.
July 28th	Moonlight Madness 7–10 p.m.
August	Back to School
August 6, 7, 8, 9th	Nicollet County Fair
August 22nd	Neighborfest
September 11, 12th	Sidewalk Sale 8 a.m.–9 p.m. Friday 8 a.m.–5 p.m. Saturday
October 30th	Halloween Dress-up
November 27th	Big Second Annual Turn On
December	Christmas Hours
13th	Hospitality Sunday 1–5 p.m.
20th	Sunday opening
7–23rd	Open every weekday night
24th	Close at 4 p.m.
31st	Close at 4 p.m.

for this project brought in $20,000. Plans were underway to extend the lights and decorations to the retail areas along Third Street, but another $2,500 was needed, for which the Council had been soliciting $100 donations from businesses in St. Peter. In coordination with these activities, Ann organized cooperative advertising Christmas flyers to be placed in shopping bags, following the motif of the street designs and promoting the downtown merchants and local seasonal events.

In the fall of 1985 (their first fall), JJ's participated in the Welcome Wagon service, for which they paid $90 to be included and have coupons printed. The service welcomed approximately 850 new and transfer students at Gustavus Adolphus. There was no response from this promotion.

At Christmas, JJ's sponsored a "men's night," during which cheese, wine, and soda were served to men shopping for Christmas gifts. JJ's helped these men shop by maintaining lists prepared by women shoppers and kept on file at JJ's for their husbands or friends. In addition, JJ's had an anniversary sale each year at the beginning of April. For several of their events, they utilized joint ads with a local men's clothing store.

For their numerous special events and regular awareness builders, Beth and Ann used newspaper and radio advertisements: the *St. Peter Herald* and *Valley*, the *Mankato Free Press*, KRBI, and KEEZ. The *Herald* was used for specials, perhaps twice a month; ads were placed in the *Valley* and *Free Press* about once a month. KRBI, the only local St. Peter radio station, was used for ads with the Retail Council (sometimes free ads were available with the Council) about once a month, while KEEZ, from Mankato, was occasionally used on a "saturation" basis, when ads were aired at regular intervals over a week's time. A description of these media and other media available in the area is provided in Exhibit 22.6. In addition to these media, residents also watched or listened to several Minneapolis-St. Paul television and radio stations.

Accounting Records and Statements

Limited financial records were maintained at the store. Essentially, these consisted of cash register tapes, a checkbook, vendor files for unpaid and paid invoices, and a spreadsheet journal form on which daily entries were made for the operations. The spreadsheet journal was given periodically to a licensed public accountant's firm.

The accounting firm used the spreadsheet journal as a source for updating the store's computerized general ledger. Then, a balance sheet and income statement were prepared. During 1985, monthly statements were issued for seven of the nine months after the new owners took over. Only three statements were issued for 1986: May, Preliminary End-of-Year, and Final End-of-Year. In 1987, only the balance sheet for March and the income statements for January, February, March, and the first-quarter had been furnished to the store owners. Selected statements from the accountant are provided in Exhibits 22.7 through 22.10.

One reason for the infrequent issue of statements was that the store owners agreed to pay the accounting firm by letting the accountant's wife charge purchases, offset against the accounting fees. Although this arrangement worked well in the beginning, it seemed that control over the issuance of statements had been transferred to the licensed public accountant.

The store owners were concerned about maintaining the vendor files so as not to miss taking a discount. With approximately two dozen vendors used as their sources of merchandise inventory, the method used to pay vendors relied upon a combination of memory and calendar entries. One of the owners had primary responsibility for handling vendor invoices.

When an invoice was received it was reviewed for accuracy, the payment date (giving cognizance to any discount period) was entered on the calendar, and then the invoice was filed in the unpaid-vendor file (actually, a stack of bills on the desk). On a daily basis, or nearly so, the calendar was reviewed to determine what bills needed to be paid. Such entries on the calendar resulted in the unpaid-vendor's file being searched for the appropriate invoice. Then, a check was issued.

The owners admitted that this was not a foolproof system. Occasionally a vendor invoice did not get paid on time—and even worse, they feared missing a discount, because both partners understood that missed discounts translated into a high effective interest cost.

EXHIBIT 22.6 **Available media**

Medium	Reach	Costs
Newspapers		
Mankato Free Press	27,000 daily except Sunday	All rates on monthly basis; ads appear 6 days/week, 24 times/month Column inch: 1–19 = $8.01/in. 20–49 = 7.17/in. 50–99 = 6.89/in. 1/4 page (3x10) = $215.10 1/2 page = 413.40 full page = 851.41
St. Peter Herald	3,500 weekly	If a home gets the Herald, it does not get the Valley; rates are all on a per-ad basis. Ad appears in both Herald and Valley.
Valley	12,000 weekly	Basic rate: $5.70/col in. Yearly: 100 in/yr = $5.28/col in. 300 = 5.06/col in. 900 = 4.85/col in. 3000 = 4.64/col in. 1/4 page (31x$5.70) = $176.70 1/2 page = 353.40 full page = 706.80
Reporter Mankato State University T/Th only during year W only in summer	on campus distribution	$3.50/col. in. 3.25/col. in. if over 75″ 2.50/col. in. in summer 1/4 page = $ 58.50 1/2 page = 122 full page = 243
Gustavian Weekly Gustavus Adolphus College Printed on Fridays, not printed during summer	on campus	Rates not available
Television		
KEYC-TV	35 miles NE and 100 miles SW min.	TAP (Total Audience Participation), spots spread throughout viewing time. 44 spots/wk = $596 Prime time (7pm–10pm) 104 spots/yr = $99/spot 10 p.m. news $89/spot 6 p.m. news 79/spot Many other packages available.
Cable TV MTV USA 97% penetration rate	48,000 residents greater Mankato area	TAP, 30 sec., 3:30–midnight 100 spots = $600 (2–3 per night) $7/ad if less than 100 50% higher for 60 sec. ads

Plays in many pizza and restaurant bars, wired to all dorms.	production = $150 for 30 sec. 175 for 60 sec. To develop jingle, starts at $100 for background music, more for lyrics.

Radio

KRBI
St. Peter
	30 mile
	radius
		30-second ads = TAP
		Per-year cost: 1–52 spots = $9.05/ad
		            53–156 = 7.70
		            157–312 = 7.00
		            313–624 = 5.75
		            625–1248 = 5.40
		Weekly cost: 10–20/wk = 7.50/ad
		            21–30 = 7.25
		            31–60 = 7.00
		            61–80 = 6.60
		            81–100 = 6.30
		            101+ = 5.95
		Noon-hour rate: $12.10/ad/30 sec.
		                  19.50/ad/60 sec.
		Copywriting help available.

KDOG Mankato Music: top 40, rock, some jazz	45 mile radius	TAP 6am to midnight, 30 sec. ads. 300/yr = $6.50/ad 20/wk = 9.25 21–30/wk = 8.50 Prime time morning or afternoon = $9.00/ad.
KEEZ Mankato Music: top 40, light rock, "classics"	200 mile radius	TAP 6am to midnight, 30 sec. ads. 14 spots/wk = $147 35 spots/wk = 332.50 Morning drive: 25% increase 13 week commitment: 10% decrease Annual contracts, 10 sec. spots, and copywriting help available.
KTOE Mankato Music: older songs, easy listening, Minnesota Twins games	75 mile radius	TAP 6am to midnight, 30 sec. ads. 14/wk = $10/spot 35/wk = 8.50 49+ = 7.50 150/yr = 7.00 600/yr = 6.25 Prime time: 25% increase; packages available. Special for ads during MN Twins games, including tickets.
KYSM North Mankato Music: country	FM: 55 counties AM:n/a	TAP, 30 sec., special promotion: 30/month for 3 months = $6.00 50 = 5.50 75 = 5.25 (393.73/mo.) 15 sec. = $4; 60 sec. = $8
XL-93 Mankato Music: light rock, mellow	80 mile radius	$8.50 prime time, 30 sec. spot 8.00 for equal number of ads/wk Special: 60 sec. for 30 sec. price = $8.50

EXHIBIT 22.7 **JJ's income statements—1985 and 1986**

	1985	1986
Income		
Sales—clothing	$47,055	$83,746
Sales—taxable	2,290	5,058
Less: returns and allowances	665	864
Total gross sales	48,680	87,940
Direct Cost of Sales		
Purchases	32,054	57,593
Freight	415	178
Store supplies	1,044	1,407
Laundry and alteration	0	31
Cash short or long (−)	0	0
Total direct cost of sales	33,513	59,209
Total gross profit from sales	$15,167	$28,731
General Operating Expenses		
Advertising and promotion	$ 1,601	$ 3,452
Accounting and legal	89	0
Bank and credit card charges	217	333
Contributions	0	316
Dues and subscriptions	90	112
Insurance	273	270
Interest	445	902
License and permits	0	0
Rent expense	3,555	4,740
Utilities and telephone	980	1,214
Office supplies and postage	183	421
Travel and market	169	429
Repairs and maintenance	306	645
Miscellaneous expense	283	105
Depreciation expense	677	922
Amortization expense	297	400
Total general expenses	9,165	14,261
Net profit before partners' salary	6,002	14,470
Less: partner salary—Beth	4,169	3,300
Less: partner salary—Ann	3,100	3,300
Current profit or (loss)	$(1,267)	$ 7,870

The owners paid rent on a monthly basis, based on a flat fee; there was no per-square-foot charge, or percent-of-sales charge. They were committed to a one-year lease. They had also borrowed $5,000 in March 1987 for inventory, and consequently had a lien against the inventory. In order to ease the burden of payments, they paid Jane Johnson on the 15th and Ann on the 15th, while Beth took her payment

---

EXHIBIT 22.8 **JJ's balance sheet—1985 and 1986**

	1985	1986
Assets		
Current assets		
Cash on hand	$ 133.87	$ 626.89
Change fund and petty cash	0.00	120.00
Checking account	2,748.36	6,308.56
Accounts receivable	0.00	0.00
Inventory	12,718.83	14,290.15
Total current assets	15,601.06	21,345.60
Fixed assets		
Store equipment	4,511.07	4,511.07
Less accumulated depreciation	677.00	1,599.00
Covenant not to compete	2,000.00	2,000.00
Less accumulated amortization	297.00	697.00
Goodwill	2,000.00	2,000.00
Total net fixed assets	7,537.07	6,215.07
Total assets	$23,138.13	$27,560.67
Liabilities and Partner Equity		
Current liabilities		
Accounts payable	$ 302.17	$ 81.14
Sales tax unremitted	53.82	95.14
Total current liabilities	355.99	176.28
Long-term debt		
Note payable—Jane Johnson	6,261.39	5,041.52
Note payable—bank	0.00	700.00
Total long-term debt	6,261.39	5,741.52
Total liabilities	6,617.38	5,917.80
Owner equity		
Owner equity—Beth	8,876.75	6,812.39
Owner withdrawal—Beth	0.00	0.00
Owner equity—Ann	7,644.00	6,959.88
Owner withdrawal—Ann	0.00	0.00
Current profit or (loss)	0.00	7,870.60
Total owner equity	16,520.75	21,642.87
Total liabilities and owner equity	$23,138.13	$27,560.67

on the 30th of each month. However, in some months when sales were particularly low, the owners did not take a salary at all. They were making double payments to Jane, in order to retire that responsibility as soon as possible. In so doing, they kept careful records of their payments.

EXHIBIT 22.9 **JJ's income statement—1987**

	January	**February**	**March**
Income			
Sales	$6,943.43	$7,977.31	$8,259.66
Taxable sales	447.83	541.83	533.00
Sales returns and allowances	(150.00)	(194.22)	(211.82)
Total sales	7,241.26	8,324.92	8,580.84
Cost of Goods Sold			
Purchases	4,544.32	5,537.44	5,715.23
Freight	29.91	23.46	35.73
Store supplies	406.48	198.05	145.61
Laundry and alterations	4.55	0.00	0.00
Total cost of goods sold	4,985.26	5,756.95	5,896.57
Total gross profit from sales	$2,256.00	$2,565.97	$2,684.27
General Operating Expenses			
Advertising	$ 634.18	$ 156.66	$ 353.19
Bank and credit card charges	38.97	1.37	19.66
Contributions	5.00	12.00	90.00
Interest—Jane Johnson	42.01	41.12	40.23
Interest—Bank	5.59	0.00	0.00
Rent	395.00	395.00	395.00
Utilities and telephone	81.14	120.65	126.25
Office supplies and postage	2.00	32.64	47.00
Travel and market	69.68	26.00	130.05
Repairs and maintenance	0.00	0.00	23.89
Miscellaneous	12.78	0.00	0.00
Total operating expenses	1,286.35	785.44	1,225.27
Less: partners salaries			
Partner salary—Beth	500.00	350.00	350.00
Partner salary—Ann	500.00	1,259.00	350.00
Current profit or (loss)	$ (30.35)	$ 171.53	$ 759.00

GOALS FOR THE FUTURE

While the owners had no explicitly stated goals for their business, they had thought about a "best case" scenario. They wanted, eventually, to buy the building in which the store was operating, and perhaps to expand the store, or at least to move the wall backward to expand the sales floor area of their store.

For Ann, whose husband farmed, a dream was to be able to earn enough from the store to renovate their fifth-generation family farm home. With the farming economy as restricted as it had been in this rural area, these were not easy times. This was all the more reason to have well-planned and well-implemented promotional programs to stimulate demand.

EXHIBIT 22.10 **JJ's balance sheet—1987**

Assets
  Current assets
    Cash $ 87
    Cash on deposit   282
    Inventory   25,514
       Total current assets   25,882

  Fixed and other assets
    Goodwill   2,000
    Store furniture and fixtures   4,848
    Covenant not to compete   2,000
       Total other assets   8,848
       Less: accumulated depreciation/amortization   2,296

  Net fixed assets   6,552

  Total assets $32,434

Liabilities and Partnership Equity
  Liabilities
    Accounts payable $ 81
    Unremitted sales tax   91
    Note payable—Jane Johnson   4,719
    Note payable—bank   5,000
       Total liabilities   9,891

  Partnership equity
    Partner equity—Beth   10,748
    Partner equity—Ann   10,895
    Current profit or (loss)   900
       Total partnership equity   22,543

  Total liabilities and partnership equity $32,434

CASE 23 ————————————————————————————————

The Dallas Morning News

As they contemplated the situation facing *The Dallas Morning News* (MN), Mr. Burl Osborne (President and Editor), Mr. Jeremy Halbreich (Executive Vice President and General Manager), and other members of the MN's top management knew that they faced important and difficult decisions as they developed a strategic marketing plan into the 1990s. Further, these executives realized the necessity of their daily 10:00 a.m. meeting to review and adjust their strategic and tactical decisions.

The dynamics of the now soft Dallas-Fort Worth market plus the actions of the rival *Dallas Times Herald* (TH) and other media competitors for both readers' attention and advertisers' dollars, assured Osborne and Halbreich that developing a new five-year strategic marketing plan for the MN would be a challenging enterprise.

The trade press loved the continuing battle waged between the MN and the TH. For years the duel had been largely nip-and-tuck, but in the first half of 1985 the MN had gained a significant circulation advantage in the TH's long-time strength—Dallas County (see Exhibit 23.1). Some industry analysts suggested the battle in Dallas for newspaper supremacy was over—won by the MN.

In 1986, after 16 years in Dallas, the TH's corporate parent, Times-Mirror, sold the TH to the MediaNews Group for $110 million effective September 1, 1986. In announcing the sale, Mr. Robert Erburu, Chairman and CEO of Times-Mirror commented, "Times-Mirror is very proud of the achievements of the *Dallas Times Herald*, but we believe that its sale at this time is consistent with our corporate strategy and is in the best interest of the long-term future of the *Times Herald*."

From the other side of the sale, Mr. Dean Singleton, President of MediaNews, boasted, "If I didn't think the *Times Herald* could beat the *Morning News*, I wouldn't have bought it."

Under Mr. Singleton's direction, the TH filed a circulation fraud suit in federal district court in Chicago against the MN, naming the Audit Bureau of Circulation as co-defendant. The MN promptly filed a countersuit against the TH also claiming circulation fraud and suggested that the TH's legal action was designed primarily to cloud the circulation issue.

In November 1986, Texas Attorney General Jim Mattox announced that he had began an investigation of both papers circulation practices. Mr. Mattox quickly found no wrongdoing at the TH. On the other hand, in February 1987, Mr. Mattox

EXHIBIT 23.1 **Circulation (In thousands) of Dallas newspapers, 1978–1987**

		Daily			Sunday	
	City zone[1]	SMSA	Total	City zone[1]	SMSA	Total
1987[4]						
MN	n/a	n/a	388	n/a	n/a	541
TH	n/a	n/a	240	n/a	n/a	338
Hhlds						
1986						
MN	239	313[2]	390	320	425[2]	522
TH	182	216[3]	245	254	305[3]	348
Hhlds						
1985						
MN	230	297[2]	369	295	384[2]	476
TH	183	214[3]	241	257	303[3]	346
Hhlds	679	1,290[2]		679	858[3]	
1984						
MN	207	267[2]	331	258	339[2]	421
TH	193	224[3]	252	259	304[3]	346
Hhlds	656	1,239[2]		656	826[3]	
1983						
MN	206	261	321	248	320	397
TH	210	253	268	271	330	355
Hhlds	647	n/a		647	n/a	
1982						
MN	195	242	295	237	298	368
TH	200	241	254	261	317	341
Hhlds	628	n/a		628	n/a	
1981						
MN	188	232	284	230	287	356
TH	194	230	244	263	315	338
Hhlds	607	1,138		607	1,138	
1980						
MN	188	229	279	225	279	346
TH	195	232	245	263	316	339
Hhlds	592	1,105		592	1,105	
1979						
MN	185	226	277	220	271	341
TH	199	235	247	264	314	336
Hhlds	538	989		538	989	
1978						
MN	189	225	277	223	271	345
TH	204	238	249	267	316	338
Hhlds	522	954		522	954	

[1] City Zone is Dallas County. The SMSA is an 11-county area made up the following counties: Collin, Dallas, Denton, Ellis, Hood, Johnson, Kaufman, Parker, Rockwell, Tarrant, and Wise.

[2] In 1984 the MN switched from SMSA to a CMSA which consists of a 9-county area (the SMSA less Hood and Wise).

[3] In 1984 the TH switched from SMSA to a PMSA which consists of a 6-county area (the SMSA less Hood, Johnson, Parker, Tarrant, and Wise).

[4] 1987 figures are unaudited.

Sources: 1977–1986—ABC Audit Reports. 1987—*Adweek*, 5/18/87, p. 3. *Sales & Marketing Management*, 1978–1986.

formally notified the MN that he would continue his investigation of the MN to determine if the paper had violated the state's deceptive trade practices. MN officials contended that Mr. Mattox's actions were in retaliation for the MN's coverage of his conduct in office, questionable campaign contributions, and the MN's endorsement of his opponent in the fall 1986 election. The TH had endorsed Mr. Mattox.

More recently, the attorney general indicated that he would examine the circulation practices of both newspapers. Further, his investigation would not begin until after new ABC circulation figures were available.

At the TH, Mr. Singleton, Mr. Art Wible (Publisher), Mr. David Burgin (Senior VP and Editor), Mr. John Wolf (Senior VP, Marketing/Advertising) and other members of the TH's top management team were experienced and aggressive competitors. They could be counted on to continue to generate aggressive marketing actions as they attempted to swing the tide to their advantage.

HISTORY OF THE DALLAS MORNING NEWS

> Build the News upon
> the rock of truth
> and righteousness
> Conduct it always
> upon the lines of
> fairness and integrity
> Acknowledge the right
> of the people to get
> from the newspaper
> both sides of every
> important question
>
> G.B. Dealey

The words above are inscribed on the facade of the present MN building. This admonition is an excerpt from a speech delivered in 1906 by Mr. G. B. Dealey, founder of the MN, at the dedication of an employees' library. This statement sets forth the philosophy that has guided the newspaper since its inception.

Mr. Dealey began his newspaper career with *The Galveston News* in 1874 at the age of 15 as an office boy. Because of his initiative and enthusiasm, he was asked to travel to north Texas in 1882 by Col. A.H. Belo (owner of *The Galveston News*) to begin researching a plant site for a new newspaper. Mr. Dealey recommended the growing railhead community of Dallas as the best location.

On October 1, 1885 the MN published its first edition as a subsidiary of *The Galveston News*. In 1894 Mr. Dealey was promoted from Business Manager to General Manager of the MN and in 1920 he was elected President. In 1926 Mr. Dealey purchased the MN and a Dallas radio station from the Belo family. In addition, he reorganized the company and changed its name to the A.H. Belo Corporation. Mr. Dealey served as Publisher of the MN from 1926 until his death in 1946 at the age of 86.

In 1981, the Belo Corporation sold shares of common stock in an initial offering on the American Stock Exchange (later the stock was moved to the New York Stock Exchange). Mr. Dealey's descendants remain the largest stockholders in Belo. The corporation was ranked as the 27th largest U.S. media company in 1986 by *Ad Age*. The principal business activities of Belo are newspaper publishing and network television broadcasting.

Belo's principal newspaper property is the MN. In addition, the company owns Dallas-Fort Worth Suburban Newspapers, Inc., a group of seven community newspapers located in the suburbs of the Dallas-Fort Worth metroplex. The corporation also owns five network affiliate television stations in Dallas, Houston, Sacramento, Tulsa, and Hampton-Norfolk, Virginia.

In 1984, newspaper publishing contributed 55 percent of Belo's revenues and 35 percent of profits. Broadcasting contributed roughly 45 percent of revenues and 65 percent of profits. In 1985 newspaper publishing contributed 57 percent of revenues and 39 percent of profits. Total operating revenues (millions) for 1986—$397.2; 1985—$385.1; 1984—$354.2; 1983—$242.6; and, 1982—$203.4.

THE RIVAL: THE DALLAS TIMES HERALD

The TH is presently owned by the MediaNews Group Corporation, headquartered in Dallas. MediaNews was ranked as the 74th largest media company in 1986 by *Ad Age* before the company acquired the TH. MediaNews's principal business is newspaper publishing. Currently the corporation owns 22 small- and medium-sized dailies plus the TH, which is the largest.

In 1985, the company reported revenues of $150 million. The privately held company was founded in 1983 by Mr. Dean Singleton and Mr. Richard Scudder when they jointly purchased the *Gloucester County Times* in Woodbury, New Jersey. Since the company's establishment, it has followed an aggressive acquisition strategy.

Dallas Times Herald Strategy—1970s

In the mid-1970s, executives at the TH had become increasingly uneasy about growth trends in the Dallas market and the handicaps of an afternoon delivery. The population was growing at a very rapid rate and, at the same time, becoming more affluent demographically. TH executives worried that the MN's traditionally upscale appeal and positioning would allow the MN to dominate among the more affluent new residents who were arriving in large numbers. Further, the majority of the newcomers preferred a morning newspaper.

The trend in Dallas and across the country toward more white-collar, service-oriented jobs was running against the long-run viability of many afternoon dailies. Many considerations favored morning delivery—for example, morning newspapers enjoyed reduced competition with evening television, home-delivery was cheaper, a larger geographic area could be served, classified advertising was more attractive, and a.m. papers had higher pass-along readership.

In developing a marketing strategy for long-term growth in this environment, TH management decided on two major actions. First, they targeted three reader groups—newcomers, females, and young adults. This strategy built on traditional TH strength among females and young adults. In addition, this strategy was seen as an investment in the future and one safe from MN retaliation. TH executives felt that the MN would be restricted by pressure from its establishment and rural base to maintain the status quo. Further, an assessment of the likely aggressiveness of the MN's top management suggested complacency. As one TH executive noted, "Times Mirror looked at *The Morning News* as some kind of country bumpkin who was fat and dumb."

Second, the TH became an all-day newspaper. On September 12, 1977, the TH published its first weekday morning edition. The MN no longer had a morning monopoly. This move by the TH sent a clear message to the MN that the level of competition was escalating.

The Dallas Morning News Responds

Early in 1979, in a move aimed at adding some research insights into their marketing strategy, the MN retained Yankelovich, Skelly, and White to conduct a profile study of the Dallas market. The "All Market Study" sampled the entire Dallas/Fort Worth area and was to be repeated every two years. Based on the findings the MN would develop a plan to improve readership among the 25–34 and 35–44 age groups; gain the Sunday circulation lead in the SMSA, publish the majority of all retail advertising linage, and strengthen its classified share. However, before priorities were set and a schedule for implementation was developed, MN management wanted to carefully study their options and find a replacement for their retiring editor.

Commenting on the "All Market Study," Mr. Jeremy Halbreich (at that time Marketing Director at the MN) stressed that,

> The study tells us not only who is out there, more than just the demographics of the market. It tells us what the people in our market are interested in, what is important to them, what are their social, civic, economic, and education concerns, their likes, their dislikes and their lifestyles. And, of course, it tells us about their reading and other media habits.

Based on the Yankelovich study, management at the MN initially concluded that they should bolster coverage of the following areas: business, fashion, sports, arts and entertainment, plus local, state, national, and international news.

While the MN was studying the market and developing plans, the TH continued to press forward with changes designed to strengthen its product. (See Exhibit 23.2 for a summary of the MN-TH marketing battles.) On August 8, 1979, the TH introduced a redesigned format to project a more upscale image. The somewhat trendy and liberal design instituted in 1972 was replaced by a more classic and conservative look. TH management had hoped the new logo would create a sense of credibility and stability. Importantly, TH management sought to give the paper "the look of a morning newspaper."

EXHIBIT 23.2 **Marketing battle summary**

The Dallas Morning News	*The Dallas Times Herald*
1978	
Launched "Fashion! Dallas" section for Wednesday paper.	Upcoming morning edition heavily advertised/promoted.
Established Ft. Worth News Bureau.	Expanded Sunday edition.
Introduced/expanded sports in "Sports Spectrum" (later discontinued).	Expanded coverage of Ft. Worth.
Expanded business coverage.	Saturday Real Estate section added.
	Sunday Travel section added.
	Sunday fashion section "Style" added (one week before MN's "Fashion! Dallas").
	Expanded Business News coverage.
	Introduced/expanded sports in "Sportsweek" (later discontinued).
1979	
Promoted lead in circulation over TH in comparative ads.	Redesigned format—more up-scale, classic, and conservative.
Radio advertising sarcastic and comparative.	Promoted redesigned format and expanded coverage begun in 1978.
Began expansion of investigative reporting staff and coverage.	Improved investigative reporting.
1980	
Expanded coverage of news throughout the state.	Distribution reorganized: morning distribution taken from independent distributors and brought in-house, afternoon distribution remained unchanged.
Expanded local news.	
Expanded sports.	
Fashion added to Sunday as well as Wednesday edition.	Morale among distributors plummets and many move to MN.
Lifestyles/Arts section added to Sunday edition.	Sales promotion lower prices: newcomer discounts, complimentary copies distributed to hotels, etc.
Television listing/events added.	
"Business Tuesday" added 5/1/80.	"Parade" magazine dropped, replaced with TH's own "Westward." Price increase from $.15 to $.25 daily, classified ad rates raised as well.
6/1/80 price increase from $.15 to $.25 daily, no change in ad rates.	
1981	
Expanded national/international news coverage.	Weekend "package" sold for $3.50, same as MN price, but includes Friday, as well as Saturday and Sunday.
50% discount to new subscribers for one month.	

EXHIBIT 23.2 **Continued**

Ad rates increased: daily rates same as TH, Sunday 50% less than TH, classified from $.35 to $.40 per line.

Redesigned graphics (masthead unchanged) to make paper "uncluttered and easy to read."

MN answers circulation fraud charges to ABC satisfaction.

Ann Landers column moves from TH to MN.

Weekend "package" expanded to include Friday.

Expanded sports coverage with "Sports Day" section.

"Parade" magazine added to Sunday paper.

Upgraded Sunday "Arts & Entertainment" section.

Launched "La Vida American" series on Hispanic life in America.

"Texas & Southwest" section introduced to expand coverage of state news.

Expanded national/international news coverage.

New subscribers promotion: for 3 months—7-day service for the price of 3-day service.

Returned distribution to independent distributors.

Ad rates increased: daily became same as MN, Sunday 50% more than MN, classified from $.40 to $.45.

Requested investigation of ABC circulation figures for MN.

After 23 years, Ann Landers column leaves TH.

Increased community involvement: programs honoring high school students, athletes, the arts (long considered a MN strength).

1982

Advertising rate increase, (causes most advertisers to choose one newspaper).

Advertising market share increases (Exhibit 23.19).

Heavily promoted sportswriter Skip Bayless moves to TH for big dollars, two new sports writers promoted—no apparent loss in circulation.

Advertising rate increase, advertising market share decrease due to advertisers being able to afford only one paper—many chose MN.

Distribution brought back in-house and improved.

Expanded circulation discounts and sampling.

Afternoon delivery outside Dallas county discontinued.

7–11 promotion: cup of coffee and the TH for $.38.

Sportswriter Skip Bayless hired away from MN (see Exhibit 23.17).

Other "big names" added to editorial staff.

"Mid-cities" section for local community coverage introduced (later dropped).

Introduced Wednesday fashion section, "Unique."

Discounted ad rates and offered selective rebates.

Circulation and ad lineage are up (see Exhibit 23.18).

1983

Special "Energy Report" added to Wednesday business coverage.

Economy emphasis added to Thursday business coverage.

Increased metro news coverage.

Weather news coverage expanded.

Sunday "TV Guide" quality improved.

Arts & Entertainment coverage expanded to 7 days.

Blackie Sherrod, TH sportswriter, lured to MN, effective 1/1/85.

7-11 promotion: Free Sunday MN with coffee at $.25.

"Sports Day" recognized as one of the top-ten best sports sections in the U.S.

Saturday Real Estate classified section introduced.

Promotions emphasized, especially games/contests.

Distribution back to independent dealers because of low circulation for morning edition.

1984

MN requested investigation of ABC circulation figures for TH.

Price increase of weekend package (Friday, Saturday, Sunday) to $5.00, matching TH.

Obtained exclusive rights to run Michael Jackson concert tickets.

Extensive, extra coverage added for the Republican convention held in Dallas.

MN "Sunday Magazine" upgraded to magazine-quality paper.

Major management changes occur at all levels.

Half-price subscriptions sold by telephone.

"Living" section redesigned and Arts/Entertainment added.

"Community Close-Up" offers advertisers 8 different geographic zones.

"Unique" society section moved from Wednesday to Sunday, and "Style" moved from Sunday to Wednesday.

"Perspectives" and "Living" dropped as separate Sunday sections, "Arts & Leisure" added.

12/31/84 Last day for acclaimed sportswriter Blackie Sherrod who moves to the MN.

1985

Blackie Sherrod joins the sports staff (see Exhibit 23.20).

Offset printing began in the new North Plant in Plano.

International component added to the Monday business section.

50% discount offered for the second ad run in a one-week period.

Subscription promotion: "3 months for the price of 2."

Sunday magazine "Westward" replaced by "Dallas City."

EXHIBIT 23.2 **Continued**

National, retail, and classified ad rates increased 11%.	Promotions to increase single-copy sales. Classified ad rates cut 20%, 15% discount offered to agencies on classified linage.

1986

Pulitzer prize awarded to two MN staff writers, finalist in three other categories: general news reporting, feature photography, spot news photography.	June: Times-Mirror announces sale of TH to MediaNews for $110 million (see Exhibit 23.21). Sale completed September 5: ■ 109 full-time employees removed ■ Four news bureaus closed ■ "Dallas City" magazine dropped ■ Section headings redesigned, more people-oriented information added, more/better color—TH became more "USA Todayish" ■ Focus on local news Friday "Entertainment," Sunday "Unique," Sunday "Arts & Entertainment," Wednesday "Fashion" sections dropped. Sunday "Datebook" entertainment section added, including gossip, events, movie reviews, etc.

In response to the TH's design changes, the MN reacted strongly through the vehicle of television commercials and print ads. For example, a 30-second television MN commercial portrayed the two newspapers as men buying clothing. The neat, slim, decisive man (MN) bought confidently and conservatively. On the other hand, the overweight, disheveled man (TH) was unable to choose between various styles and bought an unusual assortment. The voice-over sarcastically observed: "Some papers change their looks as often as some people change their clothes. At *The Dallas Morning News*, we know who we are."

The MN also began running a series of aggressive ads in the advertising trade press. These ads served to boost morale at the MN where management had been in a reacting posture for some time. The ads also served to irritate management at the TH.

In the fall of 1980, with time to analyze the results of the Yankelovich study and circulation trends, and with new leadership in place in the news department, senior executives of the MN consolidated their conclusions and set both short- and long-term objectives for their newspaper.

The overall objective was a significant increase in both the absolute and perceived margin of leadership in the market, in terms of product quality, circulation, and advertising leadership.

Management at the MN decided that the pathway to dominance consisted of strong, broadly based product improvement accompanied by appropriate marketing and promotional activities, as the foundation for circulation growth. The executives felt that circulation growth obtained by following this strategy, while requiring more time, would be more enduring than growth obtained by heavy discounting, contests, or other short-term promotions. Further, it was agreed that a well-promoted high-quality product that could assist circulation growth also would help to achieve increased advertising market share.

Since initially the greatest need was seen to be in improving Sunday readership, much emphasis would be placed on product improvement that could be reflected in the Sunday package.

Additionally, it was felt that greater margins of leadership in certain "franchise" areas of readership—business, sports, fashion, local and lifestyles news—was essential. Because much planning for a special business section already had been done, it was decided the first product change to be introduced would be in business.

On November 11, 1980, one of the priorities MN management identified through the Yankelovich research resulted in a new section—"Business Tuesday." Yankelovich data had clearly indicated that business news was critical to defending the MN's morning franchise. To produce the new section with greatly expanded local and regional coverage, the size of the business staff was doubled. A new design which included new headline faces, graphics, and indexes was added to give the section a crisp appearance.

The new expanded business coverage concentrated on Tuesday was part of the MN's overall strategy to substantially increase business coverage seven days a week. Growing financial linage prompted the MN to give their business section a high priority.

The MN launched "Business Tuesday" with major advertising support. Trade and consumer promotions began six weeks prior to the launch of the section. Radio and television spots plus outdoor were used extensively to promote the section. A four-week sampling program exposed thousands of nonsubscribers to the section.

Advertising had become a year-round, integral part of the MN's marketing strategy. In 1980, part of the MN's marketing strategy was to focus on building Sunday circulation. Sunday had long been the TH's strong suit and management at the MN wanted to change the situation. To target its Sunday promotions, the MN selected radio as the most appropriate medium. A fixed jingle ("Sunday isn't Sunday without *The Dallas Morning News*") was created to build familiarity, and live feeds were inserted to provide specifics.

Other strategies were implemented to improve MN's market standing or negate gains of the TH. See Exhibit 23.2 for specific activities through the mid-80s.

During 1983, independent research studies indicated that the MN was not only able to defend its leadership position with upscale readers but had made some progress with younger readers. The MN also performed well in retail, classified, and other advertising linage categories.

As a result of larger advertising volume and larger newshole, the MN consistently published a larger product. The MN ran more pages in classified, business, sports, local news, fashion, and the real estate sections.

In May 1985 the March ABC figures were released. These figures indicated a substantial circulation lead for the MN. The MN figures were up significantly over the previous period while the TH figures dropped substantially. The MN featured this advantage in trade advertising (see Exhibit 23.3).

THE EFFECTS OF A CONTINUING SOFT DALLAS ECONOMY ARE FELT DURING 1987

In the first half of 1987, the effects of the sluggish economy were felt at both newspapers. Many advertisers reduced their budgets in response to the economic slowdown. To make matters worse, two major retail advertisers, Joske's and Safeway, closed their Dallas operations. Joske's was bought out by Dillard's and Safeway closed their north Texas division, which included Dallas. As a result, ad linage at both newspapers fell below 1986 volumes.

Operating expense increases also put pressure on management to take steps to maintain profitability. For example, average newsprint costs increased by 6 percent effective January 1 and were upped again 7 percent effective July 1.

During March the TH announced several advertising rate changes and deals designed to help reverse their declining share of newspaper advertising linage. To bolster classified, the TH introduced a guaranteed results program called "Super Seller Classified." The TH offered two lines for two weeks for $12 with an additional two weeks free if the merchandise advertised did not sell in the initial two weeks.

To build linage the TH offered single-location department store retailers a special concession. If the retailer would run the same dollar volume in the TH in 1987 as they had in 1986, they would receive a major reduction in their line rate. The net effect for the advertiser was a significant increase in linage at no cost increase over 1986.

The TH also offered a special pick-up advertising deal. If the advertiser ran four ads in a week, the second and third ads ran at a discount and the fourth ad was free. The first ad ran at the regular rate, the second at 50 percent, the third at 25 percent, and the fourth ad was free. On the other hand, in May, the MN offered pick-up discount *only* on Sunday ads that were repeated during the next week in the business section. A second placement of a Sunday MN ad ran at 75 percent and a third ran at 55 percent.

In addition to their "Community Closeup" total market coverage product, the TH introduced a zoned advertising product "Community" in May. "Community" covered six zones with an editorial section designed to be attractive to small advertisers. Ads could be placed Wednesdays or Thursdays in any combination of the six zones.

In April, the MN received three Robert F. Kennedy Awards. These Awards included the grand prize for a series on discrimination in Dallas County jury selection.

What's the real difference between the two Dallas dailies?

Over 125,000 papers. Every day.

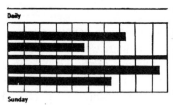

The latest circulation figures* are out. And the news is record-breaking!

As of March 31, 1985, the Audit Bureau of Circulations (ABC) shows The Dallas Morning News not only has the largest daily and Sunday circulation of any newspaper in Dallas history, but it also shows we lead the Times Herald by more than 125,000 papers every day of the week!

Over 125,000 more papers every single day. That's a stack of newspapers over a mile high!

Our readers have made The Morning News the biggest circulation winner in Dallas newspaper history.

So to reach more of Dallas, advertise with the overwhelming circulation winner, The Dallas Morning News. Call Harry M. Stanley, Jr., senior vice-president, at **(214) 977-8550.**

The Dallas Morning News

*Source: Audit Bureau of Circulations (ABC) FAS-FAX Report for the period ending March 31, 1985. Computations by The Dallas Morning News.

EXHIBIT 23.3 *Dallas Morning News* advertisement

In May both newspapers fired employees and announced cost-containment measures. The MN terminated 68 full-time and 27 part-time jobs, eliminated year-end bonuses and placed strict reductions on controllable expenses such as travel. MN cuts affected all areas except circulation, advertising, and editorial. The TH laid off 47 workers for an indefinite period and froze the wages of the paper's 1,150 full-time employees. Further, the TH reduced some salaries. The TH staff reductions affected all areas except the newsroom.

THE DALLAS/FORT WORTH MARKET

Population and Employment

The North Central Texas Council of Governments estimated the Dallas/Fort Worth nine-county CMSA population had increased 24.4 percent between April 1, 1980 and January 1, 1987. The population of the CMSA on January 1, 1987 was estimated to be 3,649,887. The breakdown by counties in the CMSA was as follows: Collin 6.3 percent; Dallas 48.7 percent; Denton 6.5 percent; Ellis 2.1 percent; Johnson 2.5 percent; Kaufman 1.4 percent; Parker 1.6 percent; Rockwell .6 percent; and, Tarrant 30.3 percent. (Exhibit 23.4 presents maps that indicate county locations.)

Although the rate of increase had slowed somewhat since the boom period of 1983-85, a relatively healthy increase was forecasted through 1988. Compounded annual growth rates between 1980 and 1987 by county were as follows: Collin 7 percent; Dallas 2 percent; Denton 7.9 percent; Ellis 3.5 percent; Johnson 4.4 percent; Kaufman 4.1 percent; Parker 4.1 percent; Rockwell 6.7 percent; and, Tarrant 3.9 percent.

Sales Management's projections through 1988 painted a continuation of earlier growth. By the end of 1988 D/FW population was forecasted to increase 14 percent over 1983. Projected growth broken down by countries within the overall market indicated that the most rapid growth would occur in the suburban counties. Growth by county was estimated to occur as follows: Collin +25.3 percent; Dallas +11 percent; Denton +24.9 percent; Ellis +16.1 percent; Kaufman +16.3 percent; and, Rockwell +24.1 percent. The Fort Worth-Arlington portion of the D/FW market (Johnson, Parker, and Tarrant counties) was projected to grow at a 14.6 percent rate between 1983 and 1988.

Average household effective buying income was projected to grow by 69.2 percent to $44,618 by 1988. Again, the strongest Dallas market growth was forecasted to occur in outlying Denton, Rockwell, and Collin counties. Johnson, Parker, and Tarrant counties (the Fort Worth portion of the market) were forecasted to grow at a slightly faster rate than the overall D/FW market.

The D/FW Area of Dominant Influence (ADI) ranked as the 8th largest ADI in the United States in 1987. Arbitron estimated the TV household population distribution as follows: children's ages 2-11, 15.2 percent; teens 12-17, 9.2 percent; 18-34, 31.8 percent; 35-49, 20 percent; and 50+, 23.8 percent.

DALLAS PMSA

DALLAS/FT. WORTH CMSA

DALLAS/FT. WORTH A D I

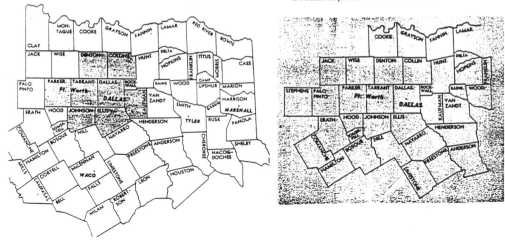

EXHIBIT 23.4 **Maps of Dallas/Ft. Worth**

The D/FW economy was based on a diverse mix of employers and had shown resistance to economic downturns. A ranking of the largest revenue generators compiled by the MN revealed that the top five firms included a convenience store chain, a steel manufacturer, a semiconductor firm, an oil field services company, and an airline.

Top corporate employers included some of these same firms, plus a defense contractor, a telephone company, two department stores, and a grocery chain. In addition, federal, state, and local governments; schools and universities; and hospitals employed a large number of area residents.

JC Penney announced the relocation of their corporate headquarters to Dallas from New York. This move would bring 4,000 JC Penney employees into the Dallas area.

Media Competitors

In addition to the TH, the MN had to contend with a host of other media vehicles that sought to attract the attention of consumers and advertisers. These competitors applied constant pressure on the MN as they sought to expand their position in the market.

In Fort Worth, the *Star-Telegram* was increasingly aggressive in competing with the two Dallas papers in the mid-cities area. The September 1986 ABC statement indicated that the daily circulation of the paper was 258,500 and 306,500 on Sundays. Compared to 1981, the *Star-Telegram* had grown 15.3 percent daily and 21.0 percent Sunday.

The *Star-Telegram* had taken a number of steps to improve its product plus to consolidate and expand its position in the Fort Worth and Tarrant County market. Corporate ownership by Capital Cities Communications placed considerable resources and expertise at the disposal of the *Star-Telegram*.

The Wall Street Journal did well in the D/FW market. *USA Today* and *The New York Times* carried on significant marketing efforts in attempts to wedge their way into the attractive D/FW market.

Three network affiliate television stations were important forces in the Dallas market. These stations were KXAS (NBC), KDFW (CBS), and WFAA (ABC). In addition, four Dallas independent stations held reasonably high shares of the viewing audience. These stations were KRLD, KTXA, KDFI, and KTVT. Average cost data for 30-second spots per household rating point during the second quarter of 1987 was $99 for day time, $130 for early news, $288 for prime time, $213 for late news, and $137 for late evening. The average rating for the top three local stations in November 1984 was 6 for day time, 11 for early news, 13 for prime time, 15 for late news, and 8 for late evening. Finally, cable television penetration stood at 38 percent of the ADI in July 1986.

The top five radio stations in Dallas based on average quarter-hour audiences were WBAP with 67,000; KVIL with 50,000; KRLD with 50,000; KKDA with 37,000; and, KMEZ with 34,000. Second-quarter 1987 cost-per-rating-point estimates for 60-second spots in morning drive-time were $134 for men 25-54 and $142 for women 25-54.

In addition to nationally distributed magazines (some with regional and single-market coverage capabilities), Dallas had five significant city magazines. These publications were *D Magazine, Dallas/Fort Worth Home & Garden, Dallas Business, Perspectives,* and *Texas Monthly. D Magazine,* for example, had a circulation of 81,000 and a one-time, four-color page cost of $4,590. A package buy of *Newsweek, Sports*

Illustrated, *Time*, and *U.S. News & World Report* for coverage of the D/FW market cost $12,590 at the three-time rate for a four-color page. Circulation of the package was 165,200.

Outdoor and direct mail also provided competition for advertising dollars. The cost of a #50 showing of 30 sheet posters in Dallas through Foster & Kleiser (a major outdoor company) required 56 illuminated posters and 8 nonilluminated and cost $18,176. (A #50 showing reaches 85 percent of the adult population with an average frequency of once every other day for a 28-day period.)

Suburban newspapers in both the north and south areas of the Dallas market had become more aggressive in the past two years. To the north, Harte-Hanks owned a group with newspapers in Plano, Lewisville, Allen, and other communities. To the south, a group with weeklies and biweeklies in DeSoto, Cedar Hill, Lancaster, and other towns provided local coverage of these suburban communities.

CURRENT OPERATION OF THE DALLAS MORNING NEWS

Circulation Trends

Historically, the MN had been much stronger than the TH in total circulation. From the outset, the MN had viewed itself as more of a regional newspaper and bent its efforts toward that end. Partially as a result of these efforts, state circulation had always been a strength (the MN is the only paper distributed to all 254 counties in Texas). The MN also had significant circulation in neighboring areas of Oklahoma and Louisiana.

The TH, on the other hand, had historically been stronger in Dallas county both daily and Sunday. Most of the circulation figures in Exhibit 23.1 reflect these historical strengths.

However, in 1984 the MN reversed the long-standing trend and took over the daily lead in Dallas county. In 1985 and 1986, the MN opened up a significant advantage in Dallas county daily and, for the first time, lead the TH on Sunday in Dallas county. At the same time, the MN was extending its total circulation lead.

MN's penetration could be enhanced if newcomers and out-of-town visitors could be identified and introduced to the *News*. Single copy sales represented another opportunity as did reaching and servicing apartment dwellers. Any new strategy undertaken had to balance resources required and likely benefits. Additionally MN was looking for programs which were (1) insulated from competitive response, and, (2) provided measurable results.

Pricing Trends

The MN has used its pricing policies for both advertising and circulation as a marketing weapon in the past to gain an advantage over its competition. Exhibit 23.5 presents data on single copy and subscription pricing of the two papers between 1978 and 1987.

EXHIBIT 23.5 **Single copy and home delivery subscription pricing MN and TH 1978–1987**

		Single Copy	
		Daily	**Sunday**
1981–1987		$.25	$.75
1980			
	12/1 MN	.25	.75
	11/1 TH	.25	.75
	5/1 TH	.25	.50
	5/1 MN	.25	.50
1979		.15	.35
1978		.15	.35

Monthly Home Delivery

		Full week	Sunday only	Saturday Sunday	Friday Saturday Sunday
1987	7/1 MN				$6.50
1986	10/1 TH				5.75
	6/1 MN				6.00
1985	12/1 MN	$9.00			
	10/1 MN				5.50
1984	10/1 MN	8.00			
	10/1 TH	8.00			
	6/1 MN				5.00
1983	12/1 MN		7.25		4.50
1982	1/1 TH		7.25		5.00
	6/1 MN				4.00
1981	9/1 MN		Drop	Drop	3.50
1980	12/1 TH	6.25		Drop	3.50
	12/1 MN	6.25	$3.00	$3.50	
1979	11/1 MN	5.25	2.50	3.00	
	12/1 TH	5.25		3.00	
	7/1 TH	4.50			
1978	4/1 MN	4.50			
	MN	3.50	1.75	2.25	n/a
	TH	3.40	n/a	2.25	n/a

In terms of advertising space charges, the MN followed a strategy of pricing above the TH in absolute terms but below the TH on a CPM basis. This applied to all three categories of ad rates—general, classified, and retail. However, the recent TH advertising discount programs had brought the two papers much closer together on a CPM basis for many important advertisers. Exhibits 23.6 and 23.7 present comparisons of the retail rates of the two newspapers in 1985 and 1987, respectively.

EXHIBIT 23.6 Retail advertising rates per column inch—1985

Contract Size

The Dallas Morning News

	Daily	Sunday		Daily	Sunday		Daily	Sunday
Open ...	$54.80	$63.65	1,200 ...	$44.77	$50.97	14,300 ...	$42.18	$48.38
50	47.61	54.08	2,400 ...	44.24	50.45	19,000 ...	41.66	47.35
100	47.09	53.81	3,600 ...	43.99	49.94	23,800 ...	41.14	47.09
150	46.58	53.30	4,800 ...	43.47	49.16	28,600 ...	40.63	46.83
200	45.28	52.27	7,100 ...	43.21	48.91	33,300 ...	40.36	46.58
500	45.02	51.49	9,500 ...	42.95	48.64	38,100 ...	39.85	46.31

The Dallas Times Herald*

	Daily**	Weekend**	Sunday		Daily**	Weekend**	Sunday
Open....	$50.00	$50.50	$56.00	5,500 ...	$38.25	$38.75	$43.75
50	43.00	44.50	50.00	7,325 ...	38.00	38.50	43.50
100	42.00	42.50	48.00	9,750 ...	37.75	38.25	43.25
180	41.25	41.75	46.75	15,500 ...	37.25	37.75	42.75
240	41.00	41.50	46.50	18,500 ...	37.00	37.50	42.50
565	40.25	40.75	45.75	25,000 ...	36.25	36.50	42.00
1,300 ...	39.50	40.00	45.00	29,000 ...	35.75	36.25	41.50
2,350 ...	39.00	39.50	44.50	34,000 ...	35.50	36.00	41.25
3,125 ...	38.75	39.25	44.25	39,000 ...	35.25	35.75	41.00

Frequency Contracts

The Dallas Morning News			The Dallas Times Herald			
	Daily	Sunday		Daily**	Weekend**	Sunday
7 Times	$47.09	$53.81	6 Times	$48.35	$49.55	$55.25
12 Times	45.28	52.27	12 Times	41.00	42.00	47.00
24 Times	45.02	51.49	24 Times	40.00	41.00	46.00
36 Times	44.24	50.45	36 Times	39.25	40.00	45.00
52 Times	43.99	49.94	52 Times	38.75	39.00	44.50

*TH rate card also included the following contract rates: 25, 75, 135, 320, 425, 750, 1,000, 1,750, 4,150, 13,000, and 22,000.

**Daily—Monday thru Thursday; Weekend—Friday and Saturday.

Source: Rate Cards effective 1/1/85 for TH; 9/1/85 for MN.

Advertising Linage

Historically the MN had led the TH in total advertising linage based in part on the MN's considerably stronger classified performance. In 1986 the MN ranked second in the United States in full-run advertising linage (5,476,495 inches). In first place was the TH's former sister paper the *Los Angeles Times* with 5,637,854. In terms of total 1986 classified linage, the MN led the nation by a substantial margin.

EXHIBIT 23.7 **Retail advertising rates per column inch—1987**

Bulk Rate Contract Size

The Dallas Morning News				*The Dallas Times Herald*		
	Daily	Saturday	Sunday		Daily*	Weekend*	Sunday
Open ...$57.60	...$59.90	.....$69.38		Open ...$57.60	...$58.10	......$64.45
50 ... 50.70	... 52.73	..... 58.95		50 ... 49.50	... 51.20	...... 57.60
100 ... 50.15	... 52.16	..... 58.65		100 ... 48.35	... 48.95	...... 55.25
150 ... 49.61	... 51.59	..... 58.10		180 ... 47.50	... 48.10	...... 53.80
200 ... 48.22	... 50.15	..... 56.97		240 ... 47.20	... 47.75	...... 53.55
500 ... 47.95	... 49.87	..... 56.12		425 ... 46.60	... 47.20	...... 53.00
1,200 ... 47.68	... 49.59	..... 55.56		750 ... 46.10	... 46.60	...... 52.40
2,400 ... 47.12	... 49.00	..... 54.99		1,300 ... 45.50	... 46.10	...... 51.80
3,600 ... 46.85	... 48.72	..... 54.43		2,350 ... 44.90	... 45.50	...... 51.20
4,800 ... 46.30	... 48.15	..... 53.58		3,125 ... 44.60	... 45.20	...... 50.95
7,100 ... 46.02	... 47.86	..... 53.31		4,150 ... 44.35	... 44.90	...... 50.65
9,500 ... 45.74	... 47.57	..... 53.02		5,500 ... 44.05	... 44.60	...... 50.35
14,300 ... 44.92	... 46.72	..... 52.73		7,325 ... 43.75	... 44.35	...... 50.10
19,000 ... 44.37	... 46.14	..... 51.61		9,750 ... 43.50	... 44.50	...... 49.80
23,800 ... 43.81	... 45.56	..... 51.33		13,000 ... 43.15	... 43.75	...... 49.50
28,600 ... 43.27	... 45.00	..... 51.04		18,500 ... 42.60	... 43.15	...... 48.95
33,300 ... 42.98	... 44.70	..... 50.77		25,000 ... 41.75	... 42.05	...... 48.35
38.100 ... 42.44	... 44.14	..... 50.48		34,000 ... 40.90	... 41.45	...... 47.50
				39,000 ... 40.60	... 41.15	...... 47.20

Frequency Contracts

The Dallas Morning News				*The Dallas Times Herald*		
	Daily	Saturday	Sunday		Daily*	Weekend*	Sunday
7 Times ...$50.15	$52.16	$58.65		6 Times ...$48.35	$49.55	$55.25
12 Times ... 48.22	50.15	56.97		12 Times ... 47.20	48.35	54.10
24 Times ... 47.95	49.87	56.12		24 Times ... 46.10	47.20	52.95
36 Times ... 47.12	49.00	54.99		36 Times ... 45.20	46.10	51.80
52 Times ... 46.85	48.72	54.43		52 Times ... 44.60	44.90	51.20
				78 Times ... 43.10	43.70	50.55

*TH Daily—Monday through Thursday; Weekend includes Friday and Saturday.
Source: Rate Cards effective 1/1/86 for TH: 9/1/86 for MN.

Exhibit 23.8 presents data on the top ten retail accounts linage during 1984 and 1986. The two papers were relatively evenly split on most of the top retail accounts. In 1986 the MN did significantly better with Sanger Harris, Dillard's, and Joske's. The TH garnered a significantly larger share of Montgomery Ward and K-Mart's ad budgets.

The data in Exhibit 23.9 indicate the percentage of various categories of ad linage garnered by the MN. The MN strengthened its position 1986 versus 1977 in eight categories out of nine.

EXHIBIT 23.8 **Newspaper linage data, 1984/1986—top-10 retail accounts**

1984		**1986**	
Account	**MN Linage (percent)***	**Account**	**MN Linage (percent)***
Sears 2,392,765 (50.4)		Sears 3,147,455 (50.3)	
JC Penney 2,179,724 (50.6)		Mervyn's 1,952,393 (50.0)	
Sanger Harris 2,227,646 (54.8)		Montgomery Ward . . . 1,635,471 (46.1)	
Mervyn's 1,893,423 (50.0)		Theaters 1,714,549 (49.8)	
Dillards 1,921,227 (57.6)		Sanger Harris 2,095,616 (61.1)	
Theaters 1,501,854 (48.9)		Dillards 1,910,888 (56.5)	
Montgomery Ward . . . 1,271,890 (43.0)		JC Penney 1,699,466 (51.5)	
K-Mart 814,701 (30.6)		Target 1,368,479 (50.0)	
Tom Thumb/Page . . . 1,259,003 (49.5)		K-Mart 897,987 (34.0)	
Skaggs Alpha Beta . . . 1,224,172 (50.4)		Joske's 1,439,828 (56.1)	

Source: Media Records 1984, 1986

*Percentage indicates percent of all lineage placed in combined total of MN and TH which was placed in MN.

Readership

The traditional readership strength of the MN had been among older adults with higher income and educational levels. The TH's strength had been among younger, middle and lower socioeconomic adults. These basic trends had accounted for the MN's stronger performance in the financial and apparel categories. At the same time, the TH had been stronger in the general merchandise category.

EXHIBIT 23.9 **MN percentage of yearly full-run advertising linage by categories 1977–1987**

	Total	Retail	Classified	General	Financial	Dept Store	Home	Food	General merchandise	Apparel
1987[3]	58	55	60	56	62	56	59	50	47	74
1986[2]	57	55	60	54	62	54	62	47	45	70
1985[1]	55	53	59	55	61	53	57	46	46	65
1984	55	52	58	56	60	54	53	46	45	65
1983	55	53	57	54	60	54	55	49	45	66
1982	53	50	55	52	56	54	53	50	46	66
1981	53	50	57	51	56	51	52	48	38	66
1980	52	49	56	49	58	50	53	49	23	67
1979	52	49	55	50	55	50	53	50	35	65
1978	51	49	53	50	56	50	53	50	26	66
1977	51	49	55	49	59	47	52	49	30	69

[1] 1985 MN linage (inches): Total = 5,778,657; Daily = 3,631,492; Sunday = 2,147,165.

[2] 1986 MN linage (inches): Total = 5,476,495; Daily = 3,464,704; Sunday = 2,011,791.

[3] 1987 *Partial year figures* for four months January through April **only**.
    MN linage (inches): Total = 1,609,906; Daily = 1,019,640; Sunday = 590,266.

Source: Media Records, 1977-86.

In terms of editorial philosophy, the TH had been characterized as more liberal in its political stands and aggressive in its investigative reporting on certain issues. The MN had traditionally been more conservative and establishment-oriented in its editorial views.

Exhibits 23.10–23.13 present 1986 data taken from a research studies conducted by Scarborough for the MN and by Savitz for the TH. These data indicate some of the strengths and weaknesses of the newspapers.

EXHIBIT 23.10 **Daily readership of Dallas newspapers by adults in the Dallas/Fort Worth ADI***

	Total adults	*Morning News*	*Times Herald*
Total adults	3,103,600	22.7%	19.7%
Age			
18–24	495,500	20.7	18.8
25–34	807,600	21.8	21.0
35–44	625,100	22.3	23.0
45–54	400,100	24.9	19.9
55–64	351,000	26.5	17.3
65+	424,300	21.9	15.0
Education			
College grad+	612,100	35.5	22.9
Some college	702,400	24.0	19.9
High school grad	1,046,200	21.1	20.1
Some HS	590,900	14.1	17.7
Grade school	152,000	8.5	9.5
Household income			
$75K+	196,300	39.0	24.9
$75–50K	353,700	30.2	23.3
$35–49,999	573,400	24.8	21.6
$30–34,999	354,500	22.7	21.5
$25–29,999	393,600	23.2	21.8
$20–24,999	409,600	19.5	22.8
$15–19,999	338,400	16.1	14.6
$10–14,999	242,400	16.7	11.1
Less $10,000	241,700	12.9	9.9
Race			
White	2,649,400	22.0	18.7
Black	372,300	26.5	25.4
Other	81,900	25.3	24.3
Marital status			
Married	1,998,700	23.0	19.5
Single	514,300	26.4	22.7
Divorced/separated	357,300	19.5	20.5
Widowed	233,300	16.0	13.4

*Average weekday readers. The Dallas/Fort Worth ADI is a 34-county area.

Source: Scarborough Research Corporation, 1986.
        Sample size—2,583.

EXHIBIT 23.11 **Sunday readership of Dallas newspapers by adults in the Dallas/Fort Worth ADI***

	Total adults	*Morning News*	*Times Herald*
Total adults	3,103,600	28.6%	25.9%
Age			
18–24	495,500	27.6	28.4
25–34	807,600	28.9	27.1
35–44	625,100	27.7	29.8
45–54	400,100	30.2	27.2
55–64	351,000	34.0	19.3
65+	424,300	25.1	19.0
Education			
College grad+	612,100	44.1	27.1
Some college	702,400	34.2	24.8
High school grad	1,046,200	24.8	27.5
Some HS	590,900	15.8	24.0
Grade school	152,000	16.0	22.0
Household income			
$75K+	196,300	40.3	28.5
$75–50K	353,700	41.1	29.5
$35–49,999	573,400	31.4	29.0
$30–34,999	354,500	26.7	26.5
$25–29,999	393,600	26.9	26.3
$20–24,999	409,600	22.7	29.0
$15–19,999	338,400	24.2	23.5
$10–14,999	242,400	24.1	18.3
Less $10,000	241,700	20.0	15.0
Race			
White	2,649,400	28.2	24.6
Black	372,300	30.7	33.9
Other	81,900	31.5	31.0
Marital status			
Married	1,998,700	28.3	25.3
Single	514,300	32.9	30.9
Divorced/separated	357,300	28.5	25.7
Widowed	233,300	21.5	20.2

*Average Sunday readers. The Dallas/Ft. Worth ADI is a 34-county area.

Source: Scarborough Research Corporation, 1986.
    Sample size—2,583.

Financial Data

Despite the heavy promotional, editorial, and other costs that resulted from the intense competition with the TH, the MN continued to be a very profitable operation. Exhibit 23.14 presents a five-year income statement for the MN. Total revenue had grown significantly over the five-year period as had both advertising and circulation revenues.

EXHIBIT 23.12 *Times Herald Daily* reader profile

	Reader	Dallas adult		Reader	Dallas adult
Age			**Lived in Dallas**		
18–24	17.5%	16.0%	Less than 2 years	9.2%	13.6%
25–34	28.2%	27.7%	2–5 years	8.1%	6.0%
35–49	27.9%	26.1%	5–10 years	13.6%	14.9%
50–64	17.1%	18.2%	10+ years	69.1%	65.5%
65+	9.3%	12.0%	**Occupation**		
18–49	73.6%	69.8%	Manager/administrator	11.4%	11.3%
25–49	56.1%	53.8%	Professional/technical	19.0%	16.1%
Median age	37.3 yrs.	38.6 yrs.	Sales	10.7%	11.3%
Household income*			Clerical	10.7%	12.5%
$25,000+	67.8%	68.1%	Craftsman/service	21.3%	19.0%
$35,000+	49.2%	48.3%	Housewife	8.8%	10.2%
$50,000+	23.9%	24.3%	Other	2.9%	1.2%
$25–50,000	44.0%	43.8%	Unemployed/retired	15.2%	18.4%
Median income	$34,600	$34,100	**Residence**		
Marital status			Rent	33.0%	30.6%
Married	59.1%	61.2%	Own	67.0%	69.4%
Single	40.9%	38.8%	**Presence of children**		
Sex			Has children	45.6%	56.6%
Male	51.0%	47.6%	No children	54.4%	43.4%
Female	49.0%	52.4%	**Race**		
% of women who work	62.7%	61.5%	White	78.3%	82.0%
			Black	15.5%	11.7%
			Hispanic	4.5%	4.7%
			Other	1.7%	1.6%

*Household Income percentages do not reflect those respondents who refused to answer.

Source: 1986 Dallas Times Herald Continuing Market Survey, conducted by Savitz Research Center, Inc.

Marketing Budget

The 1987 marketing budget for the MN was forecasted to be approximately $4,810,000 (roughly a 9 percent increase over 1986). This budget does *not* include marketing personnel salaries or the expenses for public relations events.

The overall budget was allocated by expense categories over 1986 and 1987 roughly as follows:

	1986	1987
Radio	40%	32%
Media production services	20	14
Outdoor	18	11
Television	7	23
In-paper	7	11
Print	4	6
Office supplies, travel, postage, misc.	4	3
Total	100%	100%

EXHIBIT 23.13 *Times Herald Sunday* reader profile

	Reader	Dallas adult		Reader	Dallas adult
Age			**Lived in Dallas**		
18–24	17.6%	16.0%	Less than 2 years	9.4%	13.6%
25–34	28.7%	27.7%	2–5 years	8.8%	6.0%
35–49	26.9%	26.1%	5–10 years	13.8%	14.9%
50–64	17.1%	18.2%	10+ years	68.0%	65.5%
65+	9.7%	12.0%	**Occupation**		
18–49	73.2%	69.8%	Manager/administrator	10.9%	11.3%
25–49	55.6%	53.8%	Professional/technical	16.6%	16.1%
Median age	37.1 yrs.	38.6 yrs.	Sales	11.9%	11.3%
Household income*			Clerical	11.5%	12.5%
$25,000+	69.2%	68.1%	Craftsman/service	21.7%	19.0%
$35,000+	48.1%	48.3%	Housewife	10.0%	10.2%
$50,000+	24.0%	24.3%	Other	2.3%	1.2%
$25–50,000	45.2%	43.8%	Unemployed/retired	15.1%	18.4%
Median income	$34,100	$34,100	**Residence**		
Marital status			Rent	31.8%	30.6%
Married	60.3%	61.2%	Own	68.2%	69.4%
Single	39.7%	38.8%	**Presence of children**		
Sex			Has children	46.1%	56.6%
Male	49.2%	47.6%	No children	53.9%	43.4%
Female	50.8%	52.4%	**Race**		
% of women who work	62.8%	61.5%	White	80.9%	82.0%
			Black	13.3%	11.7%
			Hispanic	4.1%	4.7%
			Other	1.7%	1.6%

*Household Income percentages do not reflect those respondents who refused to answer.

Source: 1986 Dallas Times Herald Continuing Market Survey, conducted by Savitz Research Center, Inc.

The bulk of the MN's media advertising was directed to potential readers, subscribers, and users of classified. In addition, the MN utilized the trade press (e.g., *Advertising Age, AdWeek, Editor & Publisher*) to reach potential advertisers. Roughly 65 percent of the MN's media advertising was aimed at increasing the paper's circulation, 10 percent focused on promoting the use of display advertising, and 25 percent promoted classified usage.

Exhibit 23.15 presents a representative advertisement directed at advertisers. Exhibit 23.16 presents a 30-second radio commercial promoting the MN's sports coverage.

The MN's public relations department's nonsalary budget for 1987 was approximately $1,000,000 (roughly a 4 percent increase over 1986). Examples of significant line items in the MN's public relations budget included the G.B. Dealy Awards, the MN's Tennis Classic, the MN's Basketball Classic, and Newspapers in Education program.

EXHIBIT 23.14 **Income statement—*The Dallas Morning News:*
January 1–December 31, 1982–86***

	(In thousands)				
	1982	**1983**	**1984**	**1985**	**1986**
Revenue:					
Advertising revenue	$113,409	$139,233	$164,574	$186,133	$186,599
Circulation revenue	11,542	14,427	20,563	22,331	23,876
Other revenue	447	608	784	1,441	738
Total revenue	$125,397	$154,268	$185,921	$209,905	$211,213
Expense:					
Editorial					
Payroll	$4,117	$6,256	$8,568	$9,725	$10,634
Expense	3,258	3,756	4,647	4,979	5,487
Production					
Payroll	12,475	13,661	15,743	20,750	23,337
Expense	3,097	3,270	3,331	4,120	4,697
Newsprint, ink, supplies....	43,627	49,496	61,074	69,900	66,116
Transportation					
Payroll	1,169	1,513	1,755	2,010	2,264
Expense	454	473	504	539	547
Circulation					
Payroll	2,921	4,121	6,789	7,807	7,994
Expense	5,586	5,878	7,133	7,989	8,020
Advertising					
Payroll	5,398	6,270	8,245	9,070	9,657
Expense	1,611	2,027	2,047	2,211	2,336
Administrative					
Payroll	3,026	3,648	4,621	4,991	4,521
Depreciation	7,232	8,243	9,034	11,473	12,872
Expense	15,358	16,512	18,995	20,515	23,234
Total expenses	$109,329	$125,124	$152,486	$176,079	$181,716
Operating income..........	$16,068	$29,144	$33,435	$33,826	$29,497
Operating ratio	12.81%	18.89%	17.98%	16.11%	13.97%
Other income	88	221	408	412	398
Other expenses	(137)	(245)	(281)	(521)	(540)
Income before taxes	$16,019	$29,120	$33,562	$33,717	$29,355
Income tax (current +					
deferred)	8,155	12,530	13,637	15,857	15,429
Net income	$7,864	$16,590	$19,925	$17,860	$13,926

*The data presented in this table have been disguised.

STRATEGIC PLAN FOR THE 90s

At tomorrow's 10:00 a.m. meeting, specific objectives, strategies, and anticipated competitive response were to be discussed. Mr. Osborne, Mr. Halbreich and
others in MN's top-management group understood that the battle for Dallas newspaper supremacy was still being waged.

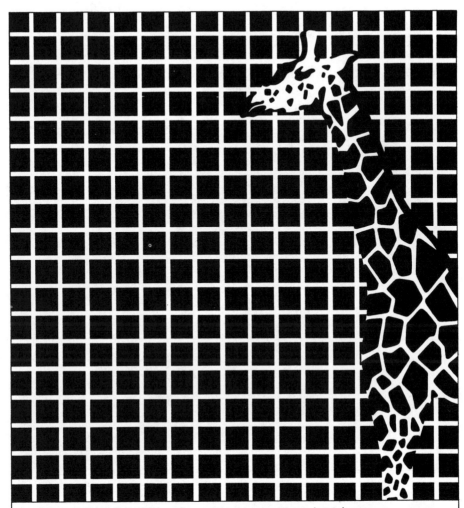

EXHIBIT 23.15 ***Dallas Morning News*** advertisement

EXHIBIT 23.16 **Dallas Morning News sports 30-second radio commercial**

	[Up-tempo music]
[Singers]	To follow the action . . . on the field . . . on the court . . .
[Umpire]	"Let's play ball!"
[Singers]	For the latest report
[SFX]	(Crack of bat hitting baseball & roar of crowd.)
[Singers]	on your favorite sports
[Fan]	"Knock the ball out!"
[Singers]	Hey Dallas! You've got all the moves! 'cause Dallas reads the *Dallas Morning News!*
[Announcer 1]	For Ringolsby's baseball column For late breaking scores For digging into the dugout For Rangers' action. I read the *Morning News!*
[Announcer 2]	Nobody beats the *Dallas Morning News* in the morning!

SKIP & BLACKIE

TWO GREAT WRITERS IN ONE GREAT PAPER.

Morning

Dallas Times Herald.

SKIP BAYLESS

Thumbs up for Cowboys

The thumb, of course, is the runt finger. Short, stubby, always getting in the way of hammers and kitchen knives and your right guard's helmet. Thumbs aren't fit for Super Bowl rings, as Pittsburgh found out, but the metacarpal, phalangeal joint is a necessary evil. One can't throw a football or give a thumbs-up without one. Which brings us to

BLACKIE SHERROD

Shake, rattle and bankroll

Even before the shake had hit the fan, Rafael Septien ran his bill up to $200. While the Dallas and Buffalo stalwarts were loosening up, Septien and Isiah Robertson crossed paths near the Cowboy bench area, shook hands and stopped to exchange pleasantries. When the Dallas kicker and the Buffalo lineback finished their chat, they shook hands

EXHIBIT 23.17 **Skip and Blackie *Dallas Times Herald* advertisement**

EXHIBIT 23.18 *Dallas Times Herald* **advertisement**

The next time a Times Herald ad rep calls on you, ask him to fill in the blanks.

1. _____	14. _____	• **1.** SANGER HARRIS	**14.** PFAU TIRE CO.
2. _____	15. _____	**2.** SEARS	**15.** HAVERTY'S
3. _____	16. _____	**3.** MONTGOMERY WARD	• **16.** WEIR'S
4. _____	17. _____	• **4.** J.C. PENNEY	• **17.** NEIMAN MARCUS
5. _____	18. _____	• **5.** DILLARD'S	• **18.** PAGE SUPER DRUG
6. _____	19. _____	• **6.** JOSKE'S	• **19.** ECKERD'S
7. _____	20. _____	**7.** WOOLCO	**20.** WINN DIXIE
8. _____	21. _____	**8.** TARGET	**21.** KROGER
9. _____	22. _____	• **9.** SAFEWAY	**22.** AMERICAN AIRLINES
10. _____	23. _____	•**10.** TOM THUMB	• **23.** LIGHTS FANTASTIC
11. _____	24. _____	**11.** K-MART	•**24.** SKAGGS DRUGS
12. _____	25. _____	**12.** MINYARDS	**25.** RICK FURNITURE
13. _____		• **13.** SKAGGS ALPHA BETA	

The 25 top Dallas advertisers according to the Times Herald. | **The 25 top Dallas advertisers according to Media Records.**

Very recently, the Times Herald ran an ad claiming that "22 of the top 25 Dallas newspaper advertisers place more ad dollars in the Times Herald than in the #2 paper."

Yet, somehow, they failed to list them.

Because the only way their claim could be construed to be true is that the number 22 represents *their own* top 22 advertisers. Media Records, an independent auditing firm that measures advertising in *both* Dallas papers, presents us with quite a different list.

Asterisks indicate advertisers who run a majority of their advertising with The Dallas Morning News. Through October. The Dallas Morning News leads in total full run advertising linage among these top 25 advertisers by 1,255,488 lines.

Source: Media Records. October, 1982.

In black and white, it shows that The Dallas Morning News carries the majority of advertising linage in 13 of the 25 top advertisers in this market. More than half place more advertising with us than with them. And we're not counting just our own advertisers, we're counting everyone who advertises in a newspaper in Dallas.

An important difference that shows up rather clearly in round numbers. Through October of this year, The Dallas Morning News has run over 10.3 million *more* lines of total full-run advertising than the evening paper. Over 3,500 more pages of advertising. And in the critical full-run

retail advertising category, we lead by over 3.2 million lines.

Those are the facts. Now if a Herald ad rep wants to explain their ad to you, we've given the rep the space.

Just one more reason why nobody beats The Dallas Morning News in the morning.

EXHIBIT 23.19 *Dallas Morning News* advertisement

Blackie Sherrod, the dean of Texas sports writers, has made his move to the pages of SPORTS DAY. Now you've got Galloway, Casstevens *and* Sherrod. Read them today.
To subscribe call 745-8383 or toll-free 1-800-442-7044.

The Dallas Morning News

EXHIBIT 23.20 *Dallas Morning News* advertisement

"How I Got A Job At The Dallas Times Herald"

— *Dean Singleton*

On September 1, 1986, a native Texan named William Dean Singleton finally got the job he'd dreamed of. He paid $110 million to become owner of the *Dallas Times Herald*.

I interviewed at the Times Herald in 1970. They told me I was too young and inexperienced to get hired. But they also told me to come back in a few years. Well, I guess you could say I'm back.

Dreams.

I left Texas 10 years ago with the dream of building a newspaper group. Forty newspapers later, I realized the dream wouldn't be complete until I brought it home.

Texas is my home. I grew up in a working class family in Graham and my family still lives here in Texas. Probably no place in America has the same pride and self respect. And in my opinion, Dallas is the center piece. It's a city of winners where dreams come true. And I've still got plenty of dreams. Even our family dog's name is "Possible Dream"

Risks.

By coming here, I'm taking certain professional risks. In a city like Dallas, if you succeed you're a genius. If you don't succeed you're a nobody. Sure, I'm putting my name and reputation on the line, but I'll tell you, it's a lot more satisfying to overcome challenges than to dodge them.

Balance.

Since my early days in newspapers, I've found that having the right advertising in a paper is almost as important as writing the news itself. So I'm intrigued at the prospect of working with advertisers and business people who have dealings with our newspaper. I'm interested in knowing what makes a retail store click. What makes an auto dealer

successful. I want my newspaper product to provide the very best environment for advertisers and readers alike.

Improvement.

The Times Herald is an excellent newspaper the way it is right now, a Pulitzer Prize winner. One that delivers the Dallas market. But our goal is to be the number one news paper in Dallas. It'll take time and a lot of hard work before we get there. But the only place I know where success comes before work is in the dictionary.

Growth.

When you look at the Dallas advertising market, one thing is very clear; the Times Herald has a major share. In fact it's one of the top ten newspapers nationally in total full run ad linage. But one of my goals for the years ahead is to dramatically increase that market share as our circulation grows. By all accounts, our circulation is making steady gains and, according to the latest syndicated research, more readers in Dallas already read the Times Herald than any other newspaper. Advertisers know that includes a tremendous number of people who read only the Dallas Times Herald. So the Times Herald is virtually a must for any advertiser who wants to reach the Dallas market.

Responsibility.

I'm a big advocate of local news coverage. And the only way to do a good job of covering the community is to be a part of it. With the owner and management team right here in Dallas, the Times Herald can be at the forefront of every major decision in the community.

Flagship.

The newspaper group I'm bringing to Dallas is among the top ten nationally in number of dailies owned. But the Times Herald is the biggest newspaper in our group and it prob

ably always will be. So it's the one place we'll put a majority of our efforts.

I'm moving my newspaper operations to Dallas because I think it's best for the Times Herald and our readers. It's also nice to be able to bring new business to Dallas. Mayor Taylor called to tell us that himself.

Involvement.

I'll often be here, but I'm not going to run the newspaper. With talented individuals like Art Wible as our publisher, Dave Burgin coming on as editor and John Wolf heading up our advertising and marketing efforts, I couldn't ask for brighter, more experienced leaders to help the Times Herald win in Dallas.

Competition.

Obviously, I think we can be the biggest and best newspaper in Dallas. I mean, why would I pay $110 million for a newspaper I didn't think I could win with. I'm a newspaperman not a land developer.

I bought the Times Herald because it's been around for more than a hundred years. It has hundreds of thousands of enthusiastic readers every day. A major share of the advertising market. And more Pulitzer Prizes than any paper in our part of the country. It's a great newspaper that's getting even better. I just figured buying it was the only way I'd ever get a job here.

Commitment.

When I bought this newspaper, it created a special bond for me. I live here now. So the Times Herald is a lot more than a new addition to my group. It's my morning paper, the first thing I read every day. And I want the same things out of it you do. That's why I promise you the very best Dallas Times Herald in history. You have my word on it.

Dallas Times Herald

EXHIBIT 23.21   *Dallas Times Herald* **advertisement**

MHA Safe Deposit, Ltd.

Late in 1983, Robert D. Hall, Jr., President of MHA Safe Deposit, Ltd., sat at his desk, looked into the nearly empty lobby, and reflected on the past year's performance. MHA had been in full operation now for about eight months and safe

This case was written by Patrick H. McCaskey, Associate Professor of Marketing, Millersville State University and Dharmendra T. Verma, Professor of Marketing, Bentley College. It is intended as a basis for classroom discussion rather than to illustrate effective or ineffective handling of an administrative situation. Copyright © 1986 by Patrick H. McCaskey and Dharmendra T. Verma. Used by permission from Dharmendra T. Verma and Patrick H. McCaskey.

deposit box rentals were well below even the most pessimistic projections of Vault Management Corporation (VMC), the firm that had helped them get off the ground.

"We started out with high expectations," Bob Hall declared. "VMC packaged and sold the concept of private safe depositories in the form of limited partnerships to groups of investors in Cleveland, Long Island, San Diego, Boston, etc. In each place they acted as a prime contractor, so to speak. Their revenue projections, box rentals, and charges were similar in each of these areas. Since there was no long history of experience with box rentals, I think these projections were predicted on the original three or four successful vaults that were built in the late 1970s."

"It's still too early to tell how the other VMC-sponsored vaults have performed, but our experience has been disappointing. The VMC projections called for rentals of over 500 boxes within the first four months at an average annual fee of almost $600. Actually, in our first four months of operation our total revenues were approximately $25,000 and we had rented a little over 50 boxes, and the average fee was closer to $300 because we added a number of small boxes—the majority of the people who have rented boxes so far have rented the smallest and cheapest boxes we have!"

Bob continued, "The concept of commercial safe depositories seems very viable and a lot of national publicity has been generated in *Time, Business Week*, and other national publications. In the last two or three years, a number of vaults have been built all over the West Coast and in Florida, Arizona, New Mexico, Oklahoma, Texas, Illinois, and Ohio—at least in the major cities in these areas. We know there is a market out there but our problem now basically is how to reach enough prospective customers to turn MHA into a profitable operation."

HISTORY OF PRIVATE SAFE DEPOSIT COMPANIES

Private safe depositories were originally started shortly after the Civil War. Initially they were used by war profiteers as a safe, secure place to put their gold and silver. Early advertisements indicate that annual rents ranged from $20 to $100 according to size and location. Even at these prices, however, the business grew quite rapidly and by 1900 there were approximately 7,500 private safe depositories in the U. S. The following is from an offering circular from the Union Safe Deposit Vaults in Boston dated December 16, 1867:

> The possessor of papers of value who stowes them into an oven, or up a chimney, or into a closet, or hides them under a bed or a carpet, is almost sure to lose them by accident, fire or robbery; few office safes are proof against burglars during the absence of their owners at night and on holidays; papers in portable safes have been frequently charred, sometimes consumed by the conflagration of the building, and boxes of securities piled into the vault of a bank which receives them without record or acknowledgement and under protest, are exposed to many dangers, and cannot under any circumstances be so well protected as in the Union Safe Deposit Vaults, constructed, arranged, and guarded for the express purpose of receiving and keeping deposits.

Around the turn of the century, branch banking came into existence. However, instead of building new buildings, many banks bought existing safe deposit companies. These moves had two effects—it put the banks in the safe deposit box business, and put the private safe deposit companies out of business. By 1915, their numbers had shrunk to a mere 35! Banks, however, perceived the safe deposit box business as peripheral to their main purposes, and retained the service primarily as a "loss leader." As a result, prices charged to customers for box rentals remained relatively unchanged for more than a century. Currently banks continue to offer safe deposit boxes in most of their offices as a secondary service for their customers.

In the late 1970s, a slow revival of the private safe depository concept began. The new demand, especially for larger boxes, was spurred by a rising crime rate, increased buying of silver and gold, and appreciation of collectables (antiques, stamps, artwork, etc.). Commercial vault companies were eager to fill some of the gaps left by the scarcity of large-size bank safe deposit boxes. Distributors of safes were also thriving. To justify prices of $150 to $2,000 per year to rent boxes, private vault operators offered services not available at banks: privacy from the government, longer hours—some stayed open 24 hours a day seven days a week, and offered tighter security. In addition, many offered pickup and delivery services.

The following news reports are examples of the publicity generated by commercial safe deposit ventures.

Besides appealing to individuals, the private vault companies are also attracting business and professional clients, especially attorneys and investment advisors. Documents such as wills and securities certificates can be stored and retrieved with a minimum of planning. . . . Some companies that keep critical data like accounts receivable and inventory on computer tapes are stashing back-up copies in their safe-deposit boxes as protection in case of fire or theft. (*Inc.,* May, 1982, p. 27).

Business Week in a March 22, 1982 article reported:

By midyear, according to the newly formed National Association of Private Security Vaults Inc., at least 60 nonbank stores are expected to be operating throughout the U.S., with an additional 40 anticipated by year end and 100 more possible in 1983. "The surface hasn't even been scratched," declares Alvin Arnell, president of Vault Management Corp., a consulting firm in Garden City, New York. Some observers foresee thousands of private vault operations, adding 5 million boxes to the 60 million already maintained by banks and thrift institutions. . . . The main attraction of the business appears to be its possibilities as a tax shelter. Many of the ventures are limited partnerships with doctors and lawyers, aimed at taking advantage of accelerated depreciation and investment tax credits. . . . Promoters claim that a private vault should achieve 60 percent occupancy and break even on cash flow in a year. . . . The risks in vault ventures can be substantial. States are looking into the need for regulation, and some markets could become saturated quickly. Banks could heat up some competition if they reprice their services to justify adding boxes and installing more larger sizes.

The Christian Science Monitor on January 21, 1982 reported:

"Banks have stepped up their orders for safe deposit boxes," says Mr. Rosberg, of the Mosler Company. "We've received considerably more orders than we had two years ago. And the orders are for larger boxes. The mix is changing toward the larger sizes." "Industrywide, orders are up about 60 percent over the past two years," he says.

VAULT MANAGEMENT CORPORATION

Sensing a growth opportunity, Vault Management Corporation (VMC) was formed by an enterprising New York financial advisor in May 1981 to identify investor groups in major cities and to prepare for them a complete plan for the establishment of private safe deposit companies through limited partnerships. VMC conducted preliminary market research studies in the various geographical areas, aided in site selection and in the initial design, construction, and installation of the facilities, and assisted in the planning and management of the safe depository (see Exhibit 24.1). For these services VMC was to be paid a one-time fee, and additional

---

EXHIBIT 24.1 **Vault Management Corporation information sent to investors**

Vault Management Corporation

THE CONCEPT

Vault Management Corporation has been organized to provide individual investor groups with a complete "turn-key" operation from initial market research through ongoing facility operations.

The principals of VMC recognized that investor groups, who are looking for a competitive return on their investment, are usually involved in other enterprises. These investors require an ongoing assistance from professionals to insure that every phase of activity is properly cared for and completed.

From extensive marketing surveys to daily operation of the facility, every step must be planned and meticulously executed. This planning involves accounting for everything: from site selection, building codes, local and federal regulations, internal operating systems, security design, box mix selection, client billing, access controls, advertising, marketing, merchandising and sales promotion.

The only way to make the facility operate profitably is to be able to control every aspect of the operation.

PLANNING—The Key To Success

Opening a private safe depository facility requires more than just deciding to go into the business. Despite the highly favorable economic and psychological climate for safe depositories, operating a private safe depository involves far more than a good market.

Security, procedures, location, appearance and intelligent handling of every development step is a vital aspect to creating and sustaining business.

THE APPROACH

With the decision to open a private safe deposit facility, Vault Management Corporation will consult with you and/or your investment group. This initial discussion addresses itself to the overall structure of the private safe deposit facility covering the following topics.

- **Attitudes and Goals**
- **Investment Requirements**
- **Location and Physical Site**
- **Methods of Structuring the Offering**
- **Return on Investment**
- **Operating Procedures**
- **Pricing Policies**
- **Additional Income Sources**
- **Personnel Requirements**

Once your investment group decides to proceed with the project, Vault Management Corporation will enter into a management service contract for the services specified in this brochure. Under this contract Vault Management Corporation receives a first year management fee plus a continued participation in the revenue of the private depository.

ongoing fees equal to a varying percentage of the partnership's annual gross revenues. At the time of the establishment of MHA, VMC had established nine private safe depository facilities at various locations around the country. Most of these were still in the planning and organizational stages.

MHA SAFE DEPOSIT, LTD.

VMC entered into an agreement with MHA Financial Corporation to organize a limited partnership. As a result of this agreement, MHA Safe Deposit, Ltd. was formed early in 1982 as a Massachusetts limited partnership "to construct, install and operate the Safe Depository" in the greater Boston area. The general partners were two individuals who had considerable experience in financial services and investments advising.

MHA was capitalized at approximately $800,000 in limited partnership investments. The facility site chosen was a former stone church building located in Newton Centre, Massachusetts, a relatively affluent, upscale community on the outskirts of Boston. The building was being rehabilitated for office and commercial use, and the partnership had leased approximately 6,800 square feet of space on the first floor. The renovations to the building were completed in time for an early January 1983 opening. It was widely agreed that the facilities and locations were both attractive and highly functional (see Exhibit 24.2 and 24.3). Robert D. Hall, Jr., a bank and financial marketing consultant was appointed President of MHA.

MARKETING RESEARCH

To support its proposal for the funding of a Massachusetts private safe depository, VMC conducted a market research study in the Boston (Newton) area in November 1981. This study was included in the offering prospectus for the limited partnership and it was similar to studies conducted in other cities.

> The basic purpose of the market research program is to identify the potential market, determine the feasibility of such a facility (private safe depository) within a given area and establish the marketing mix that will attract the customers willing to pay for such a service. The stimulation of the business activity through such a marketing mix should result in substantial rentals and ultimate profit. The market research program undertaken employed two major elements: (1) market segmentation—breaking of the potential market into parts, acknowledging the fact that the service being offered is not homogeneous with respect to demand for the service, nor in its response to our marketing (advertising) efforts, and (2) geographic segmentation—the determination of the specific areas that could be serviced by the proposed facility.

Newton Centre was the proposed site of the facility and a travel circle represented by a radius of six miles was seen as its drawing range. This area contained an estimated population of 311,178 (representing 124,541 households), and was well serviced by several major highways. Within the six mile circle were over 50 identifiable communities, including many of Boston's more affluent suburbs. Within this service area over 50 banks were contacted and surveyed.

> The objective was to assess the availability of, and demand for, safe deposit boxes. As a result of this survey of the marketplace it was determined that there was a definite shortage of safe deposit boxes and lockers. Of the institutions surveyed, 68.5 percent indicated that they did not have large safe deposit boxes or lockers available. Of the facilities responding, several indicated that they did not have any boxes at all. A total of 44,319 boxes was estimated to exist in the trade area by extrapolating the average number of boxes per institution in the area.

The consumer survey was conducted by telephone.

> Contrary to previous efforts in taking (sic) the market in the field, we determined that because of the demographics of the area, the time of the year, and the specific

---

EXHIBIT 24.2 **MHA Safe Deposit, Ltd.—Langley Place facility**

Langley Place
surrounds itself with the finest of shops within the prestigious atmosphere of Newton Centre. Retail and commercial businesses at Langley Place will feel at home as a vigorous neighbor to the nearby Chestnut Hill Mall.

Conveniently located at the junction of Beacon Street, Centre Street and Langley Road, Langley Place is midway between the Newton Exit off the Mass Pike (US90), Route 9 (Boston-Worcester Road), and Route 128 (I-95), as well as points North and South.

Added convenience is the short walk across the street to the MBTA Green Line rail service to downtown Boston and Riverside Station off Route 128 (I-95).

Municipal parking, on and off street, is available adjacent to Langley Place.

Any corporation planning to move or expand should earnestly consider the business impact of the environment, excellence of facility and accessibility of location. Blending the finest qualities of all three, Langley Place is now offered to you for occupancy.

Preserving the beauty and exquisite drama of the original exterior neo-Romanesque architecture, fifteen-inch-thick Roxbury Puddingstone walls surround an all-new interior, containing the very latest concepts in space engineering and functional design.

Artful in marriage, both original woodwork and new materials blend to make each office warm, inviting and productive.

Making each floor so unique is the variety of square footage available. Within the old bell tower, fully electronic elevator service swiftly carries passengers to each of five new floors.

Constructed within the majestic A shape roof area of the Church nave, the size of the floors vary, providing flexibility for companies preferring to lease complete floors. Office tenants have the choice of 1,500 square foot penthouse space to the entire 8,000 second floor.

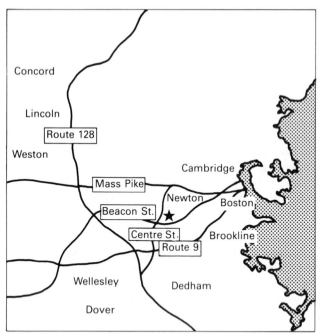

EXHIBIT 24.3 **MHA Safe Deposit, Ltd. location**

restrictions imposed by both factors, that a phone survey was more feasible. . . . statistically, one out of every five persons contacted by phone responded to the survey's questions.

A total of 255 consumer surveys were finally obtained, which was two-tenths of one percent of the total number of households. Over 95 percent (average of respondents of Questions 1–9) of those questioned responded. The remainder of the questions also received a high response percentage. . . . Population projections are accomplished by dividing the total number of surveys taken into total number of households (124,541 ÷ 255 = 488). Therefore, each response to a survey question is equal to 488 projected responses.

Question 1 of the Consumer Survey indicated that 129 families of the 255 surveyed presently rent boxes. Projecting this to the total number of boxes presently being rented we multiply the 129 responses by 488. This provides a total of 62,952 households renting boxes. Taking the 24 percent of those responding to Question #2, (those who rent more than one box), the total number of boxes being rented by the population within the service market area is 78,060.

Based on our projections, the survey indicated that there were 33,741 more safe deposit boxes being presently rented by residents of the surveyed area than were actually available within that area. This leaves us to conclude that:

■ Because of the proximity of the market service area to major business centers in Boston proper, residents of the area are utilizing safe deposit facilities outside their residential area.

- Since the area is a well-established community, the residents are utilizing banking and other financial service centers outside of their residential area. These connections were likely established prior to the expansion of bank branches within their community.
- Results of the bank survey indicated large waiting lists and long periods of time required to obtain larger boxes from financial institutions in the surveyed area.

The consumer survey report offered the following conclusions:

> The introduction of a private safe depository in the area will certainly change the existing traditional patterns and habits of the populace of the area. This conclusion was substantially indicated by the results of the market survey. The initial concern, prior to taking the survey was the ultraconservatism of the area and the effects of a new concept because of this conservatism. Yet, the overwhelming response to such questions as, "Would you be interested in renting a safe deposit box if offered one?" (Question 3), "Would you be interested in finding out more about the facility?" (Question 9), certainly indicated positively that traditional ways would be set aside in order to avail themselves of a more convenient and available facility.
>
> Seven-day opening, extended hours, and high security certainly would influence a large portion of the marketplace to use such a facility. In short, the availability of a specialized facility has become a necessity to the household population of the market area. The numerical results certainly justify the construction of a private facility that would offer the community a responsible, secure, private, and convenient method of storing valuables and collectibles.

Exhibit 24.4 presents consumer responses to specific survey questions.

EXHIBIT 24.4 **Consumer telephone survey***

1. Do you presently rent a safe deposit box?   Yes = 51%
2. Do you rent more than one box?   Yes = 24%   (N = 129)
3. If your answer to question 1 is no, would you be interested in renting a safe deposit box?
   Yes = 25%   (N = 126)
4. Could you use a safe deposit box larger than the one you are now renting?   Yes = 18%
   (N = 129)
5. Have you recently attempted to rent a larger safe deposit box?   Yes = 8%
6. Were you successful in renting a safe deposit box suitable to your present needs?
   Yes = 67%   (N = 21)
7. Would you feel secure about renting a safe deposit box that was not located in a bank, but located in a secured commercial vault?   Yes = 64%
8. Are you familiar with companies that presently provide safe deposit boxes and vaults in private safe depositories?   Yes = 11%
9. Would you be interested in finding out more about such private safe depositories and the security they offer for your personal valuables and collections?   Yes = 41%

a) Who would make the decision in your family to rent a safe deposit box or vault?
   Husband: 17%   Wife: 13%   Joint and others: 70%

b) How often do you find it necessary to visit your safe deposit box?   (N = 129)
   Once a week: 14%   Once a month: 29%   Longer Intervals: 57%

10. Would it be beneficial if you had access to your safe deposit box seven days a week?
    Yes = 60%   (N = 129)

a) What would be convenient hours?
   Weekdays: Normal business hours: 41%   Longer hours: 59%
   Weekends: Normal business hours: 71%   Longer hours: 29%

11. Would it be beneficial if you had access to your safe deposit box on legal holidays?
    Yes = 50%   (N = 129)

12. Would you like the opportunity of returning valuables to your safe deposit box or vault
    on the weekend?   Yes = 70%   (N = 129)

13. Would you feel comfortable placing your valuables in a private vault if there were
    armed guards on duty 24 hours a day?   Yes = 73%

14. Would the private safe deposit company's having a charter or license from a state
    agency influence your renting a safe deposit box or vault?   Yes = 54%

15. If you were provided with free safe deposit box insurance (face value $10,000), would
    this influence your decision to rent a safe deposit box?   Yes = 70%

16. Would you require additional insurance for box contents?   Yes = 30%

17. Would you schedule items in the safe deposit box on your regular policy?   Yes = 57%

18. Would you need a larger safe deposit box?   Yes = 19%

19. Would you need a vault?   Yes = 17%

20. Do you have objects that you would like to put into a safe depository but would not fit
    into any of the box or vault sizes commonly available at banks?   Yes = 15%
    (N = 129)

21. Would you rent a safe deposit box or vault especially designed to meet your individual
    requirements?   Yes = 60%

22. How far would you travel to a safe deposit facility that provides protection for you and
    your valuables?
    1 mile: 26%   2 miles: 22%   3 miles: 5%   4 miles: 5%   5 miles: 19%
                                over 5 miles: 9%

23. If we could provide you with a safe deposit box right now, would you rent one?
    Yes = 14%

24. Would you put a deposit on a safe deposit box or vault if it were offered to you today?
    Yes = 11%

25. Age of respondents (Age range and percent of respondents)
    20–30: 25%   41–55: 10%   61–70: 13%
    31–40: 21%   56–60: 27%   70 or older: 4%

*Total respondents to each question numbered N = 255 unless otherwise indicated.

SAFE DEPOSIT BOX AND REVENUE PROJECTIONS

In addition to the market survey, VMC made available detailed planning on
the number of boxes that would be required as inventory over a period of three years.
Their forecasts on box rentals, cash flow analysis, and revenue and cost projections

EXHIBIT 24.5 Projections for September–December 1982

Box size	Number installed	Rental fee*	Least optimistic		Average optimism		Most optimistic	
			Number rented	Revenue	Number rented	Revenue	Number rented	Revenue
3"x10"	30	$ 144	21	$ 3,024	23	$ 3,312	24	$ 3,456
5"x10"	30	240	20	4,800	22	5,280	24	5,760
10"x10"	204	400	135	54,000	149	59,600	154	61,600
10"x15"	159	640	126	80,640	145	92,800	154	98,560
15"x16"	84	800	78	62,400	84	67,200	84	67,200
22"x16"	8	1,200	8	9,600	8	9,600	8	9,600
38"x10"	9	1,280	4	5,120	5	6,400	5	6,400
33"x16"	7	1,520	5	7,600	5	7,600	5	7,600
38"x16"	7	1,680	4	6,720	4	6,720	4	6,720
63"x10"	6	1,280	4	5,120	5	6,400	4	5,120
Totals	544		405	$239,024	450	$264,912	466	$272,016

* For the year ending December 31, 1982, the partnership may offer discounts and/or commissions that could amount to as much as 20 percent of the rental fee for each box. This has been reflected in the table.

were based on three possible scenarios representing different assumptions regarding the rates of safe deposit box installations and rentals. These rental rates were then translated into appropriate cash flow/income statement projections. Exhibit 24.5 represents their forecasts for the last four months of 1982 based on the assumption that the facility would be operating by September 1982.

Exhibit 24.6 provides a summary of the projections on box rentals and Exhibit 24.7 includes cash flow projections under one of the three assumptions used by VMC.

EXHIBIT 24.6 **Projected box rentals and revenues (VMC estimates)**

| | | Number of boxes rented year end | | | | | | | | |
| | | Least optimistic | | | Average optimism | | | Most optimistic | | |
Box size	Average rental fee	1983	1984	1985	1983	1984	1985	1983	1984	1985
3"x10"	$162	71	95	120	80	100	140	80	108	150
5"x10"	270	70	95	120	80	100	140	80	108	150
10"x10"	450	438	572	722	502	606	275	502	645	900
10"x15"	720	437	572	722	459	600	760	459	645	900
15"x16"	900	334	476	601	334	500	642	334	538	750
22"x16"	1350	18	25	30	18	28	38	18	30	42
38"x10"	1440	14	19	24	17	20	28	17	21	30
33"x16"	1710	14	19	24	17	20	28	17	21	30
38"x16"	1890	14	19	24	16	20	28	16	21	30
63"x10"	1440	8	13	18	8	10	18	8	13	18
Total number of boxes		1,418	1,905	2,405	1,531	2,004	2,572	1,531	2,150	3,000

Revenue projections by VMC based on average rental fees

	Least optimistic	Average optimism	Most optimistic
1983	$ 949,122	$1,011,150	$1,011,150
1984	1,286,910	1,350,900	1,450,566
1985	1,624,860	1,741,320	2,026,620

For the years ending December 31, 1983, 1984, and 1985, the partnership may offer promotional incentives up to 10 percent of the rental fee. This has been reflected in the above table.

MHA'S MARKETING STRATEGY

Location, Facilities, and Services

Bob Hall reacted enthusiastically regarding the Newton Centre location. "We're in a beautiful location. The Chestnut Hill Mall is three miles from here, and we're looking at families with 60 percent and up tax bracket within a 15-minute ride all around us. There appears to be good word-of-mouth around here, and we do get some walk-in traffic."

EXHIBIT 24.7 **Projected cash flow***

	1982	1983	1984	1985
Sources of Cash				
Advance by general partner	$ 35,000	$ —	$ —	$ —
Limited partner investment	800,000	—	—	—
Refund of security deposit				30,600
Operating revenues*	264,912	1,011,150	1,350,900	1,741,320
Total cash receipts	$1,099,912	$1,011,150	$1,350,900	$1,771,920
Uses of Cash				
Partnership formation costs	$ 146,000	$ —	$ —	$ —
Construction costs	523,500	160,000	120,000	80,000
Operating expenses:				
Rent	35,000	122,400	124,380	131,180
Salaries	91,500	242,000	256,200	292,820
Advertising & promotion	60,000	80,000	60,000	40,000
VMC fee	32,649	72,944	76,800	104,479
Facility management fee	15,895	60,666	81,054	104,479
Other	57,750	78,554	81,250	84,275
	$ 292,794	$ 656,564	$ 679,684	$ 757,233
Other uses of cash:				
Reimburse general partner	35,000	—	—	—
Security deposit	30,600	—	—	—
	$ 65,600	0	0	0
Total disbursements before partnership distributions	$1,027,894	$ 816,564	$ 799,684	$ 837,233
Cash Distributions				
General partners	$ —	$ 20,202	$ 60,606	$ 335,757
Limited partners	—	181,818	545,454	564,243
Total cash disbursements	$ 0	$ 202,020	$ 606,060	$ 900,000
Net Cash Flow	$ 72,018	$ (7,434)	$ (54,844)	$ 34,687
Cash beginning	0	72,018	64,584	9,740
Cash ending	$ 72,018	$ 64,584	$ 9,740	$ 44,427
Percent return to limited partner	0%	22.73%	68.18%	70.53%

*These revenue projections are based on average optimism level of box rentals. Operating revenues, construction costs, and fees, as well as percent return to limited partners are slightly different for the least optimistic and most optimistic levels of rentals. 1982 projections assume a September 1982 starting date for the operation of the safe depository.

MHA is open six days per week, from 8:30 AM to 8:30 PM. Access, however, is provided 16 hours a day, 365 days a year, if prior arrangement is made during normal business hours. The office is located in a converted stone church building in the center of town with a municipal parking lot across the street. The decor is modern with extensive use of glass in the common areas, and privacy (one-way) blinds in the conference rooms and booths. Customers are offered, at no charge, the use of large, well-appointed conference rooms in the vault area. These rooms allow the customer to conduct business or review the contents of their box in private. Some customers were thought to be using MHA as a night depository for their day's receipts. They could then prepare their deposit for the bank in the morning in MHA's comfortable and secure setting.

MHA has taken extensive measures to insure the safety of their boxes. The main vault is inside the three-foot thick walls of solid stone that were used to build the original church. Banks have been, traditionally, concerned with holdups. As a result, their alarm and security systems are centered on the teller areas. The vaults are often not alarmed and secured only by their walls and possibly a time lock vault door. In MHA's case the vault is awash with alarms and an extensive alarm system envelops the entire perimeter of the facility.

To gain access to their box a customer must pass through a rigidly controlled security process. First, they must sign a signature card. This is then compared with the individual's card on file. The individual is then admitted to a bulletproof glass-enclosed vestibule. Once in there the customer must key into a touchpad his/her secret code number. If the computer approves the access code as the one chosen by the customer and on file, it then opens a door on the other side of the vestibule and admits the customer to the vault area. To gain access to the box the customer must then use their box key at the same time as the vault attendant uses the attendant's key in a dual lock system. Exit from the vault area is through a separate two-door vestibule controlled by the vault attendant.

Bob Hall referred to the services offered by MHA as being similar to a "Swiss bank" in confidentiality. "We do not require the individual's real name or social security number. A post office address is acceptable, as is a pseudonym. A bank, on the other hand, requires identification and—this is especially important—if a box holder dies, banks frequently protect themselves against possible lawsuits by sealing the box until a Department of Revenue agent can be present for a box inventory. In some states, such as Texas and New York, banks are required by law to do so. With us, a subpoena would have to be issued for the pseudonym on the box—this fictitious name could be known only to you and whoever else you choose to inform. In addition, we automatically give the customer $10,000 insurance with every box. Bank deposit insurance does not cover the contents of safe deposit boxes in case of burglary or any other loss. This was dramatized by the recent robbery of the contents of safe deposit boxes in a Medford, Massachusetts bank—none of the boxes were insured."

MHA offers customers a wide range of box sizes. Boxes start at 3″x5″x18″ and increase in many increments to 63″x10″x18″. They also offer bulk storage for such items as rugs, paintings, furs, etc. For commercial customers they have a media vault which is used to store computer tapes, disks, and microfilm. All of the MHA facilities are environmentally controlled to provide the best and safest temperature and humidity for storage. Both vaults are protected against fire by a Halon gas system. Most banks do not control temperature and humidity in their vaults or protect against fire.

However, some problems have been encountered in the use of boxes with 18″ depth. Bob Hall explained, "The majority of banks in the country offer 24″ deep boxes. The reason we have 18″ boxes is because of an arrangement that Vault Management Corporation had with a manufacturer in Florida who happens to manufacture 18″ boxes. They got a nice package deal on all these safe deposit boxes they put together throughout the United States providing they specified 18″ boxes. We could not have purchased the boxes on our own for the same price as Vault Management was able to negotiate. We've had some people bring in big stamp books and find that they don't quite fit unless they're stood on end, and people are not always happy about that."

To assist customers in understanding the specific advantages of MHA over

---

EXHIBIT 24.8 **MHA Safe Deposit, Ltd. promotional literature**

Take the MHA Challenge: Compare a Bank's Safe Depository with MHA Safe Deposit, Ltd.

	MHA Safe Deposit			Your Bank		
	YES	NO	MAYBE	YES	NO	MAYBE
Total privacy (no SS# or name req.)	X					
Boxes likely to be sealed at death		X				
Boxes likely to be opened by court		X				
Open 7 days/week; 365 days/year	X					
Extended daily hours (av. 16 hrs.)	X					
$10,000 insurance on box contents	X					
Added insurance coverage offered	X					
Separate computer tape storage vault	X					
Box rent less than most insurance costs	X					
Round-the-clock guard protection	X					
Vault exceeds federal banking requirements	X					
Vault carries highest UL rating available	X					
Both vault and building alarmed	X					
UL-certified central alarm station	X					
Limo service (armed escort) on request	X					
Bulk storage for oriental rugs, etc.	X					
Controlled environment (air, temp., etc.)	X					
Week, month, annual rental	X					
10 different box sizes offered	X					
Selection of larger boxes (1½′ to 5′ or more)	X					
Custom made boxes on request	X					
No waiting for boxes to become available	X					

When you rent a safe deposit box, you get what you pay for. Take this with you and compare your bank's boxes with MHA. At MHA you buy insurance against loss . . . insurance to cover monetary value . . . total privacy . . . immediate accessibility . . . superior protection against loss or theft.

Does your bank offer you all these advantages—or just a cut rate price?

other safe deposit box alternatives, Bob Hall designed "The MHA Challenge"—a comparison checklist of services (see Exhibit 24.8).

Pricing

MHA offers a broad range, in both size and price, for its boxes and lockers (see Exhibit 24.9). In addition to these, 60 3"x5"x24" boxes were added by Bob Hall for $60 per year on a three-year lease, thus keeping the initial price for the smallest box to $180. Virtually unlimited bulk storage space is offered to box renters at an additional charge of $1 per cubic foot per month. Media storage for computer tapes and disks is provided with unlimited access during business hours and access by appointment at all other times. This space is rented for $2 per month per tape and $15 per month per disk pack, with a three-month minimum rental period. Archival tape and disk storage is offered at a lower price.

EXHIBIT 24.9 **Safe deposit box pricing**

Box size	Annual rental	Locker size	Annual rental
3"x10"	$ 180	22"x16"	$1,500
5"x10"	300	38"x10"	1,600
10"x10"	500	33"x16"	1,900
15"x10"	800	38"x16"	2,100
15"x16"	1,000	63"x10"	1,750

Box renters are also charged a one-time, fully refundable, key deposit of $75. This money is held in escrow for the period while the box is rented to provide for any costs that might be incurred if it became necessary to drill out the lock in case the key is lost.

Bank safe deposit boxes, when available, rent for substantially less. Small boxes generally rent for $20, and the largest, most expensive boxes, are under $500 per year. Other media storage vaults charge $.25 per tape per month, but also charge an in-out fee of generally $1 every time you wish to remove and return a tape.

Since opening, MHA has offered several price promotions. A direct mail campaign was run through the local American Automobile Association which reached their 200,000 members in the area. A coupon was included in the mailing along with an article that talked about the biggest threat facing the traveler being theft of his goods left behind at home. A short-term rental of a small box was offered at $25 per week or $35 per month. In addition, free bulk storage was offered in a 2'x2'x2' box.

Brochures were distributed through two local savings banks that offered discounts. Bob Hall explained, "In order to develop immediate credibility for our operation, we entered into a referral relationship with several local banks. For example, any customer from Mutual Bank or West Newton Savings who comes in and says,

'We're from Mutual Bank or West Newton Savings,' receives a discount on their box rental, and we pay a small commission to the bank."

A conscious effort was made in the literature developed by MHA to demonstrate how the usage of the insured box at MHA could lead to substantial reductions in the cost of personally arranged property insurance (See Exhibit 24.10). This is possible because of the extensive security measures taken by MHA in protecting their vault from outside intrusion.

EXHIBIT 24.10 **Cost reduction data**

Value of insured property	$60,000
Estimated annual premium (Computed at $18.00 per $1,000 evaluation)*	1,080
Cost in secured private safe depository (Computed at $2.00 per $1,000 evaluation)*	120
Annual savings	960
Safe deposit box rental (Depends on size of box)	600
Annual savings (Total)	360

*Insurance premiums quoted by a Boston-based insurance company.

Bob Hall felt that the high prices were a key reason for their low level of box rentals, but his boxes were already in place, and operations were predicated on financial plans and projections generated from the existing pricing structure. Moreover, price reductions had been tried at other locations and had produced mixed results. Bob elaborated,

> During our initial open house we had over 500 people come in. I would say 99 percent of them had boxes already, and were shocked by the price. They came in, and when they learned of our prices they said thank you and walked out. People who already have boxes are price conscious. Many people who don't have a box will say to us, "How does that compare to a bank's price," because they don't know. In hindsight we could have sold 500 boxes had our prices been maybe just a little bit lower. In an attempt to deal with this initial price resistance, I added a number of small 3"x5"x24" size boxes at $180 for 3 years. All these are now rented.
>
> MHA has tried to overcome the pricing issue with a demonstration of the other features that we offer, features that make our product unique and, hopefully, much more desirable than a bank's safe deposit facility. And there are those nagging instances when customers appeared to be quite price inelastic . . . . We had a customer come in the other day. He just pointed to the box and said, "I want that box. How much?" He was told; he left, and returned with $500 in twenty-dollar bills. He opened his briefcase, and well, it was just filled with cash! I think the primary thing we have to sell is the privacy, the Swiss bank concept. To me, the market is that man or woman making $75,000 a year and up, but, who is also looking for a way to keep his or her earnings a secret

from everyone—including the IRS. I think our big calling card is the hours and privacy. I don't know how we're going to reach them, and I'm looking to buy a mailing list.

Promotion

At the outset, extensive publicity was generated. "The concept seemed new and fresh," Bob emphasized, "and we've had some very good publicity. We've had a big colored feature article in the *Boston Globe's* Sunday magazine section. We've had some publicity in the *Boston Herald*. We've had a substantial article in *Banker & Tradesman*, and coverage in *Boston* magazine. I've been on a couple of talk shows. I've spoken to about seven Rotary Clubs and Lions Clubs and other groups about the facility. So, we've been on the speaking circuit."

In the early stages, heavy use was made of advertising. Local newspapers were used as was the *Boston Business Journal, Banker & Tradesmen*, and *Boston* magazine. Bob explained, "We were late in our scheduled opening of the facility; however, we started advertising in October for a January opening date. During November and December, we spent $35,000 on promotions. Advertising produced people, but the people who came in as a result of the advertising all had boxes. I didn't seem to produce much in the way of people who didn't have boxes!"

Efforts were made to reach specific target markets. MHA advertised in the Suffolk Downs newspaper (a local race track). Restaurant owners in the area were contacted by direct mail. A short-term box rental was offered through the regional AAA newsletter for travelers who might want to safeguard valuables while gone. Bob Hall elaborated, "The tough thing is we've done a lot of advertising, but for all the creativity that's been involved, and the money that we've spent, it hasn't worked for us the way it should."

Personal selling has been used primarily in the effort to close sales with individuals on site, and to generate business for the media vault storage with commercial customers. Bob Hall explained, "I may be driving along and see ABC Computer Company, I'll either go in and see if I can talk to the data processing manager, or I'll get their name and try to set up an appointment. I use the *Business to Business* book from the phone company to develop leads. We've hired a salesman, but the fact that we work on straight commission didn't go over too well. We've made arrangements with a young lady that sells office supplies. She provides us with leads on a commission arrangement. When she is out calling on her customers she is going to ask what they do for storage and give them our literature."

To assist in personal selling and direct mail solicitation, numerous brochures and other printed material have been developed. To identify and communicate with potential customers their unique services, MHA developed the "MHA Challenge." Bob Hall reflected, "Area banks seem to be changing their approach of using safe deposit boxes as loss-leaders. For example, the bank across the street from us has expanded its number of boxes, added larger ones, increased their fees, and extended their hours! We know there is a market out there, but how do we reach them? How do we get to the doctors and lawyers and financial consultants who are in the upper income brackets? How do we reach the coin dealers, the stamp collectors, and the small businessmen dealing in cash transactions? That seems to be the market."

CASE 25 ———————————————————————

AT&T and the Residential
Long-distance Market (A)

Monica Barnes stood gazing out the window of her 7th floor office in AT&T Communication's (AT&T-C) Atlanta regional office. Her attention was focused on the house that shared the block in downtown Atlanta with the AT&T-C building. When AT&T had decided to build on this location, the owners of the existing house had refused to sell, forcing AT&T-C to build on two sides of and close to the house. The contrast between the stately, traditional, old Southern home and the tall, concrete and glass, modern office building was indicative of the transition period through which AT&T and the telecommunications industry were now moving.

On January 8, 1982, AT&T and the Department of Justice had signed an accord that dropped the government's 1974 antitrust charges against AT&T, scrapped the 1956 antitrust settlement that had barred AT&T from engaging in unregulated businesses, and called for the spin-off of AT&T's 22 Bell operating companies (BOCs or Baby Bells). Judge Harold Greene had formally approved the Modification of Final Judgment on August 24, 1982, giving AT&T until February 24, 1983, to submit a detailed divestiture plan, and until February 24, 1984, to execute the plan.

The two years since January 1982, had been extremely hectic for AT&T. The firm had been continually in courts or before Congress dealing with a myriad of suits and proposed bills that attempted to stop or alter the planned breakup. The plan had actually been implemented on January 1, 1984, with "old" AT&T being split into eight parts—seven new regional holding companies completely separate from AT&T and the "new" AT&T. (AT&T-C was the division of the new AT&T which was responsible for the provision of long-distance services.) However, the new AT&T still faced many changes and uncertainties as it pursued full implementation of the divestiture plan.

Monica turned from the window and began reviewing her notes from the meeting she had just finished with her boss, David Lawrence, the District Manager in charge of residential marketing for the 14 states in the Southern region. Lawrence had asked Monica to prepare a marketing plan for the region that was designed to

This case was prepared by Lew G. Brown, Bryan School of Business and Economics, University of North Carolina at Greensboro, under the supervision of Robert S. Harris, School of Business, University of North Carolina at Chapel Hill, with support of a grant from the AT&T Foundation. It is intended as a basis for classroom discussion rather than to illustrate effective or ineffective handling of an administrative situation. Some facts have been altered to protect confidentiality of company information. Appreciation is expressed to the AT&T-C staff in the External Affairs and Marketing Divisions of the Southern Region and to the Consumer Marketing Division in Basking Ridge, NJ, for their support on this project. Distributed by the North American Case Research Association. All rights reserved to the author and the North American Case Research Association. Used by permission from Lew G. Brown and the North American Case Research Association.

get residential customers to select AT&T-C as their primary interexchange carrier (PIC or Primary Carrier) as the "equal access" provisions of the judgment were implemented.

HOW LONG-DISTANCE WORKS

Exhibit 25.1 depicts the normal operation of long-distance service. A local subscriber wanting to place a long-distance call using AT&T-C would simply dial "1" plus, if necessary, the area code and then the seven-digit number of the subscriber being called. As depicted in the Exhibit, AT&T-C has "trunk-side" access to the local telephone company's (LEC) switching office. However, if the customer wishes to place a call using another common carrier (OCC), such as MCI or Sprint, the subscriber must first dial a seven-digit number to gain access to the common carrier's switching office. Then the subscriber must dial a five-to-seven digit identification number; and then, the normal seven-to-ten digits. The customer has thus used the local telephone company's "line-side" connection to reach the common carrier's switching office.

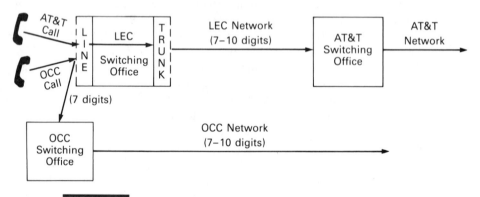

EXHIBIT 25.1 **Trunk-side vs. line-side access for long-distance calling**

The common carriers argued that because their customers had to dial additional digits which resulted in inferior technical quality and features due to the line-side access, the common carriers were at a disadvantage in competing with AT&T-C for long-distance customers.

HOW EQUAL ACCESS WORKS

The judgment signed by Judge Greene in August 1982, had included the provision that local telephone companies must provide "to all long-distance carriers

. . . exchange access . . . equal in type, quality, and price to that provided to AT&T and its affiliates." This stipulation had come to be known as "equal access." It had been included in the judgment as a result of Judge Greene's finding that the other common carriers were "disadvantaged" due to AT&T-C's "superior" connections to the local distribution networks of the Baby Bells and the other independent telephone companies. Under the provision for equal access, common carriers would have the right to purchase trunk-side access, just as AT&T-C, so that their customers would dial the same number of digits and use similar local telephone company access lines as an AT&T-C customer.

The services offered by the local telephone companies are categorized into five groups called "feature groups." These feature groups allow long-distance carriers the option of offering different types and levels of service to their customers. The group of services involved in equal access is denoted as "feature group D." In addition to the need to dial fewer digits, feature group D allows rotary-dial telephones as well as touch-tone telephones to use the service (before equal access, only customers with touch tone phones could use a common carrier) and provides answer supervision and automatic number identification services which are important in accurate billing.

It is important to note that the judgment only required that equal access be made *available* to all long-distance carriers. It did not require any long-distance carrier to make any particular feature group available to its customers. A common carrier might decide not to offer feature group D to customers served by a particular exchange office (called "end-office").

Customers served by an equal access end-office would access a long-distance carrier in one of 4 ways:

First, a customer would be able to designate a primary carrier. Once a primary carrier has been selected by the customer, any long-distance call dialed normally (1 + area code + number) would be automatically routed to that carrier. For example, if GTE Sprint had been selected by the customer as the primary carrier, all normal long-distance calls would be routed to the Sprint switch; and Sprint would bill the customer for those calls. It should be noted that the customer would first have to establish an account with a common carrier in order to be able to use its services.

Second, although a customer had designated a primary carrier, the customer would still be able to place long-distance calls using another long-distance carrier. This nonprimary long-distance carrier must have subscribed to equal access in that exchange area and have decided to accept "access-code" traffic. The customer would dial 1 + 0 + a three-digit long-distance carrier code (1+0+XXX) before dialing the normal area code and local number. The "XXXs" represent the vendor access code. For example, a customer who had designated MCI as his/her primary carrier would still be able to place calls using AT&T-C by following the above dialing procedure and using AT&T-C's access code. This procedure obviously allows customers the ability to "shop" for long-distance services and rates if they so desire and if common carriers have elected to provide equal access in the customer's area.

Third, operator-assisted calls would still be available by dialing 1+0+XXX. AT&T-C was the only carrier offering operator assistance although others might do so in the future. Local operators were available by dialing 0. They usually were AT&T-C employees under contract to the local telephone company.

Fourth, customers might continue to reach common carriers by dialing a seven-digit access code and a personal identification number if a common carrier chose to continue to provide feature group A and/or B service in an area (the same procedure as that in effect prior to equal access).

EXHIBIT 25.2 **Equal access schedule (1984)**

Date	Place of first equal access (city end-office)
July 15, 1984	West Virginia (Charleston, S. Charleston)
August 19, 1984	Minnesota (Minneapolis-Orchard)
August 24, 1984	California (San Francisco-Almeda)
	Nevada (Virginia City, Silver Spring, Carson City, Butte, Churchill)
August 25, 1984	Colorado (Denver)
August 27, 1984	Georgia (Atlanta-Toco Hills, Courtland St.)
	Alabama (Mobile-Springhill)
August 30, 1984	Indiana (Indianapolis-Trinity, Melrose)
August 31, 1984	Texas (Houston-W. Ellington)
	Illinois (Chicago-Wabash, Dearborn)
September 1, 1984	Massachusetts (Eastern-Back Bay)
	New York (Metro New York City)
	New Jersey (Hackensack, Clifton)
	Pennsylvania (Philadelphia-Pennypacker, Locust)
	Delaware (Wilmington)
	Maryland (Baltimore-Liberty, Columbia)
	Washington, D.C. (Metro)
	Virginia (Norfolk)
	Ohio (Cleveland, Columbus)
	Michigan (Detroit)
	Wisconsin (Stevens Point, Milwaukee)
	Oregon (Portland)
October 1, 1984	Washington (Seattle)
October 22, 1984	Florida (Jacksonville)
October 28, 1984	Kentucky (Louisville-New Albany)
November 17, 1984	Utah (Salt Lake City)
November 26, 1984	Louisiana (Shreveport-Monroe)
	Tennessee (Memphis)
December 1, 1984	Rhode Island
December 16, 1984	Idaho (Roberts, Moore, Howe, McKay, Island Park, Arco, Idaho Falls)
December 29, 1984	Idaho (Boise)

Source: Federal Communications Commission.

The judgment required equal access "cutovers" to begin by September 1, 1984. "Cutover" is defined as the date that long-distance calls begin to go, on a "dial-1 basis," to the designated primary carrier. By the end of 1984, 134 exchange offices would be converted to equal access. An additional 1,900 would convert in 1985, and an additional 2,400 would convert in 1986. Beyond 1986, additional offices would convert at an estimated rate of 500 per year. Conversion would take place by end-office (denoted by the first three digits in the seven-digit telephone number). Since local telephone companies would convert office by office and some offices would take longer or be more complicated to convert, there would be no uniform pattern for cutover. Thus, a city served by nine exchange offices might have those offices converted at different times throughout the 1984 to 1986 period. Small-end offices (those serving less than 10,000 lines) and other offices that might be uneconomical to convert would not have to be modified, subject to court approval. This schedule of 1984 cutovers shows the date and place where equal access will first become available (Exhibit 25.2). As of these dates, in these places subscribers may designate the interexchange carrier that will carry all of their long-distance calls; subscribers will be able to reach another interexchange carrier by dialing five digits $(1+0+XXX)$. As equal access becomes available, each interexchange carrier will pay equal costs for access to local exchanges. With the phased implementation of the full schedule (July 1984 to September 1986), AT&T and its competitors will compete for subscribers on an equal basis.

As noted above, local telephone customers would have the opportunity to select a primary carrier. The process for this selection prior to cutover was called presubscription. The specific steps to be followed in the presubscription process were to be established by each local telephone company. As of March 1984, those steps had not yet been finalized. However, there was a published general time frame that would be followed. An illustrative time frame is shown in Exhibit 25.3.

As noted in Exhibit 25.3, local customers would be notified by the local telephone company 90 days prior to the cutover for their end office of their right to choose a primary carrier. In addition, the customers would have a 180-day period

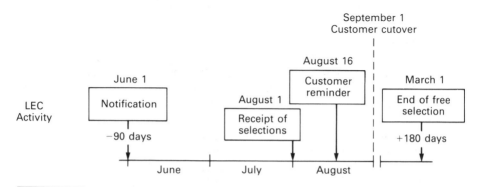

EXHIBIT 25.3 **Example of cutover time schedule**

following cutover during which they could select a primary carrier or change their original selection without any charge. Following the end of this 180-day period, customers would be required to pay a minimal charge, perhaps five dollars, to choose a primary carrier. New customers entering the system during or after the cutover process would be required to select a primary carrier as a part of opening their account.

Long-distance carriers could act as the customer's agent in the selection process. The customer could contract with the long-distance carrier for long-distance service. The long-distance carrier could then notify the local telephone company of the customer's selection.

One question that had not been resolved in the judgment dealt with how to handle those customers who, for whatever reason, failed to designate a primary carrier by the end of the 180-day period following cutover. This question was not minor in that some estimates stated that up to 90 percent of customers might fail to make a choice.

In December 1983, Judge Greene had issued an opinion in response to Ameritech's (a regional company) motion that it be allowed to route all "undesignated" traffic to AT&T-C by *default*. In that opinion, Judge Greene noted that the decree, subsequent opinions, and the Department of Justice supported the position that undesignated traffic should be routed to AT&T-C. The decree provided that customers were to be given the option of selecting an alternate carrier, but did not *require* them to make a selection. The judge noted the arguments of AT&T-C's competitors that such a situation would "perpetuate that company's [AT&T] dominant role in the interexchange market; and that Ameritech's proposal therefore conflicts with the bedrock principles underlying the decree." Judge Greene noted, however, that the alternatives to allocating undesignated traffic to AT&T-C by default had practical difficulties themselves.

A first alternative involved the *allocation* to all participating carriers of customers who have not actively chosen a long-distance company. The court argued that this alternative was entirely unsuitable since the purpose of the antitrust laws was to protect the competitive process, "not to assure positive results for competitors." The opinion also noted that many of the long-distance carriers might not be prepared to serve all the customers who might be allocated to them either due to technological problems or to the inability of customers to meet the firms' service requirements. Further, the court noted the difficulty of carriers, which the customers had expressed no desire to use, sending bills to those customers. Even if these problems could be overcome, the court noted the problem of establishing a fair allocation formula. For these reasons, the court would not require allocation of undesignated traffic.

However, the court, while refusing to impose the allocation requirement on the operating companies, did not prohibit allocation if a local telephone company wished to use this method. In fact, Northwestern Bell had indicated it would randomly allocate undesignated customers to carriers in proportion to each carrier's share of those customers who did choose a primary carrier.

A second **alternative** known as *blocking* had been proposed. Advocates of this method had suggested that when a caller who had not presubscribed nor dialed a carrier-access code attempted to place a long-distance call, the caller would be referred to a recording. The recording would instruct the caller to dial the local telephone company's business office or an "800" number to obtain additional information. The caller would be given the access codes of several long-distance companies which would allow him/her to select a carrier. However, the caller still might not be able to complete the call if he/she did not have an account with the carrier. Attempts to complete a call in this way would also be complicated by holiday or emergency situations or by language or education problems.

The court noted that the blocking procedure could cause substantial inconvenience to customers and that, while the court wished to promote competition, it could not do so at the expense of the public interest. The court also noted that having AT&T-C as a carrier of last resort was in the public interest and should be encouraged. Judge Greene, therefore, refused to require blocking.

The court granted Ameritech's motion allowing the routing of undesignated traffic to AT&T-C with the requirements that the local telephone companies inform their customers of their options during the 90-day presubscription period and also provide the opportunity to designate a carrier, free of charge, during the 90-day period following cutover. Customers receiving new service who had previously failed to designate a primary carrier or who were new to the exchange area would not be assigned automatically to AT&T-C. They would be given the information on options and could be "blocked" until a primary carrier was chosen.

Judge Greene added:

> The court recognizes, of course, that this ruling may be of substantial assistance to AT&T. For the reasons stated, that is a result that cannot initially be avoided without exorbitant costs to the public. It does not follow, however, that the court, consistent with the promotion of competition, should not require the operating companies to make reasonable efforts to acquaint customers with their options with regard to interexchange service or that it should not take steps to preclude AT&T from receiving the calls of undesignated customers in perpetuity. Such measures are, indeed, entirely appropriate.

In a footnote, the court noted that some 20 percent of telephone customers receive new service annually. Therefore, any advantage accruing to AT&T-C from the court's action "should be largely dissipated in a relatively short period of time."

Thus, Judge Greene had approved the *default* procedure. Although the Judge's ruling had supported AT&T-C's position on the handling of undesignated traffic, AT&T-C still found itself facing a situation in which almost all of its customer base would be "up for grabs" over the next 2-1/2 years.

THE RESIDENTIAL LONG-DISTANCE MARKET

The U.S. residential long-distance market in 1984 included 80 million customers. Of these, some 60 million were connected to the Baby Bells, with the remainder connected to independent telephone companies.

AT&T-Communications

AT&T-C's total 1984 revenues from both business and residential long-distance markets were expected to total $36 billion. AT&T-C's residential revenue was, like its business revenue, highly concentrated in a small segment of large-volume users. Exhibit 25.4 presents information on this revenue distribution.

EXHIBIT 25.4 **Residential revenue distribution**

Monthly expenditures on interstate long distance	Percent of households	Percent of revenue	Interexchange calls/month
$ 0– 10	74	20	0– 3
10– 25	17	29	4–10
25– 50	7	26	11–20
50–100	2	16	21–40
100+	1	9	41+

Source: AT&T-C. Data based on market analysis using 1st quarter 1983 average data.

Total interstate and intrastate residential revenues for AT&T-C for 1984 were expected to total $13.8 billion, with the interstate portion of that market expected to grow at 8 percent per year over the next five years. (Intrastate calls refer to long-distance calls that begin and terminate within the same state. The equal access decisions applied only to interstate service. Therefore, theoretically, only interstate service revenues were at risk in the equal access process. However, the common carriers were beginning to offer intrastate service, thereby threatening those revenues as well.)

The interstate residential revenues at risk in the equal access process in 1984 totaled $327 million. This figure would rise to $11.7 billion by 1989—two-thirds of the residence market revenue.

AT&T-C's Southern region's 14 states included approximately 18 million of the 80 million residential long-distance customers. In 1984, residential long-distance billings in the region were estimated to total $2.6 billion. The 14 states in the region were North and South Carolina, Georgia, Florida, Louisiana, Alabama, Mississippi, Tennessee, Kentucky, Oklahoma, Missouri, Kansas, Arkansas, and Texas.

AT&T-C continued to be classified by the Federal Communications Commission (FCC) as the only "dominant" carrier. Thus, it was subject to more regulation than the common carriers. In addition to having its authorized rate of return capped at 12.75 percent, all capital construction plans, service offerings, and price changes had to be approved by the FCC. Further, AT&T-C had to have its intrastate services approved individually by the 50-state public utility commissions. In contrast, the common carriers were generally under no such requirements. Therefore, it took

AT&T-C longer to implement changes and those changes were "telegraphed" to the competition due to the regulatory processes.

Further, the common carriers were receiving a discount relative to AT&T-C for access to local telephone companies' networks. The access fees were levied to compensate the local telephone companies for nonusage-sensitive costs. However, the access fees were levied on a per-minute of usage basis. The base access charges for common carriers were 55 percent less than AT&T-C's; and in practice, the discount could even be greater. The common carriers used this cost differential to their advantage in pricing against AT&T-C.

However, the advent of equal access would put cost pressures on the common carriers. Carriers purchasing equal access would have to pay the same rates as AT&T-C. However, due to AT&T-C having to continue to serve less profitable customers, some analysts estimated that its rates would continue to be 10 percent higher that those of its competition. Common carriers also could continue to offer lower levels of service at reduced costs as they had done, even in equal access areas. To some extent, this capability would depend on the price differentials eventually offered by the local telephone companies for the various feature groups.

Competition

While there were 400 common carriers serving the long-distance market, six (MCI, GTE Sprint, ALLNET, ITT, U. S. Telephone, and Satellite Business Systems) accounted for 88 percent of the $3.2 billion of common carrier's sales in 1983. The remaining companies were primarily resellers of AT&T-C's WATS services. The Common Carriers served 3.8 million customers. (See Exhibit 25.5.)

EXHIBIT 25.5 **Profile of major common carriers—1983**

	Revenues* (in billions)	Percent	Subscribers* (in thousands)	Percent
MCI**	$1.52	48	1,550	41
GTE Sprint	.75	23	920	24
ALLNET	.18	6	150	4
ITT	.17	5	95	3
U.S. Telephone	.14	4	80	2
SBS	.07	2	90	2
Other	.37	12	915	24
Totals	$3,200	100	3,800	100

*Includes both business and residence markets.

**MCI serves 85% of the country with its network; 30% of MCI's revenues comes from its residence long-distance voice service.

Source: AT&T-C Residence Market Management.

Both MCI and GTE Sprint appeared to be in the long-distance service market for the long run. Between them, they had announced plans to spend $2 billion on their networks in 1985. These expansion plans, however, at a time of rising access costs and price cutting to attract customers, would be predicted to bring on financial pressure in the short term.

Both firms also appeared to be adopting a strategy of offering the same services as AT&T-C. MCI had dropped its monthly minimum fee and had introduced an initial-minute charge with a lower per-minute night rate for additional minutes (similar to AT&T-C's pricing). It had also contracted with the operating companies to offer immediate directory assistance at 45 cents per call (5 cents less than AT&T-C's charge) and, along with Sprint, was offering volume discounts on customers' monthly bills.

News reports on the equal access process indicated that the common carriers saw that process as a major opportunity to take market share from AT&T-C and would be aggressive in trying to do so. An article in the March 12, 1984, edition of the *Philadelphia Enquirer* quoted W. G. McGowan, Chairman of MCI, as saying, "The most significant thing in our business is going to be that equal connection." M. J. Goodman, President of Allnet Communications noted that, "It's going to be the best opportunity for market redistribution in over 100 years." The article also noted that some firms might pursue niche strategies. For example, some firms might provide service only between two particular cities, seeking to capture the high volume, profitable traffic.

THE ASSIGNMENT

David Lawrence had attended the first public relations strategy meeting on AT&T-C's presubscription marketing strategy on February 15, 1984. This meeting had involved all the district managers in charge of residential marketing from each of AT&T-C's regions and had dealt with development of marketing and public relations strategies for the first cutover which was scheduled for Charleston, West Virginia, with a tentative date of July 15, 1984. This date meant that customers in the affected area could begin to be notified as early as April 15, 1984, that they would be required to choose a long-distance carrier.

David Lawrence had returned from the meeting and scheduled a meeting with Monica Barnes. He had indicated to Monica that even though AT&T-C would receive undesignated traffic due to Judge Greene's ruling, the corporation's objective was to secure an *active* selection of AT&T-C as the primary carrier. Although no decision had yet been made as to whether the marketing strategy and implementation for the choice process would be carried out at the national or regional levels, Lawrence wanted to be prepared with a regional strategy. The tight schedule involved left no time to wait until a final decision was made.

David had asked Monica to prepare the broad outlines of a marketing strategy for the 14 states in the southern region. He was not interested at this moment in end-office specific plans, but rather wanted a general plan on which end-office plans could be based. Specifically, he was interested in a recommended plan specifying which residential customers would be contacted, through which channels, when, with what messages, and how often during the 90-day presubscription process and, if necessary, the 180-day period following cutover. He was also interested in cost estimates for any plan that might be proposed. While Lawrence would not be responsible for overall media planning, he was interested in any suggestions or themes she might propose that he could refer to the AT&T-C offices responsible for media planning. He had asked to have the proposal by March 1.

Market Research

In anticipation of the upcoming equal access process, AT&T-C had conducted market research in 1983 to determine the important attributes of long-distance service from the customer's point of view. Five general attributes had been delineated: price, ubiquity, service quality, servicing, and innovation. Exhibit 25.6 presents a summary of the research findings.

EXHIBIT 25.6 **Residence market differentiation research: important attributes of long-distance—1983**

Attribute	Residence perception	Percent ranking attribute as most important
Price	Price performance	55
Ubiquity (widely available)	Customer able to call anywhere, anytime	22
Service quality	Lack of static, echo, disconnections	15
Servicing	Efficient, responsive customer representatives and operators	6
Innovation	New applications and services	2

Source: AT&T-C. Data based on market analysis using 1st quarter, 1983, average data.

In addition to the results presented in Exhibit 25.6, the research had found that 52 percent of those surveyed did not associate the name AT&T with long distance. Consumers also tended to overestimate both AT&T-C's and competitors' strengths. Differences in prices between AT&T-C and the competition were perceived to be larger than they actually were. Both MCI's prices and service quality were perceived as lower than they actually were.

The research also allowed the identification of certain dominant market subsegments, as shown in Exhibit 25.7.

EXHIBIT 25.7 **Dominant market subsegments in AT&T-C residence market**

Subsegment	Number of customers (In millions)	Revenue (In billions)
College	12.5	$1.3
Just moved	15.0	2.6
Working women	43.0	3.4
Military	3.5	0.3
Hispanics	8.0	0.5
Mature adults (50+)	41.0	4.0

Note: Segments are not mutually exclusive and cannot be added together.

Source: AT&T-C Residence Market Management.

Market research studies had also been started in early 1984 in order to provide a bench mark for judging the results of marketing efforts. The research had focused on the 31 markets that would be subject to cutover in 1984. Approximately 11,000 residence customers were interviewed by telephone by an independent company.

Respondents were asked to rate long-distance companies they were aware of on a variety of attribute statements using a 1-to-5 scale with 1 meaning poor and 5 meaning excellent. The attribute statements had been grouped into four categories for analysis: price, quality, ubiquity, and servicing. Exhibit 25.8 presents a listing of the statements. Exhibit 25.9 presents some results of the bench mark studies.

In the same survey, the mean rating for AT&T-C on the attribute, "Having Competitive Prices," was 3.35. For MCI, the mean rating was 4.25.

The bench mark survey had also asked respondents to name any suppliers of long-distance service. The percentage of respondents having *unaided* recall for AT&T-C was 57 percent; for MCI, 53 percent; and for Sprint, 40 percent. Interestingly, 31 percent listed the local Baby Bell as being the provider of long-distance service.

Respondents had also been asked about how much they knew about the companies. The percentage of respondents who indicated they knew a lot about AT&T-C was 26 percent; about MCI, 8 percent; about Sprint, 6 percent.

Respondents had also been asked to rate 20 characteristics of long-distance suppliers on the degree of importance of those characteristics to them. Top ratings were as follows:

- Getting good quality for the price you pay—80%
- Ability to call anytime, (to) anywhere—79%
- Ability to call anytime from anywhere—78%
- Providing accurate and reliable itemized billing—77%
- Having excellent sound quality—75%
- Paying no monthly service charge—74%
- Being an established, dependable company—69%

EXHIBIT 25.8 **Bench mark attribute statements**

Price	Servicing

Price

Having competitive prices

Having discounted rates available during convenient time periods

Quality

Having excellent sound quality

Getting good quality for the price you pay

Being an established and dependable company

Ubiquity

The ability to call anytime, to or from anywhere

Having the ability to make international calls

Servicing

Having to pay no monthly service charge

Providing accurate and reliable long-distance itemized billing

Having a trained and knowledgeable customer service force

Having long-distance directory assistance

Providing accurate and reliable information about long-distance rates and services

Having a long-distance operator available anytime you need one

The ability to make person-to-person, collect or "bill to third party" long-distance calls

Innovation

Having the ability to make credit card calls

- Having competitive prices—68%
- Having an operator available when you need one—67%
- Providing reliable information about rates/services—67%

The three lowest ratings were for:

- Having international calling capability—29%
- Ability to make time payments on bills—26%
- Having a telephone credit card—22%

EXHIBIT 25.9 **Respondents giving "excellent" rating to selected suppliers on long-distance attributes 1984**

Attribute	Percent giving excellent rating		
	AT&T-C	MCI	Sprint
Quality	55	27	21
Price	32	32	25
Servicing	54	23	19
Ubiquity	72	31	25

Source: AT&T Communications.

With regard to contacting customers, Monica was aware of recent estimates that each direct mail piece cost between $.60 and $1.20 and each telemarketing call cost between $4.50 and $5.00. She was also aware of the on-going customer contact possibilities provided by the Residential Service Center (RSC) operation staffed by customer service representatives who handled in-coming calls from residential customers about bills or service.

Monica Barnes' Position.   Monica realized the importance of the assignment she had been presented both in terms of AT&T-C and in terms of her own development. AT&T-C found itself in a very uncertain period. The firm had been required to act and react in very short time periods on matters involving millions and even billions of dollars in actual or potential revenues and costs. Employees at all levels had been required to stretch their efforts, often beyond their actual duties, in order to manage the workload.

Monica had joined AT&T-C five years earlier after completing her MBA at Rutgers. Although AT&T-C did not have what it formally called a management development program, Monica had participated in a series of assignments in the marketing area to familiarize her with the overall marketing function and thereby prepare her for a future management role. She had begun working at AT&T-C's headquarters in Basking Ridge, New Jersey, in a support role in marketing management. She had then designed sales strategies for the company's work with securities firms. Then, she had worked in sales operations on sales force productivity issues. In early 1983, she had been assigned to the Atlanta office to help establish the residential marketing function in the southern region.

As she prepared to begin outlining her work, she thought about the different points of view and expectations persons in other areas of AT&T-C would have relative to her proposal.

Network personnel were interested in maintaining network utilization and the network investment program. If utilization fell because of lost customers, Network's plans to invest in new facilities aimed at generating high value-added services targeted for the business community might have to be modified or postponed.

Finance personnel would be concerned about the cost of any programs aimed at equal access marketing as well as AT&T-C's relative cost position with respect to other carriers. They would also be concerned about a loss in volume and its effect on revenue (a 1 percent drop in volume nationwide would result in a 5 percent decrease in net income). See Exhibit 25.10 for overall financial information.

External affairs personnel would feel equal access was a success if the common carriers were moderately successful so as to supply the regulators with evidence that the market was truly competitive. This would help in their battle to end the unequal regulation of AT&T-C.

The Legal staff would be concerned that common carriers, who were ordering private-line circuits from AT&T-C to serve their new customers, be treated in a nondiscriminatory manner.

Finally, marketing personnel would worry about *any* "victory" for a common

---

EXHIBIT 25.10 **AT&T pro forma income statement for 1984***

	MTS** amount	WATS** amount	PLS** amount	Total interstate
		(In billions)		
Total revenues	$17.35	$ 6.25	$ 3.84	$27.44
Expenses:				
Maintenance	.59	.21	.48	1.28
Depr. and amort.	.58	.19	.22	.99
Commercial and marketing	1.05	.37	.27	1.69
Traffic and oper. rents	1.55	.31	.31	2.17
Relief and pensions	.42	.13	.21	.76
Misc. and other taxes	1.31	.46	.40	2.17
Access charge	10.65	4.19	1.45	16.29
Federal taxes	.43	.14	.18	.75
Total expenses	$16.58	$ 6.00	$ 3.62	$26.10
Net earnings	$ .77	$ .25	$ .32	$ 1.34
Average net investment	$ 6.04	$ 1.94	$ 2.48	$10.46
Earnings ratios	12.72%	12.79%	12.78%	12.75%

*October, 1983—With original access charge plan (including proposed rate changes)

**MTS—Measured telecommunications service. This is the category that reflects typical long-distance service. Each call is billed on the basis of distance, duration, and time of day.

WATS—Wide area telecommunications service. AT&T's bulk rate, public, switched long-distance telephone service. WATS users are billed partially on the basis of the number of hours of usage and partially on a per-call basis.

PLS—A telecommunications channel or service that is leased in its entirety by AT&T for the sole use of one or more specific customers between two or more specific points.

Source: AT&T (FCC filing, October 3, 1983).

---

carrier, even in an individual market area, being seen as evidence that the common carrier's were as good as AT&T-C. Such an event might give impetus to the common carriers' nationwide efforts.

Monica reflected that, for a company that did not even have a consumer marketing function 18 months ago, things had gotten awfully complicated. There were many factors to consider and many forces to balance in her plan.

CASE 25

AT&T and the Residential
Long-distance Market (B)

Monica Barnes sat in David Lawrence's office listening to the conference call coming over the speakerphone. Each listened intently as their counterparts in AT&T-C headquarters in Basking Ridge, New Jersey, and at other locations around the country discussed the latest Federal Communications Commission decision involving the equal access process.

The conference call was being held on June 15, 1985. Although the entire equal access process (see Case A) had been marked by uncertainty, confusion, and changes, this latest FCC decision seemed especially improbable. Monica glanced at David. She knew that neither of them was sure how much more of this they could take. The cliche, "the straw that broke the camel's back," had suddenly taken on new meaning.

Monica rose from her chair and paced beside David's desk. "Well, now I have heard everything," she exclaimed, "not only does the future change in this business, but now the past even changes!"

THE END OF DEFAULT

This latest series of events in the 2-1/2 year cutover process had begun on May 31, 1985, with an order by the FCC that put an end to the default provision under which the equal access process had been operating generally for almost a year.

In the FCC order, issued on June 12, 1985, the commission began by reviewing the history of the default provision, noting the Modification of Final Judgement provisions and summarizing Judge Greene's subsequent rulings on default. Since Judge Greene's 1983 ruling on default, the FCC had heard and considered the petitions of those who argued that the default provision gave an unfair competitive

This case was prepared by Lew G. Brown, Bryan School of Business and Economics, University of North Carolina at Greensboro, under the supervision of Robert S. Harris, School of Business, University of North Carolina at Chapel Hill, with support of a grant from the AT&T Foundation. It is intended as a basis for classroom discussion rather than to illustrate effective or ineffective handling of an administrative situation. Some facts have been altered to protect confidentiality of company information. Appreciation is expressed to the AT&T-C staff in the External Affairs and Marketing Divisions of the Southern Region and to the Consumer Marketing Division in Basking Ridge, NJ, for their support on this project. Distributed by the North American Case Research Association. All rights reserved to the author and the North American Case Research Association. Used by permission from Lew G. Brown and the North American Case Research Association.

advantage to AT&T-C. The FCC subsequently had upheld the default process but had ordered that subscribers be allowed a six-month's period following the cutover date to select a primary carrier without charge.

The equal access process continued in 1984 and early 1985 with all local telephone companies except Northwestern Bell (NWB) using the court-approved default process. However, parties continued to petition the FCC to reconsider its previous findings on the default process. On March 8, 1985, the FCC had found that there was insufficient evidence to decide on the default question and had requested further comment and suggestions on alternatives.

The May 1985, decision on which the June order was based, resulted from the additional comments received. The FCC noted that the majority of the commenters favored a *pro-rata* allocation plan. The commenters had argued that the default process preserved AT&T-C's monopoly power and that the NWB experience had demonstrated that allocation was workable and was stimulating a 20 percent increase in the number of customers choosing a long-distance company relative to local telephone companies that used default. Further, it was noted by the Department of Justice that the allocation process had proven to be cheaper than default to implement.

The NWB system called for two ballots. A customer was notified of the equal access conversion 90 days prior to cutover and given a ballot on which to indicate preference for a primary carrier. Customers who failed to return their ballots were sent a second ballot approximately 50 days before the cutover giving them another chance and indicating the primary carrier to which they would be assigned if they still made no selection. Undesignated customers were so assigned if they failed to return the second ballot and were given the 180-day period to change to another long-distance company without charge. The allocation of customers to primary carriers following the first ballot was a random process with the percentage of unallocated customers being allocated to a primary carrier being based on the percentage of customers who selected it in the first round.

AT&T-C had argued that default was proper, cited the findings in the judgment, and stated that, "As a matter of law and of fact, the customers involved here are already AT&T's customers, and were intended under the decree to remain so until they select another company as their primary carrier." AT&T-C had also submitted independent survey data of customer knowledge, attitudes, and actions to support its position.

In the May 1985 ruling, the commission found that the routing of all default traffic to AT&T could *not* be justified by a "strong showing of necessity." The FCC's prior concerns about customer burdens under allocation had been dispelled by NWB's experience. As a result, the FCC found the default procedure to be unreasonable and discriminatory and prescribed a *pro-rata* allocation plan that was *required* of all local telephone companies.

The FCC's plan followed the NWB plan with one general exception. The commission had received requests that the time period allowed for selection be extended or altered. The FCC plan allowed flexibility in this aspect of the process.

The local telephone companies would be allowed to send a second ballot with the allocated primary carrier designation to their customers as early as 40 days prior to but no later than 90 days after cutover.

No alternatives to the allocation process would be allowed. The FCC plan also suggested that local telephone companies and primary carriers develop clear and detailed information to be provided to customers on the selection process and required that local telephone companies provide information with the second ballot with respect to how the allocation process will work.

Carriers were required to implement the plan on a retroactive basis for all cutovers that took place on or after May 31, 1985. However, the FCC realized that it would take some time to implement the new plan and allowed local telephone companies to continue to default customers to AT&T during the transition period. The customer would then be subject to allocation once the local telephone company implemented its plan.

In addition to the basic NWB plan, the FCC also allowed customers to directly contact the primary carrier and make arrangements with it for service. The primary carrier could provide the local telephone company with a list of customers who had contacted it by the initial (first) ballot deadline. Any verbal commitments had to be followed up with a request for a statement signed by the customer to be sent to the local telephone company not later than the first bill.

Finally, the FCC required that non-presubscribed customers in areas that had been converted prior to May 31, 1985, should receive from local telephone companies another ballot within 90 days of May 31. If the customers still did not return the ballot, they would be allowed to remain with their long-distance carrier.

Thus, AT&T-C not only found the default procedure terminated for all cutovers on or after May 31, 1985, it also found that customers with pre-May 31 cutovers, whom had already been defaulted to it by not choosing a long-distance carrier and whom it was serving, would now be asked to choose again.

BACK TO THE DRAWING BOARD

David turned to Monica. "Well, I'm sure there will be lots of questions and probably more interpretations of this order, but I guess you had better take a look at our marketing strategy in light of the allocation process to see what, if anything, we should change."

Despite the problems, Monica felt that she had some recent market research results that might help (See Exhibits 25.11 and 25.12).

The bench mark market research studies carried out in early 1984 had been followed by "selection" studies as the 31 cutover areas went through the equal access process later in 1984. Selection studies were carried out approximately 12 to 13 weeks after the equal access announcement in each specific market by an independent firm hired by AT&T-C.

Monica opened the research report and read again the executive summary.

EXHIBIT 25.11 **Marketing research "selection studies"**

Executive Summary
Status of Choice and Notification

■ 83% of residential long-distance users in these 31 markets were aware of the announcement asking them to choose a main long-distance company. Respondents in heavy long-distance usage households, with higher incomes and in white-collar positions show higher levels of awareness.

■ Of those aware of the election, 63% have made a decision on a main long-distance supplier. This translates into slightly over half, 52% of long-distance users interviewed. A higher portion of heavy users, upper-income and white-collar workers had made a choice.

■ Of those making a decision, 63% chose AT&T and 36% decided on an OCC. This means out of the total interviewed, 33% selected AT&T and 18% chose an OCC. Nonchoosers and those not aware account for 48% of the total interviewed. A portion of nonchoosers, 5% of the total, did not make a decision as a way to stay with AT&T. Combined with those who actively decided on AT&T, brings the level of AT&T choice to 38%. MCI was the OCC most frequently chosen, selected by 13%.

■ Compared to AT&T choosers, those selecting an OCC tended to be younger, better educated, more often employed full time and in white-collar jobs, have a higher average household income and be heavier users of long-distance.

■ Actual customer response to the equal access election somewhat reflects their behavior as predicted in the preannouncement research. At the bench mark study, conducted prior to the equal access announcement, 41% claimed they would definitely or probably not go with another carrier. This compared with the 33% who actively chose AT&T at selection (or the 38% choosing AT&T both actively or passively). In the preannouncement study, 21% were current subscribers or definite or probably adopters of an OCC. In the selection survey, 18% had chosen an OCC.

■ In the earlier research, 37% were undecided as to whether or not they would subscribe to another carrier. This compares to 48% following the announcement who were either unaware or still undecided. It appears, then, that the predicted level of both AT&T retention and OCC adoption were only slightly overstated at the time of the bench mark research.

■ 79% of respondents who had decided on a carrier notified their chosen supplier. This amounts to 41% of all respondents interviewed. In other words, nearly six out of ten long-distance users, at one week after cutover, had still not notified a carrier of their choice.

■ Among AT&T choosers, 72% had notified. This represents 24% of all respondents choosing and notifying AT&T. The notification level is higher among OCC choosers: 91% who chose an OCC notified. Out of total respondents, this represents 17%. Twelve percent of all respondents chose and notified MCI.

	Percent of total respondents		Percent of choosers who notified
	Chose	**Chose and notified**	
AT&T	33	24	72
OCC	18	17	91
MCI	13	12	93

■ Notifiers of any supplier, whether AT&T or an OCC, tended to be slightly older, better educated, more frequently in white-collar positions, have slightly higher incomes than defaulters, and be heavier users of long distance.

■ Among all non-notifiers, including "not aware" and "not chosen," in the nonallocation markets, 77% know they will default to AT&T. This represents 31% of all respondents. In Minneapolis, 43% thought they would be assigned to AT&T.

■ Combining respondents who would be likely to default to AT&T (not aware, not chosen, not notified) with those already choosing and notifying AT&T totals a maximum selection rate of about 82% for AT&T at the time of the survey one week after cutover.

■ In the 31 markets studied, the level of notification ranged from 21% to 74%. The highest levels of notification occurred in Minneapolis (74%), the only allocation market in the study, and Charleston (60%), the first market to be subjected to the equal access election. Out of the 31 markets studied, 13 showed more than 20% choosing an OCC, 10 had an OCC penetration between 15% and 20%, and 8 markets had less than 15% selecting an OCC. In 8 markets AT&T choice exceeded 40%. In 10 markets AT&T choice was between 30% and 40% and in 12 markets, between 20% and 30%. Only one market, Baltimore: Liberty, showed an AT&T choice level under 20%. Markets showing a high OCC penetration level did not necessarily show a correspondingly low AT&T choice level.

■ Aside from the 18% who had selected an OCC in response to the equal access notification, another 3% of total respondents predicted they would definitely subscribe to one. This could mean a likely penetration level of 20% or 21%. Another 8% of total respondents claimed probable intention to subscribe, indicating that the OCCs could possibly obtain an eventual 28% to 29% share of market.

Factors Influencing the Selection Process

■ The main reasons for choosing AT&T related to previous experience and satisfaction with the company. Cheaper pricing, including no minimum and discount rates, was the major reason for selecting an OCC. OCC choosers also mentioned the influence of advertising, company sales efforts, and friends' recommendations.

■ OCC choosers tended to consult a greater variety of sources with greater frequency than did AT&T choosers in helping them choose a long-distance supplier: an average of 1.81 compared to 1.53. OCC choosers relied more heavily on various types of advertising, word of mouth and contact with the company. Over a quarter of AT&T choosers (28%) consulted no sources in making their decision.

Mail brochures were used considerably more often in making the decision of a long-distance supplier than had been anticipated in the bench mark study. In the earlier study, 15% predicted they would consult a mail brochure. In making their selection, 47% said they consulted a mail brochure. Company representatives, referrals, and editorial sources were used less frequently than originally anticipated.

■ 40% of OCC choosers claimed to have requested information from long-distance suppliers. This compares to only 19% of AT&T choosers who sought information. OCC choosers even sought information from AT&T with greater frequency than those who chose AT&T: 11% compared to 7%.

■ Only 24% of AT&T choosers claimed to have been aware at the time they made their decision of at least one of the three promotional campaigns* intended to encourage AT&T selection. And only 6% reported that knowledge of the promotion had some influence in their decision of AT&T as main supplier.

Among all respondents, AT&T "Opportunity Calling" was the most familiar of these programs, remembered by 44%. One-third recalled the "Reach Out America" promotion. Recall was lowest for the "Reach Out (State Name)" in those markets where it ran.

Awareness and Attitudinal Changes

■ Seven out of 10 respondents named AT&T as a supplier of long-distance on an unaided basis. Nearly as many, 67%, claimed awareness for MCI. About half could name Sprint on an unaided basis. Awareness increased at about the same level for all three of the major long-distance suppliers.

Percent unaided recall for	Bench mark	Selection	Change
AT&T	57%	70%	+13%
MCI	53	67	+14
Sprint	40	54	+14

Aided awareness appeared nearly universal for both AT&T (98%) and MCI (93%). A large majority were also aware of Sprint on an aided basis: 88%.

The former confusion existing between AT&T and the local Bell Company appears to be largely resolved. In the bench mark survey, 31% named their local telephone company as a supplier of long distance. This decreased to only 2% in the selection study.

■ While awareness increased about equally for all three major suppliers, the increase in the depth of this awareness was more dramatic for AT&T than for either MCI or Sprint.

Percent who know a lot about	Bench mark	Selection	Change
AT&T	26%	37%	+11%
MCI	15	18	+ 3
Sprint	11	12	+ 1

Choosers of MCI and Sprint claimed to know as much about AT&T as did those who chose AT&T.

■ Slightly more respondents in the selection survey than in the bench mark study perceived AT&T as the "best provider" of long distance. There was virtually no change in perceptions of MCI and impressions of Sprint were slightly more negative.

Percent who view as best provider	Bench mark	Selection	Change
AT&T	35%	39%	+ 4%
MCI	8	9	+ 1
Sprint	6	3	− 3

■ Respondents were asked to rate 20 characteristics of long-distance suppliers on their degree of importance. Over three quarters of respondents gave the top-importance rating to:

> Getting good quality for the price you pay—80%
> Ability to call anytime, (to) anywhere—79%
> Ability to call anytime from anywhere—78%
> Providing accurate and reliable itemized billing—77%

Two-thirds or better gave a top-importance rating to:

> Having excellent sound quality—75%
> Paying no monthly service charge—74%
> Being an established, dependable company—69%
> Having competitive prices—68%

Having an operator available when you need one—67%

Providing reliable information about rates and services—67%

Perceived as least important are having a telephone credit card (22%), ability to make time payments on long-distance bills (26%), and international calling capability (29%).

OCC choosers tended to rate price-related characteristics more highly while AT&T choosers gave higher importance ratings to ubiquity and service attributes.

■ There were no dramatic changes occurring between bench mark and selection in the percentage rating these characteristics as very important. The most substantial increases occurred on service and image attributes:

Ability to make person-to-person, collect calls   +7%

Providing reliable information to make wisest selection   +5%

Being an established, dependable company   +4%

Providing reliable information about rates and services   +4%

Having directory assistance   +4%

International calling capability   +4%

Importance ratings decreased on only one attribute: having discounted rates at convenient times (−2%). The importance ratings on other pricing attributes remained relatively unchanged.

■ Respondents were asked to rate the performances of the three major suppliers on their delivery of the same 20 long-distance supplier attributes. As it did in the bench mark study, AT&T continued in the selection survey to outperform both MCI and Sprint on all but price-related attributes.

Eight out of ten respondents rated AT&T as excellent on:

Ability to call anytime, (to) anywhere—81%

Ability to call anytime from anywhere—79%

Being an established, dependable company—79%

Two-thirds or better gave AT&T an excellent rating on ability to make person-to-person, collect calls (74%), directory assistance (71%), excellent sound quality (67%), and accurate, reliable billing (67%).

AT&T performed below both MCI and Sprint on having competitive pricing: 24% compared to 49% for MCI and 32% for Sprint. On quality for price and discounted rates, AT&T's ratings were below MCI's but superior to Sprint ratings.

No more than 50% gave MCI an excellent rating on any characteristic. The highest ratings for MCI were on price-related attributes. Sprint received excellent ratings from no more than a third of respondents.

■ The percent of respondents rating AT&T and MCI as excellent increased from the bench mark to the selection wave on all characteristics. The average overall increase in excellent ratings were about equal between these two carriers, about seven percentage points. The most significant increases for AT&T occurred on sound quality (+13%), immediate credit for wrong numbers (+13%), ability to make person-to-person, collect calls (+11%), providing accurate information for wisest selection (+11%). The two latter attributes were the ones to see the most dramatic increases in importance ratings as well.

Excellent rating increases for MCI were most substantial on no monthly service charge (+18%), ability to call anytime from anywhere (+13%), providing accurate information to make wisest selection (+10%), and having discounted rates (+9%).

Sprint showed fewer, and smaller, increases in excellent ratings and showed decreases in some areas.

---

* Campaigns were "Opportunity Calling," "Reach Out America," and "Reach Out (State Name.)" The latter ran in all but three markets.

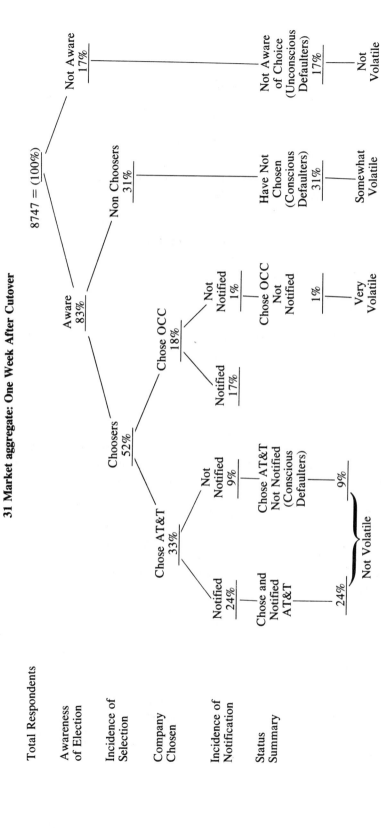

31 Market aggregate: One Week After Cutover

Total Respondents

Awareness of Election

Incidence of Selection

Company Chosen

Incidence of Notification

Status Summary

8747 = (100%)

Aware 83%

Not Aware 17%

Choosers 52%

Non Choosers 31%

Not Aware of Choice (Unconscious Defaulters) 17%

Chose AT&T 33%

Chose OCC 18%

Have Not Chosen (Conscious Defaulters) 31%

Not Volatile

Notified 24%

Not Notified 9%

Notified 17%

Not Notified 1%

Somewhat Volatile

Chose and Notified AT&T 24%

Chose AT&T Not Notified (Conscious Defaulters) 9%

Chose OCC Not Notified 1%

Very Volatile

Not Volatile

AT&T TOTAL AT WEEK ONE AFTER CUTOVER (NOTIFIERS AND DEFAULTERS): 82%

EXHIBIT 25.12 **Status of notification and default**

CASE 26 _____

American Greetings

"We're in touch" and the corporate rose logo identify the world's largest publicly owned manufacturer of greeting cards and related social-expression merchandise, American Greetings (AG). In 1981, President Morry Weiss announced the formulation of a corporate growth objective to achieve $1 billion in annual sales by 1985, which would represent a 60 percent increase over 1982 sales of $623.6 million. The battle for market share dominance between the two industry leaders, Hallmark and American Greetings, had escalated and intensified. Previously, the two leading firms peacefully coexisted by having mutually exclusive niches. Hallmark offered higher-priced, quality cards in department stores and card shops, and American Greetings offered inexpensive cards in mass-merchandise outlets. However, in 1977 American Greetings formulated a growth strategy to attack the industry leader and its niche.

THE GREETING CARD INDUSTRY

In 1985, Americans exchanged more than 7 billion cards—around 30 per person, marking the highest per capita card consumption ever. With the average retail price per card of a dollar, that made "social expression" a $7 billion business. According to the Greeting Card Association, card senders gave 2.2 billion Christmas cards, 1.5 billion birthday cards, 850 million valentines, 180 million Easter cards, 140 million Mother's Day cards, 85 million Father's Day cards, 80 million graduation cards, 40 million Thanksgiving cards, 26 million Halloween cards, 16 million St. Patrick's Day cards, and about 10 million Grandparent's Day cards. Everyday, nonoccasion cards now account for more than half of all industry sales, and they're on the rise. People living in the northeast and the north-central parts of the country buy more cards than average, and Southerners 30 percent fewer. People who buy the majority of them tend to be between 35 and 54 years of age, come from large families, live in their own homes in the suburbs, and have an average household income of $30,000. Changes in society—demographic and social—are fueling the growth of alternative cards. These changes have included increases in the numbers of blended families, single-parent households, working women, divorces and remarriages, and

This case was prepared by Daniel C. Kopp and Lois Shufeldt. It is intended as a basis for classroom discussion rather than to illustrate effective or ineffective handling of an administrative situation. The authors would like to acknowledge the cooperation and assistance of American Greetings. This case was presented at the North American Case Research Association's annual meeting in November 1987. Used by permission from Daniel C. Kopp.

population segments which traditionally have included the heaviest greeting card users—35 to 65 year olds.

Women purchase over 90 percent of all greeting cards. Women enjoy browsing and shopping for cards, and tend to purchase a card only if it is appropriate, when the card's verse and design combine to convey the sentiment she wishes to express. However, because an increasing number of women are working, these women are shopping less frequently and buying less impulse merchandise.

The growth rate for the industry has been 5 to 6 percent annually over the past several years. Sales of unorthodox cards aimed at 18–35 year old baby boomers have grown 25 percent a year. However, sales of greeting cards for the past few quarters have been lackluster. The industry is mature; sales are stagnant at about 7 billion units. According to *Chain Store Age*, the channels of distribution have been moving away from speciality stores to mass merchants.[1] Now, department stores are cutting back square footage and dropping cards altogether. Mass market appeal now has growth—one-stop shopping. Hallmark has been pushing its Ambassador line through mass merchants such as Wal-Mart and Target, in addition to diversifying into other areas.

AG is concentrating on the social expressions business: it has launched a massive national television advertising campaign to firmly position itself in all aspects of the greeting card industry. On the other hand, Hallmark, whose recent acquisitions are unrelated to the social expressions industry, is shifting its emphasis. Irvine O. Hockaday, Hallmark's CEO, said recently that he prefers outside businesses to contribute 40 percent of total Hallmark revenues, instead of the 10 percent it now contributes. Cards accounted for 64 percent of AG's 1985 sales. According to some industry experts, Hallmark is now playing follow the leader in card innovations and character licensing.

Overall slowdown in retail traffic has resulted in reduced sales. Generally, there is a soft retailing environment. The retailing industry is overstored and promotion oriented, which may result in retailers asking greeting card suppliers for lower prices to assist them in keeping their margins from shrinking. Retailers are losing their loyalty to manufacturers that supply a full line of products—cards, gift wrap, etc., and are looking instead for the lowest cost supplier of each, according to Kidder, Peabody & Company.[2] The competition in the industry has become and will continue to be intensified, especially in the areas of price, sales promotion, distribution, and selling.

More new cards have been introduced in 1986 than in any other previous year, according to the Greeting Card Association. More "feelings" type of cards, such as the "In Touch" line by AG, have been introduced. Since men buy only 10 percent of all cards sold, they are the prime target for many of the new types of cards.

[1]"Who Holds the Cards in the Greeting War?" *Chain Store Age*, April 1985, p. 85–87.

[2]E. Gray Glass III, Research Reports on American Greetings and Greeting Card Industry, Kidder Peabody and Company, May 16, 1986; May 20, 1986; December 11, 1986; and January 20, 1987.

Hallmark and AG are experimenting with different styles, fabricating novel reasons for people to buy their wares and using new technology that enables cards to play tunes or talk. According to *Time*, Hallmark offers 1,200 varieties of cards for Mother's Day, while AG boasts of 1,300.[3] The product ranges from a traditional card with a picture of flowers and syrupy poetry for $1 or less, to a $7 electronic version that plays the tune, "You Are the Sunshine of My Life."

Hallmark has introduced several lines of personal-relationship-oriented cards, commemorating such milestones as the wedding anniversary of a parent and a stepparent. In 1984, Hallmark introduced its Honesty Collection, which has been discontinued, with messages that reflected the nature of modern day relationships. In May 1985, AG's primary competitor brought out its Personal Touch line of cards, with intimate, conversational prose displayed on the front with no message inside. The Greeting Card Association found that 83 percent of all card senders do something—add a snapshot or a newspaper clipping or jot a note—to personalize a card, and Hallmark has been quick to supply a vehicle to take advantage of this opportunity.

Forbes has reported that there are more than 400 firms in the greeting card industry, but the two major ones, Hallmark and American Greetings, control approximately 75 percent of the market.[4] Gibson Greetings is the third major firm in the industry. Approximate market shares for the three industry leaders have been:

Company	1977	1984	1985
Hallmark	50%	45%	40–45%
American Greetings	24	33	30–35
Gibson	5	na	8–10

Analysts expect AG to keep increasing its market share. Over the last five years, unit growth rate at AG has been 4 to 5 percent a year, against industry wide growth rate of 1 to 2 percent. Industry expert, E. Gray Glass, III of Kidder, Peabody & Company, has indicated that AG has been showing good growth at 15 percent or better annually.[5] Furthermore, *Chain Store Age* has projected that AG will continue to take some of Hallmark's market share, but that it will take a long time for AG to pass it.[6]

The New York Times has reported that Hallmark has been successful in free-standing card shops, which account for about 40 percent of all greeting cards sold.[7] Fastest growth for AG has been big drugstores and supermarket chains. Growth has

[3]"Greetings, One and All," *Time*, May 13, 1985, p. 54.

[4]"New Markets-New Products," *Forbes*, July 30, 1984, p. 102.

[5]E. Gray Glass III, Research Reports on American Greetings and the Greeting Card Industry, Kidder Peabody and Company, May 16, 1986; May 20, 1986; December 11, 1986; and January 20, 1987.

[6]"Who holds the Cards in the Greeting War?" *Chain Store Age*, April 1985, p. 85-87.

[7]"Marketplace: Greeting Cards and Earnings," *New York Times*, June 18, 1984, p. 43.

been slower at variety stores, traditional department stores, and gift shops, which account for about 30 percent of AG sales.

According to *Investor's Daily*, AG and Hallmark have been increasing their market shares at the expense of smaller card companies, which have been forced out of the market due to the high costs of selling, distributing, and marketing, as well as the lack of extensive computerized inventory monitoring systems that only large companies can afford.[8] Industry analysts, however, have predicted that small firms with a focus niche and geographic area, will continue to enter the industry and can be profitable.

Richard H. Connor, AG Executive Vice President, stated that AG has been gaining ground on Hallmark, although he wouldn't say by how much: "If you compare the businesses that are similar with both companies, we are closing the gap. Between the both of us, we have 75 percent of the market, and some of our growth must be at their expense."

Both Hallmark and AG are being challenged by Gibson, which is the fastest growing company in the industry. Gibson scored a coup with Walt Disney Productions when they secured the rights to use Mickey Mouse and his friends, who previously had been featured by Hallmark. Gibson also has licensed Garfield the Cat and Sesame Street characters, but Hallmark's line of Peanuts cards remains one of the industry's most successful.

HISTORY OF AMERICAN GREETINGS

The story of American Greetings is one of the "American Dream" of an immigrant from Poland who came to the land of promise and opportunity to seek his fortune. Jacob Sapirstein was born in 1884 in Wasosz, Poland and because of the Russian-Japanese war of 1904, was sent by his widowed mother, along with his seven brothers and one sister to live in America.

Jacob, also known as J.S., began his one-man business buying postcards made in Germany from wholesalers and selling them to candy, novelty, and drug stores in Cleveland in 1906. From a horse-drawn card wagon, the small venture steadily flourished.

J.S. and his wife, Jennie, also a Polish immigrant, had three sons and a daughter; all three sons became active in their father's business. At the age of nine, Irving, the oldest, kept the family business afloat while J.S. was recovering from the flu during the epidemic of 1918. The business had out-grown the family living room and was moved to a garage at this time.

J.S. had a basic philosophy of service to the retailer and a quality product for the consumer. He developed the first wire wall rack as well as rotating floor stands to make more attractive, convenient displays. In the 1930s the Sapirstein Card Company began to print its own cards to ensure the quality of its product.

[8]*Investor's Daily*, May 18, 1984, p. 19.

The name of the company was changed to American Greeting Publishers to reflect the national stature and functioning of the company. Their first published line of cards under the American Greetings name, the Forget Me Not Line, went on sale in 1939 for a nickel. One card, which remains the company's all-time best seller, was designed by Irving.

The company saw great expansion throughout the 1940s, as loved ones found the need to communicate with World War II soldiers. The most significant effect of this was the widespread use of greeting cards by the soldiers. In the past, cards had been primarily a product utilized by women, thus the expansion to the male market was a significant breakthrough for the card industry.

The 1950s marked the first public offering of stock and the name change to American Greetings Corporation. Ground was broken for a new world headquarters, which led the way for expansion to world markets. The company made connections with several foreign markets and acquired a Canadian plant.

In 1960, J.S. stepped down at the age of 76. His son Irving succeeded him as president. Under Irving's leadership and with the assistance of his brothers, Morris and Harry Stone (all three brothers had changed their names from Sapirstein, meaning sapphire, to Stone in 1940 for business reasons), the company has continued to expand into gift wrapping, party goods, calendars, stationery, candles, ceramics, and perhaps, most importantly, the creation of licensed characters.

Expansion into these related items has somewhat diminished AG's recession-proof profits. Greeting card sales typically increase during recessions as people refrain from gift buying and instead remember others with a less expensive card. The supplemental items now constitute one third of the company's sales, not enough to seriously jeopardize AG during down economies, but greatly augment the company's sales during good economic times.

AG's world expansion became a major pursuit throughout the 1960s and 1970s. Morry Weiss, a grandson-in-law of J.S., became the new president of AG in 1978 with Irving continuing to act as the CEO and Chairman of the Board of Directors. Morris Stone continues to serve as Vice Chairman of the Board, and Harry Stone remains as an active Board member.

OBJECTIVES

In 1981 at the first national sales meeting ever held by AG, President Morry Weiss announced the formulation of a major corporate objective: to achieve $1 billion in annual sales by 1985. During fiscal 1985, AG strengthened its position as a leader in the industry: that year marked the seventy-ninth consecutive year of increased revenue—total revenue increased to $945.7 million, while net income increased to $74.4 million. This record of success represented a 300 percent increase in total revenue during the past 10 years, 613 percent increase in net income during the past 10 years, and a 315 percent increase in dividends per share in the past 10 years, with two increases in fiscal 1985.

According to Morry Weiss, President and Chief Operating Officer:

AG today is positioning itself for transition from a greeting company to a total communications company. For years, AG was thought of only as a greeting card maker. That narrow description no longer applies to the world's largest, publicly owned manufacturer of greeting cards and related social-expression merchandise. Today we are diversified into other major product lines, including gift wrap, candles, stationery, ceramics, party goods, and calendars. In addition, we lead the industry in licensing characters, such as Holly Hobbie, Ziggy, Strawberry Shortcake, Care Bears, and Care Bear Cousins, which are featured on thousands of retail products and on television and in motion pictures.

Irving Stone, Chairman of the Board and Chief Executive Officer added:

AG is aggressively pursuing growth in our core business, concentrating specifically on increasing market share and unit volume, and continued margin. We'll grow through our retailers by providing the programs that will generate sales and make the greeting card department the most profitable area in their store. We'll grow through our consumers by understanding their needs and providing them with products they want and enjoy buying. We'll grow by constantly improving our operations and productivity through creativity, innovation, and technology.

We expect growth and are planning for it throughout the corporation. In the past four years we have invested heavily in increased capacity, plant expansion, new equipment, and new technology. Almost two years ago, we completed an equity offering that substantially strengthened our financial position; an additional offering is not expected in the near future. Today we see no problem financing our growth while at the same time increasing our dividends.

A flurry of acquisitions occurred in the 1980s. A full list of subsidiaries, as well as AG's international operations is displayed in Exhibit 26.1.

MARKETING STRATEGIES

Product

AG produces a wide product line including greeting cards, gift wrap, party goods, toys, and gift items. Greeting cards accounted for 66 percent of the company's 1986 fiscal sales. The breakdown of sales by major product categories is as follows:

Everyday greeting cards	37%
Holiday greeting cards	29%
Gift wrap and party goods	18%
Consumer products (toys, etc.)	7%
Stationery	9%

It is the belief of AG that one of the keys to increased sales is to have a product line that offers a wide variety and selection of cards, such that a consumer can always find the right card for that special person. Each year AG offers more new products

---

EXHIBIT 26.1 **American Greetings international and subsidiary operations**

United States	Continental Europe
A.G. Industries, Inc. Cleveland, Ohio Charles H. Nervig, President	**Richard C. Schulte** Director of Operations **Grako Oy** Helsinki, Finland
AmToy, Inc. New York, New York Larry Freiberg, President	Risto Pitkanen, Managing Director **A/S Muva Grafiske Produkter** Oslo, Norway
Drawing Board Greeting Cards, Inc. Dallas, Texas Selwin Belofsky, President	Aage Dahl, Managing Director **Muva Greetings B.V.** Heerlen, The Netherlands
Plus Mark, Inc. Greeneville, Tennessee Ronald E. Clouse, President	Huub Robroeks, General Manager **Susy Card** Hamburg, West Germany
The Summit Corporation Berlin, Connecticut Robert P. Chase, President	Charles Wightman, Managing Director

	Mexico
Those Characters From Cleveland, Inc. Cleveland, Ohio John S. Chojnacki, Thomas A. Wilson, Co-Presidents	**Felicitaciones Nacionales S.A. de C.V.** Mexico City, Mexico Felix G. Antonio, President

Tower Products Company, Inc. Chicago, Illinois Melvin Mertz, President	Monaco
	Rust Craft International S.A. Michel Bourda, Managing Director

Canada	United Kingdom

Carlton Cards Ltd.
Toronto, Ontario
William L. Powell, President and
   Chairman of Canadian Operations
	Rust Craft Greeting Cards (U.K.) Ltd.
	Dewsbury, England
	David M. Beards, Managing Director and
	   Chairman of U.K. Operations

Plus Mark Canada Toronto, Ontario Richard L. Krelstein, President	**Andrew Valentine Holdings Ltd.** Dundee, Scotland Alistair R.L. Mackay, Managing Director
Rust Craft Canada, Inc. Scarborough, Ontario Gary Toporoski, Vice President, Managing Director	**Celebration Arts Group Ltd.** Corby, England W. George Pomphrett, Managing Director
	Denison Colour Ltd. Guiseley, England Brian Holliday, Managing Director

than ever before. The creative department produces over 20,000 different designs to ensure the wide selection.

AG's creative staff is one of the largest assemblages of artistic talent in the world. The department has over 400 designers, artists, and writers who are guided by the latest research data available from computer analysis, consumer testing, and information from AG's sales and merchandising departments. Careful monitoring of societal changes, fashion and color trends, and consumer preferences provides further guidance to product development. AG also gives uncompromising adherence to quality—in papers, inks, and printing procedures.

AG pioneered licensing and now dominates the industry of character licensing. Their strategy has been to maximize the potential of their creative and marketing expertise. Holly Hobbie was the first licensed character in 1968; Ziggy in 1971; and Strawberry Shortcake in 1980. When introduced, Strawberry Shortcake was the most popular new character in licensing history. Sales for Strawberry Shortcake will soon exceed $1 billion in retail sales, a revenue larger than that of any other character. In 1983, AG introduced Care Bears and Herself the Elf. The product was launched with General Mills and 23 licensees supported by an $8 million advertising and promotional campaign, including a half-hour animated television special. The Care Bears license identifies ten adorable cuddlies, each with a message on its tummy.

Another licensing creation, Popples, added a new dimension to a field crowded with look-alikes. Popples literally "pop out" from a plush ball to a lovable, furry, playmate. A plush toy that folds into its own pouch, Popples enables children to make its arms, legs, and fluffy tail appear and disappear at will. Two new toys from AmToy are reaching another new and under-cultivated market: My Pet Monster and Madballs. They were the hits of the 1986 Toy Fair show. These creatures are designed to delight the millions of young boys who prefer the bizarre to the cuddly.

Forty companies initially signed up to manufacture other products such as clothing, knapsacks, and books featuring the new characters. AG and Mattel spent about $10 million promoting the characters, including a half-hour Popples television special. The licensed product industry is $50 billion strong.

According to *Forbes,* all AG licensed characters have not been successful.[9] One flop, Herself the Elf, was perceived by retailers as being too much like Strawberry Shortcake; it also missed the Christmas season because of production problems. Another failure was Get Along Gang, which tried to appeal to both little girls and boys.

Distribution

AG distributes its products through 90,000 retail outlets located throughout the free world, which has increased from 80,000 in 1983. Additionally, there has been growth in the channels of distribution where AG is dominant. Consumers have been seeking greater convenience and one-stop shopping, channels in which AG is strong—chain drugstores, chain supermarkets, and mass merchandise retailers. Thirty-nine percent of AG sales went to drug stores, with the remaining sales (in order of rank) going to mass merchandisers, supermarkets, stationery and gift shops, variety stores, military post exchanges, combo stores (food, general merchandise, and gift items), and department stores. During the last five years, sales to drug, variety, and department stores as a percent of total revenue have declined, while sales to

[9]"Making of a Popple," *Forbes,* December 16, 1985, p. 174–175.

supermarkets, mass merchandisers, combo stores, and military post exchange units have increased, and stationery and gift shops have remained constant.

Promotion

In 1982, AG became recognized nationwide, first through television commercials and then through a new-corporate identity program. The new logo is now featured prominently at retail outlets; the updated corporate rose logo is now a standard and highly recognizable feature greeting AG customers on all product packaging, store signage, point-of-purchase displays, and even the truck fleet. The year-round advertising campaign included the promotion of the major card-sending holidays and nonseasonal occasions during daytime and prime-time programming.

Supporting marketing is a promotion generator out of which flows seasonal and special displays, special signs, sales catalogues, national television advertising, media and trade journal exposure, television programming, and special events featuring AG's exclusive characters. Results can be seen in increased support for AG's sales personnel, greater consumer awareness, improved relations with retail dealers, greater visibility within the financial community, and improved relations with employees and communities where plant facilities are operating.

The aim of AG's national consumer advertising and public relations programs is to remind people to send cards, in that one of AG's chief competitors is consumer forgetfulness. AG is the only company in the industry to sponsor national consumer retail promotions. These consumer-directed programs serve to establish brand identity and generate retail store traffic.

In 1983 AG employed 1,600 full-time salespeople, in addition to 7,000 part-timers, all of whom have been directed through 15 regional and 66 district sales offices in the United States, the United Kingdom, Canada, Mexico, and France. AG employs a large force of retail store merchandisers who visit each department at regular intervals to ensure that every pocket in every display is kept filled with appropriate merchandise.

The AG sales force is meeting the unique and challenging needs of their customers: no other company in the industry has sales and marketing personnel assigned to specific channels of distribution to give retailers the advantage of working with specialists who understand their markets, their customers, and their specific marketing needs.

The success of AG's aggressive marketing programs is explained by William E. Schmitt, Group Vice President, Marketing:

> First we have the creativity to develop the best products in the industry. Every year we prove this with new characters, new card lines, and other products and programs that attract consumers and increase sales for our customers and ourselves. Second, we have a close relationship with our customers. The retailer support programs we offer—including terms, display fixtures, advertising and merchandising programs, promotional support, and inventory controls—are unsurpassed in the industry.

Programs are tailored for individual retailers to help plan their greeting card locations, department sizes, and displays. AG shows the retailers how to merchandise innovative ideas and enhance visibility by means of proven promotional programs.

Computer technology is helping AG's sales people to project retailers' needs better, which has resulted in improved sell-through of the product at retail. MIS, the data processing unit for the AG Division, is playing a vital role in increasing sales for AG's products at the retail level. In 1984, AG began implementing a computer-to-computer reordering system that allows retail accounts to control inventories and turnaround time by electronic transfer of data to AG's headquarters data center.

Good retail presentation is a key to card sales; AG has created a unique identification for the greeting cards department. It is called the Total Retail Environment, and it uses a completely planned and coordinated approach to integrate display cabinets, signage, lighting, product packaging, and even products to create a stunning new AG look. The purposes of this new system are to establish greater consumer awareness of the AG card department, to provide a distinctive look and appeal, and to provide an attractive and enjoyable place to shop.

AG also possesses the most favorable terms-of-sale program in the industry. To improve the retailer's return-on-inventory investment, AG has successful merchandising plans, retail store merchandisers, and computerized inventory controls. AG also sports a direct product profitability (DPP) concept to evaluate productivity and space allocation for products in stores. DPP takes gross margin and return-on-inventory investment analysis a step further by reflecting revenue after allowances and discounts and subtracting all costs attributable to the product, including labor and freight. AG's sales people can then demonstrate to retailers that their greeting card department returns a high rate of profit for the space allocated.

Richard H. Connor, AG Executive Vice President, recently announced:

> To increase market share, AG revamped its sales force and created one sales department that specializes in independent retail accounts and another sales department that specializes in selling to retail chains. A third department will stock and service all types of accounts. This will give greater selling strength where it's needed and lowers our selling costs.

AG has created a new retail communications network (RCTN) that conducts research that will better enable AG to identify for accounts the appropriate products to meet the needs of their customers. Data are compiled by monitoring product sales and space productivity from a chain of nationwide test stores that encompasses all demographic and geographic variables and represents all channels of distribution. The RCTN then interprets data as it would apply to an account's specifications, including type of store, size, location, and consumer profile. This total merchandising approach to achieving maximum sales and space potential is unique in the industry.

PRODUCTION STRATEGIES

AG has 49 plants and facilities in the United States, Canada, Continental Europe, Mexico, Monaco, and the United Kingdom.

AG has been concerned with reducing production costs in order to remain the industry's lowest cost producer through efficient manufacturing operations while maintaining quality and service to their customers. According to Robert C. Swilik, Group Vice President, Manufacturing, "Improved control of our manufacturing process through planning and scheduling enable us to improve productivity, reduce manufacturing costs, and reduce inventory. Increased productivity is the result of our growing sense of shared responsibility. The relationship between management and the work force is excellent."

Quality improvements have been consistently made. Some of the major improvements have been:

1. Upgraded die cutting and embossing capabilities with the purchase of nine high-speed Bobst presses costing $1 million each.
2. Added capacity to the hot stamping and thermography operations.
3. Streamlined order filling in both everyday and seasonal operations.
4. Completed a 200,000 square-foot warehouse addition to the Osceola, Arkansas, plant and began operations in an addition to the Ripley, Tennessee, plant, which increased its capacity by 20 percent.
5. Installed a Scitex system that will dramatically improve product quality and increase productivity; new electronic prepress system enables creative department to interact with manufacturing at the creatively crucial prepress stage.
6. Installed additional high-speed and more powerful presses to further improve quality of die cutting and embossing at the Bardstown, Kentucky, plant; a 300,000 square foot addition is also planned.
7. Installed new computer graphics system called Via Video for design and layout functions for a variety of in-house publications and brochures (this gives the artist freedom to create while quickly and inexpensively exploring options and alternatives, thus increasing productivity).

MANAGEMENT

In 1983, AG underwent a major management restructuring to permit top officers of the company more time to concentrate on strategic planning. The company was reorganized from a centralized structure to a divisional profit center basis. Each division has its own budget committee, while an executive management committee comprised of five senior executives approves the strategic plans for all the divisions. Strategic plans are established in one-, three- ten-, and twenty-year time frames. Corporate AG maintains strict budgetary and accounting controls.

The basic domestic greeting card business was placed under the AG Division. Foreign and U.S. subsidiaries and the licensing division have become a second unit, with corporate management a third. Restructuring has allowed corporate management to step back from day-to-day operations and focus on the growth of American Greetings beyond the $1 billion annual revenue.

According to Irving Stone:

> The prime function of corporate management is to plan and manage the growth of the entire corporation, developing capable management and allocating corporate resources to those units offering the greatest potential return on investment. Greeting cards has been our basic business for 78 years and remains today our largest business unit; there are smaller business units, which complement the greeting card business and are deserving of our attention.

American Greetings is composed of the following divisions.

American Greetings Division.   This division encompasses the core business of greeting cards and related products, including manufacturing, sales, merchandising, research, and administrative services. It produces and distributes greeting cards and related products domestically. The same products are distributed throughout the world by international subsidiaries and licensees.

Foreign and Domestic Subsidiaries.   Two wholly owned companies in Canada, four in the United Kingdom, six in Continental Europe, and one in Mexico. Licensees use AG designs and verses in almost every free country in the world. Subdivisions include:

> *Canadian Operations*—Two companies, Carlton Cards and Rust Craft.
>
> *United Kingdom Operations*—British are largest per capita senders of greeting cards in the world. Three AG companies in the UK—Rust Craft, Celebration Arts, and Andrew Valentine.
>
> *Continental European Operations*—Five companies wholly owned.
>
> *Those Characters From Cleveland*—Licensing division of AG. Characters and new television series, The Get Along Gang.
>
> *Plus Mark*—Began producing Christmas promotional products such as gift wrap, ribbon, bows, and boxed Christmas cards in an industry selling primarily to mass merchandisers.
>
> *AmToy*—Sells novelties, dolls, and plush toys.
>
> *AG Industries*—Produces display cabinet fixtures in wood, metal, or plastic for all AG retail accounts and growing list of external clients.

FINANCE STRATEGIES

Exhibits 26.2 to 26.4 contain relevant financial information for American Greetings. The financial condition of AG has been exemplary over the years. How-

EXHIBIT 26.2 Consolidated statements of financial position—February 28, 1985 and 1986 (In thousands of dollars)

Assets	1982	1983	1984	1985	1986
Current Assets					
Cash and equivalents	$ 3,367	$ 19,950	$ 62,551	$ 66,363	$ 26,853
Trade accounts receivable, less allowances for sales returns of $57,382 ($42,198 in 1985) and for doubtful accounts of $3,378 ($2,900 in 1985)	131,996	148,018	146,896	173,637	240,471
Inventories:					
Raw material	53,515	47,636	48,738	59,197	59,343
Work in process	52,214	54,756	43,929	53,728	60,179
Finished products	97,221	122,167	139,275	152,543	181,237
	202,950	224,559	231,942	265,468	300,759
Less LIFO reserve	55,051	59,345	63,455	71,828	76,552
	147,899	165,214	168,487	193,640	224,207
Display material and factory supplies	11,724	12,245	11,532	20,809	26,826
Total inventories	159,623	177,459	180,019	214,449	251,033
Deferred income taxes	18,014	24,847	26,517	33,016	36,669
Prepaid expenses and other	2,057	3,524	4,187	4,795	6,228
Total current assets	315,057	373,798	420,170	492,260	561,254
Other Assets	22,063	32,866	34,820	31,634	47,085
Property, Plant and Equipment					
Land	3,380	5,427	6,621	6,822	7,523
Buildings	110,479	118,598	133,868	143,671	165,241
Equipment and fixtures	115,927	133,731	158,507	182,101	222,718
	229,786	257,756	298,996	332,594	395,482
Less accumulated depreciation and amortization	75,052	83,745	95,092	108,591	130,519
Property, plant and equipment—net	154,734	174,011	203,904	224,003	264,963
Total Assets	$491,854	$580,675	$658,894	$747,897	$873,302

Liabilities and Shareholders' Equity					
Current Liabilities					
Notes payable to banks	$ 4,564	$ 29,836	4,647	$ 4,574	$ 15,921
Accounts payable	39,016	40,568	52,302	56,840	66,685
Payrolls and payroll taxes	17,224	16,914	23,160	26,761	28,675
Retirement plans	5,696	7,405	10,362	12,612	11,697
State and local taxes	3,278	2,448	2,811	2,796	2,763
Dividends payable	1,918	2,641	3,304	4,622	5,317
Income taxes	12,177	8,841	23,672	27,465	18,988
Sales returns	9,241	16,423	17,795	21,822	23,889
Current maturities of long-term debt	6,531	6,998	6,432	4,359	4,786
Total current liabilities	99,645	132,074	144,485	161,851	178,721
Long-Term Debt	148,895	111,066	119,941	112,876	147,592
Deferred Income Taxes	15,530	21,167	28,972	47,422	64,025
Shareholders' Equity					
Common shares—par value $1:					
Class A	12,293	27,996	28,397	28,835	29,203
Class B	1,413	3,080	3,070	3,046	2,982
Capital in excess of par value	37,690	76,851	80,428	87,545	93,055
Cumulative translation adjustment	(3,829)	(7,179)	(9,158)	(13,688)	(16,801)
Retained earnings	180,217	215,620	262,759	320,010	374,525
Total shareholders' equity	227,784	316,368	365,496	425,748	482,964
Total Liabilities and Shareholders' Equity	$491,854	$580,675	$658,894	$747,897	$873,302

Source: American Greetings.

EXHIBIT 26.3 Consolidated statements of income—Years ended February 28 or 29 (In thousands of dollars except per share amounts)

	1981	1982	1983	1984	1985	1986
Net sales	$489,213	$605,970	$722,431	$817,329	$919,371	$1,012,451
Other income	9,052	17,634	20,252	22,585	26,287	23,200
Total Revenue	498,272	623,604	742,683	839,914	945,658	1,035,651
Costs and expenses:						
Material, labor and other production costs	222,993	276,071	310,022	339,988	377,755	416,322
Selling, distribution and marketing	140,733	179,021	217,022	246,456	274,095	308,745
Administrative and general	61,033	76,494	96,012	112,363	123,750	131,928
Depreciation and amortization	10,863	12,752	13,890	15,507	18,799	23,471
Interest	13,548	21,647	24,086	16,135	15,556	19,125
	449,170	565,985	661,032	730,449	809,955	899,591
Income Before Income Taxes	49,102	57,619	81,651	109,465	135,703	136,060
Income taxes	22,587	24,776	37,069	49,807	61,338	61,635
Net Income	$ 26,515	$ 32,843	$ 44,582	$ 59,658	$ 74,365	$ 74,425
Net Income Per Share	$ .97	$1.20	$1.54	$1.91	$2.35	$2.32

Source: American Greetings.

EXHIBIT 26.4 **Selected financial data—Years ended February 28 or 29 (Thousands of dollars except per share amounts)**

Summary of operations	1976	1977	1978	1979	1980	1981	1982	1983	1984	1985	1986
Total revenue											
As reported	$255,770	$277,985	$315,644	$373,487	$427,469	$498,272	$623,604	$742,683	$839,914	$945,658	$1,035,651
Adjusted for general inflation*	511,223	525,318	560,333	615,852	633,535	650,499	737,611	827,715	906,904	979,399	1,035,651
Material, labor and other production											
costs	114,190	118,252	131,769	161,654	190,135	222,993	276,071	310,022	339,988	377,755	416,322
Depreciation and amortization	6,329	6,982	7,544	8,453	10,070	10,863	12,752	13,890	15,507	18,799	23,471
Interest expense	4,970	5,423	3,935	5,911	9,716	13,548	21,647	24,086	16,135	15,556	19,125
Net income											
As reported	14,601	16,787	19,926	22,911	25,638	26,515	32,843	44,582	59,658	74,365	74,425
Adjusted for specific inflation*					23,024	17,495	21,349	34,817	52,298	63,860	63,630
Net income per share											
As reported	.53	.62	.73	.84	.94	.97	1.20	1.54	1.91	2.35	2.32
Adjusted for specific inflation*					.84	.64	.78	1.20	1.67	2.02	1.98
Cash dividends per share											
As reported	.13	.15	.19	.22	.25	.26	.27	.31	.40	.54	.62
Adjusted for general inflation*	.26	.28	.34	.36	.37	.34	.32	.35	.43	.56	.62
Fiscal year end market price per share											
As reported	5.07	4.69	5.25	5.75	5.69	5.50	9.63	18.69	23.69	33.06	35.62
Adjusted for general inflation*	9.83	8.68	9.08	9.12	7.99	6.87	11.03	20.60	25.16	33.75	35.05
Purchasing power gain from holding net monetary liabilities*		16,787		22,911	9,750	9,391	9,366	4,739	1,784	1,438	1,843
Increase (decrease) in value of assets adjusted for specific inflation compared to general inflation*					9,625	(15,935)	(4,981)	2,693	(10,605)	(16,067)	(5,642)
Translation adjustment*							(3,867)	(4,701)	(2,289)	(5,881)	(3,653)
Average number of shares outstanding	27,292,484	27,292,484	27,292,036	27,293,376	27,302,686	27,314,594	27,352,342	28,967,092	31,240,455	31,629,418	32,059,851
Average consumer price index	161.2	170.5	181.5	195.4	217.4	246.8	272.4	289.1	298.4	311.1	322.2
Financial position											
Accounts receivable	$ 53,258	$ 48,920	$ 54,634	$ 67,651	$ 76,629	$114,051	$131,996	$148,018	$146,896	$173,637	$240,471
Inventories	52,581	53,741	71,581	98,075	112,279	133,836	159,623	177,459	180,019	214,449	251,033
Working capital	99,643	90,308	98,188	119,421	135,443	167,772	215,412	241,724	275,685	330,409	382,533
Total assets	233,572	247,503	256,297	305,746	344,395	433,204	491,854	580,675	685,894	747,897	873,302
Capital additions	15,150	7,630	20,586	25,205	34,516	22,768	26,720	33,967	46,418	43,575	61,799
Long term debt	66,048	41,855	45,929	54,845	75,994	113,486	148,895	111,066	119,941	112,876	147,592
Shareholders' equity											
As reported	122,608	135,370	150,242	167,168	186,043	205,550	227,784	316,368	365,496	425,748	482,964
Adjusted for specific inflation*					421,248	422,991	432,781	518,955	559,395	602,350	642,767
Shareholders' equity per share	4.49	4.96	5.51	6.12	6.81	7.52	8.31	10.18	11.62	13.35	15.01
Net return on average shareholders'											
equity	12.5%	13.0%	14.0%	14.5%	14.6%	13.7%	15.4%	17.1%	17.8%	19.2%	18.5%
Pre-tax return on total revenue	10.2%	11.7%	13.3%	12.0%	11.2%	9.9%	9.2%	11.0%	13.0%	14.4%	13.1%

Source: American Greetings.

*In average fiscal 1986 dollars.

ever, AG's financial performance in 1986 was disappointing, with revenue growth estimated to be at 7 percent and earnings to be similar to those of 1985. AG's revenue and earnings growth rate for the previous five years increased at compound annual rates of 17 percent and 29 percent, respectively. AG's stock declined sharply after the disappointing financial report.

According to the research department of the Ohio Company, the reasons for the change in sales and revenues were attributed to:

1. Weak retail environment—decline in retail traffic.
2. Heavy investment in display fixtures—intense competition has forced larger investments than anticipated.
3. Reduced licensing revenues—short life cycle of products and greater competitive pressures reduced licensing revenues.
4. Increased accounts receivables and inventory due to slower collections and weak ordering by retailers.
5. Increased interest expense due to increased accounts receivable and inventory levels.

Irving Stone remarked about the company's finances:

> In fiscal 1986, the retailing picture was a rapidly changing mosaic, featuring a generally poor environment marked by a substantial drop-off in store traffic. As a result, sales of many of our products, which are dependent upon store traffic and impulse buying, fell below our expectations. Nevertheless, total revenue increased for the eightieth consecutive year, primarily due to increased greeting card sales. This is a proud record that few business enterprises can match. While this increase established a new corporate revenue milestone, it did not meet our performance goals, and earnings were flat for the first time in ten years.

FUTURE OF AG

Although AG has had significant growth in the past, events in its external environment are clouding the long-term picture.

Again, from Irving Stone:

> We foresee opportunities to expand our business and profitability. Recent management restructuring provides key officers with the time necessary to concentrate on long-term strategic planning in order to identify specific opportunities, seize upon them, and transform them into bottom-line results. Much growth potential lies ahead in our basic greeting card business, both domestically and internationally. We will strengthen our growing number of subsidiaries, improve efficiency, and increase productivity. Sales increases and expanded distribution in all channels of trade are key objectives. Licensing will continue to flourish, extending our horizons further and further.

Morry Weiss further added: "Our future growth plans include aggressively pursuing growth in our core business, concentrating specifically on increasing market share and unit volume, and continued margin improvement."

However, according to William Blair and Company, AG's earnings growth will moderate significantly from the high-earning growth rate over the past five years.[10] This is due in part to cyclical factors in the economy, but also because of slowdowns in expansion of market share, licensing revenues, and more intense competition. Furthermore, there are two conflicting trends for AG's operating margins: gains should be made from increased productivity, but the increasing competitive nature of the industry with increased promotion might well erode such productivity increases.

Furthermore, according to industry expert, E. Gray Glass, III of Kidder, Peabody, & Company, there are some positives in the industry such as demographics and promising Christmas sales.[11] However, major concerns exist which include:

- Aggressive price competition that was only modest in the past (mark up for greeting cards is 100 percent between factory and retail outlet).
- High account turnover as retailers look for most profitable lines, and card companies fight intensely for large chain retail accounts (AG recently acquired the Sears' account while Hallmark secured Penney's).
- Increased cost pressures due to increasing advertising and distribution (racks, point-of-purchase, etc.) costs (Hallmark will spend in excess of $40 million in television and magazine ads for Hallmark merchandise and benefits of sending cards. AG will spend $33 million).
- Market share gains at the expense of other firms which come at high cost to the winner.
- Growth rate of past five years will not be matched over the next five years.
- New, viable, and growing competitors will emerge.
- Investment decisions will have to be made more carefully.
- Speculation exists that Hallmark may be formulating some counterattack strategies.

Merrill Lynch recently reduced AG's earnings estimates for fiscal 1987 and 1988 because of the above conditions, difficulties in production and shipment of the Christmas line to retailers, and higher than expected new business expenses.[12] Needless to say, the executive committee of AG is concerned about the future growth potential and is in the process of formulating long-term objectives and strategies.

---

[10]Research Report on American Greetings, William Blair & Company, March 27, 1986.

[11]E. Gray Glass III, Research Reports on American Greetings and Greeting Card Industry, Kidder Peabody and Company, May 16, 1986; May 20, 1986; December 11, 1986; and January 20, 1987.

[12]Research Report on American Greetings and Greeting Card Industry, Merrill Lynch, September 1986 and December 1986.

CASE 27

Immanuel-St. Joseph's Hospital

In May 1987, Jerry Crest, president of Immanuel-St. Joseph's Hospital, was reviewing a proposal by the hospital's radiology division to lease a Magnetic Resonance Imaging (MRI) unit for use by the hospital. The annual leasing cost of the proposed unit was nearly $225,000, not including operating expenses. Mr. Crest was concerned about having the most modern equipment available to provide excellent health care, about the image of the Hospital in relation to its marketing strategy, and about the cost and rapid technological evolution of MRI equipment.

Immanuel-St. Joseph's Hospital (ISJ), located in Mankato, Minnesota, was the largest hospital in the south central Minnesota market area. ISJ was licensed for 272 beds and was currently set up for 180 beds. There were about 25 other hospitals in the area, ranging from 8 beds to 80 beds in size. In the state of Minnesota, there were in 1987 about 178 hospitals, with 25 in the metropolitan area of the "Twin Cities" of Minneapolis and St. Paul. About half of Minnesota's population of four million was located in the Twin City area. Minnesota was considered by health professionals in the United States as one of the leading states in quality of health care. The famous Mayo Clinic, with more than 1,000 physicians, 10,000 staff members, plus two large, fully-staffed, hospitals was located in Rochester, Minnesota, 80 miles southeast of Minneapolis and 80 miles east of Mankato. The University of Minnesota Medical School and hospital, located in Minneapolis, 78 miles northeast of Mankato, had an eminent reputation for quality medical care and advanced health care technology.

Nationwide, hospital utilization had been declining. Data published by the American Hospital Association showed 6,872 hospitals in the United States in 1985 compared to 6,965 in 1980. The same source indicated that in the state of Minnesota there had been 185 hospitals in Minnesota in 1980. This decline was attributed in the health care industry to financial incentives to reduce hospitalization, improved health care requiring less hospitalization, a rapid increase in hospital costs, and an adjustment to earlier over-building of hospitals. As a result of these trends, larger regional hospitals were actively competing for patient referrals from physicians and smaller hospitals in their market areas.

The ISJ medical staff of 100 doctors was organized by departments and divisions as follows:

Department of Family Practice—17 physicians

Department of Medicine—37	Department of Surgery—46
Divisions	*Divisions*
Internal Medicine—14	General Surgery—9
Dermatology—1	Ophthalmology—7
Neuropsychiatry—7	Otorhinolaryngology—2
Radiology—6	Orthopedic Surgery—10
Pediatrics—5	Urology—2
Oncology—2	Anesthesiology—3
Allergy—1	Pathology—7
Occupational Medicine—1	Obstetrics and Gynecology—4
	Dentistry—2

ISJ had a total of 700 employees, including the president, three vice presidents, and 25 nonmedical department heads. As a private, nonprofit hospital, ISJ had a Board of Directors with 17 members. The Chairman of the Board, Dr. Charles H. Brady, was a urologist and member of the medical staff. Jerome Crest, President of ISJ, also was a member of the Board. Mr. Crest had a master's degree in Hospital Administration and had worked in that profession since 1968. Prior to coming to ISJ as president in 1984, he had worked in hospitals in Alexandria, Minnesota, and in Minneapolis. The other 15 Board members were business and professional persons, farmers and homemakers, who served without compensation. There was also a Finance Committee, a Planning and Marketing Committee, and a Physical Facilities Committee. These committees were made up of physicians, board members, hospital staff members, and other citizens, who also participated as a nonpaid community service.

Although the number of patients admitted to ISJ in fiscal 1986 (year-end September 30) declined to 8,365 from 8,601 in fiscal 1985, the days of patient care increased from 43,004 in 1985 to 44,217 in 1986 (see Hospital Service Report, Exhibit 27.1). The number of outpatients (people seen or treated but not hospitalized) and occupational therapy treatments had increased between 1985 and 1986, and outpatient numbers were increasing even faster in 1987.

Revenues of ISJ had increased from $22.2 million in 1985 to $23.8 million in 1986, with the largest percentage increase being in outpatient revenues (see Statement of Income and Expense, Exhibit 27.2). Total assets had increased from $23.8 million to $24.9 million, and total liabilities had decreased from $11.4 million to $11.1 million (see Balance Sheet, Exhibit 27.3). ISJ's debt to equity ratio was lower than the .963 that was reported as average for hospitals similar to ISJ.

In addition to the hospital revenues included in the financial statements, the Hospital Auxiliary Board earned a profit of $28,306 in 1986 from the following enterprises conducted in ISJ:

Gift Shop and canteen	$11,766
Television sets	13,510
Baby pictures	3,030
	$28,306

EXHIBIT 27.1 **Immanuel-St. Joseph's—Hospital service report**

	1985	1986
Adult and pediatric patients admitted	8,601	8,365
Adult and pediatric days of care	43,004	44,217
Adult and pediatric average daily census	118	121
Births	1,253	1,149
Surgical procedures	11,188	11,541
Ambulatory day surgery (included in surgical cases above)	2,323	2,381
X-ray procedures (diagnostic and therapeutic)	26,312	25,630
Laboratory tests	130,122	131,985
Physical therapy treatments	12,975	11,491
Emergency department visits	12,062	13,344
Referred outpatients	25,925	27,702
Occupational therapy treatments	10,030	23,400
Respiratory therapy treatments	22,719	23,044
Pharmacy—prescriptions filled	161,605	176,998
Cardiac rehabilitation treatments	1,456	1,419
Dietary instructions	1,657	1,952
Renal dialysis treatments	2,555	2,334
Chemical dependency unit		
Inpatient days	1,992	1,840
Outpatient treatments	1,623	2,108
After-care visits	1,341	1,069

The auxiliary spent during 1986 a total of $10,295 on a Pacer Tread Mill, an Ear Oximeter, a nursing conference, and coloring books for pediatric patients. Future purchases planned by the auxiliary included a Hemodialysis machine, two new birthing beds, and an ultrasound therapy unit. The Auxiliary Board, consisting of 12 members (including five officers), coordinated volunteer services, of which 17,450 hours were performed at ISJ in 1986. These activities included the volunteer work of "Pink Ladies"(mature women) and "Candystripers" (teen-age girls).

MARKETING STRATEGY

ISJ strategy emphasized marketing its own medical staff primarily to other physicians and secondarily to the public. The preferred method was marketing by product line. In addition, a need was recognized to market nonacute care programs directly to the public.

The trading area for Mankato, Minnesota, included a population of about 250,000 people, of which 50,000 lived in Mankato and North Mankato. Some of the most productive agricultural land in the world was located in this area of south central Minnesota. Trends in the farm economy were toward larger acreages for greater operating efficiency, and fewer farmers, resulting in the decline of some

---

EXHIBIT 27.2 **Immanuel-St. Joseph's Hospital—Statement of income and expense for fiscal year ending September 30, 1986**

	Preceding year	Current year
Operating Revenue		
Inpatient	$16,901,183	$17,898,678
Outpatient	4,657,556	5,232,321
Outside services	656,878	734,667
Total revenue	$22,215,617	$23,865,666
This amount was reduced, however, by patients unable to pay their full bills, contracts with third-party payors, charity and allowances in the amount of:	127,208	937,584
Net revenue	$22,088,409	$22,928,082
Other revenue (purchase discounts, cafeteria and vending sales, etc.)	$ 308,978	$ 223,804
Income from investments and other supplementary income	140,609	122,348
Total revenue	$22,537,996	$23,274,234
Operating expense		
Salaries and benefits	$12,863,993	$13,560,884
Supplies, etc.	6,643,350	6,853,427
Depreciation	1,273,750	1,307,194
Interest	656,008	626,040
Total expense	$21,437,101	$22,347,545
Net surplus	$ 1,100,895	$ 926,689

In addition to operating revenue, the plant fund increased its available surplus through investment of funded depreciation and donations and gained $430,261, as opposed to the prior year of $479,296.

---

rural communities. While the Mankato area was seeking to develop more jobs in light manufacturing, international trade, education, and tourism, the entire southern Minnesota area was heavily dependent on agriculture.

ISJ offered the broadest services in its region of the state and had an accessible location in town. It was believed that some patients, particularly older patients, preferred the smaller town of Mankato to the larger metropolitan medical centers. On the other hand, the highway network made it relatively easy for people who preferred Mayo or University of Minnesota to travel to those places.

The goal of ISJ was to provide high-quality health care for the lowest possible cost. "We have about the lowest hospital rates and costs in the state," remarked Jerry Crest. ISJ's average daily patient revenue, in the six months ended December 1986,

EXHIBIT 27.3 **Immanuel-St. Joseph's Hospital—Balance sheet for fiscal year ending September 30, 1986**

	Preceding year	Current year
We own the following:		
Current assets		
Cash in bank and on hand	$ 1,674,397	$ 1,704,046
Accounts receivable (less reserve for losses)	4,097,735	4,550,754
Inventories	858,617	880,831
Prepaid expenses and miscellaneous receivables	262,168	549,702
Total current assets	$ 6,892,917	$7,685,333
Plant assets		
Land, building and equipment (less depreciation)	$11,510,866	$11,090,104
Restricted funds and investments	5,207,204	5,763,534
Deferred financing fees (less accumulated amortization)	131,718	122,105
Construction in progress	57,613	284,211
Total plant assets	$16,907,401	$17,259,954
Total assets	$23,800,318	$24,945,287
We owe the following:		
Current liabilities		
Accounts payable	$ 781,121	$ 876,163
Accrued expenses	573,438	607,339
Accrued vacation payable	797,294	799,844
Due to third-party payors	291,137	251,390
Total current liabilities	$ 2,442,990	$ 2,534,736
Plant liabilities		
Mortgage payable	17,317	—
Bonds payable (less unamortized bond discount)	8,761,009	8,475,595
Interest payable on bonds	103,884	100,266
Retirement payable	31,238	33,860
Total plant liabilities	$ 8,913,448	$ 8,609,721
Total liabilities	$11,356,438	$11,144,457
The difference between what we own and what we owe is: Current assets minus current liabilities	$ 4,449,927	$ 5,150,597
Plant capital (the community's paid-up ownership in buildings and equipment)	7,993,953	8,650,233
Total	$12,443,880	$13,800,830

was $435, which was the lowest in the national, state, regional, and special data as included in the HAS/Monitrend Report in which ISJ participated (see Exhibit 27.4). The average daily patient expense for ISJ in that reporting period was $384, which was $99 below the median and the lowest of the hospitals included in the report.

"An up-to-date image of quality is one of the most important factors in the selection of a hospital by a physician for a patient," according to Mr. Crest. ISJ sought to keep Mankato patients and to attract patients from clinics and physicians in its market area. About 80 percent of the patients in the market area did come to ISJ. The other 20 percent went, about equally, to Mayo or University of Minnesota, about 15 percent because of preference and about 5 to 7 percent because of the need for specialized treatment not available at ISJ or other local hospitals. Jerry Crest believed that people would usually wish to go to the hospital recommended by their own physician and would prefer to be as close to home as possible and still get high-quality health care for their particular need. As a general-service hospital, ISJ admitted and treated all kinds of patients, except for the few requiring specialized treatment at Mayo or University of Minnesota.

Marketing strategy for ISJ included maintaining and developing relationships with physicians in the area, expansion of specialty services to include diabetes, cardiology, cancer, and psychiatric services, and seeking to utilize the most modern technology available. Negotiations were being held with Physicians Health Plan (PHP), a large Health Maintenance Organization based in Minneapolis, to establish an affiliation between PHP and ISJ through a Southern Minnesota prepaid health plan involving other area hospitals and physicians. These steps were expected to strengthen ISJ's position as the leading hospital in south central Minnesota and to increase the number of patients referred to ISJ.

A cancer program study at a cost of $25,000 and a customer survey at a cost of $18,000 were among the new marketing activities. Marketing, including surveys, was projected to cost a total of about $197,000 for the year 1987–1988, compared to a current annual marketing cost of about $60,000.

HIGH TECHNOLOGY AND CAPITAL INVESTMENTS

ISJ Hospital had recently acquired several new items of equipment and was already installing another. Two new laser units had been installed in the outpatient department, at a cost of $100,000, for use by the ophthalmologists during eye surgery. A computerized nurse communication system had been installed at a cost of $1.2 million; this system simplified the recording of patient charges for services and the management of inventories, especially in the pharmacy. A computerized Mail (message) Registry System for physicians was to be implemented during the current year.

A new QCT Bone Mineral Analysis unit had been obtained to detect osteo-porosis (loss of bone mass). The QCT was purchased at a cost of $15,000 with funds

HAS/MONITREND™·
FOR

IMMANUEL-ST JOSEPH'S HOSPITAL
MANKATO MINNESOTA 56001

	YOUR INST 6 MONTH AVERAGE	GROUP MEDIANS (SIX MONTH AVERAGE)				VARIANCE FROM MEDIAN	C O D E EXTENSION
		NATIONAL (A) 930 163 INST	STATE (B) 328 16 INST	REGIONAL (C) 2104 37 INST	SPECIAL (D) 16142 80 INST		
1 UTILIZATION (EXCLUDES NB NURSERY)							
2 OCCUPANCY PERCENT	63.78	55.53 3	48.41 4	51.95 4	58.51 3		
3 AVERAGE LENGTH OF STAY	5.21	5.83 1	4.83 3	6.00 2	6.01 1	-.62 A	
4 AVERAGE LENGTH OF STAY MED&SURG	4.81	5.43 1	4.52 3	5.25 2	5.74 1	-.62 A	
5 PATIENT DAYS % OVER AGE 65	24.18	44.91 1	40.91 L	47.78 L	45.06 L		
6 DISCHARGES % OVER AGE 65	18.01	32.99 1	30.76 1	33.63 L	34.75 L		
7 LENGTH OF STAY OVER AGE 65	7.00	7.75 2	6.12 3	7.66 1	7.90 1	A	
8 DISCHARGES PER BED PER MONTH	3.75	2.92 4	3.08 4	2.62 4	2.97 4	.83 A	
9 ER&CLINIC VISITS / CALENDAR DAY	43.62	51.29 2	26.70 3	29.51 4	51.58 2		
10 SURGICAL VISITS / CALENDAR DAY	17.28	11.28 4	8.71 3	9.19 4	14.36 3	6.00 A	
11 PERSONNEL							
12 FTE / ADJ. OCCUPIED BED	3.68	4.06 1	4.14 1	4.06 1	3.86 2	-.38 A	
13 PAID HOURS / ADJ. PATIENT DAY	20.78	22.92 1	23.35 1	22.92 1	21.77 2	-2.14 A	-10,488
14 WORKED HOURS / ADJ. PATIENT DAY	18.05	20.49 1	20.98 1	20.61 1	19.64 1	-2.44 A	-11,956
15 PERCENT WORKED HOURS TO PAID HOURS	86.85	89.28 1	88.14 1	89.66 1	89.51 1		
16 PAID NURSING HOURS / PATIENT DAY	9.16	9.16 2	9.73 1	9.29 2	8.92 3	A	
17 OVERALL AVERAGE HOURLY SALARY	9.45	9.50 2	10.47 1	9.37 3	9.11 3	-1.02 B	-$103,884
18 NURSING UNITS AVG. HOURLY SALARY	10.02	9.94 3	10.66 1	9.86 3	9.50 3	-.64 B	-$21,211
19 EMPLOYEE BENEFITS % SALARY	16.07	16.68 2	16.86 2	15.87 3	16.97 2		
20 FINANCIAL							
21 INPT REVENUE / PATIENT DAY	435.14	611.90 1	582.95 1	593.97 L	566.91 1		
22 EXPENSE / ADJ. PATIENT DAY	383.98	476.20 1	462.93 1	468.58 1	431.28 1	-98.96 P	-$464,886
23 SALARY EXPENSE / ADJ. PATIENT DAY	198.35	221.67 2	239.48 1	219.96 1	196.35 2	-43.13 B	-$211,337
24 PHYSICIAN REMUN / ADJ. PATIENT DAY	5.13	15.36 1	9.01 1	12.06 1	13.91 1	-3.88 B	
25 INPT REVENUE / STAY	2269.10	3563.81 L	2994.66 1	3388.35 L	3436.07 L		
26 EXPENSE / ADJ. DISCHARGE	2002.33	2601.82 1	2366.52 1	2641.23 1	2611.30 1	-384.19 B	-$360,784
27 OUTPATIENT REVENUE PERCENT	23.46	21.68 3	22.81 3	21.05 3	20.90 3		
28 DEDUCTIONS FROM REVENUE PERCENT	-5.00	-19.81 H	-13.72 4	-17.31 4	-19.00 4		
29 DAYS NET REVENUE IN NET ACCTS REC	69.45	72.36 2	66.21 3	65.00 3	76.84 2	A	
30 DAYS GROSS REV IN GROSS ACCTS REC	76.00	74.56 3	76.00 2	71.61 3	74.91 3	A	
31 DAYS EXPENSE IN ACCTS PAYABLE	38.26	32.15 3	36.31 3	32.03 3	30.77 3	A	
32 QUICK RATIO	2.67	2.47 3	1.82 3	2.46 3	2.53 3	A	
33 CURRENT RATIO	3.27	2.90 3	2.06 3	2.85 3	3.02 3	A	
34 OPERATING DAYS CASH ON HAND	32.13	31.31 3	11.74 3	31.65 3	23.04 3	A	
35 OPERATING RATIO	.93	.97 2	.98 1	.96 2	.96 2	A	

EXHIBIT 27.4   **HAS/Monitrend report for ISJ**

provided by the ISJ Hospital Auxiliary. It would be used in connection with a new CT scanner.

A new CT 9800 scanner was being installed and was expected to be in operation by November 1987. CT, or computerized tomography, combined x-ray equipment with a minicomputer and sophisticated software to show details of internal body parts and formations that x-rays would not reveal. CT (sometimes known as CAT, for computerized axial tomography) had been hailed as a landmark development in health care when it was introduced on an operational basis for hospitals in 1973. ISJ obtained a CT system in 1982 and considered it essential for quality health care, even though it was expensive. Patient usage had supported the investment in the CT system. CT technology was rapidly changing, however, and the new CT 9800 system being installed at ISJ at a cost of $730,000, was considered necessary for several reasons. First, the scan could be done in two seconds (one-fourth the time of the old CT), thus improving the clarity of images involving moving body parts, and on infants and children. The CT 9800 would collect 16 times as much data per second as the older model, allowing for a faster and more accurate diagnosis. There were also some other operating improvements in the new CT that would improve patient service and reduce maintenance.

Capital investment for a laboratory to support a proposed new cardiology program was projected at $1 million. Capital costs for a proposed expansion of the emergency room and outpatient surgical facility was projected at $3 million, and for remodeling the obstetric delivery rooms at $150,000. These capital costs were intended to be met by bonding in order to conserve cash. In addition, it appeared that Magnetic Resonance Imaging capability could be leased by ISJ for an estimated initial capital cost of about $100,000, plus lease payments.

MAGNETIC RESONANCE IMAGING (MRI)

MRI was regarded in the health professions as a relatively recent high-technology development that was just as dramatic as CT had been several years earlier. MRI had initially been far too expensive for widespread use, just as CT had been at the start.

MRI was a new way to look inside the body, without using x-rays. It could produce 2- or 3-dimensional images of what was going on inside a patient's body. MRI used a magnet large enough to surround a patient's body, radio waves, and a computer.

MRI was important because it could lead to early detection and treatment of disease. MRI pictures were extremely precise—so precise that physicians could often get as much information from MRI as they would from looking directly at the tissue. For this reason, MRI had the potential to reduce the number of certain diagnostic surgeries.

MRI used no x-rays. Under normal conditions the protons inside atoms of the human body spin randomly. In the use of MRI:

- The magnet creates a strong, steady magnetic field, causing the protons to line up together and spin in the same direction.
- A radio frequency (RF) signal is beamed into the magnetic field, making the

protons move out of alignment. When the signal stops, the protons move back into their aligned position and release energy.

- A receiver coil measures the energy released by the disturbed protons. The time it takes for the protons to return to their aligned position is also measured. Those measurements provide information about the type of tissues of which the protons were a part, as well as the condition of the tissue.

- A computer uses this information to construct an image on a TV screen, showing the distribution of protons of certain atoms, usually hydrogen. The screen image could then be recorded on film or tape for a permanent copy.

Because MRI could target specific atoms, it could see right through bone, and clearly define soft tissue. MRI was especially valuable diagnosing the following disorders and diseases:

- Brain and nervous system disorders
  1. Multiple sclerosis can be seen in its earliest stages.
  2. Tumors can be distinguished from surrounding tissue.
  3. Disease in the base of the brain and interior of the spine can easily be examined.
  4. Hydrocephalus (abnormal fluid in the skull) can be detected.

- Cardiovascular disease

  1. MRI can see right into the heart and blood vessels.
  2. Blood flow can be measured, and the effects of plaque in the arteries can be seen.

- Cancer

  1. MRI can be used to detect cancer of the uterus, ovaries, and prostate.
  2. It can help detect cancer of the liver, pancreas, lymph nodes, bladder, kidneys, and vocal cords.

- Organ Disease

  1. Images are so precise that many organs, including the liver, spleen, pancreas, and adrenal glands, can be seen in great detail.

- MRI can be used to monitor the success of treatment for disease. Future uses of MRI include:

  1. Assessing damage after a stroke or heart attack.
  2. Evaluating organs for transplants.
  3. Identifying disease before structural evidence is present.

CT still shows bone structures better than MRI, so CT was not being replaced by MRI technology. The ISJ Radiology Division wanted to have both CT and MRI because they could provide much better diagnosis of patients than CT alone. Some surgery could be avoided with MRI. When surgery was needed, MRI could make it more precise.

At a Planning Committee meeting on May 19, 1987, Jerry Crest and Dr. Joe Eckert, an ISJ radiologist, presented a description of MRI and a proposal to lease an MRI unit for ISJ Hospital (see Exhibit 27.5). The proposal included reference to an analysis done by the American Hospital Association (AHA) for ISJ, projecting a demand for 6 to 12 MRI scans per week if an MRI unit were available at ISJ

EXHIBIT 27.5 **Magnetic resonance imaging**

A New Technology

Magnetic Resonance Imaging (MRI) uses a powerful magnet, radio waves, and a computer to obtain pictures. It does not use x-rays or ionizing radiation as does a CT scanner. MRI works by making a few of the body's hydrogen atoms resonate to emit a weak radio signal.

The patient lying in an MRI system is surrounded by a magnetic field about 10,000 times more powerful than the earth's. Influenced by such a powerful magnet, any weaker magnet aligns itself with the strong field. Hydrogen atoms (or protons) act just like magnets—and hydrogen is the most abundant element in the human body, particularly common in fat cells and water. When a person undergoes an MRI scan, some of his or her hydrogen atoms line up in the powerful magnetic field.

During the MRI exam, radio-frequency (RF) pulses cause some of the hydrogen atoms to flip. When the RF pulses are turned off, the protons (hydrogen atoms) return to their previous position and, in the process emit "resonance energy" radio waves.

These signals are detected by an antenna and are translated by high-speed computers into a "hydrogen map," which is an accurate picture of the tissues inside the body. With little water in its makeup, bone is essentially "invisible" in an MRI exam, making MRI excellent for imaging the brain, spinal cord, spine, and pelvic areas. Blood vessels are also seen clearly in an MRI exam: the blood gives off no detectable signals because the resonating atoms in the blood are generally pumped out of range before the antenna can detect the signal.

MRI is nonionizing, has produced no harmful biologic effects in the presently used diagnostic range, and has soft-tissue contrast 70–80 times better than that of the best x-ray CT. MRI is capable of direct imaging in any plane. In addition, it is possible to obtain multiple slices simultaneously. A multitude of techniques is available that can be tailored for different disease conditions. This makes it possible to greatly increase the sensitivity and specificity of a diagnosis.

Applications

This latest form of diagnostic imaging is becoming increasingly helpful in the diagnosis of spinal and head problems. Further, new applications are constantly being experimented with for other parts of the body and it is anticipated further appropriate uses will be identified in the not too distant future as occurred with CT scanning.

Competition

Units are currently located at Mayo (they will soon have their sixth installed), and a number of locations in the Twin Cities. There are no other units in Southern Minnesota.

Utilization Projections

Information on our patient mix and CT volume was submitted to the American Hospital Association. They applied three different utilization models to that information. From that computer modeling exercise, they project ISJ would have a demand for six to 12 MRI scans per week if a unit was available. Since most such exams are performed on outpatients, patients can either be sent to a unit in another community, or await arrival in Mankato of a mobile unit.

Current Use

Actual referral patterns by ISJ physicians reveal the following volume of referrals for MRI scans:

Orthopaedic & Fracture Clinic

1986 (12 months)	13
1987 (4 months)	9

Neurologists at Mankato Clinic

1986 (October–December)	8
1987 (January, February)	7
(March, April)	15

It is obvious from the above data, physicians on our medical staff are increasing their utilization of this modality. There were likely a few other referrals, but the above represents the bulk of our utilization.

Alternatives

We have received two proposals for bringing MRI services to the Mankato area. One is a smaller unit that would be based here full time and the other is a state-of-the-art, high-magnetic-force unit that would be brought to us weekly in a semitrailer truck. Our conclusion is the smaller unit would not be in our best interest. It is more costly, would require at least five years to pay back our investment, and would likely be obsolete well before the pay back was complete.

Mobile Proposal

The mobile unit can be leased for one to three years at a cost of $4,300 per trip. Following is a summary of the financial impact of such a unit:

AHA Computer Projections

Patients per week	11.58	9.39	6.77
Patient revenue ($550/pt)	$6,369	$5,164	$3,724
Per diem expense	4,300	4,300	4,300
Operating expenses	250	250	250
Profit (loss) per day	1,819	614	(827)
Profit (loss) annually	$94,588	$31,928	($42,978)

Approximately 20% of these patients will be hospitalized and stay an average of five days (our average length of stay), generating $2,000 in charges for that stay. About 51% of each hospital stay goes toward fixed costs and profit. Thus, each additional patient will generate about $1,020 to our bottom line. If we assume 25% of these would be new inpatients, that would add the following revenues to the above figures:

Inpatient revenue

Patients per week	11.58	9.39	6.77
5% new inpatients	.579	.470	.338
Net revenue @ $1,020/stay/year	$30,710	$24,930	$17,900

Not included in the above projections is the cost of constructing a concrete pad for the truck, and connection between the truck and hospital. We do not have cost estimates for this yet.

In addition to the above figures, there is value to the image, referral attractiveness, and general impact upon our capability of serving a larger percentage of Southern Minnesota residents that is created by this new technology.

Hospital. Dr. Eckert commented that "The history of AHA projection is invariably low." Both of the two MRI units considered were made by General Electric. While the smaller unit cost about half as much as the larger unit ($1 million compared to $2 million), the larger unit was preferred by the ISJ radiology department for several reasons. First, the larger unit would give better diagnostic images; second, the larger unit could be leased on a part-time basis (one day per week), with a beginning capital investment of about $100,000, whereas the smaller unit would have to be purchased at a cost of $1 million. It was feared that the small unit would become obsolete before the cost was recovered over a projected five-year period. MRI technology was changing rapidly. It was known that GE had a new MRI unit scheduled to come out in the fall of 1987, but cost and performance data were not yet available. There was a general provision in the proposed lease for upgrading the leased equipment, but there was no specification as to what equipment or when a change could be made. "If you can find *one* cancer, and get it," said Dr. Eckert, "it would be additional justification for having MRI capability." The Mayo hospitals and the large hospitals in Minneapolis-St. Paul all had MRI. Methodist, Ramsey, and St. Cloud hospitals, each about half again the size of ISJ but outside the ISJ service area, were soon going to add MRI. It was believed by the medical staff that few hospitals of ISJ size had MRI. "It would take about an hour to do a complete MRI," said Dr. Eckert, "and the patient would not be within the scanner during all that time." He estimated that eight or nine MRI patients could be served during an eight-hour period. The lease cost of the mobile unit would rise above the $4,300 per diem figure if the unit remained at ISJ more than eight hours, though on a less than proportional basis. No other operating cost information was available. In addition to the direct revenue expected to be generated by MRI scans, an analysis of projected increased hospital usage by patients was included in the presentation. In summing up his presentation, Dr. Eckert stated, "The biggest patient question in making a decision about a hospital is, 'Is the hospital up to date?'"

The Planning and Marketing Committee was supportive of the MRI proposal. Approval would be required by the Board of Directors, which was scheduled to meet the next day. MRI was on the agenda, together with the marketing and capital investment plans. Mr. Crest wanted to have MRI capability for ISJ Hospital, along with all of the other proposals on the agenda.

CASE 28

Volvo Bus of North America

Jan-Olof Rabe, President and Chief Executive Officer (CEO) of Volvo Bus Company of North America, sat alone in his second-floor office. Although it was only six o'clock, the December night had already dropped its curtain between the tree-lined Volvo complex and the Chesapeake, Virginia, environs. Rabe swung his chair around and stared into the darkness. Lights reflected off expensive white and blue china; coffee remaining in the cup had long been too cold to enjoy. In the distance, flashing white lights signalled to aircraft the location of three Portsmouth radio towers. Thoughts of home broke his concentration. Within a few days he would return to Sweden to meet, yet again, with the corporate board. What would they finally decide?

In many ways, Volvo Bus Company of North America paralleled the situation at General Electric's Video and Audio Division, producer of television receivers and VCRs, headquartered at nearby Portsmouth, Virginia. Both were divisions of multibusiness, multinational corporations, with plants and sales worldwide. Both, placing top priority on quality, employed advanced technology and asynchronous production lines in their production processes. Both firms had been battered by intense price competition, especially from foreign companies with U.S. plants. GE's Video Division had announced cessation of manufacturing operations nearly a year ago.

As Rabe reviewed activities of the past several months he pondered whether the Chesapeake bus operations should make a similar decision. "What went wrong?"

CORPORATE MANAGEMENT PHILOSOPHY

Volvo had always stressed quality. Assar Gabrielsson, one of Volvo's founders, wrote in the company's first sales manual in the 1930s: "Our pride, as manufacturers,

This case was prepared by Robert P. Vichas, Florida Atlantic University and Betty R. Ricks, Old Dominion University. It is intended as a basis for classroom discussion rather than to illustrate effective or ineffective handling of an administrative situation. Used by permission from Robert P. Vichas.

is that Volvo's quality and performance are the base upon which we are building our popularity."

In Volvo's quest for development of production technology and quality products, top management had adopted a guiding philosophy: to adapt the industrial environment to humans rather than mold human behavior to fit the work environment. Management permitted employees more self-determination, increased responsibility (job depth), and greater influence in deciding how their work should be performed (autonomy).

CORPORATE GROWTH AND STRATEGY

The Swedish Volvo Group (Volvo means "I Roll"), probably best known for its automobiles, manufactures not only cars, trucks, and buses, but also marine, industrial, and aircraft engines. It invested in oil and gas exploration and food-processing companies. Information in Exhibit 28.1 is broken down by legal entities, rather than by operational groups; many subsidiaries have operations in more than one section.

Truly multinational, AB Volvo, with plants in Sweden, Belgium, the Netherlands, France, Great Britain, Australia, Thailand, Malaysia, Iran, Peru, Brazil, Canada, and the United States, employs nearly 68,000 people. Corporate-wide sales in 1985 exceeded SEK86 billion (down from SEK100 billion in 1983, and SEK87 in 1984); eighty percent of sales originated outside of Sweden. World truck and bus sales accounted for SEK18 billion (approximately 1 U.S. dollar equals 7 Swedish Kronor). Income as a percent of equity reached 7.3 in 1978, 18.3 in 1983, 28.2 in 1984, and 23.7 percent in 1985.

The exhibits included with this case summarize financial characteristics of AB Volvo. Exhibit 28.1 breaks down sales and income by operating groups for 1984 and 1985; the four-line graphs in Exhibit 28.2 describe key corporate variables over the most recent ten years.

Having built its reputation on quality motor vehicles, Volvo increased automotive sales during the stable growth period of the 1960s, which, by 1971, had accounted for 75 percent of total revenue. About 70 percent of automotive revenue originated outside of Sweden; Volvo contributed between 8 and 9 percent to Sweden's total exports. Nevertheless, Volvo's world share of the automotive market amounted to little more than 1 percent.

Economic imbalance, increased competition, and weaker profits characterized the 1970s. Volvo adapted to a changing environment with a strategy aimed at creating conditions for improved profitability through growth of its traditional products and with market and product diversification.

To implement this broad strategy of growth through diversification, Volvo improved production technology and adopted a new management philosophy aimed at raising productivity and providing a more satisfying work environment. Beginning in 1972, the corporation restructured its organization along product lines. Each line

EXHIBIT 28.1 **Financial data by group company: AB Volvo, 1984–1985**

	Sales		Income before allocations, taxes and minority interests		Employees December 31	
SEK M	**1984**	**1985**	**1984**	**1985**	**1984**	**1985**
AB Volvo	4,737	5,504	1,541	885	2,196	2,425
Subsidiaries in Sweden						
Volvo Car Corporation	20,914	23,951	4,333	4,415	22,212	24,037
Volvo Truck Corporation	9,161	9,229	438	608	6,610	7,416
Volvo Bus Corporation	852	889	61	(11)	750	742
Volvo BM AB	2,615	—	66	—	5,112	—
AB Volvo Penta	1,898	1,772	173	131	1,020	1,031
Volvo Flygmotor AB	1,345	1,608	143	224	3,326	3,463
Volvo Components Corporation	5,816	6,339	92	(2)	9,072	9,818
Volvo Svenska Bil AB	5,369	6,709	243	197	695	777
Forsakringsaktiebolaget Volvia (insurance company)	273	342	21	1	—	—
Volvo Data AB	340	425	12	28	612	660
Volvo Transport AB	3,378	4,054	31	36	205	250
AB Fortos	—	188	—	58	—	130
Kockums Jernverksaktiebolag	321	184	(52)	(20)	756	300
Centro-Morgardshammar AB. . .	383	442	4	(126)	772	778
Volvo Energy Corporation	39	6	164	(31)	8	8
STC Scandinavian Trading Company AB	27,698	21,757	(330)	50	427	316
Provendor Food AB	4,947	5,393	131	154	4,946	4,989
Subsidiaries outside Sweden						
Nordic area, excluding Sweden	4,057	5,148	119	181	1,049	1,066
Europe, excluding Nordic area	6,518	7,012	227	144	2,652	2,618
North America	19,860	22,757	1,084	1,070	4,567	4,657
Other markets	2,277	2,925	203	297	1,499	2,285
Other companies and intra-group transactions	(35,746)	(40,438)	(1,057)	(687)	100	91
Group total	87,052	86,196	7,647	7,602	68,586	67,857

Note: This exhibit shows the sales, income before allocations, taxes and minority interests, and the number of employees in AB Volvo and its subsidiaries. Figures for company subsidiaries are included, where applicable.

Figures for "Subsidiaries in Sweden" include the operations of their subsidiaries in other countries.

Intra-group transactions pertain mainly to sales between group companies, to profits arising from these sales, and to dividends from subsidiaries.

The information is broken down by legal entities. This differs from the presentations dealing with operating sectors, since many group companies have operations in more than one operating sector.

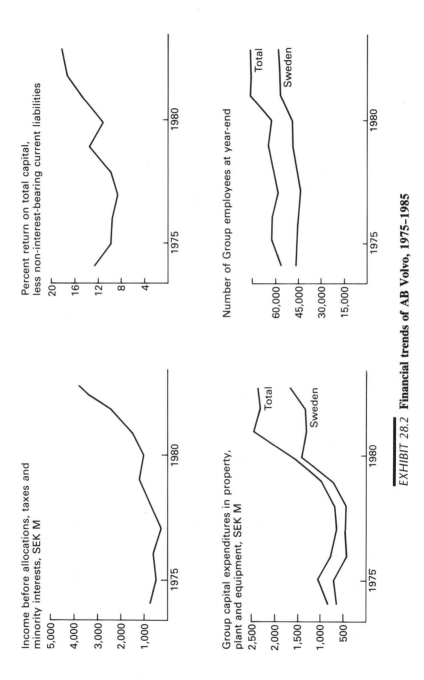

Income before allocations, taxes and
minority interests, SEK M

Percent return on total capital,
less non-interest-bearing current liabilities

Group capital expenditures in property,
plant and equipment, SEK M

Number of Group employees at year-end

EXHIBIT 28.2 **Financial trends of AB Volvo, 1975–1985**

became an independent division. Corporate headquarters reduced its staff from 1,800 to 100 persons.

Management initiated a plan to broaden product line in its transport vehicle sector, including automobiles, widen product lines in its other activities, and diversify in order to reduce dependency on automobile sales. After 1973 Volvo's worldwide profits increasingly were derived from nonautomobile activities. It further engaged in risk diversification by spreading market activities to more than 100 countries. The firm began investing in energy, food processing, and marketing brand-name food products and soft drinks.

By the 1980s, Volvo had strengthened its corporate position in traditional areas, entered new markets by establishing a presence in various countries with assembly plants, created a worldwide sales organization, and consolidated its market position in important West Europe markets. Although the Nordic countries still constituted its sales base, especially in vehicle sales, by 1983, automobile sales accounted for only 25 percent of corporate revenue.

VOLVO BUS CORPORATION (VBNA)

Volvo's bus operating sector develops, manufactures, and markets buses, bus chassis, and components. Although Sweden accounts for most production, assembly and limited manufacture take place in ten countries.

Volvo had developed a number of systems for use in mass transit, which included route networks, scheduling, staffing, computerized control, and other functions. The chassis program covered the range of 12 to 27 ton buses for use in all types of service from city traffic to tourist transportation. In 1983, Volvo introduced a completely new tourist bus of its own design, which was manufactured in Italy. In September 1985, an energy-efficient double-decker bus was delivered to London Transport, the world's largest bus operator, for test operations.

Following a five-year decline, the world market for buses stabilized in 1985. Volvo had increased its market share at the expense of competitors; in terms of unit sales, 1985 volume remained flat: 3,240 units in 1984, 3,220 units in 1985 (Exhibit 28.3). The kronor-value increase in revenue in 1985 resulted from the larger percentage of delivery of *completed* buses during the year.

EXHIBIT 28.3 **Volvo Bus operations data, 1984–1985 (All markets)**		
Item	**1984**	**1985**
Bus sales (SEK millions)	1,336	1,672
Operating income (SEK millions)	114	60
Capital expenditures (SEK millions)	47	48
Return on capital (percent)	17	8
Number of employees (December 31)	1,600	1,750

Source: Volvo, 1985 annual report.

Market	1981	1982	1983	1984	1985
			(In SEK millions)		
Sweden	192	341	308	303	318
Nordic area, except Sweden	196	199	215	262	236
Europe, except Nordic area	201	272	350	363	379
Other markets	441	216	258	408	739
Totals	1,030	1,028	1,131	1,336	1,672

EXHIBIT 28.4 **Volvo bus sales, 1981–1985**

Source: Volvo, 1985 annual report.

Exhibit 28.4 summarizes global bus sales geographically, 1981 to 1985. About 81 percent of all bus sales originated outside of Sweden; Volvo had accounted for approximately 7 percent of heavy buses and bus chassis (over 12 tons) manufactured in Organization for Economic Cooperation and Development (OECD) countries. OECD countries comprise: Australia, Austria, Belgium, Canada, Denmark, Finland, France, West Germany, Greece, Iceland, Ireland, Italy, Japan, Luxembourg, the Netherlands, New Zealand, Norway, Portugal, Spain, Sweden, Switzerland, Turkey, the United Kingdom, and the United States.

However, in West Europe the market for heavy buses had decreased by 6 percent during 1985. Despite lower demand, Volvo retained market share in Great Britain, Belgium, the Netherlands, and other countries. Its bus market shares declined in Finland from 48 to 45 percent, in Norway from 42 to 36 percent, and in Denmark from 29 to 26 percent. On the other hand, market shares rose in Sweden from 58 to 63 percent, and in Brazil from 14 to 16 percent. Higher sales in Australia, Morocco, and Algeria were due to slight market growth. By contrast, the U.S. subsidiary, Volvo Bus of North America, experienced large losses in 1984 and 1985.

THE UNITED STATES MARKET

In 1974, Volvo began construction of an automobile assembly plant on its 520 acre Chesapeake location, which had met company criteria for location, cost, and labor supply. Volvo desired a cost-effective East Coast harbor site near its main markets, accessible to an efficient highway system, with availability of skilled labor plus a surplus pool of trainable workers to permit expansion. The Hampton Roads area provided the right environment.

When auto sales dropped precipitously following the first oil crisis, plant construction was halted. The incomplete facility first functioned as an auto service center (1976–1978) for 30,000 to 40,000 automobiles. Then, in 1979, it began to serve as a job shop for customizing light trucks imported from Belgium at the rate of 2,500 vehicles per year.

Bus Manufacture

Also, in 1981, Volvo began market research on city mass transit buses in the United States and Canada. During 1983, bus prototypes were manufactured in Chesapeake, and, by 1984, the Chesapeake facility housed yet its third operation, the U.S.$25 million Volvo bus manufacturing and offices complex. Full scale bus manufacture and assembly were underway by early 1984.

The decision to establish a U.S. bus assembly division grew out of a lagged corporate response to proposals and policies of the Carter administration. President Carter favored federal subsidies to create public transportation systems in key cities. Helped by two oil crises in the 1970s, which produced sharp increases in retail gasoline prices, President Carter initially mustered congressional support for funding a mass-transit program. Statistical studies conducted in selected major cities appeared to demonstrate the need and public acceptance of massive public funding of rapid transit and ground transportation systems. A potentially lucrative articulated (i.e., long, customized) bus market, subsidized with federal money and linked with higher tariffs, did not go unnoticed by AB Volvo. House Rule 3129 (a rule passed by the House of Representatives) had already promulgated a 50 percent local content requirement (50 percent of a manufactured item must be manufactured in the United States).

In response to higher U.S. tariffs and federal financing, Volvo acted to strengthen its U.S. presence. Around the end of the 1970s, corporate management had projected a total U.S. and Canadian bus market of 10,000 units per year. Since Volvo already owned the Chesapeake property and other fixed assets, a bus assembly venture would require a lower initial capital outlay. Besides, a plant and service facility located within the United States allowed Volvo direct access to U.S. markets.

In March 1985, Jan-Olof Rabe signed a three-year contract to become the new President and Chief Executive Officer of VBNA. For a time prior to 1969, he and his family had lived in the United States. In 1969, with an engineering degree in hand, he joined the Economics Department of AB Volvo's Swedish auto division, where he remained until 1980. From 1980 to 1985, he had been general manager of Volvo's Indonesian plant, which manufactured all types of vehicles.

VBNA operated as a division of Volvo North America Corporation (VNAC), headquartered in Rockleigh, New Jersey. VNAC, in turn, was a subsidiary of AB Volvo, with world headquarters in Goteborg, Sweden, which established worldwide corporate policy and global strategies. Consequently, an AB Volvo Executive Committee decided or approved both expansion and closure. Rabe reported to VNAC and was responsible for developing operational plans necessary to implement corporate decisions.

PRODUCTION AND LABOR

The bus plant in Chesapeake was utilized to assemble 40 foot transit coaches and 60 foot articulated buses. At peak employment, more than 360 plant and office workers enjoyed above market wages and salaries at the carefully maintained facility.

Much like General Electric, Volvo demanded quality goods and quality performance from its employees; both paid quality wages.

Exhibit 28.5 shows that wages at GE and Volvo exceeded local and state-wide rates as well as the national average in all manufacturing activities. However, workers of the heavily unionized transportation and motor vehicle industries obtained basic wages about 50 percent above the typical worker in manufacturing across the United States. These wages were exclusive of fringe benefits (some of which were nontaxable), which typically added another 25 to 50 percent equivalent in wages to unionized workers. Direct labor per manufactured bus typically added up to 1,500 hours. However, due to learning curve effects, manufacture time on large orders might decline to as low as 1,000 hours of direct labor per bus.

EXHIBIT 28.5 **Comparative wage data, 1984 (Average rates in U.S. dollars per hour)**

Volvo (Chesapeake, VA, 1984)	10.00
General Electric (Portsmouth, VA, June 25, 1984)	9.97
Hampton Roads, VA area (May 1984)	8.60
Virginia—statewide (May 1984)	8.03
All U.S. manufacturing (June 1984)	8.77
Transportation equipment manufacturing (1984)	12.15
Motor vehicle and equipment manufacturing (1984)	12.65

COMPETITORS AND MARKET SIZE

By contrast, Volvo's chief U.S. competitors—both U.S. subsidiaries of German corporations—Neoplan and MAN, had located U.S. production facilities in lower-wage areas—in Lamar, Colorado, and near Charlotte, North Carolina, respectively. Aggressive marketers, Neoplan often underbid Volvo on city government contracts. Volvo management refused to compromise on quality.

Although moderately rising global revenue produced profitable business for the Volvo Bus Corporation, VBNA had suffered large losses in 1984 and 1985. In the early 1980s, a large bus in the United States would have sold for $275,000 to $300,000. By the end of 1985, that same bus would yield only $225,000 in revenue, despite higher production costs.

During 1980 to 1985, the total U.S. market had shrunk by 50 percent, and bus prices had plunged by 25 percent; four new competitors had appeared on the scene; federal subsidies had sharply declined; and VBNA could not underbid competitors. Including those on order, the Chesapeake facility had generated sales for 230 buses, 112 of which were delivered during 1985.

AT A CROSSROADS

Poor divisional performance and environmental changes favored a closure decision on one hand. A physical presence in major markets driven by a global strategy favored staying in the United States, on the other hand. Although Volvo could export its buses into the United States and Canada from its Swedish production facilities, import tariffs, local and national regulations, contract specifications, and customizing necessitated that work be done in reasonable proximity to the market. Additionally, Volvo had long ago committed itself to quality and service; and VBNA had to maintain, at a minimum, a spare parts inventory and training facilities for technicians as a condition of its contracts with purchasers.

When Swedish management reviewed its options and asked for a reassessment of the U.S. bus market, Rabe observed that projected programs of the Carter administration had highly favored expansion of a public transportation system. Volvo management, in 1979, had forecasted a total bus market of 10,000 units per year. At $300,000 1980-U.S. dollars per bus, VBNA's market share would have generated very profitable business. Management had committed itself to enter the U.S. market. The corporation had funded those plans; but the Chesapeake plant did not deliver its first bus until five years later.

Market projections and total bus sales

According to Rabe, "Buses purchased for public use are funded by local communities. Realistically, U.S. demand probably ranges between 200 and 400 articulated buses a year. Canada accounts for another 300 buses a year. We have a more difficult problem forecasting our competitors' activities. We don't have accurate cost data. Sales vary considerably each year. One manufacturer reports sales figures on number of buses produced; another adds delivered buses to work-in-progress or even adds contracts signed. There is double counting. The information is unreliable."

VBNA standing in the U.S. market

"We have most of the articulated bus market," said Rabe, "as much as 50 percent of the market." The main issue was that federal funding of a public bus system virtually disappeared under the Reagan administration, and renewed interest by Congress was unlikely for the rest of the decade. Cities, the chief customers, usually awarded contracts on the basis of lowest bids coupled with specs that drove up production costs. Volvo had to implement a plan that would allow the firm to compete profitably and still maintain high standards of safety and quality.

Internal discussions continued throughout October. In November, management asked Rabe to recapitulate the key problems. Rabe said that decreased demand largely brought about by reduced federal funding, aggressive German competitors, bid prices well below the break-even point, plus the threat of legislation that might raise the local content requirement from 50 to 85 percent were the chief challenges. Furthermore, because Volvo was already exporting more than 15 percent of bus components from its Swedish plants to Chesapeake, the proposed legislation would adversely affect sector profits.

Turning around the American bus business

One manager suggested that some of the problems stemmed from company assessments made seven or eight years ago because Europeans did not fully understand the American political system. From Watergate to Ford to Carter, it appeared to Europeans that there had been a major shift in attitudes of the American public. Because the company had been accustomed to dealing with central governments, and when President Carter encouraged public funding of mass transit, the Americans were sending mixed signals. Then they confused the world even further with the election of Reagan.

Rabe said, "We didn't fully understand the low bid process. Or the politics of bidding." The low bid system affected Volvo Bus's ability to compete. After a city requested bids on transit buses, Volvo would analyze the requirements and submit a competitive bid. Neoplan, MAN, Grumann, and others submitted bids as well. The political process mandated awarding the contract to the lowest bidder. Many specs and changes demanded by cities often were incompatible with the Volvo bus design.

"We know we have a superior design, but that doesn't enter into discussions. To meet customer specs raises manufacturing costs. A customer wants a fuel tank here instead of there, or orders a modification in the frame or body. If we move the fuel tank from the center to the left side, for instance, then everything else underneath must be redesigned. It takes workers longer to learn a new production routine. If the bid is for a few buses, our per unit costs are higher. With a big order we can recapture some of those learning costs."

"Politics dictate buying the cheapest. The approach is strictly short run. They don't consider maintenance, costs, fuel economy, comfort, safety, durability—none of these important elements that through many years of experience we have incorporated into our buses. Our buses last longer. They're efficient. In most other countries we work with negotiated bids. They consider fuel economy, availability of replacement parts, service, maintenance costs. They have a long-term approach. Our experience has been predominately with negotiated bids, and we didn't understand the American decision process."

By December 1985, management had to act to stem heavy financial losses. If retrenchment, or, worse yet, closure, was the best option, management could not just walk away from its Chesapeake operations. Closure required a carefully implemented strategy. There were many stakeholders to consider.

High-paid employees would not be able to find work with comparable salaries locally, especially after the GE layoff. Previous customers depended on Volvo Bus to supply parts and training, and pending orders might be cancelled should Volvo decide to pull out. Volvo had to maintain good relationships with its suppliers because of its other operations: Volvo Penta of America, also located in Hampton Roads, Virginia, supplied marine engines; plus the truck operation in Greensboro, North Carolina; Volvo BM, the oldest heavy-equipment manufacturer in the world; the recreational products division; and, of course, automobile sales, as well as the good name of VNAC had to be maintained. Competitors would quickly fill any vacuum left by VBNA. Volvo currently had 110 buses on order for delivery during 1986.

Rabe said, "A Volvo bus is a truly remarkable product. It's an accumulation of thousands of hours of designing, producing, and inspecting by hundreds of people. And what's so amazing is that each person puts forth an effort as if the bus they were building was their very own."

Rabe loved Volvo and was proud of its high standards and quality products. To surrender the North American market to competitors meant that Americans and Canadians would no longer have the option of riding in a safe, well-constructed Volvo bus.

The night watchman softly tapped his door, and called out, "Mr. Rabe?" Rabe put some papers into his briefcase and left his office. For a moment he stood pensively in the nearly deserted parking lot.

Once the decision had been made to penetrate the United States and Canadian markets in the 1970s, corporate momentum continued to drive the plan, long after market conditions had changed. A recognition lag and lack of belief that the environment had shifted locked the decision into place.

Rabe walked confidently to his car. He now knew what he must recommend to the Board.

EXHIBIT 28.6 Selected comparative financial data on Volvo, 1976–1985

Per share data, 1976–1985
Adjusted for share issues

	1976	1977	1978	1979	1980	1981	1982	1983	1984	1985
Dividend, SEK (not adjusted)	6	6	7	8	8	9	10	11.50	5.30	8.50
Share price at year-end, SEK (B restricted)	38	24	31	30	37	62	122	184	185	284
Direct return, percent (B restricted)[1]	6.5	10.3	9.3	11.5	9.3	6.3	3.7	2.8	2.9	3
Price/earnings ratio (B restricted)[2]	6	6	4	2	3	5	8	8	4	6
Dividend yield, percent[3]	39	65	41	24	34	35	29	22	11	17
Adjusted equity per share, SEK[4]	89	93	100	102	116	107	123	143	187	228
Income as percent of average adjusted equity[5]	7.3	4.2	7.3	14.3	9.4	9.9	13.7	18.3	28.2	23.7

[1] Dividend divided by share price at year-end.

[2] Share price at year-end divided by income per share.

[3] Dividend divided by income per share.

[4] Shareholders' equity plus 50 percent of untaxed reserves divided by the number of shares outstanding at each year end. No adjustment has been made for minority interests in 1980 and prior years, since such interests were insignificant.

[5] Income per share divided by average adjusted equity per share.

The largest shareholders in AB Volvo February 28, 1986	Number of shares	Percent of total votes	Percent of total shares
The National Pension Insurance Fund, Fourth Fund Managing Board	2,534,401	6.2	3.3
Svenska Handelsbankens Pensionsstiftelsa (pension fund)	1,410,000	4.6	1.8
AB Cardo (investment company, Investment AB Cardo from March 1986)	1,380,000	4.5	1.8
Skandia Liv and Skandia Sak (insurance company)	2,616,338	4.3	3.4
Protorp Förvaltnings AB (investment company)	1,320,100	4.3	1.7
Skandinaviska Bankers Pensionsstiftelsa (pension fund)	1,310,000	4.1	1.7
AB Custos (investment company)	1,320,730	3.4	1.7
Svenska Personal Pensionskassan (SPP) (pension fund)	3,466,364	3.1	4.5
AB Industrivärden (investment company)	1,120,000	2.5	1.4
Folksam ömsesidig Sak och Liviörsäkring (insurance group)	1,669,024	2.1	2.2
Boliden AB (industrial company, mining)	680,900	2.0	0.9
Svenska Handelsbanken Skattefondförvaltning AB (private share saving fund)	450,000	1.5	0.6
Fidelity Investments, FMR Corporation, Boston, Massachusetts	3,533,550	1.2	4.6
Säfvain AB (investment company)	351,500	1.1	0.5
The Swedish Cooperative Union and Wholesale Society	338,000	1.1	0.4

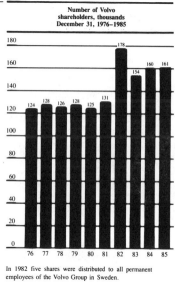

Number of Volvo shareholders, thousands December 31, 1976–1985

In 1982 five shares were distributed to all permanent employees of the Volvo Group in Sweden.

Distribution of shares, December 31, 1985
Based primarily on data supplied by Vardepapperscentralen VPC AB (Swedish Securities Register Center)

	Number of shareholders	Percent of all shareholders	Total shares owned in size class	Percent of total shares	Average shares held
Volvo shareholders owning:					
1– 100 shares	104,300	64.7	3,367,400	4.3	32
101– 500 shares	45,000	27.9	10,008,200	12.9	223
501– 1,000 shares	7,000	4.4	5,239,400	6.8	744
1,001– 10,000 shares	4,600	2.8	10,395,800	13.4	2,286
10,001– 50,000 shares	257	0.2	5,446,700	7.0	21,193
50,001–100,000 shares	39	0.0	2,709,300	3.5	69,470
100,001– shares	68	0.0	40,418,100	52.1	594,384
Share coupon and bonus issue certificates not yet exchanged, approximate			20,100		
Total	161,300	100.0	77,605,009	100.0	481

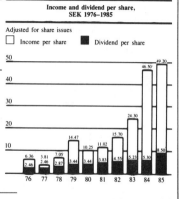

Income and dividend per share, SEK 1976–1985

Adjusted for share issues

☐ Income per share   ■ Dividend per share

EXHIBIT 28.7 **Selected financial data on the Volvo Group, 1981–1985**

Condensed consolidated statements of income

	1981	1982	1983	1984	1985
			(in SEK millions)		
Sales	48,017	75,624	99,460	87,052	86,196
Operating income	1,966	3,335	4,502	6,628	6,475
Foreign exchange gain (loss)	(246)	(721)	(226)	(551)	759
Other financial income (expense)	(295)	(369)	(331)	387	531
Income after financial income (expense)	1,425	2,245	3,945	6,464	7,765
Extraordinary income (expense)	—	235	—	1,363	—
Provision for employee bonus	—	(40)	(166)	(180)	(163)
Income before allocations, taxes and minority interests	1,425	2,440	3,779	7,647	7,602
Allocations to untaxed reserves	704	1,348	2,981	4,384	3,330
Taxes	222	508	752	1,624	1,713
Minority interests in (income) losses	(46)	(88)	158	(74)	(13)
Net income	453	496	204	1,565	2,546
Income per share, SEK	11.00	15.70	24.30	46.50	49.20

Condensed consolidated balance sheets

	1981	1982	1983	1984	1985
Cash in banks and temporary investments	5,476	7,250	11,625	11,900	14,394
Receivables and inventories	20,126	24,869	26,121	28,727	27,288
Restricted deposits in Bank of Sweden	208	221	264	1,762	2,823
Other assets	10,835	13,935	15,496	15,240	18,288
Total assets	36,645	46,275	53,506	57,629	62,793
Current liabilities	17,388	21,484	26,631	26,066	26,856
Long-term liabilities	8,535	10,904	9,706	9,005	9,285
Untaxed reserves	6,458	7,846	10,832	14,973	17,738
Minority interests	451	732	757	229	116
Shareholders' equity	3,813	5,309	5,580	7,356	8,798
Total liabilities and shareholders' equity	36,645	46,275	53,506	57,629	62,793
Capital expenditures	2,514	2,346	2,397	2,589	3,506
Research and development expenses	1,617	2,002	2,508	3,304	3,817
Number of employees, year-end	76,085	75,136	76,206	68,586	67,857
Wages, salaries and social costs	7,547	9,021	10,348	10,509	11,359
Share capital	1,394	1,698	1,735	1,940	1,940
Dividends to shareholders	251[1]	340	399	411	660[2]
Dividend per share, SEK	3.88	4.55	5.23	5.30	8.50[2]

EXHIBIT 28.8 Statements of changes in financial position: AB Volvo, 1984–1985

	1984		1985	
	(In SEK millions)			
Operations				
Net income..........................	999		961	
Depreciation.......................	30		48	
Allocations........................	499		(393)	
Increase in restricted deposits in Bank of Sweden.......................	(195)		(1,978)	
Funds provided by year's operations ..	1,333		(1,362)	
Changes in working capital components Decrease (increase) in current assets:				
Receivables, etc.	(3,646)		3,274	
Inventories	(161)		(203)	
Increase (decrease) in current operating liabilities:				
Accounts payable	(480)		23	
Advances from customers	—		51	
Amounts due to subsidiaries	2,809		923	
Other current liabilities............	(97)	(1,575)	73	4,141
Net financing from year's operations......................		(242)		2,779
Investments (increase)				
Investments in shares and participations—net	(316)		(2,992)	
Property, plant and equipment—net ...	(124)		(131)	
Long-term receivables—net..........	652	212	(576)	(3,699)
Net after investments		(30)		(920)
External financing, dividends, etc.				
Increase in short-term bank loans and other loans	531		199	
Increase in long-term liabilities.......	99		1,162	
Share issue	237			
Group contribution	1,895		2,323	
Transfers of assets and liabilities to Group companies	320		(278)	
Dividends paid.....................	(399)	2,683	(411)	2,995
Increase in cash in banks and temporary investments...........		2,653		2,075

EXHIBIT 28.9 **AB Volvo statements of income, 1984–1985**

	1984		1985	
	(In SEK millions)			
Sales.....................................	4,737		5,504	
Costs and expenses				
Cost of sales........................	3,858		4,394	
Selling, general and administrative				
expenses	692	4,550	874	5,268
Depreciation		30		48
Operating income		157		188
Financial income (expense)				
Dividends received..................	872		703	
Gain on sale of securities	10		64	
Interest income.....................	767		1,049	
Interest expense	1,038		1,392	
Foreign exchange gain (loss)	(319)	292	340	764
Income after financial income (expense) ..		449		952
Extraordinary income (expense)		1,101		(60)
Provision for employee bonus		(9)		(7)
Income before allocations and taxes......		1,541		885
Allocations		(499)		393
Income before taxes		1,042		1,278
Taxes.................................		43		317
Net income		999		961

EXHIBIT 28.10 **Statements of changes in consolidated financial position AB Volvo, 1984–1985**

	1984		1985	
	(In SEK millions)			
Operations				
Net income........................	1,565		2,546	
Depreciation and amortization	1,402		1,725	
Allocations to untaxed reserves.......	4,384		3,330	
Increase in restricted deposits in Bank				
of Sweden......................	(1,498)		(1,061)	
Funds provided by year's operations ..	5,853		6,540	
Changes in working capital				
components				
Decrease (increase) in current assets:				
Receivables, etc.	(2,559)		2,021	
Inventories	(47)		(582)	
Increase (decrease) in current				
operating liabilities:				
Accounts payable	410		(170)	
Advances from customers	(37)		9	
Other current liabilities............	47	(2,186)	513	1,791

Net financing from year's operations.......................		3,667		8,331
Investments (increase)				
Investments in shares and participations—net	(2,215)		(1,485)	
Property, plant and equipment, etc:				
Capital expenditures..............	(2,589)		(3,506)	
Disposals	348		228	
Acquisitions and sales of companies	2,934		(233)	
Long-term receivables and loans—net	457	(1,065)	4	(4,992)
Remaining after net investments		2,602		3,339
External financing, dividends, etc.				
Increase (decrease) in short-term bank loans and other loans	(985)		438	
Increase (decrease) in long-term liabilities.......................	(701)		280	
Share issue	237		—	
Decrease in minority interests	(528)		(113)	
Changes in composition of group, translation differences, etc..........	49		(1,039)	
Dividends paid....................	(399)	(2,327)	(411)	(845)
Increase in cash in banks and temporary investments...........		275		2,494

EXHIBIT 28.11 **Consolidate balance sheets: AB Volvo, 1984–1985**

	December 31, 1984		December 31, 1985	
	(In SEK millions)			
Assets				
Current assets				
Cash in banks	5,713		4,202	
Temporary investments	6,187		10,192	
Receivables, etc.	13,265		11,244	
Inventories	15,462	40,627	16,044	41,682
Restricted deposits in Bank of Sweden		1,762		2,823
Other assets				
Property, plant and equipment— net	8,199		9,565	
Investments	5,409		6,894	
Long-term receivables and loans ...	1,213		1,209	
Intangible assets	419	15,240	620	18,288
Total assets		57,629		62,793
Liabilities and shareholders' equity				
Current liabilities				
Accounts payable	6,510		6,340	
Advances from customers	1,015		1,024	
Bank loans	6,074		6,595	
Other loans.....................	3,757		3,674	
Other current liabilities...........	8,710	26,066	9,223	26,856
Long-term liabilities				
Notes and mortgages payable	4,566		4,032	
Bond loans	1,871		2,710	
Subordinated loans	673		677	
Provision for pensions	1,895	9,005	1,866	9,285
Untaxed reserves		14,973		17,738
Minority interests		229		116
Shareholders' equity				
Restricted equity				
Share capital	1,940		1,940	
Reserves	2,854		2,585	
	4,794		4,525	
Unrestricted equity				
Retained earnings	997		1,727	
Net income for year	1,565		2,546	
	2,562		4,273	
Total shareholders' equity		7,356		8,798
Total liabilities and shareholders' equity		57,629		62,793

EXHIBIT 28.12 Consolidate income statements: AB Volvo, 1984–1985
(In SEK millions except per share amounts)

	1984		1985	
Sales		87,052		86,196
Costs and expenses				
Cost of sales...................	72,062		70,388	
Selling, general and administrative expenses	6,960	79,022	7,608	77,996
Depreciation and amortization		1,402		1,725
Operating income		6,628		6,475
Financial income (expense)				
Dividends received	42		113	
Gain (loss) on sale of securities— net	96		(3)	
Interest income.................	2,052		2,223	
Interest expense	1,803		1,802	
Foreign exchange gain (loss)	(551)	(164)	759	1,290
Income after financial income (expense).....................		6,464		7,765
Extraordinary income (expense)		1,363		—
Provision for employee bonus		(180)		(163)
Income before allocations, taxes and minority interests		7,647		7,602
Allocations to untaxed reserves.....		(4,384)		(3,330)
Income before taxes and minority interests.....................		3,263		4,272
Taxes..........................		1,624		1,713
Minority interests................		(74)		(13)
Net income		1,565		2,546

CASE 29 ━━━━━━━━━━━━━━━━━━━━━━━━━━━━━━━━━━━━━━━

The Army and Air Force Exchange Service: A New Era

In 1986, the Army and Air Force Exchange Service (AAFES) was one of the largest retailers in the United States with sales of over $5.2 billion. However, the 1980s had brought increased competition in retailing both in the United States and worldwide. Additionally, there were pressures to increase AAFES' support of the military's Morale, Welfare, and Recreation (MWR) programs. Currently, 50 percent of the AAFES proceeds were used to support MWR programs. General Long, commander of AAFES, believed that some fundamental changes in the Exchange Service were required if it was to continue to be successful into the 1990s. With the widespread availability of low-priced merchandise across the United States, the competitive advantages of the Exchange Service had diminished.

The Army and Air Force Exchange Service—a worldwide retail, food, and service organization—was developed to benefit the men and women in the Armed Forces of the United States. The primary mission was to provide authorized patrons with merchandise and services of necessity and convenience at low prices. The secondary mission was to support the Morale, Welfare, and Recreation programs of the Army and Air Force. The stated objectives of AAFES that support the mission are presented in Exhibit 29.1.

EVOLUTION OF THE EXCHANGE SERVICE

Prior to 1880, traders literally followed the troops in order to sell goods to the soldiers. During the 1880s, the War Department contracted with specific traders to operate stores on the Army posts. Everything from clothing to kitchenware was sold. Because many Army posts were located far from major trading centers, traders often would sell low-quality goods at high prices. As a result, in 1889 the War Department authorized the establishment of Post Canteens that were operated under the direction of each post commander. These canteens were a combination men's club and retail store. Canteens were self-supporting, with profits going into a general post welfare fund.

In 1895, General Order No. 46 established Post Exchanges—the beginning of the modern exchange service. The name change from "canteen" to "exchange"

This case was prepared by Peter M. Ginter, Linda E. Swayne, and Tana J. Bisch. It is intended as a basis for classroom discussion rather than to illustrate effective or ineffective handling of an administrative situation. Used by permission from Peter M. Ginter.

EXHIBIT 29.1 **Objectives of AAFES**

1. To provide customers with more modern facilities comparable to what is now provided in the U.S. economy including building new facilities or renovation of existing facilities with the addition of more elaborate displays, lighting, and color schemes.
2. To develop a more clearly defined image to enhance customer and employee loyalty.
3. To provide higher quality and more specialized merchandise to meet customer demand.
4. To seek more aggressive marketing techniques.
5. To continue to generate sufficient earnings to support military MWR programs and activities.

Source: AAFES Strategic Plans & Policy Branch, AAFES Master Plan 1987, Dallas, Texas, March 26, 1986.

---

indicated the increasing retail emphasis of the system. Early exchanges operated independently. There were no standard policies or prices, and each funded its own activities. This arrangement worked well for a small domestic army but was inadequate for the 2.4 million troops that went overseas in 1918.

In 1919, a study of the exchange system indicated a lack of quality control and standard procedures. It suggested that exchanges were unprepared for modern war, but it wasn't until 1941 that the Army Exchange Service (the forerunner to AAFES), was established. It was placed within the Morale Branch of the War Department which provided broad policy guidance for operation of the exchanges.

AAFES was officially established in 1948. The Defense Department decreed that exchanges could make a small profit, a portion of which would be used to help support the military's MWR programs. In the 1950s and early 1960s, the Exchange Service was centralized and modernized. AAFES finances were consolidated enabling the profits of larger exchanges to be used to help support smaller exchanges. In addition, Congress allowed the Exchange Service to build new facilities with some of the profits instead of relying on military buildings. These new, more pleasant surroundings helped to stimulate business. In the 1960s, AAFES set up a centralized buying operation. Centralized buying helped not only to lower prices, but also to improve quality.

Operations in the 1980s

In the mid-1980s, AAFES operated in the United States and in more than twenty foreign countries as a military command under joint directives of the U.S. Army and Air Force. Modern military exchanges were similar to community shopping centers and normally included retail stores, cafeterias, snack bars, theaters, service stations, vending, personal service activities (such as laundry and dry cleaning, barber/beauty shops, photography services), concessions, and a wide variety of other activities (approximately 16,000 activities). Exhibit 29.2 provides a list of the service categories offered by AAFES.

EXHIBIT 29.2 **AAFES services**

---

1. Retail—Includes automotive equipment, jewelry, clothing, household goods, small appliances, toiletries, sporting goods, luggage, video, audio and photo equipment, computers, toys, and automobiles.
2. Food and beverage establishments—Includes snack bars, cafeterias, and ice cream parlors.
3. Theaters.
4. Military clothing.
5. Vending centers.
6. Personal services—Includes photo developing, beauty/barber shops, optical, floral, laundry/dry cleaning, fuel stations, and bakeries.

Source: HQ AAFES Public Affairs Division, AAFES-Overview Briefing, Dallas, Texas, 1986.

Fifty percent of all AAFES proceeds (profits) were turned over to military MWR activities ($114.5 million in 1986, a 32 percent increase over 1985). These funds were used by the Army and Air Force for libraries, gyms, hobby shops, child development centers, and athletic equipment. Exhibit 29.3 presents a list of MWR activities funded by the exchanges. The remainder of the earnings were retained by AAFES to build new exchanges and renovate existing facilities.

EXHIBIT 29.3 **Morale, Welfare, and Recreation (MWR) programs**

---

1. Retail—Sporting goods, video, audio and photo equipment, and computers.
2. Travel-related services (such as campgrounds, etc., not travel agencies).
3. Bowling centers.
4. Child care centers/teen centers.
5. Food and beverage establishments.
6. Libraries.
7. Recreation areas/gyms/tennis/golf.
8. Hobby shops.
9. Auditoriums.

Source: HQ AAFES Public Affairs Division, AAFES-Overview Briefing, Dallas, Texas, 1986.

A NEW RETAILING ERA

As General Long pondered the past evolution of the Exchange Service, he realized that further changes, maybe dramatic, would be required if AAFES was to continue to successfully fulfill its mission. There were clear indications that a rethinking of the marketing strategy was required.

The AAFES Commander was acutely aware that competition within the retail industry had become intense as more civilian stores offered discounted merchandise. These retail stores were direct competitors, resulting in leveling sales and reduced margins for AAFES.

In addition, Army and Air Force MWR programs and activities relied heavily on congressionally appropriated funds for their existence. For the past few years, these funds had been gradually reduced. The Commander believed that further reductions were a strong possibility, at least through 1991. Moreover, Congress was interested in reorganizing MWR activities under the direct command of AAFES. If a decision was made to place all MWR activities under the AAFES command, there would be additional pressures for the Exchange Service to support all MWR activities.

While past strategies were designed to meet the objective of providing the customers with more modern facilities (Exhibit 29.1), the commander wondered if AAFES should be placing greater emphasis on a different objective—to seek more aggressive marketing techniques. He wondered how AAFES could continue to aggressively renovate and build new facilities yet still provide sufficient support for MWR activities.

MARKETING

AAFES defined marketing as the process by which the demand for goods and services is anticipated and satisfied through the procurement, physical distribution, and sales of such goods and services. Marketing within AAFES consisted of the following programs:

1. **Sales Management Program**. This program developed the skills and resources to identify customer needs and planned the marketing of products and services to meet those needs.
2. **Merchandise Management Program**. This program provided information and policies that established the best merchandise mix to satisfy customer needs at the lowest possible price.
3. **Point of Sale Program**. This program used electronic cash registers to capture accurate, timely sales and markdown transactions for management analysis.[1]

Product

A military exchange is similar to a civilian hyperstore—a great variety of goods in one huge store. Merchandise consisted of items traditionally found in department stores (clothing, shoes, furniture, etc.), drug stores (over-the-counter drugs, pre-

[1]AAFES Strategic Plans & Policy Branch, AAFES Master Plan FY84–Fy88, Dallas, Texas, December 23, 1982.

scriptions, cosmetics, etc.), food stores, hardware stores, and garden shops. AAFES also offered a complete line of personal services (i.e., fast food, film processing, beauty/barber shops, etc.). The goal was to provide the convenience of one-stop shopping.

Service was one area of AAFES' marketing strategy that had received considerable emphasis. The AAFES' command believed that by enhancing services, customer loyalty would increase. As a result, AAFES maintained a mail order catalog, check cashing services, deferred payment plans, a liberal refund and adjustment policy, and major credit card purchase options (VISA, Mastercard, and Discover cards). In addition, all levels of management were encouraged to get personally involved in exchange operations. New items were introduced faster—from Reebok athletic shoes to Tandy (Radio Shack) computers. AAFES attempted to get new products on the shelves ahead of other retailers and prior to national advertising.

Some products, such as sporting goods, clothing, video, audio and photo equipment, and food and beverages were sold within the MWR program. For these type products, MWR was directly competing for the same customer, yet AAFES had to generate sufficient profit to support the MWR operations. Thus, AAFES often had to charge higher prices for the same products.

In order to insure quality products, AAFES developed an excellent quality assurance program. Merchandise was subjected to stringent inspection and laboratory tests. Through this program, AAFES' customers received high-quality merchandise within the price lines. In addition, AAFES conducted a vigorous consumer product safety program to detect, prevent, and respond to potential product hazards.

One major difference between AAFES and other large retail operations was that AAFES had shorter operating hours. Most AAFES facilities closed at 6:00 p.m. whereas other large retail operations were typically open till 9:00 p.m. or longer, and some stores operated 24 hours per day.

Another profitable operation for AAFES was franchises (including 102 Burger Kings worldwide, one Pizza Inn, and one Popeye's Chicken franchise). The major benefits of the franchised operations were name recognition and standardized methods and procedures. AAFES would build the free-standing unit on the military installation and manage the outlet as if it were any other franchised Burger King. AAFES hired operating labor and received all income after expenses (including the Burger King franchise fee). Income from franchised operations had been increasing at a rate of 7 percent per year for the past five years. Many exchange managers believed that developing more franchised operations would be a way to offer AAFES customers additional products and services without incurring additional operating costs.

Price

The key marketing element within AAFES was price. AAFES' overall goal was to save customers 20 percent on comparable products sold in the civilian sector. The AAFES pricing policy was considered a form of compensation to military families.

By providing savings to the customer, the military member's monthly pay was in effect increased.

Before a supplier can sell to the government (exchanges are included), the company must be evaluated and earn a place on the "approved supplier" list. Only then can the company bid on government contracts. The bidding process assures lowest-cost contracts for Exchange customers. Companies are willing to make low bids because AAFES represents a large piece of business. Thus AAFES had the advantage of low costs, plus maintained low profitability margins in order to provide low prices on all products and services.

In order to monitor the goal of 20 percent average savings, AAFES contracted with A. C. Nielsen Company to conduct annual price-comparison surveys. Prices of three hundred brandname products at the Exchange were compared with the same items at stores in the local community. More than 25,000 price comparisons were made throughout the Exchange Service. The surveys were used for analysis by AAFES to review pricing for areas not reaching the 20 percent goal. In 1986, AAFES did not meet the overall goal of 20 percent savings because of increased competition from retail discounters. Exhibit 29.4 presents the results of the Nielsen savings survey for 1986. The survey showed that AAFES provided 20 percent or more savings to the customer over other commercial retailers on many, but not all, of the items surveyed.

EXHIBIT 29.4 **AAFES savings survey—1986**

Department	Savings (In percent)
Automotive	13
Tobacco	16
Food and beverages	2
Toiletries	13
Jewelry	23
Stationary	27
Clothing	20
Household	17
Sundries	13

Source: HQ AAFES Public Affairs Division, AAFES-Overview Briefing, Dallas, Texas, 1986.

Promotion

Promotion within the retail industry often consists of multipage advertisements in local newspapers, television, and radio advertising. However AAFES, by regulation, was not allowed to use mass media advertising. Instead AAFES has relied upon word-of-mouth, post/base circulars, and the post/base newsletter or newspaper.

EXHIBIT 29.5 **AAFES logo**

In the mid-1980s, AAFES began a program to increase customer awareness among military personnel concerning the services available at the exchange by publicizing the AAFES story. This program consisted of seminars, briefings, and pamphlet distribution. Direct mail to military personnel was also utilized to expand the customers utilizing the exchange.

During this time, AAFES also became more concerned about its image. New logos, colors, packaging, signage, and advertising were being considered which would be more easily recognized and unique to AAFES (see Exhibit 29.5 for the current AAFES logo). It was hoped that changing merchandise displays, lighting, and the utilization of product demonstrations on a regular basis would create greater shopping interest. To increase customer shopping frequency, AAFES used market representatives, mall displays, and local sports and television personalities to assist in promoting its products and services. AAFES also promoted "Made in USA" merchandise and developed a direct mail program targeted at retirees, reservists and National Guardsmen.

Distribution

AAFES operated on a worldwide scale with command headquarters in Dallas, Texas (CONUS), and two overseas subordinate commands (AAFES-Europe and AAFES-Pacific). Another major element of AAFES was catalog sales. In 1986, CONUS made up approximately 58 percent of total sales, while, AAFES-Europe comprised about 28 percent, AAFES-Pacific about 13 percent, and catalog sales about 1 percent.

Within the United States, there were five Exchange regions—the West, Southwest, Midwest, Northeast, and Southeast. Each region was divided into four to five areas headed by a general manager who directed operations. Each area was made up of four to nine military installations where the exchange manager was the senior official. The exchange manager was responsible for all exchange activities at the installation. A map of the Exchange Service in the United States is shown in Exhibit 29.6.

EXHIBIT 29.6 **U.S. Exchange System**

In the mid-1980s AAFES began a $183 million program that was designed to provide an integrated, flexible, and centrally controlled distribution system. The development program was undertaken to consolidate and upgrade existing distribution facilities and create a major new centralized distribution facility on the East Coast. Interacting data systems were to be developed to maintain timely and comprehensive information to support merchandising, inventory control, physical distribution, accounting, and sales management. Information would be maintained that would allow for the identification of the most cost-effective combinations of freight and handling costs.

The distribution development program goal was to enable AAFES to maintain the proper level and mix of stock and ensure that merchandise was available to the customers when they needed it through the most cost efficient channel. AAFES, in the past, had nagging problems with stock-outs, and distribution costs were high. The program was expected to be completely operational by 1990.

Exchanges operate only on military posts and bases in the United States and abroad. Within the military installation, the exchange may be a free-standing building centrally located or located "away from the congestion" or located in whatever makeshift space was available. In the 1980s, appropriated funds were no longer available to AAFES for construction of new exchanges. Thus, facility construction was limited to upgrading only those facilities badly needing improvements.

The AAFES Consumer Profile

In order to fulfill its mission, AAFES must satisfy a broad range of customer interests. AAFES has served approximately seven million customers per year. The composition of these customers is presented in Exhibit 29.7. Military dependents (family members) constituted the largest single customer group. The support of military dependents has brought considerable change in merchandise and services offered by AAFES.

Rank and age were also important demographic characteristics of AAFES customers. Over 80 percent of AAFES customers were enlisted personnel, earning

---

EXHIBIT 29.7 **Composition of AAFES customers**

Customers	Number (In millions)
Active-duty military personnel	1.4
Military reservists	1.0
Military retirees	0.9
Military dependents (family members)	3.8
Total	7.1

Source: AAFES Commander, AAFES & You, Pamphlet, Dallas, Texas, May 1982.

relatively low salaries. Basic pay and allowances by rank, as shown in Exhibit 29.8, indicated the wide variation in income for exchange customers.

The average age of AAFES customers is 26 years; 52 percent were married and had an average of two children. For the most part, these customers desired "value" items such as household goods, recreational merchandise, infant and children's clothing, adult fashions, and sportswear—all at low prices. At the same time, AAFES must serve the needs of the officers and their families who may want higher-quality items.[2] AAFES' mission is to serve *all* its customers which means that merchandise and service must attempt to satisfy a broad range of interests.

The most recently available broad-based analysis of customer opinion was a 1979 AAFES survey of active duty military personnel. The results of this survey are presented in Exhibit 29.9. The two main improvements customers recommended were lower prices and greater clothing selection, including more budget clothing. Surprisingly, larger stores and newer facilities were not recommended.

OPERATIONS

Fiscal year 1985 was disappointing for AAFES. Although sales increased one percent over 1984, net earnings were down 28 percent from the prior year. Competition from civilian stores was keen as there was aggressive expansion by many large retail chains. Exhibit 29.10 provides a list of the major U.S. retailers and the percentage change in sales from 1985 to 1986. These retailers represent the primary U.S. competition for AAFES.

Increased competition resulted in numerous discounts and early markdowns by military exchanges. As a result, AAFES exceeded its planned markdowns by $15 million in 1985. Sales and markdowns meant added savings for the AAFES customer but significantly reduced net earnings. In addition, the strong dollar overseas in early 1985 encouraged customers stationed at foreign posts to shop in the local community.[3]

AAFES sales increased over 5 percent to $5.2 billion in 1986 and net earnings increased about 34 percent to approximately $229 million. Retail sales (excluding gasoline) increased 7 percent while gasoline sales were down 20 percent from the previous year. Food sales showed strong growth of 19 percent primarily due to the increase of Burger King facilities. Service sales increased by 8 percent, while overall vending sales declined 2 percent. Reduced markdowns, 4 percent below 1985, and greater acceptance of AAFES-branded products impacted favorably on gross profit. Operating expenses increased 12 percent over the previous year due to the expansion of Burger King and implementation of credit. While operating expenses overseas were hurt by the weaker dollar, the relatively weak dollar helped to bring customers

[2]HQ AAFES Public Affairs Division, AAFES-Overview Briefing, Dallas, Texas, 1986.

[3]Alexander, Conners, Exchange Manager, AAFES-Weisbaden, Germany, Interview.

EXHIBIT 29.8 **Air Force monthly pay and allowances by pay grade and years of service—January 1, 1987**

Pay grade	Under 2	2	3	4	6	8	10	12	14	16	18	20	22	26
Commissioned officers														
O-10	5378.10	5567.70	5567.70	5567.70	5567.70	5781.00	5781.00	5900.10	5900.10	5900.10	5900.10	5900.10	5900.10	5900.10
O-9	4766.70	4891.50	4995.60	4995.60	4995.60	5122.50	5122.50	5335.80	5335.80	5781.00	5900.10	5900.10	5900.10	5900.10
O-8	4317.30	4446.60	4552.20	4552.20	4552.20	4891.50	4891.50	5122.50	5122.50	5335.80	5567.70	5781.00	5900.10	5900.10
O-7	3587.40	3831.30	3831.30	3831.30	3831.30	4002.90	4235.10	4235.10	4446.60	4891.50	5227.80	5227.80	5227.80	5227.80
O-6	2658.90	2921.40	3112.50	3112.50	3112.50	3112.50	3112.50	3112.50	3218.10	3727.20	3917.70	4002.90	4235.10	4593.30
O-5	2126.40	2497.20	2669.70	2669.70	2669.70	2669.70	2750.70	2898.30	3092.70	3224.00	3514.80	3621.30	3747.60	3747.60
O-4	1792.50	2182.80	2328.30	2328.30	2371.50	2476.20	2645.10	2793.90	2921.40	3049.50	3133.80	3133.80	3133.80	3133.80
O-3	1665.90	1862.40	1990.80	2202.90	2308.20	2391.30	2520.60	2645.10	2710.20	2710.20	2710.20	2710.20	2710.20	2710.20
O-2	1452.60	1586.40	1905.60	1905.60	1969.80	2011.20	2011.20	2011.20	2011.20	2011.20	2011.20	2011.20	2011.20	2011.20
O-1	1260.90	1312.80	1586.40	1586.40	1586.40	1586.40	1586.40	1586.40	1586.40	1586.40	1586.40	1586.40	1586.40	1586.40
Commissioned officers with more than 4 years active duty as enlisted or warrant officer														
O-3E	0.00	0.00	0.00	2202.90	2308.20	2391.30	2520.60	2645.10	2750.70	2750.70	2750.70	2750.70	2750.70	2750.70
O-2E	0.00	0.00	0.00	1969.80	2011.20	2074.80	2182.80	2266.20	2328.30	2328.30	2328.30	2328.30	2328.30	2328.30
O-1E	0.00	0.00	0.00	1586.40	1694.70	1757.10	1820.70	1884.00	1969.80	1969.80	1969.80	1969.80	1969.80	1969.80
Enlisted members														
E-9	0.00	0.00	0.00	0.00	0.00	0.00	1974.00	2018.70	2064.30	2111.70	2158.80	2200.80	2316.60	2541.90
E-8	0.00	0.00	0.00	0.00	0.00	1655.70	1702.80	1747.50	1793.10	1840.20	1882.80	1929.00	2042.40	2270.10
E-7	1155.90	1247.70	1294.20	1339.20	1385.10	1429.20	1474.80	1520.70	1589.40	1634.70	1660.30	1702.20	1816.50	2042.40
E-6	994.50	1083.90	1129.20	1177.20	1221.00	1265.40	1311.90	1379.40	1422.60	1468.50	1491.00	1491.00	1491.00	1491.00
E-5	872.70	950.10	996.00	1039.50	1107.60	1152.60	1198.50	1242.60	1265.40	1265.40	1265.40	1265.40	1265.40	1265.40
E-4	814.20	859.50	909.90	980.70	1019.40	1019.40	1019.40	1019.40	1019.40	1019.40	1019.40	1019.40	1019.40	1019.40
E-3	766.80	808.80	841.50	874.80	874.80	874.80	874.80	874.80	874.80	874.80	874.80	874.80	874.80	874.80
E-2	738.00	738.00	738.00	738.00	738.00	738.00	738.00	738.00	738.00	738.00	738.00	738.00	738.00	738.00
E-1	658.20	658.20	658.20	658.20	658.20	658.20	658.20	658.20	658.20	658.20	658.20	658.20	658.20	658.20
E-1 with less than 4 months—590.70	608.40	608.40	608.40	608.40	608.40	608.40	608.40	608.40	608.40	608.40	608.40	608.40	608.40	608.40

Note—Monthly pay limited to $5900.10 by Level V of the Executive Schedule

Basic allowance for subsistence

Officers (including commissioned officers, warrants and aviation cadets) — $112.65 per month

Enlisteds	**E-1 —4mos.**	**All others**
When rations in kind are not available	$5.61	$6.07
When on leave or granted permission to mess separately	4.96	5.37
When assigned under emergency conditions where no government messing is available	7.43	8.03

Pay grade	Monthly basic allowance for quarters Without Dependents		With Dependents
	Full	**Partial**	
O-10	$570.00	$50.70	$701.10
O-9	570.00	50.70	701.10
O-8	570.00	50.70	701.10
O-7	570.00	50.70	701.10
O-6	523.20	39.60	636.00
O-5	493.80	33.00	585.90
O-4	452.70	26.70	535.50
O-3	366.60	22.20	446.40
O-2	295.20	17.70	382.60
O-1	253.20	13.20	343.20
E-9	334.50	18.60	456.00
E-8	309.90	15.30	424.80
E-7	264.60	12.00	395.10
E-6	234.90	9.90	358.50
E-5	217.20	8.70	318.50
E-4	188.40	8.10	275.40
E-3	183.00	7.80	253.20
E-2	155.40	7.20	253.20
E-1	141.60	6.90	253.20

EXHIBIT 29.9 **Survey of customer satisfaction**

	Satisfied	Dissatisfied
Variety/selection		X
Quality of merchandise	X	
Prices		X
Up-to-date stock		X
Ease of finding items	X	
Meets needs of enlisted personnel		X

Source: AAFES Strategic Plans & Policy Branch, AAFES Master Plan FY84-FY88, Dallas, Texas, December 23, 1982.

EXHIBIT 29.10 **Major U.S. retailing companies by sales**

Company	1986 sales (In millions)	Percent change from 1985
Sears, Roebuck	$44,281	9
K-Mart	23,812	8
Kroger	17,123	7
J. C. Penney	14,740	7
American Stores	14,021	1
Wal-Mart Stores	11,909	41
Federated Department Stores	10,512	5
May Department Stores	10,328	9
Dayton Hudson	9,259	12
Southland	8,620	0
Winn-Dixie Stores	8,580	7
A & P	7,072	10
F. W. Woolworth	6,501	9
Lucky Stores	6,441	3
Supermarkets General	5,508	11
Albertson's	5,380	6
Zayre	5,351	33
Melville	5,262	10
Wickes	4,770	70
Carter Hawley Hale Stores	4,090	3

Source: Business Week, April 17, 1987.

---

back to the military exchanges and helped earnings. A five-year financial summary for AAFES is presented in Exhibit 29.11.

Financial Projections

AAFES financial projections for 1987 through 1991 were optimistic. Sales were forecasted to increase 4 percent per year, net earnings were forecasted to increase an average of 7 percent per year, and expenses to increase 3 percent per year. However,

---

EXHIBIT 29.11 **AAFES five-year financial summary (In millions of dollars)**

	FY 82	FY 83	FY 84	FY 85	FY 86
Direct sales	$4,264.0	$4,386.0	$4,470.1	$4,484.8	$4,717.4
Concession sales	354.7	383.9	411.0	433.2	469.4
Combined sales	$4,618.6	$4,769.9	$4,881.1	$4,918.0	$5,186.8
Gross profit	$1,010.6	$1,050.1	$1,047.9	$1,080.4	$1,254.0
Concession and other income	94.0	96.6	131.8*	118.3	127.3
Selling, general and administrative expense	901.7	925.8	943.4	1,027.6	1,152.4
Net earnings	$ 202.9	$ 220.9	$ 236.3*	$ 171.1	$ 228.9
Dividends	$ 103.0	$ 111.5	$ 118.2	$ 87.0	$ 114.5
Dividends per service member (Dollar amount)	$ 78.28	$ 84.59	$ 87.71	$ 64.49	$ 84.38
Current assets	$ 990.0	$1,057.2	$1,121.1	$1,163.5	$1,228.7
Current liabilities	461.5	485.1	493.4	494.4	599.8
Working capital	$ 528.6	$ 572.1	$ 627.7	$ 669.0	$ 628.9
Fixed assets (Net)	452.5	489.6	525.0	601.8	712.8
Total assets	1,538.4	1,681.7	1,799.1	1,888.2	2,129.8
Total liabilities	496.6	525.1	529.7	533.3	661.9
Net assets**	$1,041.8	$1,156.6	$1,269.3	$1,354.8	$1,467.9
Ratio of current assets to current liabilities	2.1	2.2	2.3	2.4	2.0
Percent of net earnings to average net assets	20.5	20.1	19.5	13.0	16.2

Arithmetic differences are due to rounding.

*FY 84 Other Income/Net Earnings include $12.0 million extraordinary income.

** A significant amount of the assets of AAFES were originally donated by the U.S. Government. These assets were not placed on the balance sheet and have never been depreciated.

---

the AAFES cash position was projected to weaken through 1990 because of the costs of the distribution program. Exhibit 29.12 shows AAFES financial projections, which were based on corporate objectives, anticipated economic conditions, historical trends, inflation, the value of the U.S. dollar, and the financial benefits associated with implementation of the new distribution system. Exhibit 29.13 shows AAFES capital requirements projections.

MANAGEMENT

AAFES was operated as a military command with a functional organization structure. Exhibit 29.14 presents AAFES' organizational chart. The commander of AAFES was responsible to a Board of Directors established by the Secretaries of the Army and Air Force through the respective Chiefs of Staff. The Board consisted of

EXHIBIT 29.12 Financial operating projections FY 1985–1991 (In millions of dollars)

	Actual FY 85		Estimated FY 86		FY 87		FY 88		Long-range forecast FY 89		FY 90		FY 91	
	$	%	$	%	$	%	$	%	$	%	$	%	$	%
Sales	4,484.8	100.00	4,664.9	100.00	4,921.8	100.00	5,123.6	100.00	5,343.9	100.00	5,584.4	100.00	5,841.3	100.0
Gross profit	1,080.4	24.09	1,239.1	26.56	1,326.1	26.94	1,396.2	27.25	1,464.2	27.40	1,532.9	27.45	1,603.4	27.45
Concession income	76.7	1.71	82.5	1.77	86.9	1.77	90.8	1.77	94.7	1.77	98.8	1.77	103.0	1.76
Other income	41.6	0.93	41.8	0.90	40.0	0.81	41.2	0.80	42.5	0.79	43.8	0.78	45.1	0.77
Total Income	1,198.7	26.73	1,363.4	29.23	1,453.0	29.52	1,528.2	29.83	1,601.4	29.97	1,675.4	30.00	1,751.5	29.98
Personnel costs	755.9	16.86	833.7	17.87	889.8	18.08	927.9	18.11	967.2	18.10	1,008.1	18.05	1,049.6	17.97
Other expenses	188.8	4.21	214.4	4.60	233.6	4.75	242.2	4.73	251.7	4.71	262.0	4.69	273.3	4.68
Depreciation	82.9	1.85	85.9	1.84	96.8	1.97	101.5	1.98	105.2	1.97	109.3	1.96	114.0	1.95
Total Expenses	1,027.6	22.91	1,133.9	24.31	1,220.2	24.79	1,271.7	24.82	1,324.1	24.78	1,379.4	24.70	1,436.9	24.60
Net Earnings	171.1	3.81	229.5	4.92	232.8	4.73	256.6	5.01	277.3	5.19	296.1	5.30	314.6	5.39
ROI (percent earnings/ net assets)	13.04		16.25		15.23		15.54		15.54		15.36		15.12	

*Numbers may not add up due to rounding.

EXHIBIT 29.13 **Capital requirements projection FY 1985–1991 (In millions of dollars)**

	Actual FY 85	EST FY 86	EST FY 87	FY 88	Long-range forecast		
					FY 89	FY 90	FY 91
Part 1: Sources and Applications							
Cash	(41)	(23)	(42)	(31)	(50)	(2)	49
Inventory	895	890	956	978	1,004	1,034	1,068
Net fixed assets	602	724	867	993	1,139	1,218	1,307
Sinking funds	174	189	142	146	151	156	161
DPP/credit	109	111	118	123	129	135	141
Other assets	110	135	141	150	160	170	181
Total Assets	1,849	2,026	2,182	2,359	2,533	2,711	2,907
Vendor accounts payable	301	294	306	319	327	336	347
Employee benefits payable	91	106	109	118	127	137	147
Other liabilities	101	118	151	175	190	199	215
Dividends payable	1	38	29	32	35	37	39
Total Liabilities	494	556	595	644	679	709	748
Capital requirements	1,355	1,470	1,587	1,715	1,854	2,002	2,159
Part 2: Reconciliation of Capital Requirements							
Net assets (Start of year)	1,269	1,355	1,470	1,587	1,715	1,854	2,002
+Earnings	171	230	233	257	277	296	315
−Dividends declared/estimated	85	115	116	128	139	148	157
Net assets (ending)	1,355	1,470	1,587	1,715	1,854	2,002	2,159

*Numbers may not add up due to rounding.

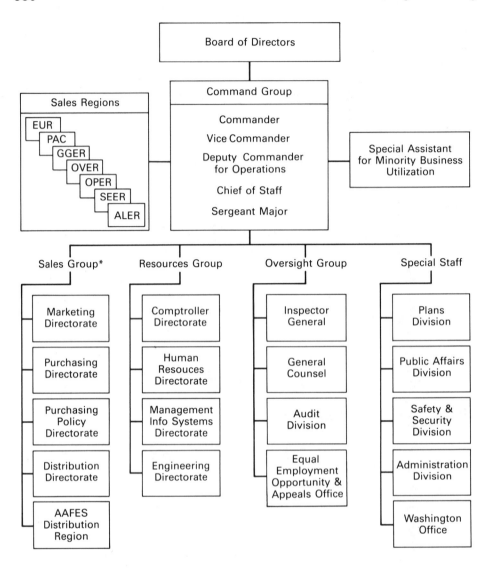

*Sales Group elements report directly to
the Deputy Commander for Operations.

EXHIBIT 29.14 **Army and Air Force Exchange Service organization chart**

seven Army and seven Air Force members plus the AAFES commander. The Board met four times per year and the chairmanship of the board alternated, usually at three-year intervals, between the Comptrollers of the Army and Air Force.

Functions of each organizational group are outlined in Exhibit 29.15. Within each sales region there were typically marketing, accounting and finance, human resources, general counsel, administrative, purchasing and distribution, engineering,

---

EXHIBIT 29.15 **Organizational responsibilities**

Command Group—Directs AAFES organization within the guidelines established by Congress, Department of Defense, and the Army and Air Force. Establishes corporate policy and philosophy.

Special Staff—Responsible for representing the AAFES Commander in the Washington, D.C. area with Congress, Department of Defense, and other governmental and commercial industry representatives. Provides administrative support, responsible for all planning aspects, public affairs programs, safety and security programs.

Oversight Group—Responsible for independent evaluations of the economy, effectiveness and efficiency with which management responsibilities are carried out, EOC program, morale and discipline matters affecting performance, and legal matters.

Resources Group—Responsible for financial management and accounting activities, engineering guidance, personnel and management information systems.

Sales Group—Selecting, purchasing and controlling inventory, equipment and supplies, distribution maintenance, purchasing policies, and marketing functions.

Source: HQ AAFES, AFESR 2–3: Organization & Functions, Dallas, Texas, October 1986.

---

and public affairs departments. Store managers retained responsibility for individual unit operations and were provided flexibility within broad sales policies. Management's primary concern was with providing service and convenience to the military community and sufficient earnings to support MWR programs.

POSITIONING STRATEGY

The AAFES commander believed that some fundamental decisions had to be made to better position AAFES in light of changes that have taken place in the retail industry. Historically, customers perceived AAFES as the most desirable place to shop, eat, and obtain various other services. Competition had been limited and low prices compensated for any shortcomings.

Recently the situation had changed dramatically. Large chains offering convenience, service, and low prices were readily accessible to the customer. Wal-Mart, Target, K-Mart, hyperstores, warehouse clubs, fast-food, and automotive parts discounters were in direct competition with AAFES. Many of the exchange customers no longer believed that AAFES was the only place to shop.

General Long advocated that AAFES was in direct competition with large retail discounters and would have to adopt marketing strategies that were successful in that sector. The Commander reviewed the differences and similarities of AAFES and civilian retail operations. He concluded that the primary difference between AAFES and other large retail operations was twofold. First, AAFES had a limited customer base. Secondly, AAFES operated under direct governmental supervision and must support MWR programs. Most other aspects of the operation seemed very similar to civilian U.S. retail operations. As the Commander pondered these similarities and differences, he thought about the strategies that would be appropriate for AAFES to fulfill its primary and secondary mission. Did AAFES no longer have a role in the compensation of military personnel? How could the exchange be positioned to compete against civilian retail stores? These and other questions needed to be carefully considered before recommendations were made to the AAFES Board.

CASE 30

Humana Inc.

Humana Inc. is an international company that provides an integrated system of health care services that includes hospital care, prepaid health care and indemnity insurance plans, and medical care centers where independent physicians deliver primary medical care. At the end of fiscal 1985, their operations included 86 hospitals, 148 MedFirst clinics, and 359,200 members insured by Humana Care Plus. The company had 43,800 employees with corporate headquarters in Louisville, Kentucky. Its hospitals are primarily situated in the Sunbelt states (see Exhibit 30.1) and were once grouped into five regions, but they have since been condensed to four regions.

Humana Inc. was founded in 1961 by David A. Jones and Wendell Cherry, two young attorneys in Louisville. In the company's infancy the legal name was Extendicare which was derived from the words "extended care" and clearly identified the company's original business—nursing homes. In 1968 the company constructed its first hospital in Huntsville, Alabama. During the next decade the company embarked on major projects of building and acquiring hospitals, owning over 40 by 1977. The nursing homes were sold so that the company's attention and energy could be focused on managing hospitals. The name was changed to Humana in 1974 to reflect the company philosophy in terms of its dedication to humankind's health needs. In 1978, Humana acquired American Medicorp, a multihospital system, which resulted in the company doubling in size and becoming the largest chain of proprietary hospitals.

This case was prepared by Lorraine Justice, Terry Wheeler, and Jeff Totten. It is intended as a basis for classroom discussion rather than to illustrate effective or ineffective handling of an administrative situation. Used with permission from Lorraine Justice.

● Humana Hospitals
▲ Humana MEDFIRST Markets
■ Humana Care Plus Markets

■ ● Anchorage, Alaska
● Geneva, Switzerland
● London, England
● Mexico City, Mexico

EXHIBIT 30.1 **Locations of Humana facilities**

Over the years, Humana has enjoyed financial success (see Exhibit 30.2). This performance was a direct result of acquiring or building new hospitals and selling unprofitable ones. Humana has been listed on the New York Stock Exchange since 1971. From 1972 to 1982, Humana outperformed *Fortune* magazine's top 100 largest diversified service companies. Earnings per share increased 34.6 percent, gaining the company a position in the top four. Humana was number one on this list for total return to investors with an annual average of 36.7 percent. This performance has greatly added to the company's ability to acquire outside capital in an industry where vast amounts of investment capital are needed to finance health care advances. Michael M. LeComey of Merrill Lynch, Pierce, Fenner & Smith stated in the *Wall Street Journal,* "with Humana, investors are dealing with what I believe may be the most aggressive and smartest major company in the United States. That's a lot to say about any company, but Humana's success and the absolutely uncanny accuracy of its corporate strategy make it a supportable statement."

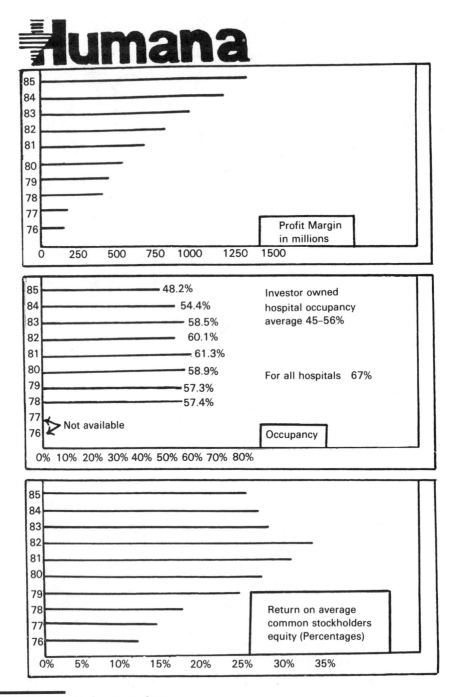

EXHIBIT 30.2 **Performance chart**

MANAGEMENT PHILOSOPHY

The twenty-five year success record of Humana is largely attributed to its management philosophy. In 1981, top-level management recognized the need to explore alternatives in health care delivery at a time when the hospital business was thriving. In the company's 1981 Annual Report, David A. Jones, Chief Executive Officer, said: "The world is turning, the system is evolving, and those who do tomorrow what they did yesterday are likely to be caught short." Now, five years later, health care is in a period of unprecedented change. That foresight in 1981—the early recognition for the need to change—has given Humana an unparalleled opportunity for market leadership. Management's philosophy is to constantly pay close attention to the way the environment is changing so that the company can anticipate the changing needs of customers. Humana is not the same company it was 20 years ago or even one year ago.

MISSION STATEMENT

It is no longer business as usual in the health care industry—public policy is changing; advances in medicine and technology are proliferating; the number of elderly people is multiplying; consumers are demanding increasingly higher quality, lower-cost services; competition within the industry is burgeoning, employers are aggressively managing their health care benefits, and the impetus of overall cost containment and government regulation is throwing added weight behind the push for change.

This convergence of powerful forces creates enormous opportunity for a company that respects the best in traditional health care and is committed to responsive, effective innovation. Within this dynamic environment, Humana's commitment remains clear:

> The mission of Humana is to achieve an unequaled level of measurable quality and productivity in the delivery of health services that are responsive to the needs and values of patients, physicians, employers, and employees.

The company's strategy is threefold: insistence upon excellence and productivity, the creation of an integrated health care system, and exploring new services that address the needs and values of customers.

CURRENT SITUATION

Humana's three divisions include the hospital division, health services division, and group health division. In addition, considerable emphasis was being placed in developing Centers of Excellence and research efforts.

Hospital Division

Humana's 86 hospitals in the hospital division are located in the United States, London, Geneva, and Mexico City. The hospital division's efficient and effective operation provided the earnings that enabled the company to invest in the rapid expansion of the other two divisions. When the company's fiscal year began on September 1, 1984, they were still known primarily as a hospital company. When it ended on August 31, 1985, the company had achieved recognition as an integrated system of health care services.

Health Services Division

Humana MedFirst is the company's health services division. The clinics work with the basic building block of the health care system—the doctor's office. These clinics, totaling 148 at the end of fiscal year 1985, are the nations largest network of primary medical care centers. They offer high quality, affordable care at convenient locations and hours. The private physicians who practice in the offices remain independent owners of the medical practice. Humana supplies the office space, administration, and support services on a contractual basis.

Group Health Division

Humana Care Plus is the group health division product that was formed three years ago in anticipation of government and business initiatives to halt increasing health care costs. The theme of Humana Care Plus is "The health care plans from the health care professionals." This health insurance program for growing companies provides a solution to rising health care costs, a two-year rate guarantee, a choice of plans to meet the employee's needs, freedom to choose the physician, quality hospital care, comprehensive quality and cost management, personal service, and simplified claims processing.

Center of Excellence

A Center of Excellence is Humana's concept of the highest ideals of medicine, i.e., excellence in patient care, medical education, and the search for new knowledge. This concept was introduced in 1982 as a way to encourage and support physicians interested in clinical research and medical education in Humana Hospitals. The centers are referral and consultation centers with state-of-the-art technology, supporting services, and education and research programs that sustain the physicians' and the hospital's reputation for excellence. After a Center of Excellence is designated in a certain specialty, the Humana Institute receives a grant from the Humana Foundation to support research and educational activities. Continued funding is based on the performance of these programs. This major commitment to fund medical education and clinical research for practicing physicians is a pioneering effort for the investor-owned hospital industry. At fiscal year-end (August 31, 1985), the program had grown to 19 centers, representing 12 specialities: pulmonary, diabetes, cardiovascular, neurology, orthopedics, ophthalmology, obstetrics, gynecology, spinal injuries, burn treatment, digestive treatment, and urology.

Research

The recent decline in federal spending on medical research has produced a financial dilemma for scientists, research-oriented doctors, and the nation's academic medical centers. The federal cuts clearly signal the government's unwillingness to shoulder its accustomed medical research burden. This reluctance opened the way to support from successful private health care firms with financial resources and medical facilities sufficient to share the load. Clinical investigation, requiring high-quality hospital care, is a research area in which these firms are beginning to have an impact. Humana's support of clinical investigation of the artificial heart is a notable example of this trend. The totally artificial heart was a research effort caught in a squeeze between the rising costs of hospitalization and a declining level of National Institute of Health (NIH) funding when researchers decided to move the project into the clinical stage in 1982. Dr. William C. DeVries at the University of Utah was the first surgeon to perform a permanent artificial heart implant in a human on December 1-2, 1982. He joined the private practice of Dr. Allan Lansing, Medical Director of the Humana Heart Institute International in Louisville. The research and operations performed by Dr. DeVries at Humana Heart Institute International were the second, third, and fourth in the initial series of seven clinical trials authorized by the Food and Drug Administration. Humana's funding of this program is a reflection of the company's commitment to clinical preeminence, research, and education.

HEALTH CARE INDUSTRY PROBLEMS

Declining Inpatient Business for Hospitals

During the past few years, major changes in American health care have taken place. There has been a nationwide and industrywide decline in the number of people using hospitals as inpatients. People are using outpatient services if possible, in lieu of being admitted to the hospital. This results in the hospital's acuity level dramatically increasing—those who do become inpatients need more services and care. Therefore, the problem is twofold: less patient days to produce revenue and a higher acuity level which requires more sophisticated equipment, technology, and highly trained staff members. Many experts feel that hospital usage peaked in 1975. In 1982, admissions and total inpatients dropped for the first time, despite an aging, highly susceptible population.

The current average occupancy rates for investor-owned hospitals run from a low of 45 percent to a high of 56 percent compared with a 67 percent average for all United States hospitals, also a record low. The American Hospital Association reports that in 1984, hospital admissions dropped 4 percent nationwide. During this time period, only one key indicator increased—hospital-run outpatient clinics. In this critical time for the industry, investor-owned chains are slowing the acquisition and construction of new hospitals.

Competition

Today people want more information, second opinions, and more choices in health care. These factors would stiffen the competition in any industry and certainly have in health care. The days when a hospital is just a hospital are ending. Building blocks for integrated health care systems are being assembled with the four largest investor-owned chains—Hospital Corporation of America, National Medical Enterprises, American Medical International, and Humana—being dominant on the scene. The Big Four have been growing rapidly, making a healthy profit. They own, lease, or manage acute-care hospitals, substance-abuse centers, nursing homes, home health services, and free-standing facilities of all kinds. Over the past two years, they all began marketing health insurance plans. Most have experienced, however, a decline in profits in recent years and the trend seems downward.

The investor-owned hospital chains operating acute care hospitals produce seven billion dollars in revenue annually. Investor-owned competition is greatest in five Sunbelt states where state regulation is the least and population growth is the greatest. Hospitals are also usually situated in the more affluent suburbs; Humana certainly holds true to this. Multihospital systems now comprise 30 percent of the nation's hospitals. This form of ownership is expected to increase to 80 percent by 1995. They have formed bank-like holding companies to control a variety of operations. Other nonprofit facilities have established for-profit subsidiaries to increase revenues and draw greater amounts of capital.

The not-for-profit community hospitals, the not-for-profit hospital coalitions, and other investor-owned chains are major competitors of Humana. The advantages that the investor-owned chains enjoy are management expertise, access to capital, economies of scale in purchasing, sophisticated information systems, and quality assurance programs. They are also invaluable resources for each other.

Other competitors include outpatient surgery centers, urgent care centers, HMOs, and physicians. Some experts estimate that 50 percent of the nation's 20 million surgeries could be done on an outpatient basis. Outpatient surgery centers numbered 330 in 1985 and projections are that there will be over 800 clinics in 1990. Urgent care centers totaled 55 in 1978, 652 in 1982, 1,800 in 1984, and are expected to total 4,975 in 1990 with $3.5 billion in revenues. Health Maintenance Organizations (HMOs) offer prepaid health care at a fixed price from free-standing clinics operated by doctors. Another threat is that Medicare and Medicaid programs may allow reimbursement for HMOs. A study in 1984 conducted by the Health Care Finance Administration revealed that hospital utilization decreased by 50 percent after patients joined HMOs. Competition with doctors offices has also surfaced. Many physicians now have their own labs, x-ray, EKG, EEG, and ultrasound equipment. (In past years, patients were referred to hospitals for this type of testing.)

Although competition is a problem in the health care industry, it has, like in other industries, resulted in increased quality at competitive prices.

Rising Health Care Costs

More than 10 percent of all money spent in the United States for goods and services is spent for health care. The upward spiral of health care costs, as measured by percentage of GNP, is expected to increase as follows:

Year	GNP
2033	20.0%
2000	15.0%
1990	12.0%
1983	10.8%
1975	8.6%
1965	6.1%

The growth of health care expenditures has become an issue of national concern. The media, both popular and professional, have devoted expanded coverage to the situation. While growing dollars spent on health care have contributed to the financial success of Humana, the burdens this staggering growth has placed on individuals, the government, and employers (who are primarily responsible for paying the nation's health care bills) have been widely recognized. Many employers have increased the deductible and copayment amounts their employees must pay for health care causing inpatient utilization to shrink. Answers to the spiraling health care cost problem will not come easily. Difficult decisions must be made by employers, government, health care providers, and employees alike. As both a major employer and a leading health care provider, Humana will play an important role in the development and implementation of these solutions.

Technology

Advances in technology, with its appropriate use and assessment of clinical applications, are extremely important. Replacing obsolete equipment is a major undertaking. Technology is evolving at an intense pace which makes it almost impossible for health care administrators and physicians to remain current with the equipment and methods that provide the most cost-effective diagnosis, treatment, and management of patients. For example, the general public is not aware of the high cost of equipment—a CAT scan alone is priced at approximately $1 million!

Humana has responded to this problem by implementing a formal technology assessment program whereby technological change throughout the medical field is continually monitored and made available to those who need it.

Medicare Reimbursement

Health care subsidies are diminishing. That's the hard fact on the doorstep of the American public, which for years has received well-intended subsidies that disguised the true cost of health care, encouraged excessive use, and resulted in a staggering national medical bill. The government now pays hospitals to treat Medicare patients on the basis of diagnoses which have predetermined prices; if the treatment costs less, the hospitals keep the difference, but if it costs more the hospitals absorb the additional cost. For example, the average Diagnosis Related Group (DRG) for a back problem in a hospital in Milwaukee County is roughly $2,900.[1] This amount is paid regardless of the total charges and the hospital cannot bill the patient for the difference.

This "diagnosis related group" method of reimbursement began to affect hospitals treating Medicare patients in October 1983. It has created incentives for efficiency since high-cost hospitals will receive basically the same payment as low-cost hospitals. Thus, efficiency and cost effectiveness have become important to hospitals. There are some serious questions being raised by this reimbursement method. The concern is that patients are being "hustled out of hospitals sicker and quicker." For example, in Milwaukee, Wisconsin area hospitals, the average length of stay for Medicare patients has dropped dramatically from 1982 to 1985. The following statistics show several examples:

Diagnosis	1982	1985
Heart Failure	12 days	9 days
Cataract Surgery	3–4 days	0 days (outpatient)
Stroke	19.2 days	11 days

How will Medicare change in the future? Strong majorities of the Arthur Andersen & Co. ACHCE panelists anticipate that the qualifying age will be higher, that coverage will be based on the patient's income level, that all beneficiaries will be covered for catastrophic illness, and that they will be paying higher premiums, deductibles, and coinsurance. It is also the panel's consensus that assignment of benefits will be mandatory for physicians and that a voucher system will be implemented.

Doctor Surplus

There is a nationwide oversupply of some medical specialties. Residency programs are being cut back but probably not enough to reduce the surplus in the near

---

[1] *The Milwaukee Journal,* August 11, 1986, page 4A.

future. The projected increase for the general population in the next decade is .8 percent per year, practicing M.D.'s and D.O.'s (doctor of osteopathy) will proliferate more than twice as fast—an average annual rate of 2.1 percent. The nation's physician population ratio will climb from the current 212 per 100,000 to 252 per 100,000 (that's only 396 people per active physician).

For-profit Health Care

An investor-owned hospital is owned by private investors. It gets capital from the investors and it pays taxes. A nonprofit hospital, in contrast, may be privately owned (by a religious group) or publicly owned (by the government) and pays no taxes, yet produces the same revenues.

Profits make Humana a self-supporting company and a major contributor to the economy through payment of property, sales, franchise, federal and state income taxes. All hospitals need profit. Many so-called nonprofit hospitals make a profit, but label it a "surplus." Nonprofit really refers to their tax status. These facilities are not required to pay income, property, and most other taxes. But, all hospitals must take in more than they pay out or they eventually will have to close their doors. Changing the general public's negative impression of the for-profit status (i.e. making money from sick people), has begun, but has some distance to go.

Indigent Care

Hospitals that do not receive tax subsidies for the indigent still provide emergency care for those who cannot pay. Indigent care has been a substantial financial burden for everyone—hospitals, tax payers, communities, etc.

Recent legislation set in place a comprehensive plan of health care assistance to the indigent sick. In Texas, reimbursement for indigent care from the county will be available. However, the effects of the bill on county property taxes are not yet known.

In May 1983, Humana leased the University of Louisville hospital and guaranteed to provide necessary hospital care to indigent residents of Jefferson County, Kentucky, in return for the government's payment of an annual fixed sum guaranteed by Humana to increase no faster than tax receipts. In addition to arranging for Humana to lease the hospital and establishing a trust to fund the hospital care of the county's poor people, the agreements set up an affiliation between Humana and the University of Louisville School of Medicine, which is benefiting both financially and academically through improved programs. Louisville's innovative public-private arrangement offers other communities in the country a model for dealing with the question of access to care for people who cannot afford to pay. All local hospitals continue to accept emergency patients without regard to their ability to pay, while government has contracted with Humana to provide care for nonemergency indigent patients. Together with ACCESS, a Humana-funded family physician center that is open 365 days a year and accepts patients without regard to ability to pay, the agreement to operate Humana Hospital-University makes Louisville perhaps the first city in America to solve its indigent care problem.

Physician Attitudes

Physicians seem to be somewhat resistant to change when it affects their practice of medicine. For example, some see the multihospital systems as "big business" and therefore a threat. Some question the objectives of the peer review organizations and feel the new Medicare reimbursement system is a potential bombshell due to the financial strain. Older physicians have problems adjusting to the pattern of practice in an HMO. Most doctors are in agreement that the medical malpractice liability problem is potentially disastrous due to the possibility of limiting high-risk specialties. A new relationship is emerging from the need to change the long-standing partnership between physicians and hospitals. Both the physician, whose pattern of practice is threatened and who is facing an over-population of doctors, and the hospital, suffering from decreasing census, find themselves in a declining marketplace. For both to survive, they must plan and work more closely than at any previous time in their history. This new relationship must evolve through coordinated strategic planning by the hospital and the physician community. It must be based on trust that a partnership will emerge for the benefit of the hospital, the physician, and the patient.

Further compounding these problems are the changing attitudes and needs of the consumer. In the 1960s, insurance companies and federal and state programs such as Medicare and Medicaid, covered the majority of consumer health care costs. Also during this time, health care costs were minimal when one compares them to today's spiraling prices. The national economy was relatively stable and employers were more apt to provide policies as fringe benefits.

As the 1970s came along, health care costs began rising, and the nation's population grew older and needed more care. These were also times of record unemployment which brought about a near crisis for those who relied heavily upon employer-provided health insurance. People became increasingly dependent upon the federal and state programs, and thus, these programs required an even larger proportion of the government budget. Hospitals felt the crunch because an increasing number of customers were incapable of paying for their services. This meant that bad debt losses had to be passed on to the paying consumer in terms of higher prices.

In the 1980s, health care costs rose even higher as the cyclical trends in unemployment continued and the average age of the U.S. citizen increased. Also, the Federal deficit reached an all-time high and government spending came under closer scrutiny. The days of free-flowing government funds were gone. The Medicare and Medicaid programs were receiving fewer funds, thus putting an even greater hardship on the consumer. Insurance companies, after experiencing an ever-increasing number of claims began covering fewer high-risk clients. They also required the customer to pay a larger deductible and began working more closely with the employers.

Today the customer is being called upon to pay an increasing proportion of the health care cost. In short, he or she became more dollar conscious and as a result, the customer is more apt to ask for a second opinion before having surgery, will stay in the hospital for shorter periods, and will shop around for the best possible health care at the lowest possible price.

HUMANA MARKETING

In the past, marketing in the health care industry was basically in the form of public relations, nonproduct specific, and general positioning/image building. Examples of these activities include sponsorship of community events, educational programs, newsletters, hospital tours, exhibits, and health fairs.

Humana began its marketing efforts other than public relations with the inception of its customer relations department in 1981. Initially the purpose of this department was market research in the form of patient satisfaction questionnaires. All patients who were discharged from Humana hospitals received a questionnaire that asked specific questions regarding nursing care, ancillary services, dietary, housekeeping, business office—and that *all important* question: "Would you return to this hospital should you need hospital services in the future? If not, please explain." The results of a six-month study revealed that 96 percent of Humana patients were very satisfied with the services. But, the company's executives looked very closely at that 4 percent who said they would not return. The patients indicated that the facilities, equipment, and medical care were good, but that employees needed to work on caring, understanding, smiling, communicating, and having a positive attitude. They said the employees needed to respond to patients' fears and apprehension. This research showed that caring is integrally a part of excellent health care service. With this valuable information, the top executives gave the company's education department the project of developing a human relations training program for all employees. The program was developed and began in 1982. It is called "Humana Care" and is now a companywide employee education and sensitivity training program. It focused attention on excellence in the human aspects of providing good health services. Stated simply, Humana Care means that each employee treats patients as if they were members of the employee's own family.

Another Humana marketing strategy was aimed at name recognition. All Humana facilities now have the company name and location rather than individual names as in the past. The hospital name changes were gradual and were associated with special events, e.g. construction, replacement hospitals, anniversaries. In 1985, the Health Services Division's MedFirst was changed to Humana MedFirst. The insurance product name is Humana Care Plus. This added to Humana's overall name recognition and the integration of its businesses. Humana has become a national brand name.

Marketing strategies for Humana at this time are product oriented. Some of the programs that are available for the facilities to utilize include, but are not limited to, day surgery, cardiovascular, obstetrics, physicians practice building, burn service, cancer, chemical dependency/substance abuse, diabetes, emergency, industrial medicine, ENT, gastroenterology, home health, infertility, neurology/neurosurgery, ophthalmology, orthopedics, pediatrics, psychiatry, pulmonary, rehabilitation, research, senior citizens, spinal, urology, wellness, and women's programs. An example of a women's program, Breast Diagnostics, is seen in Exhibit 30.3.

EXHIBIT 30.3 **Breast Diagnostic Center**

I. Research highlights

Consumer research

Points-of-difference (versus outpatient mammography)

- "Someone is responding to our needs, and this is a need. Someone is concerned about us."
- "Experts" due to specialization.
- Perceived as present state-of-the-art and commitment to remain so in the future.
- Benefits of separate facility:
  More convenient, time savings,
  Hospital is for sick people, center is for education and testing,
  Perceived as less expensive than the hospital,
  Less red tape and bureaucracy.
- Current education is perceived as inadequate—few women believe they are competent in performing their breast self-exam.

Physician reaction

- High degree of sensitivity in some locations.
- Overall perception of the service offered is very favorable.
- A strong education program tends to legitimize the center.

II. Product definition

Multi-Modality Technology	Mammography: gold standard, highest use for screening and diagnostic
	Ultrasound: screening for young or pregnant, diagnostic for symptomatic
	Other: procedures of local interest or innovations Humana may wish to investigate
Education	Education important to consumers and essential for physician acceptance.
	MammaCare preferred due to its exclusivity and perceived superiority over other education packages currently available.
Physicians	Radiologists dedicated to the concept and willing to commit necessary time and interest.

Primary care referral base, that must be worked with through design and implementation phase with emphasis on potential referrals from program.

Staffing

All-women staff with strong technical and people skills. "Primary care" technologists that follow patient through screening modalities and education.

Facility

A wellness, noninstitutional, homelike environment.

Sufficient floor space to accommodate basic model and with expansion capabilities when volumes dictate.

Pricing

Below market, presuming volume. (Test for price elasticity is planned.)

Positioning

"A special place for women."

"Not a cancer clinic."

"Specializing in early detection and education of breast disease."

The *most* important phrases consistently identified in consumer research.

If we are to achieve screening volumes, we must avoid strong consumer promotion of the treatment side (cancer clinic), even though expertise in this area is a natural spin-off.

III. Criteria for successful breast diagnostic center

1. A population base large enough to support a Center: 30,000–50,000 females age 35–64; 180,000–300,000 total population base.

   This is a general guideline based on U.S. age distribution studies. Because of variables, calculations should be made on a market-to-market basis.

2. A radiologist who is committed to building volumes. Many excellent radiologists are not widely experienced in mammography and prefer not to do large volumes. Because the radiologist is so important to the success of the center it is essential that he/she be interested in the center and is willing to promote it. Indications of commitment would include special training or willingness to seek special training in mammography or ultrasound.

3. Approximately 2,000 square feet of space. The center should be located in an area easily accessible for outpatients and the radiologists. The ground floor of a medical office building or an area of the hospital with a separate entrance is most desirable. Outside signage should be easily identifiable from the parking lot.

4. Purchase of the newest low-radiation-dose mammography and dedicated breast ultrasound equipment.

5. Wellness-oriented feminine decor that will set Humana Breast Diagnostic Centers apart from the competition. The special decor and amenities that go with it will help direct business to facility by word-of-mouth.

6. A base of primary care physicians to support the center. OB/GYN's, internal medicine, and family practitioners with offices located on the hospital campus are an important source for patients. Hospitals that have or plan to establish a number of services oriented to women are prime candidates for breast diagnostic centers.

7. A public relations director, agency, or individual responsible for initiating news media coverage and building understanding and support among local women's groups.

8. A commitment to an extensive marketing campaign to educate women and physicians about the service and promote its use.

IV. Overview

The Concept	A *dedicated unit* for the education and early detection of breast disease—
	Environment: wellness-oriented, feminine decor
	Technologies: mammography and ultrasound
The Need	Breast cancer is the leading cause of cancer deaths among women.
	Early detection increases 5-year survival rate from less than 50 percent to 90 percent.
	The American Cancer Society (ACS) has established guidelines for routine mammography on all women 35 and older. Less than 5 percent currently comply with mammography screening guidelines.
The Target	To attract women with no known breast disease, asymptomatic—to screen for early detection based primarily on ACS mammography guidelines (46 percent of all females)
	versus
	Past breast diagnostics was dedicated almost solely to diagnosing symptomatic patients, after lump was found and survival rate was less than 50 percent (2 percent of all females).

The Strategy	Consumer	Educate, motivate and build awareness/preference for BDC
	Physician	"Pull" through education and detailing "Push" through consumer pressure
The Objective	Primary	Leadership position among area physicians, consumers and media. Especially important in women's programs.
	Secondary	Financial viability from Center operation and spin-off business—related and unrelated

---

Humana has moved toward centralizing all marketing activities by reorganizing the corporate marketing department. Under the direction of the vice president, corporate marketing will be divided into marketing management for the three divisions and marketing services. The objectives are as follows:

- Improved strategic focus
  Comprehensive marketing planning
  Increased Humana awareness
  Greater Humana benefit orientation

- Enhance strategic linkage
  Marketing congruence between divisions
  Marketing congruence within divisions

- Increased ability to respond to change
  Within the organization
  To competition
  To other influences

- Greater marketing leverage
  Improved marketing service resources
  Improved program quality
  Improved program coordination
  Improved supplier management
  Competitive advantages

- Improved personnel interaction
  Between divisions
  Within divisions
  Between marketing functions

- Identification of new business opportunity
  Strategic fit
  Marketing leveragability

The forces bearing down on the health care industry are coming from every direction—government, business, health maintenance organizations, preferred provider arrangements. Combinations of these are having a distinct effect on how, when, and where consumers select health care providers.

The current marketing strategy for Humana is:

Target market—patients in the Humana service areas who have the ability to pay for services (insurance or private pay).

Product—health care services, i.e. hospital care, primary medical care clinics, group health insurance programs, outpatient surgeries, diagnostic testing and therapy.

Place—metroplex areas are the current emphasis as all three divisions can function efficiently and effectively in such an environment.

Price—must be affordable and competitive in each geographic area.

Promotion—on the company level, it must be a "one image" campaign; on a local level, it must be geared to the specific needs of the customers.

Humana is obviously a leader in health care and has performed well in its 25 years of operation. The health care industry is, however, in a frightening period of change. Decisions made today will have far reaching implications.

CASE 31

Tissot: Competing in the Global Watch Industry

One sunny afternoon in May 1985, Dr. Ernst Thomke drove his Porsche through the Jura mountains; he was on his way to Bienne for a Tissot strategy session. After more than a decade of declining sales, layoffs, and factory closings the popular business press was proclaiming the return of the Swiss watch industry. Much of the credit for the resurrection had been given to Thomke, President of Ebauches SA, one of the Asuag-SSIH companies, and initiator of a new, low-priced Swiss fashion watch: the SWATCH.

Thomke believed that the predictions of a revived Swiss watch industry were premature. He had accepted the considerable task of giving the Asuag brands, and particularly Tissot, a hard look to formulate new strategies to bring the Asuag group profitability in the second half of the 1980s and beyond. Specifically, his goal was to increase Asuag-SSIH total volume from seven million to 50 million units. As his Porsche sped through the countryside he considered the past and future trends for the global watch industry and he asked himself, "How can Tissot grow and profit?"

In 1985, the future trends for the global watch industry were anything but clear. Over the past 15 years, the industry had experienced radical changes. Innovation in products, production, and marketing were all key factors in the volatility that marked a period of rapid entry, often followed by rapid exit, of new competitors and the departure of some established producers.

In 1970, the global watch industry was dominated by Swiss watch manufacturers. By 1975, the competitive field had expanded and key players came from Switzerland, Japan, and the United States. By the early 1980s, the United States had all but disappeared as a contender and Hong Kong was the world's largest exporter in units in the industry with 326.4 million watches and movements in 1984. Japan ranked second in number and value of units produced. Between 1970 and 1984, the Swiss dropped to third place in unit volume as their assembled watch exports dwindled from 48 million to 17 million pieces. However, Switzerland continued to rank first in value of watch exports, Sfr. 3.4 billion in 1984 (Exhibit 31.1).

This case was prepared by Susan W. Nye, Research Associate, under the direction of Jean-Pierre Jeannet, Visiting Professor. It is intended as a basis for classroom discussion rather than to illustrate effective or ineffective handling of an administrative situation. Copyright © 1985, by IMEDE (International Management Development Institute), Lausanne, Switzerland. Used by permission from Jean-Pierre Jeannet and IMEDE.

EXHIBIT 31.1 **Watch production, export, and activities**

**Total production of watches and watch movements worldwide
1960–1984* (In millions of pieces)**

1960	1970	1975	1980	1982	1983	1984
98	174	220	300	330	370	n/a

**Watch production by country 1960–1983
(Percentage of worldwide unit production)**

	1960	1970	1975	1980	1982	1983
Switzerland	43.0	42.0	32.0	18.4	10.8	9.3
Japan	7.2	13.7	14.0	22.5	24.7	26.1
Hong Kong	—	—	—	18.5	30.0	35.0
United States	9.7	11.5	12.5	4.0	—	—
E. Germany	20.5	14.5	16.7	15.7	14.8	13.2
France	5.6	6.3	7.6	3.3	2.9	2.2
W. Germany	8.0	4.7	4.3	2.2	1.2	1.1

**Watch exports—watches and movements
1960–1984 (In millions of Sfr.)**

	1960	1970	1975	1980	1982	1984
Switzerland**	1,159.2	2,383.7	2,764.3	3,106.7	3,091.9	3,397.3
Japan	16.4	399.3	835.1	1,911.1	1,908.5	2,876.2
Hong Kong	—	63.1	246.1	1,855.6	1,779.0	2,091.2
France	26.2	78.1	209.3	265.0	218.3	233.7
Germany	83.6	129.6	140.2	171.7	175.4	231.4

**Watch exports—watches and movements
1960–1984 (In millions of pieces)**

	1960	1970	1975	1980	1982	1984
Switzerland**	42.6	73.4	71.2	51.0	45.7	46.9
Japan	0.1	11.4	17.1	48.3	63.6	94.7
Hong Kong	—	5.7	16.1	126.1	213.7	326.4
France	1.3	4.4	9.5	9.8	8.4	6.2
Germany	3.8	4.1	9.5	4.5	4.7	5.5

Exports as a percentage of total pieces produced 1960–1984

	1960	1970	1975	1980	1982	1984
Switzerland	97	97	97	97	97	97
Japan	2	48	57	72	80	n/a
Hong Kong	—	100	100	100	100	100
France	24	40	57	***	***	***
W. Germany	48	50	***	***	***	***

Assembled watches as a percentage of watches and movements exported (Value)						
	1960	**1970**	**1975**	**1980**	**1982**	**1984**
Switzerland	81.3	86.1	87.9	85.9	91.5	92.9
Japan	51.6	83.6	92.1	90.6	87.6	85.0
Hong Kong	97.1	100.0	96.6	95.4	96.9	96.7
France	87.7	93.8	93.8	88.7	91.5	94.4
Germany	91.1	88.7	90.6	89.0	92.0	94.8

Assembled watches as a percentage of watches and movements exported (Pieces)						
	1960	**1970**	**1975**	**1980**	**1982**	**1984**
Switzerland	73.7	73.6	71.7	55.9	59.3	55.2
Japan	29.0	64.8	78.1	75.5	67.5	60.6
Hong Kong	98.2	100.0	98.1	94.4	95.6	92.1
France	n/a	89.5	90.4	81.6	79.0	94.4
Germany	89.3	88.9	85.5	69.0	74.4	72.6

*Does not include other timepieces such as penwatches, etc.

**Including nonassembled movements.

***Not available—because of re-exports, exports are larger than production.

Source: Swiss Watch Federation.

THE WATCH INDUSTRY IN SWITZERLAND

The Swiss watch industry was concentrated in the Jura along the western border of Switzerland. The Swiss had conquered the world market with mechanical watches and had developed a reputation for fine craftmanship, elegance, and style. Swiss companies produced 80 percent of the watches selling for Sfr. 1,200 or more, and virtually all top-priced watches. A large portion of these watches were still mechanical.

Until the early 1970s, Swiss watchmaking was intensely specialized and fragmented, with a rigid structure that had remained unchanged for centuries. Major changes began in the 1970s with several mergers involving sizable firms and important initiatives in both horizontal and vertical integration.

The Swiss watch industry was essentially a group of industries. Traditionally, the Swiss had operated on a two-tier system, components manufacturing and assembly. In 1934 the Swiss government had instituted laws that made it illegal to open, enlarge, transfer, or transform any watchmaking facilities without government permission. Exports of components and movements were also illegal without permission, as was the export of watchmaking machinery. These regulations were instituted to protect the Swiss watch industry against foreign competition. The government began deregulating the industry in 1971 and in 1985 these laws were no longer in effect.

Swiss watch firms generally fell into one of three categories. First, there had been a large number of "one-man-and-a-boy" and other small enterprises that produced components, movements, or put purchased parts into cases. These firms marketed on the basis of long-established personal contracts. Included in this category were the piece work assemblers. A significant portion of inexpensive mechanical watches were assembled by Jura farmers during the winter as in-home piece work. Second were the well-established, privately owned watchmakers that produced expensive, handmade watches. And finally, there was the Asuag-SSIH organization which was a group of companies representing approximately 35 percent of total Swiss exports of watches and movements (Exhibit 31.2).

Watches and movements declined from 11.9 percent to 7.2 percent of total Swiss exports from 1970 to 1980. At the start of 1970 there were 1,618 watchmaking firms in the industry. This figure had fallen to 634 by 1984. Between 1970 and 1984, the full-time labor force producing watches shrank from 89,500 to 31,000. Layoffs due to the shrinking demand for mechanical watches were exacerbated by

---

EXHIBIT 31.2 **Exports by technology segments—1960–1984**

Mechanical watch and movement exports
(Percentage of total units exported 1960–1984)

	1960	1970	1975	1980	1982	1984
Switzerland	100.0	99.6	98.1	80.4	50.8	29.4
Japan	100.0	n/a	n/a	33.6	16.5	8.5
Hong Kong	—	n/a	n/a	28.7	15.1	7.6
France	100.0	94.4	98.2	75.5	60.7	45.1
Germany	100.0	85.8	84.7	50.7	29.2	16.8

Electronic watch and movement exports
(Percentage of total pieces exported 1960–1984)

	1960	1970	1975	1980	1982	1984
Switzerland	—	0.4	1.9	19.6	49.2	70.6
Japan	—	n/a	n/a	66.4	83.5	91.5
Hong Kong	—	n/a	n/a	71.3	84.9	92.4
France	—	5.6	1.8	24.5	39.3	54.9
Germany	—	14.2	15.3	49.3	70.8	83.2

Mechanical watch and movement exports
(Percentage of total value exported 1960–1984)

	1960	1970	1975	1980	1982	1984
Switzerland	100.0	98.5	94.0	69.2	51.1	46.6
Japan	100.0	n/a	n/a	22.2	11.4	9.8
Hong Kong	—	n/a	n/a	32.0	28.2	16.9
France	100.0	91.1	96.2	56.2	34.3	24.0
Germany	100.0	85.1	84.4	51.8	26.4	15.2

Electronic watch and movement exports
(Percentage of total value exported 1960–1984)

	1960	1970	1975	1980	1982	1984
Switzerland	—	1.5	6.0	30.8	48.9	53.4
Japan	—	n/a	n/a	77.8	88.6	90.2
Hong Kong	—	n/a	n/a	68.0	71.8	83.1
France	—	8.9	3.8	43.8	65.7	76.0
Germany	—	14.9	15.6	48.2	73.6	84.8

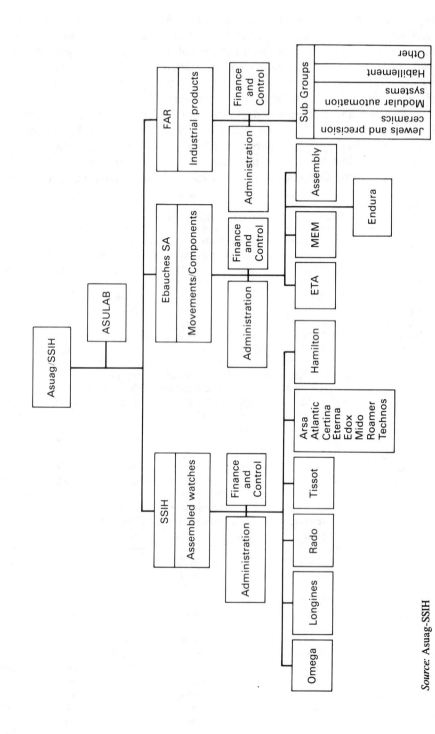

Source: Asuag-SSIH

EXHIBIT 31.3 **Asuag-SSIH organization—1983**

automation, rationalization, and concentration initiated throughout the Swiss watch industry.

ASUAG-SSIH

Company Background

In an effort to rejuvenate the industry, a consortium of seven Swiss banks orchestrated a merger between SSIH and Asuag in 1982. They provided the merger with a capital and cash infusion totaling more than Sfr. 700 million. In return the bank gained 97 percent ownership of the combine and planned to sell shares to the public when it returned to profitability, estimated at five to ten years. During 1984, with sales totaling Sfr. 1,582.4 million and after tax profits of Sfr. 26.5 million, the industry began to turn around. In February 1985, it was announced that control would be returned to private investors.

Asuag, short for Allgemeine Schweizer Uhrenindustrie, had been the largest producer of watches and watch components in Switzerland, accounting for about one-third of total Swiss watch exports and 25 percent of production in Switzerland. Asuag was founded in 1931 when the Swiss government orchestrated the consolidation of a wide variety of small watchmakers to strengthen the industry during the worldwide depression. The combined organization, Asuag-SSIH, is shown in Exhibit 31.3.

Movements were produced by the twelve subsidiaries of Ebauches SA, including ETA. ETA was the largest Swiss movement manufacturer. ETA produced a full range of movements, but was best known as a producer of high-quality, expensive, ultra-thin watch movements used for luxury watches. Ebauches' companies sold 65 percent of their production volume to the Asuag-SSIH brands. Ebauches' sales had dropped from 51.1 million to 32.1 million pieces between 1973 and 1984. During this period the world market for movements had grown from 215 million to 350 units. Ebauches' world market share dropped from 23.8 to 9.2 percent.

Asuag's brands of finished watches included: Longines, Eterna, Certina, and Rado. Rado was the largest selling mid-priced Swiss watch with annual sales of about one million units. Fifty-five percent of Asuag's production was in finished watches. Asuag began losing money in 1977, reporting an accumulated net loss of Sfr. 129 million in 1982.

Société Suisse de l'Industrie Horlogère (SSIH) had been the second largest watch company in Switzerland, responsible for 10 percent of total output. SSIH was made up of a diverse group of companies producing watches and movements in all price categories. SSIH group companies included Omega, Tissot, and Economic Time.

SSIH had encountered severe financial problems in the late 1970s. In 1977, the Zurich-based trading group Siber Hegner & Co. AG, a major international distributor of Swiss watches, including Omega and Tissot provided SSIH with a capital infusion of Sfr. 32.5 million. A rescue plan was devised that deemphasized the lower-price end of the market. Siber Hegner management concentrated on electronic quartz models which sold at prices above Sfr. 235. Tissot watch prices were pushed upwards and Tissot models were sold in the Sfr. 235 to 1,500 range. Omega watches were priced above Sfr. 600 at retail. Companies producing at the low-price end of the market were sold off and inexpensive watch production was reduced from 69.2 to 19.7 percent of total. At the same time, the product mix was shifted and electronic watches increased from 8.9 percent of total in 1976 to 47.9 percent of total sales in 1980. Siber Hegner provided a cash infusion for research and development and a worldwide advertising campaign. Acquisitions and joint ventures were arranged to improve integration, although management, production, marketing, and sales remained decentralized.

Initially, the industry picked up, with profits in 1979 allowing for the first dividend payment since 1974. However, profitability was short lived and in June 1981, SSIH announced a loss of Sfr. 142 million for the year ending March 31, 1981, giving the company a net loss of Sfr. 27.4 million. A consortium of Swiss banks in an effort to bail out the company provided cash and credit valued at almost Sfr. 230 million in return for 96.5 percent equity in the recapitalized company.

Tissot SA

Thomke described Tissot, and most Asuag-SSIH watches, as a "branded commodity." The individual companies produced their products under recognized brand names, but Thomke felt that the watches had been poorly developed in terms of brand image and personality. Thomke believed the weak image had led to the decline in Tissot sales (Exhibit 31.4). His goal was to create a workable brand strategy and identity for Tissot. In May 1985, Thomke believed that Tissot had gained the reputation of an "inexpensive" Omega.

The company produced about 400,000 watches in 1984, for watch sales of Sfr. 42 million. The average retail price for a Tissot watch was about Sfr. 375. Strongest sales volume was from watches in the Sfr. 300–700 range. Retail prices ranged from Sfr. 175 to 800 for stainless steel and gold-plated watches. A second smaller line of gold watches sold for between Sfr. 1,000 and 5,000. Tissot watches were sold in Europe: Switzerland, West Germany, Italy, Scandinavia, and the United Kingdom. Tissot was also sold in Brazil, South Africa, Hong Kong, Singapore, and Japan. Tissot had been withdrawn from the U.S. market in the 1970s but Thomke wanted to reintroduce it to the United States as soon as possible.

Tissot production was limited to assembly. Employment at the factory had declined from a high of 1,200 to 200. All components and movements were purchased from Asuag-SSIH or independent companies. At the start of 1985, Tissot workers were assembling a product line of some 300 styles, each produced in a woman's and man's model and in a number of different metals and combinations. Thomke had already assigned ten engineers at Tissot to review the product line and production process.

Tissot shared Omega's distribution at both the wholesale and retail level. Almost all Omega wholesalers were independent distributors. A total of 12,000 retail stores, mostly jewelry stores, and a few "high-class" department stores carried Tissot watches. The majority of its watch sales came from the top 3,000 stores. Ex-factory prices ranged from Sfr. 60 to 2,000. Both wholesalers and retailers provided advertising and promotion support, but all promotion activities had to be initiated by Tissot.

Thomke was aware that if he wanted to build a strong image for Tissot, he would have to increase his marketing and promotion expenditure. Asuag-SSIH set targets for Marketing and Profit Margins (MPM) for each brand. Thomke felt that a 50 percent margin would give a brand adequate funds for marketing and profit. Only his latest product, SWATCH, came close to that figure, followed by Rado with almost 30 percent. A target MPM of 15 percent had been set for Tissot for 1984, but Thomke had learned that the actual margin had been closer to 10 percent.

Thomke believed that the MPM had been squeezed by wholesalers because of the slow turnover for Tissot watches. Wholesalers demanded a margin of 28 to 45 percent for Tissot watches. Explaining the situation, Thomke said, "Tissot has never recovered the sales and market share it lost to Seiko and Citizen in the 1970s. Sales to retailers have slowed considerably and consumer demand is down. To encourage wholesalers to keep Tissot in inventory, the company granted more liberal wholesaler margins, at the expense of marketing funds and profits."

Thomke felt that it was still possible to build up the brand and re-establish a strong wholesale network. However, he realized that this was an expensive proposition. He was prepared to invest 18 to 20 percent of sales in promotion, but to have any effect, he needed a promotion budget of Sfr. 12 million for Europe alone. Thomke estimated that the company could spend Sfr. 6 to 8 million in Germany, Tissot's largest market in 1985. This figure would be divided with one-half targeted for media advertising and the rest for point-of-sale promotion. If handled correctly, promotion activities would give Tissot the strong image that Thomke felt was essential to successful watch sales.

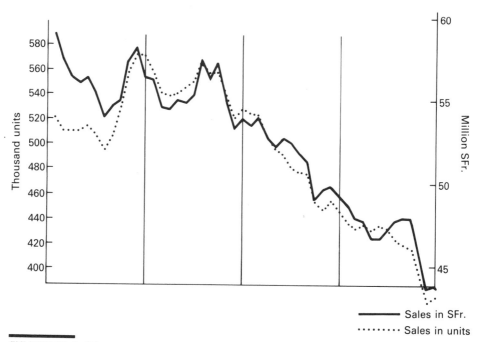

EXHIBIT 31.4   **Tissot world sales 1981–1984**

WATCHMAKING TECHNOLOGY

Designing a Watch Collection

Watches covered a broad spectrum in terms of style and price, ranging from sport watches for informal or daytime wear, to luxury dress watches which were pieces of jewelry. It could take three years to bring a watch from the drawing board to the market. A watch collection was made up of as many as 30 to 40 lines. Each line had up to 1,000 models. A watch line was differentiated by case shape, design, and the movement. The differences between models were cosmetic variations in color and types of materials or due to slight variations in technology, such as day/date calendars or self-winding mechanisms.

Watch cases were made in precious metals, standard steel, brass, and plastic. The cases of many expensive luxury watches were decorated with semi-precious and precious stones, such as lapis-lazuli, diamonds, and sapphires. Watch cases were made in two or three pieces. Two pieces, the back and front were standard and held the watch together. For better watches a separate rim held the crystal in place. The rim provided designers with more flexibility when developing new models and gave the watches a finer finish.

Watch crystals were pieces of thin glass or plastic that protected the hands and dial and came in three types. The most inexpensive were plastic, followed by mineral glass and sapphire glass. Sapphire glass was very hard and could not be scratched or chipped.

Straps or bracelets held the watch on the wrist and came in a variety of materials. Straps came in leather, plastic, and cloth ribbons. Bracelets were made from precious metals, standard steel, brass, and plastic. Precious and semi-precious stones were often set into the bracelets of luxury watches. Up until the 1970s, most watches were sold with leather straps. In the past 15 years fashion tastes had changed and most watches were purchased with bracelets.

Timekeeping Technology

Every watch was composed of four basic elements: a time base, a source of energy, a transmission, and a display. The movement was the watch's time base. Movements came in two major categories: mechanical and electronic. Mechanical movements were driven by the release of energy from an unwinding spring. Electronic watches ran on an electric battery. Energy was transmitted through a series of gears, a motor or integrated circuits to the hands in analogue watches. These hands moved around the dial to display time. Integrated circuits were used to transmit time to digital watches, and time was displayed numerically in a frame on the watch case (Exhibit 31.5 and 31.6).

Mechanical Watch Movements

The movement was a complex set of 100 or more tiny parts. While all mechanical watch movements operated on the same principle, there was a great deal of variety in watch quality. Friction and wear had to be minimized to insure long term accuracy of the tiny moving parts. To minimize friction, jewels were placed at all the movement's critical pivot and contact points. Fifteen was the standard number of jewels but high-quality movements might contain as many as thirty. Contrary to

---

EXHIBIT 31.5   **Watchmaking technologies**

Inside a mechanical watch

The time base is composed of a spiral balance wheel whose movement back and forth recurs, for instance four times per second.
The source of energy is a taut spring.
The transmission consists of a train of pinions and wheels.
The display consists of hands moving around a dial.

Components of a mechanical watch

The movement-blank
The ebauche, the key part of the watch, serves to carry the main spring, the wheel pins, and the regulating parts. The cocks provide the support at the other end of the pins and pinions. Finally, the wheels and pinions intermesh to provide the transmission moving the hands. The plate, the cocks, the wheels together make up the movement-bland of a watch in its unassembled stage.
In addition, the movement of a watch includes the regulating pieces. The whole assembly is inserted into a watch case with glass, dial, and crown for winding up the watch and setting the time. The whole thus constituting the finished product.
Despite the minute dimensions and the finishing and precision required for each unit, mass production reaches a rate of as much as 4,000 to 10,000 complete movement-blanks (depending on calibre) per day and per assembly line.

The regulating parts
The regulating parts carry out the function of time base. They include the balance-wheels, the hairspring, and the assortment. These parts regulate the working of the watch, keeping constant control of the amount of energy provided by the main spring and transmitted to the display by the wheel assembly.
Their production calls for extreme precision to micrometer* standards and a high degree of know-how for handling the tiny delicate pieces.

The jewels
The jewels, synthetic rubies, are used to support the pins of the wheel and thus diminish friction and wear. Shaping them with the aid of a diamond paste has taken centuries to develop and achieve precision to a scale of a tenth of a micrometer. A new technology for doing this using laser beams has made it possible to speed up the predrilling of the holes in the jewels.

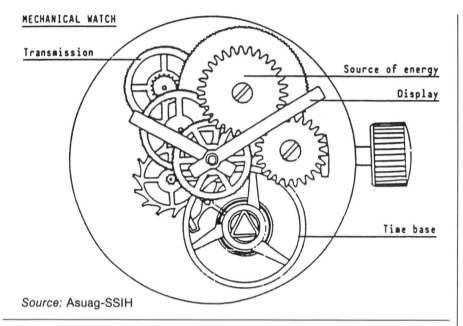

MECHANICAL WATCH

Transmission

Source of energy

Display

Time base

Source: Asuag-SSIH

Inside an electronic watch (analogical or digital)

The time base is composed of a quartz crystal vibrating at, for instance, 32,768 times per second.

The source of energy is an electric battery.

The transmission is provided by conductors and integrated circuits (analogical and digital watches), a motor synchronized with a train of pinions and wheels (analogical watches).

The display is provided by hands moving around a dial in the case of analogical watches; figures appearing in a frame in the case of digital watches.

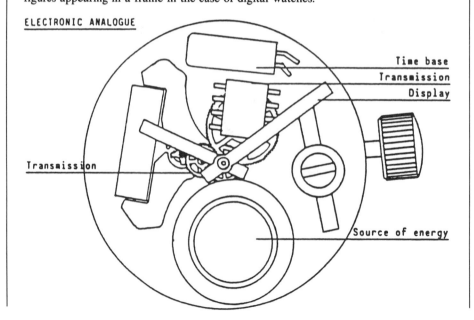

ELECTRONIC ANALOGUE

Time base
Transmission
Display

Transmission

Source of energy

ELECTRONIC DIGITAL

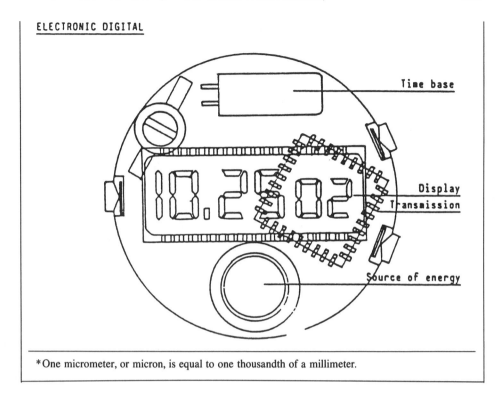

*One micrometer, or micron, is equal to one thousandth of a millimeter.

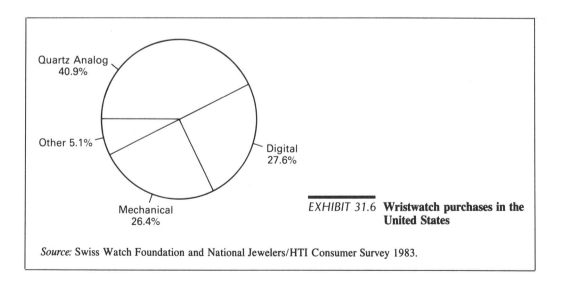

EXHIBIT 31.6 **Wristwatch purchases in the United States**

Source: Swiss Watch Foundation and National Jewelers/HTI Consumer Survey 1983.

popular belief, adding more jewels did not necessarily indicate increased quality, or cost to production. These internal jewels were synthetic and relatively inexpensive. It was the overall care and craftsmanship that went into the watches that created the expense and not the jewels themselves.

The precision and accuracy found in high quality jewel-lever watches required micro-mechanical engineering expertise. A variety of modifications could be made to a spring-powered watch which added to the complexity of the interior design but not the basic mechanism. Refinements, such as improved accuracy, miniaturization, water resistance, and self-wind technology, rather than radical new developments had occurred. Calendars and chronographs, as well as watches with start/stop mechanisms were also possible.

Pin-lever watches, also called "roskopfs" after their inventor, had metal pins instead of jewels on the escapement mechanism gear teeth. Roskopf's original goal in inventing this watch had been to make the movement so simple that watches could be made affordable to everyone.

Electronic Movements

A Swiss engineer, Max Hetzel, invented the first electronic watch in 1954. This development was largely possible due to advances in miniature batteries and electric motors during World War II. Initially, electronics did not represent a big departure from mechanical technology, nor offer substantially better accuracy. While the energy source was replaced with electronics, the transmission and regulating components remained unchanged.

The tuning-fork watch, developed in the 1960s, represented a significant change to the traditional principles of determining time. A small battery in the watch sent an electric current to the tuning-fork and stimulated it to vibrate at 360 cycles per second. The vibrations were transmitted to a set of gears which drove the hands on the watch face. Tuning-fork watches (if properly adjusted) were accurate to within one minute per month.

The quartz crystal watch began appearing in the marketplace at the end of the 1960s. An electric current was passed through a quartz crystal to stimulate high frequency vibration which could be converted into precise time increments. Microcircuitry subdivided the crystal's frequency into an electric pulse which drove the watch. The pulse operated a tiny electric stepping motor or was transmitted through conductors and integrated circuits to drive the gears and watch hands.

In 1972, digital watches appeared for the first time. These watches had no moving parts and the conventional face and hands were replaced with digital readouts. Early digital watches used light emitting diodes (LED) to show the time. With this technology, users pressed a button for time display. LED watches required a great deal of power and batteries lasted no longer than one year. Liquid crystal diodes (LCD) also came on the market in 1972. These watches displayed the time continually. These watches were considerably more conservative in energy usage, and batteries lasted from three to five years or longer.

Early electronic watches were not fully water- and shock-proofed and the batteries often malfunctioned in hot, humid climates. However, within a short period of time, technological advances led to electronic watches that were waterproof to depths of 30 meters, shockproofed and able to withstand tropical climates.

Designing electronic watches for women had initially created problems, as well as opportunities. To create models that fit a woman's smaller wrist required considerable miniaturization of the movement and battery. Creating smaller movements led to increased design flexibility. Improvements in miniaturization and advancement in large-scale integrated circuits (LSI) and battery technology allowed manufacturers to add special functions without excessive bulk. Watches began to take on the appearance of multifunction instruments. Runners, skin divers, sailors, and other sports enthusiasts bought watches that could provide them with waterproofing and sophisticated chronograph functions. Travelers were afforded the opportunity to buy watches with multitime-zone functions and alarms. Watches were also available with calculators and radios, and progress was being made toward a television watch.

Watch Production

Movements, hands, cases, and bracelets were assembled to produce a complete watch. Mechanical watch quality was dependent on the care taken in assembly as well as the quality of the individual components. High-quality mechanical movements were made by hand and a combination of semi- and highly skilled craftspeople were needed. Mechanical watch assembly was done in batches. Highly skilled workers were essential at the final stages of production, for finishing and adjusting to produce high-quality, finely finished, accurate movements and watches.

While the term, pin-lever, refers specifically to the replacement of jewels with metal pins, roskopf's were made from lower-quality grade materials. Labor requirements for roskopf's were reduced with semi- or unskilled labor working in batch production.

Electronic movements for analog watches combined micromechanical and electronic engineering. The electronic regulating mechanism simplified the production process which could be run in an automated setting with semi-skilled labor. Movements for digital watches were radically different from analog watches. These watches had no moving parts and time was programmed onto a silicon chip. Unskilled labor could be used for digital watches that were assembled in batches on automated assembly lines.

Both mechanical and electronic watch reliability was tied to the number of inspections the manufacturer made. For mid-priced and expensive watches 100 percent inspection occurred at several points during the process. Tests were made for water- and shock-proofing as well as accuracy.

Costs of production were a function of a company's degree of integration and automation, material costs, and the local wage rates. Material costs were based on the quality of the watch produced. With roskopf watches labor constituted a significant portion of variable costs, but as the watches moved up-market the materials, fine stainless steel, sapphire crystals, and eventually precious metals and decorative jewels played the major role in the watch's ex-factory price. Watchmakers could improve their variable costs by assembling at volumes above 10,000 pieces. Assemblers producing 100,000 to 500,000 units per year could benefit from component supplier discounts that were as high as 20 to 25 percent. Beyond this point, cost improvements could only be realized with new production processes, automation, and robotics. Wages for the Swiss watch industry averaged Sfr. 12 per hour. Most Swiss watchmakers sought a 30 percent gross margin. In Japan, average hourly wages for factory workers were Sfr. 7.20. Japanese producers had an average gross margin of 40 percent. In Hong Kong manufacturers kept their ex-factory prices low with inexpensive, but highly productive piece-work labor, averaging under Sfr. 10 per day, fewer inspections, and cheaper materials. Gross margins of approximately 10 to 15 percent were typical for Hong Kong manufacturers (Exhibit 31.7).

SEGMENTING THE GLOBAL WATCH INDUSTRY

Price Segments

Price has been a traditional means of segmenting the watch market into three categories. The first group were low price "C" watches and included all watches sold at retail for under Sfr. 120. Roskopf watches and inexpensive digitals competed in this market. These watches accounted for 33 percent of the total value of the global watch sales and 86 percent of unit volume. The mid-price or "B" watches ranged from Sfr. 120 to 700 at retail. This sector represented 25 percent of sales in Swiss francs and 12 percent of total units for 1984. Electronic watches dominated both the "C" and the "B" price segments.

The third category were the top-priced watches. The retail price of "A" watches ranged from Sfr. 700 to 5,000. Manufacturers of luxury watches "AA" class, sold to a small exclusive group willing to pay several thousand Swiss francs for a special custom-design jeweled watch. Precious stones and/or metals used in the watch face and bracelet accounted for the major portion of the "A" and "AA" watch prices. This was particularly true for electronic watches where movements averaged Sfr. 18. About 27 percent of the value of total watches and 2 percent of pieces sold worldwide were from the "A" tier. "AA" watches accounted for 16 percent of global

---

EXHIBIT 31.7 **Breakdown of production costs**

Estimated cost breakdown for Swiss watch with ex-factory price of Sfr. 390

Case	70
Bracelet	90
Dial	50
Crystal	18
Movement	18 (50 for mechanical)
Hands	5
Total materials costs	251
Assembly and quality control	25
Margin	114
Ex-factory	390
Wholesalers margin	260
Retailers margin	650
Consumer price	1,300

Estimated cost breakdown for Japanese watch with ex-factory price of Sfr. 250

Total variable costs	150
Margin	100
Ex-factory	250
Wholesalers margin	60–90
Retailers margin	310–340
Consumer price	630–700

**Estimated cost breakdown for watch made in Hong Kong with
ex-factory cost of Sfr. 80**

Case and dial	15
Bracelet	15
Crystal	15
Movement	18
Hands	2
Total materials costs	65
Assembly and quality control	6
Manufacturer's margin—10%	8
Ex-factory	80
Wholesalers margin	30
Retailers margin	55–110
Consumer price	165–220

Source: Asuag-SSIH and interviews with industry experts.

watch sales in Swiss francs, but less than 5 percent of total units. Mechanical watches still dominated the high-priced segments (Exhibit 31.8).

Evaluating timekeeping technology was difficult for consumers. When shopping for watches, consumers choose a particular price level and expected a certain level of technical proficiency, style, and intangibles such as prestige. Quartz technology

EXHIBIT 31.8 **Watch purchases by type in the United States at retail prices**

Retail price	Percent all watches	Percent Quartz analog	Percent digital	Percent mechanical
$1,000 or more	.8	.5	.7	1.5
$300–$999	2.4	4.0	.7	1.5
$100–$299	23.5	38.0	8.9	14.6
$50–$99	33.5	33.5	31.9	35.4
$25–$49	39.8	24.0	57.8	47.0

Source: National Jeweler/HTI Consumer Survey 1983.

had changed the price/accuracy ratio. Before the electronic watch, accuracy was bought with expensive, finely engineered jewel-lever watches. With the introduction of electronics, watches with accuracy of plus or minus 15 seconds per month could be purchased for as little as $9.95.

Geographic Segments

Technologies and price have had an impact on the world market for watches. Historically, the United States has been the major importer of finished watches. The United States was often the launching ground for new products and success in this market indicated the strong possibility of global success. The strong dollar and improving U.S. economy in 1984–85 had had a positive impact on the sales and profits of Swiss and Japanese watch companies. Europe and Japan were also strong markets for watches in all price categories. However, throughout the 1960s and 1970s new opportunities for watch sales opened up in the oil producing countries in the Middle East and in less developed countries (LDC).

In the 1960s, watch producers began to move into the LDC with inexpensive roskopf watches. This market was taken over by inexpensive digitals in the early 1970s. However, the initial success of the cheap digital in this market was short lived and consumers returned to mechanical watches. The miniature batteries in the quartz watch were very expensive in these regions, sometimes more than the original cost of the watch. By 1984, this problem had been solved and inexpensive electric watches again dominated the LDC market.

A new opportunity for watch manufacturers developed in industrialized countries with young children providing a new and growing market for inexpensive watches. Until the 1960s, most children received their first watch in their mid- to late teens, often as a gift. Roskopf watches opened up the market to children in the seven to ten year range. A significant portion of these purchases were novelty watches, with cartoon and storybook characters which were sold as gifts for young children. (Exhibit 31.9).

EXHIBIT 31.9 **Consumer buying in the United States—breakdown of watch purchases by age**

Total jewelry and watch purchases by age group

Age	Percent
55 + years	23.6%
35–54	45.0
25–34	23.0
18–24	8.4

Distribution of watch and jewelry purchase prices by age of purchaser

Retail price	18–24 years	25–34 years	35–54 years	55 + years
$1,000 and more	1.3%	1.5%	3.3%	1.2%
$300 to $999	11.3	8.8	9.0	10.4
$100 to $299	27.3	25.3	26.7	27.6
$50 to $99	20.7	24.8	25.3	28.5
$25 to $99	39.4	39.6	35.7	32.3

Source: National Jeweler/HTI Consumer Survey 1983.

The market for expensive watches moved to the Middle East in the early 1970s. The rest of the world was caught in a recession, largely due to escalating oil and gas prices, and demand for high-priced luxury items fell off. Buyers in the oil producing countries had both the money and the interest to purchase luxury goods. The Swiss were particularly adept at meeting the changing fashions and tastes of this new luxury segment and provided expensive, luxury watches with lapis-lazuli, coral, diamonds, and turquoise (Exhibit 31.10).

EXHIBIT 31.10 **Major importers of Swiss watches and movements (In millions of pieces)**

	1960	1970	1975	1980	1982	1984
Hong Kong	1.9	10.0	11.3	12.5	4.1	4.9
United States	12.4	19.2	12.0	5.9	3.6	4.6
Germany	1.3	2.9	5.0	4.9	3.6	4.0
Italy	1.2	2.6	2.6	2.5	2.3	3.0
France	0.2	0.7	0.8	1.6	1.9	2.2
Japan	0.2	1.0	1.6	0.7	0.7	2.0
United Kingdom	1.7	6.1	6.3	3.2	1.9	1.9
Saudi Arabia	0.2	3.4	1.1	1.0	1.2	0.9
Arab Emirates			1.4	1.9	1.3	0.8
Spain	0.8	2.5	1.9	1.3	1.1	0.8
Total 10 largest markets	19.9	48.4	44.0	35.5	21.7	25.1
Total worldwide	41.0	71.4	65.8	51.0	31.3	32.2

Major importers of Swiss watches and movements (In millions of Sfr.)

	1960	1970	1975	1980	1982	1984
United States	250.6	482.2	348.6	379.7	407.8	598.7
Hong Kong	76.6	242.6	257.6	401.6	344.1	351.5
Italy	70.1	153.9	194.0	256.4	287.7	300.3
Germany	48.2	135.3	195.6	241.7	212.4	246.6
Saudi Arabia*	12.2	92.0	84.0	201.9	271.9	233.1
France	10.6	38.6	75.6	123.3	152.0	169.8
Japan	14.1	88.0	172.5	109.0	120.3	167.1
Singapore	38.3	45.1	58.3	79.7	106.2	150.3
United Kingdom	43.1	131.3	176.6	125.3	127.2	139.9
Arab Emirates*			59.4	71.7	94.9	82.1
Total 10 largest markets	563.8	1,409.0	1,622.2	1,990.3	2,124.5	2,439.4
Total worldwide	1,146.3	2,362.2	2,720.3	2,917.5	3,011.0	3,298.8

Major importers of Japanese watches and movements
(In millions of pieces)

	1980	1982	1983
Hong Kong	14.2	23.0	28.3
United States	7.5	10.3	11.8
Germany	3.4	2.7	3.1
Italy	0.8	0.8	1.1
France	1.1	1.9	2.6
Canada	0.8	0.7	1.0
United Kingdom	1.1	1.7	2.2
Saudi Arabia	2.1	2.8	3.9
Arab Emirates	0.6	1.3	1.4
Spain	0.5	2.0	2.1
Total 10 largest markets	32.1	47.2	57.5
Total worldwide	48.3	63.6	76.0

Major importers of Japanese watches and movements
(In millions of Sfr.)

	1980	1982	1983
United States	316.9	372.9	403.4
Hong Kong	383.7	471.0	580.8
Italy	40.9	33.3	47.6
Germany	142.4	94.4	88.0
Saudi Arabia	107.3	94.8	158.3
France	72.0	73.0	95.5
Canada	44.6	39.6	51.1
Singapore	18.3	29.9	23.0
United Kingdom	54.3	56.0	56.7
Arab Emirates	24.5	42.4	58.9
Total 10 largest markets	1,205.0	1,306.4	1,563.2
Total worldwide	1,918.5	1,925.4	2,224.7

Major importers of watches and movements from Hong Kong
(In millions of pieces)

	1980	1982	1984
Canada	2.9	8.6	10.2
United States	32.6	81.7	119.2
Germany	11.5	15.6	20.5
Italy	4.6	5.2	8.0
France	6.6	4.8	4.2
Japan	5.9	8.2	12.4
United Kingdom	9.7	10.4	12.6
Saudi Arabia	2.4	6.4	7.1
Arab Emirates	1.4	3.9	6.2
Spain	4.2	9.5	14.8
Total 10 largest markets	81.8	154.3	215.2
Total worldwide	126.1	213.7	284.1

Major importers of watches and movements from Hong Kong
(In millions of Sfr.)

	1980	1982	1984
United States	469.4	591.3	671.7
Canada	56.7	63.3	57.8
Italy	62.7	34.9	40.8
Germany	194.9	129.4	145.9
Saudi Arabia	58.9	102.3	100.5
France	88.5	34.2	22.8
Japan	69.5	65.1	84.7
Singapore	43.8	46.8	34.2
United Kingdom	139.0	82.6	76.3
Arab Emirates	25.7	59.6	57.0
Total 10 largest markets	1,209.0	1,209.4	1,291.5
Total worldwide	1,859.7	1,779.6	1,915.3

*Saudia Arabia with Arab Emirates in 1960 and 1970.

Source: Swiss Watch Federation.

TRENDS IN WATCH DISTRIBUTION

Wholesale Distributors

Watch distributors played an essential role in linking the manufacturer to the retailer. Distributors generally sold one or perhaps two noncompeting brands. Wholesalers expected exclusive distribution rights for the brand for a given region. Distributors maintained a sales force to sell to and service retailers. They purchased watches outright and maintained a local inventory.

Manufacturers expected their distributors to participate in promotional activities. Distributors attended trade fairs and contributed to advertising, mailing expenses, and point-of-purchase display materials.

The distributor was responsible to find and oversee adequate watch repair services. Watch repair was a key issue for watches in the "B", "A", and "AA" categories. This service need had led to a close working relationship between the producer, distributor, and retailer. The distributor found and licensed watch repair services and jewelers with watch repair capabilities. For especially difficult repairs the distributor helped arrange for work to be sent back to the factory. With inexpensive, "throw-a-way" watches, repairs were less critical or nonexistent. Importers of "C" level watches had greater freedom in channel selection. Mass merchandisers, drug stores, and even supermarkets were used to distribute watches to end-users. Some of these watches were sold with a guarantee, and rather than repair, a replacement was offered.

Most watch manufacturers had agreements with independent distributors. The Japanese and some of the private Swiss firms operated wholly or partially owned marketing and sales subsidiaries in their foreign markets. Twenty-five to thirty-five percent was the standard markup granted wholesalers and importers of Japanese and Hong Kongese watches. This figure increased to 40 percent or more for importers of most Swiss watches.

Retailers

A wide variety of retailers sold watches to the end-user, including jewelry and department stores, mass merchandisers, and mail order catalogues.

An estimated 40 percent of worldwide watch sales came from jewelry stores. Watch manufacturers benefitted from the jeweler's selling expertise and personal interaction with consumers. Watches sold in exclusive jewelry and department stores benefitted from the store's deluxe or fashion image. Fine gold, mechanical watches were a natural extension of the jeweler's product line and most were capable of minor watch repairs and cleaning. When electronics were initially introduced, some jewelry stores resisted the new technology. Electronics were not within the jeweler's extensive training. Within a short period of time, however, customer demand and refinements to the technology moved quartz watches into jewelry stores worldwide.

Jewelry stores had been the traditional outlet for watch sales until the mid-1950s. The rapid growth in roskopf and later in inexpensive digital watch sales was accompanied by channel diversification and watches moved into new outlets: drug stores, department stores, and supermarkets. Retail watch sales in the U.S. had been influenced by channel diversification and in 1983 less than 30 percent of watches sold in the U.S. were purchased in jewelry stores (Exhibit 31.11).

Stock turn for a "B", "A", or "AA" watch could be as low as two times per year at retail and phasing out older models and cleaning out the pipeline could take 2 or 3 years. "C" watches generally moved more quickly, with 4 to 6 stockturns per year.

Jewelry stores and department stores were accustomed to a 50 to 55 percent markup. Mass merchandisers' margins varied and went as low as 25 percent.

EXHIBIT 31.11 **Watch type purchased by outlet in the United States**

	Percent analog	Percent digital	Percent watches
Jewelry store	34.3	12.0	27.6
Department store	26.3	27.6	26.2
Discount store	14.7	23.1	16.7
Catalog showroom	14.7	10.4	10.3
Mail order	14.7	11.2	5.4
Wholesaler	2.5	1.5	3.1
Drug store	2.0	6.0	5.1
Flea market	*	*	2.4
Other outlets	3.0	7.5	6.2

	Cost of purchases in main outlets				
	$1000+	$300–999	$100–299	$50–99	$5–49
Jewelry store	70.0%	69.4%	49.1%	34.6%	27.2%
Department store	*	6.9	16.7	22.5	27.9
Discount store	2.5	1.7	5.8	9.7	10.5
Catalog showroom	5.0	5.2	8.9	9.4	7.3
Other outlets	22.5	16.8	19.5	23.8	27.1

*Less than 1%.

Source: National Jeweler/HTI Consumer Survey 1983.

COMPETITORS IN THE GLOBAL WATCH INDUSTRY

Timex

Timex, a U.S. company, began selling inexpensive, mechanical watches in the late 1950s. Most Timex watches fell into the "C" range, with prices ranging from under Sfr. 15 to just over Sfr. 250.

The company developed into a manufacturer of mass-produced, hard alloy pin-lever watches. Manufacturing was mechanized, simplified, and standardized. When the company's pricing plan called for a 30 percent mark-up at the retail level, jewelry stores refused to carry the watches. Timex moved into mass outlets such as drug, department, and hardware stores, and even cigar stands. The number of outlets for Timex watches in 1985 was estimated between 100,000 and 150,000. This figure was down from a high of 2.5 million in the 1960s. By the late 1960s, 50 percent of all watches sold in the United States were Timex. In 1985, Timex had capacity to produce 15 million watches.

Timex had an advertising budget of approximately Sfr. 20 million, most of which was spent on television sports events. Timex produced a large number of

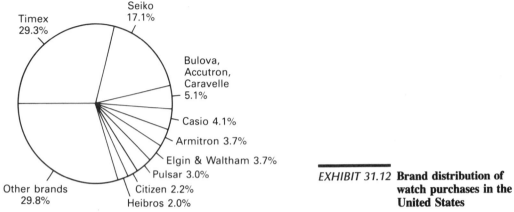

Timex
29.3%

Seiko
17.1%

Bulova,
Accutron,
Caravelle
5.1%

Casio 4.1%

Armitron 3.7%

Elgin & Waltham 3.7%

Pulsar 3.0%

Citizen 2.2%

Heibros 2.0%

Other brands
29.8%

EXHIBIT 31.12 **Brand distribution of watch purchases in the United States**

Source: Swiss Watch Foundation and National Jewelers/HTI Consumer Survey 1983.

styles, but did not promote any single model or style. The company was known for its "takes a licking and keeps on ticking" slogan, promoting Timex durability.

Timex began limited production of digital watches in 1972. By the mid-1970s, the company was feeling pressure from new entrants from Japan and from other U.S. companies. Sales support for mechanical watches was withdrawn and Timex attempted to increase its digital capacity and to gain electronics capabilities rapidly. As a mechanical watch manufacturer, Timex had been fully integrated, but used outside sources for electronic components. The company's initial entries to the digital market were poorly received and sales declined to Sfr. 1 billion in 1979. Throughout the 1970s, the company faced significant losses that amounted to Sfr. 260 million by the end of 1982. These losses were expected to escalate.

In the 1980s, Timex moved into consumer electronics, computers, home health care products, and refocused its watch business to try to halt its profit slide and plant closings. In 1981, Timex invested in a British home-computer company founded by inventor Clive Sinclair. The computer had little capacity but had the lowest price on the market. In 1982, fierce price competition in the home-computer market squeezed margins and the price was cut in half to approximately Sfr. 100. The company also lost sales to competitors such as Commodore which offered more power for about Sfr. 180. Timex management viewed the watch industry as splitting into two parts: jewelry and wrist instruments. Timex reported that its development plans would emphasize the wrist-instrument business with multifunction watches.

Texas Instruments, Inc.

In 1975, a number of U.S. electronics companies entered the industry with digital watches and circuits for electronic movements. Finding themselves with excess capacity, an estimated 100 chip producers entered the watch market. Most started as suppliers of movements and components and integrated forward into production and assembly of complete watches. In the early days of digital watch sales, demand far outstripped capacity. In spite of this fact, the electronics companies continually pushed price down in a market share war that eventually destroyed this attempted entry into the watch business.

Texas Instruments (TI) was the largest of the semi-conductor and computer companies to enter the watch industry. Its consumer electronics division began in the early 1970s with hand-held calculators. The company then broadened this line with watches, home computers, and educational products.

Watch manufacturing at TI began in 1976, when its first LED, plastic-cased watch with Sfr. 40 price tag was introduced. One month later the price was cut in half. TI developed a digital watch that could be made from TI-built parts on automated equipment. Prices were set to undercut the mechanical watch competition with a goal to gain a large piece of both the U.S. and global market. Prices were set to reflect budgeted, future volumes.

While TI had surprised the competition with reduced prices, it was caught off-guard with advances in digital display readouts. To provide a full line of products the company imported seven out of 13 of its basic lines from Hong Kong, including its multifunction watches. The corporation reported Sfr. 6.4 billion in sales in 1979, Sfr. 800 million of which came from consumer goods. The division showed a pretax profit of Sfr. 4 million down from pretax $28 million in 1978. Profits continued to slide and TI moved out of the watch industry in 1982.

Casio Computer Company

In 1974 Casio, a Japanese computer company, entered the market and claimed 12 percent share of all Japanese watches sold within five years. Casio watches were sold in the "C" price range. Casio manufactured its watches in highly automated factories. Its product line was limited to digital watches, many of them multifunctional with stop watches, timers, and calculators. Casio management has been quoted as saying, "People should own at least three watches." In 1985, Casio was selling an estimated 30 million watches per year. The Casio name was clearly linked worldwide with multifunction watches.

Casio's first entry into the digital market was priced at Sfr. 180 and initial sales were weak. As the company's watch prices began to fall, sales doubled annually from 1974 to 1980.

Casio was among the first electronic watch producers to determine that the electronic watch's greatest appeal was technical rather than aesthetic. The company urged its department and mass merchandise store retailers to display its watches in the camera, calculator, or stereo department, rather than the jewelry department. Casio management felt that sales personnel at these counters understood electronic equipment better than jewelry salespeople and could therefore answer customer questions.

The Hong Kong Watchmakers

Hong Kong entered the watch market in a major way in 1976, specializing in inexpensive electronic and mechanical watches. Hong Kong watch manufacturers did not sell under their own company or brand name. Private-label watches were produced and sold in minimum lots of 1,000 to 2,000 pieces per model.

Ten major producers accounted for an estimated 70 percent of total volume, but as many as 800 "loft workshops" were also operating. These production facilities could be started at low cost and run with minimum overhead. Hong Kong was the world's largest watch exporter, and was responsible for 326.4 million units in 1984; total value was Sfr. 2,091.2 million.

Most watch production in Hong Kong was limited to assembly. Inexpensive components and movements were purchased in large lot sizes. Hong Kong manufacturers kept their design costs minimal or nonexistent by producing copies and near-copies of watches displayed at trade fairs and in jewelry stores. Average ex-factory prices were Sfr. 25 for a mechanical, Sfr. 60 for quartz analog, and Sfr. 12 for electronic digitals. Hong Kong watch prices began to fall rapidly in the late 1970s. Simple watches selling for Sfr. 18 to 20 in 1978 dropped to Sfr. 12 in one year and margins shrunk to less than Sfr. 1.

Counterfeiting was a fairly common practice among small Hong Kong manufacturers. A counterfeit copied the original watch design and was marked with the brand name. This practice was generally avoided by the large producers who beginning in the early 1980s, were seeking entry into the international watch establishment. Counterfeiting was a significant problem faced by European and Japanese producers. Unlike technological innovations, it was very difficult to establish patents or copyrights on designs. Firms could begin to protect their brand name by establishing a company or joint venture within Hong Kong.

SWATCH WATCH SA

SWATCH was a plastic, quartz, analog watch. SWATCH was sold at Sfr. 15 ex-factory and Sfr. 50 at retail in Switzerland. Prices outside of Switzerland were slightly higher and the top price was $30 in the United States. The product was available in 12 styles, which changed twice per year, in a woman's and a man's model.

SWATCH WATCH was an Asuag-SSIH company under the direction of Ernst Thomke. It was founded in 1985 when it was split off from its original producer ETA. SWATCH WATCH remained within the Ebauches group of Asuag-SSIH. Within two years of its introduction in 1982, the brand had hit sales of 3.5 million units. Sales for 1985 were expected to reach 7.5 million units. In 1985, SWATCH management was concerned that the company's already constrained capacity could become an increasingly significant problem over the next few years. The product was produced on a fully automated and robotised assembly line and the hands were the only component purchased from an outside source. The company had enjoyed rapid decline in production costs per watch. Thomke had met and surpassed his original target production cost of Sfr. 10 per watch.

From introduction it had been positioned for active people, a sport or fashion accessory and not as a time piece. The watch sold in jewelry and department stores. The company had spent heavily on promotion and advertising, budgeting approximately Sfr. 5 per watch for marketing expense and profits.

SWATCH invested Sfr. 20 million in marketing efforts and was expected to spend Sfr. 30 million in 1985. SWATCH was sold in 19 industrial countries and approximately 50 percent of all SWATCHes were sold in the United States. In the majority of markets, independent distributors were employed. However, SWATCH WATCH USA was a wholly owned subsidiary that controlled distribution in the United States. SWATCH WATCH USA played a significant role in the creation of marketing strategy and planning for the watch.

Seiko

Seiko, part of the K. Hattori Company, began marketing an electronic, quartz watch in 1969 and emerged as the market volume leader in the global watch industry within ten years. In 1984, the company reported annual sales of Sfr. 3.8 billion for watches and clocks. Seiko-brand watches fell within the "B" category. But the company competed in the "C" segment with the Alba and Larus labels, high "C" or low "B" segment with the Pulsar label, and "A" segment with the Jean Lassale brand. In 1984, the company sold 55 million watches; 22 million under the Seiko brand.

Seiko had been using assembly line production since the mid-1950s. Following the example of the Detroit automobile factories, its engineers designed assembly lines and unskilled laborers were employed in most production. The firm was fully integrated: manufacturing key components, jewels, and even watchmaking machinery. Seiko was among the first to initiate large-scale production and sales of electronic watches.

Seiko had been protected from foreign competitors in its domestic market. Only expensive watches, about 5 percent of total units and 20 percent of total value of Japanese purchases, were imported. Almost all of the low- to mid-priced watches purchased in Japan were produced by Seiko and one of its two domestic competitors, Citizen and Casio. Japanese companies produced some low-priced movements for Hong Kong manufacturers. However, movements for "B" watch production were not exported to Hong Kong.

Seiko used the United States as a market for initial entry, where they gained a reputation that they then sold worldwide. The company offered fewer than 400 quartz and mechanical models in the United States, but over 2,300 worldwide. These models included analog, digital, and multifunction watches. Plans called for an expansion of the number of styles sold in the United States and a broadening of the price range at the upper and lower ends of the market.

Seiko owned sales subsidiaries in all of its major markets. Seiko watches were sold in jewelry and department stores. It had also established service centers in all of its major markets. This service allowed the customer to bring or mail a repair problem directly to the company, bypassing the jeweler. Seiko spent as much as Sfr. 80 to 100 million annually in worldwide advertising, mostly television, to sell its quartz watches. Seiko had created a strong brand image based on its quartz technology and accuracy.

While Seiko was a formidable competitor for the Swiss watch industry, Japanese consumers were a major market for Swiss luxury watches. Throughout the 1970s and 1980s, Swiss luxury watches were considered a status symbol in Japan. In 1981, Seiko moved into the luxury market, at home and abroad, when it purchased a small Swiss watch producer Jean Lassale. The company's plan was to combine Swiss design and elegance with Japanese engineering and technical skill in electronics.

By 1970, both Seiko and its Japanese competitor, Citizen, had diversified into new businesses with internal development, mergers, and acquisitions. Included in the expanded product line were consumer electronic products such as computers, software, calculators, high-speed printers, miniature industrial robots, office equipment, and machine tools and even fashion department stores. As Seiko faced the 1990s, these product lines were expected to become an increasingly important part of the companies' total sales and profits. In 1970, clocks and watches represented 99 percent of Seiko sales; but by 1983 that share had dropped to 40 percent. Top executives at Seiko expected this figure to continue to decline to 30 percent by 1990.

Longines SA

Longines was well-known internationally but losing money when it was acquired by Asuag in 1974. Longines was developed into the group's premiere, or top-priced, brand and began contributing to profits in 1976.

After joining Asuag, Longines' prices began to climb as the company edged its way into the high-priced "A" watch segment. The first Swiss manufacturer to produce electronic watches in 1969, Longines' product mix was 50 percent electronic. In 1985, average price for Longines watches was Sfr. 4,500 to 5,000.

Longines produced at levels of about 500,000 watches per year. Investments were made in more efficient machines to reduce dependence on skilled labor and the number of different types of movements and other precision parts was cut back. Longines continued to make about 30 lines, each with many variations.

Longines put all of its promotion money behind its leader model, the "Conquest." Management felt that the top-priced "Conquest" best represented the overall style of the collection. "The Longines Style" campaign was supported with an advertising and promotion budget of 10 percent of total sales and this sum was matched by Longines agents. Advertisements were placed in international and local media.

In 1984, Longines introduced a new watch line, the Conquest VHP. VHP stood for "very high precision" and the watch promised accuracy within one second per month. The gun-metal-colored titanium and gold watch contained two quartz crystals. The first was the timekeeper and the second compensated for vibrations and effects of the weather. The watch sold for Sfr. 1,650 at retail and initial response from the marketplace was very positive. Advertising for the new line stressed the watch's Swiss origin with the heading "Swiss Achievement."

Rolex

Rolex, with its prestigious "Oyster" line was perhaps the best known of the Swiss luxury watch manufacturers. Rolex was a private company, owned by a foundation. The company was responsible for about 5.5 percent of Switzerland's watch exports by value, with estimated annual export of 400,000 units, valued at Sfr. 700 to 800 million. Rolex did not disclose its domestic sales.

Ninety percent of all Rolex watches were produced with mechanical movements housed in gold or platinum cases. The "Oyster" line was described as a premium sports watch. "Oyster" watch prices ranged from Sfr. 800 for stainless steel watches to Sfr. 14,000 for solid gold watches. Production was semi-automated and Geneva housewives made up a large part of the semi-skilled labor. Skilled workers were required for hand-assembly in the final stages of production. The company always allowed production to lag slightly behind demand.

Throughout the turbulent 1970s, the company had stayed consistently with the luxury sport watch market. Rolex limited advertising to the higher-priced "Oyster" line. Rolex also had a second line, "Cellini," of high-priced luxury dress watches. The company resisted entry into the electronic age; only 10 percent of the Rolex line was electronic. There was some speculation that in the next three to five years quartz watches would rise to 30 percent of total output. In 1983, quartz production was limited to watches under the Tudor brand, at the low end of Rolex's market and were priced below Sfr. 1,200. The Tudor watches were not advertised and did not bear the Rolex name. In 1985, Rolex categories included three "Oysterquartz" models.

Rolex employed wholly owned marketing subsidiaries in 19 countries. The Geneva headquarters worked through the subsidiaries to license jewelers to sell and service its watches. The subsidiaries provided sales and service support to local retailers and watch repairers. Maintaining adequate service coverage was important in an era of throw-away watches. For example, the New York subsidiary licensed 70 watch repairers to service Rolex watches. Distribution to retail outlets was based on a quota system. Subsidiaries were also used to maintain tight control over retail prices, Rolex did not permit any discounting. Promotion and advertising expenditures were estimated at 10 percent of sales. This expenditure was matched by the wholesalers and retailers.

Piaget SA

Piaget SA was founded by George Piaget in 1874, and in 1985 was still a family business directed by the founder's grandsons and great-grandsons. The company's workshops produced approximately 15,000 handmade watches each year at prices ranging from Sfr. 4,000 to 400,000. The company carried a large collection of luxury watches for both men and women, producing approximately 1,200 models.

Only gold and/or platinum were used to encase the watch movements, and many of the watches were decorated with precious stones. Both mechanical and quartz models were included in the Piaget collection. Piaget was the only producer of luxury dress watches that was fully integrated. The company produced the world's thinnest mechanical watches: 1.2mm for a hand-wind model, and 2mm for an automatic. Historically, the Piaget line was limited to dress watches, but the company entered the sports watch market in 1980.

Worldwide, Piaget watches were carried by 400 retailers. They tended to be the most prestigious stores in their areas and were located to be accessible to potential luxury watch buyers. Whenever possible, the watchmaker preferred retailers to carry only Piaget in their luxury dress watch line. Annual advertising expenditure for Piaget was estimated at Sfr. 3 million, excluding the United States. About 55 percent of this expense was paid for by Piaget, and the rest was contribution from distributors and retailers.

Other Swiss manufacturers producing luxury dress watches included Audemars-Piguet, Patek-Philippe and Vacheron & Constantin. All three were smaller than Piaget, producing less than 15,000 watches per year and followed similar strategies.

Ebel

Ebel was founded in 1911 by Eugene Blum. The company described its transition in the 1970s as a renaissance.

In 1974, the third generation of Blums, Pierre-Alain, took over the company. When Pierre-Alain Blum became President, Ebel's 50 employees were making private label watches. With new management, Ebel began to take a closer look at the customers of its chief client Cartier. Within a short period of time, Ebel began branded watch production and employment grew to 500 people. In 1984, sales were estimated between Sfr. 150 and 170 million.

The company's growth came about with the development of a unique one-piece watch case and bracelet construction that became the base for the Ebel collection. Ebel's goal was to design and maintain a "classic," timeless collection, and the company did not plan to make major annual changes to its line. Ebel watches sold at retail Sfr. 1,000 to 15,000. The company had five models and realized 90 percent of its sales from the top three. The company's goal was to create a strong brand image. Using its leader model, Ebel promoted its watch lines with the slogan "Architects of Time."

Ebel began production of electronic movements in 1978. With that change in technology the company enjoyed a boost in sales. In 1985, Ebel was assembling 300,000 units per year. The company maintained tight control over its suppliers. Ebel had production and development contracts with its movement supplier and partial ownership of its case and bracelet manufacturers. The company still assembled private-label watches for Cartier. In 1975, sales to Cartier had represented 90 percent of sales, 10 years later these sales represented less than 50 percent of total. It was estimated that Cartier sales provided about 25 percent of Ebel's profits in 1984.

Blum maintained close personal contact with the end customer, making frequent visits to jewelry stores. His goal was to keep a close eye on stock levels at jewelry stores and avoid a build up of stock in the distribution channels. He also wanted to insure that the jewelry store's image was in line with the Ebel image.

In addition to its "Architects of Time" media advertising, Ebel also used sports sponsorship as a means of building an image with the public. Ebel became one of the first watch companies to actively use sporting events for its watch promotion. Ebel sponsorships included a soccer team in Geneva, tennis, and golf matches.

In the 1980s, Ebel was broadening its business activities. It expanded its product line by becoming the distributor for Schaeffer pens. Ebel also entered the clothing business with the American firm of Fenn, Wright, and Manson. They opened a boutique in Geneva and others were in the planning stages. Finally, Ebel was the agent for Olivetti computers for the French speaking part of Switzerland. The distribution company employed 12 people including programmers.

Recent Entrants to the Watch Industry

A new group of outsiders and newcomers has entered the global watch industry. Many of these companies (or current ownership) have been operating for 10 years or less. With few exceptions, these "watchmakers" subcontracted all production and assembly, mostly in Switzerland. The watches were then positioned in the market as high-fashion pieces.

Raymond Weil.   Included in this group was Raymond Weil, founded in 1976. Within 10 years the company had reached annual sales levels of approximately 300,000 quartz watches, at prices ranging from Sfr. 500 to 1,700. All work was subcontracted to companies and individual component manufacturers and assemblers in the Jura region of Switzerland. The company employed 15 people for design, marketing, sales, and administration. One-third of all wholesale activities were captively held.

Weil's success in the watch industry was attributed to the company's sense of style and fashion. A new collection was introduced each year with six woman's and six man's watches. Weil was constantly responding to changes in consumer tastes and the latest trend. His 1985 spring collection was named for a hit movie, *Amadeus*, a biography of the life of Mozart. Raymond Weil had a limited budget for its advertising and promotion expenditures, relying on a few well-placed messages and style to sell its products.

Cartier.   These watches were classic in design and limited to 15 different models. Cartier subcontracted its watches from Ebel. The Cartier watch lines included models that sold for as much as Sfr. 100,000. Most Cartier watches were quartz and sold at prices ranging from Sfr. 1,200 to 25,000. Selling at a level of 450,000 units per year, the watch was an addition to the company's collection of accessories and jewelry. The watches were sold through the company's specialized retail stores and independent boutiques, jewelry, and fashionable department stores all over the world. Watch advertising and promotion expenses were minimized because the company's name was well recognized in the marketplace and the watch fell under the umbrella of the company's other accessories.

Gucci.   These watches were sold by an independent entrepreneur who licensed the Gucci name. These "A" watches were sold at Gucci shops and by independent jewelers and high-fashion department stores and boutiques. Annual volumes for Gucci watches were estimated at 400,000 units. The company did not advertise heavily and relied on the Gucci name for prestigious name-brand identity.

Summary

Thomke knew that there were a number of options open to him to bring Tissot from its current status of a "branded commodity." He estimated that relaunch in Europe would be a minimum of Sfr. 12 million. Costs for reintroducing Tissot to the United States would be even greater. To afford these marketing expenses, Tissot marketing and profit margins would have to improve and sales volumes would have to grow. Thomke knew he could shift prices and was considering pushing Tissot prices downward to the bottom of the "B" group. A downward price shift would require a considerable increase in volume if the Tissot brand was to be profitable. The producer's margin decreased as watches moved down market to the "B" and "C" segments. Thomke knew that producers of expensive watches that had a strong positive image with consumers could command high ex-factory prices. This provided the luxury watch firms with considerable margins for marketing expenditures and profit.

Thomke believed that to operate profitably a watch had to capture at least 10 percent of its market segment. He wanted to produce a workable brand strategy that would allow Tissot to gain at least 10 percent of its segment. Thomke had several key factors to consider. The fast-paced technological changes of the 1970s had slowed and the traditional watch-buying market was maturing. However, he saw that nontraditional approaches had allowed new entrants such as Raymond Weil and SWATCH to successfully gain footholds and profits in the global watch industry.

CASE 32 ————————————————————

SASSAFRAS!

"Will this meeting please come to order? We have a lengthy agenda to cover this morning," Janet Ellison, incoming Chairperson of the Cookbook Committee shouted over the laughter and chatter emanating from the meeting room. The 1986–87 Cookbook Committee, which had been appointed in April 1986, only two months earlier, was now ready to take over the marketing and office management activities from the old committee.

After talking about office hours and office procedures, and revisions in policies, Janet had come to the last item on her list. She turned to Julie Jones, the new Cookbook Marketing Chairman and said, "Julie, why don't you brief the other committee members on some of the matters we've been discussing?" Julie, armed with pages of notes started, "We have quite a task ahead of us! As you all know, SASSAFRAS! sold extremely well in its first year. The sales momentum created because our book was new has to be sustained. Making our cookbook stand out from all the others is going to become more difficult since SASSAFRAS! is only one of many attractive community cookbooks on the market. And we can't rely on orders from our League members to boost our sales figures." "I agree completely," added the Retail Sales Coordinator, "I think our League members are burned out on buying SASSAFRAS!. Most of our members have already purchased copies for their mothers, their mothers-in-law, their grandmothers, their friends, etc. They don't know who else to give copies to!" Julie continued, "What we need to do is develop some unique, creative and effective marketing strategies to ensure that SASSAFRAS! continues to sell as well as or better than it did in its first year of publication. Who has some thoughts?"

BACKGROUND AND HISTORY: FROM IDEA TO FINAL PRODUCT

SASSAFRAS! was a community cookbook developed and marketed by the Junior League of Springfield, Missouri, Inc. It was in a second printing of 10,000 books—this having been accomplished less than a year after it was first published in April 1985.

This case was prepared by Professors Mary K. Coulter and Ronald L. Coulter of Southwest Missouri State University. It is intended as a basis for classroom discussion rather than to illustrate effective or ineffective handling of an administrative situation. Copyright © 1987 by Mary Coulter and Ron Coulter. This case was presented at the Case Research Association meeting, 1986. Distributed by the Case Research Association. All rights reserved to the authors and the Case Research Association. Used by permission from Ronald L. and Mary K. Coulter and the North American Case Research Association.

SASSAFRAS! was developed with the intent of it becoming a long-term, successful fund raiser for the Junior League of Springfield (JLS). JLS, a nonprofit organization, was devoted to developing and training women as volunteers to work to improve their local community. The League did this by providing financial support for programs and trained volunteers for various community projects.

JLS had two other fund-raising activities in addition to SASSAFRAS!. These were the annual Charity Ball and the Plaid Door Thrift Shop. Both had been fund raisers for a number of years: the Charity Ball for 27 years and the Plaid Door for 10 years. Money raised by these activities supported community programs that the League reviewed and approved annually. Examples of community projects that had been supported in the past included the local public television station, the local ballet company, the regional opera, the Girl's Shelter, a public school drug abuse awareness program, etc. Other money for league operations and project support came from annual dues ($50), required member contributions (including a $50 donation to the Plaid Door and a $40 donation to the Charity ball; as of yet there was no financial requirement by the membership for SASSAFRAS!), and other individual and community organization donations.

JLS, a member of the Association of Junior Leagues, was one of over 266 leagues across the United States and internationally. Several of these leagues (149) published a cookbook as a part of their fund-raising activities.

SASSAFRAS! began as an interest group of JLS. Interest groups were considered a vital part of any league since they provided research in areas of interest to the membership. The Cookbook Interest Group was sanctioned in May 1982, and immediately began the task of researching the feasibility of publishing a cookbook. On August 20, 1982, just 3 months after getting the go-ahead, the interest group presented a 26 page proposal to publish a cookbook to the Ways and Means Committee of the JLS. The proposal was developed by (1) studying resource material from the headquarters of the Association of Junior Leagues, (2) attending two seminars conducted by national cookbook publishers, and (3) consulting with several chairpersons of other successful League cookbook committees. After studying the proposal, the Ways and Means Committee recommended it be presented to the JLS Board of Directors. It was presented and accepted by the Board who then recommended that the proposal be introduced to the general league membership at its next meeting.

At the January 1983 meeting, the membership approved the motion, "that JLS adopt the publication of a cookbook as a long-term fund raiser with a commitment of 20 volunteers and $50,000 funding." The hard work and effort by the Cookbook Interest Group had paid off. As one of the members put it, "Our idea and dream, our cookbook, can now become a reality."

A Cookbook Committee immediately was appointed and began working in late January 1983. The committee members prepared and sent 425 "recipe packets" to every JLS member. Approximately 3,000 recipes were submitted by league members and "friends" of the league. Each recipe was copied, coded and filed, making it ready for testing. The committee felt a strong responsibility to emphasize the importance of recipe testing.

During 1983–84, most of the committee's time was spent conducting and monitoring recipe testing. More than 5,200 testings and nearly 31,300 tastings were completed and evaluated, resulting in the selection of over 700 recipes to be included in the cookbook.

The committee also made the decision to contract with an advertising and marketing agency to develop the title, theme, and general format of the cookbook. In May 1984, a title and design for the book was approved. The Cookbook now had an identity. The Committee believed the name SASSAFRAS! provided that "just-right" flair needed to make the cookbook stand out.

During 1984–85, the committee rewrote, edited, titled, typeset, proofread, and pasted up the 726 recipes to be included in the cookbook. SASSAFRAS! was developed around the theme of being The Ozarks Cookbook. In the Ozarks, the distinctiveness of the sassafras tree was legendary because all of the tree's parts were usable—bark, roots, and leaves all provided products used even today. The sassafras tree was often characterized as "all things for all people." The name *SASSAFRAS! The Ozarks Cookbook* was chosen to reflect the region's heritage. In fact, the logo that depicted this theme was presented quite clearly and dramatically on the cover of the cookbook. Recipe titles, suggested menu selections, and narrative throughout the book carried out the theme. Special features included the following:

- Professionally designed book featuring 408 pages, full-color pictures of selected recipes, plus sepia landscapes of the Ozarks.
- Introduction by Janet Dailey, best-selling Ozark novelist.
- 726 outstanding recipes selected from more than 4,000 submissions—each double-tested for quality, accuracy, and ease of preparation.
- Durable, full-color 6 1/2 by 9 1/2 inch hard cover, spiral bound to lie flat.
- 12 sections with mylar divider tabs, individual indexes and large easy-to-read print.
- Special "Ozarks Outdoors" section featuring recipes suitable for picnics, tailgate parties, camping, river floating.
- Comprehensive cross-referenced index.

A description of these features was used in press releases, retail and wholesale brochures, and any time the book was being promoted.

On January 15, 1985, a camera-ready manuscript was mailed to the publisher. Three months later on April 10, 1985, the first copies of SASSAFRAS! arrived. A gala introduction for the cookbook was ready to go.

The SASSAFRAS! Debut

Martha Stewart, a well-known authority on cooking and entertaining, was brought to Springfield as a guest of JLS to present a lecture/demonstration and also to help promote the April 1985 Charity Ball (which had as its theme, of course, SASSAFRAS!). Media coverage for the cookbook included a press conference, three local television interviews with the chairperson of the SASSAFRAS! committee, public service announcements, and local newspaper and magazine articles. Even Willard Scott of NBC's *Today Show* featured the book in one of his broadcasts. Sales from April 18, 1985 (date of first actual sales) to May 31, 1985, totaled 2,585 retail books and 1,329 wholesale books for gross revenues of $51,000.

1985–86 OPERATIONS

Once the fanfare surrounding the book's introduction was over, it was down to business for the 1985–86 SASSAFRAS! committee. Exhibit 32.1 shows the committee structure. There were basically two areas of organized activity: marketing procedures and office (i.e. bookkeeping and shipping) procedures. The first year of operations was primarily a year of experimenting with ideas and approaches. Some worked well and others did not.

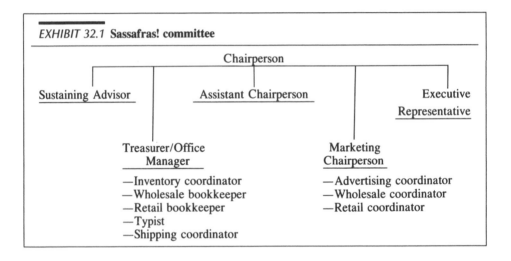

EXHIBIT 32.1 **Sassafras! committee**

Chairperson

Sustaining Advisor — Assistant Chairperson — Executive Representative

Treasurer/Office Manager
—Inventory coordinator
—Wholesale bookkeeper
—Retail bookkeeper
—Typist
—Shipping coordinator

Marketing Chairperson
—Advertising coordinator
—Wholesale coordinator
—Retail coordinator

Marketing Procedures

The marketing group, which consisted of the marketing chairperson, advertising coordinator, wholesale coordinator, and retail coordinator, was charged with the responsibility of developing and implementing all marketing plans. Part of their activities was the need to define target markets, to develop appropriate methods of promotion to these target markets, and to define the most efficient channels of distribution. Both wholesale and retail sales of the cookbook were emphasized although the committee believed that long-run success of the cookbook was dependent upon building a strong, continually growing wholesale sales base.

Because of the initial success of the book (7,129 books were sold between the release date of April 20, 1985 and August 31, 1985, with gross revenues of $70,595), the marketing group had its work cut out for it to market the book most effectively during the 1985–86 year. The initial momentum created because the book was new had to be sustained. Several marketing activities, both wholesale and retail, were planned and implemented.

Wholesale. Wholesale sales of SASSAFRAS! were made to retailers at a standard 40 percent discount from the suggested retail price of $14.95. The retailer could then sell the book at any desired price. During local wholesale sales trips in 1986, committee members observed price tags on SASSAFRAS! ranging from $11.95 to $17.95. However, most retailers sold the book at the suggested retail price.

Wholesale accounts included bookstores, department stores, kitchen/cookware stores, country craft stores, gift shops, and assorted other types of retail outlets. The largest wholesale account for SASSAFRAS! was Silver Dollar City, an entertainment attraction with an 1870s atmosphere, located about 45 miles south of Springfield near Branson, Missouri.

During the first year of operations, there were mass mailings of the cookbook's wholesale brochure to potential accounts (in August 1985 and March 1986). Wholesale mailing lists were initially developed by utilizing telephone books, lists provided by the publisher of SASSAFRAS!, and personal (League members') suggestions. Emphasis was placed on saturating retail outlets in the local market both in Springfield and in the two prime tourist markets adjacent to Springfield—the Branson lakes area and the Lake of the Ozarks area. Announcement letters and 725 wholesale brochures with order cards were mailed initially after the SASSAFRAS! introduction to businesses within the local area as well as regionally (i.e. the rest of Missouri, Arkansas, Kansas, and Oklahoma). Special offers, such as providing a SASSAFRAS! wooden plank crate for use as a point-of-purchase display, were occasionally made to existing wholesale accounts. Another offer used to encourage Christmas and tourist season sales was free shipping for a designated period of time. In June 1985, there were 74 active (i.e. purchasing regularly) wholesale accounts and by April 1986 there were 145 accounts.

Exchanging lists of best wholesale accounts with other Junior Leagues was a common practice and the committee approved participating in these exchanges. Wholesale brochures and order cards were mailed to retailers found on these lists in hopes of opening new accounts.

The wholesale coordinator was responsible for servicing active accounts, developing new accounts, and updating wholesale address files. Her job was demanding and time consuming. When asked to describe what she did, she stated, "This job is fun but challenging! Our two biggest sales pushes are during the summer when we are encouraging retailers to order for Christmas and during the spring when we're encouraging tourist and summer sales. During other times, I try to follow up on leads for new accounts and keep our noncomputerized address files current. It's enough to keep me and probably someone else very busy."

Even with all of the wholesale marketing efforts, the marketing group had never been able to get the cookbook placed in any large department store chains and had not been able to successfully penetrate market areas outside of the Ozarks region.

In October 1985, the committee began to discuss the possibility of placing SAS-SAFRAS! with cookbook distributors. Book distributors played an important role in the national distribution and marketing of cookbooks. Because of its attractive appearance and initial sales success, several distributors had already expressed an interest in carrying SASSAFRAS! in their lines. Distributors received a greater purchase discount (from 45 to 52 percent depending on the distributor) than the retailer and then made money by selling to retailers. Going with a distributor would mean less profit per book for JLS but could provide a wider distribution of the cookbook and hopefully generate more sales volume to increase overall profit. Distributors would include the cookbook in their product line which they represented and sold to retailers. Each distributor had a catalog that they sent to retail stores and they also attended gift shows throughout the year where they displayed the cookbooks in their line. After much discussion about the advantages and disadvantages, the committee decided to contract with three well-known, reputable cookbook distributors because they believed doing so would broaden the SASSAFRAS! sales base. Some committee members, however, still expressed concern about the loss of control over sales.

Retail.   Retail sales were described as sales of SASSAFRAS! made by JLS to individuals with JLS receiving the full retail price of the book. Retail sales provided the most profit per book for JLS because there was no price discount, but such sales would soon become more difficult, especially as the membership of JLS and the local market became saturated. However, promotional activities were developed to sell as many books at the full retail price as possible. These promotional activities were of two types: in-league promotions and other types of retail promotions.

In-league promotions were targeted toward the 461 JLS members. One of these promotions was a continuing offer of one free book for every 20 sold. Exhibit 32.2 shows through October 1985 how successful this offer had been. Retail sales kits, which included copies of retail order forms and sales receipts, were available to any League member to sign out and take to sell the book at school, art groups, office, church, etc. Around Christmas time, free gift wrapping and a six-books-for-the-price-of-five special were offered to League members. This particular promotion was also successful in terms of sales generated. A springtime promotion was planned that offered a free dinner for 12 to the individual who sold the most cookbooks between February 1, 1986 and May 1, 1986. This offer was a disaster—only 21 people participated and only 79 books were sold.

EXHIBIT 32.2 **Free book offer**

1 free book earned by	30 people who sold	759 books
2 free books earned by	8 people who sold	385 books
3 free books earned by	2 people who sold	129 books
4 free books earned by	1 person who sold	89 books
56 free books earned by	41 people for a total of	1,362 books sold

Other promotional activities (not in-league) were tried throughout the year. In November 1985, sales letters were sent to the names on the retail mailing list that contained names and addresses of people who had previously purchased the book. This promotion was not at all successful in generating new or repeat orders.

Order forms included in the back of the cookbooks (see Exhibit 32.3) were a different story. These were effective in generating retail sales. Between four and five (in some weeks there were as many as 10) of these order forms were received and processed weekly. However, continuing success with the order forms was dependent upon continuing to reach new households.

Sales by committee members at various community events and locations throughout the year were also tried with mixed results. A booth set up at a large regional shopping mall was quite successful, but there were some concerns and questions about competing with the bookstores in the mall who carried SASSAFRAS!. Booths at the Ozark Empire Fair during August 1985 and at a university basketball game in February 1986 were not at all successful for sales. Only nine books were sold in the fair and only three books were sold at the basketball game, but the com-

Sassafras!

Mail to: SASSAFRAS!
        2574 East Bennett
        Springfield, Missouri 65804

Please send _____ copies of SASSAFRAS! @ $14.95 each _____
Postage and handling .... @   2.00 each _____
Gift Wrap (enclosure card to read) _____
_____ @   .75 each _____
                                              TOTAL_____
☐ Check ☐ Money Order ☐ Visa or MasterCard (see over)
Make check or money order payable to SASSAFRAS!
Name _____
Address _____
City _____ State _____ Zip _____
Proceeds from the sale of these books shall be returned to the community through projects approved or sponsored by the Junior League of Springfield, Missouri, Inc.

- -

Sassafras!

If using Visa or MasterCard, please fill in the following:

Name _____

Address_____ Phone (_____)_____

City _____ State_____Zip_____

Charge to my: ☐ [VISA] Visa   ☐ [MasterCard] MasterCard

Account Number: [| | | | | | | | | | | | | | | |]

Expiration Date: _____
                         (Month)   (Year)

Customer's Signature: _____

EXHIBIT 32.3 **SASSAFRAS! order form**

mittee felt community exposure at these events was beneficial. A new professionally designed retail brochure was printed for future use in promoting retail sales.

"Our new brochure is really attractive. Now all we have to do is get it into the most effective places without upsetting our wholesale accounts so we can see increased retail sales," explained the retail sales coordinator.

Office Management

As with any new enterprise, office policies and procedures had to be established. A community cookbook consultant was hired in June 1985 to give assistance and advice to the Cookbook Committee on the development of effective office management. Guidelines regarding hours of operations, credit checks, refunds, damages, local deliveries, shipping, etc., were outlined and used by the committee during the 1985-86 year. As new situations arose, the committee revised and/or added new policies and procedures.

Publisher Arrangements. The choice of a book publisher was as serious a decision as all of the other selections facing the Cookbook Committee. Proposals were solicited from three publishers recommended by the community cookbook consultant. Quality of materials and cost of service were important factors in the decision. The publisher chosen for the first edition of the cookbook agreed to comply with the quality specifications for a set price. In addition, the publisher provided a limited number of support services such as drop-shipping and warehouse storage space. The contract called for printing 10,000 copies. Because of the initial sales success, the Cookbook Committee was faced in October 1985 with making a reprint decision. The quality of materials and cost of service from the initial publisher had not been as expected, so another publisher was desired for the second printing of 10,000 copies. Again, proposals were solicited from three publishers. By now, the Cookbook Committee had some experience in negotiating contracts. Quality specifications were particularly important since the committee believed the quality image and reputation of the cookbook was at stake. A different publisher, one who had several Junior League cookbooks under contract, was selected. A mutually acceptable contract with storage, shipping, and cost terms was worked out over a two month period. By February 1986, the first shipment of the reprint had arrived at SASSAFRAS! offices.

Facilities. All cookbook activities, both marketing and office, took place at Junior League headquarters in an old, renovated, elementary school building. SASSAFRAS! had its own offices consisting of two very large adjoining rooms with desks, chairs, tables, a shipping counter, closets, and limited storage space for cookbooks. From the very beginning of operations, SASSAFRAS! had its own phone line and answering machine. Since the SASSAFRAS! office was open only one day per week from 9 a.m. to 1 p.m., the answering machine was an important communication link between customers, both wholesale and retail, and the office. Most individuals who called left messages.

Committee Members. The Cookbook Committee structure was described earlier and shown in Exhibit 32.1. The committee consisted of volunteers who made a one year commitment to a project. However, some committee members could decide to serve on the SASSAFRAS! committee more than one year, which would provide more continuity for operations.

Financial Information

A summary of books sold, gross revenues, and net profit is shown in Exhibit 32.4. The suggested retail price for the book was $14.95. The marketing group did not plan to increase the price in the foreseeable future. A summary of total retail and wholesale sales for seven months is shown in Exhibit 32.5.

EXHIBIT 32.4 **December 30, 1985 financial summary**

Books sold	10,040
Gross revenues	$117,836
Net profit	$44,807

The Junior League did not release information on costs.

EXHIBIT 32.5 **Cookbook sales by category**

	Retail	Wholesale	Distributor	Other*	Total
June, 1985	241	773	—	36	1,050
July, 1985	231	1,001	—	24	1,256
August, 1985	112	492	—	24	628
September, 1985	247	791	—	12	1,050
October, 1985	170	378	—	—	548
November, 1985	274	240	—	—	514
December, 1985	473	559	—	—	1,032

*"Other" includes special promotions and/or intra-league committee sales.

INDUSTRY INFORMATION

Cookbooks were second only to the Bible as steady bestsellers. The first printed cookbook, published in 1474 in Rome and entitled, *De honesta voluptate et valetudine* (roughly translated as "Of Honest Indulgence and Good Health"), went through 53 editions in four languages within 100 years. "Cookbooks are still big business."[1] An industrywide survey estimated $208 million in gross sales in 1984—a figure up 15

[1]"Cookbooks are Still Big Business," *Publisher's Weekly*, September 20, 1985, p. 41.

percent from 1983. Cookbooks ranged from the old classics (e.g. *Better Homes and Gardens New Cookbook* and *The Betty Crocker Cookbook*), to community cookbooks developed and marketed by Junior Leagues all over the country, to universities presenting cookbooks of culinary delights of days-gone-by.

Many publishers wondered how long the phenomenon of widespread interest in cookbooks would last. The pressures of competition were becoming increasingly intense. In 1984, an average of over two cookbooks were published daily. This translated to an annual output of 833 new titles in 1984 while in 1973 only 365 cookbooks were published. "Cookbooks represent one of the fastest growing subject fields," claimed Andrew Grabois, product manager of *The Subject Guide.*[2] They were second only to computers as a popular field of books.

Many publishers have expressed concern about the saturation point for cookbooks. However, there was still a certain degree of optimism about the cookbook market. This optimism rested on a number of factors including:

- Shelley Hurley, the cookbook buyer at B. Dalton, reported that sales have increased 10 percent to 18 percent each year over the last four years.
- At Waldenbooks, cookbooks ranked seventh among the 50 bestselling categories in 1984, reported Dara Tyson, manager of public relations and promotions.
- Editors reported that cookbook proposals revealed a greater pool of talent than ever before.
- Cookbooks were increasingly found on national bestseller lists.
- *The Silver Palate Good Times Cookbook* (Workman) had sales figures totaling 298,000 copies only three months after its release.
- Jason Epstein, Vice President and Editorial Director of Random House, summed up the industry's guarded optimism best: "People in this country have been irrevocably exposed to good food. The process will slowly be democratized and will eventually translate into the sale of more and more cookbooks—unless something goes drastically wrong with the economy."[3]

Certainly the most dramatic change in cookbook publishing over the last few years has been the "advent of the big beautiful book."[4] Consumers were looking for lavish cookbooks—ones which could bring glamour, excitement, and pleasure into their lives. Cookbooks had to look zippier, be more stylish, and present materials in a visual way. Even with price tags ranging up to $45, there had been positive consumer response to these highly visual lifestyle cookbooks.

American regional cookery was a popular subject matter for cookbooks. The ample selection of titles, and climbing sales figures attested to the enormous demand for and continuing success of these cookbook types. The public was eager for books devoted to specific regions of the country. This interest in regional cooking ignited

[2]Ibid, p. 42.
[3]Ibid.
[4]Ibid.

an almost unbelievable explosion in community and charitable cookbooks being published over the past decade. The best-selling community cookbook was published by the Junior League of Baton Rouge, Louisiana. *River Road Recipes*, first published in 1959, had over one million copies in print. This cookbook was highly successful because of the authentic regional recipes and the descriptive narrative that provided a taste of the region.

One firm that specialized in helping organizations publish fund-raising cookbooks noted that its marketing research showed that five years ago, one out of ten women collected cookbooks. This figure was now up to three out of ten women and one out of ten men collected cookbooks. Privately published community cookbooks varied in quality and many contained international, not just local recipes. However, the more successful titles had reached an audience beyond their immediate region.

The proliferation of cookbooks contributed to the birth of specialty bookshops around the country. Most were located in prime tourist areas and depended upon tourist clientele as well as local clientele for support. According to these specialty booksellers, word-of-mouth was the single most effective means of promoting a cookbook. These booksellers also recognized the positive impact of local advertising and media appearances by the author.

Consumer preferences also impacted upon the design and ultimate success of cookbooks. The perceived value (enough recipes, enough pictures, etc.), price accessibility (price of competitive titles, price resistance of consumers on prices above $22.95, etc.), and format novelty (does it look worth the money, is it different in any way, etc.) all influenced the purchase decision. What it all signified, though, was defining who bought which cookbooks and why. One interesting discovery about the marketplace that came from an informal study of food editors was their belief that consumers currently tended to be as eager to read cookbooks as to cook from them.

Although competition among cookbooks is becoming quite intense, opportunities still exist for commercial success of well-planned and well-developed products. The challenge lies in knowing the marketplace, the strengths and weaknesses of the product, and then making appropriate decisions regarding marketing activities. Will SASSAFRAS! be able to maintain its momentum and meet the challenges it faces? The Junior League of Springfield, Inc. is determined to make SASSAFRAS! a success.

CASE 33 ───

┌───┐
│   │
│   **Kraft, Inc.**   │
│   │
└───┘

Some of America's best-known brand names in food products are produced by Kraft. These include Kraft, Velveeta, Parkay, Miracle Whip, Philadelphia, Cracker Barrel, Sealtest, Light n' Lively, Breyers, and Breakstone's. The company's products are sold to stores and restaurants in 130 countries by over 5,000 salespeople. Kraft ranks second only to General Foods in the food processing industry. The company is truly an industry giant that grew from very humble beginnings.

Even as Kraft has changed, so has the food processing industry. In the 1980s, Kraft and its competitors have realized that the recent and projected slow population growth in the United States means that most future gains in market share must come at the expense of one another. As a result, the industry is being restructured through mergers and acquisitions as the major firms seek to strengthen their competitive positions. In order to remain at the top of the industry, Kraft's top managers must make correct strategic decisions regarding the company's product mix and the manner in which to structure the organization in order to best compete in the changing industry environment.

HISTORY OF THE COMPANY

James L. Kraft came to Chicago from Canada in 1903 and began wholesaling cheese from a rented, horse-drawn wagon. His four brothers—Fred, Charles, Norman, and John—joined the prospering business. By 1914, they were selling 31 varieties of cheese under the brand names Kraft and Elkhorn.

Kraft merged with a rival company, Phenix Cheese, in 1928. Kraft-Phenix accounted for 40 percent of U.S. cheese production and also had operations in Canada, Australia, Britain, and Germany. The company was acquired in 1930 by National Dairy. The new company ranked as one of America's largest, with annual sales of $375 million. For the next four decades, Kraft functioned as a separate entity in Chicago, while National Dairy functioned primarily as a holding company from its headquarters in New York City.

James L. Kraft died in 1953 at age 78. In 1969, the National Dairy company name was changed to Kraftco. Corporate headquarters was moved from New York City to the Chicago suburb of Glenview in 1972. In 1976, the company name was changed to its current title, Kraft, Incorporated.

Kraft, Inc. merged with Dart Industries in 1980 to form Dart & Kraft, Incorporated. Dart Industries had gone through significant restructuring of its business units during the few years preceding the merger with Kraft. In 1985, Dart & Kraft, Inc. operated in four major business segments, as seen in Exhibit 33.1. Results for 1985 were marked by strong growth for Kraft, Hobart commercial equipment, and the Wilsonart decorative laminate businesses. Success in these segments offset profit declines at Tupperware, Duracell, West Bend, and KitchenAid. Dart & Kraft ranked 34th among the 1985 *Fortune* 500 Industrials with annual sales of $9.9 billion and net income of $446 million.

EXHIBIT 33.1 **Dart & Kraft, Inc.—1985**

Business segments	Strategic business units
Food products	Kraft, Inc.
Direct selling	Tupperware (plastic storage, preparation, and servingware for food)
Consumer products	Duracell (batteries) KitchenAid (home appliances) West Bend (small appliances and physical fitness equipment) Health Care businesses
Commercial products	Hobart (foodservice cooking equipment, cookware washers, refrigeration products, and supermarket weighing and wrapping equipment) Wilsonart (decorative laminates and disposable plastic and rubber items)

Dart & Kraft acquired nine businesses at a cost of $300 million during 1985. These included Frusen Gladje superpremium ice cream; Invernizzi S.P.A., an Italian cheese company; and the Westman Commission Company, a full-line foodservice distributor. Top management expected these and the other 1985 acquisitions to be compatible with their strategy of maintaining a mix of high-quality, primarily consumer-oriented businesses. John Richman, Chairman and Chief Executive Officer, stated in the company's 1985 Annual Report that such acquisitions were likely to continue in 1986. In early 1986, the company signed an agreement to acquire Vulcan-Hart Corporation, a leading producer of gas cooking equipment, which was expected to add further competitive strength to Dart & Kraft's food equipment business.

Dart & Kraft recently took actions directed toward divesting most of the company's small health-care operations and on January 31, 1986, the sale of KitchenAid to Whirlpool Corporation was consummated. Mr. Richman stated in his annual letter to the stockholders that this sale was opportunistic, rather than the result of strategic reappraisal. The sale resulted in an after-tax gain of $41 million to be recorded in the first quarter of 1986.[1]

Dart & Kraft's strategy in early 1986 was summarized by Chairman Richman and President Batts as follows:

> As to the longer term, our strategy will not be dramatically different. Contrary to the current industry trend, we continue to believe that there are benefits to be derived from our particular type of controlled and related diversification. For example, our ability to balance the cash-generating capacity of our retail food business and Tupperware with higher-growth, cash-using businesses like Duracell is an important benefit.[2]

OPERATIONS AT KRAFT, INC.

Michael A. Miles was President and Chief Operating Officer of Kraft, Inc. in 1985. Kraft's mission statement from that year is presented in Exhibit 33.2. Mr. Miles had publicly identified five strengths and three weaknesses of Kraft. The five strengths and supporting reasons for them were as follows:

1. Huge mass and resources—Kraft is one of the four largest food businesses in the world, and second only to General Foods in the United States.
2. Growth markets and growth categories—from 1979 to 1983, per capita consumption of cheese in the United States increased 23 percent, pourable dressings 14 percent, and premium ice cream 18 percent.
3. Extremely strong brand names and market share positions—Kraft is either the leader or a strong contender in virtually all of the major categories in which it competes.
4. Excellent customer relations—research indicates Kraft has the best reputation for quality in the food industry and that only Procter and Gamble compares with Kraft in sales-force skill and effectiveness.
5. Worldwide infrastructure—the human and financial resources are in place to support new business initiatives anywhere in the world.

Mr. Miles also reported the following weaknesses:

1. No recent track record of success in developing significant new products.
2. Too conservative; need more challenges.
3. Increasing competition.

---

[1] Dart & Kraft, Inc. 1985 Annual Report, p. 31.
[2] Ibid., p. 4.

EXHIBIT 33.2 **Kraft, Inc. mission**

Mission summary

Kraft's mission is to become the leading food company in the world, based on achieving superiority versus competition in a balance of these factors:

- Outstanding overall quality of people, products, and business plans
- Return on management investment (ROMI)
- Rate of growth in unit sales and operating income
- Innovation.

Customers

Kraft's businesses will be built on the fundamental concept of achieving superiority versus competition in:

- Identifying the wants and needs of customers, both end-consumers and trade
- Providing high-quality products and/or services to meet those needs in unique or advantageous ways
- Marketing those products/services to reinforce their appeal and achieve superior acceptance.

Industries/markets channels of distribution

Kraft will compete in any segment of the food business, in any geographic market, and in any channel of distribution, where:

- Participation can make a material long-term contribution to sales and income, while generating returns at or above corporate targets.
- The combination of product quality, management quality, and innovation provides us with a sustainable competitive advantage—or the prospect of same in a reasonable time frame.

Competition

Kraft has mass and resources that enable it to compete with any company in the world, and will utilize these resources to the fullest legal, ethical, and moral extent.

Kraft will engage any competitor in any geographical market, category, or channel of distribution of interest, where the combination of product quality, management quality, and innovation provides us with a sustainable competitive advantage.

Kraft will defend its established businesses ferociously.

People/organization

Kraft recognizes that the quality of its people is the critical element in achieving the success of its mission.

Kraft's human resources policies and practices will be built on a standard of excellence and a total commitment to equal opportunity and fair treatment.

Kraft will promote based on merit and from within wherever possible.

Business style

Kraft's business style will be characterized by:

- Overarching commitment to quality
- Openness, honesty
- Initiative
- Innovation
- Aggressiveness
- Action orientation
- Competitiveness
- Efficiency
- Risk acceptance
- Superior analysis and planning
- A standard of excellence in people.

What we say we do, we *do* do.
James L. Kraft

Source: Kraft, Inc. planning document.

In addition, Mr. Miles outlined five broad strategies Kraft was currently pursuing:

1. To protect and build the existing businesses—for branded products, increased spending on advertising—competitive pricing and more emphasis on advertisable product improvement—for commodity products, being the lowest-cost producer.
2. To gradually weight the business mix toward branded, value-added products and away from commodities.
3. To augment the growth of existing branded positions by a more active new business development effort.
4. To continue to pursue expense and asset minimization in all areas.
5. To increase organizational vitality.[3]

President Miles believed that these strategies would best capitalize on Kraft's major strength: a quality reputation in producing and promoting branded food products. As these branded products were expanded, the company planned to continue the retreat from fluid milk and certain private-label items, and from its bulk cheese and edible-oil businesses in Europe.

The fifth strategy—increasing organizational vitality—involved many actions. These actions included increasing employee communications, eliminating some excess layers of middle management, and a large-scale test of doubling the size of the U.S. retail sales force. The intent of these actions was to increase the sense of urgency and the timeliness of decision making. Some employees in Kraft's Retail Food Group dubbed this the M/B/F/ program, meaning more/better/faster.

KRAFT PRODUCT LINES

The key performers during 1985–86 were the Retail Food, Food Service, and Dairy Groups. These and Kraft's other operating units and their principal products are identified in Exhibit 33.3.

Refrigerated Products Division. Kraft began the national distribution of Light Philadelphia Brand process cream cheese, another of several new products aimed at calorie-conscious consumers. The expansion of this product continued during 1986.

Grocery Products Division. Kraft experienced success with reduced-calorie versions of Miracle Whip Salad Dressing and Kraft Real Mayonnaise. Both products became the leading share brands in their categories. Velveeta Shells and Cheese Packaged Dinner, introduced in 1984, also experienced significant sales increases.

---

[3]Warren L. Batts, President and Chief Operating Officer, Dart & Kraft, Inc., presentation to the Consumer Analyst Group of New York, at St. Petersburg, Florida, February 21, 1984.

EXHIBIT 33.3 **Key performers during 1985–1986**

Group and division	Principle products
Retail Food Group	
Refrigerated Products Division	Process, natural, and cream cheese
Grocery Products Division	Salad dressings, mayonnaise, dry packaged dinners, and barbecue sauce
Venture Division	Bagels and herb teas
International Group	
Primary Operations in Canada, West Germany, Italy, Australia, the Philippines, Latin America, and Mexico	Wide variety of products representing all Kraft divisions
Dairy Group	Ice cream, ice milk, lowfat yogurt, cottage cheese, and sour cream
Foodservice Group	Distributes products from the Retail Food Group to restaurants
Industrial Foods Group	Supplies food manufacturers with edible oils and edible-oil-based products, cheese items, snack seasonings, imitation cheese, flavorings, confections, dairy and nondairy proteins, and other ingredients

---

Presto, a new Italian salad dressing, was introduced nationally during 1985. Even as volume declined, profitability on Parkay Margarine increased due to lower edible-oil costs.

Venture Division. This division completed two acquisitions during 1984—Lender's Bagel Bakery, Inc., and Celestial Seasonings, Inc. Both did well during 1985. The bagel business was geographically expanded beyond the Northeast during the year, necessitating the building of additional capacity which was scheduled for completion during 1986. Profit declined slightly in the Celestial Seasonings herb teas business due to costs incurred in creating new marketing programs and strengthening channels of distribution. In addition, four new tea flavors were added during 1985—Lemon Zinger, Raspberry Patch, Island Orange, and Cranberry Cove.

The Venture Division entered an agreement with DNA Plant Technology for the development and marketing of Vegisnax raw vegetables bred for superior taste and texture. The division also entered an agreement early in 1986 with San Francisco French Bread Company to market a line of sourdough products.

Foodservice Group. This group attempted to capitalize on the almost 50 percent of the American food dollar that is spent on meals away from home. The group accounted for 13 percent of Kraft's total sales, and experienced a 12 percent growth of tonnage sales during 1985. Many products, such as the familiar individual-serving packets of Kraft's jams and jellies, are distributed by the Foodservice Group. The group engages in extensive research and development activity. Because the company manufactures nearly 50 percent of what the Foodservice Group sells, profit is captured from both production and distribution. This group also adds value to Retail Food Group acquisitions by broadening distribution of products such as Lender's Bagels and Celestial Seasonings herb teas.

Two acquisitions were completed by the Foodservice Group during 1985—the Westman Commission Company, a full-line distributor serving seven Rocky Mountain states, and Seaboard Foods, Inc., a broadline distributor in North Carolina. Letters of intent were signed in early 1986 to acquire distribution businesses in Kansas City, Chicago, Phoenix, and the New York areas.

The Foodservice Group developed innovations to add efficiency during 1985. A portable entry terminal for sales representatives shortened order-processing time and supported next-day delivery service. A computerized restaurant management system called "Kraft Link" connected customers with the nearest Kraft Foodservice location and assisted them with menu, food-cost and sales analysis, as well as order entry and inventory control. This system also provided customers with automatic price updating, on-line order verification, and other helpful services.

Dairy Group.   This group accounted for nine percent of total company sales. The group experienced market share and profit gains in almost every product line during 1985 due to an overall 10 percent sales increase.

The group's excellent year in ice cream was enhanced by the acquisition of Frusen Gladje, a superpremium ice cream line. This line's sales tripled following the acquisition as a result of a quick move to expand its sales territory and the creation of new television and print advertising.

Kraft's all-natural premium ice cream line, Breyers, expanded into nine western states during 1985. Sealtest ice cream celebrated its 50th anniversary with a 16 percent volume increase, aided by its new Cubic Scoops flavors. Double-digit sales gains were also registered by Polar B'ar ice cream squares and Light n' Lively ice milk. Sales increases were also achieved by Light n' Lively lowfat yogurt, Breakstone's, Sealtest, and Light n' Lively lowfat cottage cheese, and Breakstone's and Sealtest sour cream.

The only Dairy Group product to show a sales decline during 1985 was Breyers yogurt. This product was improved in late summer by adding larger chunks of fruit and more graphically appealing packaging.

International Group.   This group, which accounted for 24 percent of company sales, reported lower 1985 profits. This was primarily due to poor results in West Germany, Kraft's largest European market. Other European operations did well, especially Kraft S.P.A. in Italy, where the company acquired a major interest in Invernizzi S.P.A., a Milan-based producer and distributor of natural cheeses.

Kraft Australia acquired the Everest Group, a small, regional producer of pasta, ice cream, and frozen dinners. This acquisition was designed as a base from which Kraft could diversify from its dependence on cheese in the Australian market.

Anticipating that the poor economic conditions in Venezuela were going to persist, Kraft was in the process of introducing a new line of lower-cost products there. The company sold the small business interest it had in Brazil.

Industrial Foods Group. This group accounted for seven percent of Kraft's sales. Price declines in the edible-oil market during 1985 caused a significant decrease in group profits even though sales volume increased. The industrial ingredients business, however, achieved higher sales and profits.

Two important actions were taken in the Industrial Foods Group during 1985: the industrial emulsifier business was sold because it was not achieving satisfactory return; and the decision was made to phase out the California oil refining operations by September 1986. This latter action was designed to remove Kraft from the low-return bulk oils market. The company planned to continue supplying the West Coast with higher-margin specialty oil products from its two refineries located in Tennessee and Illinois.

All of these activities in Kraft's five groups were designed to move the company toward the major goal enunciated in its mission statement: to become the leading food company in the world. As Kraft's top management strives toward this goal, the U.S. food industry is changing. The dairy industry in which Kraft competes has witnessed changes in consumer preferences and consumption patterns during recent years. In addition, the larger food processing industry of which Kraft is a part is undergoing major restructuring.

THE U.S. DAIRY INDUSTRY

Three significant developments affected the dairy industry in 1985:

1. Cheese made a major comeback after three low-growth years.
2. The dairy farmers' advertising and promotional campaign completed its first year of operation.
3. Concern within the dairy industry intensified as Congress debated the dairy provisions of the 1985 farm bill.[4]

Four firms that operated in several segments of the dairy industry accounted for 18.3 percent of total 1985 sales, down one percent from 1984: Dart & Kraft, 6.8 percent; Beatrice, 4.6 percent; Borden, 3.7 percent; and Nestle, 3.2 percent.

[4]Facts relating to 1985 events and forecasts for the dairy industry are drawn from *1986 U.S. Industrial Outlook*. Department of Commerce/International Trade Administration, pp. 40–13 through 40–19.

Fluid Milk

Per capita consumption of two major fluid items—whole milk and cottage cheese—has declined consistently during recent years. Many consumers perceive that lowfat and skim milk are more healthful than whole milk. Lowfat and skim milk are also less expensive than whole milk. As a result, milk consumption patterns have changed. From 1980 to 1984, consumption of whole milk declined 3.4 percent annually, and it declined another four percent during 1985. Skim milk consumption grew by 8.8 percent during 1985, while lowfat milk use increased 3.9 percent. During 1980 to 1984, total per capita consumption of all milk declined .9 percent, and then remained unchanged during 1985.

Estimated per capita consumption of cottage cheese decreased 1.4 percent in 1985, while per capita consumption of lowfat cottage cheese (a yogurt rival) rose 5 percent. Per capita yogurt consumption increased 12.6 percent.

The four leading processors of fluid milk achieved 19.3 percent of total sales, as follows: Southland, 6.8 percent; Beatrice, 4.6 percent; Borden, 4.3 percent; and Dairymen, a cooperative, 3.6 percent.

Cheese

Per capita consumption of all cheese declined an estimated 1.6 percent during 1985, but some product categories gained while others lost (see Exhibit 33.4). For example, per capita consumption of American cheese declined 2.4 percent while that of Italian-type varieties increased 2.9 percent. One-half of cheese production is of American cheese, while Italian varieties account for one-fourth of production.

EXHIBIT 33.4 **U.S. per capita consumption of cheeses (In pounds)**

Types of cheese	1983	1984	1985*
American	11.62	12.02	11.77
Cheddar	9.13	9.73	9.53
Other American**	2.49	2.29	2.24
Italian	5.73	5.82	5.99
Mozzarella	3.71	4.06	4.20
Ricotta	.54	.58	.61
Provolone	.90	.55	.57
Other Italian varieties	.58	.63	.61
All other cheese	5.85	5.46	5.15
All cheese	23.20	23.30	22.91

*Estimated.

**Includes Colby, washed curd, stirred curd, and Monterey Jack.

Source: U.S. Department of Commerce: Bureau of the Census, and International Trade Administration (ITA); U.S. Department of agriculture. Estimates by ITA.

Cheese substitutes fortified by the milk protein casein have appeared on the market during recent years. For example, many brands of frozen pizza contain these less costly substitutes.

Producer prices for all natural cheese dropped 1.1 percent during 1985, while those for all processed cheeses declined 1.7 percent. Four producers of natural and processed cheeses accounted for 33 percent of total sales: Dart & Kraft, 21 percent; Schrieber Food, 5 percent; Land O' Lakes, 4 percent; and Beatrice, 3 percent.

Frozen Desserts

Consumption of ice cream and other frozen desserts had been quite steady during recent years. In 1985, estimated per capita consumption of ice cream melted 2.3 percent, while sherbet declined 3.9 percent. At the same time, per capita consumption of ice milk increased 2 percent and mellorine climbed 62.4 percent. Mellorine contains soy-based products such as frozen tofu, which many consumers consider to be more healthful than ice cream.

Along with mellorine, gelatin bars and frozen fruit bars are also gaining popularity among adults as well as children. Among the major food processors, Castle and Cooke now manufactures fruit bars and General Foods produces gelatin bars.

A few years ago, a few small companies began to achieve success in the premium ice cream market. Premium ice cream has a higher butterfat content than standard ice cream, and is often produced with only natural ingredients, such as milk, sugar, and real fruit flavorings. Major food processors have now recognized the potential of this market segment. In 1983, Pillsbury acquired Haagen-Dazs, a popular regional producer of premium ice cream. In April 1985, Dart & Kraft acquired Frusen Gladje, a privately held manufacturer of premium ice cream.

In 1985, the average retail price for a half-gallon of ice cream reached $2.31, as producer prices edged up an estimated two percent. Four ice cream makers garnered 31 percent of the market for ice cream and frozen desserts: Southland, 11 percent; Dart & Kraft, 8 percent; Borden, 8 percent; and Beatrice, 4 percent.

Outlook for the U.S. Dairy Industry

Exhibit 33.5 summarizes the estimated and forecasted values of industry shipments of various dairy products for the years 1982 to 1986. The aggregate value of shipments for 1986 is expected to increase .7 percent, while total per capita consumption is expected to increase .8 percent, less than the predicted rate of population increase. Predictions for the real (inflation-adjusted) growth of specific products ranged from a 1.7 percent gain for cheese to a 1.6 percent decline for ice cream and frozen desserts.

Per capita consumption of all cheese may remain static, but consumption of Italian types is expected to increase three percent. Consumption of most other types of cheese is likely to be static or to decline.

Shipments of premium ice cream are expected to increase, thus preventing further decline in the real growth of frozen desserts. Novelty items and frozen tofu

EXHIBIT 33.5 Recent performance and forecast: dairy products (In millions of dollars)

	1982	1983	1984[1]	1985[2]	1986[3]	Percent change			
						1982–83	1983–84	1984–85	1985–86
Value of shipments[4]	39,063	40,219	40,832	42,689	43,879	3.0	1.5	4.5	2.8
Creamery butter	1,687	1,737	1,778	1,835	1,853	3.0	2.4	3.2	1.0
Cheese	10,763	10,907	11,064	12,332	12,785	1.3	1.4	11.5	3.7
Condensed & Evaporated Milk ...	4,731	5,746	5,673	5,603	5,631	21.5	−1.3	−1.2	0.5
Ice cream	2,855	2,963	3,126	3,244	3,302	3.8	5.5	3.8	1.8
Fluid milk...........	19,028	18,865	19,191	19,675	20,308	−0.9	1.7	2.5	3.2

[1] Estimated except for exports and imports.
[2] Estimated.
[3] Forecast.
[4] Value of all products and services sold by the Dairy Products industry.

Source: U.S. Department: Bureau of the Census, Bureau of Economic Analysis, International Trade Administration (ITA). Estimates and Forecasts by ITA.

will continue to serve market niches. Demand for lowfat milk, skim milk, and yogurt are expected to continue to rise while demand for whole milk will continue its decline.

The volume of dairy shipments is expected to rise .2 percent annually from 1985 to 1990, while the population increases .9 percent a year. This slow expansion will be spread unevenly among the industry's product segments.

Ice cream and frozen desserts are expected to register slight declines. Shipments of fluid milk are likely to remain unchanged because the population of the prime consuming group, children aged 15 years and under, will expand only .2 percent annually. Expansion of the butter market will prove difficult as an increasing number of people reach maturity having used very little of it.

RECENT EVENTS IN THE FOOD PROCESSING INDUSTRY

The U.S. food market tends to grow pretty much in line with population growth. The population has been growing less than one percent annually, and per capita food consumption trends have been relatively flat. As a result, there has been low overall growth in the U.S. food market during recent years. U.S. food expenditures rose 3.2 percent in real terms during 1985, compared to 2.1 percent during 1984.

The increasing number of two wage earner households in the United States has resulted in higher disposable incomes and a growing need for convenience. While Americans want more healthful meals, they have less time to prepare them, but more money to spend for them. As a result, spending for food away from home has been increasing much faster than spending for food prepared at home. Although real food-at-home spending rose faster than real foodservice sales during 1985 (+2.6% versus +1.2%), the reverse was true for the 1983 to 1985 period (+11.3% for food away from home versus +6.6% for food at home).[5]

These two trends—slow growth in the food industry and a trend toward increased food consumption away from home—indicate that it will be difficult for competitors in the food processing industry to make continued large gains in the market simply through internal growth of existing products. For this reason, several large food processors have recently begun to reposition themselves into propitious product and geographic markets and to capitalize on the trend toward eating away from home. The slow-growing market means that the majority of future market-share gains will result from taking existing market share away from competitors. Thus, the market has become, and is expected to remain, fiercely competitive. Food processors were second only to department stores in advertising expenditures during 1984 with outlays of $4.2 billion (see Exhibit 33.6).[6]

[5]"Food, Beverages, and Tobacco: Current Analysis," *Standard and Poor's Industry Surveys*, Vol. 54, No. 9, Sec. 1, February 27, 1986, p. 1.

[6]"Advertising: Special Report,"*Standard and Poor's Industry Surveys*, Vol. 153, No. 40, Sec. 1, October 3, 1985, p.1.

EXHIBIT 33.6 **Top 20 spenders on advertising—1984 (In millions of dollars)**

Company	1983	1984
Procter & Gamble	915.0	976.0
Sears	898.0	925.1
General Motors	823.5	892.3
Phillip Morris	810.6	892.0
Ford	787.2	808.5
Reynolds (R.J.)	633.0	702.0
Beatrice	288.0	680.0
Warner-Lambert	592.0	607.0
PepsiCo	488.3	595.9
Coca Cola	463.2	535.8
Sara Lee	456.0	513.0
Anheuser Busch	403.9	480.2
American Express	384.0	490.0
J.C. Penney	381.0	465.0
General Foods	395.9	431.8
Eastman Kodak	390.0	430.0
Ralston Purina	438.0	429.6
Dart & Kraft	**339.6**	**418.6**
American Home Products	409.9	412.0
General Electric	363.0	356.0

Source: Computstat Services, Inc.

Repositioning efforts also resulted in 315 mergers and acquisitions involving 260 firms in the food sector during the first six months of 1985. This is only a slight increase from the number of similar mergers during the same period of 1984.

Three 1985 mergers with a combined transaction cost approaching $14 billion achieved the most notoriety during 1985: R.J. Reynolds acquired Nabisco Brands for $5 billion; Phillip Morris spent $5.6 billion for General Foods Corporation; and Nestle S.A. purchased Carnation Company for $3 billion. In addition, Beatrice Foods agreed to a leveraged buyout that will take the company private. Food and beverage industry shipments account for about 60 percent of these four firms' annual sales, and together these companies sell 15 percent of total food and beverage industry shipments.[7] The slow growth of demand and the rapid change in consumer tastes may portend continued mergers in the food industry. In addition, food companies have been repurchasing their own stock at an unprecedented rate, partly to prevent becoming takeover targets. Stock held by the largest food processors as a percent of their total shares outstanding has increased from about two percent in 1981 to 15 percent by the end of 1985. These buybacks have added strength to the market price of these stocks. But financiers have also discovered the value of strong, established

---

[7]"Food and Kindred Products," *1986 U.S. Industrial Outlook*. U.S. Department of Commerce/International Trade Administration, p. 40–1.

brand names in the food industry. The combination of realized market strength from good brand names and the stock buybacks caused food industry stock prices to jump 60 percent during 1985, even though industry profits declined two percent.[8]

Several indicators point to a good year for food processors during 1986:

1. Cost savings resulting from lower oil prices.
2. Stable prices for food commodities are predicted.
3. The average company's bottom line could be increased by 10 percent if proposed tax legislation being considered by Congress is passed.
4. Despite recent merger activity, there is no sign that the Justice Department is becoming concerned about concentration in the industry.[9]
5. Operating efficiencies and economies of size resulting from the recent mergers and acquisitions.[10]

The following statement regarding the food processing industry appeared in a January 1986 *Business Week* article: "As recently as five years ago, when high tech was king, the packaged-food industry drew nothing but yawns. Food companies themselves were weary of low margins and slow growth. But now a new ethic has taken hold, and the industry is alive and thriving. Boring had become beautiful."[11]

The cost savings from lower commodity prices and possible tax legislation mentioned above will help companies finance the advertising costs that will continue to be necessary in this highly competitive market. It appears that those firms that can most successfully identify and satisfy the rapidly changing customer needs with strong, high-value-added brands will be the winners in this slow-growth market during coming years.

DART & KRAFT BECOMES DART AND KRAFT

In July 1986, Dart & Kraft Chairman John M. Richman surprised the investment community by announcing that he would divide the corporation into two parts: a new Kraft, Inc., consisting of Kraft's food operations and the Duracell battery business, to be headed by Richman; and a corporation (later named Premark International, Inc.) composed of Tupperware, West Bend, Hobart, and Wilsonart, which would be spun off to shareholders and headed by Dart & Kraft President Warren L. Batts. Richman felt that the Kraft-Duracell combination would be more attractive on Wall Street. He was quoted as saying in reference to the former Dart & Kraft

---

[8]Kenneth Dreyfack, "The Stage Is Set for More Megadeals," *Business Week*, January 13, 1986, p. 67.

[9]Ibid.

[10]"Food and Kindred Products," *1986 U.S. Industrial Outlook.* Department of Commerce/International Trade Administration, p. 40-1.

[11]Dreyfack, *Op. Cit.*

Inc., "over time we feel Kraft would not be recognized for the power it is in the food industry."[12]

From 1980 to 1985, Dart & Kraft Inc.'s overall operating profit grew at a compound annual rate of 4 percent, while Kraft's rate was 10.3 percent, and Duracell's was 15 percent. During the same period, Tupperware's contribution to Dart & Kraft's earnings fell from 30 percent in 1980 to about 10 percent in 1985. Premark's management must contend with Tupperware's problems, the slow growth of its other units, and the loss of cash flow from the food business.[13]

When the announced spinoff raised questions about the wisdom of the 1980 merger, Richman pointed out that a $1 investment in Dart & Kraft at the time of the 1980 merger would have appreciated to $5.34 by mid-June 1986. "The numbers tell it all," said Richman.[14]

FINANCIAL DATA

Exhibits 33.7 to 33.12 present a summary of Kraft, Inc.'s financial performance during recent years as presented in the firm's 1986 Annual Report. Inventories are valued at the lower of cost or market. In 1985, costing for virtually all domestic inventories was changed from the FIFO to the LIFO method. The FIFO method is used for other inventories, which represent approximately 43 percent of all inventories. Inventory cost includes cost of raw materials, labor, and overhead. Due to the nature of the business, management considers it impractical to segregate inventories into raw materials, work in progress, and finished goods.

[12]Ellis, James E., "Dart & Kraft: Why It'll be Dart and Kraft," *Business Week*, July 7, 1986, p. 33.
[13]Ibid.
[14]Ibid.

EXHIBIT 33.7 Summary of selected financial data (Dollars in millions, except per share)

	1982	1983	1984	1985	1986
Summary of operations					
Net sales	$7,618	$7,425	$7,628	$7,920	$8,742
Costs and expenses					
Cost of products	5,754	5,395	5,442	5,478	5,970
Delivery, sales and administrative expense	1,399	1,475	1,550	1,727	2,055
Interest expense	87	68	94	79	71
Interest income	(58)	(63)	(70)	(50)	(39)
Other income, net	(33)	(19)	(37)	(34)	(25)
Total costs and expenses	7,149	6,856	6,979	7,200	8,032
Income from operations	469	569	649	720	710
Nonoperating items	(91)	—	—	—	—
Income from continuing operations before income taxes	378	569	649	720	710
Provision for income taxes	168	252	295	312	320
Net income from continuing operations	210	317	354	408	390
Net income from discontinued operations	140	118	102	58	23
Net income	$ 350	$ 435	$ 456	$ 466	$ 413
Net income per share					
From continuing operations	$ 1.27	$ 1.92	$ 2.33	$ 2.82	$ 2.77
From discontinued operations	.86	.72	.68	.40	16
Total	$ 2.13	$ 2.64	$ 3.01	$ 3.22	$ 2.93
Dividends	$ 197	$ 210	$ 209	$ 219	$ 234
Per share	1.20	1.28	1.38	1.52 1/3	1.68
Financial position					
Current assets	$2,286	$2,476	$2,339	$2,326	$2,475
Current liabilities	1,134	1,256	1,479	1,415	2,283
Working capital	1,152	1,220	860	911	192
Property, plant and equipment, net	901	900	948	1,075	1,350
Total assets	4,709	4,998	4,882	5,091	4,749
Long-term debt	574	549	508	439	232
Shareholders' equity	2,774	2,923	2,598	2,880	1,798*
Per share	$16.89	$17.77	$18.09	$19.95	$13.29
Statistical information					
Return on equity**	12.8%	17.7%	22.7%	22.3%	21.7%
Return on total capital**	11.0%	14.2%	17.0%	18.4%	15.4%
Long-term debt to equity**	34.9%	30.6%	32.6%	23.9%	12.9%
Total debt to total capital**	28.9%	27.2%	34.0%	24.5%	34.9%
Capital expenditures	$ 257	$ 137	$ 164	$ 181	$ 209
Depreciation	$ 116	$ 96	$ 104	$ 99	$ 113
Payroll and employee benefits	$1,104	$1,118	$1,114	$1,208	$1,386
Average number of employees	50,500	49,500	47,400	50,100	51,300
Number of shareholders at year-end	78,808	74,443	70,807	72,249	70,190
Number of shares of common stock outstanding at year-end (thousands)	164,237	164,483	143,627	144,334	135,279
Average number of common and common equivalent shares (thousands)	164,265	164,887	151,589	144,898	140,970

Note: Amounts have been restated to reflect the results from continuing operations, where appropriate. In 1986, Kraft adopted the new pension accounting standards issued by the Financial Accounting Standards Board. In 1985, Kraft adopted the LIFO inventory method of accounting for substantially all domestic inventories. Number of shares and per share data reflect a three-for-one stock split in 1985.

*Shareholders' equity for 1986 reflects the spinoff of Premark International, Inc. and the repurchase of shares.

**Equity and total capital are year-end balances reduced by the net assets of discontinued operations for these ratios.

EXHIBIT 33.8 Segments of business by classes of products—five-year summary

		1982	1983	1984 (In millions)	1985	1986
Net sales	Food Products					
	Retail food	$3,259.2	$3,016.2	$3,182.3	$3,289.9	$3,365.0
	Dairy group	821.2	701.8	591.8	621.4	651.1
	Foodservice group	625.3	686.4	773.3	889.7	1,314.3
	Industrial Foods group	437.9	486.3	576.0	531.3	441.6
	International group	1,897.5	1,769.7	1,707.2	1,733.0	2,007.7
	Total	7,041.1	6,668.4	6,830.6	7,065.3	7,779.7
	Consumer Products	576.9	764.4	797.8	854.2	962.5
	Net sales	$7,618.0	$7,424.8	$7,628.4	$7,919.5	$8,742.2
Operating profit	Food Products					
	Domestic	$ 365.4	$ 413.2	$ 467.7	$ 579.9	$ 613.9
	International	137.4	165.0	168.5	150.4	190.0
	Total	502.8	578.2	636.2	730.3	803.9
	Consumer Products	46.4	65.0	93.9	82.6	29.9*
	Total operating profit	$ 549.2	$ 642.2	$ 730.1	$ 812.9	$ 833.8
Identifiable assets	Food Products					
	Domestic	$1,480.0	$1,430.3	$1,604.5	$1,607.8	$2,378.0
	International	772.7	680.9	701.1	786.4	849.6
	Total	2,252.7	2,111.2	2,305.6	2,394.2	3,227.6
	Consumer Products	493.0	576.1	661.3	757.7	849.6
	Corporate	833.8	1,182.3	875.3	891.3	672.1
	Total identifiable assets of continuing operations	$3,579.5	$3,869.6	$3,842.2	$4,043.2	$4,749.3

* After restructuring charges of $37.0 million.

EXHIBIT 33.9 **Common stock prices and dividends**

	1985			1986		
	High	**Low**	**Dividend**	**High**	**Low**	**Dividend**
First quarter	$31 1/2	$27 7/8	$.35 1/3	$53 1/2	$38 7/8	$.39
Second quarter ..	36 5/8	29 3/4	.39	65 7/8	47 1/2	.43
Third quarter....	38 3/8	33 5/8	.39	65	51 3/4	.43
Fourth quarter...	44 7/8	36	.39	58 1/2*	47 1/8*	.43

*On October 31, 1986, Kraft, Inc. spunoff the businesses that make up Premark International Inc.

EXHIBIT 33.10 **Consolidated statement of changes in financial position**

	Year ending Dec. 29, 1984	Year ending Dec. 28, 1985	Year ending Dec. 27, 1986
		(In millions)	
Cash provided from continuing operations			
Net income from continuing operations	$ 353.6	$ 408.0	$ 390.1
Items not resulting in cash flow			
Depreciation and amortization	111.3	112.2	135.5
Deferred income taxes	49.9	39.5	60.8
(Increase) decrease in working capital used in continuing operations (except cash, temporary investments, and borrowings) adjusted for translation	(73.1)	46.5	65.2
Cash provided from continuing operations	441.7	606.2	651.6
Investments			
Capital expenditures	(164.3)	(180.6)	(209.0)
Book value of properties sold	33.6	15.0	12.5
Business acquisitions and divestitures, net	(153.4)	(64.8)	(562.3)
(Increase) decrease in investments and long-term receivables	28.5	(62.2)	45.8
Other, net	9.9	5.7	11.3
Cash used for investments	(245.7)	(286.9)	(701.7)
Financing			
Dividends paid	(208.5)	(219.3)	(234.0)
Purchase of treasury stock	(531.7)	—	(597.7)
Decrease in long-term debt	(33.9)	(72.3)	(114.9)
Increase (decrease) in short-term borrowings	164.6	(135.0)	485.9
Cash used for financing	(609.5)	(426.6)	(460.7)
Cash provided from discontinued operations	167.9	65.6	356.0
Decrease in cash and temporary investments	$(245.6)	$ (41.7)	$(154.8)

EXHIBIT 33.11 Consolidated balance sheet (Dollars in millions, except par value)

	Dec. 28, 1985	Dec. 27, 1986
Assets		
Cash, time deposits and certificates of deposit	$ 160.9	$ 194.1
Temporary investments, at cost that approximates		
market	315.6	127.6
Total cash and temporary investments................	476.5	321.7
Accounts and notes receivable, less allowances of $27.4 in		
1986 and $19.1 in 1985	734.4	941.7
Inventories	1,115.3	1,211.3
Total current assets	2,326.2	2,474.7
Investments and long-term receivables	284.4	246.5
Prepaid and deferred items	115.7	139.6
Property, plant and equipment		
Land	32.6	45.1
Buildings and improvements	495.6	584.6
Machinery and equipment	1,249.5	1,504.7
Construction in progress	90.9	87.8
Total cost	1,868.6	2,222.2
Less—accumulated depreciation.....................	(794.1)	(872.1)
Property, plant and equipment, net.................	1,074.5	1,350.1
Intangibles, net of accumulated amortization of $55.9 in		
1986 and $35.5 in 1985	242.4	538.4
Net assets of discontinued operations..................	1,047.4	—
Total assets	$5,090.6	$4,749.3
Liabilities and Shareholders' Equity		
Accounts payable	$ 434.3	$ 551.4
Short-term borrowings	130.0	615.9
Accrued compensation	169.4	193.7
Other accrued liabilities	333.5	447.7
Accrued income taxes	321.4	356.0
Current portion of long-term debt	26.0	118.3
Total current liabilities	1,414.6	2,283.0
Long-term debt	438.7	231.5
Deferred income taxes	228.6	284.8
Other liabilities	128.5	152.0
Shareholders' equity		
Preferred stock, $5.00 par value; authorized		
150,000,000 shares; issued—none	—	—
Common stock, $1.00 par value; authorized		
600,000,000 shares; issued 164,735,955 shares	164.7	164.7
Capital surplus...................................	317.5	33.2
Retained earnings	3,191.8	2,810.9
Treasury stock, 29,457,022 shares in 1986 and		
20,402,106 shares in 1985, at cost................	(503.3)	(1,074.9)
Unearned portion of restricted stock issued for		
future services	(1.0)	(.9)
Cumulative foreign currency adjustments	(289.5)	(135.0)
Total shareholders' equity	2,880.2	1,798.0
Total liabilities and shareholders' equity	$5,090.6	$4,749.3

EXHIBIT 33.12 Segments of business by geographical area—three-year summary

	1984	1985	1986
		(In millions)	
Net sales			
United States	$5,581.1	$5,819.3	$6,278.3
Canada	673.1	638.6	628.6
Latin America	131.6	132.7	106.2
Europe and Africa	929.4	1,060.9	1,445.1
Pacific area	313.2	268.0	284.0
Net sales	$7,628.4	$7,919.5	$8,742.2
Operating profit			
United States	$ 522.6	$ 623.7	$ 644.7
Canada	81.9	70.1	67.7
Latin America	16.9	18.1	15.2
Europe and Africa	76.8	67.9	69.7
Pacific area	31.9	33.1	36.5
Total operating profit	$ 730.1	$ 812.9	$ 833.8
Identifiable assets			
United States	$2,017.1	$2,060.7	$2,864.9
Canada	217.2	227.2	218.1
Latin America	90.9	75.2	65.5
Europe and Africa	411.8	594.2	710.3
Pacific area	229.9	194.6	218.4
Corporate	875.3	891.3	672.1
Total identifiable assets of continuing operations	$3,842.2	$4,043.2	$4,749.3

CASE 34 _____

| Circuit City Stores Inc. |

Ed Kopf, director of planning for Circuit City Stores Inc., had just finished reviewing a consultant's report which concluded that Circuit City should once again offer products through mail order. More specifically the consultant recommended that Circuit City introduce a high-gloss mail-order catalog containing top-of-the-line, high-margin consumer electronic items.

The potential benefits of mail-order sales were attractive. Mail order seemed to offer a quick and inexpensive means of expanding geographically as well as increasing Circuit City's penetration in its existing markets. Mail-order sales also would allow Circuit City to extend its product lines to include high-margin but low-volume items that were not feasible to carry in all stores. In addition, there would be promotional synergies between mail order and retail store operations.

The consultant believed that this was an opportune time for Circuit City to reintroduce mail-order selling. There were currently no dominant mail-order catalogs specializing in Circuit City's merchandise lines. Furthermore, Circuit City had demonstrated an ability to satisfy diverse consumer markets. Circuit City's advanced point-of-sale (POS) system, which supplied on-line communications between all Circuit City operations and its corporate offices in Richmond, could give the company a competitive advantage in processing orders. Also, no existing consumer electronics mail-order firm could match Circuit City's buying power. Strategically, catalog sales would allow Circuit City to take advantage of growing consumer acceptance of in-home shopping. And, it would put the company in a position to test new technologies in in-home shopping that many experts believed would significantly affect retailing in the near future.

Despite the consultant's enthusiasm, Ed had more than a few misgivings. If Circuit City were to offer a "high-end" catalog, as the consultant recommended, how would a high-price product offering affect Circuit City's "low price" image and promotion strategy? How would a "skim" marketing strategy fit with one of Circuit City's greatest competitive strengths, its ability to underprice and outpromote the competition by concentrating on volume? Circuit City had succeeded by mass marketing products with a broad-based appeal; would the company know how to promote more exclusive products to the electronics buff?

On the other hand, if Circuit City were to offer a catalog featuring items comparable to current in-store offerings, would it generate new business or would

This case was prepared by James Olver under the supervision of Eleanor G. May, Professor of Business Administration, The Darden Graduate School of Business Administration. Copyright © 1985 by The Darden Graduate Business School Sponsors, Charlottesville, Virginia. Used by permission from Eleanor G. May.

it cannibalize the existing customer base? Would the catalog prices have to match in-store prices? What would the catalog offer that other local retailers didn't?

Regardless of the type of product offered, other issues would have to be resolved before deciding whether to enter the mail-order business. How would mail order fit into the volatile consumer electronics market? Today's prices and technology might be hopelessly outdated before the completion of the catalog's life. Would consumers buy high-ticket consumer electronics without having the opportunity to test the product or at least to see it? Would they be confused by differences between the product and service offered in the retail stores and those available through the catalog? How would the product be serviced? An important question for Circuit City was whether there were better opportunities in areas other than mail order. Should the company get involved in what could be presumed to be a sideline, during a time of very rapid growth?

COMPANY BACKGROUND

Circuit City was the largest specialty retailer of name-brand consumer electronics and appliances in the United States. Through its outlets centered in the Southeast, Circuit City sold large and small appliances, audio, and video equipment, and advanced consumer electronics (ACE). Circuit City sought to dominate the markets it entered and often achieved more than a 35 percent share of market in consumer electronics sales. Circuit City was the largest-volume member of NATM (National Appliance and Television Merchants), the industry's largest buying group. Tremendous buying power, coupled with what the company's chairman, Alan Wurtzel, called a "critical mass" of convenient local outlets, allowed Circuit City to offer broad selections and low prices, as well as local repairs and optional extended warranties on most products.

Circuit City's promotional activities were well suited to its guaranteed-lowest-price strategy (within 30 days of purchase a customer received a refund of the difference if another retailer in the market area offered the identical merchandise for a lower price than that paid at Circuit City). Frequent storewide sales with names like "Midnight Madness," "Price Slasher," and "The Thing" contributed to Circuit City's tremendous sales volume, which averaged around $5.6 million per store—about 10 times that of the typical consumer electronics specialty store, by Circuit City estimates. Promotions were backed by full-page newspaper ads and inserts (FSI) packed with sale-priced items, primarily at the lower-price end of each product category, (See Exhibit 34.1). In most markets, promotions were supported also by television and radio advertising that the smaller local specialty stores typically could not afford to match. Circuit City's gross advertising expenditures in 1984 were 5.9 percent of sales.

Until 1979, Circuit City Stores Inc., then operating under the name Wards Company, Inc., had offered consumer electronics through mail order, first under the name Dixie Hi-Fi, which was the name used by Wards in its discount audio outlets located in the Southeastern states. Fair trade laws had allowed Dixie Hi-Fi

EXHIBIT 34.1 **Example of Circuit City newspaper advertisement**

to sell audio equipment through the mail at prices significantly lower than those at the retail stores in most areas, resulting in roughly $5,000,000 in annual mail-order sales. The layout of the Dixie catalog emphasized a "low cost, no nonsense" approach: black-and-white sketches of the items were accompanied by detailed descriptions of the product and its technical specifications.

In the early 1970s, Wards operated several retail consumer electronics and appliance chains of its own, plus the Dixie mail order/discount outlet business, and leased departments in several discount department stores. During the recession of the mid-1970s, Wards suffered severe losses when several of the department store chains from which it leased went bankrupt. Between 1977 and 1981, the Dixie Hi-Fi discount audio stores, and Custom Hi-Fi and Sight and Sound consumer electronics

EXHIBIT 34.2 **Balance sheet**		
Years ended February 28 or 29	**1984**	**1985**
	(In thousands)	
Assets		
Cash	$ 21,761	$ 45,230
Accounts and notes receivable	8,318	10,544
Merchandise inventory	47,346	73,688
Other current assets	1,642	1,749
Total current assets	79,067	131,211
Property and equipment, net	21,566	43,984
Deferred income taxes	1,568	1,531
Other assets	7,701	14,647
Total assets	$109,902	$191,373
Liabilities and Stockholders' Equity		
Current installments of long-term debt	$ 277	$ 1,477
Accounts payable	25,545	37,016
Accrued expenses and other liabilities	6,550	8,160
Accrued income taxes	621	13,432
Total current liabilities	32,993	60,085
Long-term debt	15,187	27,885
Other liabilities	1,297	1,652
Deferred revenue	4,141	5,733
Excess of value received over cost of assets acquired, net	7,707	6,843
Stockholders' equity		
Preferred stock of $20 par value	591	590
Common stock of $1 par value	9,882	10,861
Capital in excess of par value	6,826	27,064
Retained earnings	31,278	50,660
Total stockholders' equity	48,577	89,175
Total liabilities and stockholders' equity	$109,902	$191,373

stores were consolidated as Circuit City. The resulting entity offered consumer electronics at Dixie's low prices, with the superior service, selection, convenience, and aesthetic appeal of Custom Hi-Fi and Sight and Sound. In addition, the chain of discount appliance stores, Wards Loading Dock ("name brand appliances at forklift prices"), was revamped, consumer electronics product lines available in the Circuit City stores were added, and the stores were renamed Circuit City Superstores. With the demise of the fair trade laws and the tremendous success of the Circuit City format, mail order was abandoned in favor of vigorous expansion with retail outlets. In 1984, the corporate name was changed from Wards to Circuit City to diminish confusion and to more clearly describe the firm.

The strategy paid off handsomely. Sales revenues had grown at a compound annual rate of 43 percent between 1982 and 1985, while profits had increased almost sevenfold in the same period (see Exhibits 34.2 to 34.4).

EXHIBIT 34.3 **Statements of earnings**

Years ended February 28 or 29	1983	1984	1985
		(In thousands)	
Net sales and operating revenues	$245,914	$356,708	$519,214
Cost of sales, buying, and warehousing	176,755	253,887	370,765
Gross profit	69,159	102,821	148,449
Selling, general, and administrative expenses	58,194	79,140	109,031
Interest expense	1,758	1,372	1,409
Total expenses	59,952	80,512	110,440
Earnings before income taxes	9,207	22,309	38,009
Provision for income taxes	3,700	10,300	17,775
Net earnings	$ 5,507	$ 12,009	$ 20,234
Earnings per common share (in dollars)	$.62	$1.23	$1.94

EXHIBIT 34.4 **Sales and earnings**

Years ending February 28 or 29	Net sales	After tax earnings
1985	$519,214,000	$20,234,000
1984	356,708,000	12,009,000
1983	245,914,000	5,507,000
1982	176,169,000	2,935,000
1981	131,881,000	2,701,000
1980	119,609,000	2,286,000
1979	111,534,000	2,570,000
1978	90,799,000	2,052,000
1977	72,360,000	1,250,000
1976	61,185,000	1,362,000

Circuit City's retail operations in 1985 included 35 Circuit City stores, 13 Superstores, 12 Lafayette stores on the East Coast, and 33 leased departments in Zody's Department Stores on the West Coast (see Exhibit 34.5). The company had nearly 3,800 employees and 377,000 square feet of selling space (see Exhibit 34.6). In 1985, Circuit City was involved in a program of upgrading the Circuit City stores (to Superstores if there was sufficient space, to "mini" Supers if there was a space limitation) and opening free-standing Superstores to replace the Zody's units.

EXHIBIT 34.5 **Number of retail units**

Fiscal year ending February	Superstore	Circuit City	Lafayette	West Coast	Total
1985	13	35	12	33	93
1984	8	38	11	41	98
1983	7	36	8	50	101
1982	7	31	8	51	97
1981	4	37	0	41	82
1980	4	36	0	35	75
1979					70
1978					70
1977					61

EXHIBIT 34.6 **Space and employee data**

	Square feet selling space	Sales per square foot	Number of employees
1985	376,607	$1,371	3,796
1984	360,792	989	2,057
1983	349,389	704	1,664
1982	308,754	571	1,323
1981	230,936	571	1,052
1980	215,570	555	957
1979			943
1978			824
1977			610

CIRCUIT CITY STORES

Whether in Superstore or regular format, the Circuit City store layout emphasized an expansion of "The Four Ss" to five: the fifth "S" was for "Speed." As the 1985 Annual Report noted, "Circuit City has long recognized that retailing is part theater. The Superstore has been carefully designed to dramatize and to deliver efficiently to the customer exceptional *Savings*, outstanding *Selections*, and high quality *Service* before and after the sale—all with *Speed* and guaranteed *Satisfaction*." The effect of this combination was particularly dramatic in the 30,000- to 40,000-square-foot Superstores, which had up to 14,000 square feet of showroom space, 15,000 square feet of warehouse, plus space for service and sales support. (Other Circuit City stores and the Lafayette stores had a minimum of 4,000 square feet of selling space and 1,500 square feet of storage.)

Upon entering a typical Superstore building, the customers walked by large picture windows behind which repairmen could be viewed working on Circuit City products. Adjacent was "Kiddie City," a playroom to occupy children while parents shopped. Inside the showroom, the customer was confronted by an impressive array of television and video equipment, appliances, and consumer electronics grouped by product category, each featuring a wide variety of price/performance choices. The TV and appliance areas occupied 5,000 to 10,000 square feet. Appliances included washers and dryers, refrigerators, freezers, dishwashers, and microwave ovens. One wall in the television area was lined from floor to ceiling with sets of various sizes and descriptions. In front of these were aisles of shelves stocked with other television and video equipment and accessories such as VCRs, cameras, and videodisc players. A vast assortment of tape decks, phonographs, receivers, tuners, amplifiers, and speakers, sorted by price/performance characteristics, were displayed. A listening room was available where the audiophile could test the stereo equipment; an adjacent, separate area contained car stereos. The advanced consumer electronics products and accessories included tape recorders, radios, handheld TVs, telephones and other communication devices, and portable stereo equipment. A limited line of home computer hardware and software had been carried, but by 1985 this merchandise had been discontinued.

All models of most products were set up for the shopper to try out. But, in contrast to most catalog showrooms, a knowledgeable and eager salesforce was available to answer questions and offer advice both about the product and about the sales terms. Once a purchase decision was made, the salesperson entered the order on a POS computer terminal on the showroom floor, which simultaneously placed the order to the warehouse, updated the inventory, recorded the name and phone number of the customer, the size and type of his order, and the name of the salesperson, and computed the salesperson's commission.[1] Daily summary reports allowed store managers to evaluate sales and profit performance both of salesmen and of product categories (see Exhibit 34.7).

After the salesperson placed the order, the customer took the order slip to the cashier where payment was made or credit was arranged. Small accessories,

---

[1]According to *Mart* magazine (June 1985) the median salary for a floor salesperson selling this type of merchandise in appliance/TV stores, home electronics stores, specialty stores (i.e., telephone, computer, video, hi-fi), or department stores and mass merchandisers was $18,061 in 1984. Of the respondents that pay commissions, 40 percent pay between 1 percent and 3 percent, 13 percent between 4 percent and 9 percent, and 47 percent, 10 percent or over.

EXHIBIT 34.7 Example of "Daily Processed Sales Summary" for store 0817

Salesman	# Tickets	Merchandise (In dollars)	Gross margin percent	Extended service plans Dollars	Extended service plans Percent	SPIFF (In dollars)
A	15	1,412.41	33.7	97.88	6.9	38.25
B	17	3,098.32	18.8	0	0	24.00
C	9	265.44	10.6−	169.97−	64.0−	8.50
D	11	2,377.64	22.1	0	0	44.00
E	1	24.00−	100.0−	0	0	.00
F	1	64.29	.0	0	0	.00
G	2	357.00	11.5	0	0	1.00
H	14	1,044.75	27.3	88.94	20.0	38.25
I	16	1,490.54	32.5	83.26	6.1	60.25
J	2	118.88	.0	0	0	6.00
K	1	599.00	28.9	0	0	20.00
L	7	141.16	20.2	0	0	.75
M	19	1,363.61	31.6	89.79	7.2	24.50
N	2	140.65−	70.8−	0	0	2.00−
O	13	3,452.89	21.0	229.91	6.7	47.00
P	1	.00	.0	69.97	0	.00
Q	2	298.00	23.2	0	0	2.50
R	8	95.33	27.9	0	0	1.50
S	9	125.72	18.6	0	0	1.25
T	16	172.83	10.3	2.50	1.5	1.00
U	13	3,823.67	21.4	0	0	27.00
V	7	218.07	31.1	1.00	.5	4.50
W	10	135.92	15.4	17.66	13.0	2.50
X	18	4,302.56	19.4	225.88	5.3	34.75
Y	8	138.49	15.9	0	0	3.50
Z	2	21.18−	100.0−	29.97	141.5−	.00
AA	10	1,420.51	29.0	27.94	2.4	24.50
BB	15	3,124.98	21.7	129.88	4.2	36.50
CC	23	1,713.63	29.8	38.03	2.2	25.75
DD	13	29.31	14.4	0	0	5.25
EE	20	1,558.40	27.9	91.73	5.9	25.00
FF	21	2,388.33	19.8	0	0	10.25
Total	326	$35,145.85	22.7%	$1,054.37	3.0%	$516.25

Category of sales	Sales	Cost of sales	Gross margin percent	Extended service plans Dollars	Extended service plans Percent
Merchandise					
Video	$13,215.58	$10,602.86	19.8	413.55	3.1
Major	8,765.57	7,209.69	17.7	204.73	2.3
Audio	8,236.33	5,594.88	32.1	121.22	1.5
ACE	5,088.34	3,879.57	23.8	211.26	4.2
Other	159.97−	127.98−	20.0−	103.50	64.7−
Sub-Total	$35,145.85	$27,159.02	22.7	$1,054.37	3.0
Delivery	41.97				
Installation	.00				
Service Parts	.00				
Service Labor	.00				
VCR Membership	.00				
VCR Rental	56.50				
Service Charges	12.00				
Grand Total	$35,256.32	$27,159.02		$1,054.37	

such as tapes and batteries, were available next to the cashier. After the sale was consummated, the customer walked to the warehouse to pick up the order.

Although Circuit City often did not carry "top-of-the-line" models because of the company's reliance on volume, most departments had something for the vast majority of consumer electronics customers. Overall, Circuit City merchandise sales were about 50 percent video, 30 percent audio, 10 percent appliances, and 10 percent ACE. In addition to the merchandise sales, less than 10 percent of the revenues came from sales of services, including delivery, extended warranty, and repair services.

Offering a selection of ACE products, particularly home computers and accessories, was difficult, however. Circuit City stores and Superstores had carried in prior years some of the more popular lines, such as the Commodore, Texas Instruments, and Atari home computers and video systems. Rapid technological innovation in these products made demand and prices particularly unstable, and the wide range of options and accessories available (e.g., computer software) made it difficult to stock an adequate inventory. As a result, these ACE products had not been backed by Circuit City's 30-day lowest-price guarantee. One attempt by Circuit City to cope with product proliferation and obsolescence was an in-store "catalog" through which customers could order software and accessories that were not stocked in the stores. The catalog, actually a computer printout of product names and prices without any descriptive information, had to be updated weekly.

MAIL-ORDER FEASIBILITY STUDY

In the summer of 1984, Circuit City decided to reexamine the issue of mail-order catalog sales. A consulting firm was employed to examine trends in mail-order merchandising and in attitudes toward mail order of consumer electronics, and to recommend a course of action based on Circuit City's competitive strengths, broad strategic considerations, and a cost/benefit analysis. If mail order looked promising, the consultant was asked to develop an implementation plan that would include recommended product offerings, positioning of the catalog, development of a customer base, and the relationship between store and mail-order operations.

THE MAIL-ORDER MARKET

For purposes of the analysis, "mail order" was limited to mail, telephone, or catalog-desk orders of merchandise, and excluded telephone solicitation; it also excluded types of transactions in which the product ordered was immediately available to the customer. For example, store sales by catalog showrooms such as Best Products would not be included, while sales at Sears and Penney catalog order desks would be. By this definition, mail-order sales had been increasing nationally at an average annual rate of about 10 percent for the prior five years, roughly twice the growth rate of traditional retail outlets. The Direct Marketing Association estimated that Americans purchased about $40 billion worth of merchandise through the mail in 1983; other estimates ranged from $25 to $100 billion, depending on the definition of "mail order."

There were in 1983 between 4,000 and 5,000 mail-order catalogs for consumer goods; about 6.7 billion catalogs were mailed both by mail-order firms and by other retail firms. The market segments most relevant to Circuit City were classified as "Audio-Video" and "Consumer Electronics/Scientific," with approximately 230 catalogs in Audio-Video and 190 in Consumer Electronics/Science. Mail-order sales in 1982 for these two categories were estimated at $515 million, roughly 22 percent higher than in 1981.[2] The consultant's report noted that the largest competitors in

[2]Total sales in 1984 of major appliances were reported by *Merchandising* magazine to be nearly $17 billion; for video equipment $12 billion; for audio, $7 billion; and for ACE (including personal computers), $5 billion.

EXHIBIT 34.8 **Example of 47th Street Photo catalog page**

these areas had roughly 10 percent of the sales share of their market segment, and no major U.S. retailer had entered either segment.

Marketing strategies in both of the segments relevant to Circuit City varied widely from firm to firm. Some firms, such as 47th Street Photo, were discount operations targeting a fairly broad-based audience (see Exhibit 34.8). Others, such as Sharper Image and Markline, featured list-price specialty products that would appeal to a select clientele (see Exhibit 34.9 and 34.10). Copy and layouts reflected the theme of the catalog and the characteristics of the target audience.

Mail-order merchandisers were able to target audiences with desired demographic, psychographic, and purchase-pattern profiles, through specialized mailing lists. As a result, some catalogs projected the image of an exclusive specialty shop yet

EXHIBIT 34.9 **Example of Sharper Image catalog page**

A. Emerson's compact TV/video cassette player is a great Markline value at only $499!

This 10-inch color TV has a built-in video cassette player that's loaded with features. The AC/DC television has automatic fine tuning and color control. The video cassette player features 3-speed automatic playback, automatic rewind and replay, and speed search. It can even freeze a single frame for stop-action viewing. Unit measures 14x11.5x13.9".

EMVCT120 Emerson TV/Video cassette player
$499   (S&H $20)

SPECIAL VALUE!
"Big" screen TV/VCR in one unit!

At last, here's a VCR and 19" television you can tote around in one piece. The VCR is built right into the base of this 19", 105 channel, cable ready, high resolution monitor. Tote Vision (shown on p. 25) features TV/VCR wireless remote control of all functions. Allows up to 8 hours of record/playback time with auto playback speed selector. This direct-drive, front loading system has automatic rewind. 3 playback speeds, memory, LED indicators, visual cue/review search function and more. Ideal as a compact home entertainment center. Size is 62x22¾x22¼".

TOCB1900 Tote Vision
(was $799.00) **NOW $699.00**
(S&H $25)

New
B. Go on tour with your favorite entertainer.

Bring the sound of live concerts inside your home or car with the Sony AC-DC Powered Digital Compact Disc Player. This remarkable Sony design combines state-of-the-art technology & quality in this miniaturized compact disc player. Features ultra-thin, three-spot laser pick-up system with a digital filter, minimizes noise and improves high frequency reproduction. Elastic damper arm with pick-up absorbs vibration and improves tracking. Features automatic music sensor for instant repeat or advance track selection up to 99 tracks forward or reverse. Auto off. Supplied with AC adaptor, DC adaptor, cassette adaptor, mounting plate and patch cords.

SXD160 Sony Portable CD Player
$279.95   (S&H $4.50)

MARKLINE
Customer Service
1-800-225-8390

EXHIBIT 34.10 **Example of Markline catalog page**

generated large sales volumes. There was little evidence that a mass-appeal approach necessarily resulted in greater sales.

CONSUMER TRENDS

The consultant noted four broad consumer trends that had been credited with contributing significantly to the overall growth in mail order. These highlighted a growing demand for more specialized mail-order services:

- As a result of increased emphasis on developing and maintaining personal individuality, consumers were demanding more choices than stores could display or stock.
- A higher proportion of women in the work force meant less time for shopping but increased household disposable income.
- Awareness of and demand for hard-to-find items had increased consumers' interest in alternatives to in-store retailing.

- Consumers' desire for more leisure time for self-development and creative expression was leaving less time to search for a particular item or service.

TECHNOLOGICAL DEVELOPMENTS AND FUTURE TRENDS

Technological developments had complemented, and perhaps accelerated, the movement toward greater acceptance of in-home shopping. For example, passive direct-response systems, such as toll-free 800 phone numbers, contributed to the growth in mail-order sales. An experimental cable TV channel, offered "info-mercials"—five- to ten-minute descriptions of particular products. Catalogia, Inc., consolidated a national network of 3,000 electronic multi-catalog retail shopping systems into a central data base, through which consumers could obtain the names of catalogs where a desired product was available. Sears and J.C. Penney had experimented with videodisc catalogs.

Teletext data transmission offered information varying from stock prices to weather reports; retailers could use teletext to present products to consumers. The Source, CompuServe, and Dow Jones Information/Retrieval were all examples of teletext services available in the United States. All three national television networks had competing teletext systems in test market. Unlike other commercial teletext systems, which used computer terminals as vehicles, the network systems embedded a digital signal in the television vertical blanking interval (the technology used in captioning for the deaf). The signal could be read using a relatively inexpensive decoder, allowing the user to access, on the television, "pages" of information at will. When coupled with an 800 number for ordering, placing an order simply involved turning on the TV and dialing the phone.

One of the most promising and controversial technologies under development was videotex, a two-way interactive system that could operate through either home computers or cable TV. Unlike teletext, videotex subscribers could transmit as well as receive information. Videotex applications already included in-home financial transactions, electronic mail, reservation bookings, and retail sales transactions. Videotex, in use in Europe since 1976, was available commercially or publicly in several European countries and in Canada. In the United States, many of the largest communications, retailing, banking, and computer companies had been attempting to determine how to develop a dominant position in the business and/or consumer end of the videotex market. The list of firms involved in individual or joint ventures included CBS, Knight-Ridder, Times-Mirror, Time Inc., Cox Cable, Warner/AMEX, AT&T, Honeywell, Digital, IBM, and Chemical Bank, as well as Sears, Dayton Hudson, J.C. Penney, Melvin Simon, and Federated Department Stores.

Industry observers differed widely concerning time horizons for videotex development and adoption, as well as its eventual impact on retailing. There were several barriers to widespread consumer adoption, such as the cost of videotex terminals and user mistrust of the technology, as well as technological problems that needed to be resolved. Nonetheless, the consultant believed that videotex and related technologies had potentially significant ramifications for retailing, and it was important that Circuit City be prepared to adopt these technologies as they developed.

FURTHER CONSUMER RESEARCH

It was clear that some consumers were willing to order some types of consumer electronics through the mail. In order to learn more about this market segment, the consultant had conducted a focus-group interview to determine the issues deemed important by mail-order customers.

These issues were then addressed in more detail in a survey of consumer electronics mail-order customers. A questionnaire (Exhibit 34.11) was mailed to 1,500 subjects chosen at random from the mailing list of a prominent consumer electronics mail-order firm. About a 30 percent response was received.

FOCUS GROUP FINDINGS

Most of the ten focus group participants had had some experience with mail order. Two of the attendees reported poor experiences—slow delivery or defective products—but this had not prejudiced them against using mail order.

There were three frequently cited advantages of store purchases over mail order:

- The opportunity to see, hear, and touch the merchandise
- The opportunity to take the purchase home immediately
- Greater confidence in warranty and repair availability

For the most part, participants saw little or no value in the information and recommendations provided by in-store salespeople. Salespeople were described variously as:

- Order-takers only
- Unpleasant to deal with
- Low-paid and low-skilled
- Not well-versed in the characteristics of their own and their competitors' products
- Insensitive to the consumer's needs

Focus group participants seemed most likely to consider mail order if the following conditions were met:

- Merchandise could be returned unconditionally
- The company offering the catalog was known to the consumer
- The catalog offered brand-name products
- The desired product was unlikely to be damaged in shipping
- The product had a relatively low markup

EXHIBIT 34.11 **Survey instrument used for mail-order survey**

October, 1984

Dear Sir or Madam,

The enclosed survey is an important part of a project to analyze how people make choices when purchasing consumer electronics. I would appreciate it if you would take just a few minutes to complete and return this questionnaire. Your response is extremely important.

A postage-paid return envelope is enclosed. Please mail your responses as soon as possible. Thank you for your help.

Sincerely,
Susan Quillen

Please Note: For this survey, the terms "mail order" and "mail-order catalog" refer to the purchase of products from catalogs you have received through the mail (orders can be placed either by telephone or by mail).

1. For each of the products listed below, please check those which your household has purchased in the last three years, and indicate whether or not you purchased them through mail-order catalogs. (Check all that apply.)

	Bought in the last 3 years		Bought through mail order	
Computer peripherals	Yes ____	No ____	Yes ____	No ____
Computer software	Yes ____	No ____	Yes ____	No ____
Microwave oven	Yes ____	No ____	Yes ____	No ____
Portable stereo	Yes ____	No ____	Yes ____	No ____
Portable TV	Yes ____	No ____	Yes ____	No ____
Stereo system/components	Yes ____	No ____	Yes ____	No ____
Telephone	Yes ____	No ____	Yes ____	No ____
Video game systems	Yes ____	No ____	Yes ____	No ____
Video tape/disc player	Yes ____	No ____	Yes ____	No ____

2. If you have purchased any of the above products in the past three years, please circle the product you bought most recently (if you purchased more than one product at that time, circle the most expensive item). If you have not purchased any of the products in Question 1 in the last 3 years, please skip to Question 4:

3. Question 3 concerns the product you circled in Question 2.
   A) How much did you pay for the product?

   Under $20 ____ $20-$50 ____ $50-$200 ____ $200 ____ $500 ____   over $500 ____

B) Which of the following sentences best describes your knowledge of this specific product before you purchased it?

I had owned or tried the product before. _____

I had seen the product demonstrated but never tried it myself. _____

I had seen the product myself but never saw it demonstrated. _____

I had seen only pictures of the product. _____

I had never seen the product or any pictures of it. _____

C) In deciding where to buy, did you compare prices or features . . .

. . . by speaking with store salespeople?	Yes ____	No ____
. . . by inspecting products in a store?	Yes ____	No ____
. . . in mail order catalogs?	Yes ____	No ____
. . . by telephone?	Yes ____	No ____
. . . by word-of-mouth?	Yes ____	No ____
. . . through advertising?	Yes ____	No ____
. . . by reading Consumer Reports?	Yes ____	No ____

D) Which of the following sentences best describes your use of mail-order catalogs in this purchase decision?

I never looked at this product in mail-order catalogs. _____

I looked in mail-order catalogs but wouldn't consider buying it through them. _____

I considered buying it through a mail-order catalog, but chose to buy it through a store instead. _____

I bought the product through a mail-order catalog. _____

E) Why did you choose the method of purchase indicated in Question D?

_____

F) If you purchased through a mail-order catalog (if not, proceed to question H); how did you place your order?

Over the telephone _____ Through the mail _____

Why did you choose this method? _____

G) If you purchased through a mail-order catalog, did you seek additional information on the product over the telephone?

Yes _____ No _____

H) How important were each of the following considerations in your decision of where you bought the product? (Circle one in each row.)

	extremely important	somewhat important	slightly important	not at all important
— low price	1	2	3	4
— informative salespeople	1	2	3	4
— convenient location	1	2	3	4
— ease of purchase	1	2	3	4
— past experience with the store/catalog	1	2	3	4
— reputation of the store/catalog	1	2	3	4
— availability of repairs	1	2	3	4
— liberal return policy	1	2	3	4
— friendly sales people	1	2	3	4
— credit availability	1	2	3	4
— extensive product line	1	2	3	4

Question 4 concerns your use of mail-order catalogs for any type of product.

A) Approximately how many products have you purchased through mail-order catalogs in the past two years? (check only one)

None _____ 1-2 _____ 3-5 _____ 6-10 _____ more than 10 _____

B) How many different mail-order catalogs have you ordered from in the past two years?

None _____ 1-2 _____ 3-5 _____ 6-10 _____ more than 10 _____

C) Please indicate your experience with the following mail-order catalogs:

	Have bought from	Have considered buying from	Have not considered buying from	Am not familiar with
Circuit City	_____	_____	_____	_____
Crutchfield	_____	_____	_____	_____
L.L. Bean	_____	_____	_____	_____
Land's End	_____	_____	_____	_____
Lubin & Sons	_____	_____	_____	_____
Radio Shack	_____	_____	_____	_____
Sears	_____	_____	_____	_____

5. Question 5 will only be used for statistical purposes and is completely confidential.

A) Your current age:

Under 18 _____ 18 to 24 _____ 25 to 34 _____ 35 to 54 _____ 55 and over _____

B) Your sex: Male _____ Female _____

C) Your marital status: Single _____ Married _____

D) Number of household members (including yourself) 18 years of age and over:

None _____ 1 _____ 2 _____ 3 _____ 4 or more _____

E) Number of household members (including yourself) under 18 years of age:

None _____ 1 _____ 2 _____ 3 _____ 4 or more _____

F) Your residence is located in which type of area:

Urban _____ Suburban _____ Rural _____

G) Do you own your own home?

Yes _____ No, I am renting _____

H) Your highest level of education: (check one only)

Have not received high school diploma _____

High school graduate _____

Some post high school education _____

College graduate _____

University work beyond Bachelor's degree _____

I) What is the occupation of the head of your household: (check one)

Professional/Technical/Managerial _____

Sales/Clerical _____

Skilled Labor _____

Semi/Unskilled Labor _____

Retired _____

Student _____

Other, please specify _____

J) Your total household income:
   Under $5,000   ____
   $15,000 to $25,000   ____
   $25,000 to $35,000   ____
   $35,000 to $50,000   ____
   $50,000 and above   ____
                           THANK YOU!

Participants reported that generally they researched products prior to purchase, particularly in the case of expensive items. They were likely to seek recommendations from friends and family, *Consumer Reports*, and in-store demonstrations, and they were likely to compare prices among catalogs. Many indicated that they often visited specialty shops in the evaluation process, but would purchase the item wherever they could secure the lowest price.

MAIL SURVEY FINDINGS

The demographic profile of the questionnaire respondents corresponded closely to that found among other consumers who used mail order. When compared with the general population, however, respondents tended to be:

- Concentrated between 25 and 54 years of age
- Largely male
- Surburban
- College graduates
- More likely to be employed in professional/managerial positions
- From households with incomes over $25,000

Demographics varied by product purchase category. Younger, less affluent subjects had bought proportionally more stereo components and portable stereos. ACE purchases, such as computer accessories, on the other hand, were concentrated among the more educated, affluent, professional respondents. Homeowners were more likely than nonhomeowners to have purchased appliances, but were less likely to have purchased a home stereo.

Respondents who reported using mail order for their most recent consumer electronics purchase had also ordered proportionally more mail-order products in the prior two years, and had ordered through more different catalogs than had other respondents. It appeared that consumers were most familiar with catalogs that had an image or product offering similar to that of catalogs they had purchased from in the past. For example, in general, respondents who were most familiar with Lands End (a catalog including a wide assortment of active sportswear) were also familiar with L.L. Bean, and to a lesser extent with Sharper Image, but were less familiar with Circuit City. Circuit City customers, on the other hand, were generally quite familiar with Radio Shack, and somewhat with Sharper Image, but were less familiar with L.L. Bean. Reported familiarity with Lubin & Sons, a fictitious name included to check reliability of the answers, was very low.

The percentage of respondents who had used mail order was highest among the better educated consumers, aged 35 to 54 years. This held across a variety of catalogs as well as for mail order in general, although Sears mail-orderers were more middle-income, and Lands End and L.L. Bean had sales concentrated at both the high and low ends of the income scale. With the exception of Spencer Gifts, purchase experience increased with education.

Preferences for certain sources of product information varied according to respondents by age and education. Younger respondents relied more on friends, salespeople, and hands-on experience in purchase decisions. Those aged between 35 and 54 years were less inclined to shop around, either by visiting stores, checking ads, or asking advice. They were more likely to buy through catalogs, and more often sight unseen, than those either younger or older. Better-educated consumers were most likely to use catalogs as a means of comparison, and were less concerned with helpful salespeople, familiarity with the store, or store reputation. They placed proportionally more orders by phone, and asked for additional information when placing orders.

In deciding where to purchase a product, in-store shoppers placed more importance on convenient location and availability of repairs than did mail-order shoppers. They also relied more on past experience with the retailer than did those who purchased through catalogs. Mail-order purchasers, on the other hand, were relatively more concerned than were in-store shoppers with the retailer's reputation, return policies, price, breadth of product line, and ease of purchase.

EXHIBIT 34.12 Consultant's report—most recent consumer electronics/appliance purchase

Most recent purchase	Percentage who bought it through mail order	Percentage who had considered buying it through mail order	Percentage who had owned/tried the product before buying	Percentage who had never seen the product before buying
Stereo	72	11	30	28
Software	61	23	13	42
Telephone	46	23	32	39
Portable stereo	38	23	38	29
VCR	37	26	29	25
Peripherals	36	40	34	15
TV	9	44	36	26
Video games	9	46	64	0
Microwave	6	38	41	0

The consultant compared the relative importance of several purchase criteria across various types of consumer electronics and appliance purchases (see Exhibit 34.12, 34.13. and 34.14). It appeared that stereos and peripherals were deemed suitable for mail order, but only after first examining the product in a store. Telephones, portable stereos, and computer software seemed to be considered "safe" mail-order categories, even if the product had not been pretested in a store. Other products, such as televisions, video games, and microwave ovens, were not often purchased through the mail. The consultant believed the results indicated particular concern about dealer

---

EXHIBIT 34.13 Consultant's report—consumer electronics/appliance purchases in the past three years

| | Percentage who had bought: | |
Product category	Through mail order	Not through mail order
Stereo component system	34	32
Telephone	24	44
Computer software	21	14
Computer peripherals	15	36
Portable stereo	9	27
VCR	6	18
Video game system	5	21
Television	3	36
Microwave oven	1	34

EXHIBIT 34.14 Consultant's report—purchase decision criteria by product

| | Decision criteria | | | |
Product purchased	Informative salesperson	Convenient location	Outlet reputation	Availability of repairs
Microwave oven	44*	31	44	69
Stereo	31	10	58	32
VCR	31	24	31	23
Peripherals	28	9	17	30
Television	21	21	37	33
Telephone	19	26	34	34
Video games	18	64	27	18
Software	17	20	30	20
Portable stereo	10	15	25	14

*To be read: "Of the respondents whose most recent consumer electronics/appliance purchase was a microwave oven, 44 percent rated 'informative salespeople' as 'extremely important' in their purchase decision."

reliability and service when purchasing TV's and microwaves. Purchasers of video games, on the other hand, apparently were more interested in convenience, which was interpreted to mean getting the product quickly.

CONSULTANT RECOMMENDATIONS

We see a clear opportunity for Circuit City to build a prominent position in the consumer electronics segment of mail-order catalogs. There are, however, two basic strategies the Circuit City catalog could pursue.

First, Circuit City could develop a catalog with a similar format to its store operations; namely, guaranteed lowest price, low- to middle-line products across a wide spectrum of product categories, and high-volume sales with modest profit margins. The primary advantage to this approach is that it matches the strengths that Circuit City has built and demonstrated successfully. However, we believe that the following disadvantages make this strategy unattractive for implementation:

- This strategy has the greatest potential for cannibalizing current Circuit City sales, rather than adding incremental sales.
- The guaranteed lowest price would be extremely difficult to administer because the catalog would face price competition in virtually every part of the United States.
- There is a strong possibility that this strategy would fail to take full advantage of the higher margins mail order makes available through low overhead.
- If Circuit City wanted to modify the catalog's product mix in the future, it would be difficult to try to upgrade the quality and prices of a catalog that has already built a discount image and reputation.

Conversely, a catalog that carried a top-of-the-line group of products not only avoids the disadvantages described above, but also offers several advantages to Circuit City:

- Circuit City would be able to build purchasing power in top-end products by expanding its base of sales for those items (this would allow Circuit City to offer some of these items in their high-volume retail stores as well as in the catalog).
- Circuit City would have an opportunity to try new and different products on a limited basis without having to bump existing store products in favor of more uncertain items.
- This approach would place Circuit City in a market segment where the number one catalog (Sharper Image) has sales only a fraction of Circuit City's and where Circuit City could price lower than its major competitors without having to offer "rock bottom" prices.

To pursue this aggressive strategy in the top-of-the-line catalog market, we suggest that Circuit City develop their catalog along the following lines:

A. Products

1. The catalog should contain a select number of consumer electronics products from the top end of Circuit City's current audio, video, telephonic, computer, and recording product categories. These products might not be available in Circuit City stores, and as such would supplement rather than compete with existing Circuit City sales. These products would represent approximately 90 percent of the catalog's contents.

2. The catalog would also contain a few specialty, "one-of-a-kind" or "gadget" electronic items (video watches, for example). These would be high-margin, gift/impulse items and would compose 10 percent of the catalog. However, at Christmas time, a larger proportion of such items should be included in the catalog.

3. At least 20 percent of the products in each issue of the catalog should be new items. This approach assures that the catalog remains interesting to the consumer.

B. Prices

1. Catalog prices should be slightly lower than competing specialty electronics/audio stores and catalogs. This should be feasible because of Circuit City's tremendous buying power. While top-of-the-line products can command price premiums, if consumers find identical products in different catalogs, lowest price determines which catalog gets their order.

2. The catalog should not pursue a lowest-price guarantee, thus allowing margins well above those in the Circuit City stores, and avoiding the disadvantage discussed above.

3. Catalog prices should include shipping costs, to insure that the face value of the Circuit City catalog price is the actual price paid by the consumer.

C. Layout

1. The name of the catalog should suggest exclusivity and high technology, with only a small reference to its association with Circuit City. This approach takes advantage of potential Circuit City name recognition without confusing the catalog with Circuit City's discount image. Examples of appropriate types of names are as follows:

   a. THE CUTTING EDGE a division of Circuit City
   b. UPTOWN ELECTRONICS a subdivision of Circuit City
   c. SELECT CUSTOMER ELECTRONICS a subsidiary of Circuit City

2. The outside dimensions of the catalog should be somewhat smaller than most catalogs (approximately 7"x10" overall) because when catalogs are stacked on the consumer's coffee table, this smaller catalog will be placed on top of the larger 8 1/2" x 11" catalogs published by Sharper Image, Markline, etc.

3. The cover design should be uncluttered and clever. It should promote general interest rather than specific products. These covers will encourage

the customer to open the catalog (clearly a critical step) and will help distinguish the catalog from other electronic catalogs that tend to print simply a barrage of products on their catalog covers.

4. The catalog should be relatively brief (between 24 and 48 pages), with four-color, high-gloss print, and with no more than two or three items per page. This format strongly supports an image of top quality and exclusivity.

5. The description of each item should be as brief as possible for easy browsing, but appropriate to the price and complexity of the specific item.

D. Distribution

1. The catalog should be mailed to a select number of Circuit City customers, based on their past history of buying top-end items or having spent a certain amount of money in the store, perhaps $500. This will limit the number of catalogs that will be sent, and more importantly, insure that they are sent to segments of Circuit City customers that are most likely to purchase from the catalog.

2. The catalog should also be sent to people nationwide who have previous experience with consumer electronics through the mail, or who meet certain demographic characteristics as determined by our research. These people can be reached through one or more of the following methods:

   a. Renting mailing lists from companies such as American Express, Crutchfield, or Sharper Image.
   b. Placing advertisements with clip-out coupons for a free catalog in select national and/or regional magazines and newspapers.
   c. Producing television ads that promote one product, but that include an opportunity to call in for a free catalog.

3. The initial mailing should be at least one million pieces, sent in late September/early October on a staggered basis (200,000 each week for five weeks). One million catalogs must be printed to achieve economies of scale in printing costs. The staggered mailing will help Circuit City administer the flow of orders since most of them will come soon after the catalog arrives in the customer's home.

4. The catalog should be updated on a quarterly basis, again with staggered mailings, to allow product-line changes and to replace catalogs that have been discarded or forgotten.

E. Services

1. Customers should be able to order items via mail, through a toll-free 800 number, or through a store. The first two are conveniences that catalog customers will expect. Use of the POS system would be an added convenience that Circuit City can provide as well, allowing store salespeople to sell catalog items not available in the stores.

2. Telephone salespeople should be trained to provide additional product information, encourage sale of related items, and promote extended warranty plans, in addition to taking orders. These talents will encourage consumers to purchase technical items that cannot be described fully in a few paragraphs; they will also allow Circuit City to achieve some of the trade-up and warranty sales often precluded by catalogs.

3. A 60-day, "no questions asked," return policy should be provided. A strong return policy is a major selling point for catalogs.

This strategy is highly aggressive and would entail significant start-up and operating costs. It will also provide significant returns to Circuit City. Based on only a 2 percent response rate on one million catalogs at an average of $120 per order (as seen in comparable catalogs), Circuit City would realize sales of $2.4 million.

We feel that Circuit City is particularly well suited to succeed with this aggressive approach for the following reasons:

■ Circuit City is substantially larger than the major players in the consumer electronics end of the mail-order industry (compare Circuit City's sales of $246 million to Sharper Image's sales of only $35 million).

■ Circuit City has the buying power to allow higher margins than other competitors in this segment. Thus, even if pricing becomes the major form of competition, Circuit City should be able to win out.

■ Circuit City already has some experience with catalogs and substantial experience in consumer electronics sales. Besides being a substantial plus in and of itself, its retail stores also give Circuit City immediate access to a substantial list of potential catalog customers.

CONCLUSIONS

Ed Kopf, who had been Director of Marketing when the study of mail order was commissioned, realized that this subject was one of important concern for long-range planning. He saw the need to watch the developments of in-home shopping, but was unsure of their economic implications for Circuit City.

He knew that some firms whose business was primarily mail order, reported significantly higher profit ratios than did the average retailers. Firms that distributed principally through stores and that had treated mail order as an add-on usually were not able to develop detailed cost data to determine the bottom line profitability of mail order. Indications were, however, that the profit results were not so successful for retail store firms that added mail-order operations as for the firms that had always concentrated on mail order.

The costs to develop and distribute a mail-order catalog were reported from one source to be 40 cents per copy, with 1.5 million mailed. The return (number of orders) ranged from below 2 percent to 5 percent of the mailings. A rule of thumb had been established in the business that a 2 percent return was needed to break even. To obtain a high number of returns when a firm began a catalog operation, it was necessary to "rent" names from other mail-order firms through list brokers. The cost of names printed on pressure-sensitive labels ranged from $2.50 to $10.00 per thousand, depending usually on the quality of the list.

Ed wondered whether the Circuit City warehouse system could handle the mail orders, or whether it would be necessary to set up a separate warehouse for fulfillment of mail orders. But his biggest concern was when the time would be right for Circuit City to enter the rapidly growing mail-order market. And, if the firm were to decide to embark on this venture, what should be the extent of the merchandise offered and where should responsibility for the project lie in the Circuit City organization?

CASE 35

Rockwood Manor

Dan Chapman, administrator for Rockwood Manor retirement facility, sat in his Spokane, Washington, office contemplating a recommendation to his Board of Directors on how Rockwood could meet the apparent demand for housing to accommodate the active elderly in Spokane County. He knew the Board would ask several important questions. What is the size of the market for retirement facilities? What kind of housing facilities do the active elderly want, and how should those facilities be priced?

Dan had observed the increase in the elderly both nationally and locally. Many of the newly retired were healthy, active people who looked forward to a physically active lifestyle. Although they did not wish to move into a dormitory-style facility, they did want to get out from under the burdens of maintaining a home. They wanted to be free to move about as they pleased, yet have a private secure place they could call home.

In his tenure at Rockwood, Mr. Chapman had also observed that seniors were concerned about financial matters. Some wanted to build an estate for their children while others felt they should spend their hard-earned money on themselves. The current pricing schedule for rooms and health care at the Manor accommodated these two viewpoints. He was not sure how pricing would be handled in a different housing/service configuration.

This case was prepared by Professor William R. Wynd, Eastern Washington University. It is intended as a basis for classroom discussion rather than to illustrate effective or ineffective handling of an administrative situation. Used by permission from William R. Wynd.

NATIONAL TRENDS

The nation's population of the elderly is on the rise. According to *U. S. News and World Report*, "One of every five Americans is 55 years or older, and that figure will climb to one in every three and one-half over the next 40 years."[1] This increase is attributed to several factors. One is a decline in the death rate of 2 percent annually since 1970, due largely to improved public health care measures. A declining birth rate over the last decade has also contributed to a higher proportion of the elderly in the population. Projections indicate that by the year 1990, 30 million people will be over age 65, accounting for 28 percent of the U.S. population.

Elderly households are increasingly well-off financially when they reach retirement. Women currently account for an estimated 49 percent of the work force and, with the increased number of women working, the income from a second pension is by far one of the most important factors in the maintenance of an upward trend in income among the elderly.

Business Week recently reported a study speculating that spending by the elderly since the mid-1970s may have been extensive enough to depress the national personal saving rate.[2] Those elderly currently 65 and older make up about 16 percent of all adults, but they received more than half of all interest income and close to one-third of all capital gains reported to the IRS in 1982. Furthermore, while the average family held $18,695 in liquid assets in 1983, families headed by persons 65 to 74 years of age averaged $30,666.

With an average age of 74, the nation's elderly can expect at least 10 more years of life. Common sense would indicate a tendency to spend their discretionary income. Most are in reasonably good health (though they hate to climb stairs), their spouse is still living, and they have the time to enjoy a wide variety of leisure activities.

Indeed, the elderly are apparently spending more of their money on housing and transportation. The Department of Labor publishes three budgets for a retired couple made up of hypothetical lines of goods and services that were specified in the mid-1960s to portray three relative levels of living: lower, intermediate, and higher. The categories include food, housing, transportation, clothing, personal care, medical care, and other family consumption. In 1981, the percentage spent by the nation's elderly on housing, transportation, and clothing increased as income increased.

Although a growing elderly population constitutes a potential market for a wide variety of goods and services, the segment represented by active, affluent seniors is being increasingly cultivated by a wide variety of providers. A.T. Sutherland, advertising manager for *Modern Maturity* indicates that the maturity market (aged 50+) accounts for 25 percent of all consumer expenditures purchasing 3 percent of all domestic cars, 30 percent of all food consumed at home, 25 percent of all cosmetics and bath products, 25 percent of all alcoholic beverages, 41 percent of

---

[1]Mary Gallean, et al., "Life Begins at 55," *U. S. News and World Report*, September 1, 1980, pp. 51–60.

[2]"Misdirected Advertising Prevents Marketers from Taking Bite from 'Golden Apple' of Maturity Market," *Maturity News*, October 26, 1984, p. 19.

all toaster ovens and food processors, 37 percent of all slenderizing treatments and health spa memberships, and 31 percent of all automobile tires.[3]

Contrary to the belief that many senior citizens are inclined to migrate to the Sunbelt region, evidence shows that many seniors prefer to live in the home they have lived in for years. Change becomes less appealing as time passes. Hence, many elderly wish to remain in familiar surroundings for as long as they can. According to the U.S. Department of Housing and Urban Development, 70 percent of the population 65 and over live in their own homes, 5 to 7 percent live in retirement homes, 18 to 20 percent live in apartments or government subsidized housing, and 5 percent live in institutions.[4]

Those elderly who opt to sell their homes have a wide variety of new concepts available to them, including condominium retirement settings, mobile home courts, and group homes as well as the traditional retirement center facilities. If they change living location they are often drawn toward urban centers with lower populations where the cost of living is usually more reasonable.

THE SETTING

Spokane, Washington, is one of the nation's most beautiful cities and has many attractions as a retirement community. Located in northeastern Washington state, Spokane was the site of the 1974 World's Fair. Conservative and rural in nature, the region is among the nation's most fertile wheat producing areas. Most of the urban population is employed in wholesale and retail trade, financial services, and health care, servicing a number of sparsely populated counties in northeastern Washington and northern Idaho. Most Spokanites reaching retirement age stay in Spokane. Taxes, costs of maintaining a household, low crime rate, and availability of doctors and sophisticated medical facilities are among the attractions.

According to the 1970 census, 44,400 of the 287,487 total county population were aged 60 or over. The 1980 census counted 54,436 of the 341,058 total county population as aged 60 or over. The number of persons 60 or over increased by 9,996 in the 10 years between the censuses. Exhibit 35.1 is a bar chart showing the 1980 population in Spokane County with projections for 1985 and 1990. The population by age group and sex is shown in Exhibit 35.2.

ROCKWOOD MANOR

Rockwood Manor is a residential health facility that offers a full spectrum of services to meet the housing, nutrition, health, social, and spiritual needs of older persons. It is operated by a nonprofit corporation related to the United Methodist

---

[3]"Are the Elderly the Key to the Savings Puzzle?" *Business Week*, December 31, 1984, p. 17.

[4]U.S. Department of Housing an Urban Development, Office of Policy Development and Research, *Characteristics of the Elderly*, Washington D.C.: Government Printing Office, February 1979, pp. 1-73.

EXHIBIT 35.1 **Spokane County—1980 census and population projections for
1985 and 1990**

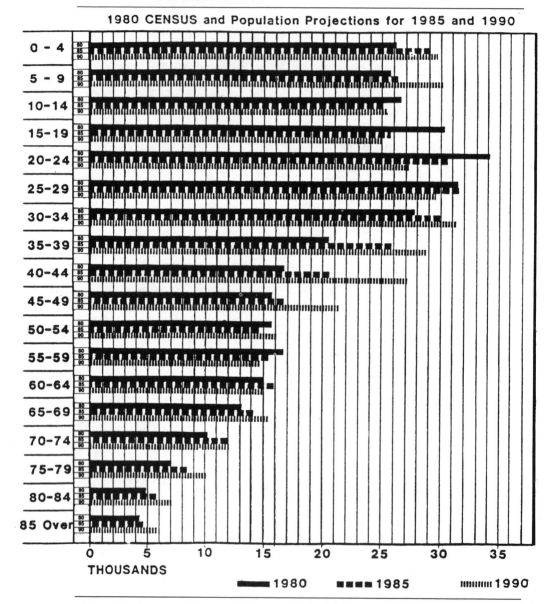

1980 CENSUS and Population Projections for 1985 and 1990

Source: Population, Enrollment, and Economic Studies Division, Office of Financial Management
(November 1982).

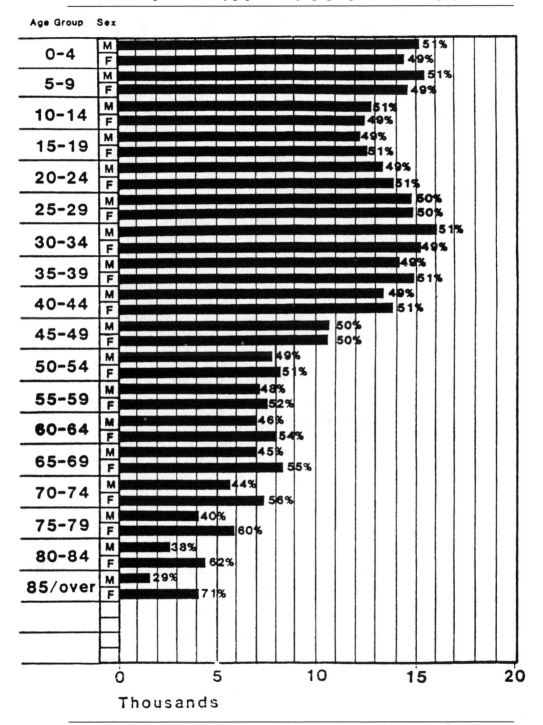

EXHIBIT 35.2 Spokane County population by age group and sex—1990 projection

Age Group   Sex

Thousands

Source: Population, Enrollment, and Economic Studies Division, Office of Financial Management (November 1982).

Church but receives no financial assistance from the church or any other organization. Residents purchase the privilege of living in a unit of their choice. Prices are based upon the charge for a standard living unit of 300 square feet. Living units may be purchased for cash or under terms of a time payment contract. A minimum down payment is required for a living unit under terms of the contract. The balance, plus interest on the declining balance, is amortized for a term of 84 months. In addition, residents pay a monthly services fee.

Residents of Rockwood Manor must be independently ambulatory and able to care for themselves at the time of admission. There is a per diem charge for infirmary care beginning with the eleventh day of confinement during any one month. The amount of this per diem charge is equal to the audited cost of a day's care in the infirmary. If a resident becomes a permanent patient in the infirmary, and his living unit is paid for in full, he may then surrender his living unit to the corporation, in which case he will then receive the infirmary care for the current monthly services fee of a standard living unit. There are currently 44 infirmary beds that are 85 percent occupied.

Rooms are also available for those residents who are not bed patients but who need assistance in the activities of daily living such as bathing and dressing. These rooms are attended by a special corps of aides under the supervision of the director of nursing services. A per diem charge is made for this intermediate health care.

A resident may cancel his contract by giving sixty days notice in writing, except during illness. If the living unit has been paid for in full, the unearned balance is refunded upon the resale of the unit.[5] If the unit has been purchased under terms of a time payment contract, no refund is made. A time payment contract terminates with death.

Rockwood manor enjoys a reputation of being one of the finest retirement homes in the region. Its physical plant is clean, neat, and well maintained. Its personnel are pleasant, helpful, and professional. These image factors combine to keep its 225 apartment high rise filled to capacity.

THE MARKET

An increasing elderly population represents a diverse market for a wide variety of retirement centers. Traditional retirement centers have almost always been operated by not-for-profit organizations, usually church affiliated. These centers normally sign a contract with the resident for lifetime care and promise no one will be asked to leave due to financial problems.

According to a survey by the national accounting and consulting firm of Laventhol and Horvath, the future of the nation's life care/continuing care retirement

---

[5]Unearned balance is calculated by dividing the amount paid by the tenant by the number of months the tenant is expected to live as shown by actuarial tables in use by major life insurance companies. The quotient is multiplied by the number of months the tenant occupied his/her unit. This amount is kept by Rockwood, the remainder (unearned balance) is returned to the tenant.

industry is rapidly changing as entrepreneurs enter the expanding market.[6] These newer facilities, though still in the minority, offer a variety of possibilities. Some still offer the life care contract, but with totally or partially refundable entry fees. Others concentrate on renting units. They have no entry or endowment fees and health care is usually provided strictly on a pay-as-needed basis.

Increasing costs and a growing market have brought together investors and not-for-profit organizers. An increasingly common partnership occurs when an investor group finances the development in return for the tax advantages. When these are exhausted, the not-for-profit organization purchases the development for fair market value.

Marketing for the typical life care center development usually precedes construction by a full year. Most developments presell half their units and achieve 66 percent occupancy within six months after completion and 95 percent within 18 months.[7]

A recent survey of establishments listed in the Yellow Pages of the Spokane County Telephone Book under the heading "Retirement and Life Care Communities and Homes" indicated a capacity of 1,031 living units and 711 infirmary beds. Occupancy of living units was nearly 100 percent. Infirmary beds were filled to 80 percent of capacity.

Competition in the current Spokane market to serve relatively high-income retirees comes from two other not-for-profit organizations and one recently constructed for-profit condominium apartment complex with minimum health care. One retirement complex most similar to Rockwood Manor just announced a duplex/multifamily addition designed for the active elderly. Their existing and planned units are either apartments, condominiums, or duplex units. Although the existing facilities were full and often enjoyed a waiting list, what additional capacity would do to occupancy rates was a matter of conjecture. The latest development would add an estimated 250 new units.

PRICING/COST CONSIDERATIONS

Dan Chapman had a real problem with pricing. He knew that some people prefer to "pay as you go," some wanted to pay the full costs up front, and others wanted something left for their estate after they passed on. He knew that prices depended on a number of factors, not the least of which was the construction costs of the units and how long they would be occupied. He felt that the initial purchase price must include the right to occupy an apartment in Rockwood Manor with the attendant advantages of housekeeping, food services, and medical care. The current purchase price for a unit in the Manor was $36,000 for a 600 square-foot apartment and $54,000 for a 900 square-foot unit. A modest monthly fee for singles and for doubles was also charged. This fee covered utilities, meals, linen, and cleaning services.

---

[6]Aaron M. Rose, "Entrepreneurs Reshaping Lifecare," *Modern Healthcare*, July 1984, pp. 148–153.
[7]Ibid.

EXHIBIT 35.3 **Construction costs—single family detached housing***

	House	Garage	Total cash costs	Total value with land
1250 sq. ft.	$68,750	$10,368	$107,249	$112,249
1000 sq. ft.	55,000	7,776	86,155	91,155
750 sq. ft.	41,250	5,184	65,060	70,060

Pro-rata land value in each case is assumed to be $5,000. Below is a detailed illustration of costs associated with construction of a 1000 square foot cottage unit.

1. Construction costs 1000 sq. ft. x $55	$55,000
2. Garage (18 x 24) 432 sq. ft. x $18	7,776
3. Contingencies = 5% (1, 2, 4, 5)	3,671
4. Architect & engineering = 10% (1, 2, 5)	6,675
5. Pro-rata recreation facilities:	
$5,000 per unit set back 3 years PV@8%	3,969
6. Management = 5% (1, 2, 5)	3,337
7. Taxes = 7.8% (1, 2, 4, 5)	5,727
Total out-of-pocket cost	$86,155
Pro-rata land value	5,000
Total land and building value	$91,155

*Construction costs for condominium units would average 12 percent less, including garages.

Cost of construction varies with the size and density of units. Apartment units are least expensive followed by condominium units with common walls and shared open spaces. Single family "cottage" units were most expensive to construct.

A local architectural firm provided rough estimates of the cost of several sizes of single family homes with garages. Economic life of the homes was considered to be 50 years, at which time they would be renovated for about $35,000 (current price) and their economic life extended for another 35 years. The land on which the units would be built was owned free and clear. About 50 undeveloped acres bordering the existing facility were owned by Rockwood Manor (See Exhibit 35.3).

CASE 36 ———————————————————————————

Ryan's Family Steak Houses, Inc.

Ryan's Family Steak Houses, Inc. had experienced tremendous success since beginning operations in 1978. The management of the firm had guided Ryan's to an enviable position as an operator of steak house restaurants for the family trade. Much of the success was credited to tight managerial control over expansion and a desire to serve a quality product for a reasonable price. The reputation of the company within its segment of the overall restaurant business was outstanding, and the favorable financial performance of the firm was reflected in the compound growth in revenue of 96 percent and net earnings of 90 percent since the first year of operations.

The managers of the firm were aware that its success was based on concentrating operations in the growing economy of the southeastern portion of the United States. However, the region not only provided a favorable business climate for a firm admired for its steady growth, it also held the largest number of family steak house restaurants. Competition in the area was strong, but in spite of this the managers of Ryan's consistently had been able to open the new units planned each year. In 1985, it planned to open fourteen new company-owned units and three franchised units, and the firm was on schedule as it reached the mid-year mark.

The reputation of family steak houses in other areas of the country was far below that enjoyed by firms operating in the Southeast. This difference in customer perception was also characteristic of cafeterias such as those operated under the familiar names of Morrison's, Piccadilly, and Luby's. As a region, the Southeast also held the largest concentration of cafeterias. The reason for these differences in the level of acceptance by consumers in the various regions of the country were difficult to understand; especially when it is obvious that cafeterias can cater to regional tastes and preferences.

Ryan's had established its position in the Southeast market by gradually expanding outside its initial base in Greenville, South Carolina. New units had been opened in smaller cities throughout the state until 1982, when company officials decided to test larger metropolitan areas. Atlanta was selected as the starting point for this expansion, by the end of 1984 Ryan's was operating in eight states extending south from Kentucky to Florida and west to Alabama.

Investors in this expansion of the firm were obviously pleased by the growth in the number of restaurants operated by the firm as well as by the gains in earnings per share. Ryan's went public in 1982, and has traded over the counter at a price earnings ratio well above the norm for the restaurant industry throughout its period of public ownership. Earnings have been reinvested in the business, rather than paid out in dividends. Thus, the investors look to the continued expansion in the number of restaurants owned or operated by Ryan's as the basis for the value of the firm. At this juncture, the managers of the firm must consider further extension of operations outside the Southeast to meet this expectation.

HISTORY

Ryan's Family Steak House opened its first restaurant in Greenville in 1978. Alvin McCall founded the new company on the relatively simple concept that success could be attained by providing customers with a quality product for a reasonable price. Superior service and overall good customer relations were also stressed as a way to distinguish Ryan's from other restaurants emphasizing budget steak operations. The company philosophy was probably best stated by T. Mark McCall, Alvin McCall's 27-year-old son and Vice President of Operations, when he said that:

> We make less per customer than other restaurants, but we feed more customers. We serve the highest quality product—USDA, grain-fed steak from Colorado. We're built around doing the best in every area—we don't cut quality. We swallow losses if we have to, but we put out the best no matter what it costs. Ultimately, it all flows to the bottom line.

From the beginning of operations until 1982, Ryan's expanded each year by opening new restaurants in South Carolina. In 1982, the elder Mr. McCall realized that the firm could not continue to expand unless additional capital was obtained from external sources. At this time, each new unit cost approximately $900,000, including $185,000 for the basic equipment required for operations. To obtain the additional funding required for expansion, the company offered the public 500,000 shares of common stock at $25.25 per share; this netted the firm $7 million in needed funds. As described in the prospectus connected with the public offering, the newly raised capital was to be put to use in the expansion of the company, primarily outside the state of South Carolina. This growth plan outlined in the offering has continued to attract the attention of outside investors and the additional capital provided has allowed the continued expansion of the firm. From 1982 through 1984, Ryan's opened exactly the number of units that had been planned, and the firm was on target for new openings during 1985. During this period, revenue grew from $9,789,000 to $32,874,000, while net income increased from $974,000 to $3,345,000.

OPERATIONS

A typical Ryan's unit is a 7,500 square-foot structure with simple decor which has remained relatively unchanged since the opening of the first unit in 1978. The buildings are all freestanding and the newer units seat approximately 345 people.

Management is in the process of expanding the seating of the previously built units from the current size of 250 to approximate the size of the newer restaurants. Tables and chairs are arranged in one large room with a salad bar acting as the main focal point.

The highest quality USDA grain-fed steak is the primary menu item and major emphasis is placed on the quality of this entrée. Less than 4 percent of the budget is spent on advertising—well below industry norms—and food costs are typically 45 percent of total costs. This figure is seven percentage points above the industry average; however, Ryan's management has no intention of lowering the amount spent on food. The company does not run specials or promotions and primarily relies on word-of-mouth advertising.

Customers place orders for entrées, which range in price from $1.29 for a hamburger to $6.99 for a prime-rib dinner, on a cafeteria-style line. The average check is $4.50. Food orders are brought to the tables and waitresses refresh coffee and beverage orders, but tables turn every 35 minutes on average. The average restaurant in the chain has gross revenues of close to $1.5 million annually and serves 6,500 customers a week, figures indicative of a volume-oriented operation.

At year-end 1984, the company was operating in eight states including franchised operations in four states. The managers of Ryan's intended to limit any future expansion of franchising to the state of Florida. This decision was based on the desire of management to maintain the image of a food product of high quality upon which the company was founded.

The expansion outside South Carolina was best described as "slow and steady." McCall believed the poor reputation of his competitors in the family steak house business hurt the overall industry. This was an obvious concern to management since expansion had become a central feature of the plans for the company. The general perception of the public in many regions of the country was that the quality and selection of food at budget steak houses was inferior to that of traditional restaurants and cafeterias.

New site location was based on strict demographic studies and took existing real estate prices into account. Typically a selected site would have 50,000 or more people within a three-mile radius. The dinner business is directed toward the low-middle and middle-income groups with the realization that families with the head-of-household holding down a blue-collar position are the primary clientele and a staple element in Ryan's success. Ryan's has consciously avoided locations that are situated within a city's "restaurant row." A major reason for this policy is the cost of real estate for such sites and the potential for rivalry that can develop when competitors are located beside one another. It may be surprising that this unusual site location strategy did not require offsetting advertising expenditures, but this had been Ryan's experience in its successful introduction of new restaurants.

McCall has made a great effort to instill pride in the 2,000 employees involved in the operation of the company-owned units. All employees are given full health coverage which includes dental, travel accident, and life insurance. Paid vacations are also enjoyed by every worker. The compensation of the managers of the various company-owned units consists of a base salary plus bonuses that reflect unit sales.

The bonus often makes up 50 percent of the overall compensation of managers, which McCall feels is an excellent way to motivate superior performance. In addition, options on stock purchases are granted to managers and higher level executives, and McCall is considering the institution of a stock purchase plan that will be available to all employees. He believes such a plan will encourage managers to feel that they are in business for themselves, and McCall hopes that all employees will adopt this philosophy.

INDUSTRY REVIEW

During 1984, the number of restaurants in the United States increased by almost 3 percent. The Department of Agriculture estimated that by the end of the year there were 253,854 separate commercial eating places in operation. These provided a wide selection in respect to menu, location, and other features that cater to consumer circumstances, tastes, and preferences. Among this number of eating places were 124,433 restaurants and lunch rooms, 123,769 fast-food outlets, and 5,640 cafeterias, accounting for sales of approximately $100 billion out of a total $159 billion expended on food services away from home. The number of commercial eating places accounting for the $100 billion in sales has grown by an average of 1.5 percent over the last seven years, although the volume of sales by these establishments grew by an average of approximately 16 percent during the same period.

The pattern of growth in the number of the various establishments and their sales differed: the number of restaurants and lunch rooms increased by an average of less than 1 percent, while the number of fast-food outlets increased by over 3 percent; during the same period of time the number of cafeterias decreased by an average of a little less than 3 percent. Sales of each of these three types of establishments increased over the seven years, with restaurants and lunch rooms increasing by somewhat less than an average 14 percent, fast-food outlets by an average 19 percent, and cafeterias by an average of approximately 9.5 percent. Estimates of the growth in the number of meals served and the value of those meals in dollar terms would not be quite as dramatic because of price level increases during this seven-year period.

It might also be noted that the number of restaurants catering to certain types of food segments grew at a faster pace than others. For example, the fastest growing types of restaurant in 1984 included those that served Oriental food and higher priced full service menu items. Both types of operations showed a 10 percent increase over the previous year, a year in which the rate of growth in restaurant establishments increased by just less than 3 percent. Restaurants that emphasized chicken items on their menus and pizza restaurants also grew well above the average, increasing their numbers by 7 and 6 percent respectively. Those restaurants serving seafood, steak, barbecue, and Italian food items all grew at a rate less than the overall average.

The most common specialty restaurant serves pizza, although the 31,000 of these establishments is somewhat less than the 39,000 generic sandwich shops. The other popular specialty restaurants include 8,500 seafood restaurants, 11,900

Mexican restaurants, 12,500 Chinese restaurants, 4,000 Italian restaurants, and 1,300 French restaurants. There were approximately 7,700 restaurants serving a steak menu in 1984; these included 840 higher priced steak houses and 3,600 family steak houses. The remaining steak houses were unclassified in respect to their type. An additional 12,300 restaurants catered to the family trade with a full menu, while an additional 1,700 restaurants provided a full menu at upscale prices.

An examination of growth in particular regions of the country reveals the influences of population migration and local taste preferences. During 1984, no region experienced a decline in growth in the number of restaurants. The slowest growing regions increased 1 percent. The fastest growing regions in 1984 included the South Atlantic states (5.4%), the Pacific region (4.3%), and the states in the region of the Rocky Mountains (3.5%). The quicker rate of growth in the South Atlantic was attributed primarily to an increase in the number of hamburger and pizza restaurants. Hamburger restaurants account for 9.5 percent of all restaurants in the region while pizza restaurants accounted for 9 percent. The South Atlantic region also had the largest number of seafood restaurants of any region, and these made up almost 5 percent of the total restaurants in this area of the country.

Steak restaurants comprised approximately 2.6 percent of the total restaurants in the United States in 1984; however, these were distributed unequally among the various regions of the country. The highest concentration of steak restaurants was in the East South Central region, where approximately 3.9 percent of the total restaurants had a steak menu. The South Atlantic and West North Central regions contained the next largest concentrations of steak restaurants, with 3.5 and 3.4 percent respectively. The New England, Middle Atlantic, and Pacific states held the lowest proportionate number of steak houses, with such restaurants making up 1.8 percent of the total number in these regions.

Family steak houses made up the largest proportion of all steak restaurants in those states that had the largest number of steak restaurants. The states of Alabama, Kentucky, Mississippi, and Tennessee that made up the East South Central region of the country had 62 percent of these restaurants classified as family-type steak restaurants. The next largest proportion—57 percent—was found in the South Atlantic states, followed by the states of Illinois, Indiana, Michigan, Ohio, and Wisconsin that made up the East North Central region of the country. The proportion of the the steak restaurants in the family category made up 51 percent of the total number. The lowest proportion of steak restaurants in the family category—33 percent—existed in the New England states, followed by the Middle Atlantic, West North Central, and Pacific states, each with 36 percent of the steak restaurants in the family steak house category.

Many observers believe that the United States is close to a saturation point in the number and capacity of restaurants. It has been noted that a new restaurant is more likely to draw customers away from existing establishments, rather than creating its own new demand. Under these circumstances success depends upon operating strategies that clearly distinguish the restaurant from others in the field, providing the customer with choices among restaurants, improving productivity to glean greater profits from fewer sales, and consolidating the restaurant's position in its market. The most recent growth in the overall restaurant industry is largely the product of restaurant chains catering to the mass of consumers with specialty operations. These chains have greater opportunity to effect the operating strategies that can cope with market saturation.

In today's market, restaurants are less frequently the destination of their patrons, so the chains compete with one another by pre-empting convenient locations that capture customers engaged in other activities. Another factor that seems to be shaping the nature of the restaurant business is the recent trend to more home entertainment and consequently eating at home. Firms operating restaurant chains have become quite imaginative under these circumstances, making their locations more attractive to the casual customer. New restaurant concepts abound, and more recent trends include catering to tastes in lighter, fresher food items; pleasant experiences in more informal settings that borrow from European motifs and earlier days of the American experience; and more casual dining that has come to be described as grazing on appetizer-styled food items in larger variety.

These trends in the conduct of restaurant business have produced only minor changes in the basic structure of the industry. The essentially fragmented nature of the business, brought about by the need to locate in proximity to a targeted clientele, can be only partially offset by chain operations that permit some consolidation of activities. Therefore, restaurants still compete in a fashion that fits the model of monopolistic competition and suits niche strategies, although some economies of scale can be attained in supporting activities. What chain operation has permitted is the deployment to wider markets of distinctive competencies and proprietary advantages held by corporations, overcoming the limitations of time and space in respect to the variety of eating-out experiences that can be enjoyed by the American public.

The raw materials and supplies essential to restaurant operations have remained in the hands of traditional suppliers. Some firms entering the restaurant business as chain operators have principal lines of business that are related to some of these raw materials. In most cases, however, these items make up only a small part of overall requirements.

Franchising of restaurants has played an important part in the overall industry, and it is a typical aspect of chain restaurant operation. A U.S. Department of Commerce report on the impact of franchising in those segments of the industry where this is a practice states that sales of company-owned restaurant operations will total $17.9 billion dollars in 1985, while sales from franchised operations will reach $30.9 billion by year end. According to this report, franchising has become a powerful force partly because economic factors have made growth through company-owned units difficult for many businesses. With rising costs of construction and training, and with franchising enlarging its share of retail receipts, the Commerce Department predicted an increased trend toward multiunit ownership by franchisees and the increased granting of rights to develop large regional areas to such licensees.

CONSUMER TRENDS AND COMPETITION

Ryan's Family Steak House has suffered the consequences and reaped the benefits of many of the features of the changing restaurant business during its existence. These included the change in consumer preference for food items during the six years of Ryan's existence. The health conscious attitude of the public had carried over to the diet that many Americans were adopting. The concern over consumption of large amounts of red meat had prompted many restaurants, fast-food varieties included, to offer "lighter" menu options. The introduction of salad bars in restaurants was an indication that owners were aware of the trend and had taken action to increase the appeal of their outlets. Manifestation of this change was evident in the creation of new chain operations, such as D'Lites of America, which emphasized the fact that all menu items carried less caloric and fat content. D'Lites, based in Atlanta, had embarked on an aggressive franchising plan and by mid-1985 had better than 50 units operating, while only being in business for three years. Ponderosa Steak Houses, Inc. had taken what management had termed a new direction in 1983 with the installation of a $20,000 salad bar unit with heating and cooling capabilities. This move was expected to allow the company more flexibility in the entrees offered. Specials such as country fried steak and meat loaf could be utilized to increase the appeal to customers. The Ponderosa management believed this move was consistent with the nutritional concerns of the public and would serve to set Ponderosa apart from other chains that offered a standard salad bar.

Large corporations were also becoming involved in the trend to open new restaurants featuring a more nutritional appeal. General Mills Corporation started a new chain, The Good Earth, which emphasized salads and pita bread sandwiches. Along similar lines, R.J. Reynolds opened an alternative to heavier menu items, the Fresher Cooker, in the past two years. The biggest question facing firms opening operations centered around the soup, salad, and sandwich idea was how large a market was available. Although the estimates varied, there were many who felt the market for such restaurants was as large as the fast-food hamburger market.

As indicated previously, the chain operation of restaurants is the dominant feature of the changing industry. The portion of market share taken by these operations has grown over the years; in 1970 the portion of market share of the top 100 chain companies was 24 percent; by 1982 this had grown to 47.7 percent. Any list of major chain restaurants would be dominated by those in the fast-food categories, but this is not the exclusive realm of chain operator. One list (with many intermediate exclusions) includes the firms in Exhibit 36.1.

Many of the listed firms compete either directly or indirectly with Ryan's. All compete with one another in providing an opportunity for individuals and families to enjoy a meal prepared away from home, depending upon the immediate tastes and preferences of customers at a particularly limited location. If the particular restaurant of a firm at a given location offers a specialty menu, it may not compete with the restaurant of another firm offering a different menu, in spite of the close proximity

EXHIBIT 36.1 Selected restaurant operations

Firm (Representative Businesses)	1984 sales (In millions)
McDonald's	$3,366
Pepsico (Taco Bell, Pizza Hut)	2,002
Pillsbury (Burger King, Steak & Ale)	1,877
Transworld (Hardee's, Quincy's)	1,341
General Mills (Red Lobster, York Steak)	1,288
W.R. Grace (Restaurant Group)	1,076
Wendy's International (Wendy's, Sisters)	939
Marriott (Big Boy, Roy Rogers)	635
Morrison	476
Sizzler's Restaurants International	451
Ponderosa (Steakhouse, Casa Lupita)	422
USACafe (Bonanza, Culpeppers, Shakey's)	421
Luby's Cafeterias	175
Ryan's Family Steak Houses	32

of the two operations. Two restaurants that would otherwise be close substitutes in respect to taste and preferences of customers would be noncompetitive if located in different cities. In this same respect, the restaurants of the same firm, with identical menus do not compete because of the separation of locations. Some firms that more directly compete with Ryan's Family Steak House are discussed in more detail below.

Ponderosa, Inc.

This Dayton, Ohio firm is mainly involved in the operation and franchise of a chain of steak houses in the United States, and it remains among the largest of these chains. It also has been developing Casa Lupita Mexican restaurants and overseas steak house operations, with the long-range goal of expanding its franchising base in order to even out earnings. In 1984, the firm operated 444 restaurants and franchised an additional 220; this number was down somewhat from the previous year when the company owned and operated 450 restaurants and franchised 243. The steak house portion of the business is significantly concentrated in Ohio, Pennsylvania, New York, Illinois, and Michigan. It features steak, prime rib, hamburgers, chicken, and seafood entrées, an all-you-can-eat salad bar, hot soups, beverages, desserts, and breakfast. The ESI Meats unit of the firm processes and distributes meat and related products throughout the United States. These latter products include salad dressings, steak sauce, and baked goods.

In 1982, the firm opened the first of its international steak houses in Watford, England. The firm intends to expand its international operations to other overseas locations in competition with the York Steakhouse operations of General Mills, as well as with the European chain operations of Berni Steak House, Beefeater

Steak Restaurants, and Cavalier Steak Bar in the United Kingdom. Other chain steak house operations on the European continent include the well-known Churrasco Steak Houses and the French operations of Hippopotamus and Couste-Paille and the German Maredo and Block House. Elsewhere in the world, steak is a menu item in many small, owner-operated establishments.

USACafes

This Dallas, Texas company is the most recent phenomena in the family steak house business. It was created in August 1983 as a subsidiary of Bonanza International to operate the franchised Bonanza Restaurants, and later in the same year it was spun off as an independent entity. More recently the firm has declared its intention to become a multiconcept franchiser and it has become an aggressive acquirer of restaurants that fit that bill.

As far as steak house operations are concerned the firm has attempted to reshape the image of its restaurants. It is moving from its previous emphasis on a budget, Western-theme steak house attractive to a blue-collar clientele, toward a more diverse menu that would be attractive to the broader middle class. This has involved the remodeling of the restaurants and changing menus to include broiled fish, broiled chicken, and fresh vegetables offered on a salad bar that the firm has called Freshtastics. As a result, the average weekly sales of a Bonanza unit went from $14,117 in 1983 to $14,934 in 1984, with weekly sales in the first quarter of 1985 averaging $16,500.

USACafes operates its Bonanza steak houses in 43 of the United States, Puerto Rico, Canada, and Australia. All are franchised, except for two in Dallas and one in Oklahoma that are retained as sites for employee training and test marketing of new services and products. The major markets that the firm hopes to penetrate more fully in its repositioned configuration include the northwestern portion of the United States, Canada, Pennsylvania, New York, Kentucky, Tennessee, Wisconsin, and Minnesota.

The attempt to diversify the restaurant operations of the firm included the acquisition of a small Colorado-based barbecue chain called Culpepper's, which USACafes hopes to expand as a delivery and drive-through chain in other portions of the country. These "Ribby" outlets would deliver ribs, beef, and chicken with assorted vegetables to make up an entire meal. The cost to build one of these outlets is $175,000, in contrast to the $800,000 to $900,000 cost of a Bonanza restaurant.

Still another development activity involved signing an option in 1984 to purchase a franchise to operate Primo Delicafes, Jan Drakes's Garden Cafes, and several other quick service outlets designed for shopping mall operation. The same year saw the purchase of a 36 percent interest in Shakey's Pizza and an attempt to take over the Ponderosa corporation. USACafes acquired somewhat less than 5 percent of the shares of Ponderosa at about $12 a share and sold it recently for approximately $19.25, when this play to rapidly expand steak house operations failed.

Sizzler Restaurants International

   Sizzler Restaurants International, after being spun off from Collins Foods in 1982, instituted a renovation plan designed to enlarge seating capacity and give the units a more open garden-like atmosphere. In May 1983, Sizzler acquired seventeen Rustler Steak House units from the Marriott Corporation. The revenues and profits for the Rustler units have shown a steady increase from 1983 through the end of the 1985 fiscal year, ended April 30, 1985. In June 1985, Sizzler purchased privately owned Tenly Enterprises of Rockville, Maryland. Tenly operated a chain of 85 restaurants, comprised of the remainder of the Rustler chain exclusive of the 17 Western units previously purchased by Sizzler. Tenly had recorded modest profits with the operation on sales of $65 million. Renovation of the cafeteria-style Rustler restaurants would not be completed until late 1985. The Tenly acquisition expanded Sizzler's operations in New York, New Jersey, Pennsylvania, Maryland, and the District of Columbia. At fiscal year-end 1985, 45 percent of the company's revenues were from California with no other state accounting for more than 10 percent. The acquisition of Tenly created net interest expense of $500,000 for the 1986 fiscal year and created $8 million of long-term debt for the previously debt-free firm.

Morrison's

   Owners of cafeteria operations such as Morrison's were seeing similar changes in trends of food choices by customers as those experienced by operators of steak houses. Morrisons' operations were concentrated in the Southeast with one-third of the units located in Florida. Menu changes had included the addition of Mexican dishes as well as more expensive items like steak and lobster.

   Along with menu changes, Morrison's was offering a take-out option to its customers. This tactic was being used primarily in newly constructed units and it had experienced only mixed success. The percentage of take-out sales to total unit sales varied from 10 percent to 25 percent among the company stores. The management at Morrison's felt that in order for this part of the business to run effectively it was necessary to limit the number of menu items and provide separate parking facilities for take-out customers.

   The need to provide a separate parking area for a take-out operation was impossible in the Morrison's restaurants located in shopping malls. However, the slowdown in shopping mall construction forced the company to begin developing free-standing units. This meant the firm was now having to compete for the same real estate as family steak houses and other chain operations.

   Realizing the need to expand the geographic scope of operations from the Southeast, Morrison's management test marketed in Ohio, Illinois, and Oklahoma in 1984. The results of the test indicated that cafeterias were generally viewed negatively and these types of operations had a problem of identity in the mind of the consumer. These negative opinions were coupled with the fact that numerous menu changes had to be instituted for the different regions to suit local tastes. Management

EXHIBIT 36.2 **Ryan's Family Steak Houses income statement (In thousands)**

	1978	1979	1980	1981	1982	1983	1984
Revenues							
Sales by company-owned restaurants	$563	$3,476	$5,344	$7,937	$9,434	$19,153	$31,995
Revenues from franchised restaurants	—	15	—	16	124	299	436
Interest and other income	5	20	66	95	231	390	443
Total Revenues	568	3,511	5,410	8,048	9,789	19,842	32,874
Cost and expenses							
Company-owned restaurants							
Food and beverage	244	1,715	2,633	3,847	4,528	9,081	15,039
Payroll and benefits	118	694	1,089	1,564	1,876	3,786	6,525
Depreciation and amortization	18	84	126	175	222	477	902
Other operating expenses	67	311	497	647	792	1,710	2,878
General and administrative expenses	35	161	262	392	515	889	1,539
Interest expense	11	61	106	160	144	81	—
Total costs and expenses	493	3,026	4,713	6,785	8,077	16,024	26,883
Earnings before income taxes	75	485	697	1,263	1,712	3,818	5,991
Income taxes	5	194	299	602	738	1,695	2,646
Net earnings	70	291	398	661	974	2,123	3,345
Net earnings per common share	.01	.04	.05	.08	.10	.15	.23

assessment of the test effort were generally unfavorable. Morrison's had opened only six new units in each of the last two years but management predicted the company would be opening twelve new units in each of the forthcoming years.

Luby's Cafeterias

Another regional cafeteria operation, Luby's, Inc., operates exclusively in the Southwest with 82 out of 94 units being located in Texas. The company earned a net income of $17.4 million on its sales of $175 million in 1984. The management of the firm was becoming increasingly aware of the strong regional reputation of the company, which led it to develop plans for expansion. The firm has not performed any test marketing in other regions. However, with such a large concentration of restaurants in the oil-dependent state of Texas, management was anxious to expand the geographical scope of its operations.

CONCLUSION

Mr. McCall realized that growth was an essential component in the success of Ryan's up to the present time. The Southeastern market, especially the markets in South Carolina and Georgia, had supported the largest share of restaurant units for Ryan's, and he did not doubt that the firm and its business had a strong regional association. The family steak house segment of the restaurant industry was not as welcomed by the population in other regions. This concerned Mr. McCall and the other managers of the firm. They felt that the existing units could support faster customer turnover and enlarged seating capacity to accommodate 325 to 350 patrons as one way to expand revenue.

Although Ryan's had included a soup and salad bar in all of the current units, a new idea had been proposed. To augment the traditional, beef dominated menu the management had developed a plan to install a much larger hot and cold bar. The new addition would offer several different meats and vegetables as well as desserts and fresh bread. An initial examination of this proposal indicated that it would cost $55,000 to install such a new super bar in a typical Ryan's operation. Management's desire to maintain uniformity among the units would require installations in each existing restaurant. With 41 company-owned restaurants expected to be in operation by the end of 1985, the more than $2 million cost of such a project was something to be examined closely.

Company officials realized the cost of food, which Ryan's spent more on by a large margin than competitors, would present a problem if inflation in food prices should suddenly occur. If this happened at the same time as the $2 million capital outlay for the new bars, the profit margin of the firm would be squeezed and the gains made by the firm in the first six years would be frustrated.

The notion of operating a nationwide chain of restaurants is an obvious attraction to Mr. McCall and the investors in the business. This is not quite as easy to accomplish in the family steak house business as it is with the chain operation of hamburger, pizza, or chicken outlets. Franchising has been the key element in each of these three types of business. Mr. McCall's views on franchising has been stated previously, and he will not be easily swayed from this opinion.

The ability to maintain an aggressive expansion of company-owned units is the principal ingredient in the growth strategy of the firm. Alvin McCall had been an

EXHIBIT 36.3 **Ryan's Family Steak Houses balance sheet**			
	1982	**1983**	**1984**
		(In thousands)	
Assets			
Current assets			
Cash and cash equivalents	$3,192	$ 7,086	$ 2,220
Receivables	18	55	126
Inventories	152	237	389
Prepaid expenses	17	20	7
Total current assets	3,379	7,398	2,742
Property and equipment			
Land and improvements	1,128	2,060	3,985
Buildings	3,133	5,801	9,284
Equipment	1,621	2,886	6,939
Construction in progress	32	960	2,378
Total property and equipment	5,914	11,707	22,586
Less accumulated depreciation	600	1,060	1,929
Net property and equipment	5,314	10,647	20,657
Other assets, principally deferred charge	102	246	500
Total assets	$8,795	$18,291	$23,899
Liabilities and Shareholders Equity			
Current liabilities			
Accounts payable	$ 645	$ 597	$1,446
Income taxes	238	86	86
Accrued liabilities	96	168	287
Current maturity of long-term debt	28	24	27
Total current liabilities	1,097	875	1,846
Long-term debt	1,302	829	802
Deferred franchise fees	30	38	22
Deferred income taxes	218	520	1,055
Shareholders' equity			
Common stock at $1.00 par	1,262	4,116	4,320
Additional paid-in capital	3,896	8,800	9,396
Retained earnings	990	3,113	6,458
Total shareholders' equity	6,148	16,029	20,174
Total liabilities and equity	$8,795	$18,291	$23,899

EXHIBIT 36.4 **Ryans' Family Steak Houses statement of changes in financial position (In thousands)**

	1981	1982	1983	1984
Sources of Working Capital				
Net earnings	$ 661	$ 974	$2,123	$ 3,345
Items not affecting working capital:				
Depreciation and amortization	176	229	495	951
Deferred income taxes	—	128	302	535
Funds provided by operations	837	1,331	2,920	4,831
Proceeds from issuance of common stock	—	3,729	7,758	524
Increase in deferred franchise fees	30	—	8	—
Disposals of property and equipment	—	1	—	—
Tax benefit from exercise of nonqualified stock options	—	—	—	276
Income tax expense, pro forma	600	—	—	—
Total sources of working capital	1,467	5,061	10,686	5,631
Uses of Working Capital				
Additions to property and equipment	21	3,037	5,793	10,879
Increases in other assets	—	59	179	336
Reduction of long-term debt	5	27	473	27
Decrease in deferred franchise fees	—	—	—	16
Distribution to partners	1,483	—	—	—
Provision for costs of exchange offer	10	—	—	—
Total uses of working capital	1,519	3,123	6,445	11,258
Increase (decreases) in working capital	$ (52)	$1,938	$4,241	$(5,627)

integral part of a similar growth situation during his association with the Quincey's steak house chain. Quincey's was also based in South Carolina and had expanded rapidly during the six years of Mr. McCall's involvement. He sold his interest in Quincey's in 1977, as one of the founding partners. The normal agreement to eschew participation in a similar business for a stipulated period was avoided in this sale, and Mr. McCall made it clear in the agreement that he reserved the privilege to start what became Ryan's Family Steak House during the following year.

Mr. McCall's experience with the Quincey's chain undoubtedly would be invaluable at this point in the growth-life of the Ryan's chain as the firm faces decisions critical to its future. Ryan's has been in operation for approximately seven years; one year longer than the number of years Mr. McCall was associated with Quincey's. He will need to draw on the experience from each of those years as the firm shapes its strategy for the near future.

CASE 37 ————————————————————————————

Knickers in a Twist

After Peter Barnett left Shiplake College, Henley-on-Thames, Oxon, he became involved in the wine trade. He worked both in his native England and in France where he visited most of the wine growing regions. Personality differences with his employer led to his dismissal necessitating a major career decision for Peter. His family had a tradition of being self-employed. Therefore, Peter decided that he also should try his hand at being his own boss. However, Peter was not sure what kind of business he should start.

One evening Peter was discussing his dilemma with his father and a lawyer friend of his father. After examining several possibilities, Peter was still not committed to any particular business. His father's friend noted that Peter seemed to have his "knickers in a twist"—a term meaning that someone is confused or undecided. Peter latched onto this term and decided that he would start a business called Knickers in a Twist. Now all he had to do was decide what his product would be, who would manufacture it, who would buy it, etc. Peter also had to decide whether this business should be created or whether he should consider other options.

PLANNING FOR KNICKERS IN A TWIST

Peter believed that the title for his proposed company was unique, and he felt that it would catch the interest of potential investors, suppliers, etc. However, he knew that any interested persons would also want facts, figures, and projections before they agreed to invest in his company or sell his product. He began his business plan with an introduction explaining his ideas and his business.

Introduction

Since leaving school in 1979, I have been gaining experience in the workplace and developing a good idea that would lead me onto bigger and better things. The phrase "Knickers in a Twist" came up in a conversation with a practicing barrister. The actual marketing idea of putting knickers (ladies underpants) in a twist within a tube is mine. One of my aims is to make buying and giving underwear fun.

With such an enormous market in knickers, it is evident that the consumer is always on the lookout for something new and different. According to my research,

This case was prepared by Robert L. Anderson and John Dunkelberg. It is intended as a basis for classroom discussion rather than to illustrate effective or ineffective handling on an administrative situation. Used by permission from Robert L. Anderson.

there has never been a product called Knickers in a Twist. Marks and Spencer, the department store, controls a large portion of the underwear market; however, they by no means dominate the market. This market is vibrant and fashion conscious, more so now than ever before. It is my opinion that the market is at a point where it requires a new, interesting, and significantly different marketing idea. I believe K.I.A.T will fit very well into a gap in the up-market section.

Buyers are always on the lookout for something new and interesting. I feel, therefore, that I am very much in the right place at the right time with the right product. I believe that I have a product of genuine and exciting potential to place in a large and receptive market.

Strengths and Weaknesses of K.I.A.T.

Peter wanted to provide as much objective information as possible about his proposed business, so he realistically identified what he thought were his company's strengths and weaknesses.

Strengths. The strengths of Knickers in a Twist include the following:

- The small size of the company allows flexibility and the ability to react quickly to market developments.
- The nature and presentation of the product will make it possible to change the buying pattern from women buying for women to men buying for women.
- The company will not be tied to an integrated manufacturer.
- Personal service will be provided to the customer at all times.
- The company should be able to develop new products quite rapidly.
- It should be possible to protect the product by acquiring a trademark for the name Knickers in a Twist.

Weaknesses. There did not seem to be too many weaknesses associated with the proposed company; however, Peter did identify the following possible weaknesses:

- The small size of the company could cause some problems.
- The company would suffer initially from the lack of resources.
- Peter acknowledged that his lack of experience might be a problem during the early startup stages.

Companies Associated with K.I.A.T.

Before Knickers in a Twist could begin operations, many suppliers, distributors, attorneys, accountants, etc., would need to agree to provide their products or services to the company. Exhibit 37.1 is a list of people and companies selected by Peter and the reasons for their selection.

EXHIBIT 37.1 **Potential suppliers**

Supplier	Location	Reason selected
Accountants	Dearden Farrow 1 Serjeants' Inn London EC4	In top 20 listing of accountants.
Solicitors	Prettys Elm House 25 Elm Street Ipswich	Highly reputed firm in East Anglia.
Graphic designers	First Impression 91A Drayton Gardens London SW10	One of the few firms in London specializing in small business design.
Lingerie design consultants	Aura St. John's Studios Richmond	Consultants to Berlei, Next and Undies.
Packaging materials	AMT Ltd. Amton House Cheltenham	Reliable and recommended.
Designers and producers of display	P.M. Crafts Ltd. Hertfordshire	Leader in its field.
Manufacturing	Belfiore Ltd. Malta	Manufacturer for other companies.
Cotton suppliers	Perido Leicester	Supply Next and Marks & Spencer.
Packagers	Remploy Ltd. 68 Queensland Rd. Islington	Assemble many household goods.
Elastic suppliers	Charnwood Elastics Leicester	Suppliers to Marks & Spencer.

Products

The company would initially sell only one product, cotton knickers. However, Peter knew that other products would have to be developed later if his company was to grow.

The Brief.   The knicker is designed by Aura, a leading lingerie design firm whose designs fill the shelves of well-known highstreet shops. The design is known technically as high-leg mini, which is sexier than most types of knickers (see Exhibit 37.2). While the name Knickers in a Twist provides the company with a marketing edge, the company will not be successful unless the product is different and well made. In conjunction with Aura, K.I.A.T. has designed a brief that is similar to one

FXHIBIT 37.2 **Knickers in a Twist design**

currently marketed on the Continent but not seen much in England. The knickers will come in two colors, lemon and aqua, and two other colors, peach and white, will be introduced later.

Additional products. After the company has achieved a measure of success with its knickers, it might add the following to its product line: silk briefs (a deluxe version of the original cotton brief), mens' boxer shorts, mens' ordinary underwear, briefs and bras to match, swimwear, bikinis, and hosiery.

Packaging and Display

The packaging of the briefs should compliment the name of the product; therefore, Peter decided to twist two different color knickers and package them in a transparent tube measuring 6 inches in length and 2 inches in diameter (see Exhibit 37.3). A three color label, using the distinctive Knickers in a Twist logo, will be placed on each tube. The tubes will be placed in a plastic dispenser (see Exhibit 37.4) which can hold 20 tubes. The dispenser is designed to convey the same theme as that of the product it dispenses—namely up-market, eye-catching design likely to encourage impulse buying.

An exciting new concept from Peter Barnett, the new name in fashion accessories. Two pairs of high-leg mini-brief knickers in fashion colours twisted into a convenient sized tube sold from a dispenser.

EXHIBIT 37.3 **Knickers in a Twist packaging**

EXHIBIT 37.4 **Knickers in a Twist display**

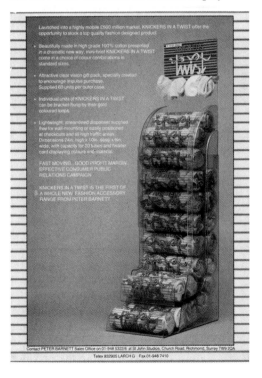

Production Strategy

Initial manufacturing of the briefs will take place in Malta. It is less expensive to have the material shipped to Malta and have the finished product returned to England than it is to manufacture the product in the United Kingdom. The production company, Belfiore Ltd., has agreed to manufacture the briefs in lots of 32,000 in colors specified by Peter. The finished briefs will be returned to England where they will be packaged by Remploy, a government-subsidized company that employs the handicapped. Once packaged, the tubes will be shipped to retailers, thereby reducing the need for warehousing finished goods. At some point in the future, Peter hopes to be able to have the briefs manufactured in the United Kingdom.

Pricing

A tube of knickers will have a suggested retail price of £4.95 including Value Added Tax (VAT). Peter knows that the final price charged for his product will be determined to a large extent by the market. The following are prices charged by other sellers of similar products.

Marks & Spencer	Pack of 3	£2.99
Underwoods	Pack of 3	3.50
Sock Shop	Tube of 3	3.99
Selfridges	Single brief	2.99
Richard Shops	Single brief	1.99
Debenhams	Single brief	.99

Peter believes that quality and the novelty aspect of his product will allow him to charge a higher price than his competitors (see Exhibit 37.5 for additional price and profit information).

Promotion

Even high-quality, cleverly packaged knickers will not sell themselves. They must be promoted in such a way that customers will choose Knickers in a Twist over comparable products. Peter intends to use the following promotion techniques: attend trade fairs, offer discounts for bulk purchases, obtain free editorials and comments in journals, try to get free publicity in newspapers and on TV, use mail order, and have retailers promote the product.

EXHIBIT 37.5 **Gross profit at various prices**

Recommended retail price	Cost per tube	Price to dealer	Gross profit
£4.95	£1.20	£1.87	£.67
4.90	1.20	1.85	.65
4.85	1.20	1.83	.63
4.80	1.20	1.81	.61
4.75	1.20	1.79	.59
4.70	1.20	1.77	.57
4.65	1.20	1.75	.55
4.60	1.20	1.73	.53
4.55	1.20	1.71	.51
4.50	1.20	1.69	.49
4.45	1.20	1.67	.47
4.40	1.20	1.65	.45
4.35	1.20	1.63	.43
4.30	1.20	1.61	.41
4.25	1.20	1.59	.39
4.20	1.20	1.57	.37
4.15	1.20	1.55	.35

The Market

Peter had done the work required to develop a quality product. Now he had to convince himself and others that there was enough market demand for Knickers in a Twist. Peter knew from secondary sources that about £580 million were spent annually for women's underwear, and he knew from the information in Exhibit 37.6 that briefs were becoming a larger portion of the entire market (see Exhibit 37.7 for additional market data).

EXHIBIT 37.6 **Lingerie products as a proportion of the total market**

Sector	April 1985	April 1986
Bras	28%	29%
Briefs	23	25
Nightdresses	15	14
Slips	12	12
Housecoats	12	10
Corsetry	8	8
Vests	2	2

EXHIBIT 37.7 **Percent of people who bought various types of underwear in the last 12 months**

Item	All	Age					
		15-19	20-24	25-34	35-44	45-54	55-64
Brassieres	66%	67%	93%	81%	77%	68%	58%
Corsets/girdles	19	1	4	6	14	23	38
Nightwear	42	29	52	47	48	51	42
Pants/Knickers	76	69	84	85	89	78	69
Slips—full length	19	3	1	11	20	31	31
half length	27	13	35	34	35	37	25
Suspender belt	6	8	12	8	7	7	3
None of these	5	13	1	3	2	8	9

Competition

Peter is confident that his product would do well in the underwear market; however, he also realizes that he has to overcome several entrenched competitors. Since there is more room for innovation and differentiation at the middle to upper end of the market, competition is fiercest at the lower end of the market. Knickers in a Twist would be positioned at the higher end of the market, thereby eliminating some of the competition. Peter is convinced that good design and high quality with novelty packaging and logo will enable K.I.A.T. to compete successfully with other retailers. Advertising and location of the dispenser near the checkout counter will also give his product a competitive edge.

Distribution

Peter had considered a number of different channels of distribution before settling on selling through retailers. Once Knickers in a Twist becomes a profitable, recognized product, Peter might consider selling by direct mail or using his own salesforce to distribute the product. Peter has approached the retailers listed in Exhibit 37.8 who show some degree of interest in the product.

Personnel and Location

Since all aspects of the business will be subcontracted to other companies, Peter will not need any employees for the first few months. He expects to hire a part-time bookkeeper within the first six months, and he might establish his own direct sales force if the product sells well. Knickers in a Twist will have no employees other than Peter for the first few months; therefore, office space is minimal. At present, Peter shares an office with the design consultant, Aura, in Richmond.

EXHIBIT 37.8 **List of retailers approached**

Debenhams	Very interested, though for technical reasons and coming in too late for Christmas will not purchase in 1986. They are interested in taking K.I.A.T. in 1987.
Sock Shop	Very interested, however, because of heavy commitments in 1986 will not be able to do any business until 1987.
Trust House Forte (retail sales)	Very keen and receptive to the idea; however, they would like to see the finished product before making a buying decision.
Harrod's	Will retail the knickers.
Harvey Nichols	Will retail the knickers.
Underwoods	Same as Trust House Forte
Selfridges	Same as Trust House Forte
Fenwicks	Same as Trust House Forte
Owen & Owen	Same as Trust House Forte
British Home Stores	Same as Trust House Forte

In addition to the above stores, Peter would also like to do business with the following retailers and mail order companies:

Undies	Empire Stores
House of Fraser	Grattan
Asda Group	International Import & Export Company
Jenners, Scotland	Texplant
Sears Stores	Great Universal Stores

Financing

Peter did not know exactly how much initial capital he would need to start his business. He knew that the cost of two knickers in a tube would be £1.20, and since his initial production run would be 16,000 tubes, he would need at least £19,200. To cover manufacturing costs and other ancillary expenses, Peter estimated that he would need £25,000. With that figure in mind, Peter approached several commercial banks with a request that they make him an essentially unsecured loan. Because he lacked experience and collateral, Peter was unsuccessful at his attempt to borrow £25,000. Peter learned of the government's Small Business Loan Scheme which guaranteed up to 70 percent of a bank loan for new businesses. Using this loan guarantee and his father as a cosignor, Peter was able to secure a £25,000 overdraft.

Knickers in a Twist's lenders wanted to know how many firm orders the company had and when the company would start showing a profit. Peter told the bank that he had firm orders for 5,000 tubes of knickers, and he estimated breakeven to be at 18,417 tubes (see Exhibit 37.9). Peter expected to reach the breakeven point in the first full year of business.

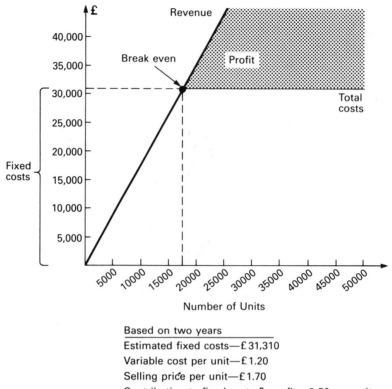

EXHIBIT 37.9 **Estimated breakeven**

The Decision

Peter has done the work necessary to start a new business. He incorporated the business as Knickers in a Twist Ltd. (he expected to change that to Peter Barnett Ltd.) and has agreements with suppliers and manufacturers. He has a £25,000 overdraft and retailers who have agreed to sell his product. Finally, he has enthusiasm, optimism, and considerable energy. Now Peter Barnett must decide if he should formally start Knickers in a Twist Ltd.

CASE 38 ——————————————————————————————

Guest Quarters—Frequent Flyer

In January 1986, John Vernon, Vice President of Marketing for Guest Quarters, a firm of all-suite hotels, decided that Guest Quarters should join at least one of the "frequent flyer" programs conducted by the major airlines. He knew that some action needed to be taken immediately to increase occupancy and profits at Guest Quarters, particularly the new units in Tampa, Florida and Charlotte, North Carolina. The newest hotels, the ones that lenders looked to in making determinations of financial strength, were experiencing problems in developing the kind of acceptance that Guest Quarters had gained in its older locations. Despite the fact that almost no data substantiating the benefits or costs of frequent flyer programs were available, Mr. Vernon believed that participation in such a program could help remedy the firm's situation. However, many options were open as to how and when to implement this strategy.

BACKGROUND

Guest Quarters, the pioneer in the all-suite segment of the hotel industry, was founded in 1972 when real-estate developer George Kaufman bought a garden apartment complex in Atlanta, Georgia. Originally positioned as temporary housing for relocated families, it evolved into a new concept: the all-suite hotel. By 1985, Guest Quarters had grown to a total of nine properties: three in the Washington, D.C. area, two in Atlanta, and one each in Houston, Tampa, Charlotte, and Greensboro. Two other units were under construction in Bethesda, Maryland (bringing to four the number of units in the Washington, D.C. area) and in Austin, Texas. Since 1972, Guest Quarters had experienced a compound annual growth rate in revenues in excess of 25 percent. The 1984 operating margin was 37 percent. All-suite properties typically delivered gross margins in a range between 35 percent and 60 percent, compared with 25 percent for standard hotels.

The Guest Quarters product concept was originally that of a "home away from home," blending the convenience of a hotel with the space and freedom found in a personal residence. The first Guest Quarters in Atlanta (Roswell Road) continued to present this image, catering to salespeople and middle-management executives who had extended assignments in the Atlanta area and also serving as temporary housing for executives' families who had been transferred to Atlanta.

This case was prepared by Eleanor G. May, Professor of Business Administration, The Darden Graduate School of Business Administration. Copyright © 1986 by The Colgate Darden Graduate Business School Sponsors, Charlottesville, Virginia. Used by permission from Eleanor G. May.

In the newer Guest Quarters units, however, the service package was closer to that of a full-service hotel with food and beverage operations, common areas for meetings, and so on. Guest Quarters suites typically consisted of a living room, dining area, and a fully equipped kitchen, in addition to a bathroom and one or two bedrooms. To make them more distinctive and more homelike, each suite was decorated with original prints and live plants.

Guest Quarters targeted primarily the business traveler. In 1985, 70 percent of all Guest Quarters revenues were generated from the individual corporate traveler, while an additional 25 percent of revenues were derived from guests attending meetings or conventions. Recent research conducted for Guest Quarters indicated that the typical Guest Quarters customer spent more time on the road than did the typical traveler.

Guest Quarters rates varied according to location, depending on the competition and on the level of luxury and amenities of the building and the suite, but in general a Guest Quarters suite was priced equivalent to a single room in a full-service hotel. One bedroom suite per diem rates varied from $85 to $150; two bedroom suites ranged from $90 to $235 (see Exhibit 38.1 for a full list of rates).

In many ways Guest Quarters resembled a holding company of nine independent hotels rather than a chain of similar units. The geographic expansion of the firm had been determined by the availability of real estate rather than by a coordinated plan to position the hotel for a particular market. Growth of the company had occurred both by acquiring existing buildings and by constructing new ones. The hotels varied in size from 101 suites at New Hampshire Avenue in Washington, D.C. to 335 suites at the Galleria in Houston. There was no standard facility design and individual suites varied in size and layout by facility. Properties also varied in

EXHIBIT 38.1 **Room rates, 1985**

Location	One-bedroom suite		Two-bedroom suite
	Single	**Double**	**Double**
Washington area:			
Alexandria	$ 97	$112	$134
Pennsylvania Avenue	130	150	235
New Hampshire Avenue	130	150	235
Houston	105	125	185
Atlanta area:			
Perimeter Center	120	140	182
Roswell Road	88	99	109
Greensboro	70	85	90
Charlotte	95	107	145
Tampa	110	120	160

physical appearance as well as the service available. Exhibit 38.2 describes some of the variations among the locations.

The Guest Quarters service package varied by facility. In 1985, restaurants, suite (room) service, meeting and banquet facilities were found at most locations.

EXHIBIT 38.2 **Guest Quarters service packages**

| | Services | |
| | Size (sq. ft.) | |
Suites		**Availability**
Studio	484	Alexandria only
1 bedroom	600–800	All locations
Executive suite	900	Greensboro only
2 bedroom	996–1,560	All locations
3 bedroom	1,350	Roswell Road only
Penthouse	1,400	Alexandria only

Dining room

Available at all locations except New Hampshire Avenue, Pennsylvania Avenue, and Greensboro.

Lounge

Available at Perimeter, Charlotte, Tampa, and Houston. Included in dining room at Roswell Road and Alexandria. Not available at New Hampshire Avenue, Pennsylvania Avenue, and Greensboro.

Suite service (room service)

24-hour service available at Perimeter, Charlotte, Tampa, and Houston. 7 a.m. to 11 p.m. service available at Roswell Road, Alexandria, New Hampshire Avenue, and Pennsylvania Avenue. Continental breakfast only at Greensboro.

Swimming pool (on site)*

Available at all locations except Pennsylvania Avenue.

Jacuzzi and sauna (on site)*

Available at Perimeter, Charlotte, Tampa, and Greensboro only.

Fitness/Exercise area (on site)*

Available at Perimeter, Charlotte, Tampa, Houston, and Greensboro.

Airport parking/courtesy car

Varies by location.

*Some locations have affiliations with off-site facilities.

Additional special services, such as a lending library of bestsellers, cable television, exercise facilities, secretarial services, and a grocery shopping service, were also available depending on location.

In the spring of 1985, the average Guest Quarters occupancy rate ranged from 73 percent at Pennsylvania Avenue to 43 percent at Charlotte. Furthermore, like all hotels that catered to business travelers, Guest Quarters occupancy rates were much higher Monday through Thursday than Friday through Sunday. (See Exhibits 38.3 and 38.4 for details of occupancy and demand.) Occupancy rates were major indicators of profitability for hotels as a result of the low variable cost per room—$2 to $3 per night. Many of the corporate travelers, however, were allowed corporate discounts, and thus did not pay the full "rack" rate.

EXHIBIT 38.3 Average daily occupancy by hotel, January–June 1985

Hotel	Mon.	Tues.	Wed.	Thurs.	Fri.	Sat.	Sun.	Avg.
Washington area:								
Alexandria	70%	69%	71%	67%	59%	56%	57%	64%
New Hampshire Avenue	66	69	74	68	51	53	57	62
Pennsylvania Avenue	79	83	84	78	61	66	66	73
Houston	54	56	54	48	35	33	39	46
Atlanta area:								
Perimenter Center	80	81	83	77	37	36	49	53
Roswell Road	71	77	76	62	45	48	56	62
Greensboro	73	72	71	73	56	56	59	66
Charlotte	46	55	59	50	32	33	28	43
Tampa	66	78	79	70	42	39	42	59
Average	67%	71%	72%	66%	46%	46%	50%	60%

GUEST QUARTERS MARKETING

National marketing and advertising promotions for Guest Quarters were conducted out of headquarters in Washington, D.C. Exhibit 38.5 shows the total marketing and sales budget for Guest Quarters for 1986. The national marketing staff consisted of the Director of Marketing, Mickey Rowley, who reported to John Vernon. Mr. Rowley's responsibilities included developing all print and media advertisements, designing and administering direct mail campaigns, managing the 800 reservation number, acting as the national sales director, and supervising the Guest Quarters regional sales office in New York. As National Sales Director, Mr. Rowley took salespeople to implement sales "blitzes" in cities where Guest Quarters did not have hotels. In this capacity, he also managed national accounts and developed joint promotions with such companies as Hertz Car Rentals and Ask Mr. Foster Travel Agency.

EXHIBIT 38.4 **Seasonal demand by hotel, January–June 1985**

| | Peak | |
Hotel	Month/day	Occupancy rate
Washington area:		
Alexandria	April, Saturday	100%
New Hampshire Avenue	June, Tuesday	87
Pennsylvania Avenue	June, Tuesday	87
Houston	May, Monday	72
Atlanta area:		
Perimeter Center	June, Tuesday	97
Roswell Road	June, Wednesday	87
Greensboro	April, Thursday	94
Charlotte	March, Wednesday	76
Tampa	March, Tuesday	99

EXHIBIT 38.5 **Marketing budget—1986**

Advertising	$1,330,000
Regional sales offices	229,000
Toll-free telephone service	313,000
Sales payroll at hotels	790,000
Sales expense at hotels	258,000
	$2,920,000

One direct mail campaign had been very effective. Guest Quarters had mailed 500,000 cards to major credit unions giving 20 to 40 percent discounts on weekend stays at Guest Quarters. The credit unions distributed the cards to their members as a benefit of membership. Mr. Vernon claimed that in one hotel 18 percent of one month's revenue had been generated through this campaign.

Guest Quarters advertised in all in-flight magazines, in every other issue. It advertised about 20 times a year in the *Wall Street Journal.* Guest Quarters also arranged "trade-out" with Cable News Network. CNN provided Guest Quarters with free advertising in return for hotel accommodations.

The regional sales office in New York City, staffed by two people, was responsible for calling on headquarters of major accounts and large travel agencies. The staff arranged free accommodation for travel agents on tours, for which airlines, hotels, and car rental agencies donated travel accommodations. John Vernon, however, questioned the effectiveness of promoting to travel agencies. He believed that at least 80 percent of business travelers either knew where they wanted to stay or received recommendations from someone they knew.

Each Guest Quarters hotel had a "marketing" or sales staff of four people. The staff, which consisted of a director of marketing, two directors of sales, and a secretary, was responsible for calling on all potential customers in its area—it had a free reign in providing discounts to attract sales.

THE LODGING INDUSTRY

In 1985, there were 54,000 lodging establishments in the United States with a capacity of 2.7 million rooms; average occupancy during 1985 was just over 64 percent. The industry was considered mature, changes in demand usually occurred only when the general economy shifted. However, a significant oversupply of rooms had developed in a number of metropolitan areas. Industry experts predicted that by 1992 there would be 3.1 million rooms and thus the oversupply would continue. Demand was forecasted to increase at the rate of 1 to 3 percent per year, keeping pace with the 2 percent supply increase, therefore, maintaining occupancy rates at the mid-60 percents.

The maturity of the lodging industry had led to consolidation among firms in an attempt to maintain the historical double-digit growth rates and to gain economies of scale. For instance, in 1985, Marriott acquired Howard Johnson's and Holiday Inn purchased both Residence Inns and Embassy Suites.

Industry segmentation had also accelerated as large chains perceived a need to differentiate themselves if they were to maintain their market shares. The all-suite segment had grown rapidly as part of this trend. The 300 all-suite hotels represented less than 2 percent of the total room inventory in 1985, but industry experts predicted that this supply would grow at a rate of 20 to 25 percent annually in the next few years. By 1990, there would be an estimated 1,000 all-suite facilities offering almost 150,000 suites. In addition to Guest Quarters, all-suite chains included Embassy Suites, Residence Inns, L'Hermitage, Lexington, and Park Suite Hotels. Several large hotel chains like Doubletree Inns and the Radisson Hotel Corporation were experimenting with all-suite properties, and Marriott was poised to enter the market. Exhibit 38.6 describes the major participants in the all-suite segment of the industry in 1985.

Advertising and promotion in the lodging industry was not standardized among firms either by type or amount. Hyatt, for example, was conducting a $2 million nationwide print and broadcast advertising campaign, while Marriott was spending $16 million on its "honored guests" awards program. Promotions and advertising typically were not carefully evaluated because of the unavailability of accurate, broad-based consumer data.

Some lodging executives thought that a major problem in the industry was the lack of product differentiation. It was believed that, within a similar price range, guests perceived that many hotels looked alike and offered similar benefits. James Collins, Senior Vice President for Marketing at Hilton Hotels Corp., said, "We all have happy people [employees], we all have good facilities, we all have good service."

EXHIBIT 38.6 **Composition of the suite hotel industry, 1985**

Company name	Average room rate	Existing		Under construction		Announced plans
		Number of sites	Number of rooms	Number of sites	Number of rooms	
Amberley Suites	$52.50	2	354	3	450	Open 20 properties by 1988
Double Tree Suites	$82.50	1	221	1	220	Open 30 properties by 1990
Granada Royale/ Embassy Suites	$70–$75	43	9,260	37	7,950	Open 150 to 200 properties by 1988
Guest Quarters	$87–$120	9	1,729	1	189	Open 3 to 5 properties per year
Hawthorne Suites	$70	6	554	0	0	Open 200 properties nationwide
Hotel Corp of Pacific	$60–$100	19	4,463	0	0	
L'Hermitage	$154	7	1,089	1	80	
Lexington	$39–$69	13	2,184	2	240	Open 5 to 7 properties per year
Marriott		0	0	0	0	Will become major competition in 1986
Park Suite Hotels	$70	8	1,857	3	885	Open 12 to 15 properties per year
Quality Inns	$45–$85	0	0	5	700	Open 300 properties during next 5 years
Radisson Hotels	$75	1	150	3	759	
Residence Inns	$65	55	6,448	25	2,500	Open 500 properties by 1990
Royce Hotel Suites	$75–$100	2	305	14	2,100	Open an average of 2 per month
Totals		166	28,604	95	16,073	

In evaluating the marketing efforts in the lodging industry, Michael Levin, President and Chief Operating Officer of Days Inn of America, stated. "I call it marketing by necessity—for survival."

AIRLINE FREQUENT FLYER PROGRAMS

Airline frequent flyer programs were born in the 1979–1980 recession. Airline industry profit performance, which had been adversely impacted by deregulation, was further damaged by decreasing load factors, the air traffic controllers strike, and by increases in both interest rates and fuel prices. The airline industry traditionally suffered under the burden of high operating leverage; therefore, it was extremely important for the airlines to try to maintain volume. Prior to this time, airlines attempted to maintain volume through special fares and through other promotional programs designed to increase customer loyalty and repeat business.

American Airlines was the first airline to develop a frequent flyer program—the "AAdvantage program," introduced in 1981. Such programs offered flyers "mileage points"—awards of free travel on future flights—for miles traveled on the airline beyond a certain minimum. Other airlines soon followed suit, and the programs expanded as other travel businesses (hotels, rental cars, cruise lines) recognized the benefits to be derived from frequent traveler programs and became affiliated with one or more airline programs. The programs gained momentum in 1983 when United Airlines offered extra bonus coupons to flyers as part of an effort to regain business lost during the strike. By 1985, each of the 12 major trunk-line carriers had developed frequent flyer programs. These programs included 16 hotels, 9 rental car agencies, and 17 associated airlines. Exhibit 38.7 lists the major airlines' programs and their hotel and rental car affiliations as of January 1986.

There were a number of factors that could affect the future of frequent flyer programs and of the airline industry:

- Intense competition within the airline industry.
- Costs of implementing and operating frequent flyer programs.
- Availability of marketing information.
- Ethical problems surrounding frequent flyer programs.
- Tax liability issue surrounding frequent flyer programs.

The airline industry as a whole had not fully recovered from the downturn that accompanied the recession and the oversupply of seats after deregulation. Although fuel prices and interest rates had fallen, load factors remained low. Furthermore, no abatement was expected in the level of industry competition. Deregulation had resulted in the major airlines revamping their route structures as they had their competitive strategies. A fairly common strategy was to establish "hubs" at additional locations in order to provide tie-ins to a greater number of destinations.

EXHIBIT 38.7 **Frequent flyer program affiliations, January 1986**

Airline	Hotels	Car rentals
American Airlines	Inter-Continental Sheraton	Avis
Continental	Marriott	Thrifty
Delta	Preferred Hotels Marriott	National Alamo
Eastern	Marriott	Hertz Dollar General
New York Air	Resorts International	Avis
Northwest Orient	Stouffer Hilton Omni/Denfey Preferred Hotels Radisson/Colony	National Thrifty
Pan Am	Inter-Continental Sheraton	Hertz
Piedmont	Stouffer	Hertz
Republic Airlines	None	Hertz National
TWA	Hilton Marriott	Hertz
United Airlines	Hyatt Westin Meridien Kempinski	Hertz Budget
Western Airline	Sheraton Village Resort Condominiums	Budget

Expansion by the major airlines had served to further aggravate the problem of excessive seat capacity. Industry load factors slipped 1.5 percentage points in 1985, to approximately 55 percent, the lowest level in five years. Price wars led to a 22 percent drop in yield per passenger mile and a decline in operating profits. Industry sources believed that the fare structure would continue to deteriorate, and operating profits for 1986 were expected to fall approximately 8.5 percent from 1985 levels to $700 million.

There appeared to be little evidence as to whether frequent flyer programs were a cost effective method of maintaining customer loyalty. While the airlines were not forthcoming about the revenues and expenses associated with frequent flyer programs, it was clear that the programs were costly both to develop and to operate. Frequent flyer programs were, in effect, price-cutting measures. Each of the major airlines provided similar bonuses to their customers, and so the industry as a whole ended up simply offering the customer, in effect, rebates on tickets, reducing the airlines' gross margins. The long-term profitability of the programs had yet to be determined, and the absolute effect was not easy to quantify, because a major part of the cost was postponed until redemption. There were no figures on how many people actually cashed in their bonuses. Nor was it known how many people used free tickets for flights they would have taken anyway, or how many took an unplanned trip to use their free ticket.

It was also unclear whether frequent traveler programs actually influenced business travelers' decisions. For instance, the head of travel administration for Bankers Trust International was doubtful about the efficacy of such programs. According to him, most frequent business travelers are well-paid executives who do not have the time to worry about changing their plans to win free mileage points. However, a straw poll by *Economy Magazine* taken among bankers suggested otherwise. Many respondents to the poll said that they were members of schemes for Pan Am, American Airlines, or TWA—some bankers belonging to more than one. Those bankers who belonged to programs said they would be influenced in favor of using an airline to which they belonged, when there was a choice.

Apparently, the only quantifiable public information on participation in frequent flyer programs was in a 1985 study of the frequent flyer as a lodging guest conducted by Market Facts, Chicago, for the American Hotel and Motel Association. The study surveyed 1,055 travelers who were selected from among a representative panel of 30,000 men and women on the basis of their travel histories. Only 30 percent of the respondents were involved in some type of frequent flyer program; 21 percent were enrolled in some type of frequent traveler plan. No information on if and how much the frequent-flyer programs had increased business was available from the airlines that were developing and promoting the programs.

A possible controversy concerning frequent flyer bonus programs had been raised by some employers, who questioned whether awarding bonuses to business travelers for travel that had been paid for by the employer was ethical and legal. According to proponents of frequent flyer programs, however, many businesses took the position that business travel was a significant personal inconvenience to the employee; therefore, any such benefits should accrue to the traveler. Others believed that the bonuses should go to the employer rather than the employee since the employer paid for the original ticket and therefore in effect paid for the bonus.

In addition, abuse of frequent flyer programs was occurring, such as taking a circuitous route in order to accumulate extra bonus points on a specific airline. Some flyers arranged trips to their advantage by not taking the most direct route and arranging stops. Many companies were taking steps to prevent such abuse. Systems and requirements were being developed to require that both time and money efficiency to be applied in flight planning. At some firms, in-house travel services have been made responsible for implementing such a policy. For others, travel agencies offered services that would guarantee efficiency in travel arrangements. Other companies were dealing with the problem by attempting to get the benefit to accrue to the business itself rather than to the individual. Such a procedure required the cooperation of the airlines, since the systems were designed originally to restrict the bonus to the specific flyer and his or her family.

A tax liability issue also cropped up. Representative Harold Ford (Democrat, Tennessee) introduced a bill into Congress requiring that frequent flyer bonuses be reported as income to the individual. According to Congressman Ford, the cost of frequent flyer programs accounted for as much as 7 percent of the $66.5 billion that corporations paid for travel.

LODGING INVOLVEMENT IN FREQUENT FLYER PROGRAMS

Hotel companies could participate in the "earnings" and/or the "awards" segment of airline frequent flyer promotions. As an earnings partner, a hotel chain offered members of a specific airline frequent flyer program the opportunity to earn mileage points when staying at one of its hotels; mileage points could also be redeemed for services at that hotel chain. In contrast, an awards partner permitted redemption of mileage points earned elsewhere (through rental cars or air travel) for lodging.

All the major upscale hotel companies were affiliated with a least one frequent flyer promotion, either through the earnings or awards portions or both. Some companies had joined as many as four. In addition, a number of smaller upscale hotels had formed a coalition called "preferred hotels" through which they participated in these programs. Typically, lodging companies participated in both the earnings and awards segments of at least two frequent flyer programs. Sometimes, some units of a chain, such as resort locations, would be exempted from the program.

Typically, the airline approached the hotel company to join a frequent flyer program. It usually was important that the locations of the hotel properties be sufficiently compatible with the airline route structure for the airline to want to have the specific hotel chain in its program.

It appeared that little or no analysis was made by the hotel companies to determine the effect of a program on profits. The decision to join apparently was a defensive measure as well as a means of gaining information about and dialogue with high frequency users.

The costs to the hotels were negotiated with the airlines. Generally, no initial "program initiation" fee was charged to the hotel company. Transaction costs to the lodging chain for the earnings portion of a frequent flyer program were based by the airline on a mileage equivalency. For example, a hotel might give 2,000 miles "credit" to the frequent traveler for each overnight stay. When the visit was recorded with the airline program, a fee was charged to the hotel (possibly one cent for each mile credited to the guest.) Miles offered by hotels to guests varied between 500 and several thousand. Hence the cost to the hotel might be 2,000 X $.01 or $20 per guest using the frequent flyer program. Some hotel chains allowed awards for each night of the stay, others gave "mileage" only once for each visit to the hotel.

Additional costs were incurred by the hotel, of course, when bonus points, which typically had not been acquired at the hotel, were redeemed for free accommodations.

It appeared that hotel chains were joining programs not in response to evidence that the program would increase profitability but because other hotel chains were participating in a program. While no hotel company provided any figures, some believed that their involvement in frequent flyer programs had improved occupancy, primarily by stimulating repeat business. None of the companies were willing to state that it induced new customers to try the hotel. Tracking was not generally utilized in the industry and most companies did not have the information required to measure the costs and benefits of participating in the program. Of the major hotel chains, only Sheraton reported experiencing incremental profits attributable to participation in frequent flyer programs.

ALL-SUITE CHAINS AND FREQUENT FLYERS

In early 1986, no all-suite hotel chain was affiliated with an airline frequent flyer program nor did it appear that any had plans to join one in the near future. According to a spokesperson at Embassy Suites, "Our marketing dollars are better spent on advertising to induce trial than on promotion such as frequent flyer programs that encourage repeat business." This opinion was typical of other companies, with the exception of Marriott. Marriott's all-suite hotels, when introduced, reportedly would be included in existing Marriott hotel frequent flyer affiliations.

Some hotel groups had opted to develop and implement their own "frequent traveler program." Holiday Inns, after reputedly losing millions on its frequent traveler program, made major changes in it, limiting its use and benefits to Holiday units. Ramada Inns was developing a "business card" plan, with restricted bonuses, and Marriott Hotels had instituted its "honored guests program."

CONCLUSION

John Vernon believed that the Guest Quarters decision to enter a frequent flyer program should be implemented promptly if the firm was to continue to be profitable. He was unsure, however, what program should be adopted and what benefits should be offered. In any event, he knew that steps had to be taken right away to increase occupancy at Tampa and Charlotte.

CASE 39

Housatonic Valley Workshop

Housatonic Valley Workshop (HVW) began as a father-and-son partnership in Oxford, Connecticut. Neither Edwin Ellner, nor his son, Peter, had any prior business experience, although Peter had just finished his junior year in the School of Business Administration at The University of Connecticut. The Ellners decided to begin the manufacture and sale of solid brass bookmarks patterned after early American weathervanes, an appropriate design for Connecticut Yankees.

By June 1986, father and son had transformed ideas into tangible equipment and patterns and spent the next several months building special tools and experimenting with various manufacturing techniques and package designs. Within six months they had expended $4,000 for tools and development, and anticipated laying out yet another $3,000 for permanent tooling. To hedge against the rising cost of brass, they acquired a $3,000 inventory of sheet brass.

Their sole product, a brass bookmark, represented a traditional design. A clasp clipped over a page; the top third, the weathervane design, protruded above the page. They planned to market 19 distinct designs, such as a horse, a rooster, an eagle, an Indian, a fish, and a mermaid.

MANUFACTURING

The Ellners designed a manufacturing process to produce these delicate items efficiently in a machine shop. Unfortunately, burrs on the product after manufacture

This case was prepared by Robert P. Vichas, Florida Atlantic University. It is intended as a basis for classroom discussion rather than to illustrate effective or ineffective handling of an administrative situation. Used by permission from Robert P. Vichas.

required hand filing. Scratched items had to be polished, which meant even more hand labor. Final products were waxed. All machine shop work was contracted out.

During the first several months of operation, quality control problems were numerous. For instance, stains, pock marks, scratches, sharp edges, and bent items would plague entire batches. To improve the manufacturing process Edwin Ellner worked closely with the machine shop and carried on aggressive negotiations to persuade the shop to provide careful attention to the work. Nevertheless, the fledging firm faced rising costs on an item it intended to market at a low price. By the end of the first year, however, with the process debugged, HVW finally could depend upon a quality supply at a cost sufficiently low to permit competitive pricing.

Attractive, yet simply designed, the package could effectively capture the attention of an impulse buyer. Glued onto a card, the brass bookmark was placed into a clear plastic package. The reverse side of the card related the story of the weathervane.

INITIAL MARKETING

By December 1986 (too late for Christmas sales), the Ellners were ready to market their product. Despite inexperience in sales and marketing, they developed a general market plan. They decided to target general-purpose gift shops, small department stores, bookstores, museums, and art galleries. To aid in-store sales, HVW designed a display board, which had a sample of each bookmark glued on it, a painting of a barn, and a weathervane.

Interest in early American folk art had been strong for some years. Weathervanes and furniture brought high prices at antique auctions. HVW believed that a select group of people interested in such art and antiques would form the customer base. Consequently, they approached stores where this type of person was thought to frequent.

Initially they made personal contacts with museums, gift shops, art galleries, and book stores where an enthusiastic response generated nearly 100 percent sales per contact. Many store clerks reacted enthusiastically and bought bookmarks on the spot for gifts or for themselves. When HVW began cold-calling on small department stores and general-purpose gift shops, response again was favorable and enthusiastic.

A family member who had spent the holidays with the Ellners returned to California in January 1987 with a sales package and managed to sell bookmarks to some California gift shops.

By February (eight months after inception) the Ellners were having second thoughts. Did the product have universal appeal? Shops in New England and New York bought them. Shops in California bought them. Friends liked them. Store clerks bought them. People who never heard of a weathervane liked and bought them.

On the other hand, the snowy New England winter did not mask the cold truth: there were no repeat orders. For example, the Yale Coop at New Haven, Connecticut had sold only one bookmark in two months. (Unfortunately, the product display had been placed in a section by the pots and pans.) Other stores had sold only three to five each.

Was the product a flop or was its introduction ill-timed? What should HVW do now? On one side, this might be a good time to cut losses and discontinue operating. Some quality control problems still plagued them. On the other, few entrepreneurs achieved success without persistence and sweat. HVN was capitalized mostly with sweat equity; the business was beset with production and marketing problems; Peter Ellner was in the last semester of his senior year. Should they quit?

HVW survived financially because the Ellners received no income from the business. The cost breakdown was:

Retail price	$2.50	(suggested)
Wholesale price	$1.25	
Production costs	$ .32	
Gross profit	$ .93	(per unit)

Typically, wholesale price for gift shops is 50 percent, for department stores 45 percent.

However, this gross profit figure was misleading. Production costs, for example, did not include labor-intensive operations involved in touching up the finished product. Neither did figures allow for refinement of the manufacturing processes. Packaging, boxing, handling and other costs also needed to be accounted. On the other hand, HVW recovered its cost for the display board from the retailer; all merchandise was shipped f.o.b., Oxford Connecticut.

Although the Ellners allowed that the key to successful marketing of their product was wide-spread distribution, they had neither the time nor resources to call personally on small individual stores whose small orders, at best, scarcely covered sales costs. On the other hand, they had no entree into large department stores.

MASS DISTRIBUTION

Then, when things seemed darkest, a trip to a giftware trade show revealed the following two avenues for mass distribution.

Manufacturer Representatives

Sales representatives typically have permanent show rooms in one to ten cities around the United States. Buyers from gift stores visit show rooms and place orders. Also, sales representatives set up booths at giftware shows. Often field representatives cover a region or the entire country. Orders are forwarded to the manufacturer for drop shipment, and the manufacturer bills customers direct. In other words, manufacturer agents perform only a sales function for which they typically charge 20 percent of the wholesale price.

Distributors

Distributors also have show rooms and booths at giftware shows; and they offer national distribution. Distributors purchase in job lots, warehouse inventory, distribute catalogs to gift stores, bill customers, carry receivables, and usually earn 36-1/2 percent of the wholesale price. Exhibit 39.1 illustrates the effect on gross profit under two retail price assumptions.

Peter Ellner summarized HVW's situation. "We're faced with both pricing and distribution questions." He asked, "Should we raise price and maintain the distribution initiative? That means we'd be locking ourselves into low-volume sales. Or should we reduce per unit profit expectations, engage a middleman, and concentrate on high volume production?"

The Ellners readily acknowledged their inexperience. Their first encounter with a slow-paying account was a bookstore, three months overdue, which still took a 10-day discount.

Exclusive Distribution

As the plot thickened, and the outlook grew darker, a third opportunity for distribution knocked—the California Connection—in the person of Mr. Kim.

Mr. Kim had set up his own giftware company about the same time that the Ellners had formed the Housatonic Valley Workshop. Already he had become an

---

EXHIBIT 39.1 **Effect on gross profit**

Assume a retail price of $2.50 per unit

	Manufacturers Representative	Distributor
Wholesale price	1.25	1.25
Middleman	.25	.46
Net Price to HVW	1.00	.79
Cost of Production	.32	.32
Gross Income	.68	.47

Assume a retail price of $3.00 per unit

	Manufacturers Representative	Distributor
Wholesale price	1.50	1.50
Middleman	.30	.55
Net price to HVW	1.20	.95
Cost of production*	.45	.45
Gross income	.75	.50

*If the price is raised, quality of the packaging may need to be upgraded, which is accounted for in the higher production costs.

effective distributor and sold large quantities of giftware merchandise to a variety of small and large outlets. His products were carried by quality stores. He advertised in *The New York Times.* He was an aggressive marketer. He was an equally aggressive person. By his manner and speech, he conveyed the impression that he was indeed in control of his situation. He spoke as though he had the entire giftware market at his beck and call. Previously he had been an automobile salesman.

Within three weeks after the Ellner relative had sold bookmarks to some California stores, HVW received a telephone call from an excited Mr. Kim, owner of a giftware factory. "Mr. Ellner," he asked, "how would you like to be rich? If you make me your exclusive distributor, I'll buy 100,000 bookmarks now and market them for you. I can get them in Macy's, Bloomingdale's, and stores all across the country. When can you fly out here? I'll pay your way."

Mr. Kim's timing was nearly perfect. The Ellners had doubts about their original decision to target an early American folk art market segment. But the February blues had yet to set in. HVW had not considered utilizing an agent or middleman, let alone Mr. Kim's services. Still, Mr. Kim had experience. He knew the market. His offer sounded almost too good to be true. They delayed making a decision.

Then Mr. Kim warned HVW that their idea could be stolen. "Someone could see the bookmark in a store, size up the manufacturer as being too small to defend itself, and make and sell the product independently. The way to defend against knock-offs," advised Mr. Kim, "is to have an experienced distributor [like himself] handle it."

Over the next three months negotiations with Mr. Kim became mired in details. At first he offered to collect orders. Then he wanted to warehouse the product and purchase it at a lower price. Finally, he wanted just bookmarks, without packaging, at and even lower price. He claimed potential purchases of 200,000 to 300,000 pieces a year. He promised to send periodically a list of customers. Finally, HVW agreed to a price of $0.95 per unit; but Mr. Kim signed a purchase order for only 5,000 pieces and later decided that he did not want even the HVW name on the product.

LEGAL ISSUES

HVW held copyrights on each bookmark design. A copyright is granted for any significantly unique product. For instance, an authentic miniature replica of Roden's sculpture, Burgher of Chalais, had been considered unique by the courts. On the other hand, in another court case, a copy of a toy cash register with plastic replacing some metal parts, and repositioned keys, was held not to be unique.

A copyright neither protects its holder from lawsuits nor guarantees success in a suit. A defendant may challenge the validity and scope of a copyright. HVW copyrights were susceptible to challenge because the bookmarks were reproductions of weathervane designs found in books. Consequently, it may be argued in a court of law that the bookmarks were not unique.

HVW's attorney suggested a patent. A patent protects the concept rather than the creation. The effectiveness of patent protection depends on the ability of the attorney to obtain an encompassing patent. The cost to HVW would range from $2,000-to-$4,000.

A copyright infringement law suit in an out-of-state case, according to HVW's attorney, would cost $2,000-to-$35,000 to litigate. Since courts have not traditionally awarded legal fees in copyright and patent suits, the attorney would require a substantial retainer fee.

However, winning or losing a law suit carried other risks as well. If HVW should win an infringement suit, the defendant may well declare bankruptcy and leave HVW with substantial legal fees and no opportunity for recovery. On the other hand, if copyrights were proven invalid in any infringement suit initiated by HVW, the Ellners (since it is an unincorporated business) could be sued for illegal restraint of trade under certain circumstances.

The HVW attorney also pointed out that due to diverse state laws, there was no guarantee that any suit would be tried in Connecticut, which would result in substantially higher legal fees. For example, California has a more liberal, long arm clause than Connecticut. The long arm clause allows the plaintiff to force a trial in his home state.

The Ellners had been in business less than a year. By late April 1987, Peter was preparing for final examinations and graduation. Edwin was devoting far more time to the business than he had originally anticipated. Prospects for the future were still uncertain. The distribution problem had not been resolved. The attorney had surfaced more potential problems than potential solutions. Solving the manufacturing problems represented the chief accomplishment of the past year. They wondered what they should do.

CASE 40

Con-Way Central Express

Jerry Detter finished the last session of the "New Employee Orientation Seminar" at the Sheraton in Ann Arbor standing in front of a banner with TEAM on it in the Con-Way Central Express (CCX) colors of orange and brown likening CCX to bailing twine. "Each strand in bailing twine," he said, "is very weak but when you twist all of the strands together you have a twine that is very strong and not easily broken." The acronym TEAM stands for Together Each Accomplishes Much. Thus TEAM sums up Jerry's belief as to why, by any measure, CCX had been so successful since its inception in 1983.

In 1986, CCX, a subsidiary of Consolidated Freightways, Inc., provided short-haul overnight freight service to points in the Midwest including the states of Michigan, Illinois, Indiana, Iowa, Kentucky, Ohio, Pennsylvania, Minnesota, and Wisconsin. Its headquarters was now located in a 7,600-square-foot office on the south side of Ann Arbor, Michigan in a commercial/light industry park. The company was founded on June 20, 1983 in a farmhouse nicknamed "Tara" which looked like it had barely survived the Civil War. CCX, which began operations in 1983 with 72 employees and 11 terminals, had 1,500 employees at 38 locations just three and a half years later. During this same period, revenues increased over twenty-five times which is even more amazing given the shakeout in the trucking industry that was causing many firms to declare bankruptcy.

THE PARENT

Consolidated Freightways, Inc. (CFI), the parent of CCX, is a large freight handler operating worldwide with five principal business lines: long-haul trucking, regional trucking of which CCX is one of three subsidiaries, air freight, international ocean container service, and specialized truckload and forwarding service. Its balance sheets for 1984 through 1986 are shown in Exhibit 40.1 and its income statements for 1983 through 1986 are shown in Exhibit 40.2.

CFI pioneered many innovations in the transportation industry, such as the use of double trailers, that today are standard in the less-than-truckload (LTL) transportation business. The latest innovation was the establishment in 1983 of the Con-Way regional freight companies; Con-Way Eastern Express (CEX), Con-Way Western Express (CWX), and CCX. The opportunity to begin the regional businesses was ripe due to the deregulation of the trucking industry which began with the passage of the Motor Carrier Act of 1980. Con-Way Eastern Express was begun by purchasing an existing carrier while CCX and Con-Way Western were formed as new companies. By the end of 1986, CFI had invested $50 million in CCX and in turn had a subsidiary that was growing very rapidly and returning excellent profits. In September 1986, *Forbes* estimated that the three regional companies of CFI would generate $15 million in profits on sales of $150 million for 1986.

Consolidated Freightways Motor Freight (CFMF), the long-haul division of CFI, accounted for about $1.5 billion in revenue in 1986. It had terminals and operated in many of the same cities as the regional subsidiaries but CFMF sold to different markets since the average length of its haul was 1,000 miles. Thus the regional units did not directly compete with CFMF.

EXHIBIT 40.1 **Consolidated Freightways, Inc. and subsidiaries—balance sheet**

	1984	1985	1986
		(In thousands)	
Current Assets			
Cash	$34,185	$31,176	$41,372
Marketable securities	107,409	77,599	94,041
Net accounts receivable	198,640	226,484	249,522
Notes receivable	11,511	13,556	24,891
Operating supplies	23,897	22,470	27,485
Prepaid expenses	37,476	46,567	48,066
Prepaid income taxes	14,478	7,845	14,057
Total current assets	$427,596	$425,697	$499,434
Other Assets			
Marketable securities for investment	$120,300	$123,056	$151,685
Notes receivable due through 1990	10,149	9,525	7,053
Operating rights and goodwill, net	19,689	18,915	20,447
Investment in tax benefit leases	8,042	7,460	5,999
Investment in CF Financial Services		4,986	5,267
Deferred charges and other assets	9,159	6,275	12,463
Total Other Assets	$167,339	$170,217	$202,914
Property, Plant & Equipment			
Land	$48,660	$54,235	$63,818
Buildings and improvements	204,918	234,694	249,577
Motor carrier equipment	446,492	515,945	574,153
Other equipment & leasehold improvements	106,699	118,889	129,335
Total	806,769	923,763	1,016,883
Less accumulated depreciation	(341,130)	(386,104)	(443,791)
Total net property	$465,639	$537,659	$573,092
Total Assets	$1,060,574	$1,133,573	$1,275,440
Current Liabilities			
Accounts payable & accrued liabilities	$229,926	$226,574	$290,810
Federal & other income taxes	5,800	584	
Accrued claims cost	38,823	35,983	47,049
Current maturities of long-term debt	19,347	9,971	6,688
Total current liabilities	293,896	273,112	344,547
Long-term debt	$62,645	$62,539	$58,700
Deferred items	$151,197	$194,128	$207,145
Total liabilities	$507,738	$529,779	$610,392
Shareholders' Equity			
Common stock, $.625 par value	$17,579	$17,647	$26,570
Capital in excess of par value	61,863	63,622	57,758
Cumulative translation adjustment	(5,839)	(8,176)	(7,120)
Retained earnings	520,183	571,926	630,228
Less treasury stock	(40,950)	(41,225)	(42,388)
Total shareholders' equity	$552,836	$603,794	$665,048
Total Liabilities & Shareholders' Equity	$1,060,574	$1,133,573	$1,275,440

EXHIBIT 40.2 Consolidated Freightways, Inc. and subsidiaries—income statement

	1983	1984	1985	1986
		(In thousands)		
Revenues				
Surface Transportation	$1,173,866	$1,480,156	$1,616,567	$1,843,177
Air Freight	181,229	224,753	265,575	281,290
Total	$1,355,095	$1,704,909	$1,882,142	$2,124,467
Costs & Expenses				
Surface Transportation				
Operating Expenses	$864,599	$1,121,968	$1,215,678	$1,353,368
Selling & Admin.				
Expenses	159,512	192,076	213,519	262,648
Depreciation	58,934	65,420	79,096	86,875
Total	$1,083,045	$1,379,464	$1,508,293	$1,702,891
Air Freight				
Operating Expenses	$137,235	$168,361	$214,589	$238,781
Selling & Admin.				
Expenses	33,077	35,889	43,423	43,825
Depreciation	2,243	2,993	3,602	3,925
Total	$172,555	$207,243	$261,614	$286,531
Operating Income				
Surface Transportation	$90,821	$100,692	$108,274	$140,286
Air Freight	8,674	17,510	3,961	(5,241)
Total	$99,495	$118,202	$112,235	$135,045
Other Income				
Investment Income	$23,618	$20,991	$22,446	$16,203
Interest Expense	(9,893)	(7,379)	(6,159)	(7,298)
Miscellaneous, net	(162)	(3,079)	(1,103)	3,440
Total	$13,563	$10,533	$15,184	$12,345
Income Before Taxes	$113,058	$128,735	$127,419	$147,390
Income Taxes	$47,594	$54,270	$48,128	$58,281
Net Income	$65,464	$74,465	$79,291	$89,109
Net Income per Share	$1.62	$1.88	$2.06	$2.31

INTRAPRENEURING

To say that Jerry Detter, the President of CCX, has charisma seems trite when one sees him in action, for he epitomizes the idea. All of the employees agree he was and continues to be the driving force that created and sustains CCX. Jerry was 38 years old when CFI asked him to start CCX. He figured he was "young enough to start over" if the project failed, but he was confident it would succeed.

Jerry joined CFI as a terminal dock worker immediately after graduating in the bottom-third of his high school class. He said he was only reading at the fifth grade level at the time and realized quickly he needed to improve himself. By the time he was 23 he was a terminal manager; by 28 he managed the largest terminal in the United States with 1,200 employees (which he was able to reduce to 900 five years later). He had been with CFI for eighteen years and was a division manager responsible for 23 terminals at the time he was selected to start CCX.

Originally, CFI proposed to buy a company rather than start a new regional carrier from scratch. The accountants said it would cost $11 million to turn the proposed acquisition around, but Jerry thought it would take four times as much. Jerry convinced CFI to start a new company and the proposed acquisition went out of business within 90 days affirming his judgment. The original concepts for the company were simple and remain so today. Overnight delivery service was to be provided at least 95 percent of the time at a competitive cost using union-free labor with superior efficiency and flexibility and with team work and profit sharing stressed. Jerry likened CCX to a speedboat which can make quick turns and adjust rapidly to the marketplace and competitors. Not only are the management concepts and style at CCX atypical of the industry but they are also unique at CFI.

At an employee orientation seminar in February 1987 that continued for two-and-a-half days, a number of comments were made by the employees regarding the company and Jerry's leadership.

> "It's great to talk to the president personally and think he really cares about your ideas."
>
> "I like the honesty of this company."
>
> "The company takes care of its equipment and provides good equipment."
>
> "The company pays above average wages with profit sharing."
>
> "CCX is intense but I like it."
>
> "There is real team work here. Everyone tries to help. The spirit and profit sharing are great."

Ninety-five percent of the drivers are former union members. Jerry encourages this because they have something to compare CCX to and are appreciative of the different climate. The employees in turn appreciate the union-free environment.

THE TRUCKING INDUSTRY

The U.S. trucking industry can be segmented in several different ways. First, there is the for-hire carrier versus the private carrier. For-hire carriers are considered part of the trucking industry while private carriers are not since they are solely owned by individual companies and in turn only transport that company's freight. Private carriers are typically not subject to the same detailed regulations as for-hire carriers. By 1980, private carriers probably numbered 100,000.

For-hire carriers can, in turn, be divided into intracity truckers and over-the-road truckers. Expenditures for local cartage in 1986 still represented 40 percent of all expenditures on motor freight service. Intrastate cartage represented 60 percent of the tonnage carried. Intracity carriers are subject to state regulation.

Over-the-road carriers are subject to federal regulation and intermodal competition. Regulated carriers can, in turn, be divided into common carriers, who provide service to the general public and contract carriers, who do not haul for the general public but provide specialized service to individual shippers. There were an estimated 193,000 self-employed truckers (contract carriers) in 1980. There were three classes of regulated carriers in 1980 based upon the annual amount of revenue they handled as shown below.

Class I—In excess of $3,000,000

Class II—$500,000 to $3,000,000

Class III—Less than $500,000

The common carriers can be regular route carriers or irregular route carriers. Regular route carriers of general freight operate through terminals where less-than-truckload (LTL) cargoes are received, sorted and consolidated into truckload lots for subsequent movement to other terminals where the same process is reversed. Such terminals also serve as points for switching cargoes between carriers. Thus regular route carriers are in the distribution business and the terminal network required to perform this service requires a much larger capital investment than is necessary for contract carriers. In addition, their terminal operations make them more labor intensive and, therefore, more costly and dependent upon good terminal management.

The trucking industry from 1978 through 1984 was relatively stable in regard to ton-miles carried and employment as shown in Exhibit 40.3.

Regulation of the trucking industry was established by the Motor Carrier Act of 1935 during the Great Depression in order to overcome destructive competition, chaotic price structures, and market forces that were thought to be unreliable for

---

EXHIBIT 40.3 **Intercity ton-miles**

Year	Number of miles (In billions)	Percent of U.S. total	Employment (In thousands)
1978	599	24.3	1212
1979	608	23.6	1249
1980	555	22.3	1189
1981	527	21.7	1168
1982	520	23.1	1128
1983	548	23.7	1133
1984	602	23.6	1212

Source: Transportation Policy Associates, *Transportation in America Regulation of the Trucking Industry.*

producing satisfactory results. It was a movement away from the free market toward socialism. The lack of stability in the industry was thought to be due to the ease of entry (little capital required), owners were free to send their trucks anywhere they wished, and each operator set his own rates.

The act provided for the Interstate Commerce Commission to control entry into the interstate market, define and limit operations within the market, and control the rates charged. The control of entry was accomplished by requiring a "certificate of public convenience and necessity" for any carrier who sought new or extended routes. This certificate required a hearing in which existing competitors in the market could contest the need for the new carrier. As might be expected, the majority of the operating rights by the mid-1970s were obtained under the grandfather clause of the act. The protective nature of regulatory policy reduced the risk that would have been encountered in a competitive industry and provided a good opportunity to grow with the general economy.

The control of operations was provided by requiring the commission to specify the nature and extent of authorized service that individual carriers could offer. As a result of this power, a congressional study in 1945 showed that 62 percent of intercity certificates had been limited to special commodities and only 32 percent of intercity carriers had general commodity authority that were subject to numerous exceptions. Furthermore, over one-third of the intercity carriers were limited in obtaining income-generating backhauls and one-tenth were prohibited from taking return loads for compensation. Route restrictions forced carriers to travel unnecessary distances often partially or totally empty. Of regular route carriers, only 30 percent had full authority to serve all intermediate points on their routes and 10 percent had no such authority.[1]

In order to facilitate the massive job of controlling rates in the interstate trucking industry, the commission encouraged regulated carriers to use rate bureaus to jointly make rates. By 1980, ten major general freight rate bureaus were operating in different parts of the country. These rate bureaus from their beginning clearly involved price fixing which was illegal under U.S. antitrust laws. Although this dilemma was resolved by the Reed-Bullwinkle Act of 1948, which theoretically preserved the right to make individual rates, in practice the delays and litigation caused by the requirement that the proposing carrier show that the proposed rate was just, reasonable, and compensatory, effectively precluded individual rate making.

Deregulation of the Trucking Industry

Deregulation of the trucking industry began in 1977 with some administrative changes and culminated in the Motor Carrier Act of 1980. This Act altered all of the three factors involved in regulation: entry policy, operating authority, and rate making. The ease of entry was facilitated in two ways; the burden of proof of public convenience and necessity was eased and the basis for protest by existing carriers

---

[1]Charles R. Perry, *Deregulation and the Decline of the Unionized Trucking Industry* (Philadelphia: Industrial Research Unit, The Wharton School, University of Pennsylvania, 1986), p. 27.

was constrained. These changes caused the number of applications for operating authority to grow from 12,700 in 1979 to 22,735 in 1980 and to over 29,000 in the twelve months following passage of the act. Grants of authority to new entrants grew from 690 in 1979 to 1,423 in 1980 and to 2,452 in the following twelve months. Two years after the passage of the act, applications were averaging about 1,100 per month, 43,000 new certificates had been issued, and about 8,000 new carriers had been granted operating authority.[2]

Rate making was altered by the act to permit carriers to take independent rate actions without the potential procedural obstacles previously put up by the rate bureaus. These obstacles included the power to delay filing the proposal and the right to notify other members of the proposed rate change prior to action being taken.

Deregulation served to weaken the elaborate set of barriers to competition among existing carriers. It also produced another incentive that enhanced competition—added capacity. The operating restrictions previously in place had tied up capacity through inefficiencies. Elimination of the restrictions freed up this capacity for productive use.

Although the rate bureaus continued to operate, a shakeout occurred in the trucking industry in the three years following the passage of the act, caused by the economic climate as well as the increased competition. Rate reductions became more common and carriers had stronger incentives to control costs including wages negotiated with the Teamsters Union. Management could no longer afford to minimize confrontation with the Teamsters.

The trend toward nonunion carriers which had begun to develop prior to the 1980 Act was accentuated after the passage of the act. In 1983, nonunion employees were 44 percent of the drivers and helpers, 42 percent of the vehicle maintenance personnel, and 69 percent of the cargo handlers. In 1983, Class I nonunion carriers were able to generate 2.5 times as much revenue per dollar of compensation as the unionized carriers. Exhibit 40.4 summarizes the costs and revenue relationships.

[2]Ibid., p. 76.

EXHIBIT 40.4 **Average Annual Pay and Productivity per Employee for Class I Carriers—1983**

	Union	Lightly unionized	Nonunion	Union to nonunion
Wages	$27,293	$21,734	$18,630	1.46:1
Benefits	4,096	1,365	897	4.57:1
Compensation	31,389	23,099	19,527	1.61:1
Revenues	52,555	57,219	81,097	.65:1
Ratio of Revenue to Compensation	1.67	2.48	4.15	.40:1

Source: ICC databank of trucking industry statistics.

The LTL motor freight industry has higher rates than the truckload segment because it is a distribution network and as such is more labor intensive. Rate increases over time have brought LTL rates to the point where they reflect the full cost of handling such freight. The competitive advantage had gone to those firms with the lowest labor-productivity costs. Many anticipate a further shakeout of the weak firms in the industry which will make those least able to control and reduce their labor costs the first to go.

The economic benefits from deregulation exceed the original government estimates by a factor of 10 ranging from $56 to $90 billion annually. Not only have transportation costs themselves been reduced but, more importantly, much of the increased efficiency is due to better management of inventory and delivery systems. In effect "just-in-time" inventory concepts were facilitated. Exhibit 40.5 shows the components of 1986 U.S. logistics cost. The performance of transportation services

---

EXHIBIT 40.5 Components of 1986 U.S. logistics cost

Distribution service		Cost (In billions of dollars)	
Inventory			
Carrying		$ 98	
Warehousing			
Public	$ 6		
Private	50		
Total warehousing		56	
Total carrying/holding			$154
Transportation			
Motor carriers			
Public carriers	54		
Private and shipper affiliated carriers	75		
Local freight carriers	76		
Total		205	
Nonmotor Carriers			
Railroads	29		
Water carriers	18		
Oil pipelines	9		
Air carriers	6		
Forwarders, brokers and agents (net)	1		
Total nonmotor carriers		63	
Shipper-related services		3	
Total transportation			271
Distribution administration			18
Total			$443

Source: Robert V. Delaney, "The Disunited States: A Country In Search of an Efficient Transportation Policy," *CATO Policy Analysis.* No. 84, March 10, 1987, p. 3.

must be consistent and dependable if investments in inventory are to be controlled. Prior to deregulation producers and distributors either built excessive inventory or operated their own trucks in order to overcome the poor service provided by many carriers. The competition fostered by deregulation has forced better service.

MARKETING

The marketing activities of CCX are managed by Bryan Millican who is 37 years old. He graduated from the University of Waterloo in Canada with a bachelor's degree in Mathematics and Computer Science and later received his MBA degree from the University of Western Ontario. He began working in the trucking industry in Canada when he was 16 and has had extensive experience in data processing and marketing. He accepted the job at CCX after talking to Jerry Detter without even knowing his salary because he liked the opportunity and the fact that CCX was open for new thoughts. He normally spends 50 percent of his sixty-hour week on the road seeing how customers perceive the marketing programs and how employees use the programs. Because of his background in computers, Bryan personally wrote many of the programs that are used locally by CCX.

CCX uses a three-phase marketing strategy. The first phase is increased market awareness that CCX is a regional carrier. The company began with terminals in the eleven major cities in the central states region. Jerry Detter wanted to get the "biggest bang for the buck." Next, more key cities were added followed by secondary cities and finally the network was spread out to encompass the entire area. One of the key factors stressed is on-time service with the goal of 96 percent of the freight being delivered the next day—CCX was operating at 97 percent in late 1986. (Regional trucking is much more sensitive to time than national trucking.) Another factor is the coverage between major freight centers within the region. Finally, financial stability or staying power is emphasized. Exhibit 40.6 shows how terminals were added from 1983 through 1986 to carry out these policies.

The second phase is the penetration of the market area. CCX is among the top 25 in the country in terms of tonnage handled; the company is proceeding toward the third phase which is domination of the midwest market with the premier service as well as coverage. CCX began with 700 points of service (terminals, pick-up points, etc.), was at 6,500 points in 1986, and is looking forward to an expansion of 15 more terminals to include 10,000 points of service in 1987. CCX's present market share is over 10 percent and Bryan Millican's goal is to have 20 percent of the market by June 1988. Jerry Detter sees a 45 percent growth in revenue in 1987 (which would put CCX among the top 20 in the country) and a 25 percent share of the market by 1990. All of this is to be accomplished with a tight administrative and selling expense budget which was 5.5 percent of revenues in 1986.

The selling strategy for CCX as developed by Bryan consists of these elements.

- Try us, test our product.

EXHIBIT 40.6 CCX terminal locations by the year added

	1983	Additions 1984	Additions 1985	Additions 1986
Michigan				
Detroit	X			
Grand Rapids	X			
Battle Creek		X		
Pontiac			X	
Holland				X
Flint				X
Jackson				X
Ohio				
Toledo	X			
Cleveland	X			
Columbus	X			
Cincinnati	X			
Dayton			X	
Akron			X	
Findlay				X
Pennsylvania				
Pittsburgh	X			
Sharon/Newcastle			X	
Erie			X	
Indiana				
Indianapolis	X			
South Bend		X		
Fort Wayne		X		
Kokomo			X	
Evansville			X	
Illinois				
Chicago	X			
Palatine		X		
Aurora			X	
DesPlaines				X
Bloomington				X
Danville				X
Wisconsin				
Milwaukee	X			
Janesville		X		
Green Bay			X	
Fond Du Lac				X
Minnesota				
Minneapolis	X			
Iowa				
Quad Cities	X			
Kentucky				
Louisville			X	
Lexington				X
Missouri				
St. Louis				X

- Identify time sensitive customers.
- Make it easy for customers to deal with us—keep it simple.
- Strive for error-free shipping.

Pricing

Since deregulation, the industry has been reluctant to raise prices because of the severe competition and the shakeout that has occurred. Many freight companies have declared bankruptcy as a result of these factors. CCX tries to differentiate itself from competition by the quality of its service—consistent, realistic next-day delivery with practically error-free shipping.

The trucking industry as noted previously had traditionally used rate bureaus for its rate base system which is not related to mileage the freight travels. Most trucking firms still use this system even following deregulation which allowed other systems to be used. Subject to the rate-base system used, the result can be different freight costs between the same terminals depending upon which direction the freight is traveling. The freight-class system when used to calculate freight costs (as used by most firms) is not based on logic. Thus the freight-class 200 is not double the 100 class but exceeds two times the 100 class.

CCX's basic pricing policy is to have a *different* pricing system. By staying out of the rate bureaus, CCX is perceived as having lower prices since they are not part of a cartel. Actually, some of CCX's rates are higher and some are lower than competition. The CCX system is based on a ZIP code model and is totally determined by mileage. An individual printout is given to each customer so there is no need for elaborate, difficult-to-use tariff guides. Savings to CCX from this simplified system are estimated to be $150,000 to $400,000 annually since no rate clerks, who are highly paid technicians, are required. Furthermore, the customers appreciate the simplicity.

There are nineteen classes of freight, as defined by the National Motor Freight Classification (NMFC) system. In CCX's pricing system, Class 100 is established as the base level of rates. Classes are based on the density of the freight, the weight of the freight, how stowable it is, and how susceptible to damage it is, its valuation, etc. For instance, rough steel plate is Class 50 and light bulbs are Class 200. In the CCX system, once the class number is established, it is easy to calculate that class's rate by using a multiplier to the Class 100 base rate. There is a minimum charge of $38 for less than 250 pounds. All of the 100,000 shipments per month are rated by the computer. All that is needed as input is the originating point based on the three-digit ZIP code, destination ZIP code, weight, and class of the freight. The average revenue per 100 pounds of freight handled by CCX is $6.50.

Jerry Detter believes that "there is no bad freight, just bad rates." The typical customer is not very analytical and judges the price based on the discount level given. On balance CCX's rates are about 5 percent above the rate bureaus since a better product is provided, but a discount is offered on each shipment since the customer expects it. CCX rarely loses a customer entirely.

The decision maker for the customer is typically the shipping and receiving manager or the warehouse manager. CCX has stressed small- to medium-sized shippers and stayed away from the big companies, although now larger accounts are being emphasized. Big companies are moving toward using one carrier and part of CFI's strategy is to be able to service this kind of account anywhere. The average CCX customer uses the company three times per week with two shipments each time at a charge of approximately $2,500 per month.

Terry Hartley is the pricing manager. He is responsible for coordinating bids, negotiating with customers, and regulatory compliance. He has two employees who work on auditing rates. The pricing manager makes 80 percent of the pricing adjustments but Jerry Detter OK's all adjustments. Of the requests for adjustments submitted, 20 percent are rejected outright. Ninety-two percent of the business is sold at the base price.

Sales

The drivers at CCX are called driver salesmen and they do actually sell. In fact, 20 percent of the business is maintained by them and they distribute 30 percent of CCX's promotional literature. In the company seminars, a list of "Things CCX Driver Salesmen Must Do To Increase CCX Revenues" is discussed with the new driver salesmen. The list includes the following twelve items.

1. *Always* be courteous.
2. Always treat the customer with professional *respect*—if ever in doubt, contact your terminal manager. Never argue.
3. *Ask for business* at every opportunity.
4. Stress *CCX Service Excellence* on every call (comments regarding service on inbound bills, testimonials, promotional materials, and CCX's on-time percentage).
5. Create *awareness* of CCX services that a customer has never used (new terminals, additional points, inbound traffic, protective service).
6. Get *multiple* bills per stop.
7. Hand out CCX promotional literature and get it up on the walls (stickers, dispatch cards, route maps, etc.).
8. 36 percent *discount* on *every* shipment—make sure every customer knows that.
9. Make customers aware of the many *features and benefits* of CCX:
   - Best service in the Central States,
   - A CFI company,
   - Very low claims ratio,
   - Professional, experienced people,
   - Easy to use,
   - Simple and very competitive pricing program,

- Union-free company,
- Coverage of thousands of points on a direct basis daily.

10. Hats and other promotional materials—use them to increase your business (scratch pads, dispatch cards with CCX telephone number, stickers, hats).
11. The 30-second sales call.
12. Leads to your account managers.

Bryan Millican believes the CCX driver salesmen know more about their company than most managers in other companies. CCX believes its sales training is the best in the trucking industry.

Exhibit 40.7 shows the organization chart for CCX. As indicated, all line responsibility flows through the terminal managers in the operations area. Bryan Millican does have a dotted-line relationship to the field account managers and does make calls on customers with them. There are one to five account managers assigned to each terminal for a total of 77. They make 9 to 10 calls per day. Generally, each account manager has about 200 accounts and calls on the large ones twice a month and the medium-sized ones once a month. Each manager has a revenue quota that increases monthly. The revenue quota for each terminal is set by a committee of Jerry Detter, Bryan Millican, Dick Palazzo, Vice President of Operations, and Kevin Schick, Controller.

Telemarketing is another important aspect of CCX's sales strategy. Pat Jannausch is the director of the Account Management Center (AMC). She is particularly good at training, due to the fact that she was a teacher before joining CCX. She has 21 people working in the center who account for 12 percent of the sales. Each person makes 35 to 40 telephone sales calls per day which averages one call per customer every six weeks. The center handles 11,000 of the company's 32,000 accounts which tend to be the smaller accounts. Once an account is obtained by the center it stays a "center account" regardless of how big it becomes. It costs about $6.50 per call. In addition, there are 250,000 direct mailings made by the center annually. Potential customers are obtained by referring to the Harris Directory and Dun & Bradstreet's Directory, by talking to recipients of freight from CCX, by referrals from driver salesmen, and by canvassing shippers of specific commodities, such as electronics firms, involved in "just-in-time" inventory systems. There is a four-week training program for AMC account managers. An income statement for the center is generated with full absorption of overhead.

Promotion

Most of the advertising for CCX is done by the parent, CFI, in the form of image advertising in trade magazines and general business magazines such as *Forbes* and *Fortune*. Due to the high cost of advertising and regional nature of CCX's operations, little advertising is done by the subsidiary. For instance, a single-page four-color ad running three times per year cost $20,000. Very little advertising is done by CCX in the yellow pages and the various industrial guides. Most of the expenditures are for

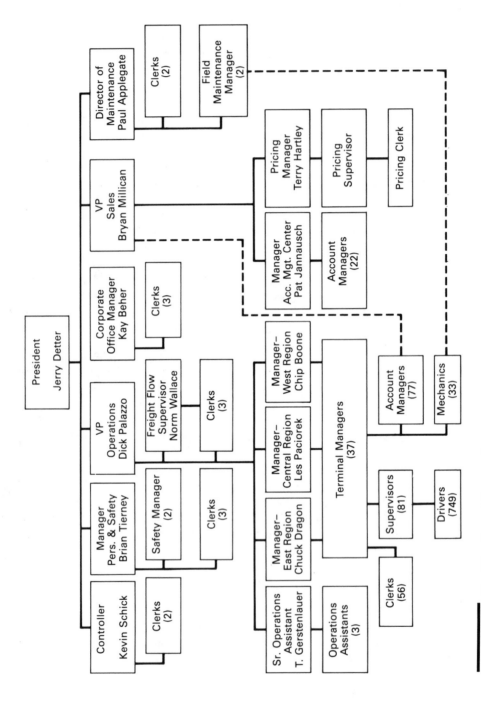

EXHIBIT 40.7 **Con-Way Central Express Organization Chart**

promotional items—literature, printed brochures and pamphlets, and some specialty items.

Bryan personally does all of the advertising layout work for all of the promotional literature used locally by CCX. Local typesetting services are used but the actual printing of the pieces is done by CFI in their central printing shop. Printing material costs about $200,000 per year. Total marketing expense for CCX, which initially ran 20 percent of revenue now runs about 5 percent and is expected to drop further.

As is probably true in any industry, there are ethical issues that arise in the trucking industry. Some carriers use entertainment in lieu of price competition. Others give gifts. As a policy, CCX gives any discount earned to the the company paying the shipping bill. Gifts are not given beyond the normal promotional material (CCX hats, model trucks, pens, etc.). Entertainment is less than 1 percent of marketing expense.

Competition

There is no more competitive area of the United States than the Central region in which CCX operates. The revenue from this region exceeds $1 billion and it is estimated by CCX that there are more than 4,000 carriers operating in the market. Exhibit 40.8 summarizes CCX's estimate of the revenue by its top thirty-five competitors in the Central States region.

Not all of these carriers are profitable. CCX estimates that the operating ratio for these 35 carriers varies from the best at 84 percent to the worst at 126 percent. Given these estimates, it is not difficult to see why bankruptcies have been common and are continuing.

According to Jerry Detter, the strongest but not the largest competitor is TNT Holland. TNT Holland was formerly known as Holland Motor Express before being acquired by TNT Pilot Freight Carriers, a subsidiary of Thomas Nationwide Transportation of Australia, in 1985. Holland had $128.7 million in revenue in 1986, having doubled in size in the last eight years. It has 30 terminals in Illinois, Indiana, Kentucky, Michigan, Missouri, Ohio, Tennessee, Iowa, and Wisconsin and

---

EXHIBIT 40.8 **Central region competition**

	Central states revenue (In thousands)	Percent of revenue
Top 10 carriers	$ 621,000	57.6
11–20	286,000	26.5
21–25	98,000	9.1
26–35	73,000	6.8
Total	$1,078,000	100.0

serves 2,854 points. Thus CCX serves 76 percent more points with 23 percent more terminals and provides service to Pennsylvania and Minnesota as well but does not cover Tennessee. Holland is currently discounting its prices.

ANR Freight System, formerly ATL (Associated Truck Lines), operates in all states that CCX does plus some others outside the Central States region. ANR has a large network of terminals and agency stations (81 in CCX's market area) and serves over 8,000 points. ANR's revenue for 1986 was $175 million which was down 5 percent for the same period in 1985. Its on-time service level was recently reported to be 80 percent with a goal of 85 percent. ANR is estimated to have 12 percent to 14 percent of the Central States market.

OPERATIONS

Dick Palazzo, Vice President of Operations, is 47 years old and has had 24 years experience with CFMF, starting as a clerk and finishing as a division manager prior to joining CCX. Dick was with Jerry Detter from the beginning and is his alter ego, for they complement each other. Dick is the sounding board for everyone, someone to tell your troubles to. He studied industrial management for the equivalent of two to three years at the University of Akron from 1959 through 1966. He typically works 60 to 70 hours a week, spending about 50 percent of his time in the field.

Terminals and Freight Assembly Centers

CCX's operational area is divided into three regions: Eastern, Central, and Western with a regional manager in charge of each region. CCX began operations without regional managers but added two in 1985 when the number of terminals increased to 27. Again a regional manager was added in 1986 when the number of terminals increased to 37.

Under these three regions are 37 terminals, which are supervised by a terminal manager aided in three instances by an assistant terminal manager, with a total of 1,410 truck doors, which handled about 625,000 tons of freight in 1986. The 749 driver salesmen are supervised directly by 81 supervisors. The terminal managers also have direct responsibility for 77 account managers and 59 clerks. The typical terminal manager spends about 10 percent of his time selling personally or with account managers. CCX would like to see 30 to 40 percent of the time spent on selling.

Each of the five normal work days, the driver salesmen pickup and deliver freight between the hours of 8 a.m. and 4 p.m. over routes determined by the mix of customers that day. Weekends are not normally worked since freight picked up on Friday will be available for delivery on Monday morning in the normal course of events. At 8 p.m. the line haul drivers drive a tractor and two 28 foot trailers either to a freight assembly center or to a meet-and-turn-point about equidistant between two terminals. There the trailers are exchanged and the driver returns to the original terminal.

In conjunction with seven of the terminals, there are freight assembly centers located at Aurora, Illinois; Indianapolis, South Bend, and Fort Wayne, Indiana; and Toledo, Columbus, and Cleveland, Ohio. Exhibit 40.9 shows a map of the CCX system indicating terminals, freight assembly centers, and meet-and-turn-points. Every night between 11 p.m. and 3 a.m. freight is brought into these centers from the various terminals, unloaded, sorted, and reloaded on to another trailer that is going to the final destination of the freight. Upon arriving at the center and after checking in, drivers, who are paid by the mile on a line haul, begin working on an hourly basis until they resume driving back to their original terminal. The loading is done on a progressive basis rather than by staging the material by delivery sequence on the dock prior to loading. The driver salesman making deliveries to customers the next day determines the final delivery sequence.

The control of line haul activities is the responsibility of Norm Wallace, the freight flow supervisor. He has three employees working for him at the central office in Ann Arbor. They develop, with the aid of the computer, the line haul report that is used to control truck operations transferring freight overnight. They balance pounds and linear feet of space, regardless of how high the freight is stacked, on each trailer in and out of each terminal by each "lane" which is the path between the terminals and/or centers. In case of an imbalance in one direction, an empty trailer will be sent along or carried back as circumstances may require. One of the key reports used in controlling shipments is the loading manifest shown in Exhibit 40.10.

Operations Control

Operations are controlled by a number of reports. The production report, known as the "244" is submitted daily (Exhibit 40.11) and weekly by each terminal. Done by hand by the terminal manager or his assistant manager, this report goes to the regional managers, Dick Palazzo, and CFI's Portland, Oregon computer center. The two operations assistants supervised by Tom Gerstenlauer, Senior Operations Assistant, check the calculations, highlight substandard items, and send a rebuttal back to the regional managers about errors and problems. This activity shows the reports are actively being used. A monthly "244" report is submitted by each terminal manager within three days after the end of the month along with a trial income and expense statement. By the 13th to 15th of the month a computer recap of the 244 is received by Dick Palazzo and in turn transmitted to the terminals with comments.

Dick monitors the morning report daily. It includes revenue, wages, labor/wages, percent overtime, equipment out of service, number of shipments that did not move, any shipments not billed, and any bills that were brought back because they were not delivered. He also monitors the Empty Miles Report which shows the empty trailers and in which lanes they occurred. The actual payroll figures are checked versus the various reports and the service factor checked on a weekly basis showing the on-time statistics. Annually, Dick sets goals for all terminals including revenue, productivity, labor, and claims.

Another element of Dick Palazzo's job is handling new terminal expansion. The regional managers do a lot of the leg work but Dick personally makes the final

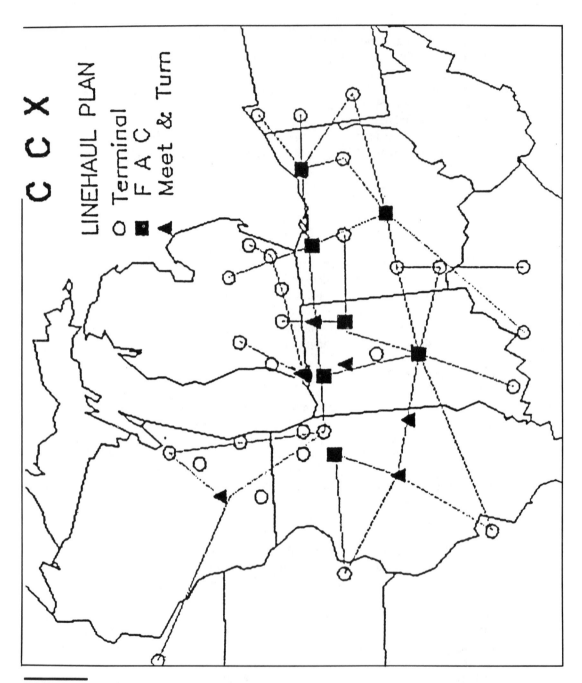

EXHIBIT 40.9 **Con-Way Central Express system map**

04145-00 (10/86)

LOADING MANIFEST

TRAILER NUMBER	MID	LOADING LOC. SIC	RESP RDC	TRAILER NUMBER	DEST SIC
	TCON			—	

DESTINATION	DATE	TOTAL WEIGHT	% CUBE	BILLS	TIME/DATE CLOSED	LOAD RELEASE NUMBER
						841501

ORIGIN	SWEPT	NAILS PULLED	HOLES REPAIRED	WHEELS CHOCKED	SPECIAL INSTRUCTIONS/REMARKS	(38 CHARACTER LIMIT)

WEIGHT CARRIED FORWARD — CUBE — BILLS

LINE NO	PIECES	WEIGHT	ID	H/M	PRO NUMBER	LINE NO	PIECES	WEIGHT	ID	H/M	PRO NUMBER
1						23					
2						24					
3						25					
4						26					
5						27					
6						28					
7						29					
8						30					
9						31					
10						32					
11						33					
12						34					
13						35					
14						36					
15						37					
16						38					
17						39					
18						40					
19						41					
20						42					
21						43					
22						44					
SUB TOTAL ▶						SUB TOTAL ▶					

LOADING DIAGRAM (IDENTIFY MARKS)

TOP VIEW — SIDE VIEW

NOSE — REAR — NOSE — REAR

SIDE — BOTTOM

MARKS
1. C/_____ D/_____
2. C/_____ D/_____

DO NOT LOAD CLASS A OR B POISONS IN A TRAILER CONTAINING MATERIAL THAT IS MARKED AS OR KNOWN TO BE FOODSTUFF, FEED OR ANY OTHER EDIBLE MATERIAL INTENDED FOR CONSUMPTION BY HUMANS OR ANIMALS.

TOTAL ▶		CUBE	BILLS

SEAL NUMBER		CHANGED SEAL NUMBER	

HEATER: ☐ YES ☐ NO	UNIT NO.
PLACARDS: ☐ YES ☐ NO	TYPE

AUTHORITY:

SPECIAL INSTRUCTIONS (TYPES OF HAZARDOUS MATERIAL) INFORMATION USEFUL TO UNLOADER CONCERNING LOAD, ETC.

EXHIBIT 40.10 **Con-Way Central Express loading manifest**

EXHIBIT 40.11 Con-Way Central Express production report

WEEKLY TERMINAL PRODUCTION and COST REPORT

40340-20 (Pa)

Terminal _Cleveland OH_ Code _XCL_ Week Ending _5-16-87_

HAND WRITTEN PREFERABLE (LEGIBLE)

FREIGHT HANDLING

FUNCTION		LABOR			TONNAGE IN CWT UNITS					PERFORMANCE				
	A Std. Hrs.	B Hrs. Worked	C Prem. Hrs.	D P/R Cost	E Inbound CWT	Outbound CWT	Reshp CWT	H Total CWT	Std. Lbs/M.H.	J Lbs/M.H.	K Cost/CWT	L $ Variance		Avg. Load
1. Direct P&D 266	128	141	12 (3V)	1904	3617	4720	xxxx	8337	6500	5913	.23	(310)		
2. Cross Dock 379	541	592	16 (31)	6895	14818	14956	4229	34063	6300	5853	.20	(657)		
3. City Liner P&D 262	933	1062	50 (W)	13155	14278	14916	xxxx	29843	3200	2810	41	(2296)		
4. Direct Peddle	xxxx	xxxx	xxxx	xxxx			xxxx	xxxx	xxxx	xxxx	xxxx	xxxx		
5. LTL Peddle 239							xxxx							
6. Frt. Not Handled	xxxx	xxxx	xxxx	xxxx			xxxx	xxxx	xxxx	xxxx	xxxx	xxxx		
7. Vol. Trlr (Over 10Mi)	xxxx	xxxx	xxxx	xxxx			xxxx	xxxx	xxxx	xxxx	.57	xxxx		
8. Weekly Total	1602	1985	78 (13)	22754	18495	19676	4229	42900	xxxx	xxxx	xxxx	xxxx		
9. LTL	xxxx	xxxx	xxxx	xxxx			xxxx	% DIRECT TONNAGE						

% OF CITY LINER AND PEDDLE CWT TO LTL CWT ___ % OF I/B AND O/B AND O/B CROSS DOCK CWT TO LTL CWT ___

OTHER TERMINAL ACTIVITIES

FUNCTION	LABOR			HOOKS	PERFORMANCE					V. LOAD FACTOR		
	B Hrs. Worked	C Prem. Hrs.	D P/R Cost	H Total Hooks	J Std. Hks/Hrs.	K Cost/Hooks	Hooks/Hrs			No. of Trailers	Trailer Type	Avg. Load
10. Hostling - Term Yard 382	15	-	177	98	6.5	1.81					SEMI$	
11. Hostling - Pig/Pike 236										237	DUBS	11421
12. Dispatch - L/H 212		xxxx										
13. Dispatch - P&D 226				22. Explanation and Comments							3706674	
14. Term. & Bldg. Repairs392												
15. Other Term. Labor *												
16. Weekly Total	15	-	177									

(* Hours entered on line 15 must be explained in this section.)

CITY LINER P&D STOPS: 2565
2.13 SpL

OFFICE

FUNCTION	LABOR			PERFORMANCE			
Std. Bills/M.H.	B Hrs. Worked	C Prem. Hrs.	D P/R Cost	Bill/M.H.	J Cost/Bills		
17. Billing 321 322	50	4 (V)	943	35	.26	xxxx	xxxx
18. Gathering 325 361	170	10 (V)	1476	15	.57	xxxx	xxxx
& Other 359 382	220	14 (3V)	1919			xxxx	xxxx
19. Sub Total							
20. Sets Checked - Terminal 422							
21. Weekly Total	220	14 (3V)	1919	220	24	10.9	

NUMBER OF BILLS

E Inbound Bills	1736
F Outbound Bills	0
G Bld for Other Term.	1736
Total Outbound Bills	404
H Total In & Out Bills	3336
U Reshp Bills	

MARKETING REVENUE

Wkly. Trl. Rev.	131936
Wkly. Qual. Rev	129390
Qual. Rev. Quota	126206
Qual. % Quota	102.5
Trl. Rev. Cwt	7.13
Trl. Rev. Pr. Yr	104982

	E Total I/B Rev.	Total O/B Rev.	Total I/O
	130592	262578
	130592	xxxx
	129529	xxxx
	104.9	xxxx
	6.64	2/1886
	106904	

% OVERTIME HOURS TO HOURS WORKED

FUNCTION	HRS. WORKED	O.T. HOURS	%
Frt. Handling	1775	153	8.6
Oth. Term. Act.	15	-	0
Office	220	24	10.9

PAYROLL TO REVENUE SUMMARY

	CURRENT WEEK	WEEK OF PRIOR YR.
N Mean Revenue	128715	105562
P Total Terminal Payroll	24850	19850
R % P/R to Mean Revenue	19.3	18.8
Std. % P/R to Rev.	20.0	-

RECEIVED
CON-WAY CENTRAL EXPRESS
MAY 19 1987
BY _____

Litho in U.S.A.

decisions and arranges for leases or purchases. A terminal is usually 50-feet wide and is leased by the door. The cost of leasing is about $150 per month per door. The cost of building a terminal is $18,000 per door. Originally all terminals were leased but nine are now owned through CFI.

The operations assistants conduct audits at each terminal with a goal of two per terminal per year. The audits cover all aspects of operations and operating statistics. The audits are written by hand in the field and are later typed with references to the master manual. The operations assistants also conduct seminars for clerical and supervisory personnel on a semiannual or quarterly basis on such topics as handling hazardous materials, outbound loading, and handling OS&D (over, short, and damaged) freight. Another assistant is to be added in 1987.

Claims control is another function of the operations department. In 1985, there were 3,580 claims for loss or damage for a total of $506,827 paid. The ratio of paid claims to shipments was 1/164. The projected claims and payments for 1986 were expected to be 5,350 and $905,000, respectively. This projection if attained would actually be 1 per 177 shipments since the total business of CCX is increasing rapidly.

EQUIPMENT AND MAINTENANCE

CCX's investment in equipment has grown substantially from the 1983 beginning as shown below in Exhibit 40.12.

EXHIBIT 40.12 Equipment owned by CCX		
	1983	**1986**
Tractors	43	621
Trailers	127	1,524
Dollies	40	410
Fork lifts	11	113
Hostlers	0	10

Each tractor costs about $40,000 and each trailer about $12,000. A tractor lasts about 750,000 miles or five years and requires a new engine at 400,000 miles. A dolly carries the front part of the double trailer much like the tractor does to the lead trailer. A hostler is a small tractor-type vehicle that is used to move trailers around a freight assembly center instead of using a road tractor.

At the end of 1986, CCX had 10 Service Shops employing 33 mechanics to service the fleet of vehicles shown above. Paul Applegate, the director of maintenance, manages the maintenance activities through two field maintenance managers who do extensive traveling. Maintenance expenditures are distributed as follows: tractors—56.1 percent, trailers—33.3 percent, washing—7.3 percent, and fork lifts—3.3 percent.

There are three maintenance meetings held each year for the whole system that are moved to different shops. A preventative maintenance program is carried out. Maintenance expenditures over $500 must be approved by Paul Applegate. Warranty claims are controlled and administered through a warranty clerk. Tractors are in use about 20 hours per day except when they are in the shop for major maintenance.

PERSONNEL AND SAFETY

Brian Tierney is the Manager of Personnel and Safety. He is 33 years old and has a degree in political science from Loyola University in New Orleans. He began working for CFI after graduation from the York, Pennsylvania consolidation center in a training program that lasted for 45 weeks, followed by nine months as office manager in Philadelphia and four years in Portland, Oregon as a member of the internal audit staff. He first met Jerry Detter in October 1977 and Jerry had kept in touch until he asked him to join CCX. Brian did the preliminary interviewing for the terminal personnel recruited from blind ads and recommendations from CFI. Brian described the organization on June 20 when the first freight was hauled as a "25 year-old trucking company with one day of experience."

Safety is very important to CCX considering that 50 million miles are driven each year. The Department of Transportation as well as state agencies have jurisdiction over trucking companies and do perform random inspections. Weekly comparisons are made by CCX regarding preventable accidents. Safety achievement awards are given yearly. The low accident frequency for 1986 is quite impressive: one per 750,000 road miles, one per 4,200 city driving hours, and 8,300 hours worked per industrial injury.

CCX has a mandatory drug testing program. Each employee is tested once a year and is given 30 days notice of the test. Less than 3 percent of new employees and less than 1 percent of present employees test positive. Rehabilitation is stressed for those who are using drugs and an unpaid leave is given to undergo rehabilitation.

About 80 percent of the work force for CCX are regular employees. The balance of the work force is supplemental employees. Since the trucking business is seasonal with July and late December being the slowest periods, most companies lay off employees during these slow times. CCX does not lay off regular employees but rather discontinues supplemental employees. Supplemental employees usually move into regular employee status after six to nine months since CCX is expanding rapidly. This period gives CCX a good opportunity to evaluate each employee and in turn for the supplemental employee to evaluate CCX as a permanent employer.

The pay levels are evaluated each June and changes made as indicated by competitive factors. Supplemental workers make $10.30 per hour. The hourly pay schedule for regular employees is shown in Exhibit 40.13. Overtime is not paid for line haul driving since the driver is paid by the mile. Overtime is paid for work in excess of eight hours per day and 40 hours per week for local operations employees even though government regulations do not require it. Employee benefits include comprehensive

---

EXHIBIT 40.13 **Pay schedule**

	Drivers	**Mechanics**
Initial rate	$10.80	$12.40
After 6 months		13.50*
After 12 months	11.70	
After 24 months	12.40	
After 36 months	13.50	

*A $.50 premium is paid to lead men.

---

health insurance covering major medical, dental, vision and hospitalization, group life insurance, pension plan, tuition refund plan, stock purchase plan, a vacation plan of two weeks per year rising to three weeks at eight years and four weeks at fifteen years, nine paid holidays, sick leave, funeral leave, and jury duty leave. Uniforms for all employees are provided by CCX which is also a valuable marketing tool since it is not common in the industry. Probably the most important benefit from the employee's standpoint is the Incentive Compensation Plan. Under this plan CCX paid bonuses of $700,000 in 1984, $2,000,000 in 1985 and $3,200,000 in 1986 with individual employees receiving the maximum or close to the maximum provided for their wage level.

Supplemental employees are screened for drugs, their driver records are checked, a road test is given, and three interviews are held before they are hired. Each new employee is given one week's training working with four drivers and a supervisor. Upon attaining regular status, employees attend an orientation seminar for three days which is conducted by Jerry Detter and his executive group. Designed to familiarize employees with the personnel policies and procedures, and benefits, the company wants to establish an effective avenue for communications.

CCX believes one of the key differences between itself and others in the industry is its emphasis on communication with its employees at all levels. CCX has an employee involvement committee made up of Dick Palazzo, Paul Applegate, Brian Tierney, and three drivers from each region. This committee meets four times per year to discuss any subject of interest. CCX has an annual meeting for all sales and management personnel (about 200 attended), to review the year's performance. Regional meetings are held four times each year including a reception and dinner on Saturday night and a Sunday breakfast followed by a four-hour meeting for all regular employees of the region. About every six weeks a Saturday morning breakfast followed by a two-hour discussion is held for the employees of each terminal. Attendance at these latter meetings is voluntary but usually about 80 percent of the employees attend. All of these meetings are designed to maintain the open communications needed in a union-free environment. In addition, Jerry Detter has a uniform and works on a dock or truck about every eight weeks to maintain first hand contact with the work force.

FINANCE

Kevin Schick is the Controller for CCX. He is 35 years old and has an undergraduate degree in accounting and finance from Marquette University and an MBA with a major in accounting from Northwestern University. Before joining CCX in April 1983, he had worked in various accounting positions.

Since the accounting activities for CCX are handled by CFI in Portland on their main frame computer, Kevin has major liaison activity between CCX and Portland. He has a small staff of two clerks, one does accounts payable and the other does capital expenditure appropriations and analysis work on spreadsheets using a PC computer thereby freeing Kevin's time for longer-term planning. He does a one year detailed financial plan plus four additional years of a strategic plan showing projected revenues, costs, capital expenditures, and net working capital. The input for this plan comes from regional and terminal managers with Jerry Detter and his executive staff setting basic parameters such as tonnage and competitors' reactions. Kevin then puts in the detail assumptions working with Jerry, and to some extent with Dick Palazzo, on a one to one basis. The plans have worked out well since about 80 percent to 90 percent of the costs can be nailed down easily. The final review of the strategic plan is with Jerry before submitting it to CFI.

Kevin says he has an entrepreneurial taste and fulfills the role of a "corporate wet blanket" which is the role often taken by the financial executive. He submits a weekly forecast compiled from various internal reports to the Portland computer center who in turn submits it to CFI's home office in Palo Alto. He also submits a "week that was" management report to Palo Alto which is really an exception report. Each month after the books are closed he prepares a monthly analysis for Jerry's signature to be sent to Palo Alto. He also does a quarterly forecast on a rolling four-quarter basis.

Kevin prepares the narrative for the capital expenditure report. One of the advantages CCX has had was easy access to capital through CFI. Both the payback method using two to three years and the net present value using 15 percent are utilized in evaluating capital expenditures. CCX remitted 5.1 percent of its revenues to CFI in 1986 to cover the "interest on funds used." He sees some tightening of capital availability from CFI occurring because other entities of CFI are requiring capital also.

When commenting on Jerry's leadership Kevin sees him as the "spiritual leader of the drivers who can crawl inside the driver's mind." He believes Jerry's biggest value to CCX is an operational mind that can visualize the future. Kevin anticipates the shakeout in the trucking industry will continue for another three or four years. The service factor will be of prime importance to the customer.

THE FUTURE

When thinking about the future, Jerry Detter is just as enthusiastic as he is in describing the path of CCX thus far. Plans are under way to lease a new building being constructed near the present home office. Phase one will include 14,000 square feet with phase two expanding to 20,000 square feet over a one-and-a-half year period. The new facility will include a training center for 72 people and a cafeteria and kitchen. CCX is paying the local Sheraton Hotel so much for the frequent training sessions that a center for CCX can be justified. Thus far over 1,300 employees have been trained. Proposed capital expenditure needs for 1987 are $20 million. He is looking for a 25 percent market share of the Midwest trucking market within a few years. After that goal is reached? Well, Jerry Detter is never short of ideas!

CASE 41

Ansafone Corporation

In April 1982, Frank Rogers, nonexecutive Chairman of Ansafone Corporation, was concerned about how the company could exploit the recently liberalised U.K. market for telephone answering machines (TAMs) and reverse its loss of £900,000 for the year ended March 31, 1982. Ansafone's main business was the leasing of TAMs. Their models ranged from simple dual tape machines to those with sophisticated remote control and extended recording capacity (Exhibit 41.1).

Connection to the public network of user-owned, rather than leased, TAMs had been permitted by British Telecom as of October 1, 1981. For the first three years this permission would be extended only to a small range of British-made products. Nevertheless, the difficulty of selling TAM rentals was already increasing.

Ansafone's sales manager, Mr. Clarke, was concerned by the recent increase in salesperson turnover, resulting, in his opinion, from "loss of confidence." The 1981–1982 turnover was around 75 percent against the normal level of around 50 percent per year. Quotas had been set on the basis of new annual rental per salesperson of £31,000, to cover costs and give a reasonable profit. In 1981–1982, however, only nine out of 110 sales staff reached this target. Mr. Clarke had accordingly raised the minimum standard from £18,000 to £24,000 retaining the target of £31,000. He also instituted a "quota club" with an annual prize for those who reached 100 percent. Statistics on sales operations are shown in Exhibit 41.2.

This case was written by Professor Kenneth Simmonds and Simon Slater of the London Business School. It is intended as a basis for classroom discussion rather than to illustrate effective or ineffective handling of an administrative situation. Certain facts have been omitted or disguised. Copyright © 1984 by Kenneth Simmonds. Used by permission from Kenneth Simmonds.

EXHIBIT 41.1 **Ansafone telephone answering machines—(April 1982)**

Model	Features	Annual rent (In British pounds)	New rentals 1981–1982 (actual)	New rentals 1982–1983 (budgeted)
6	Answering and recording, dual tape.	180	1,800	—
6A	As 6, plus choice of only answering.	230	1,050	4,700
600	As 6A, *plus* will not answer if cassette full, two-way recording, remote playback to voice or bleeper coding, dictation facility.	290	1,400	1,160
7	Voice-controlled recording; two-hour capacity. (Two-way recording, dictation, dual tape.	300	90	100
7P	As 7, plus voice coded playback.	240	1,000	1,400
S100	Simple play and answer, dual tape.	110	570	1,400
	Total		5,910 units	8,760 units

EXHIBIT 41.2 **Sales statistics**

Average TAM salesperson weekly performance

Direct approach calls	60
Demonstrations	6.6
Contracts	1.1
Enquiries	3.4
Demonstrations	2
Contracts	1

Forms of commission

(1) No salary; £4,500 advance on commission
   37 percent commission on 1st year's rental

(2) Basic £4,000; £2,000 advance on commission
   19 percent commission on 1st year's rental

Sales cost per contract 1981–1982

   Budget—£220
   Actual—£270

NEW RENTALS

About 50 percent of new rentals came from enquiries, the rest came from direct approach, starting with "cold" telephone calls. The historical conversion of enquiries to sales had been about 40 percent, but had been dropping. Exhibit 41.3 shows a recent analysis of a sample of enquiries. Enquiries themselves had also been dropping. The publicity budget had therefore been increased to £300,000 for 1982-1983 with half earmarked for advertising, £100,000 for promotion, and the rest for miscellaneous costs. Last year Ansafone had spent £50,000 on Yellow Pages advertising and £30,000 on local classified ads. Staff could see very little pattern to customers, and found it impossible to predict from nine million business telephone lines which would rent a TAM. Consequently there was no segment targetting of advertising, and cold calling took in all businesses in the area.

EXHIBIT 41.3 Sales enquiry analysis—March 1982			
	Enquiries	**Contract**	**Conversion %**
Local classified ads	75	30	40
Users	60	40	67
British Telecom	20	5	25
Yellow Pages	300	75	25
Reputation	250	50	20
Recommendation	30	15	50
Total	735	215	29

CONTRACT RENEWALS/CANCELLATIONS

Mr. Clarke was also concerned about the rising level of cancellations of contracts. In 1981-1982, Ansafone gained nearly 6,000 contracts and lost over 8,000. A feature of the rental contract was that it automatically renewed and six months' advance written notice was required for cancellation even at the *end* of the typical three-year contract. An analysis had shown that cancellations between 1981-1982 fell roughly into the following categories: bad debts/gone out of business, 2,200; closing down, 1,000; no further need, 2,000; and going for purchase substitute, 3,000; for a total of 8,200 cancellations.

Executives argued that only the "bottom end" of the customer base, the smallest and most financially insecure, were being lost, either by substitution to purchased machines or by insolvency because of the recession. Moreover, the impact on the rental income was still only marginal. Ansafone's revenue was £11.2 million for 1981-1982 although it had had to bear a write off of £1 million on new products that had not caught on. In addition, the "rental base" of rents up to renewal dates for the 48,000 outstanding contracts at December 31, 1981, totalled £21.2 million.

EXHIBIT 41.4 **Ansafone corporation balance sheet—As of March 31, 1982 (In millions)**

Funds employed	
Share capital and reserves	£6.5
Long-term loans	2.2
	£8.7
Represented by	
Land, buildings, fixtures, plant and vehicles	
(estimated current market value £2.7m)	2.3
Equipment on hire (ECMV £8.0m)	11.0
Total fixed assets:	13.3
Stock and work in progress	3.1
Debtors	2.1
Current assets:	5.2
Creditors	(2.0)
Bank overdraft (limit £9m)	(7.8)
Current liabilities:	(9.8)
Deficit on working capital	(4.6)
Net assets	£8.7

This was a definite asset, although, it did not now show on Ansafone's balance sheet (Exhibit 41.4).

In taking steps to halt the erosion, Mr. Clarke had arranged in March for rentals administration to inform sales of impending cancellations by forwarding the written notices received. Discounts of up to 35 percent on rental renewals were now authorised to be proffered, in stages, by the sales force. Commission would be paid to sales staff as if the full annual rental had been obtained.

COMPETITION

Despite spending some £300,000 annually on research and development, Ansafone had found no answer to the growing sales inroads of pirate companies. Before liberalisation, small importers had been selling TAMs illegally in the United Kingdom. Now the sale was legal although use on the public network remained technically illegal. Answercall, who entered the market in 1979 as an "illegal pirate" selling unlicensed machines from the Far East, was the most successful. It had sold around 90,000 unlicensed machines and expected to continue at an equivalent annual rate of 30,000. Its advertising claimed: "A large number of companies automatically renew their rental contracts because they have a trouble-free machine without realising that they can drastically reduce costs by buying instead." However, at least one small importer had gone into liquidation in 1981 because its sales volume did not generate enough margin to cover heavy promotional costs.

EXHIBIT 41.5 **Retail prices of competing TAMs**		
	Light usage	**Heavy usage**
Nonremote control	£ 65–£100	£100–£160
Remote control	£100–£150	£170 upwards

The heavy advertising and low purchase prices of the pirates (Exhibit 41.5), compared with Ansafone's rental-only rates and prices of the few other licensed manufacturers, had stimulated the market to an annual value of approximately £50 million. New methods of distribution had also fuelled the growth, including mail-order advertisements in *Exchange and Mart,* and a growing number of small local retail outlets, many set up by ex-TAM-rental sales staff.

SERVICE, RENTAL, AND PRODUCTION OPERATIONS

As against the competition, the Chairman could see a major strength in Ansafone's service and rental administration. The nationwide service organisation employed 157 staff and offered same-day service or replacement. This service cost Ansafone £29 per installed machine in 1981–1982, but was considered essential for businesses relying on TAMs. In comparison, competitors selling through distributors offered only a one-year warranty, then an annual maintenance contract at £30 per annum. Moreover, the customer had to send the machine in for service or repair and would be without a TAM during that period. Competitors claimed, though, that only 2 percent of machines were expected to give trouble once in a useful life of five to six years. Ansafone's rental administration employed a staff of 70 costing about half as much as the service organisation, and was also regarded as extremely well-organised and administered. Both service and rental units were "capable of absorbing new products, more contracts, and new conditions of business, such as hire purchase."

Manufacture of new products was also an alternative. Ansafone manufactured all TAM equipment from basic components, buying in tape transport mechanisms from a large U.K. manufacturer. Manufacturing staff were now down to 40, one-fifth the number of two years earlier. As most were engaged in refurbishing used rental machines, there were few economies of scale in new manufacture. New Ansafone TAMs cost on average £200 in direct labour and materials. The solid design of the models that had previously been specified by British Telecom made it hard to reduce these costs. There were also about £800,000 of factory overheads currently arising. But the facilities were modern and bright and capable of carrying four or five times the output.

CASE 42

Apple Computer, Inc.
Targets Desktop Engineering

Matthew Robertson was reviewing the first quarter sales figures for the Macintosh II. It seemed amazing to him that the most challenging problem Apple faced today was how to keep up with the demand for Mac IIs. The corporate first quarter results were impressive. Not only were sales up 57 percent compared to first quarter results a year ago but net earnings increased more than 200 percent.

EXHIBIT 42.1 **Apple Computer, first quarter sales and earnings**

	1987	1988	% Change
Sales	$662 million	$1.042 billion	+ 57%
Net Earnings	$ 58 million	$ 121 million	+ 209%

The phone rang suddenly and broke Matthew's concentration. "Hello Matthew, this is Jan." "Hi Jan, how's it going?" "Crazy, of course. Listen I'm not going to be able to make this afternoon's meeting. Can we reschedule for tomorrow morning—first thing?" "Sure, no problem. I was just looking over the quarterly report. Have you seen it?" "I heard it was great, but did you hear that Sun has finally introduced their low-end workstation?" "Yeah, we've got a lot to talk about, don't we? Look, I'll let you go Jan, see you tomorrow."

Matthew looked around his office and saw the mountains of information he had been collecting and analyzing for the past three weeks. Tomorrow morning he'd compare notes with his other team members, Janice Latham and Tom Kelly, and together they would come up with a program for Apple's formal entry into the engineering workstation market. Introducing the Mac II to Apple's new market would be a lot like his previous assignment as a member of the tremendously successful Desktop Publishing Market Development Team (MDT), but it would also be more challenging, Matthew thought. And Matthew realized *he* was now responsible for the success of this team—desktop publishing had been pioneered by Apple, but the engineering workstation market was already established. The competition would be ready.

This case was prepared by Robert O. Lewis, Linda E. Swayne, and Peter M. Ginter. It is intended as a basis for classroom discussion rather than to illustrate effective or ineffective handling of an administrative situation. Some facts have been altered to protect confidentiality of company information. Used by permission from Linda E. Swayne.

APPLE COMPUTER'S BACKGROUND

Apple manufactures and markets two principal lines of personal computers, related software, and peripheral products. The first, which fueled the company's growth into 1986, was the Apple II product line. This line was geared to the educational (preschool through high school) and home computing markets. The second and the platform for the future growth of Apple was the Macintosh product line. Macintosh was developed for the business market (productivity and desktop publishing) and the higher educational market. See Exhibit 42.2 for a chronological history of Apple. Apple had not escaped the industry-wide computer slump of 1984–85. However, through a well-organized restructuring, Apple emerged in 1986 as a leaner, more market-sensitive company and went on to record sales and profits.

EXHIBIT 42.2 **Chronological history of Apple Computer, Inc.**

March	1976	Apple Computer was founded by Steven Wozniak (26) and Steven Jobs (21). They produced a hobbiest computer that contained 16 times the memory of any other such computer. It was priced at $666.66. Officially formed on April Fools' Day.
Jan.	1977	Jobs, Wozniak, and Mark Markkula incorporate Apple Computer and draft the first formal business plan.
April	1977	Apple II is introduced.
Dec.	1977	First year sales $774,000.
Feb.	1980	Annual sales reach $100,000,000.
Dec.	1980	Apple offers public stock.
Aug.	1981	IBM introduces the PC.
Jan.	1983	The Lisa is introduced. The forerunner of the Macintosh.
Dec.	1983	Apple annual sales reach $1 billion.
April	1983	John Sculley becomes President and CEO.
Jan.	1984	Fully automated Macintosh factory begins operation. Less than 1% of the cost of a Macintosh unit can be attributed to labor.
March	1984	Apple ships the Macintosh.
June	1985	Steven Jobs is removed from operations at Apple.
Dec.	1985	Annual sales reach $1.52 billion.
Feb.	1986	Apple purchases a Cray supercomputer to assist in the design of new products.
April	1987	Apple announces a 2-for-1 stock split and a first-ever cash dividend.
May	1987	Apple introduces the Macintosh II. This machine is positioned for the power-user in markets such as corporate MIS departments and desktop publishing.
Sept.	1987	Splits U.S. sales organization into three regional divisions—Western, Central and Eastern.
March	1988	Apple begins shipping A/UX, (UNIX software interface for engineering workstations).

When founded in 1976, Wozniak and Jobs had very specific ideas about what they wanted. The first business plan was written by retired Intel founder, Mark Markkula. The original corporate objectives and key strategies are included in Exhibit 42.3.

In 1987, Apple's CEO, John Sculley, set corporate objectives that included achieving $4 billion in sales by 1990, spending $300 million on research and development by 1990, and maintaining the entrepreneurial spirit of a small company. He and the Apple employees were committed to the corporate mission: "To produce innovative products that place the individual, not the mainframe, at the center of the computing universe."

Organizational Structure

Apple's organizational structure was designed to meet the corporate objective of maintaining the entrepreneurial spirit of a small company. It is best described as a hybrid design—neither centralized or de-centralized, it's actually a network. The

---

EXHIBIT 42.3 **Apple's corporate objectives and strategies—1976**

Objectives

- Obtain a market share greater than or equal to two times that of the nearest competitor.
- Realize equal or greater than 20% pretax profit.
- Grow to $500 million annual sales in 10 years.
- Establish and maintain an operating environment conducive to human growth and development.
- Continue to make significant technological contributions to the home computer industry.
- (Possible) Structure company for easy exit of founders within five years.

Key Strategies

- It is extremely important for Apple to be the first recognized leader in the home computer marketplace.
- Continually market peripheral products for the basic computer, thereby generating sales equal to or greater than the initial computer purchase.
- Allocate sufficient funds to R&D to guarantee technological leadership consistent with market demands.
- Attract and retain *absolutely* outstanding personnel.
- Rifle-shot the hobby market as the first stepping stone to the major market.
- Maintain significant effort in manufacturing to continually reduce cost of production.
- Grow at the same rate that the market grows.
- Design and market the computer to be more economical than a dedicated system in specific applications, even though all features of the Apple are not used.

Source: John Sculley, *Odyssey: Pepsi to Apple,* New York: Harper & Row, Publishers, Inc., 1987.

network stems from the Board of Directors and the single layer of upper management (six senior executives). It is given structure with functional areas like operations, marketing, finance, etc. Senior members of the functional departments will recognize a problem or opportunity that needs to be addressed. Knowledge of the problem (or opportunity) comes from either a member of a functional department or someone in the network. Then modular groups are set up to solve that specific problem or develop that opportunity, and later disbanded when the task is completed and reformed into other groups to take on new projects.

The marketing functional area stems from the corporate marketing and sales managers, to one of the three regional marketing managers, then to separate managers within the region for Education, Retail, and Direct Sales. Reporting to the sales managers are sales representatives of varying capacities as well as sales support people.

Apple believes that the network is a superior format because it is a natural way for communication to flow. Inside the network, idea exchange is not inhibited by functional boundaries or management levels. Creativeness, flexibility, innovation and individuality are all fostered in the network schema. The high-technology industry is subject to rapid change, therefore the company and its personnel must be able to quickly share ideas about any change, develop alternatives, make a decision, and implement it. Another chief advantage of the network design is its efficiency. In 1987, Apple's annual sales per employee figure was roughly $450,000—based on 1987 sales that included a 25 percent boost in employment. Therefore the network structure allows Apple to operate leaner and achieve a corporate objective—to preserve its entrepreneurial spirit.

Through this network, Apple has identified the engineering workstation market as a lucrative target for the future. A task group was formed to analyze the situation and develop strategies to be implemented through the marketing channels. They would also recommend the direction for product development to meet the future needs of the identified target market.

Organizational Philosophy

Apple considers itself to be a "Third Wave" company (as opposed to a "Second Wave" company which sees the future as an extension of the past and therefore focuses on ritual) and focuses on the individual. Exhibit 42.4 illustrates the difference between a "Third Wave" and "Second Wave" company.

APPLE AND THE MICROCOMPUTER INDUSTRY

With a revenue increase of 40 percent in 1987, Apple Computer is in a strong position in the computer industry. Analysts project 1988 revenues to approach $3.8 billion, another 40 percent increase (see Exhibit 42.5).

The key to this success was the introduction of the Macintosh II, a machine that is equal to or better than (depending on the application) the high-performance

EXHIBIT 42.4 **Contrasted management paradigms**

Characteristic	Second Wave	Third Wave
Organization	Hierarchy	Network
Output	Market share	Market creation
Focus	Institution	Individual
Style	Structured	Flexible
Source of strength	Stability	Change
Structure	Self-sufficiency	Interdependencies
Culture	Tradition	Genetic code*
Mission	Goals/Strategic plans	Identity/directions/values
Leadership	Dogmatic	Inspirational
Quality	Affordable best	No compromise
Expectations	Security	Personal growth
Status	Title and rank	Making a difference
Resource	Cash	Information
Advantage	Better sameness	Meaningful difference
Motivation	To complete	To build

*Note: Genetic coding is a term describing how a third-wave company refers to the past only for a sense of direction.

Source: John Sculley, *Odyssey: Pepsi to Apple,* New York: Harper & Row Publishers, Inc., 1987.

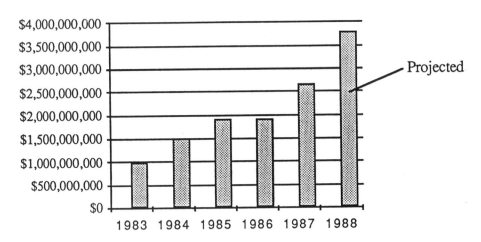

Source: Apple Computer, Inc., Annual Report 1987; Hypercard Supplement

EXHIBIT 42.5 **Apple Computer annual sales**

machines offered by IBM, Compaq, and other similar microcomputer manufacturers. The Mac II features superior color graphics, extremely fast processing speed, and an advanced 32-bit architecture with the ability to run multiple operating systems. One operating system of importance to the engineering marketplace is UNIX. The Macintosh II can be configured to operate this complex system while maintaining its friendly user interface.

The power of the Mac II gained the awareness of MIS professionals, many of whom had regarded the original Macintosh as a "toy." With the introduction of the Mac II, many business/MIS decision makers realized that Apple could compete with IBM and would remain a key player in the computer industry. The user interface Apple had touted was now on a powerful system and, to give Apple even more credibility, IBM copied it in the form of the OS/2 presentation manager (operating system).

On March 18, 1988, Apple filed suit against Microsoft Corporation and Hewlett-Packard for copyright violations concerning the Macintosh Operating System. The suit directly charged that Microsoft's Windows 2.03 software copied the Macintosh interface.

According to technical analysts, the Macintosh operating system is at least two years ahead of IBM's OS/2 in the evolutionary process (capabilities, upward expansion, and available software), and Apple's future depends on its ability to maintain that lead. Currently IBM maintains the lead in the industry although that lead has eroded considerably from August 1987 to January 1988 (See Exhibit 42.6).

EXHIBIT 42.6 **Microcomputer market share**

	8/87	1/88
IBM	66%	47%
Apple	8%	17%
Compaq	6%	12%
Compatibles	20%	24%

However, when marketing research surveys potential buyers (those planning to buy within the next year), over 60 percent indicate that they plan to purchase an IBM computer (see Exhibit 42.7). Among respondents who have considered purchasing a specific brand, some have not tried the brand (see Exhibit 42.8). Of those respondents who have tried the brand they intended to buy, the percentage who actually bought that brand is somewhat less that the trial (see Exhibit 42.9).

[1]Jim Forbes, Daniel Lyons and Gregory Spector, *PcWeek*, March 22, 1988, page 1.

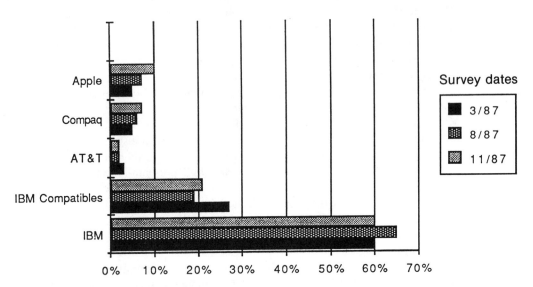

Source: Richard Stromer, *PcWeek,* January 12, 1988, p. 138.

EXHIBIT 42.7 **Share of year-ahead planned purchases**

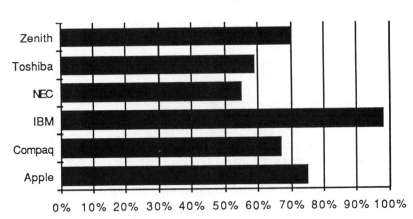

Source: Richard Stromer, *PcWeek,* March 22, 1988, p. 146.

EXHIBIT 42.8 **Percentage of respondents considering a brand who have
tried that brand**

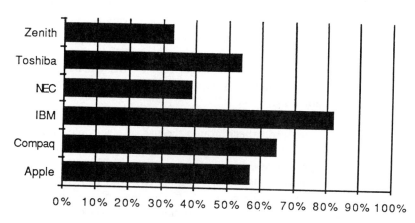

Source: Richard Stromer, *PcWeek*, March 22, 1988, p. 146.

EXHIBIT 42.9 **Percentage of respondents who have tried a brand and have purchased that brand**

TARGET MARKET

Apple's primary markets are designated higher education, business, government, K-12 education, and international. International sales currently account for nearly 30 percent of the company's annualized revenue. Apple has designated desktop engineering as the next target market.

The engineering workstation (desktop engineering) market consists of the various engineering fields—electrical, chemical, mechanical, civil, industrial, and architectural. Apple had segmented the market into two principal submarkets—the engineering workplace and engineering higher education. The UNIX workstation market is not limited to the United States, or engineers, and independent research has projected the world-wide market potential to be more than $20 billion by 1990. Apple has beefed up its international presence, implementing a strategy called *multilocal focusing* in recognition of this and other growing markets. Multilocal is Apple's term for regionalizing corporate communications as well as the ability to customize the product line for the end-user.

Apple's present objective is to secure a strong foundation within the two market segments in the more narrow scope of the engineering workstation market. Apple plans to leverage resources for long-term growth and development of the two targets. Once Apple has established itself as a major workstation manufacturer, they will expand the objective to include all UNIX environments and applications.

Workstation Defined

In 1987, the U.S. engineering-specific workstation market, only eight years old, accounted for over $3 billion in sales. An engineering workstation is a microcomputer that is positioned in the market between a minicomputer and the traditional personal computer. A workstation has become a high-performance personal computer that typically uses a programming language called UNIX, which is a sophisticated operating system that controls the workstation and communicates with other computers of different manufacture.

UNIX is the preferred system because it supports networking (tying many different computers together through the use of electronic hardware and software), allows the use of more than one application at a time, has full graphics support, and is not a proprietary system (meaning that with some adjustments most any computer can operate UNIX, allowing the use of any application software program written under UNIX). Engineers use this system to perform tasks that range from scientific analysis to product design simulation. With the decreased cost of computing, engineers and scientists are realizing the benefits that were once limited to the mainframe computer. And the computers can now sit on their desk.

COMPETITION

Sun Microsystems, IBM, Digital Equipment, and Apollo Computer make up the principal competitors in the engineering market. Hewlett-Packard is expected to bring its Spectrum computer to the UNIX marketplace soon. Apollo Computer pioneered the engineering workstation market in 1980. In 1985, it had a 40 percent market share that has since eroded to around 18 percent. Revenues and market share information are illustrated in Exhibit 42.10.

IBM

The machine IBM has positioned for engineers is the Model 80. It is based on the 80386 Intel microprocessor with a speed of up to 20 megahertz (a measure of raw processing speed). It operates with OS/2 and DOS system software, however, the computer has proprietary hardware set up to reduce the cloning potential (competitors who copy or purchase the same parts that IBM uses).

The Model 80 can be categorized into IBM's new computer line as the Personal System 2 (PS/2). As of March 1988, IBM reported sales of 1.5 million PS/2 units and the Model 80 represents roughly 82,500 units sold. Due to the markets' resistance to proprietary hardware, IBM has instituted tough quotas for its dealer network (many of the same dealers carry the Apple line). This has resulted in almost wholesale pricing—the Model 80 started out retailing over $10,000 but now sells for approximately $7,000.[2]

[2]*PcWeek*, March 29, 1988, p. 10-11.

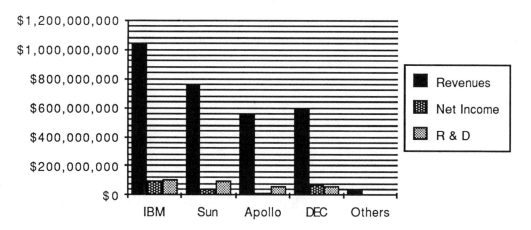

Marketshare

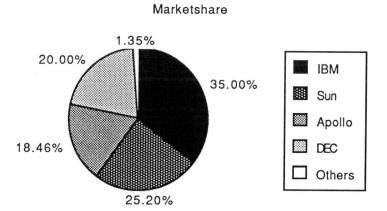

Compiled from *Business Week,* March 14, 1988, page 134 and *Datamation,* Nov. 15, 1987, pages 61–76.

EXHIBIT 42.10 **Major competitor revenue and market share—1987**

John Akers, IBM's Chairman, has instituted a complete reorganization to reestablish IBM as the most profitable company in the world. Analysts expect the changes to help IBM become more innovative and to move products out into the market more quickly. "IBM has been taking too long bringing systems to the market," said Michael Geran, VP for Nikko Securities International, a New York brokerage firm. "This is an evolutionary step by IBM to use an organizational change to speed up product releases and get closer to the marketplace."[3]

Sun Microsystems

Sun manufactures a line of computers that range from desktop supercomputers to low-end workstations. These computers have all been positioned into the engineering market. Sun has not had the means to expand beyond that market. The company announced in February 1988 that their Triad Strategy was to be comprised of three different computers all featuring the UNIX operating system and a user-friendly graphic interface similar to the Mac interface. Sun is well known for its marketing savvy (oriented toward personal selling) in the engineering market and is one of the fastest growing computer manufacturers.

With a UNIX operating system, Sun was seen as a "safe buy." But Sun is not without weaknesses; it is apparently vulnerable to manufacturing inefficiency (most of the system components are purchased) and has had a lack of financial clout.[4] Sun recently announced the sale of a 20 percent block of stock to AT&T.[5] Analysts view this as a sign of the impact of larger companies entering and expanding the market. The smaller companies will have to rely on their responsiveness to changing technology and market needs in order to succeed or survive.

AT&T is not new to computers; they lost between $800 million and $1.2 billion in 1986 alone and laid off thousands of employees. AT&T was the original developer of the UNIX operating system and had seen many companies profit from it while they were regulated by the government and not permitted to sell computers until the early 1980s. Industry analysts expect several effects of the agreement between Sun and AT&T. Sun will gain the distribution channel AT&T was using (dealers), and Sun will get financial resources to fuel its rapid growth. Analysts consider the price for Sun's 20 percent block of stock to be a bargain at $300 million, giving AT&T the opportunity to recoup previous losses.[6]

Sun's newest computer, the Sun 386i, uses a 80386 Intel microprocessor that is also purchased by IBM, Compaq, and others for use in their high-performance machines. The Sun 386i will be positioned against the IBM Model 80, Compaq 386, and the Macintosh II. Using a "386" processor will allow the Sun system to run DOS applications within the UNIX operating system software, giving the user access to all programs written for the IBM world. Jeff Elpern, manager of sales development for alternative distribution channels for Sun, has been quoted as saying that MicroAge, Entre Computer, and other independent dealers have been signed to distribution agreements. Mr. Elpern expects to have 100 dealers signed by the end of June 1988. Andrew Neff, an analyst with Bear, Stearns & Co., a New York investment company,

[3]Steven Burke, *PcWeek*, February 9, 1988, p. 127.
[4]"Mid-Range Shootout: Mini/Micro Survey,"*Datamation*, November 15, 1987, p. 61-76.
[5]*PcWeek*, January 12, 1988, p. 1.
[6]Ibid.

said "Last year, it was IBM who was getting eaten up by Compaq at the high end and by everyone else at the low end. Now it's Compaq's turn." (Note: reference to IBM's "high-end" is equivalent to the "low-end" Sun workstation.)[7]

William O'Shea, Executive Director of AT&T's Information Technology Division, stated, "It is key that we recognize the existence of DOS and OS/2 and that we operate effectively in environments that include those systems as well as UNIX."[8]

Apollo Computer

While Apollo established the workstation market, recent competition with more financial resources and better marketing expertise has contributed to Apollo's decline. Sales are still increasing, however, not at a rate in proportion to the growth of the market. Apollo's low-end workstation is the DN 3000. Their principal market for this system is the previous Apollo customer.

Digital Equipment Corporation

Apple Computer and Digital Equipment Corporation (DEC) have reached a marketing agreement for strategically aligning their products. Analysts expect DEC to concentrate on the high-end of the engineering market and Apple to focus on the low- to middle-end.

Compaq

Currently Compaq is positioning its "386" machine as superior in performance, quality, and value compared to the IBM models. They've been very successful. It is unknown what impact the Sun entry into the broad dealer channel will have upon Compaq's strategy.

Hewlett-Packard

The HP Vectra RS/20 computer is based on the 80386 microprocessor and operates on DOS similar to the IBM models.

The HP Spectrum is reported to use a RISC processor (Reduced Instruction Set Computing), a type of processor where 20 percent of all computer instructions are executed in 4/5 the time of a normal processor. It is reported that the price will be near that of a low-end workstation, and that it will operate UNIX and run DOS similar to the Sun 386i. The graphics interface used on this computer is the subject of the Apple lawsuit.

[7]Kenneth Siegmann, *PcWeek*, March 29, 1988, p. 139.
[8]Steven Burke, *PcWeek*, March 29, 1988, p. 139.

THE MEETING

Tom Kelly, a software engineer and software market analyst, and Janice Latham, a hardware engineer and hardware analyst, were seated with Matthew as they began to discuss the decisions they would have to make.

Apple's marketing research team in conjunction with their product development team had determined that an unmet need existed in the engineering workstation market. Research indicated that engineers would request a computer that would do more than scientific applications especially if they were already using a high-end system or were seeking a system for subordinate engineers. Exhibit 42.11 illustrates engineer preferences when selecting a workstation.

EXHIBIT 42.11 **Ranked criteria for workstations by engineers**	
Power, benefits, features	1
Support	2
Compatible/networkable	3
Learning curve	4
Cost effectiveness	5

Apple also recognized that MIS directors relied on input from engineers concerning workstation requirements but MIS directors were still responsible for the results of the purchase decision. Exhibit 42.12 indicates the purchasing criteria used by MIS directors. Jan and Tom agreed that the surveys were fairly representative of customer attitudes.

EXHIBIT 42.12 **Ranked criteria for workstations by MIS directors**	
System quality/reliability/performance	1
Compatibility/networkable	2
Vendor reputation/financial strength	3
Application software availability	4
Price	5

Matthew reminded them that the market for engineering workstations was $3 billion in 1987. Projections for the low-end segment of the workstation market were $1.1 billion in sales for 1988, $1.15 billion in 1989, and $1.3 billion in 1990. Jan said, "Those projections seem conservative to me. Looking over this quarter's sales figures, we are selling all we can make, yet we don't know if we're meeting our potential." "You're right," Matthew responded, "we don't even know the real potential of this market. It might be just like desktop publishing where we found that any small business could benefit from using the product. Every engineering application could conceivably be performed on the Mac II and there are numerous types of engineers. . ." (see Exhibit 42.13).

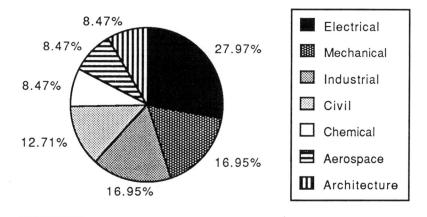

EXHIBIT 42.13 **Engineers by discipline**

Next, Matthew brought up the point that support was ranked highly by engineers. Apple's primary salespeople would come from the dealer organization. Jan said, "There are different kinds of engineers, each with a certain need, and they're different primary markets. Yet electrical engineers are electrical engineers although some are employed in business, some in government, and some in higher education. I think we're kidding ourselves if we believe our dealer network can easily handle the more sophisticated installations."

"I can see that and yet we can't ignore the dealer network," commented Matthew. "I can't think of a way to reach as many engineering prospects as we did desktop publishing prospects."

Apple uses a direct sales force primarily to sell to large corporations (approximately 100 accounts), all universities, and to the dealer network. The dealer network is divided into two types-retail accounts and independent resellers. The retail accounts are usually national chains like Computerland and MicroAge. The independent resellers are individual stores that combine a retail plan with an outbound sales program.

Something else was bothering Tom, "Take a look at this computer comparison from *PcWeek* for low-end engineering workstations. Everybody's here except us."

"We should have been there! The Mac II has virtually the same performance as those in the article," said Jan. "We have the 68020 processor with a 2 mips rating and look at this price comparison." (See Exhibits 42.14 and 42.15).

Matthew concentrated on another hurdle Apple would have to overcome. "Our image is very strong as a home computer marketer and the Macintosh seems to

---

EXHIBIT 42.14 **Computer performance comparison**

IBM Model 80	Compaq 386	Sun 3/50	Sun 386i	Apollo DN 30
16 mhz 80386	20 mhz 80386	16 mhz 68020	25 mhz 80386	16 mhz 68020
1.5 mips*	2 mips	2 mips	3 mips	2 mips

*mips (million instructions executed per second) is a benchmark used to compare processing power.
Source: PcWeek, March 29, 1988, page 139.

EXHIBIT 42.15 **Price comparison**

	IBM Model 80	Compaq 386	Sun 3/50	Sun 386i	Apollo DN 30	Mac II
Price	$7,000	$7,000	$7,995	$8,500	$8,295	$6,500
Price/mips	$4,500	$3,500	$4,000	$2,800	$4,000	$3,250

Source: PcWeek, March 29, 1988, page 139.

---

suffer from an image of being so easy to use it must lack power and sophistication." Jan jumped in, "several participants in my hardware focus group study kept saying they didn't believe sophisticated software was available, even though they knew the hardware was powerful." "Even Seymour Cray, the Cray supercomputer designer, uses a Mac II to design his new systems. But it's expensive to change attitudes," exclaimed Tom.

"Our marketing budget for the engineering workstation segment has tentatively been set at $16 million. That has to be allocated for the workstation in all our primary markets—engineers in business, government, and higher education," replied Matthew. He went on, "as I see it, we have three challenges: the image of the Macintosh as a toy, the perception that sophisticated software packages are not available, and the sales of engineering workstations through our current dealer network. Corporate expects us to make the Mac II a major player in the workstation market."